COLLECTED
VERSE PLAYS

The Warlords, Part One
The Warlords, Part Two
The Tragedy of Prince Tudor
Ovid Banished
The Rise of Oliver Cromwell

NICHOLAS HAGGER

First published by O Books, 2007
O Books is an imprint of John Hunt Publishing Ltd.,
The Bothy, Deershot Lodge, Park Lane, Ropley, Hants, SO24 0BE, UK
office1@o-books.net
www.o-books.net

Distribution in:

UK and Europe
Orca Book Services
orders@orcabookservices.co.uk
Tel: 01202 665432 Fax: 01202 666219 Int. code (44)

USA and Canada
NBN
custserv@nbnbooks.com
Tel: 1 800 462 6420 Fax: 1 800 338 4550

Australia and New Zealand
Brumby Books
sales@brumbybooks.com.au
Tel: 61 3 9761 5535 Fax: 61 3 9761 7095

Far East (offices in Singapore, Thailand, Hong Kong, Taiwan)
Pansing Distribution Pte Ltd
kemal@pansing.com
Tel: 65 6319 9939 Fax: 65 6462 5761

South Africa
Alternative Books
altbook@peterhyde.co.za
Tel: 021 447 5300 Fax: 021 447 1430

Text copyright Nicholas Hagger 2007

Design: Stuart Davies

ISBN-13: 978 1 84694 026 2
ISBN-10: 1 84694 026 5

A CIP catalogue record for this book is available from the British Library.

Printed in the UK by 4edge Ltd, Hockley. www.4edge.co.uk

COLLECTED VERSE PLAYS

The Warlords, Part One
The Warlords, Part Two
The Tragedy of Prince Tudor
Ovid Banished
The Rise of Oliver Cromwell

NICHOLAS HAGGER

BOOKS

Winchester, UK
Washington, USA

"A poet, like a paraglider, soars
Among the clouds, beneath the blue sky, looks down
From the One that's behind his fluffy verse.
An artist understands what the Whole is
And reveals Truth to universal man."
The Tragedy of Prince Tudor, 4.3

By the same author

The Fire and the Stones
Selected Poems
The Universe and the Light
A White Radiance
A Mystic Way
Awakening to the Light
A Spade Fresh with Mud
A Smell of Leaves and Summer
The Warlords
Overlord (4 volumes)
The One and the Many
The Tragedy of Prince Tudor
Wheeling Bats and a Harvest Moon
The Warm Glow of the Monastery Courtyard
The Syndicate
The Secret History of the West
The Light of Civilization
Collected Poems 1958-2006
Classical Odes
Overlord (one-volume edition)
Collected Short Stories, 1966-2006
The Secret Founding of America
The Rise and Fall of Civilizations

CONTENTS

PREFACE TO
COLLECTED VERSE PLAYS

These four verse plays, written between 1994 and 2000 and presented together in one volume for thematic comparison, develop my preoccupation with the forces that shape national power and with the abuse of power. They represent my revival of verse drama in our time – single-handed in the sense that I operated in isolation – following the efforts of Eliot, Auden and Fry between the 1930s and 1950s. They were written as a kind of sideline while I was deeply engaged in producing books in other disciplines and very busy.

Looking back now, I am struck by the scale of what I was trying to do in my unnaturalistic settings. To put the last year of the Second World War on stage in two parts with 219 speaking parts (and four choruses of four, i.e. 234 characters in all) – even the abridged version has a cast of 94 – and then to put the entire English Civil War and Puritan Revolution with a cast of 38, and 31 or more minor parts – what did I think I was doing? I was clearly not writing with budgets in mind. (The ideal budget for actors' wages is a cast of two.) Like Goethe in *Faust*, Parts 1 and 2, I was trying to catch a historical trend that required an epic sweep: the shift from Britain to the United States as ruler of the world stage and the marginalising of Britain that took place in 1944/5, the consequences of which have shaped our own time; and the degeneration of the libertarian Cromwellian vision into regicide (which is called tyrannicide) in 1648/9, echoes of which can be found in the Blair government's reform of the Lords in the UK in our own day, and will be found in future British governments forced to implement the world-government agenda.

These plays develop my preoccupation with the forces that shape national power, and represent different treatments of the abuse of power. Whereas Montgomery in the two Parts of *The Warlords* sees his nation lose power to a world government-in-waiting that wants Stalin to reach Berlin first, and Prince Tudor observes with dismay the break-up of the kingdom whose crown he is waiting to inherit, my latest two historical plays take the exploration of the abuse of power into new areas. Augustus, who rules the Roman world, banishes Ovid to silence his criticisms – a fate that can befall any artist who stands up to supreme power. Cromwell, on the other hand, rises to supreme power as Protector – in effect, Augustan dictator – of England,

Scotland and Ireland with the help of international interests keen to replace Charles I. With Augustus and Cromwell, the focus shifts from the victims of supreme power to the perpetrator. The four victims in the four verse plays – Montgomery, Prince Tudor, Ovid and Charles I – are all defeated by a world government which is hidden in the case of Montgomery, Prince Tudor and Charles I and naked in the case of Ovid.

In fact these four plays explore one theme: world government, the imminent prospect of which I have investigated very fully in *The Syndicate* (published in 2004). In *The Warlords* (written in 1994/5) Montgomery is blocked by Eisenhower's Rockefellerite world-government superiors from taking Berlin as they want Stalin to found an East-European empire there. In *Prince Tudor* (written in 1998) the two factions of the world government are set to abolish the British monarchy and the Prince is confronted with having no kingdom to rule – a predicament that will become a reality if the new European constitution is ratified by four-fifths of the EU's member nation-states for this would replace all member nation-states by a superstate under which they would all be substates. In *Ovid Banished* (written in 1998/9) Augustus, the leader of the world government of the day, banishes Ovid, the poet, for knowing too much about a plot against his rule and (arguably) for questioning his policy towards the barbarians. Ovid, the (partly inadvertently) dissident artist, has to live among non-Latin-speaking barbarians for the rest of his life. In *The Rise of Oliver Cromwell* (written in 2000), the world-government Rosicrucians and Jews of Amsterdam fund Cromwell's army in return for a pledge to kill Charles I – so that the Jews can return to England from which they had been banned since their expulsion in 1290. (See my book *The Secret History of the West*, ch 2 for full details and for the letters between Mulheim Synagogue and Cromwell.) Again, there is an attack on the integrity of the nation-state, which has been mirrored by Cromwellian New Labour today. One way or another, world-government thinking defeats an English General, an English Prince, a Roman poet and an English King.

All four plays deal with plots or conspiracies, and counter-plots: in *The Warlords* the world-government Syndicate's 1944-5 plot to allow Stalin to take Berlin and advance towards world government via the Yalta negotiations, and the resistance of Montgomery and Churchill; in *Prince Tudor* a world-government Syndicate plot to replace the British monarchy and sovereignty with a European republic and split England into smaller states within a United States of Europe, and a counter-plot to defend the monarchy by eliminating a threat; in *Ovid Banished* an imperial world-government plot to reintroduce morality in Rome and a counter-plot to replace the Claudian imperial line with the Julian line; and in *The Rise of Oliver Cromwell* an internationalist, potential world-government plot between Cromwell and Dutch Rosicrucians to overthrow the king, and Charles I's resistance and counter-plot to escape.

All four plays are based on meticulous research and are factually accurate. They therefore dovetail with *The Syndicate* and its companion volume *The Secret History of the West* and flesh out a picture of a secretive, shadowy world government that intrigues against the West, swallows its sovereign independence, censors artists and breaks down national barriers. Within the tentacles of world government individuals such as Montgomery, Prince Tudor, Ovid and Charles I put up heroic resistance but barely understand the forces that crush and defeat them.

This issue is the most important issue of our time, yet my fellow-writers have totally ignored it. Indeed, most are unaware of it. A friend (Kingsley Shorter) wrote to me in 1966 of our time at Oxford, "I see now that you were perhaps fighting for your life when most of us didn't even know there was a war on." History has repeated itself – the same could be said of today.

As to the technical side, I began *The Warlords* before writing my epic *Overlord*. *Overlord* is in strict iambic pentameters. *The Warlords* allows anapaests and dactyls, even paeans (4-syllable feet), and the verse is consequently loose. The act of writing *The Warlords* tautened my verse so that it was more classical by the time I came to *Overlord*. The last three plays reflect this tautening. In all the four verse plays I have sought to use verse, including dramatic monologue and rodomontade, to catch characters making existential decisions and choices in unnaturalistic settings, appealing to the imagination, evoking the scenery in words as the settings are not realistic.

Two of these plays are contemporary – *Prince Tudor* and *The Warlords*, which is set in my lifetime but is further back in time – and two are clearly historical. In a sense, all four plays are historical verse plays. The *genre* of the historical verse play presents historical subject matter to draw an analogy, and make a point, about a contemporary political theme. This *genre* was perfected by Shakespeare, who commented on contemporary events through such historical plays as *Henry IV*, Parts 1 and 2, *Richard II*, *Julius Caesar*, and *Hamlet*. Shakespeare has to be the model for a contemporary revival of the verse play. In all his plays Shakespeare was able to achieve his range and depth by foregoing realistic scenery and appealing to the imagination to supply scenic details by suggesting them through his words. Shakespeare invited the audience to imagine the scenery and surrounding nature, such as the house-martins round the eaves (Banquo's "temple-haunting martlets"); and Lear's heath. Through his use of language he stimulated the imagination into "seeing" the scenery. In this Shakespeare followed the unnaturalistic method of Sophocles whose Greek plays depended on his words for their scenic effects.

The unnaturalistic Sophoclean-Shakespearean verse play was abolished in 1642 as a result of the Civil War, which closed the theatres. Cromwell finally banned dramatic performances in 1655. Drama returned with the Restoration, but with the exception of Dryden's *All for Love* (1672), which is about Antony and Cleopatra, prose took over. After that there were dramatic poems (rather than poetic dramas) by Byron, Shelley and Yeats, but the unnaturalistic drama that employs pictorial language in place of scenery was not revived until Eliot's *Murder in the Cathedral* in 1935, which has some elements in common with this *genre*. The true revival of the verse play had to wait 350 years until the 1990s (in my own work, beginning with *The Warlords*, first published in 1996) launched a new movement in verse drama.

This movement has coincided with the work at London's Globe Theatre, with which I have been privileged to have a link. From early 1998 I urged Mark Rylance, then Artistic Director at the Globe and (then) my co-trustee of the Shakespeare Authorship Trust's library at Otley Hall, at that time my Tudor house in Suffolk, to put on contemporary verse plays. Shakespeare and his contemporaries wrote plays about contemporary or nearly contemporary events, I said at some length; some plays at the Globe should now similarly include works with a contemporary analogy or angle. My suggestion was not taken up but I was asked to have the entire casts of the Globe productions of *As You Like It* (1998), *Julius Caesar* (1999), and *The Tempest* and *Hamlet* (2000) to stay at Otley Hall for up to three days each. During these four visits I must have encountered more than 120 actors and speakers of verse, including the Masters of Verse and directors who have had experience of putting verse on stage. These visits led to an exchange of views on the revival of verse drama.

I found these visits of immense benefit. I took part in their rehearsals: I was Antony's standard-bearer in the final battle of *Julius Caesar* on nearby ploughed fields, a Doctor of Philosophy at the University of Wittemberg instructing Hamlet and Horatio on the Lutheran philosophy of the 1580s, and the priest who married Gertrude and Claudius before the beginning of *Hamlet,* presiding over a candlelit "altar" in the summerhouse after dark wearing an Elizabethan frockcoat with the entire Globe cast as congregation before me. The *Hamlet* actors rehearsed the players' scene in the enclosed space of Otley Hall's Linenfold Room to see if it could be performed in such a small space – the effect on the court, of whom I was one, was extremely intimate – and there have been times when I have felt like Hamlet coaching the players. We were all aware of the ghosts of the players of the 1590s watching our activities with approval. Elizabethan plays may have been performed in the "plahouse" wing at Otley Hall, which was dated by dendrochronology I commissioned to 1588 and appears to be an early version of a Fortune-style square-yard theatre with a north-south alignment (which guaranteed afternoon sun on the west side on open-air theatre days). Plays seem to have been performed indoors in the Banqueting Hall, then my bedroom, or outdoors in the Elizabethan courtyard (now under the rose-garden). The actors' "tiring-room" (attiring-room) below the Banqueting Hall, where the actors prepared themselves behind the open-air stage, was my study. The "rehearsal theatre" that the Tudor rooms and grounds of Otley Hall became during these visits was as inspiring to me as Lady Gregory's Abbey Theatre and Coole Park evidently were to Yeats.

I recall good discussions with Giles Block and Tim Carroll, Masters of Verse of *Julius Caesar* and *The Tempest* respectively, when, sitting in the Literary Room at Otley Hall, we focused on what the verse is doing in verse dramas and how to treat the verse in Shakespeare's plays. We agreed that Shakespeare tried to hear – and catch – the human voice. The iambic pentameter is the basic unit of verse drama. To this day people tend to speak in iambic pentameters in everyday life. Although Shakespeare varies the iambic pentameter, adding half a foot with a feminine ending, for example, and including irregularities that enable him to catch the struggle of thinking while it is happening to create a natural effect in which the structures, philosophy and imagery heighten the language, the discipline of the iambic pentameter is always there in the blank verse. It is a mistake to free it too often, to break a pentameter in half with a central pause or to stress an unstressed word so that a line sounds like a 4-stress line. Nevertheless, the pentameter must be varied so that it does not become monotonous. The aim of the Master of Verse or director is to allow the characters to communicate naturally through it while preserving the beauty and on occasion rhetoric of the language.

Essentially the iambic pentameter is a medium for sincerity. People fully express their feelings in verse and conceal them in prose. Verse is perfectly suited to an age in which characters tell us the truth about themselves, whereas prose is more suited to characters who lie to us about themselves and each other, as did the characters of the mannered Restoration sexual comedies.

Giles Block was fond of quoting the 18th-century Goldsmith's *The Citizen of the World; or, Letters from a Chinese Philosopher, Residing in London, to his Friends in the East* (1762): "We speak to conceal rather than reveal our feelings." In other words, the mind of prose censors the heart. In my four verse plays I have revived the soliloquy, in which characters tell the truth and reveal their feelings. In my verse plays I want to get behind the social façade to the inner thoughts. I am therefore a devotee of the iambic pentameter which conveys sincerity.

I am using verse to revive the timeless, unnaturalistic bare-stage setting of Sophocles and Shakespeare and to paint the scenery in words that suggest the context of the situation as well as react to it. Speech should combine the naturalness of the iambic pentameter with heightened language and imagery that can accommodate switches into soliloquy. Speech has various modes. It is partly transactional – it is designed to achieve a particular goal such as to sell someone something or wheedle something out of someone or persuade someone of the rightness of a particular idea or course of action – but it is also partly responsive: it responds to people and their situation. A manipulative character will use speech transactionally part of the time and may let us know in soliloquy what his real feelings are; a sincere speaker, on the other hand, may express emotion through verse. Speech can also be partly (on occasion) descriptive as it dwells on verbal scenery through an image.

Verse can therefore be more mannered than the grunts and inarticulate "ums" and "ers" of hesitant contemporary speech, and yet still be natural, as the Elizabethans (notably Marlowe) discovered. In the best verse drama, the rhetoric of verse carries the meaning along through image and gracefully poised pentameter while seeming natural to the audience.

The structure of *The Rise of Oliver Cromwell* needs some comment, for it is more fluid and more panoramic than *Ovid Banished*. The scenes are shorter and flow into each other more rapidly, as if influenced by cinematic techniques. The reason for this is the dynamic view of action held by Universalism. Universalism sees a perpetual present, a process, and a rapid unfolding of events, and the many scenes within each act are a consequence of this Universalist vision. As I have written elsewhere, the Universalist view of a work of art is idiosyncratic (ie peculiar to itself), like the Romantic or Classical view of a work of art.

All four plays are in fact Universalist plays. They deal with the universal theme of the manipulation of power and the shortcomings of world government, which at its best is a desirable utopian end if approached with the right state of mind – or heart. Augustus and Cromwell both lack this right state of mind – hence the shortcomings of their governments. As I have written elsewhere, Universalism combines the Romantic and the Classical – social, rational debate with a dynamic sense of growth – and a Universalist structure is ideal for showing Ovid and Charles I enmeshed in a process that is both ever-changing and yet constantly limiting.

The historical play is more difficult to write and more demanding on the dramatic poet than is a verse translation, in which the characters and plot are given to the translator who can as a result concentrate totally on his use of language without worrying about characterization, plot or structure. (In his translations of Sophocles, Euripides and Seneca, Ted Hughes was able to take the characters, plot and structure as already given. Ted Hughes, also a translator of excerpts of Ovid's *Metamorphoses*, wrote me a number of letters and cards, and had he lived he would have been extremely interested in *Ovid Banished*, which I told him I was writing.) The historical play lends itself to foregoing natural scenery more than the contemporary play, as T. S. Eliot discovered. The verse of *The Confidential Clerk* and *The Elder Statesman* sits awkwardly beside the realistic settings in which they were produced: the 1950s drawing-rooms with curtains. It was a mistake for him to move away from the Sophoclean-Shakespearean bare stage of *Murder in the Cathedral*.

Two other verse dramatists in the present movement that has revived verse drama have written historical plays: Peter Oswald, dramatist of *Augustine's Oak*, and Tony Harrison, whose play on Cromwell approves of Cromwell and his changes, and is written from the other side of the fence. So far as I am aware, Prince Tudor is the only contemporary-set (as opposed to historical or translated) unnaturalistic verse play. *Ovid Banished* and *The Rise of Oliver Cromwell* offer a new historical verse drama for our time. The challenge now is to write unnaturalistic contemporary plays in verse, as did Shakespeare's contemporaries.

For years I have mused over verse plays on Alexander the Great, Suez, J. F. Kennedy and the 1984 British miners' strike. Perhaps one day I will get round to these. If any theatre company is receptive and would like to commission one of them, please get in touch. It will be helping to keep the revival of verse drama going in our time.

17 January, 2 February, 20 March, 6 April 2006

THE WARLORDS

From D-Day to Berlin

A Verse Drama in Two Parts

DRAMATIS PERSONAE

CHARACTERS IN ORDER OF APPEARANCE

A   Gen. Dwight D. Eisenhower, Supreme Commander of the Allied Expeditionary Force

B   Gen. Sir Bernard Montgomery, Commander-in-Chief, British Twenty-First Army Group

B   King George VI

B   Winston Churchill, British Prime Minister and Minister of Defence

SA   Field Marshal Smuts, South African Prime Minister

B   Field Marshal Sir Alan Brooke, Chief of the Imperial General Staff, War Office, and Chairman of the Chiefs of Staff Committee.

A   Lt-Gen. Omar N. Bradley, Commanding General, US Twelfth Army Group

A   Lt-Gen. George S. Patton, Commanding General, US Third Army

B   Major Kit Dawnay, Military Assistant to Montgomery

B   Corporal, batman to Montgomery

B   Paul, deputy chef to Montgomery

B   Lt-Gen. Sir Miles Dempsey, General Officer Commanding-in-Chief, British Second Army

C   Lt-Gen. H. D. G. Crerar, General Officer Commanding-in-Chief, First Canadian Army

B   Group Captain J. M. Stagg, RAF, Eisenhower's meteorologist

B   Air Chief Marshal, Sir Arthur Tedder, Deputy Supreme Commander AEF

I   Kay Summersby, Eisenhower's driver and mistress

B   Admiral Sir Bertram Ramsay, Naval Commander-in-Chief, AEF

B   Air Chief Marshal Sir Trafford Leigh-Mallory, Air Commander-in-Chief, AEF

B   Rear Admiral George Creasy, Ramsay's Chief of Staff

B   D-Day soldier

A   Lt-Gen. Walter Bedell Smith, Chief of Staff to Supreme Commander, AEF

A   Lt-Commander Harry Butcher, Eisenhower's Naval Aide

G   Field Marshal Erwin Rommel, Commander of Army Group B

G   Lt-Gen. Hans Speidel, Rommel's Chief of Staff

G   Lucy Rommel, Rommel's wife

FDBe   Chorus of the Occupied

G   Adolf Hitler, Supreme Commander of the Armed Forces and Commander-in-Chief of the Army

G   Martin Bormann, Chief of Nazi Party Chancellery

B   Capt. Johnny Henderson, Montgomery's Aide-de-Camp

B   Howard Marshall, BBC representative

G   Grand Admiral Karl Dönitz, Commander-in-Chief of the Naval High Command (OKM), later President of the Reich (Hitler's successor)

G   *Reichsmarschall* Hermann Göring, Commander-in-Chief, Air High Command (OKL)

G   Gen. Burgdorf, Hitler's chief adjutant

B	Capt. John Poston, Montgomery's Aide-de-Camp
F	Gen. Charles de Gaulle, leader of the Free French
F	French aide
B	Chorus of Londoners
A	*John Eisenhower, Eisenhower's son
G	Gen. Alfred Jodl, Chief of the Operations Staff (OKW)
G	Gen. Rudolf Schmundt, Hitler's ADC
G	Stenographer
G	Field Marshal W. Keitel, Chief, Armed Forces High Command (OKW)
G	Field Marshal Gerd von Rundstedt, Commander-in-Chief West (OKW) from 4.9.44
B	Air Marshal Sir Arthur Coningham, Air Marshal Commanding RAF Second Tactical Air Force
B	John (Jock) Colville, formerly one of Churchill's private secretaries, a fighter pilot
G	Chorus of Auschwitz prisoners
G	Col. Heinrich Borgmann, one of Hitler's adjutants
B	Air Chief Marshal Sir Arthur Harris, Air Officer Commanding-in-Chief, RAF Bomber Command
B	Lt-Gen. Frederick Browning, Commander of First Allied Airborne Army (whose daughter later married Montgomery's son)
G	Col. Count Claus von Stauffenberg, Chief of Staff to Commander of the Replacement Army, conspirator
G	Major John von Freyend, Keitel's adjutant
G	*Col. Heinz Brandt, conspirator
G	Gen. Erich Fellgiebel, conspirator
G	Dr. Joseph Goebbels, Minister of Propaganda, Gauleiter of Berlin
G	Albert Speer, Reich Minister of Arms and Munitions
G	*Walter Funk, Economics Minister
G	Major Otto Remer, Commander of the Guard Battalion *Grossdeutschland*
G	Gen. F. Olbricht, deputy to Col-Gen. Fromm
G	Lt Werner von Haeften, Stauffenberg's Aide-de-Camp, conspirator
G	Col.-Gen. F. Fromm, Commander-in-Chief of the Home Army
G	*Col. Mertz von Quirnheim, Olbricht's Chief of Staff, conspirator
G	Col.-Gen. Ludwig Beck, Head of State designate after the *coup* of July 20.
G	*Lt Ewald Heinrich Kleist, conspirator
G	Lt-Gen. Erich Hoepner, conspirator
G	Hauptmann Bartram, Fromm's adjutant
G	*Lt-Col. Gehrke
G	Sergeant
G	Firing-squad, including soldier
B	Bill Williams, Head of Intelligence to Montgomery, ex-Oxford history don
G	Heinrich Himmler, SS *Reichsführer*, Chief of the Gestapo, Chief of Police, Minister of the

Interior, Commander of the Reserve Army, Commander of Army Group Vistula

G   Ernst Kaltenbrunner, Head of SS *Reich* Security, Head Office (RSHA)

G   Dr. Erwin Giesing, one of Hitler's physicians

G   *Franz von Sonnleithner, Ribbentrop's Foreign Ministry liaison official with Hitler and Hitler's interceptor of foreign messages at Rastenburg

G   Dr Roland Freisler, chief judge, the People's Court

G   Field Marshal von Witzleben, conspirator

G   Count Yorck von Wartenburg, conspirator

G   *Maj-Gen. Helmuth Stieff, conspirator

G   *Gen. Paul von Hase, Commandant of Berlin, conspirator

G   *Lt-Col. Bernardis, conspirator

G   *Capt. Klausing, conspirator

G   *Lt. von Hagen, conspirator

G   Dr. Kurt Hanssen, Public Prosecutor

G   Cameraman

G   Hangman and Executioner

A   *Gen. Humphrey Gale, Chief of Administration, SHAEF

A   Gen. Allen, Chief of Staff, 12th US Army Group

B   James Gunn, artist

A   Lt-Gen. Courtney H. Hodges, Commanding General, US First Army

R   Marshal Josef Stalin, Secretary-General of the Communist Party of the Soviet Union and premier of the Soviet state, co-ordinator of First, Second and Third Belorussian and First Ukrainian Fronts

A   Maj. Chester Hansen, aide to Bradley

A   Maj.-Gen. Sir Francis de Guingand, Chief of Staff to Montgomery

B   Gen. Archibald Nye,Vice Chief of the Imperial General Staff, deputy to Brooke

B   *Gen. Freddy Morgan, Eisenhower's Deputy Chief of Staff, SHAEF

B   Maj-Gen. K. W. D. Strong, G-2 Division (Intelligence) SHAEF

B   Gen. John Whiteley, Chief of Operations, SHAEF

G   Gen. Günther Blumentritt, von Rundstedt's Chief of Staff

B   Maj.-Gen. R. E. Urquhart, Commander of First British Airborne Division

R   Marshal Georgi Konstantinovich Zhukov, Commander on the ground under Stalin of First, Second and Third Belorussian and First Ukrainian Fronts, and direct Commander of First Belorussian Front

R   Marshal Konstantine K. Rokossovsky, Commander of First Belorussian Front

R   Vyacheslav Mikhailovich Molotov, Soviet Foreign Minister

R   Gen. Antonov, Chief of Operations and first deputy Chief of the General Staff

R   Paulina Molotov, Molotov's wife and reputedly Stalin's mistress

A   Gen. George C. Marshall, Chief of Staff of the US Army

G   Gen. Ernst Maisel, chief law officer to Burgdorf

G   Manfred Rommel, Rommel's son

G	Field Marshal Walter Model, Commander-in-Chief West and Commander of Army Group B
B	Dai Rees, golfer
A	Brig-Gen. Everett Hughes, a friend of Eisenhower's
A	Gen. Kean, Chief of Staff to Hodges
A	Lt-Gen. William H. Simpson, Commanding General, US Ninth Army
G	Gen. Heinz Guderian, acting Chief of the General Staff of the Army
G	Count Helmuth J. von Moltke, conspirator, founder of the Kreisau Circle
G	*Father Alfred Delp, Jesuit, conspirator
G	*Col. Franz Sperr, conspirator
G	Eva Braun, Hitler's mistress and later wife
G	Ilse Braun, sister of Eva and Gretl Braun
G	Col.-Gen. (later Field Marshal) Ferdinand Schörner, Commander of Army Group Centre
G	Chorus of Berliners
R	Gen. Vassily Chuikov, Commander of Eighth Guards Army, First Belorussian Front
R	Gen. Malinin, Zhukov's Chief of Staff
G	SS Guard
G	Gen. Walther Wenck, Guderian's Chief of Staff
G	Major Bernd Baron Freytag von Loringhoven, Guderian's adjutant
G	Capt. Gerhard Boldt, Loringhoven's Aide-de-Camp
G	Gen. Fegelein, Chief of Waffen SS, Himmler's personal representative to Hitler, married to Gretl Braun, Eva Braun's sister
G	Chorus of Dresdeners
G	Lt-Gen. Helmuth Reymann, Military Commander of Berlin
G	Dr. Theodore Morell, one of Hitler's physicians
G	Magda Goebbels, Goebbels' wife
G	SS *Brigadeführer* (Brig-Gen) Heinz Lammerding, Himmler's Chief of Staff
A	Lt Tex Lee, Eisenhower's office executive
G	Col.-Gen. Gotthard Heinrici, Commander of Army Group Vistula after Himmler
G	Gen. Theodore Busse, Commander Ninth Army
G	Col. Refior, Reymann's Chief of Staff
A	Aide to Gen. Marshall
R	Gen. S. M. Shtemenko, Chief of Operations
R	Lavrenti Beria, Head of the NKVD (state security)
R	*Georgi Malenkov, Secretary of the Central Committee of the Communist Party
R	*Anastas Mikoyan, Minister of Trade and Industry
R	*Marshal Nikolai Bulganin, representative of the Supreme Command for Soviet fronts
R	*Lazar Kagonovich, Transport Minister
R	*Nikolai Voznesensky, in charge of the economy
R	Marshal Ivan Stepanovich Koniev, Commander of First Ukrainian Front
G	Gen. Hans Krebs, Chief of the General Staff of the Army after Guderian

G	Maj-Gen Walter Buhle, organiser of the Reserve Army
R	Vassiliev Kokorin, Russian air force officer, nephew of Molotov
G	Pastor Dietrich Bonhoeffer, conspirator
G	Ex-prisoner
G	SSman
G	Guard
A	Maj-Gen. Alexander Bolling, in charge of 84th Division
G	Staff 1 and 2, Ministry of Propaganda
G	Rudolf Semmler, assistant to Goebbels
G	Joachim von Ribbentrop, German Foreign Minister
G	Col. Eismann, Heinrici's Chief of Operations
R	Russian soldier
R	Lt-Gen. N. K. Popiel, Chief of Staff, First Guards Tank Army
G	Traudl Junge, Hitler's secretary
G	Gerda Christian, Hitler's secretary, later chief secretary
G	Johanna Wolf, Hitler's secretary
G	Christa Schröder, Hitler's secretary
G	Chorus of Berliners
B	Major Peter Earle, Liaison Officer, formerly Military Secretary to the Vice Chief of Imperial General Staff
B	Dr. Robert Hunter, Montgomery's physician
G	Klaus Bonhoeffer, Dietrich Bonhoeffer's brother-in-law, conspirator
G	*Rüdiger Schleicher, also Dietrich Bonhoeffer's brother-in-law, conspirator
G	Albrecht Haushofer, poet, conspirator
G	*Herbert Kosney, conspirator
G	12 other prisoners, and SS Guards
S	Count Folke Bernadotte, Vice-Chairman of Swedish Red Cross and nephew of King Gustav V
G	Lt-Gen. Helmuth Weidling, Commander of 56th Panzer Corps, later Commandant of Berlin Defence Region
G	Capt. Kafurke, Weidling's Intelligence Officer
G	Gen. Hasso von Manteuffel, Commander of Third Panzer Army
G	Heinz Lorenz, Hitler's press officer
G	Walter Wagner, municipal councillor, registrar of marriages
G	*Constanze Manziarly, Hitler's vegetarian dietician
G	Major Willi Johannmeier, soldier
G	Arter Axmann, Head of the Hitler Youth
B	Ernie, a British private
G	Belsen men and women
G	Lt-Col. Weiss, Burgdorf's adjutant
G	Professor Haase, one of Hitler's physicians

G	Hans Bauer, Hitler's personal pilot
G	Major-Gen. Wilhelm Mohnke, Commander of Waffen SS units near Chancellery
G	Major Otto Günsche, Hitler's SS adjutant and bodyguard
G	*Heinz Linge, Hitler's valet
R	Lt.-Gen V. A. Glazunov, Commander of 4th corps
G	Col. Theodor von Dufving, Weidling's Chief of Staff
G	Heidi Goebbels, Goebbels' daughter
G	Sgt. Misch, SS guard
R	Lt-Col. Matusov, staff officer to Chuikov
R	Lt Kiselyov, company commander
R	Private Vladimir Abyzov, soldier in Kiselyov's unit
G	Heinersdorf, Senior Executive Officer, Ministry of Propaganda
G	Gen.-Admiral von Friedeburg, Commander-in-Chief of the German Fleet
G	Gen. Kinzel, Chief of Staff, German Army North
G	Rear Admiral Wagner, Flag Officer to the Admiral of the Fleet
G	Major Friedl, Gestapo
C	Lt-Col Trumbell Warren, Montgomery's Personal Assistant
B	Col. Joe Ewart, Montgomery's German-speaking Intelligence Officer
G	*Col. Pollok, holder of German codes
B	Chorus of Londoners
F	*Gen. de Lattre de Tassigny, commander of First French Army
B	*Gen. Sir Harold Alexander, Commander-in-Chief of all Allied Forces in Italy
B	*Clement Attlee, British Prime Minister from July 1945
B	*Anthony Eden, British Foreign Secretary
B	Capt. Pim, in charge of Churchill's Map Room
A	President Harry Truman, US President after Roosevelt
A	Aide to Truman
A	Averell Harriman, US Ambassador to Moscow

*Non-speaking part.

A	American
Be	Belgian
B	British
C	Candian
D	Dutch
F	French
G	German
I	Irish
R	Russian
SA	South African
S	Swedish

MAIN CAST

An example of how the main speaking parts can be spread between a cast of 33 (based on what is approximately feasible rather than what is desirable in terms of resemblance).

Eisenhower + Bernadotte
Montgomery + Weidling
Churchill + Hunter
Brooke + Hansen + Loringhoven + Wagner
Bradley + firing-squad + Chorus + Lammerding + Fegelein + Pim
Patton + Remer + Gen. Marshall + Guderian + Haase + Matusov
Dawnay + Browning + Olbricht + Model + Buhle + Glazunov
Henderson + Ramsay + Coningham + Reymann + Kokorin
Chef + Speidel + Fromm + de Guingand + Heinrici + Dufving
Dempsey + Keitel + Kaltenbrunner + Lee + Refior + Lorenz + Beria
Stagg + Howard Marshall + Borgmann + Hanssen + Wenck + Dietrich
    Bonhoeffer + Kiselyov
Tedder + Rundstedt + Wartenburg + Strong + Himmler
Kay Summersby + Eva Braun + Jean Gordon + Junge
Leigh-Mallory + Colville + Dr. Morell + Urquhart + Hughes + Koniev +
    Weiss + Sokolovsky
Rommel + Stalin + Friedeburg
Bedell Smith + Dönitz + Speer + Allen + Busse + Earle
Butcher + Jodl + Haeften + Freisler + Maisel + Mohnke
D-Day soldier + aide to de Gaulle + stenographer + hangman + Dai Rees
    + Simpson + Krebs
Bormann + Rokossovsky + Crerar
Williams + Witzleben + Moltke + Bolling + Boldt
Göring + Dr. Giesing + Malinin + Whiteley + Manteuffel + Harriman
Hitler + Truman
Burgdorf + Bomber Harris + Blumentritt + Zhukov
George VI + Poston + Manfred Rommel + Nye + Hodges + Antonov + Semmler + Popiel +
    Günsche
De Gaulle + Stauffenberg + Chuikov + Schörner + Goebbels
Aide + Sergeant + Cameraman + Kean + SS Guard + Shtemenko
Lucy Rommel + Magda Goebbels + Paula + Ilse + Chorus + Marlene
    Dietrich + Christian
6 Chorus of the Occupied/Londoners/Auschwitz prisoners/Berliners/
    Dresdeners + Schröder + Wolf + Belsen men and women + SS guards
    + firing-squad + Heidi + Misch + Kinzel + Freyend + Friedl + Manfred

+ Klaus Bonhoeffer + Schleicher + Haushofer + Kosney + any other non-speaking parts.

Total 27 cast + 6 chorus, etc. = 33. This can be reduced to 30; it is better if it is increased.

SCENES

*Asterisked blocks are candidates for excision if the two
Parts are put on as one play. See Appendix for abridged version.

Recommended intervals: Part One, at the end of Scene 4, on page 112;
Part Two, at the end of the Belsen scene, on page 275.

PREFACE TO THE WARLORDS, PARTS 1 AND 2

The Warlords puts the last year of the war on stage. Its two Parts are therefore necessarily long and rival the length of Goethe's *Faust,* Parts One and Two.

At one level *The Warlords* has been written as a celebration of the 50th anniversary of VE Day (8 May 1995) and, besides creating imaginatively realised, living, solid characters who move in and out of known events I have wanted to leave the audience with a clear, historically accurate – and verifiable – picture of the main issues. The Second World War dominated my childhood; I lived in the path of the air raids and the flying bombs. The men in the assault craft were heroes for my generation, and my awe of their bravery in leaping into water under fire on D-Day with men dying all round them has, if anything, increased over the years. There is still great interest in what happened. After fifty years an event passes into history and people who were once living take on the force of historical characters and appear to represent historical forces. I met both Churchill and Montgomery, and it is with reverence that I now present them in terms of the drives and forces which shaped our lives.

I have found the medium of verse liberating; I have been acutely aware that the sweep of my settings would be impossible in the medium of realistic prose drama. This revival of contemporary verse drama is essentially practical; it gets the job done better than prose could by escaping the constraints of realistic settings and by reviving monologues, soliloquies, asides. As Marlowe and Shakespeare found, and as Goethe also discovered in *Faust,* Parts One and Two, verse drama can range over battlefields and heaths and get inside the soul of characters.

The verse in *The Warlords* varies the strictness of iambic pentameters (⏑–) by including trochees (–⏑), anapaests (⏑⏑–) and dactyls (–⏑⏑) where feeling requires a loosening, and even tribrachs (⏑⏑⏑), bacchiuses (⏑––), cretics (–⏑–) and sometimes amphibrachs which reverse cretics (⏑–⏑). On rare occasions there may be 4-syllable feet such as paeons (–⏑⏑⏑ or ⏑⏑⏑–) or Aeolic choriambs (–⏑⏑–).

A verse dramatist writing today follows in the footsteps of Marlowe, who developed blank verse (which Surrey had imported from Italy and which Sackville and Norton first used dramatically in *Gorboduc* in 1561), and Shakespeare, and their historical plays *Tamburlaine the Great* and *Henry the Fourth* (both in two parts); Webster, whose *The White Devil* draws on the history of Renaissance Italy, and Dryden's *All for Love;* and more recently Eliot's *Murder in the Cathedral* and Fry's *The Lady's not for Burning.*

Every historical dramatist has a source. Marlowe used an English version by P.F. of the German *Historia von D. Iohan Fausten* of 1587; Shakespeare North's Plutarch and Holinshed's *Chronicles;* Webster a German newsletter written from the Fugger banking house in Augsburg; and Dryden Plutarch's *Life of Antony* as well as Appian's *Civil Wars* and Dio's *Roman History.* I have assembled a library on the Second World War of a couple of hundred books. The British accounts of the last year of the war (such as Nigel Hamilton's) support Montgomery, the American accounts (such as Stephen Ambrose's) Eisenhower. I have tried to be even-handed, and to show both sides. I have gone to some pains (notably visiting Normandy, Berlin, Warsaw, Auschwitz and Munich, and many other such places on the Continent) to achieve historical accuracy and veracity. I went with the view, recently confirmed by the eye-witness Traudl Junge (whose book *Until the Final Hour* came out in 2002 shortly before she died), that Hitler dictated his will to her *before* his wedding to Eva Braun rather than after (as some books assert). Generally speaking, the dialogue reflects established events, while the soliloquies provide imaginative interpretation based on documentation.

My interpretation of the characters has been based on documentary evidence. To focus on some of this, a number of books on the occult influences on Nazism show that Hitler must be seen in relation to the Thule Society and the occult practices of Dietrich Eckart, which included forays into black magic; and that there was at least a suppressed Satanism in the Nazi drive against Jehovah, the Jewish god. Several books show that after the bomb plot Hitler declined into a shuffling, trembling human wreck who was but a shadow of his former dictatorial self. His fascination with the spear of Longinus has been documented in Trevor Ravenscroft's *The Spear of Destiny* and there are several books on the Nazis and the occult, the most sober and academic of which is Nicholas Goodrick-Clarke's *The Occult Roots of Nazism,* the most interesting Nigel Pennick's *Hitler's Secret Sciences.* The first was Pauwels and Bergier's *The Morning of the Magicians,* and the most comprehensive is Francis King's *Satan and Swastika: The Occult and the Nazi Party.* All these books look back to Hermann Rauschning's *Hitler Speaks* (1939) in which the Nazi Governor of Danzig describes his conversations with Hitler between 1932 and 1934, and H.G. Baynes's *Germany Possessed* (1941). Lawyers wanting convictions and executions at the Nuremberg trials suppressed some of the occult material as it might have given the defendants cause to plead diminished responsibility.

That Hitler was shown the *Protocols of the Elders of Zion,* which he mentioned as a Jewish work in *Mein Kampf,* by Rosenberg, to whom Eckart introduced him around 1920, is documented in many books, for example Lucy S. Dawidowicz's *The War Against the Jews, 1933-45.* The Final Solution to kill the Jews was decided on at the Wannsee Conference of January 1942, chaired by Heydrich, but it had its roots in the early 1920s and is heralded in *Mein Kampf.* (For the eschatalogical connotations in the word "Final", which led Malraux to speak of "le retour de Satan", see Dawidowicz, p18.) How Hitler saw the Jews can be found in a number of books, including the chapter "Jehovah as Satan" in Dusty Sklar's *The Nazis and the Occult*. The Allies' knowledge of events in Auschwitz from May 1941, and certainly in March and June 1944, is documented in Martin Gilbert's *Auschwitz and the Allies*.

Montgomery was at heart a very religious man. His father was a clergyman, he always went to church when he could, he wrote of "the Lord mighty in battle" and, according to his deputy chef (who travelled with him from Broomfield House to Luneburg Heath and with whom I have had a long discussion) he always went to bed at 9 p.m. to pray in his caravan. It was generally known in "A" Mess that Montgomery could not be disturbed on any account after 9 p.m. because he was in prayer, obtaining God's Providential guidance for the huge decisions he faced. For some years he lived simply in a caravan close to Nature, both on North-African sand and European grass, and he did not smoke or drink, and thus represented the puritanical tradition.

That the Jewish Paulina Molotov, the Soviet Foreign Minister's wife, became Stalin's mistress after his wife died is suggested in Larisa Vasilyeva's *Kremlin Wives*. Files in the KGB archives show that Niels Bohr gave Stalin nuclear secrets via Beria's agents Vasilevsky and Terletsky, as reported in *The Sunday Times* of 26th June 1994.

Eisenhower's relationship with the Irish driver Kay Summersby is documented in her book (written under her later name, Kay Summersby Morgan), *Past Forgetting: My Love Affair with Dwight D. Eisenhower*. It is not known if she told the whole truth; but if she did then Eisenhower was sexually impotent during the whole war. I have chosen not to believe this entirely.

The conflict between the Christian Montgomery, the occultist Hitler and the materialist Stalin goes deeper than social disquiet and raises metaphysical considerations of good and evil. After fifty years the time has come to present Hitler's racism in its true context, de-demonising Hitler but not hiding his involvement with the occult, without which the Holocaust cannot be understood. (Indeed, failure to address Hitler's occult beliefs about Jehovah is the main reason why the Holocaust has so far not been understood.) Philosophers who study the universe seek to reconcile the opposites of war and peace within the total scheme, as did Tolstoy, and Montgomery's belief in a Providential power for good that orders events in a fallen world offers such a reconciliation.

The Warlords honours the men who delivered us from evil and enslavement by a totalitarian dictatorship and shaped the world we know. The last year of the war threw up so many issues that have dominated the last fifty years: the Russian domination of Eastern Europe; the atomic bomb; the rise of American world power; the decline of British world power, which can be dated back to the demotion of Montgomery on 1st September 1944; the dream of a united Europe; the Final Solution of the Jewish problem which saw five million Jews killed; and the need for a world government. Against a background of conflicting ideologies, philosophies and historical forces, *The Warlords* explores the warlords' leadership, and, I hope, present an eternal image of the relationship between power and good.

The Warlords can be produced as two separate plays or as one play with excisions (see Appendix). Asterisked blocks are candidates for excision.

13 February 1995; revised 2 February 2006

LAY-OUT OF THE
FÜHRER BUNKER, BERLIN

(Numbers indicate areas referred to in *The Warlords*)

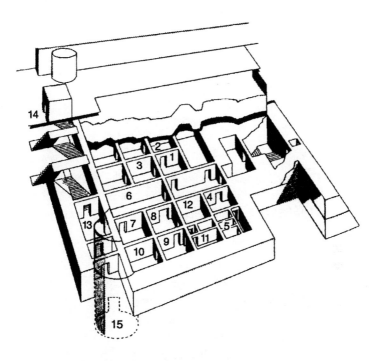

1. Telephone switchboard
2. Dr. Morell's room
3. Orderly officers' social room
4. Blondi's room (Hitler's dog)
5. Toilets
6. Reception room or ante-room in corridor
7. Conference room
8. Refreshment room or ante-room by Hitler's office
9. Hitler's office or study/living room with picture of Frederick the Great
10. Hitler's bedroom
11. Hitler's and Eva's bathroom
12. Eva's bedroom
13. Emergency exit to
14. Garden exit, and
15. Dome-shaped tower

THE WARLORDS

PART ONE

SCENE 1.

D-DAY

(*15 May 1944. St. Paul's School, lecture theatre.* EISENHOWER, MONTGOMERY, KING GEORGE VI, CHURCHILL, SMUTS and BRITISH CHIEFS OF STAFF *sit on chairs in the first row.* GENERALS *and their* STAFF *sit on wooden benches behind. Several hundred are present. Blackboard, map.*)

Eisenhower.   Today we present the plan for Operation
Overlord so that every commander has
A last chance to understand the strategy.
It is vital we are honest. It is the duty
Of anyone who sees a flaw to say so.
I now invite General Montgomery,
Allied Land Forces Commander, to come forward.

(MONTGOMERY *rises in battledress. He speaks in a tone of
quiet emphasis, addressing the audience. As he starts there
is a hammering on the door and* PATTON *swaggers in and sits
down. Montgomery looks round angrily.*)

Montgomery.   General Eisenhower has charged me with the
Preparation and conduct of the land battle.
There are four armies under my control.
First American, Second British: assault.
Third American, First Canadian: follow-up.
The enemy. Last February, Rommel took command
From Holland to the Loire. It is now clear
That his intention is to deny any penetration.
Overlord is to be defeated on the beaches.

To this end he has thickened his coastal crust,
Increased his infantry, and redistributed
His armoured reserve. Fortress Europe has
Become more and more formidable. There are
Sixty German divisions stationed in France,
Of which ten are *élite* Panzer divisions,
And four of these are in the Normandy area,
(*Pointing with pointer*) At Caen, Lisieux, Rennes and
    Tours. Rommel
Is an energetic and determined commander,
He has made a world of difference since he took over.
He will try to force us off the beaches
And secure Caen, Bayeux and Carentan.
The Allies *must* seize and hold fast these three
Nodal points, in which case Rommel will revert
To his Alamein tactics of counter-attacks.
Now there are several hundred of you here,
And I want to give you all a clear idea
Of the problem we face, and the solution.

(*Later.*)

Montgomery.   So, to sum up, the plan is straight forward
And simple. We hold the enemy at Caen,
Like a boxer holding off his opponent
With his left fist, and then with our right flank
We deliver a terrific surprise blow
From the peninsula around Cherbourg, through Rennes,
To Paris and the Seine, like a boxer
Swinging with his right and hitting his opponent
In his solar plexus, and send him reeling against
The ropes – the river Seine. Is that completely clear?
We're *not* knocking him out at Caen with our left,
We're holding him off with the British and Canadians.
The knock-out comes with our right, the Americans.
I remind you, these phase lines show where we expect
To reach in the ninety days after D-Day.
Now morale is very important. The soldiers
Must go in seeing red. We must get them
Completely on their toes, with absolute
Faith in the plan, infectious optimism

And offensive eagerness. Nothing must stop them.
If we send them into battle in this way
Then we shall succeed, and we'll show Hitler
Who is really Overlord of Europe.

(Later. Audience standing and chatting. The KING, CHURCHILL *and* BROOKE *talk.)*

Churchill.   It was like Henry the Fifth before Agincourt:
              Confident, optimistic, but grave.

Brooke.   He
              Has pressed me for *Overlord* since forty-two.

Churchill.   He returned to Britain a hero, the conqueror of Rommel.
              There's been nothing like the popular acclaim
              Since Wellington returned from Waterloo.
              When he began going round the country
              Speaking to thirty thousand men in a day,
              Wearing the beret of a tank soldier
              And being cheered for his charisma, I
              Thought he really might be after my job.

King.   I thought he was after mine.

Eisenhower.   I hope not mine.

Churchill.   Monty would make a good Prime Minister.
              A Prime Minister must be popular,
              He must be a showman who can represent
              All things to all people, secure support,
              Speak simply on many levels at once,
              Be understood in factory and office alike,
              Be a reconciler who holds together
              Conflicting views, coalitions of opinion.
              He must appear honest, he must inspire,
              He must speak boldly and be identified
              With a clear view, and be known for a plan,
              Lead from a position well understood
              And promise a better tomorrow, over the hill,
              For a leader is lost when he stops looking ahead.
              A Prime Minister is a General in a beret

Who takes the troops with him by oratory
And the dash he cuts in his battledress.

(*Laughter.*)

A leader is how his people see him.
He is their expectations in terms of which
They may be disappointed. He must strive
To be their dream, even though he is quite other,
And the man within privately scoffs at what
They hang on him, the image they want him to be.
A leader is an actor who plays for applause.

(*Laughter.* EISENHOWER *moves away.*)

Bradley.   A brilliant presentation, clear and convincing.

Patton.   You were very confident, you radiated confidence.

Eisenhower   (*joining them*). Without notes, you were totally in charge,
                  A very convincing estimate of the situation.

Montgomery.   Ike, you handled it well. You said little
                  But what you said was on a high level.

Bradley.   You inspired your King to speak. That was unexpected.

Montgomery.   What he said was just right, short but just right.

Patton.   Smuts was pessimistic about German ruthlessness,
                  But Churchill made a stirring speech at the end.

Montgomery.   He was more full of life than the last occasion.

Eisenhower.   He looked quite dejected then, and when he spoke
                  He said "I am *now* hardening to the enterprise."
                  That shocked me, I realised he had not
                  Believed that *Overlord* would succeed till then.

Montgomery.   He does now. He has faith in the plan now.

(17 May. Broomfield House study, Montgomery's TAC HQ. MONTGOMERY and DAWNAY.)

Dawnay.

A letter from Churchill's military assistant,
General Ismay. Churchill was "much concerned"
By some of the statements made at Monday's
Conference, for example, two thousand clerks
Are to be taken to keep records, and at
D plus twenty there will be one vehicle
To every 4.84 men. Ismay writes:
"The Prime Minister would like to have a discussion
With you and your staff on the whole question
Of the British tail", before dinner on Friday.

Montgomery.

It's interference. But I'll have to see him.

(19 May. Broomfield House study.)

Montgomery.

I understand, sir, that you want to discuss
With my staff the proportion of soldiers to vehicles
Landing on the beaches in the first flights.
I cannot allow you to do so. I took
An unsound operation of war as I
Told you in Marrakesh on New Year's Day,
With the organisation of command and frontage wrong,
And recast it into a clear plan that
Everyone can have faith and confidence in.
Nothing has been left to chance or improvisation.
The staff have done a terrific job preparing
The invasion. After months of meticulous planning
The whole of southern England is an army depot.
There are queues of tanks and lorries and guns
All waiting to be shipped, all checked by SHAEF.
The work is now almost completed. We
Have just enough vehicles, the right number.
All over England troops are moving towards
The assembly areas, prior to embarkation.
To make a change now would cause tremendous
Disruption, and shake their confidence in the plan.
In the last two years I have won battles
At Alamein, Tripoli, Medenine,
Mareth, Wadi Akarit, Sicily,

	And Southern Italy. The invasion of Normandy
	Has the confidence of the men. Besides commanding
	A British army I will command a Canadian
	And two American armies. Do you want to come
	Between a battlefield General and his men, his staff?
	I could never allow it, never. If you think
	That is wrong, you have lost confidence in me.
	And you must find someone else to lead the expedition.
Churchill.	Get the troops ashore, that's the main thing to me.
	I will make it an issue of confidence if you don't
	Allow me, as Prime Minister, to have my say.
	I want the invasion to succeed, I must
	Be sure we have made the right preparations.
Montgomery.	You cannot talk to my staff. At this stage
	For you to address the Twenty-first Army Group
	Would be unwarranted interference.
	I cannot allow you to do so. My staff
	Advise me and I give the final decision.
	They then do what I tell them.

(CHURCHILL *breaks down and weeps.* MONTGOMERY *offers Churchill his handkerchief.*)

Churchill.   I'm sorry, Monty.
I'm tired and overstrained, I don't mean
To interfere.

Montgomery.   Let's go next door, where I
Will present my staff.

(GENERALS, BRIGADIERS *and* COLONELS *are drawn up in a line.*)

Churchill.   I'm not allowed to talk
To you gentlemen.

(*Later.* CHURCHILL *is leaving.* MONTGOMERY *and* HENDERSON.)

Churchill.   I've signed your Ten Chapters book. Read it out.

Henderson   (*reading*). "Chapter Five. On the verge of the greatest
Adventure....I record my confidence
That all will be well and the organisations
And equipment of the army will be worthy
Of the valour of the soldier and the genius
Of their chief, Winston S. Churchill."

(*22 May. Broomfield House caravan.* MONTGOMERY *and* KING *walking outside.* CORPORAL, CHEF.)

Montgomery.   We only use the House during the day
For meetings and formal dinners. Only the chef
Sleeps in, the rest of us sleep in tents in the field
Round my three caravans which are TAC HQ,
And we eat in the dining marquee. We have
To toughen the minds of the men, and their physique,
Get them used to living in the battlefield.
I'm afraid there are no exceptions. Tonight,
Sir, you will sleep in my caravan, in there.
My batman will bring you water. Corporal
Fetch hot water from the kitchen.

Corporal.   Sir. Sir, the new chef
Would like a word. (*Exit.*)

Montgomery.   Yes, Paul.

Chef.   I'm standing in
For Sergeant Wright. Is tonight's menu to be
Different? I mean, is rationing suspended?

Montgomery.   No, we have strict food rationing, this is
The Army, not Windsor where game, fresh fruit,
Vegetables, rabbits, I have heard, are brought
By loyal subjects for your family, sir.
Here like any commoner the King makes do.
There can be no extra rations because
The King has come.

Chef   (*embarrassed*).   Very good, sir. (*Exit.*)

Montgomery.	We eat
	At half past six in the House. My bedtime's nine.
King.	Can I bath?
Montgomery.	No, sir. The water supply was hit
	In the Portsmouth bombing raids, it's been off since
	We moved here. We receive water from a wagon
	That calls, or take jerry cans to an army
	Tanker. The men cannot take canvas baths,
	Nor we.
King.	What are those trenches?
Montgomery.	Toilets, sir.
	As there is no water, we don't use the House.

(DAWNAY *appears.*)

I'll meet you by the cedar, on the lawn.

(THE KING *goes gingerly into the caravan as the* CORPORAL *arrives with water.* MONTGOMERY *turns away with* DAWNAY.)

Kit, I shall want to give the King my *Notes*
On High Command in War, and a photograph
Of myself. Can you get them ready? Wavell,
Auchinleck, Marshall, Mountbatten, Fraser,
Mackenzie-King and Smuts have had copies
And so should the King who, not long ago,
Was in favour of appeasing Hitler
And did not want Churchill to be PM.
It will be educative. You have heard me say,
I have three superiors – God, Churchill, Brooke
In that order – and to none other defer.

(*During the next week.* MONTGOMERY *speaking to troops. He addresses the audience.*)

Montgomery	(*beckoning*). Gather closer, you're too far away. That's better.
	Now all of you are soon going to be involved
	In D-Day, when we invade France

And deliver the enemy a terrific blow
From which he will not be able to recover.
Now I am travelling about and meeting all
The troops who will be going, and I say to you
We have spent several months perfecting our plan,
Everything is prepared, nothing is left to chance,
And I will only move when I know it's safe.
We have to fight, but I don't want to lose lives.
We have done everything we can on the organisation.
Now it's up to you, and you can do it.
I know you can do it, and I believe in you.
And you have seen me and met me, you've seen
I wear a beret, the same as you, and you
Can now believe in me. I've already
Beaten the Germans in seven battles,
I know how to beat Rommel yet again,
And with your help and the Lord Mighty in Battle
On our side, we will drive the Nazis out of France
And out of Germany and win the war.

(*1 June. Broomfield House dining-room.* MONTGOMERY *at dinner with his four army commanders:* DEMPSEY, CRERAR, BRADLEY, *who is shy and quiet, and* PATTON, *who is boastful. A convivial atmosphere.*)

Montgomery.   It's done, I've written it in my betting book.

Dempsey.   And I bet General Bradley five pounds that the war
With Germany will end by November the first.

Bradley.   You're on. I'm optimistic, but I'm not
That unrealistic.

Montgomery.   That's in my betting book.
And that's my target date to end the war
By reaching Berlin by November the first.
(*Rising.*) Commanders, thank you for flying down here
And attending our final conference before D-Day,
Our final look at the plans, and for staying on
For this last supper before the historic invasion.
It has been a very convivial occasion.
And though I only drink water or orange juice,

I want to toast you and the success of
Your four undertakings. To the success
Of *Overlord*.

Patton.   I suppose I should reply
As the oldest army commander present,
And previously Bradley's boss. If everything moves
As planned there will be nothing for me to do
As Bradley will be doing it. I would like to toast
The health of General Montgomery, and declare
Our satisfaction at serving under him.

(*The* FOUR COMMANDERS *rise and toast* MONTGOMERY.)

(*Aside*.) The lightning did not strike me for my lie.
I have a better impression of Monty
But Dempsey's a yes-man and Crerar doesn't impress.

Montgomery   (*aside*). Bradley is diffident and he abhors
The swaggering Patton, who is a sabre-rattler,
Ignorant of battle but good at thrusting.
Dempsey is imperturbable, but I have doubts
About Crerar as a battlefield leader.
(*Aloud*.) Here we are, leading the greatest invasion
In history, and I am reminded of
A scene in *Antony and Cleopatra*
Before Actium when Lepidus is carried out.

Patton.   That will be Brad, the quiet ones drink the most.

(*2 June. Broomfield House dining-room.* MONTGOMERY *dining with* EISENHOWER.)

Montgomery.   A Commander has to be many-sided.
He must assess a situation and
Make a clear plan and communicate it clearly
To all his subordinates. He must have great
Authority and inspire trust. He must make
Men eager to follow his commands. He must take
Account of ever-changing situations
And simplify the complexity so
It is comprehensible. A Commander

Is like an artist who reveals the One
Behind the surface many, in all its forms,
The unity behind multiplicity.
A Commander reveals the aim behind a war
At every twist and turn of a long campaign.
And the men sit in their camp and do not know
How definite the Commander has to be.

(*Silence.*)

Eisenhower.   Bushey Park is like an armed camp, canvas
Tents under every tree, GIs sitting
And all round a red wall, sentries at the gate.
Today I wrote my Order of the Day
At Southwick House. It begins: "Soldiers, Sailors
And Airmen of the Allied Expeditionary Force:
You are about to embark on the Great Crusade,
Toward which we have striven these many months,
The eyes of the world are upon you."

Montgomery   (*reading*).   "You will bring about
The destruction of the German war machine,
The elimination of Marxist tyranny
Over oppressed people of Europe, and
Security for ourselves in a free world."
It's very eloquent. You know, Ike, you're
Just the man for the job.

Eisenhower.   I support you
Firmly, Monty.

Montgomery   (*aside*).   I like him immensely.
He has a generous lovable character,
And I would trust him to the last gasp.
I do like him tremendously. He is
So very genuine and sincere.
(*Aloud.*)   Ike,
I'm having trouble with Churchill. Last night
Ismay rang, Churchill wishes to visit
The Portsmouth area this weekend. If he comes
He'll be a bore and may attract attention.

Why in hell doesn't he go and smoke his cigar
At Dover Castle and fix the Germans'
Attention to Calais. He also wants
To go to sea in a cruiser and see the assault
And the bombardment on D-Day. He'll be
An embarrassment and a liability,
And he is too valuable to take such risks.
If anything happens to him we will be
In a bad position. He needs good sense
To control his fighting spirit. Can you stop him?

Eisenhower.	I don't know, I can try. Let's go back now
To Southwick House and question the Met men
About the weather for June the fifth.

(*Saturday June 3, evening. Southwick House mess room.* EISENHOWER, *his* COMMANDERS
and RAF Group Captain STAGG. *Bookcases and French windows, large map.*)

Stagg.	Bad news. High pressure is giving way to a low
As a depression over Iceland spreads south.
The weather on June the fifth will be overcast
And stormy with Force Five winds. It's getting worse.

Eisenhower.	Thank you. Please leave the room. (Exit Stagg.) Well,
	what do we think?
	What do you think, Monty?

Montgomery.	 I have laid the plan
And prepared the armies. It is for you
As Supreme Commander to say if the armies should go.
A decision to cancel must be made
Twenty-four hours before the landings as
The invasion fleet of five thousand ships
Will assemble then.

Tedder.	 I don't think we should go.
You can't have an invasion through mountainous seas –
Look what happened to the Spanish Armada –
And low cloud which does not allow air cover.

Montgomery.	I am in favour of going. Everything is ready.

A huge operation is co-ordinated.
The morale of the men has been lifted.
If we don't go now, we must wait a month,
And morale will flag, and the Germans may find out.
They think we have an army around Dover,
Operation Fortitude may be discovered.

(*One hour later.* EISENHOWER *with* STAGG *and the others.*)

Eisenhower.   No irrevocable decision has been made.
                 The American Navy with Bradley's troops
                 Should leave for Omaha and Utah beaches,
                 Subject to a possible last-minute cancellation.
                 I will make the final decision at the weather
                 Conference at eight tomorrow morning.

(*4 June, 1 a.m. Eisenhower's trailer off Pitymoor Lane, near Southwick House.* EISENHOWER *looking at the sky.* KAY SUMMERSBY *in the doorway.*)

Kay.   Dwight, you should sleep.

Eisenhower.   No, I'm looking at the sky.

Kay.   I don't like to see you so bleakly depressed.

Eisenhower.   Not depressed, just with those men on the sea.

(*4 June, 4.30 a.m. Southwick House, mess room.* EISENHOWER *and* STAGG.)

Stagg.   Sea conditions will be slightly better than
                 Expected, but low cloud will ground air forces.

Ramsay.   The sky is practically clear, when do
                 You expect cloud and wind?

Stagg.   Five hours from now, sir.

Ramsay.   I think we should go.

Eisenhower.   Leigh-Mallory?

Leigh-Mallory.	I'm against.
	Air forces could not carry out the plan.
Montgomery.	Some of the air programme would be cancelled,
	But most could go ahead. We must go, for
	Each hour's delay makes the troops' ordeal worse.
Eisenhower.	Tedder?
Tedder.	I must disagree with Monty.
	We need full, and not partial, air support.
Eisenhower.	*Overlord* is being launched with ground forces
	That are not overwhelmingly powerful.
	We need the help of air superiority
	Or the landings will be far too risky.
	If air cover cannot operate we must postpone.
	That is my casting vote. Any dissentient voices?
Montgomery	(*aside*). The sky is clear, dawn glows, yet we postpone
	Because of dissenting meteorologists,
	But I have myself revered air supremacy,
	And there must be unity of purpose and decision
	Under the Supreme Commander. Be silent.
	(*Silence.*)
Eisenhower.	D-Day is not June fifth.
	(*Pause.*)
	Monty, perhaps
	You and I should walk down to the Golden Lion.
	Fruit juice?
Montgomery	(*aside*). I must watch Tedder. He and Ike
	Swapped houses near Bushey Park. Ike began in
	Park House on the golf course, but found it large
	And the lane too narrow. Tedder moved out
	Of Telegraph Cottage for him. They are
	Neighbours, and Ike feels he must reflect his view.

(4 June. La Roche Guyon. ROMMEL *and his Chief of Staff General* HANS SPEIDEL.*)*

Rommel.
There won't be an invasion in this weather.
The Straits of Dover are even worse than here.
If they come they won't get off the beaches.
It's my wife's birthday. I'm going to take
A short vacation, I shall drive to Herrlingen
And give Lucy her present, these new shoes,
Then visit the *Führer* in Berchtesgaden
And press him to move Panzer Group West to
The coast rather than hold it in reserve
As von Schweppenburg and Rundstedt want.
We need three more divisions in all.
Look after the *château* for me.

(4 June, 7 p.m. Broomfield House. Wind and rain. EISENHOWER *and* MONTGOMERY *over dinner in the dining-room.* PAUL *the chef, serving, overhears.)*

Montgomery.
If we don't go on June the sixth, we can't
Until the nineteenth, and to stand men down
And bring back ships will damage their morale
And blow their secrecy. We have to make it work.

Eisenhower.
You're right. If we have air superiority,
We have to go.

Montgomery.
Thank God you banned Churchill,
Banished him to a train near Southampton.

(4 June, 9.30 p.m. Southwick House mess room. Wind and rain. EISENHOWER, *with* MONT-GOMERY, TEDDER, SMITH, RAMSAY, LEIGH-MALLORY, BRADLEY, GEN. STRONG, STAFF OFFICERS. *Eisenhower at table, the others drinking coffee in easy chairs. Enter* STAGG.*)*

Stagg.
This afternoon we saw a break in the weather.
We now agree, the depression in the mid-
Atlantic must slow down, giving a breathing space
Of perhaps a day on June the sixth: little
Cloud, quieter seas. The rain will stop
In two or three hours.

(A cheer goes up. The rain is pouring down.)

Eisenhower	(*aside*). Rear Admiral Creasy, Air Marshal Leigh-Mallory, And Major-General de Guingand are cross-Examining Stagg. Ramsay is content. Leigh-Mallory and Tedder are anxious About the effectiveness of heavy bombers. But we can call on our fighter bombers.
Ramsay.	If *Overlord* is to happen on June the sixth The Commander of the American task force Must be told in the next half hour. If they sail And are recalled, they cannot sail again Until the tides are right and must wait till June the nineteenth.
Eisenhower	(*aside*). The lonely isolation Of making a decision with risk either way. If *Overlord* is to happen before the nineteenth I must decide now. (*Aloud.*) Smith?
Bedell Smith.	It's a helluva gamble, But it is the best possible gamble.
Eisenhower	(*aside*). I must build my decision round Monty. (*Aloud.*) Monty, do you see any reason why We should not go on Tuesday?
Montgomery.	No, I would say: Go.
Eisenhower	(*aloud*). What are the air ramifications of A decision to go? (*Aside.*) I mean to go. (*Aloud.*) Thank you. I am quite positive that the order must be given. I order the convoys to put to sea again. A final irrevocable decision Will be made at four-thirty tomorrow morning.

(5 June, 3.30 a.m. Eisenhower's trailer. EISENHOWER outside.)

Kay.	Dwight.

Eisenhower.	The wind was shaking the trailer. It's like
	A hurricane. The rain is horizontal.
	I may have to call the operation off.

(*5 June, 4.30 a.m. Southwick House. Mess room.* EISENHOWER *and* COMMANDERS *all in* battledress, MONTGOMERY *in fawn-coloured pullover and light corduroy trousers. Coffee.*)

| Stagg. | The rain will clear within a matter of hours. |
| | Look it's already happening now. |

Eisenhower	(*pacing, shooting out his chin*).
	Who's for go?
	Monty. Smith. Ramsay?

| Ramsay. | I'm concerned about |
| | Spotting for naval gunfire, but will take the risk. |

| Eisenhower. | Tedder? |

| Tedder. | I'm ready. |

| Leigh-Mallory. | Air conditions are |
| | Below the acceptable minimum. |

| Eisenhower. | Thank you, Stagg. |

(*Exit* STAGG.)

The ships are sailing into the Channel.
If they have to be called back, we must do so now.
The Supreme Commander is the only man
Who can do that.

(EISENHOWER *thinks. Time stops.*)

OK, let's go.

(*A cheer. Everyone rushes to their command posts.* EISENHOWER, *alone, sits on in immense isolation.*)

| Eisenhower | (*reflecting*). The fate of thousands of men hung on my |

words,
And the future of nations. I had power
Over the whole world, and was still; but now
It is too late to change the decision.
The invasion cannot be stopped – even by me.
Overlord now has a life of its own.
It is in the men, not me, that power resides.

*(5 June, 1 p.m. Eisenhower's trailer. EISENHOWER and BUTCHER playing checkers.)

Butcher.   I'm winning, two kings to one.

Eisenhower.   I've jumped a king
          And got a draw. It's a good omen.

(5 June, evening. Newbury. EISENHOWER and KAY, who is dressed as his driver. Blackened faces of TROOPS. Sound of planes overhead.)

Eisenhower.   There go the Hundred and First Airborne. Eighty
          Per cent casualties Leigh-Mallory reckons.
          Well, it's on. (He chokes back tears.) Let's go back to the car.

(5 June, 9 p.m. Broomfield House. MONTGOMERY by his caravan, his BATMAN and DAWNAY.)

Montgomery.   Everything possible has been done to ensure the success
          Of the landings. We've done everything possible.
          It is now in the hands of God. It'll be
          All right. I'm turning in at the usual time.
          Wake me at the usual time. No, not before.

          (He goes into his caravan.)

          It seems only yesterday that I led, in rain,
          My company in a charge at Meteren
          At the start of the First World War, and as
          I stormed the village was shot through my chest
          And knee by a sniper, and the soldier
          Dragging me to safety was shot and killed
          And fell on top of me. For three hours in
          The lashing rain I lay, bleeding. They dug

A grave, and as they picked me up and dumped me
In a greatcoat to sling me and drop me in
An orderly called "Hey, this one's still alive."
If I had died then, who'd have redrawn *Overlord*?
I feel I was saved by Providence for this moment.
(*Praying.*) O Lord, Eisenhower has entrusted to me
The conduct of *Overlord*, which is now in my hands.
I have launched the biggest invasion ever,
A hundred and seventy-six thousand men
Are now in the air or on the waves, to land
In Fortress Europe, breach Hitler's Atlantic Wall
Which is in the hands of my old adversary,
Rommel, from whom I captured this caravan.
Lord many will die on both sides, scarring your earth.
Forgive me Lord for destroying your world,
Your hedgerows, wild flowers, chestnut trees and fields,
With tanks, with flame-throwers – forgive me for
Taking part in the killing of men, but if
I don't, what will happen? Hitler will continue
His murderous campaign, his guards will press on
With the Final Solution. I have a just cause,
But Lord, let me not kill unnecessarily.
I will be cautious, to win with minimum loss.
Perception of evil is a point of view,
Lord, let me see within the harmony of the One
That shows this war has meaning in relation to Good.

(*He pauses.*)

O Lord, in this situation I must kill.
You do not want me to. I am like Arjuna
In the *Bhagavadgita*. Let me act without
Interference from my rational, social ego,
Let me act from my soul and I will be in harmony
With your will, and those who die as a result
Of my decision will die at the behest
Of your divine will. O Lord, I am troubled
At the thought of those who will die. I commit them to you,
To the whole, the One. And may you absolve me
From this necessity. For to remove Hitler
And his Final Solution men must die,

And it is worse for them not to die, and for more
To die. O Lord, Overlord.

*(6 June, 4.00 a.m. Eisenhower's trailer. EISENHOWER and KAY.)

Eisenhower.   Well, it's four o'clock, I'm going to bed.

*(6 June, 6.30 a.m. Rommel's house. Dining-room. ROMMEL arranged Lucy's presents. The phone rings.)

Rommel.   Speidel. Airborne landings in Normandy?
                      It can't be the invasion in this weather.
                      Confirm it and let me know. If it's serious
                      I'll leave immediately.

(Chorus of the OCCUPIED.)

Chorus.   The Allies have landed, there is hope again.
                      No longer shall we walk with sullen faces.
                      A spring is in our step, liberation
                      Cannot be far away, freedom from the yoke,
                      From helmeted Nazis driving by our squares,
                      From Gestapo questionings and firing-squads,
                      Freedom from the noose in public places.
                      Once again we can live without fear – soon.
                      Come, Montgomery, liberate us, but
                      Without smashing our towns and killing our men.

(* 6 June, 7 a.m. Eisenhower's trailer. EISENHOWER is reading a Western novel.)

Butcher.   Sir, good news from Leigh-Mallory. The air drop
                      Was a success, casualties were light.

Eisenhower.   Good.

                      (His face has a huge grin.)

(D-Day SOLDIER.)

D-Day Soldier.   For two nights we tossed on the choppy sea.
                      It was full of ships and craft, surely the Germans

Would see us and bomb us from the air?
The storm soaked us as we huddled on deck.
No one said much, we waited, seasick. Then
At H-hour a barrage from our Navy ships.
We scrambled down long ropes, packs on our backs,
Clutching rifles near tied gas masks, and jumped
Into assault craft, a ribbon of shore ahead
Gleaming in the early morning sunshine,
With little puffs of smoke from our Navy's shells.
Dipping, swaying, we crouched all tense and looked,
We approached through fire, bullets whipped up the waves
And clanged our sides. We nosed through floating bodies
Towards the smoke. A German plane roared down
And strafed the crowded beach, men and vehicles.
In that moment each one of us was afraid.
Yet we all showed courage. Bang! Down went the flap,
Out, we jumped into three feet of cold waves
And waded through the bullets and corpses
To the sand at the lapping water's edge,
Then dived as the plane whined down and raked our path.
"Mines," someone shouted, "stick to the matting."
We ran doubled-up under sniper fire.
The man beside me on the landing craft
Fell at my side, shot through the head. We gathered
At a muster point at the top of the beach,
And I saw a German soldier dead in a tree.
We were given provisions, and then ran on
Towards a house and fields, we advanced.

(*6 June, 10.30 a.m. Rommel's house.* LUCY. *Speidel rings.*)

Rommel.   Speidel. It is the invasion? Are you sure?
I will leave immediately.
(*To Lucy.*)   The invasion has come,
It is confirmed, out of high seas and storm,
And I was not at my post. Montgomery,
Who defeated me at Alamein, seems to know
My movements and when I am three divisions short.
The only way to repulse him was to drive
Him off the beaches into the sea. If he now has
A foothold, I fear it may be too late.

(*6 June, later. Broomfield House.* DAWNAY *and* PAUL, *the chef.*)

Dawnay.

The great one is amazingly cool. He was woken,
Given the good news, then went back to sleep.
Now he is studying the land we have taken
From the messages sent through to his caravan.
He is sitting quietly, plotting the positions.

(MONTGOMERY *in his caravan. He summons* DAWNAY.)

Montgomery.

The British and Canadians are ashore,
But the Americans cannot land on Omaha.
The cliffs are defended by Germans who were
Conducting an exercise, we found out too late.
Signal to Dempsey, ask him if he can take
Bradley's troops: "Can you take Five Corps?"

(*Later.*)

Dawnay.

Dempsey says: "No, unless you want to leave
Our people out, because it is too crowded
To go in together."

(*6 June, late morning. The Berghof, Hitler's HQ in Berchtesgaden.* HITLER *and* KEITEL.)

Hitler.

Again and again I have warned Rommel and Rundstedt
The first invasion will come in Normandy.
In March I several times warned the Generals,
On May the sixth I telephoned Jodl
That I attached particular importance
To Normandy. But Rommel and Rundstedt
Remained convinced the invasion would take place
In the Straits of Dover. Now I can attack
London with my flying bombs. Now the enemy
Is where we can get at them.

(*Silence. Exit* KEITEL. *Enter* BORMANN.)

I am not worried.
I do not believe that this "invasion"
Is anything other than a diversion.

I have always said that the main attack will come
In the Pas de Calais. I speak as Will.
The Atlantic Wall will repulse them,
There will be another Dunkirk.
We are invincible, I am a will
To conquer, I have a personal destiny
Within the historical process.

Bormann.   Providence
Has saved you to lead Germany
Through this time of trial.

(*Silence.*)

Hitler.   There must be no let up
In the solution to the Jewish problem.
By expelling Jews from their privileged positions
I have opened up their positions to the children
Of hundreds of thousands of working-class Germans,
And I am depriving the revolutionary movement
Of its Jewish inspiration: Rosenberg,
To whom Eckart introduced me, my mentor,
Brought out of Bolshevik Russia a book,
The Protocols of the Elders of Zion,
The secret plans of the international
Jewish conspiracy for world domination.
I read it shortly after Zionists
Brought America into the First World War.
It shows that the Jewish doctrine of Marxism
Seeks the destruction of all non-Jewish
National states, and plans to hand the world
To the Jews. Russia has been captured by the Jews.

Bormann.   Through Bolshevism and the Jewish Trotsky
The Jews seek to achieve world domination.

Hitler.   And to spread through Germany as the Thule Society taught.
The Jews are a race, not a religious persuasion,
They foment revolution with Freemasons
And democrats from Britain and the US.
The Final Solution is the removal

Of Jews altogether. I am the Messiah
Who will save man from the Jewish Antichrist.

Bormann.   Zionism has driven the Bolsheviks
To butcher millions in the Soviet Union.

Hitler.   And is now driving the Allies' war-efforts.
Hungary is rotten with Jews everywhere,
Right up to the highest level, and a network
Of agents and spies. We must make a clean sweep.
We must do this while we are still able to.
Two days after the Americans entered Rome,
An invasion in Normandy. It is a diversion.
But it is also impudence. Launched from Britain.
Pah, I will pay Britain back with reprisal weapons.
I have eight thousand flying bombs, each one
Twenty-five feet long with a one-ton warhead,
Each pilotless with a jet engine. Prepare
To send the first of these to London.
I will rain destruction from the sky.

(*6 June, early evening.* EISENHOWER, *pacing outside his trailer.*)

Butcher.   The landings have been successful. We have now
A hundred and fifty-six thousand ashore,
And two thousand five hundred casualties,
Mostly at Omaha. We have Bayeux,
The seat of William the Conqueror, who
Is the only man besides Caesar, and now you,
To command a successful cross-Channel assault.

Eisenhower.   We have not got Caen.

(*7 June, morning.* HMS Faulknor. MONTGOMERY *and* BRADLEY.)

Montgomery.   Welcome aboard HMS *Faulknor.* I hope
Your ship is comfortable?

Bradley.   Thank you.
Sir, I'm concerned about the operational
Situation on Omaha beach, which is not yet secure.

Montgomery.	That is why I am here. The Allied armies
	Must link up in view of the German opposition.
	Collins' Seven US Corps must fight eastwards
	From Utah and join Gerow, not go to Cherbourg.

Bradley.   That's a change to the plan.

Montgomery.   It is necessary.

(*7 June, mid-morning. HMS* Apollo. EISENHOWER *and* MONTGOMERY.)

Montgomery.   Ike, in view of the American difficulty
              On Omaha beach, on the whole US Army front
              The immediate tactical plan has been altered.
              The Utah and Omaha beach troops must link up
              Or the Panzer Divisions will obliterate Omaha.

Eisenhower.   All right, I will signal the Combined Chiefs of Staff
              In Washington to that effect, and will say
              That after that adjustment, the original conceptions
              Will be pursued.

              (MONTGOMERY *rises to move away.*)

                          Oh, Monty, I'm concerned
              That Caen has not been captured.

Montgomery.   It's clear the enemy
              Intend to hold it strongly and to drive into
              My eastern flank. Dempsey will have to envelop it
              Rather than take it by a frontal attack,
              And then pivot on Caen and swing his right flank
              As the plan provides. I am well satisfied
              With today's fighting.

              (MONTGOMERY *moves away.*)

Eisenhower.   I'm not satisfied.

Butcher.   I find
              Him insufferable. He almost made out that

Americans had messed up his plan on Omaha,
He seemed to derive some satisfaction from
Re-arranging the whole American front.
I find his self-satisfaction irritating.

Eisenhower.   He can be self-righteous and rather rigid.

Montgomery   (*aside*). I am in theory responsible to Ike
Who is in turn responsible to the Combined
Chiefs of Staff, and beyond them, to two governments,
But I look to Brooke for guidance, I am
The senior British officer in Europe and
I am responsible for my nation's interests.

SCENE 2.

NORMANDY: DEFEATING ROMMEL

(*8 June, evening. Creullet. TAC HQ, Montgomery's caravans. MONTGOMERY sitting outside with the BBC rep, HOWARD MARSHALL. Beside him, a chamber-pot.*)

Montgomery.   Our first location after landing at Sainte Croix-sur-Mer
Was a totally unsuitable place for my TAC HQ.
It was a crossroads between fields with German trenches
And under artillery fire. Colonel Russell
Must have taken it from a map. My Canadian
Assistant, Warren, scouted round and found
Me this lovely *château*. It was occupied
This morning by fifteen Germans whom he took prisoner.
So here we are. We arrived this afternoon.
I have everything except a chamber-pot.
I tried to gesticulate what I wanted,
And Madame de Druval has produced one,
After bringing vases, and look, you see its crest.
Montgomery. For my ancestors came
From Sainte Foy de Montgomery near Falaise.
Roger de Montgomery was number two
To William the Conqueror. I landed near Dives,

The spot from which William sailed. My family invaded
Britain, and now are liberating the
Conqueror's Norman homeland from the Saxon yoke.
Everything is going well. Rommel's Twenty-first
Panzer Division has arrived at Caen
And half have been destroyed, and half of the rest
Have been sent to retake Bayeux, weakening their thrust.

Marshall.
Was it over-optimistic, faulty thinking
To expect troops who landed yesterday morning,
Many seasick, to march on foot to Caen
And capture it by nightfall, without armoured
Troop carriers that follow tanks, of the kind
The Germans have? And why was the British
Tank advance so slow?

Montgomery.
                                    Everything is going to plan.

(HENDERSON *and* DAWNAY *are in the "A" mess tent.*)

Henderson
(*to Dawnay*). He's tired and on edge, nothing's gone right
But now he's in the field, all is confidence
And he has time for relaxing anecdotes
About chamber-pots.

(*8 June, later. Montgomery's caravans.* MONTGOMERY *and* DAWNAY.)

Montgomery.
Signal to Ike that while the Americans
Concentrate on linking Utah and Omaha
Bridgeheads, Dempsey will strike south of Caen at
Villers-Bocage and then Falaise.
Say I am very satisfied with the situation.

(*9 June, 11.30 a.m. Montgomery's caravans.* DEMPSEY *leaving.* HENDERSON.
MONTGOMERY.)

Dempsey
(*to Henderson*). The great one's tense and unapproachable. (*Exit.*)

Montgomery
(*to Henderson*). I have written a letter for Ike, it's addressed to
The Chief of Staff at SHAEF. I'd like you to
Catch a motor launch to Portsmouth and take

It to Southwick. Dempsey wants American
Five Corps to go with him. We're going to hold
North and west Caen, where the Germans are counter-attacking,
And push Seventh Armoured Division south of Bayeux
And then swing round left-handed and take Caen
From the rear.

(*10 June. Telegraph Cottage, near Bushey Park.* EISENHOWER, BUTCHER *and* KAY.)

Butcher.   There's no information from Montgomery
                   Who agreed to cable every night.

Eisenhower.   That's too bad.
                   How can I evaluate what's happening
                   In Normandy if I don't have any cables?
                   Monty is slow. Bradley's disappointed,
                   Taking Caen was supposed to shield his troops,
                   American troops, and now they're exposed.

Kay.   You know,
                   Montgomery is the only person in
                   The whole Allied Command whom I dislike.
                   He's like a desert rat, with his pointed nose
                   And his quick eyes which dart to either side.
                   How can you stand not hearing from him? Tell him off.

Eisenhower.   I feel angry and frustrated, cut off.
                   I need to be the field Commander in charge
                   Of Twenty-first Army Group. Then I'd know
                   What the situation is.

*(Later.)

Butcher.   Sir, there was a signal from Monty. SHAEF had it.

                   (BUTCHER *waves a cable.*)

(*10 June, 11.30 a.m. Port-en-Bessin.* MONTGOMERY, BRADLEY *and* DEMPSEY *in a field.*
Montgomery in hunting jacket.)

Montgomery.   So there are two Panzer divisions dug in

Before Caen, and Dempsey will outflank them
From Bayeux. Could you, Brad, parallel this,
Drive south towards to Caumont? This would confuse
Rommel in Caen and divert enemy troops
From Collins' attack towards Cherbourg.

Bradley.   I
Am afraid I cannot, sir. The American
Build-up is twenty-four hours behind schedule.
The Omaha beachhead is only two miles deep.
My priority is to link the two beachheads.

Montgomery   (*disappointed*). The Desert Rats will have to fight alone.
They are already advancing through the Eighth
Armoured Brigade's shield near Tilly to seize
Villers-Bocage, the western gateway to Caen.
Fifty-first Highland Division are with them,
My two most experienced divisions, which
Fought under me at Alamein.

(*10 June, early evening. Creullet. MONTGOMERY by his caravan with DAWNAY.*)

Montgomery.   Signal to Eisenhower that American
Five and Seven Corps have at last joined hands,
And that I have given Bradley the green light
For Collins to race for Cherbourg. Tomorrow
Signal both Ike and Brooke, and say that my
General object is to pull the Germans
On to Second Army so that First Army
Can extend and expand. The British will
Soak punishment so the US can break out.

(*10 June, early evening. Berghof, Hitler's HQ. HITLER, DÖNITZ and GÖRING.*)

Dönitz.   The invasion has succeeded. The Second Front
Has come.

Göring.   The Navy assured us the enemy
Would not risk his best ships in a sea invasion.

Dönitz.   Discussion of such matters is not opportune

At present. There should be more air-strikes.
The enemy flew over ten thousand on
Invasion day, our *Luftwaffe* three hundred.

Hitler.　　I have warned since March that the first invasion
Would come in Normandy, not the Pas de Calais.
No one would listen to me. Send the 9th
And 10th SS Panzers to the Normandy front.

(*He goes out to his balcony. Bavarian Alps ahead of and
below him.*)

(*Alone.*) From this high point in the Bavarian Alps
I look down on the slopes and paths of the world
And think how I have climbed to this great height
From Braunau in Austria, where I was born.
I left school without a certificate,
I lived in a doss-house in imperial Vienna,
I was a corporal in the First World War,
And saw my country humiliated, shrink
And then in Munich, in beer-cellars, the Hofbrauhaus,
I stood on tables and spoke and they echoed.
Eckart taught me I had a destiny,
After my rise to Chancellor, it was inevitable
That I would take the Rhineland, Austria
(My home country), and the Sudetenland,
Then Czechoslovakia and finally Poland;
I made my choice and carried out my free act.
I was driven not by personal ambition
But the will to purify the German race
Of all its Jewish blood. I made a pact
With the Bolshevik Devil to take Poland
And cleanse it of its ethnically degenerate past.
Chamberlain was a well-intentioned fool,
He was no match for my diplomacy.
How I despised him when he waved his paper.
I did not seek war with Britain and Russia,
But I blitzkrieged Britain and invaded Russia,
And my Atlantic war drew in Britain's supplier,
The Zionist US. I committed aggression
Against these three powers, beyond good and evil;

Because I sought to impose my vision
Of a pure race of god-men on the world,
And Jews and Bolsheviks were the obstacles.
Now two powers attack me on the west, and I
Am pressed on the east. And this Montgomery,
Who beat Rommel in North Africa and Italy,
Is now poised like some agent of the divine,
To strike and repay me for my cleansing.
But I do not believe in a moral universe,
That aggression leads to destruction, but in power.
I sought like Augustus and Constantine,
Like Charlemagne and Napoleon to rule
Europe and dominate the whole world,
Not for personal ambition, but so that the idea
I embody could find universal expression:
The supremacy of the Aryan race,
The Germanic people's mission to rule the world.
I am a German imperialist, I seek
To destroy the British Empire and inherit it,
To be crowned Kaiser of a world empire
Where German ideas are followed throughout the world,
Where God is dead as Nietzsche said, and where
Beyond good and evil, all is will to power.
I have to become the Christian Antichrist
To reject the *Old Testament* of the Jews
And the Christian code that says "Thou shalt not kill" –
Did not Napoleon reject its good –
In order to combat the Jewish Antichrist
Who seeks to destroy Germany and rule.
I have remade good in a nihilistic world.
Christians see me as the Antichrist, but I am
The Messiah who saves mankind from Jewish rule.
And so Montgomery does not frighten me.
Providence rules by power, not by what is good.
Occult Providence took me to this great height
Because I tapped its secret energy,
Providence is neutral, neither good nor evil.
So I shall continue to fulfil my destiny,
I belong to an idea that will repel
A dying Christendom and the Allies.
European civilisation is not in decline.

There is a union ahead of all its states,
Which I am bringing about. Europe will play
The central role in the coming world order.
Montgomery and I are locked in a tussle of will,
Of power, not of vengeance for evil done;
Between the Allies' world order, and mine.
I live in a universe that is not benign,
That is neutral to the wishes of humans,
In which the strong impose their will, their power,
In which the Superman takes charge for man
And sets up a structure that can survive
A thousand years. Great men with a destiny
Like Napoleon, and me, can kill millions
And remain untouched by any moral law
That was falsely invented by a dying Church.
I am the force of a *new* world order,
An idea that began in Bavaria
With Weishaupt, who was anti-Catholic
And anti-Habsburg, against all religion
And established government through the occult,
A force that Frederick knew before he died,
A force which Zionism later stole.
I will cleanse Weishaupt's power of its Bolshevik grime.
I draw from an occult Bavarian will,
That channels an energy in the universe,
I am its Messiah against both Jew and Christ.
And, with open visionary centres,
With insight that will be known in the new Age,
I will repel the Allies from Normandy,
This little diversion, just as I will repel
The main attack when it comes in the Pas de Calais
And all Zionist power that claims to be "good".

(*10 June, evening. Berchtesgaden.* HITLER, BORMANN *and* BURGDORF.)

Burgdorf.   Rommel plans to divert his counter-attack
                   From the British armour driving on Caen
                   To the American drive on Cherbourg,
                   And then return to stop Dempsey's advance
                   Which is already near Villers-Bocage.

Bormann.	Rommel is letting the British advance on Caen.

Hitler.	Caen is nearer to Paris than Cherbourg.
	I veto Rommel's plan. Army Group B
	Will attack the British bridgehead from Caen,
	Using the reinforcements we have supplied.
	Send Rommel an *Enigma* signal now.

(*12 June, 9 a.m. Creullet. Montgomery's TAC HQ.* MONTGOMERY *and* DEMPSEY.)

Montgomery.	The Desert Rats must speed up. We believe
	Three more Panzer divisions are on their way
	To reinforce Caen. Second Army must
	Seize Caen before these Panzer divisions arrive.
	Meet Erskine, the Desert Rats' commander,
	And Bucknall, and hurry them up.
	Now I must cancel my conference with Bradley.
	He has the American Chiefs of Staff to lunch,
	Marshall, King and Arnold will eat C rations and
	Hard TAC biscuits in his new HQ.
	O dear, I've got Churchill arriving for lunch,
	With Smuts and Brooke. He'll get excited and
	Ask dozens of questions when I should be
	Concentrating on the task of the Desert Rats.

(*Later, after lunch. Operations trailer.* CHURCHILL, SMUTS, BROOKE, MONTGOMERY, *who stands before a map.*)

Churchill	(*excitedly*). And the enemy are only three miles away?
	Why, German armour may roll through our lunch.

Montgomery.	That is unlikely, Prime Minister. But to resume.
	My main strategy is to draw the Germans
	Onto the British east flank so the Americans
	Can break out from Cherbourg and wheel round.
	We shall exploit all German mistakes at once.
	For example, they've concentrated their
	Panzer strength to hold Caen and block what they
	Think is a thrust towards Paris and the Seine,
	But we have an excellent chance of encircling
	Their Panzer corps and capturing prisoners.

The Allied aim is to defeat the German
Armies in the West, not break out towards the Seine.

(*Later.* CHURCHILL *and* HENDERSON.)

Churchill   (*curious*). So what is Monty's day?

Henderson.   Here in "A" Mess
                   His day is simple. He rises in time
                   For breakfast at eight and is out by nine
                   In two jeeps with four redcaps, visiting
                   Headquarters, front line troops. At four he returns
                   Takes his uniform off, puts on his grey
                   Sweater and corduroy trousers. From five
                   Till six he has his main meal. Then he sits
                   In the open air with his LOs,
                   His young Liaison Officers who act as scouts,
                   His eyes and ears for different parts of the front,
                   And report what they have seen in the battlefield.
                   They sit with mugs of tea. Each will have been to
                   A different battle zone. He took the idea
                   From the Duke of Wellington – some say Napoleon –
                   Who had eight Liaison Officers in the field,
                   And his way of fighting, in caravans near the front,
                   Is not unlike the method of Waterloo.
                   From seven he reads and thinks, he goes to bed at nine.
                   Then he must not be disturbed for
                   Any reason. I know he prays every night.
                   In his caravan. I have seen him, heard him.

(*Later* MONTGOMERY *and* BROOKE *briefly alone.*)

Montgomery.   Thank you for covering my back in London,
                   With Churchill and Tedder. I wish you could
                   Do something about Ike. His approach to war
                   Differs fundamentally from my own.
                   I am amazed he has commanded the only
                   Cross-Channel invasion since Julius Caesar
                   And the Conqueror. Of course it was my doing.

Brooke.   For a Caesar he is genial, but behind

The friendly exterior is a ruthless mind
That balances conflicting national interests
And appears to lead by compromise, but may
Favour his masters' interests, not blatantly
But indirectly, at one remove, so that
At surface level all seems reasonable
And there are sound military reasons
For what may at heart be political.
Beware of him. He has a restlessness
That latches on to any new idea
And seeks to integrate it within the scheme,
Always for a military reason, you follow.
There is something in him that reminds me of a fox.
He is a great man, and a simple one,
Both at the same time. I find it hard to understand
How a great man who leads like William the Conqueror
Can while away his time with Western novels.
There's a disparity between his decisions, what he gives out,
And his tastes, what he imbibes. Perhaps his mind
Is more advanced than his culture, or perhaps
He is quite simply, just an American.

Montgomery. He is pulling against me the whole time.

Brooke. You must remember how you were appointed.
He was made Supreme Commander because Roosevelt
Would not release Marshall, his Army Chief
Of Staff, just as Churchill did not wish to
Release me, his Chief of Staff. Eisenhower
Hoped for Alexander, but his easy-
Going nature alarmed our War Cabinet
Who, as you know, on my recommendation
Vetoed his preference and gave him you,
And you then ripped to pieces the COSSAC plan.

Montgomery. It was a bad plan.

Brooke.   But he had accepted it.
He will continue to be difficult,
But under a surface friendliness. You see.

(*Later.* MONTGOMERY *and* HENDERSON.)

Montgomery.   Now I've got Churchill out of the way I can deal
                   With Leigh-Mallory. We need his paratroop drop
                   Near Caen. Urquhart is keen to do it, but,
                   Sitting in his office, he says it must be at night
                   And our navy might fire at his planes in the dark.
                   Signal de Guingand. LM is a gutless
                   Bugger who refuses to take a chance
                   And plays for safety on all occasions. I have
                   No use for him.

(*13 June, later.* MONTGOMERY *and* POSTON.)

Montgomery   (*thinly*). What happened at Villers-Bocage?

Poston.   The Desert Rats
                   Entered the cheering village and some tank crews
                   Got out. Some Cromwells pushed on. Just outside
                   Five Tiger tanks of I SS Panzer Corps
                   Lay in wait, commanded by Michael Wittmann,
                   The ace who destroyed a hundred and thirty-eight
                   Tanks on the Russian front. He set off alone
                   And destroyed four of our tanks in the village
                   With eighty-eight millimetre shells, blocking
                   Retreat. He returned and attacked our column.
                   He destroyed the first tank, then went down the line.
                   By mid-morning his one Tiger destroyed
                   Twenty-seven tanks and twenty-eight armoured
                   Vehicles and killed eighty infantrymen.
                   His own tank was disabled but he escaped.
                   Bucknall then withdrew. Dempsey was not consulted.

Montgomery.   Rommel has given us a bloody nose.
                   My Desert Rats. I will see that Bucknall
                   And Erskine are sacked.

Poston.   And his counter-attack
                   Has taken Carentan, the junction between
                   The two American armies. He ignored Hitler.

(*Later.* MONTGOMERY *and* HENDERSON.)

Montgomery.   Now, Rommel has ignored Hitler and sent
                        His Second Panzer Division defiantly
                        Westwards and taken Carentan and mauled
                        The Desert Rats. The weather is getting worse,
                        And threatens our naval resupply, our troop
                        Reinforcements. Bradley is overstretched
                        And should delay his southern offensive.
                        We need to hold the Caen-Bayeux road and
                        Lure Rommel into counter-attacking us
                        So we can destroy his armour as at Alamein.
                        We have four hundred tanks there, and should not
                        Attack yet. We should postpone Dempsey's pincer
                        Movement to encircle the Panzer divisions.

(*14 June, morning. London. Eisenhower's HQ at 20 Grosvenor Square.* EISENHOWER.)

Eisenhower.   What's the matter with Monty? Why won't he attack?
                        The Germans should be kept off balance, but he
                        Needs supplies, and doesn't make any gains,
                        And even retreats. He hasn't taken the airfields
                        South of Caen, as he promised Leigh-Mallory,
                        And the air commanders at this morning's meeting
                        Spoke of "a state of crisis". Even Tedder says
                        The present situation has the makings of
                        A dangerous crisis. Leigh-Mallory's
                        Going to visit Monty today.

(*14 June, late morning. Montgomery's TAC HQ.* MONTGOMERY. *Enter* DE GAULLE *with a* FRENCH AIDE.)

Henderson.   An unexpected visitor.

Aide.   General de Gaulle.

De Gaulle.   I landed at Courseulles today, on the beach
                        Juno of the Canadians, with the Free French
                        And now that I 'ave returned to France, as
                        Leader of the Free French, I am in charge
                        Of all territory liberated by

Your *Operation Overlord*.

Montgomery. No you're not,
I'm in charge as Land Commander of the Allied
Expeditionary Force, which does not include the French.
France collaborated with Hitler, I remind you.

De Gaulle. That is not right –

Montgomery. I'm in charge.

(*Later.* MONTGOMERY *and* HENDERSON.)

Henderson. I've found de Gaulle. He's in Bayeux, he made
A speech to the locals and caused a traffic jam.
His staff kept shouting "General de Gaulle"
And pointing at him to create interest.
He said the Free French are reconquering
France "with the aid of the Allies". Wait till Ike hears.
Military vehicles were unable to get through.

Montgomery (*furiously*). Who does he think he is? He signed "France"
In my visitors book. He's interfering in
My running of the war. Stop him. Send him
Back to England.
(*Aside.*) He's a poor fish who gives
Out no inspiration.

(*Later.*)

Henderson. An order from Churchill. He has vetoed
Your instructions. You are "to leave de Gaulle in peace".

Montgomery (*angrily*). It's all very well for a politician in London
To say that, but we're running a war here,
And if de Gaulle is stopping our tanks getting through
Then "leaving him in peace" will be costly.

Henderson. The Resistance does look to him.

(*Chorus of* LONDONERS.)

Chorus.	What is that whine that suddenly cuts out?
	What is that crash, that devastation as
	Houses crumble, bodies are strewn in the street?
	What weapon has been unleashed upon us?
	What are these flying bombs, that without pilots
	Can be fired across the Channel at random,
	To fall anywhere, any time, with no more warning
	Than a stopped whine? We are all terrified.
	Death hovers in the air and we do not know
	Where it will strike. May it not be us. Not us.

(*15 June, 4 p.m. Creullet, Montgomery's TAC HQ.* EISENHOWER, *his* SON, *and* TEDDER *waiting. Enter* MONTGOMERY.)

| Montgomery. | Ike, I'm sorry, I didn't know you were coming. |
| | I've been visiting Bradley. |

| Eisenhower. | It's my fault. My son. |

(MONTGOMERY *shakes hands with* IKE'S SON *and greets* TEDDER.)

John can you leave us? Perhaps find something to eat?

(*Exit* EISENHOWER'S SON.)

The first flying bomb has fallen on London,
And we've come to see if there really is a crisis.

Montgomery.	Leigh-Mallory was here yesterday, he offered me
	An air bombardment along five thousand yards
	So that the army can advance behind it,
	A most encouraging development.

Eisenhower.	We arrived this morning, and, finding you gone,
	We visited Dempsey's headquarters and found
	An Army/Air conference in session.

| Tedder. | I was concerned as neither Spaatz nor Coningham |
| | Was represented. |

| Montgomery. | Yesterday I asked |

Leigh-Mallory to send his planning staff.
It came out of yesterday's meeting.

Eisenhower.   Leigh-Mallory
Has not told anyone else that he would support
An infantry attack with Bomber Command
And 8 USAF.

Tedder.   Coningham and I
Are sure this cannot be done effectively.
I have sent the airmen home, the idea is dropped.

(MONTGOMERY *stares at* TEDDER.)

Montgomery.   You disapprove of air support to armies
By heavy bombers.

Tedder.   It just will not work.

Montgomery.   Then the armies will have to fight Rommel
Without the support of SHAEF's heavy bombers
And without *all* weapons in our arsenal.
Come to the operations caravan
And I will put you both in the picture.

(*Later, in the caravan.* EISENHOWER *is taking notes.*)

Montgomery.   The conduct of war is like a game of chess.
Both players must think ahead and have a plan,
A strategy, to feint on the left and slice
Through on the right. To play by simply reacting
To the other player's moves is ragged, chaotic,
Suicidal, and yet some would have us do that.
War is fought in the mind, and the victor
Is the one who is the more mentally tenacious.
I must stress, Caen is the key to Cherbourg.
Rommel, and Hitler, must be made to believe
That the British are attempting to break out
In the east towards the Seine, so they dare not
Release the four Panzer divisions to block
The American thrust to Cherbourg. Villers-

Bocage has helped to create that belief,
It has not imperilled Bradley's drive at all,
It is the key to his success.

Eisenhower.   Monty,
We're impressed. There is no crisis.

Tedder.   The idea of a crisis was over-stressed.

Montgomery.   My Normandy strategy is succeeding.

(*16 June. Montgomery's TAC HQ.* MONTGOMERY *and* DAWNAY.)

Montgomery.   The PM said he is very anxious
The King should come over here, just to land,
Have lunch with me, and go away. I agreed
But told Simbo to keep anyone else away,
To warn Eisenhower off. I can't deal with
More than one VIP. I've told Churchill
He must not come again just yet. Anyhow,
Having agreed, I now learn Eisenhower
Wants to resurrect *Anvil* round Bordeaux.
Signal to Brooke, it is a gross distraction
From the critical battle of Normandy. Bordeaux
Will be difficult to supply and cover from the air.
The Supreme Commander should use his supreme command
To prosecute the battle in Normandy
With all available weapons.

(*Enter* HENDERSON.)

Henderson.   His Majesty the King, sir.

Montgomery.   Glad you could come,
Sir, and see the liberation of Normandy.
I don't think the people of Normandy wish
To be liberated, as that means heavy fighting
And their towns destroyed and many killed.
When they chucked their hand in they thought they could
     escape
All this, but now they find they can't. The French

Are now paying, and don't like liberation.
They want to end the German occupation
And expel the Germans without dirtying their hands.
I was saying to Churchill and Brooke –

(DAWNAY *has taken a phone call in the caravan and is gesturing.*)

Excuse me.

King.
He is polite to me, but his eyes have
An insolence, an independence that says
"I honour Churchill for what he has done,
And Brooke because he was at Sandhurst too,
But you are in truth a Hanoverian
Who did not get where you are by merit -
Have not dirtied your hands as others have -
But merely took the trouble to be born.
And your brother is a known pro-German."
Much of being a King I find tedious.
All need to bow at, cheer, salute something,
The crown I wear, and so they bow to me.
I am like a cardboard cut-out and they hang
Their wishes, dreams, aspirations round my neck
Like a Hawaian garland, and I must pass
From place to place and smile, for them, not me.
How much I sacrifice for their wishes.
But this war I am involved in, and I want
To share the discomforts and fate of my people:
We are all at risk from these new flying bombs,
From the sudden roar from the sky and explosion
That can leave Buckingham Palace a pile of stone.

(*16 June. London.* TEDDER *and* CONINGHAM.)

Tedder.
Power has gone to his head. He tells the great
Who he will see and who he will not, and when.
He keeps the Supreme Commander waiting all day
Who has just been escorted by thirteen fighters.
We sent him a message before we arrived,
He could have come back early from Bradley,
Indeed, cancelled his visit. He tells the PM

Not to come, he speaks to the King with a cold contempt.
He tells Liddell Hart he is "too busy"
To see him, he offers a Napoleonic image.
He is on a pinnacle, and it is *hubris*,
It will surely tempt the gods to fling him down,
To cause him to fall.

Coningham.   We shall see the consequences
Of what we have started.

(*17 June, morning. Margival, near Soissons, Hitler's reserve HQ, Wolfschlucht 2*. HITLER, ROMMEL *and* RUNDSTEDT. JODL, SCHMUNDT *and others*. STENOGRAPHERS.)

Stenographer.   This man is the terror of the world. Four Focke-
                     Wulf Condors flew him and his staff to France,
                     The entire fighter force along the route
                     Was grounded, anti-aircraft batteries
                     Shut down. As he drove from Metz airport to here,
                     Luftwaffe fighter planes patrolled the highway.
                     He has come to boost the Field Marshals' confidence
                     After the reverses in the battlefield.
                     All men tremble at the power his conquests brought.
                     I look forward to seeing what the man is like.
                     I am sure he will have Rommel quaking too.

Hitler.   Soissons is near the battlefield where I
                     As a corporal won my Iron Cross.
                     Rommel and Rundstedt have asked for an urgent
                     Conference on the situation in France.

Rommel.   The situation does not improve. The troops,
                     Both Army and SS, fight like tigers,
                     But the balance of strength tips against us.
                     Reinforcements are not getting through,
                     The Allied Airforce and warships bombard us
                     Every day. The British are trying to break out
                     Towards the Seine, the Americans –

Hitler   (*radiating confidence*). Are you losing your nerve?

Rommel.   I know Montgomery from the desert.

	He will press relentlessly till our cordon breaks, Then nothing will stop him. It is only days Before the front caves in. Rundstedt agrees.
Rundstedt.	I asked permission to withdraw my forces From the peninsula to Cherbourg port And fortress.
Hitler.	Yes. The fortress should hold out As long as possible and until mid-July To hinder the enemy's sea-supply. The withdrawal is part deception, as there will be A winter attack by four Panzer divisions.
Aide.	Air-raid warning.

(*The* STENOGRAPHERS *leave.* ROMMEL *and* HITLER *stand together in the air-raid shelter with* RUNDSTEDT, SCHMUNDT *and* CHIEFS OF STAFF.)

Rommel.	My *Führer*, please believe Politics will soon have to play a part, Or the situation will deteriorate Too far to be salvaged.
Hitler	(*snapping*). The time is not ripe For a political decision. One sues for peace from strength. To do so now would be to admit defeat In Normandy. I have often spoken Of my "secret weapons", and already London Has been bombarded by V-I rocket bombs And is reeling as under the blitz. Britain will now Sue for peace.
Aide.	False alarm.

(*The* STENOGRAPHERS *return.*)

Hitler.	If you can contain the enemy Diversion in Normandy, if we can defeat The expected landing in the Pas de Calais

On the beaches, as at Dieppe, then the German
Position will be one of strength.

Rommel.   To regroup,
                          I need to withdraw my Panzers, but can't
                          While the British press round Caen.

                          (HITLER *shrugs*.)

* (*17 June. Montgomery's HQ.* DEMPSEY *and* MONTGOMERY.)

Montgomery.   We'll change our plan. You launch a mock
                          Attack on our right near Caumont, and then,
                          When Rommel is looking the wrong way, unleash
                          8 Corps in a blitz attack and envelop Caen
                          From the north-east. That is *Operation Epsom*.

*(*18 June. Dempsey's HQ.* DEMPSEY *and* MONTGOMERY.)

Montgomery.   So you don't like the new plan?

Dempsey.   For 8 Corps
                          To attack Caen east of the two rivers is a risk.
                          There's too little room for our troops and artillery,
                          As I've said. I think we should go back to the first
                          Plan: attack on the right and not the left.

Montgomery.   Very well. Your left flank will be defensive.

(*20 June. London.* EISENHOWER *in an air-raid shelter with* BUTCHER.)

Eisenhower.   I'm cooped up in these cramped conditions because
                          Hitler still has the buzz-bomb rocket sites.
                          Monty should be hurrying to reach them, but no,
                          He's postponed an offensive yet again. He's slow.
                          I'm ordering *Anvil* in Bordeaux, I know
                          There will be no landings till mid-August,
                          But at least we're doing something. He's like a snail.

                          (*A whine cuts out, a crash of a doodlebug.*)

*(*22 June. Creullet. Montgomery's TAC HQ. Meeting for all Corps and Divisional*
COMMANDERS. MONTGOMERY.)

Montgomery.   The weather has been very stormy, but don't lose heart.
                I say to all you corps and divisional commanders,
                We have been successful in pulling the German reserves
                To the Caen, or eastern, sector of our lodgement area,
                And I congratulate you. This has relieved
                Pressure in the American sector,
                And as a result we now own the whole
                Of the Cherbourg peninsula except the port
                Of Cherbourg itself.

(*22 June, later. Creullet. Montgomery's TAC HQ. MONTGOMERY and POSTON.*)

Poston.   The storm has destroyed the American Mulberries,
                But only damaged ours. But nothing can be unloaded.
                All that we need to resume our offensive
                Is tossing on ships near the floating harbours.

Montgomery.   We are five days behind in our build-up,
                This delay is what Rommel needs, for he can
                Get more Panzer divisions into Normandy.
                Arrange for a signal that Dempsey's blitz attack
                Is postponed still further.

                (*Enter* DAWNAY.)

Dawnay.   A signal. Eisenhower
                Has ordered Wilson to start Anvil quickly,
                As part of the Overlord strategy.

Montgomery.   It will ruin the Allied Offensive in Italy
                And will not help me a jot. He has not consulted
                Me, the *Overlord* Commander. It's outrageous.
                And then on top of everything we have to move
                Our TAC HQ because the BBC
                Reported the King had met me in my HQ
                "In the grounds of a *château*", as good as told
                The Germans where we are. Marlborough
                And Wellington didn't have the whereabouts

Of their HQ broadcast for the enemy to hear.

(25 June. Eisenhower's HQ. EISENHOWER and BUTCHER.)

Butcher.   A signal from Monty. The blitz attack
             On Caen starts tomorrow. He says "If we
             Can pull the enemy on to Second Army
             It will make it easier for the First Army
             When it attacks southwards."

Eisenhower. At last. Signal back, "I am hopeful that
             Bradley can quickly clean up the Cherbourg mess."

**(26 June. Eisenhower's HQ.)*

Butcher.   A signal from Monty: "It can be accepted
             That Cherbourg is now in First Army hands
             And the enemy commander has been captured."
             Cherbourg was the priority in the *Overlord* plan.

             (EISENHOWER *grins.*)

**(27 June. Blay, Montgomery's new HQ. MONTGOMERY and DAWNAY.)*

Montgomery. I am sending you to England with a letter
             To Brooke which assesses the situation.
             Bradley is cautious, but the worst problem,
             Churchill apart, is the jealousies that have lost
             Us air support, I mean Tedder and Coningham,
             Who are in league against Leigh-Mallory.
             I will keep out of it, but we need air cover.
             It's a sensitive letter, I hope he can help.

(29 June. Berchtesgaden. HITLER, ROMMEL and RUNDSTEDT.)

Hitler.   I have Rommel's figures: thirty enemy
             Divisions have landed, sixty-seven more
             Are waiting to cross the sea. I have accepted
             We are now on the defensive in France.
             I blame our *Luftwaffe*, and the women
             And cooking of France, which have softened our troops.

I have said there must be attacks on ships,
Requisitioning of trucks and convoy highways
Protected by aircraft to supply Normandy.

Rommel.   Field Marshal Rundstedt speaks for me. Rundstedt.

Rundstedt.   In my view no counter-attack can be made
And we should give up our position at Caen
And withdraw out of range of the ships' artillery.
General Schweppenburg feels the same,
His assessment is here.

Jodl.   That is the first step
To the catastrophic evacuation of France.
It is better to fight the decisive battle
Where we stand.

(*29 June. London underground war rooms. Churchill's office.* CHURCHILL *and* COLVILLE.)

Churchill.   A memorandum to Anthony Eden.
"The Foreign Office have copied a telegram
For immediate distribution to the War Cabinet,
Which makes it clear that eight hundred thousand
Hungarian Jews have been deported and sent
To Birkenau near Oswiecim, where it says
A million and a half Jews from Europe
Have already been killed. What can be done? Or said?"

(*He ponders.*)

Colville.   Sir, a signal from Monty. Bradley is
Delaying his thrust until July the third
Because the storm has delayed reinforcements.
Dempsey now faces eight Panzer divisions
Round Caen. An *Ultra* signal shows
Rommel is about to attack Cheux. Monty
Welcomes the attack as part of his strategy
To hold Rommel's armour while Bradley breaks
To Rennes and St. Malo, and also Paris.

Churchill.   Stalin has said that the crossing of the Channel

And landings in Normandy are "an unheard
Of achievement, the magnitude of which
Has never been undertaken in military history".

(*Chorus of Auschwitz* PRISONERS.)

Chorus.   What will become of us? Who will help us.
We hear that Montgomery has landed,
Normandy is a long, long way away.
How many months will it be before his troops
Have captured Berlin and reached here? Where are
Zhukov's men? Last month, eight thousand were killed.
This month, some two hundred and twenty-five
Thousand, mostly Jews sent from Hungary.
We know, we've seen them, we drag the bodies
From the gas chamber into the crematorium
Next door, we burn them and bury the surplus.
Each day prisoners are taken out and shot
Before the killing wall next to block eleven,
And more are hanged on the portable gallows.
Montgomery, make haste, help us, help us.
We cannot wait more than a few more weeks.
It will be our turn soon. Help us, help us.

(*1July. Churchill's office.* CHURCHILL.)

Churchill.   Send a message to Stalin: "The first week
Of the Soviet summer offensive in Belorussia
Has been outstandingly successful.
This is the moment for me to tell you
How immensely we are all here impressed
With the magnificent advances of the Russian armies,
Which seem, as they grow in momentum, to be
Pulverising the German armies which
Stand between you and Warsaw, and afterwards Berlin."

(*1 July.* RUNDSTEDT *on phone.*)

Rundstedt.   Keitel? Rundstedt. While Rommel and I were away
The British IIth Armoured crossed the Odon.
When General Dollmann heard this, he poisoned himself.

Officially he died of a heart attack.
Caen is now undefendable. You say
"What should we do?" Make peace, you idiots.
That's what I will be advising Hitler.

(*1 July. France.* ROMMEL *and* RUNDSTEDT. *Enter COL.* HEINRICH BORGMANN.)

Rundstedt.   You are one of Hitler's army adjutants.

Borgmann.   The *Führer* has sent me to decorate you
                   With the Oak Leaves.

                   (*He decorates* RUNDSTEDT.)

                             And to give you a blue envelope.
                   (To Rommel.) The *Führer* has sent a signal, that you must hold
                   The present lines.

Rommel   (*to Rundstedt*).   What does it say?

Rundstedt.   Kluge
                   Has taken my place. I am no longer
                   Commander-in-Chief, West.

(*2 July, morning. Blay, TAC HQ. Church bells and guns, yapping from* two *puppies.*EISENHOW-
ER *and* BRADLEY *outside the map caravan. Enter* MONTGOMERY.)

Montgomery.   Ike, Brad, what a pleasant surprise. I've been to church.

Eisenhower.   I'm over here for a five-day visit
                   To send a first hand report to the Combined
                   Chiefs of Staff, and I'm glad to escape London.
                   The V-I raids mean we're living underground.
                   We've evacuated SHAEF. From our viewpoint
                   As we shelter, it looks like stalemate here.

Montgomery.   Come and see the German Panther and Tiger
                   Tanks we've knocked out and captured,
                   And then I'll brief you on my strategy.

(*Later.* EISENHOWER *and* BRADLEY *outside the map caravan.* MONTGOMERY *still inside.*)

Eisenhower.	I am stunned by the clarity and logic
	Of his plan. In London he seems too slow,
	Over-cautious, but here, I've fallen under
	His conviction, his professionalism, his
	Physical presence, his spell. He has a certain
	Charisma, and I can see you and Dempsey
	Cannot go any faster. This bocage
	Is not tank country.
Bradley.	Collins told me,
	The British were in the war nearly three years
	Before us, and took heavy casualties in
	North Africa. It's natural that they're cautious.
Eisenhower.	But the fact remains, the British have failed to expand.
	I still want, nay demand, an offensive.
	I wonder why he's not mentioned *Anvil*.

(*8 July. Blay, Montgomery's HQ.* MONTGOMERY *and* DAWNAY.)

Montgomery.	I am perplexed. Ike seemed to understand
	When he was here, but now he urges haste,
	Expresses concern at our lack of progress
	Because Bradley failed to break out on the third,
	With the Germans defending every yard of ground.
	He wants a major attack on the left. But I've just
	Launched *Charnwood*, a direct assault from the north,
	As I briefed him I would when he was here.
	He doesn't understand the battle, nor
	Does anyone at SHAEF. And he's losing his nerve.
Dawnay.	Perhaps there are political pressures
	For a swift advance to the Pas de Calais
	To capture the V-I rocket launch-sites.
Montgomery.	He's lost his nerve, just as we're taking Caen.
	I shall write to him now and say that we
	Must be quite clear as to what is vital or,
	Our sense of values wrong, we may go astray.
Dawnay.	The city of Caen, save for its southern suburb,

Is now in British and Canadian hands.

(*10 July. Blay. Montgomery's caravan.* BRADLEY, DEMPSEY, CRERAR *and* PATTON.)

Bradley   (*depressed*). I've failed in my effort to break out.

Montgomery   (*quietly*).   Never mind.
                        Take all the time you need, Brad. If I were you
                        I think I should concentrate my forces more.

Dempsey.   And what should I do now? What is my role?

Montgomery   (*to Dempsey*). Go on hitting, draw the German armour
                        On to yourself to ease the way for Brad.

Patton.   I can't wait to smash into Brittany,
                        I don't want to wait till August, I want there now.

(*14 July. London. Bushey Park. Eisenhower's HQ.* EISENHOWER. BEDELL SMITH *shows in*
BOMBER HARRIS.)

Bedell Smith.   Air Marshal Harris.

Eisenhower.   Monty needs you to provide
                        Heavy bomber assistance. Now I know
                        There have been reservations about supporting infantry
                        From the air, but we're going on the offensive
                        All along the line, we're going to gain ground and
                        Kill Germans. I've explained this to Churchill.
                        We're all excited by the prospect of an attack
                        That will be decisive. At one stroke we will
                        Knock loose our shackles.

Harris.   So the new operation
                        On the seventeenth, *Goodwood*, will break out? You're on.

(*16 July. Blay. Montgomery's HQ.* MONTGOMERY *and* HENDERSON.)

Montgomery.   I'm alarmed that Ike's signal is euphoric.
                        No commander can have done more to avoid raising
                        Expectations. I've sent Kit to the War Office,

Written seven pages to Brooke, and sent
De Guingand to brief Ike, to simplify
The complex issues, to stress with simplicity
We are making the *enemy*, not the British or SHAEF,
Believe that we are breaking out to Paris;
And that our true aim is to dent Rommel's armour,
To muck up his plans and kill enemy troops.
Rommel is the objective.

(*Enter* GENERAL BROWNING.)

Browning, sit down.

Browning.   As commander of all airborne divisions
I have dropped parachutists, and we have found
Rommel's HQ, and know where he goes to fish
And shoot pigeons. Would you like us to kill him?

Montgomery   (*aside*). How strange that what I have heard in my deepest thoughts
And do not allow to surface should now be
Externalised in this proposal. What is right?
To say Yes and help the British break out
Or say No with the Christian code? He is
My old adversary at Alamein and elsewhere,
I would rather beat him face to face, fairly
As in a duel with pistols. But fair play
Has no place in war. War is war.
(*Aloud*.)   Yes, I would.

(*17 July, morning. La Roche Guyon.* ROMMEL *and* SPEIDEL.)

Rommel.   The German front in France will collapse
In a few weeks. We have tried to convince Hitler
To surrender. He will not. Yesterday
I warned him in my dispatch of a grave crisis
And told him the proper conclusion must be drawn,
That I must speak plainly. We must now surrender
On our own responsibility and open
Independent peace negotiations with the Allies
As soon as possible.

Speidel.   I agree. But will you now
                            Join the movement against Hitler?

Rommel   (*shocked*).   No, no.
                            I have my soldier's oath, which is ancient
                            And holy in the German tradition.
                            I am a professional. I disapprove
                            Of any movement against our Head of State.
                            To make a change in Berlin is not the way.
                            The Commander-in-Chief, West, who is now Kluge,
                            Should negotiate for the Allies to march,
                            Unopposed, across the Seine and into Germany.
                            We will talk further when I return tonight.

(*17 July, 9 p.m. Blay. Montgomery's HQ. MONTGOMERY and HENDERSON.*)

Henderson.   A report that will interest you. Rommel
                            Was in his staff car on a country road.
                            Two of Broadhurst's fighter bombers strafed it.
                            The driver lost an arm, Rommel was thrown
                            Out of his car and is now in hospital
                            With a severely fractured skull and splinters
                            In his face. Your enemy is out of the war.
                            The village near where the attack took place
                            Was Sainte Foy de Montgomery.

Montgomery.   My ancestor's.
                            If I am Achilles, he was my Hector.

                            (MONTGOMERY *turns away and goes to his caravan.*)

                            (*Praying.*) Lord, my enemy has been removed from the war,
                            And if that is your will, then I thank you.
                            But if I am responsible - if he was targeted
                            By Browning's men, and the name of the village
                            Suggests this, or else it is an amazing coincidence –
                            Then I am sad, for he is a noble man
                            And deserved a better end to his career.
                            Lord, be with him now, help him to recover,
                            Remove his pain, support his family.
                            And now, Lord, I put him out of mind for good.

(*Silence.*)

I feel it may have been better for the war
If Rommel were still in charge, but I don't know why.

(*He rises and slowly takes Rommel's picture off the caravan wall.*)

SCENE 3.

STAUFFENBERG'S BOMB PLOT

(*18 July. Blay. Montgomery's HQ.* MONTGOMERY *and* POSTON.)

Montgomery.   How has the *Goodwood* battle gone?

Poston.   A day
                   Of awe-inspiring power. Four and a half
                   Thousand aircraft pummelled German positions
                   East of the Orne on the southern outskirts of Caen.
                   I saw Tiger tanks buried, set ablaze,
                   Flung upside down. Then our armour went in –
                   Not our infantry because the War Office warned
                   Dempsey casualties could not be replaced –
                   And seemed to break through, but the German defences
                   Were over six miles deep, and our tanks caught fire,
                   We lost four hundred in all. The Desert Rats
                   Were slow, the infantry lagged behind – Crerar
                   Is no commander and a poor soldier – and the day
                   Ended with only yards gained, and no breakthrough,
                   And Dempsey, with five thousand casualties
                   And no headway despite three armoured divisions,
                   Has withdrawn. *Goodwood* has been a disaster.

Montgomery   (*quietly*). I shall claim it was a tactical success.
                   I like a picador, have paralysed
                   The bull's neck muscles with my twisting lance.
                   (*Depressed.*) But Bradley has delayed his pass again.

(*19 July evening. London, Bushey Park, SHAEF's HQ.* BUTCHER *on the phone.*)

Butcher.   Ike's lying down. His blood pressure's up,
                         He's had ringing in his ears, it's the mental strain
                         Of being frustrated at Monty's slowness.
                         He's been in bed all day.

                         (EISENHOWER *appears*.)
                                             It's Tedder, sir.

Eisenhower   (*taking phone*). The British armoured units have withdrawn.
                         You say Monty stopped the armour going further?
                         How dare he.

Butcher   (*nervously*). Your blood pressure, sir, let me –

Eisenhower   (*waving him aside*). The British air commanders are disgusted.
                         You are now telling me "I told you so".
                         You say the British Chiefs of Staff would support
                         Any recommendation I make. The sack?
                         Huh huh. Let me make sure I've got that now.
                         I take over field command, Alexander
                         Replaces Monty in charge of Twenty-first,
                         Chief Big Wind, you say, will be made a peer,
                         And you take Leigh-Mallory's place and command
                         The air forces. I'll have to think about that.
                         I'll call you.

(*19 July, late evening. London, underground war rooms. CHURCHILL in blue and gold dressing-gown in bed, a canary on his head. BROOKE.*)

Churchill   (*furiously*). *Goodwood* has failed, and now Ike says
                         General Montgomery banned all the VIP visits
                         During the battle. Who is he to dictate
                         To me? To stop me? When I was Minister of Munitions
                         In the First World War, Haig always allowed me
                         To visit. I have written to Ike that I
                         Have no intention of visiting General
                         Montgomery's headquarters and that Ike
                         Should provide a Staff Officer to show me about.
                         If General Montgomery disputes my visit
                         In any way, the matter will be taken up
                         Because I have a right and a duty

To acquaint myself with the facts on the spot.

Brooke.   I will visit Monty tomorrow morning.

(20 July. London, Bushey Park, Eisenhower's HQ. BUTCHER on phone.)

Butcher.   Bedell Smith? Butcher here, sir. Ike has asked
               Me to let you know, he's been to see Monty
               In response to that signalled invitation
               To visit him alone - that meant without Tedder.
               Monty's given him a logical explanation,
               And although Ike pointed out that there will soon
               Be more American troops than British in France,
               He says there's to be no hint of what he discussed
               With you last night. Sir, I don't know what Monty
               Has done, but he sure worked some magic. Ike is now
               A changed man. He's gone fishing, he's thrown away
               His blood-pressure pills, he's more happy with
               Monty's conduct of the war in Normandy.

(20 July, 12.35 p.m. VON STAUFFENBERG with a briefcase, in Keitel's sitting-room in Hitler's headquarters in Rastenburg, Wolfsschanze, the Wolf's Lair.)

Stauffenberg   (*alone*). Now is the moment of my destiny.
               For nine months I have plotted to restore
               Germany's greatness from a tarnished regime.
               Ever since I became Olbricht's Chief of Staff,
               And Olbricht promoted me to be Chief of Staff
               To Fromm so I could activate his Reserve Army
               And impose martial law when the *Führer* dies.
               All my life has led up to this moment,
               To kill the man who has shamed Germany
               And operate *Valkyrie*; and I have been
               The leader of the plotters - politicians, Generals.
               Though I am crippled and have no right hand
               And only three fingers on my left hand, yet still
               I can carry a briefcase and prime a bomb.
               Twice I marched the troops of the Reserve Army
               To take Berlin, and twice I aborted the plan,
               The first time because Göring was not there,
               The second time because Hitler left early.

Now I have the best opportunity of all
As Hitler wants me to attend a staff conference.
It should be in the underground concrete bunker
But has been transferred to a wooden hut.
I have a wife and children. If I fail
I will put them at risk, and many others.
But I must act, this tyranny cannot go on.
Hitler's atrocities shame all mankind.
By ending the war now I will save, what? –
Twenty or thirty million lives, bring peace
And freedom to our sacred Germany.

(STAUFFENBERG *moves to disclose* VON HAEFTEN, *sitting.*)

(*To Haeften.*) Two two-pound packages of explosive.

Haeften.   They're here.

(STAUFFENBERG *stoops and breaks the fuse capsule of one of the packages with pliers held in his three fingers. The door opens. Stauffenberg starts.*)

Orderly.   Keitel wants you to hurry up.

Stauffenberg.   Coming.

(*Major* JOHN VON FREYEND, *Keitel's adjutant, appears.*)

Freyend.   Stauffenberg, do come along now.

Haeften.   You've only primed one of the packages.

Stauffenberg.   One will have to do. It should be enough.

(*Exit* STAUFFENBERG, *leaving* HAEFTEN *holding one of the packages. Stauffenberg reappears.*)

Stauffenberg.   Now I will put the briefcase close to Hitler.
I will lay the bomb under his conference table,
Then the *Wehrmacht* will have a *putsch*, and then
We will arrange to surrender to the Allies

And stop the senseless conduct of the war.

(*He enters the hut and puts the briefcase under a heavy oak table near HITLER. COL. BRANDT moves it to the other side of the table's leg.*)

Haeften.   Colonel Stauffenberg, phone call from Berlin.

Stauffenberg.   Excuse me.

(*He goes out and waits with Gen. ERICH FELLGIEBEL. They watch. The hut explodes in smoke and flame. Two bodies fly out of the open windows. One is Brandt's.*)

                    No one could have survived that.
                    I will telephone Berlin to activate Valkyrie.
                    Then von Haeften and I will bluff our way
                    Out of the compound and drive to the airfield
                    Where our Heinkel is waiting.

(*They leave. HITLER staggers out, his trousers and hair on fire. He beats out the flames.*)

(*20 July, 12.45 p.m. Rastenburg, Wolf's Lair, a corridor in the Guest Bunker. HITLER and KEITEL. Hitler's face is smoke-blackened.*)

Hitler.   I thought it might be a paratroop attack
                    So I avoided the windows for the corridor.

Keitel.   That must have been one of the Todt workmen.

Hitler.   A German workman would never lift his hand
                    Against me. I always sensed this opposition
                    To me in the General Staff. Stalin knew what
                    He was doing when he rubbed out Marshal Tukhachevsky.
                    Now, I shall make a clean sweep. Send for Dr. Morell.

(*He sits unsteadily, and takes his own pulse. His SECRETARIES appear.*)

(*Grinning.*) Well ladies, things turned out well again. Ah, Dr. Morell.

(*A few minutes later.*)

| Hitler. | I am invulnerable, immortal. |
| | My survival is a great miracle. |

Dr. Morell.	You have some badly torn skin on your legs
	And a hundred splinters from the oak table. Your face
	Has been cut by splinters, a timber has bruised
	Your forehead. Your eardrums are perforated.

Hitler.	This was the work of cowards. If they had drawn a gun
	On me I might respect them, but they didn't dare
	Risk their own lives. I shall make an example of them
	That will make anyone else think twice before betraying
	The German people. My own life is not
	Important, but anyone who lifts a hand
	Against the German State during a war
	Must be destroyed, must be executed.
	Guards, search for hidden fuse cable and for
	Additional bombs. Now I shall have lunch.
	Call in the secretaries or I will be late. I meet
	The *Duce* from his train at two-thirty.

| Dr. Morell. | You can't possibly meet the *Duce* now. |

| Hitler. | I must. What would the world's press say if I didn't? |

(*20 July, mid-afternoon.* GOEBBELS *in his office with* SPEER *and* WALTER FUNK, *Economics Minister. The telephone rings.*)

Goebbels.	My *Führer.* A failed assassination attempt?
	That is scandalous, treasonous, criminal.
	You are safe. That is Providential. A *coup*?

(*He looks out of the window.*)

Yes, my Ministry is being surrounded now.
I will deal with it.

(*He puts poison capsules in his pocket.*)

There is an attempted *coup*,
Please excuse me. Send in Major Remer.

(*Enter Major* OTTO REMER *almost immediately.*)

Remer, what is going on?

Remer.   Sir, the commandant
Of the Berlin garrison, General von Hase,
Has told me the *Führer* has been assassinated
And the SS are attempting a *putsch*. I have orders,
Which I must obey, to seal the Wilhelmstrasse
And arrest some ministers, including you.

Goebbels.   But you have an oath of personal loyalty
To the *Führer*.

Remer.   The *Führer* is dead.

Goebbels.   He's alive.
An ambitious group of Generals has begun
A military *putsch*, the dirtiest in history.
I am going to speak to the *Führer* now.
You will speak with him.

(GOEBBELS *telephones on his direct line.*)

                                    My *Führer*, it's Goebbels again.
I have *Major* Remer here.

Remer.   Jawohl, mein Führer.
Jawohl, mein Führer.

(*He hands the phone back to* GOEBBELS *who listens.*)

Goebbels.   I understand, my *Führer*.
Colonel Remer is to crush the rebellion in Berlin.
He is to obey my orders or those of Himmler
Who is Commander of Reserve Army in place of Fromm.
And General Reinecke. I will broadcast
That the *coup* has failed.

(*He turns to* REMER)

Arrest the plotters.

(*20 July, 4.45 p.m. Berlin, Bendlerstrasse, upstairs now, 2nd floor. Colonel-General* FROMM *in his office.* STAUFFENBERG, OLBRICHT, HAEFTEN, KLEIST)

Stauffenberg.   Why didn't you activate *Valkyrie*
At once, as soon as I telephoned?

Olbricht.   I was at lunch.
But that aside, the *Führer* is alive.
He is entertaining Mussolini to tea.
As soon as Fromm heard Hitler is alive
He refused to go along with us.

Stauffenberg.   Hitler
Is dead. As usual Field Marshal Keitel's
Lying. I saw his body carried out.

Olbricht.   Orders for *Valkyrie* have now been given.

Fromm   (*raging, banging fists on desk*). I am in command, I will not allow
Subordinates to do such things. You are
All guilty of insubordination,
Revolution, treason. The penalty
For all of you is death. Who ordered this?

Olbricht.   Colonel Mertz von Quirnheim.

Fromm.   Bring von Quirnheim.

(*Enter Colonel* VON QUIRNHEIM, *Olbricht's Chief of Staff.*)

I want to confirm, did you give orders
For *Valkyrie*?

Quirnheim.   I did.

Fromm   (*raging*).   You, all of you,
Are under arrest. (*To Quirnheim.*) Cancel the orders.

Quirnheim   (*sitting down*). Colonel-General, since I am under

Arrest, my freedom to move's restricted.

Fromm   (*to Stauffenberg*). The assassination attempt has failed.
Stauffenberg, you will have to shoot yourself.

Stauffenberg.   No, we are in control. It is you who's
Under arrest. Take his pistol. Guard him.

(FROMM *rises and lurches forward, lunging with his fists towards*
STAUFFENBERG.)

Fromm   (*shouting*). You haven't been my Chief of Staff three weeks
And now you've got me into trouble with –

(HAEFTEN *and* KLEIST *draw their pistols.* FROMM *sits back.*)

Stauffenberg.   Put him in his adjutant's room next door.

(*Nearly midnight.* PRO-NAZIS *let* FROMM *out of his room. There is an exchange of gunfire.*
STAUFFENBERG *is hit in his good left arm in a corridor. Stauffenberg is brought into Fromm's
room by* BECK, OLBRICHT, VON QUIRNHEIM, HAEFTEN *and* HOEPNER. *Enter Fromm with
his adjutant* HAUPTMANN BARTRAM. *Haeften points his pistol at Fromm, who cowers.
Stauffenberg, bleeding from his shoulder, indicates that Haeften should lower his pistol. He
looks at Fromm with contempt. Enter Lt-Col.* GEHRKE *and* STAFF OFFICERS. *They observe.*)

Fromm.   All of you, over there. We have you covered.
You have plotted against the *Führer*, you
Have caused him pain. This is a court martial.

Stauffenberg.   He has known of the plot for weeks and has
Done nothing to prevent it and he wants
To kill us so we can't reveal that he
Is one of us. And now he is our judge
And jury. Some trial.

Fromm.   Quiet. You will not speak
Unless addressed. I pronounce you guilty
Of conspiring to assassinate our
Beloved *Führer*, high treason. Sentence:
Colonel-General Beck, General Olbricht, Colonel-
General Mertz, this Colonel whose name I will

Not speak, Lieutenant-General Hoepner and
Lieutenant von Haeften are condemned to
Death. Sentence will be carried out at once.
Have you any last wishes?

Stauffenberg.   I alone
Am responsible for everything. These
Men are just soldiers who obeyed orders
I gave. They are guiltless.

Fromm.   No, they are guilty.

Beck.   I wish to keep my pistol for private use.

Fromm   (*nodding*). You must do it now. Here.

Beck   (*stunned at the speed*).   Goodbye, my friends.

(*Standing, he points his Luger at his temple, flinches as he pulls the trigger.
Loud report. He falls back into* STAUFFENBERG's *bloodstained arms with
blood trickling from his head wound.*)

(*Moaning.*) Another gun. Quickly.

Staff Officer.   Try this Mauser.

(*Standing,* BECK *tries again. Loud report. He falls to the floor, moaning.*)

Sergeant.   Beck is not dead.

Fromm   (*contemptuously*). He has even bungled that.
Help the old gentleman.

(*The* SERGEANT *bends over* BECK, *whose head is bleeding, and
administers the* coup de grace *in front of the conspirators, who wince.*)

Take his leather
Overcoat as your reward. Any more
Last wishes?

Hoepner.   I had nothing to do with

The plot, I wish to compose a defence.

Olbricht.   I wish to write a statement.

Fromm   (*thinking*).   Very well.

Hoepner.   Please can I see you in private.

(*Half an hour later. FROMM emerges from the room next door. HOEPNER is led away under guard. OLBRICHT stops his writing. STAUFFENBERG is sitting apparently in prayer, clutching his shoulder.*)

Fromm.   Further investigations are required.

          (*Enter a* SOLDIER.)

Soldier.   General, the *Grossdeutschland* Guard Battalion
          Has arrived under Lieutenant Schady.

Fromm   (*starting*). Thank you. Hauptmann.

Bartram.   General.

Fromm.   Go down and pick
          Ten *Unteroffizieren* from Schady's
          Men and line them in the courtyard in front
          Of the pile of sand the builders have left,
          And line his army trucks with headlights on.

          (*Exit* BARTRAM.)

(*Only a little later.* STAUFFENBERG *seems in another world.*)

Fromm   (*to Olbright*). You've written enough now.
          (*To guards.*)   Take these four down
          To the courtyard.

Stauffenberg.   Goodbye my loyal friends.
          We will rise above their guns and hold ourselves
          Erect, for our idea was right, to stand
          Against atrocities. What we thought we

Will act, our self-control will show we still
Hold our beliefs, our self-mastery in
The face of wrong. We will call others to
Complete our task. Our Germany thanks you.

(STAUFFENBERG, OLBRICHT, HAEFTEN and QUIRNHEIM are marched
under guard and stood against a mound of sand. Dim light from a row of
army lorries with hooded headlights. The FIRING-SQUAD appears.)

Fromm.   Execute them. They shame our Fatherland.

Stauffenberg (standing straight, shouting). Long live our sacred Germany.

Haeften   (shouting).   Not him.

(HAEFTEN dives in front of STAUFFENBERG and takes his bullets. The
crash of the FIRING-SQUAD reverberates. Three fall. Stauffenberg is still
standing. Perplexed, the firing-squad reloads. The crash of the firing-squad
again. Stauffenberg falls back on the sand.)

Soldier.   Did he shout "sacred" or "secret" Germany?

Fromm.   Send a teleprinter message to the Führer:
              "Attempted putsch by irresponsible Generals
              Bloodily crushed. All ringleaders shot."
              Take their bodies to the local churchyard.

(Later. Enter SPEER and REMER.)

Fromm.   I've just had some criminals executed.

Remer.   I am not pleased, we wanted to question
              These men. You must come to the Propaganda
              Ministry, and be questioned by Goebbels
              And Himmler.

Speer.   A very hasty end. Say what
              You will, these men, if wrong, were very brave.

(21 July, 1 a.m. Martial music on radio, then Hitler's voice.)

Hitler.	I am speaking to you, first, so you may know
	I am unhurt and well, and second so that
	You may hear details of a crime unparalleled
	In German history. A conspiracy
	To eliminate me has been hatched by
	A tiny clique of ambitious, irresponsible,
	Stupid and criminal officers. I was spared
	A fate which holds no terror for me, but would
	Have had terrible consequences for
	The German people. I regard this as a sign
	That I should continue the task imposed
	Upon me by Providence. The criminals
	Will all be ruthlessly exterminated.

*(*A little later.* RASTENBURG, *Hitler's room.* HITLER *and* BORMANN.)

Hitler	I will have blood, I will have sacrifice.
	Just as in Warsaw, Stroop gave me the gift
	Of the Ghetto for my birthday, so now
	I will see the conspirators on meat hooks.
	They must be hanged like cattle. On thin wire.

| Bormann. | I will attend to it. They will be filmed. |
| | I have the idea of using piano wire. (*Exit.*) |

Hitler	(*alone*). I must watch them suffer, with you my dear.
	We will receive the sacrifice of blood
	Of thousands who made me suffer like this.
	Oh Eva, you have written from Bavaria,
	I wish you were here. My spear, I will spear them.

*(*21 July, 3.40 a.m. Hitler's HQ.* HITLER *and* BORMANN.)

Bormann.	General Fromm has just been arrested, and
	The traitors' action is now at an end.
	(*Wheedling.*) A letter from von Kluge about Rommel.
	"The view of the Field Marshal is unfortunately right.
	I have spoken with the commanders around Caen
	And the regrettable evidence is that in the face
	Of the enemy air forces' complete command,
	There is no way we can counterbalance

Its annihilating effect without giving up
The field of battle."

Hitler.   They are defeatist,
            All my Generals.

(*21 July, morning. Blay. Montgomery's HQ. The dining marquee.* MONTGOMERY *alone.*)

Montgomery   (*aside*). Brooke has told me Churchill has an order
            In his pocket, dismissing me. All TAC HQ
            Know this rumour. I will meet fire with fire. Brooke
            Says Ike told him I am keeping him from France,
            Which made him furious. I will welcome him
            Although I regard his visit as meddlesome.
            He likes canaries, I will charm him with mine.
            A General must be confident to all.
            I will radiate optimism and boost his nerve.

            (*Enter* HENDERSON *and* CHURCHILL *wearing blue coat and cap.*
            It is raining outside. There is a frosty atmosphere. PAUL *the chef is listening*
            behind a tent-flap.)

            (*Aloud, shaking hands.*) Prime Minister, I'm delighted and honoured
            To welcome you to near the Cerisy forest,
            And I'm greatly looking forward to briefing you.
            Have you seen my dogs and canaries, sir?

Churchill   (*sitting*).   I have
            A canary that sits on my head. Henderson,
            Would you mind leaving us?

            (*Exit* HENDERSON *to the kitchen tent, with* PAUL. *They listen.*)

                        Monty, SHAEF – Ike and
            Tedder - want you dismissed. We've had setbacks –

Montgomery.   Setbacks? What setbacks? The battle is going
            Excellently.

Churchill.   They say we're losing the war
            And you're panicking, they want Alexander

To take over. And I'm Defence Minister
And Prime Minister, and I've a right to be here,
Monty.

Montgomery.   It's dangerous, sir.

Churchill.   Let me be the judge
Of that.

Montgomery.   There's no panic here, come into
The operations caravan and I'll show you a map.
The Germans are doing exactly what we want.
Tedder doesn't understand my plan, I don't want
To take Caen but to keep pressing on it
To bring the Germans to me, then Patton can
Swing round.

Henderson   (*to Paul*).   You should not be hearing this.

Paul.   Nor you.

(MONTGOMERY *and* CHURCHILL *walk to the caravan.*)

Montgomery.   I am not fighting the Germans and the Italians
Alone, but the Americans and British as well,
The only people I'm not fighting are
The Russians.

Churchill.   Monty, I know the feeling well.

Montgomery.   In four to five weeks you will have all France
In your pocket.

(*They enter the caravan.*)

(*Later. Enter Brigadier* BILL WILLIAMS, *Intelligence Officer. He knocks on the caravan door.*
MONTGOMERY *opens.*)

Williams.   Sir, we have gleaned from scraps of *Ultra* there's
Been a sort of revolution in Berlin.

Montgomery.	How intriguing. Sir, do you know anything About this?

(CHURCHILL *holds keys on a long chain and opens two red boxes.*)

Churchill.	There's something about it in here. See what you can find.

(MONTGOMERY *and* WILLIAMS *rifle through the dispatch-boxes.*)

Williams.	These are *Ultra* signals. Sir, have you read this?
Churchill.	No.
Williams.	This could mean a sudden end to the war.
Montgomery.	There could be a surrender this morning. The American *Cobra* attack may not be needed. We've got the Germans on the run.

(*They emerge from the caravan,* CHURCHILL *beaming.*)

Churchill.	Monty, I must be off.

(*Exit* WILLIAMS.)

Montgomery.	Whenever you get angry In the future, sir, you're to send me a telegram And find out the truth.
Churchill.	I promise I will.
Montgomery.	And this bottle of cognac is a peace offering.

(*They shake hands. Exit* CHURCHILL. *Enter* HENDERSON.)

He is volatile, he's up and down, and love
Can turn to rage, but that was very friendly.

Henderson.	You've bought yourself another month, I would say.

Montgomery.   Things will have improved by then.

(*21 July. Berlin. Prinz Albrechtstrasse,* Gestapo *HQ.* HIMMLER *visits the cellars with* ERNST KALTENBRUNNER.)

Himmler.   The Special Commission you set up yesterday
                    Already has four hundred officials who
                    Interrogate day and night the ever-widening circle
                    Of those implicated in this shameful plot.
                    Each day Kielpinski will write a summary
                    Of what has developed and send it to Bormann.
                    I would like to see your methods, how you extract
                    Confessions, so I am knowledgeable
                    If Bormann asks. Take me to a cell where I
                    Can see an interrogator at work.

Kaltenbrunner.   Hundreds of officers have been arrested,
                    Including General Fromm. We are getting names.
                    Generals include von Tresckow and Wagner
                    And Field Marshals Rommel and von Kluge.
                    Also von Stulpnagel. We suspect Canaris,
                    Moltke, Dohnanyi, and Bonhoeffer.
                    There will be thousands of names. This is how they talk.

                    (*He opens a door. There is a muffled shriek, a groan.*)

                    His legs are in metal tubes with sharp spikes,
                    That are screwed into his flesh. There are more spikes
                    In his fingertips. A helmet and blanket
                    Muffle the screams. He will talk, they all do.

Himmler   (*nodding and turning back*). The Army has been purged.
                       Guderian,
                    The new Chief of Staff, has pledged its allegiance
                    To the *Führer*. The army salute will be
                    Abolished for the party raised arm. All
                    Chiefs of Staff will be party men, and teach
                    The tenets of Hitler. This will be announced.

(*24 July. Rastenburg, Hitler's room.* HITLER *and* DR. GIESING. BORMANN *and* SONNLEITHNER *nearby.*)

Hitler.	My right ear is bleeding, my eyes flick to
	The right, I keep thinking I am falling
	To my right. But the shock has got rid of my nerve
	Complaint, my left leg does not tremble now
	But my hearing.... Cauterise my ear again,
	Ignore my pain. I stopped feeling pain long
	Ago, pain exists to make a man of you.
	(*To Sonnleithner.*) I had *both* eardrums perforated, yet
	I did not feel a thing, it happened so fast.
	That's probably how it is when you shoot yourself.
	Even if you shoot yourself in the mouth, not the brain,
	I now know you don't feel a thing.

| Dr. Giesing. | It's amazing you were not more badly hurt. |

Hitler.	Providence protected me. I am immortal
	Until I have completed my Providential task.
	(*To Bormann.*) Exhume Stauffenberg and the three others.
	They were buried in their uniforms with their medals.
	I want proof that they died, I do not trust Fromm,
	Or the Army, who may have invented
	The execution to put me off their track.

| Bormann. | I will attend to it. Rest assured, it will be done. (*Exit.*) |

*(*24 July. London, Bushey Park. SHAEF HQ, EISENHOWER *on phone.*)

Eisenhower.	Winston, you're just back from Normandy. What
	Do you people think about the slowness
	Of the situation over there? You are
	Supremely happy with the situation?
	Tedder said Monty deliberately
	Restricted Dempsey's break-out, and that he did
	Not have the slightest intention of a clean breakthrough
	To Paris. A diversion? You support him.
	(*Aside.*) He's obviously sold Winston a bill of goods.

(*25 July. Blay. Montgomery's HQ. MONTGOMERY *and* EISENHOWER.*)

| Montgomery. | How are you? |

Eisenhower.	Still suffering from high blood pressure.

Eisenhower.   Still suffering from high blood pressure.
I think it's been caused by all the sleep I've lost
As a result of the buzz-bombs. I've come to see
The start of *Cobra* but did not expect
American planes to bomb American troops
Two days running with over seven hundred
And fifty casualties. The lesson is,
Heavy bombers can't give tactical support.

Montgomery.   We're still trying to find out why this happened.

Eisenhower.   Monty, you should know there's a strong feeling in the US
That American troops are doing more than British
As Americans have suffered more casualties
And captured more prisoners.

Montgomery.   Your bigger casualties –
Ten thousand to the British and Canadian six –
Are due to American lack of skill in fighting,
For example, bombing their own side.

Eisenhower.   That's not right.
I'm under pressure from General Marshall.
There's a feeling that there will soon be more
American troops than British, that they're doing more.
I asked you to support *Cobra*, You declined.
If *Cobra* fails – and the battle is touch and go –
Then there may be criticism of your command.

(*25 July. Rastenburg.* HITLER *and* GOEBBELS *in his office, on phone.*)

Hitler.   Goebbels, I am indebted to you for crushing
The army *putsch* by the officer corps.
You are now to be Reich commissioner
For total mobilisation of resources for war.
You are to have power over all civilians
And party authorities.

Goebbels.   My *Führer*, I am honoured.
And pleased to serve you.

(He leaves Hitler's room. Outside, to his assistant.)

If I had had these powers
Earlier, when I wanted them, the war would now
Be finished. It takes a bomb under his arse
To make Hitler see reason.

(27 July. London. Churchill's underground HQ. Dinner. EISENHOWER, BEDELL SMITH, BROOKE, CHURCHILL.*)*

Churchill.   Over lunch yesterday, you expressed dissatisfaction
              With Montgomery, and I have asked you to repeat
              These criticisms in the presence of my Chief of Staff,
              And now I would like to hear his reply.

Brooke.   The criticisms which the Supreme Commander
              And his Chief of Staff have again expressed
              To the Prime Minister are defeatist and
              Do not accord with the picture I have received
              From General Montgomery today. He is fighting hard
              On the eastern flank to assist the Americans
              On the western side. I am quite certain that
              Montgomery's strategy is about to pay off,
              And anyone who doubts that knows nothing about strategy.
              If the Supreme Commander has any criticisms
              Of the way his Land Forces Commander-in-Chief
              Is directing the battle, he should return
              To Normandy and put them to his face
              And not complain to others behind his back.

Eisenhower.   I am shy of doing that in a sensitive matter.
              I want to maintain the best relations between
              The British and Americans and win the war.

Churchill.   We cannot make a public statement about
              Our strategy in making the Germans believe
              The British are trying to break out when they're not,
              As this would be read by the enemy. Silence is best.

(29 July. Bradley's HQ in France. MONTGOMERY *and* HENDERSON.*)*

| Henderson. | Ike's with Kay, his Irish driver. |

| Montgomery | (*scathingly*). You mean, His floozie. |

| Henderson. | It's her first time in Normandy. |

(*Enter* EISENHOWER, KAY SUMMERSBY *and* BRADLEY. MONTGOMERY *ignores Kay, who talks aside with Bradley.*)

| Eisenhower. | It's excellent news that Brad's armoured divisions Have caused the German front to disintegrate. |

| Montgomery. | Yesterday I took Dempsey to Brad's headquarters, Dempsey's launching his next armoured attack From Caumont and Kluge will be out of position As he expects us to thrust towards Paris. We all agreed the plan is working well. |

| Eisenhower. | Did you get my signal, that I am delighted That your basic plan has begun to unfold Brilliantly with Brad's success? |

| Montgomery | (*nodding*). Yes, I did. |

| Eisenhower | (*elated*). I've told the American censor, General Surles, That I am responsible for strategy And major activity in Normandy And that any criticism of you Is criticism of me. |

(EISENHOWER *and* BRADLEY *turn away.*)

| Montgomery | (*to Henderson*). O-o-oh, did you hear that? Now he smells triumph, he's taking the credit. |

| Henderson. | It's time to meet Bradley, sir. |

*(*1 August. Churchill's office. *CHURCHILL *and* BROOKE.)

| Churchill. | Rokossovsky is ten miles from Warsaw, |

Having advanced four hundred miles in six
Weeks, and today the Polish Home Army,
At the direction of the Polish Government-
In-Exile in London, have risen against
The Germans in their city, the Warsaw Uprising.
Koniev has taken Lvov, and other Russians
Are in North Poland and Lithuania.
I want to know what Stalin will do. Will he help
The Free Poles?

(*2 August.. Stalin's Kremlin office. STALIN on phone.*)

Stalin.   Rokossovsky? Your report? You have lost
A hundred and twenty-three thousand men
On the way to Warsaw, your troops are exhausted.
You fear a German attack from the south.
You are still outside Warsaw. Stay where you are,
Don't move on Warsaw. The Uprising is led
By a General Bór, real name Komorowski,
Who wants a pro-British democratic Poland,
He is against the Red Army and will fight you
If you go in. Sit tight and let him fight
The Germans, and when they are both worn out,
And street-fighting is no longer a danger,
Then you may go in.

* (*3 August. 10 a.m. Dempsey's HQ in France. Map. MONTGOMERY and DEMPSEY.*)

Montgomery.   Now that the plan is working, and we have Rennes,
And Patton is going to make an eastward wheel
While you, Crerar and Bradley tie Kluge down
Between Caen and Mortain, and swing his right
Flank round towards Paris, outflanking the enemy
And forcing some back to the Seine; it will be
Possible for you and Hodges to outflank
The Germans to the north in this Falaise gap.
And if Crerar strikes south towards Falaise
We can surround the enemy in a pocket.
This is the consequence of sticking to the plan
For two months, making the struggle for Normandy
The longest ever battle in the West,

Surpassing the three-week battle for France
And the twelve-day battle of Alamein.

(7 August. Forêt de Cerisy, Montgomery's new TAC HQ. MONTGOMERY and BRADLEY.)

Montgomery.   I would like a full encirclement to the Seine.

Bradley.   Sir, time is critical, that would take too long.
                     I advise a short encirclement at Falaise.
                     I can't believe that Hitler has sent in
                     Four Panzer divisions, right into our trap.
                     Kluge doesn't seem to know what we're about.
                     We should spring it as soon as we can. It will be
                     A present to Ike, who's setting up SHAEF HQ
                     In Tournières today.

(8 August.. Eight conspirators before Freisler's People's Court: VON WITZLEBEN, HOEPNER, STIEFF, VON HASE, BERNARDIS, KLAUSING, HAGEN, and VON WARTENBURG, all army men, ranks ranging from Field Marshal to Lieutenant. FREISLER is in a blood-red robe. Swastika flags.)

Freisler   (*shouting*). Witzleben, you were a Field Marshal, why
                     Are you fiddling with your trousers? You dirty old man.

Witzleben.   My belt has been taken away.

Freisler.   Can't you speak?

Witzleben.   My teeth have also been taken away.

Freisler.   Wartenburg, you wanted to tell the Court something?

Wartenburg.   Of my contempt for National Socialism.
                     Man has a moral and religious duty
                     To oppose any regime which lacks respect
                     For the sacredness of human life.

Freisler.   Enough.

(He has signalled to the cameras behind a swastika to stop filming.)

I won't have any more of these irrelevant
Speeches.

(*He signals to the cameras to resume.*)

You say you are guilty. The Court
Accepts your confession. We have now heard
The evidence. This is the last day of this trial.
The Court finds all the defendants guilty.
It denies them the honour of beheading
And sentences them to death by hanging.
Sentences to be carried out at Plotzensee
This afternoon, film to be sent to the *Führer*.

(*8 August. Later. The Plotzensee execution building, two windows under eight meat hooks on a roof beam. A black curtain. A camera, two* CAMERAMEN. *Film lights. The Public Prosecutor* HANSSEN, *sitting.* VON WITZLEBEN *is led in half-naked.*)

Hanssen.   Accused, the People's Court has sentenced you
To death by hanging. Hangman do your duty.

(VON WITZLEBEN *is led to under the first meat hook by two executioners. The grinning* HANGMAN, *one of the two, puts piano wire round his neck.*)

Witzleben.   Piano wire. And meat hooks. (*Scathingly.*) For a human being.

Hangman   (*grinning, leering*). A slow hanging.

(*The wire is shaped in a figure of 8. They lift him and throw the upper noose over the meat hook. They let him drop. The wire bites into his neck, causing a ring of blood. As his feet move they draw a curtain but leave a gap for the camera to watch.* HOEPNER *is led in, the General who escaped Fromm's firing-squad.*)

Hanssen.   Accused, the People's Court has sentenced you
To death by hanging. Hangman do your duty.

(HOEPNER *is led to under the second meat hook by the two* EXECUTIONERS. *The same process is repeated. The black curtain half drawn.*)

Cameraman 1.   Sir, we can't face any more.

Hanssen.   The *Führer* has said
                "They must be hanged like cattle." It must be filmed.
                The *Führer* wants to watch them die tonight.
                A plane is standing by to fly your film
                To Rastenburg.

SCENE 4.

MONTGOMERY'S DEMOTION

*(*13 August, 12.15p.m. Forêt de Cerisy, Montgomery's HQ. MONTGOMERY, BRADLEY *and*
DEMPSEY.)

Montgomery.   Thank you for flying up here, Brad. Now, Patton
                Has raced away and could reach Paris, the Seine,
                But you still favour the short encirclement
                At Falaise?

Bradley.   Yes sir. Once Patton starts racing,
                He can find he's going in the wrong direction
                As at Palermo. We have Germans in a trap.
                It's wiser to spring it now, rather than let
                Them out.

Montgomery.   In that case, none must cross the Seine
                Without being mauled. The plan is as follows:
                The Canadians will attack, supported by
                Heavy bombers; Dempsey will seize Falaise
                To allow the Canadians to push towards
                Trun and Argentan, where Collins will
                Arrive from the southern flank, and Patton will
                Act as long stop east of L'Aigle.

*(*15 August, 7.30p.m. Rastenburg, Wolf's Lair, Hitler's HQ. HITLER *bent, with cotton wool in his*
ears. BORMANN.)

Hitler.	Patton is rampaging through Brittany,
	The Americans have attacked us near Falaise
	All day, and still no sign of Field Marshal
	Von Kluge, and now we learn his radio truck
	Has been silent all day, and he is mentioned
	In an enemy radio signal. Either he is dead,
	Or he is surrendering to the British and
	Joining forces with Russia, an idiotic
	Notion. SS General Hausser will now
	Take over Army Group B and stop the enemy.

*(*16 August. Later.*)

Hitler.	The worst day of my life. I have not slept,
	The sedatives don't work, send my doctor.
	Now Eberbach's headquarters report that
	Kluge arrived last night in the middle of the trap,
	With no explanation for where he was yesterday.
	There are reports he has contacted the British.
	Signal he is to leave the area at once.
	I can no longer trust him. Contact Field Marshal
	Model and appoint him Kluge's successor.
	Oh my headache. Damn Stauffenberg.

(*16 August. London, Churchill's underground HQ.* CHURCHILL *and* BROOKE.)

Brooke.	In the BBC news yesterday there was a report
	That Eisenhower has taken personal command
	In France with Bradley's and Monty's army groups
	Under him. This was retracted today.
	It is clear to me that Eisenhower now wants
	To be Field Commander of the Allied army groups
	In France once he's set up battlefield HQ.
	He's now in Normandy, but Monty is
	Treating him like a VIP, he's forbidden
	Him to attend meetings with Bradley, Patton,
	Dempsey and Crerar. He's inviting trouble.
	Listen to this disturbing letter I've had:
	"Ike is apt to get very excited and talk
	Wildly at the top of his voice. He is now here,
	Which is a very great pity. His ignorance

As to how to run a war is absolute
And complete....He is such a decent chap that it is
Difficult to be angry with him for long.
One thing I am firm about; he is never allowed
To attend a meeting between me and my
Army Commanders and Bradley."

Churchill.   He's digging his grave.
He is self-willed and convinced of his mastery
Of modern battlefield warfare, and scorns
The "lesser" talents of his fellow Generals.
He has no sense of tact or diplomacy.
Someone should tell him that Eisenhower is
In charge of over a million American troops.
It is not for us to say this to him now.
It has been said already. The *Anvil*
Landings near Marseilles will affect Italy.
We have the Pacific to think of. We must
Visit the Italian front, and Monty will
Have to fend for himself, and it is up to him
Whether his character strengths or flaws will
Gain the upper hand, whether he has learned
From the advice you have given him, and his treatment of me.

(*17 August. Fougères, Bradley's HQ.* MONTGOMERY *and* BRADLEY.)

Montgomery.   We must keep a grip on the battle and not be
Carried away. Patton has charged towards Paris
Like a bull - Palermo again - and the Canadians
And the Poles are trying to close the jaws of our trap
Without Patton. We have taken a hundred and fifty
Thousand prisoners in Normandy, and another hundred
Thousand troops are in the Falaise bag. Meanwhile
Leclerc has raced off to beat Patton to Paris:
Another hole. Gerow has pulled him back.
We need to think ahead beyond the Seine,
Which we will reach tomorrow. As I see it
Twelve and Twenty-one Army Groups should keep
Together as a solid mass that need
Fear nothing. The British and Canadians
Should hug the coast and go for Antwerp and

Capture the rocket sites that threaten England.
You should form a right flank towards Aachen,
Cologne and then the Ruhr. Together we will form
A single, narrow thrust.

Bradley.   I agree entirely.

Montgomery.   I have not yet discussed the plan with Ike.
I want to put to him that the US Seventh
Army, driving up from the south of France,
Should target the Saar. Ike is not likely
To have any great objections, and he will,
I think, undoubtedly accept what we say.

Bradley   (*aside*). Does he really believe that? Wishful thinking.
He is deluding himself.

(*17 August. Later. Bradley's HQ.* EISENHOWER *and* BRADLEY; HANSEN, *Bradley's* AIDE.)

Hansen   (to *Eisenhower*). Sir, a communication from General Marshall.

(EISENHOWER *takes it and reads.*)

Eisenhower.   Hey, Brad, listen to this: "The Secretary",
That's Stimson, "and I and apparently all Americans
Are strongly of the opinion that the time has come
For you to assume direct exercise of command
Of the American Contingent." He says that
"The astonishing success of the campaign"
Has evoked "emphatic expressions of confidence
In you and Bradley". He doesn't say the same
About Monty. I'm taken aback.

Bradley.   Me too.

(*20 August. Rastenburg. Hitler's HQ.* HITLER *and* BORMANN.)

Bormann.   My *Führer*, Kluge is dead. Army doctors
Say it was a cerebral haemorrhage.
He was still shocked by the failure of his
Counter-attack on Avranches, and then Falaise.

Hitler.	It is scandalous that the Canadians have
	Taken Falaise. This was largely Kluge's fault.
	He was defeatist and pessimistic.
	But could he not have committed suicide?
	He was linked to the *putsch*, along with Speidel.
	I want a second army autopsy.
	Model is to be congratulated on
	Saving the German forces from encirclement.
	He does not know the meaning of surrender.

(*21 August. Tournières. Eisenhower's HQ.* EISENHOWER *and* BUTCHER.)

Eisenhower.	Marshall wants me to command, and I have here
	A letter from Monty to Brooke, which arrived after
	Brooke left for Italy, saying the two
	Army Groups should keep together. However Brad
	Favours an eastward drive to Germany,
	Not north via the Lowlands, and the Red Army
	Yesterday launched its offensive to Romania.
	The balance of Allied troops has changed.
	On D-Day America had fewer troops than Britain.
	Now America has twice as many,
	Now three-quarters of all forces. It is
	Impossible not to change the command structure.
	I have now decided to change the system of command
	On September the first. I will take command
	Of the two Army Groups, and Bradley's Twelve Group
	Will drive for Metz and Saar. The British can
	Go north to destroy V-bomb rocket sites
	While the Americans go into Germany.
	The Army Groups will separate. Send a cable
	To the Combined Chiefs of Staff, and a directive
	To Monty.

(*21 August, evening. Condé, Montgomery's new TAC HQ.* MONTGOMERY *and* DE GUINGAND.)

Montgomery	(*devastated*). Tomorrow the battle of Normandy will be won.
	I do not agree with the decisions reached.
	I am sending you back to General Eisenhower
	With some *Notes on Future Operations*.

You are to tell General Eisenhower that
These *Notes* represent my views and that Bradley
Has expressed his agreement with them.
Ask the Supreme Commander to lunch with me
The day after tomorrow. He should come and see me.
(*Aside.*) Eisenhower will read in the *Notes* that I want him
To abdicate command over both Army Groups.

(*Exit* DE GUINGAND. *Enter* HENDERSON.)

Henderson   (*gently*). I said you'd bought a month.

Montgomery.   But when I've just won.
Eisenhower wants to scoop the reward.
I thought he was too decent to do this.
I was wrong. This, in the hour of my greatest triumph.
It is dangerous to swap horses in mid-stream.
And when the Germans are on the run, and the war....
(*Aside.*) O Brooke, would that you were in the War Office
And not on a long visit to Alexander.

(*22 August. Condé,, Montgomery's HQ.* MONTGOMERY *and* DE GUINGAND, *who has returned from Eisenhower, and* NYE, *Brooke's deputy.*)

De Guingand.   I spent two hours with him in an apple orchard.
He wouldn't budge. The Allied Forces must split,
The British to the north, the Americans perhaps to the east.
He says the British can't count on any Americans
In the north.

Montgomery.   Procrastination. "Perhaps to the east."
I disagree with any plan which splits
The Allied force.

Nye.   Sir, as Brooke's deputy,
I beg you not to split the Allied command
While Churchill and Brooke are out of England.
The Alliance must come first.

(*23 August. Laval, Bradley's new HQ.* MONTGOMERY *and* BRADLEY.)

| Montgomery. | On August the seventeenth you agreed with me |
| | That both Armies should go north. |

Bradley	(*dropping the "sir"*). No, I did not.
	I see that the British should go north because
	Of the V-I sites, but I have always wanted
	To go east to Germany.

| Montgomery | (*thinly*). You have been got at. |
| | Yesterday, when you went to visit Ike. |

Bradley.	No. The American army has put behind it
	The poor performance at Kasserine Pass,
	Salerno and Anzio, and has a new confidence.
	We're pouring fifty divisions into Europe
	While fighting in the Pacific, we've come of age.
	We have double the troops, we want to go east
	To Germany. We can do it on our own.

Montgomery	(*sadly*). I trained you, and now you want to race off
	Like Patton. It's a mistake to split the Armies.
	It will not shorten the war but prolong it.

| Bradley. | We don't see it that way. And as regards training, |
| | I'm "the military Lincoln" in the press back home. Good day. |

(*23 August, 12 noon. Condé, Montgomery's HQ. As* MONTGOMERY *returns,* EISENHOWER *arrives with* BEDELL SMITH *and* GENERAL GALE.)

Montgomery	(to *Eisenhower*). I must see you alone and get your decision
	On certain points of principle. The staff
	Should not be present.

(EISENHOWER *and* MONTGOMERY *go alone into the map caravan.* MONTGOMERY *stands before the map, feet apart, hands behind his back, eyes darting.*)

You know I want a northward
Thrust of both Armies, who would be so strong
They need fear nothing. The immediate need
Is for a firm plan. I think it's a mistake

To split the Armies, and for you to take command
In the field. The Supreme Commander should be on high,
On a perch with a detached view of land, sea, air,
Civil control, political problems. He should
Not descend into the intricacies of
The land battle, someone else should do that.
And it is a whole time job for one man.
Today the Falaise trap is closed, we are now
Bombing the Germans caught inside. We have won
A great victory because of land control,
Not in spite of it. If American public opinion
Is the problem, let Bradley control the battle,
Put me under Bradley.

Eisenhower.   No, that's not my intention.
I don't favour a single thrust to the Ruhr.
The Germans are in confusion, I want two thrusts
With the flexibility to reinforce either,
Depending on which is succeeding the most.

Montgomery.   I don't think either will be strong enough, alone.
The British, alone, need additional forces
For the northern thrust to the V-I sites.

Eisenhower   (*deliberately*). They can have American assistance, but
It should be kept to a minimum.

Montgomery.   Who should command
The northern thrust?

Eisenhower.   There must be one commander. You.

Montgomery.   Twenty-first Army Group only has fourteen divisions.

Eisenhower.   How many American divisions would you need
For your thrust to the north?

Montgomery.   An American Army
Of at least twelve divisions on our right flank.

Eisenhower   (*speechless*). If that happened the Americans would only have

One Army, and public opinion would object.

Montgomery.   Why should public opinion make you want to take
Military decisions which are definitely unsound?

Eisenhower.   You must understand, it's election year in the States.
I can take no action which may sway public
Opinion against the President, and lose
Him the election. And so we must now separate
The two Army Groups, I must take command
Of the ground forces and send the two Army
Groups in different directions so there is
No question of the Americans being under
The operational control of a British General.

Montgomery.   Military logic does not base itself
On public opinion.

Eisenhower.   The American Army Group
Will become two armies, so we have three
In all: an Army Group of the North, of the Centre
And of the South. And I will be Generalissimo
In the field.
(*Aside*.)   He takes a narrow military view
And lacks the diplomatic sense to grasp
That I must do what Marshall and Roosevelt want,
And how they perceive public opinion is
A pressure on me I cannot ignore.
He puts my blood pressure up. I want rid of him.
The only way I'll agree to a single thrust
In the north, is if it accords with the separation
Between Americans and British my masters want.

Montgomery   (*aside*). SHAEF are behind this mess, and Bedell Smith,
Not the American election, that's an excuse.
In his heart of hearts he knows it's wrong.
(*Aloud*.) So the British are on their own in the north, but are not
Strong enough to thrust without American help,
Which must be commanded by an American.
(*Shaking his head*.) We have split the Allied effort on the day
It achieved its greatest victory in World War Two,

At its highest point when it could shorten the war.
I speak from the highest summit the Allies reached.
This is a mistake and will lengthen the war.

Eisenhower.   Bedell Smith and I will go off and draft
               A directive I will show you before it goes out.

               (EISENHOWER *leaves the caravan*.)

Montgomery   (*alone*). This is the reality of war. Meetings,
               Signals, modifications of the plan,
               Developments, bickerings, and the Generals
               Are all isolated from the main action.
               They are like instruments in an orchestra.
               Each has its own position, plays its own note,
               But together they sound a great symphony
               Like the *1812* with cannon and mortar fire
               That ends in triumph to cheers and applause.
               But each remains quite separate, alone,
               And only the score – the plan – holds them together;
               And if that is changed, there is cacophany.

(*Later*. GENERAL ALLEN, *12th US Army Group's Chief of Staff. Enter* PATTON.)

Patton.   Where is everybody?

Allen.   Gone, sir. You've just missed them.
               Generals Eisenhower, Bradley and Montgomery.

Patton.   Say, I've just thought up the best strategical idea
               I've ever had. Write it down. The Third Army
               Will cross the Seine at Melun, and the Yonne at Sens,
               And swivel north across the Marne and the Oise
               And cut off German troops fleeing from Dempsey
               And Hodges at Beauvais. In other words,
               Third Army abandons Saar and takes part in
               Monty's northern thrust.

Allen   (*thinly*).   Sounds fine to me, General.

Patton.   Tell it to Brad when he comes back. I want

	To start this tomorrow. (*Exit*.)
Allen.	I think you're too late,
	General, by just an hour.

(*Later in August. Falaise, the battlefield.* EISENHOWER *stands apart from* KAY.)

Eisenhower.	Now I, the Supreme Commander, am confronted with
	The reality to which my plans have led:
	The Falaise battlefield, covered with tanks,
	Guns, vehicles, horses and thousands of dead
	German soldiers in uniform, overhung
	Like a morning mist with the foul stench of death
	That gets in my throat and chokes and sickens me;
	A field of decaying flesh, as if the top
	Had been taken from a burial ground, exposing
	The rotting corpses of the hidden dead.
	This is an inferno, this is infernal. I loathe war,
	I despise what my plans have done,
	This victory I have won over these humans.
	I am disgusted with myself for being
	Involved in this slaughter, this massacre,
	Which falls below the standards I uphold.
	War is like a cesspit that must be cleared out,
	There is nothing for it but to wade in muck
	And inhale the sickening stench and finish the job.
	But while I do it, I hate what I am doing
	And want to keep casualties to a minimum.
	The odour of war nauseates me, Kay,
	And I feel ashamed to have ordered that these young men
	Should be bombed and strafed into lifelessness like this.
	Civilisation is not pretty when
	It resorts to war and deeds of barbarism.

(*29 August. Avernes, Montgomery's new TAC HQ.* MONTGOMERY *and* BROOKE.)

Brooke.	It's a pity this all happened while I was away.
	It will add three to six months to the war.
	But you can look back on a staggering victory,
	Perhaps the most outstanding military victory
	In the whole of human history, and all through your plan.
	Our political chief, Grigg, thinks the same.

Montgomery	(*tiredly*). We killed ten thousand Germans in the Falaise pocket
	And took fifty thousand prisoners. You
	Could walk for hundreds of yards stepping on dead flesh.
	The stench was awful, and many horses died.
	The men who got out were stragglers without vehicles
	Or equipment. It was a terrific blow.
	Paris has fallen – I declined Eisenhower's
	Invitation to go there – and Dieppe will soon fall.
	Overlord has reached a successful end.
	But what now? I go north with six or eight
	American divisions under Hodges,
	In all less than half what I have had. Patton
	Says it's a mistake for Hodges to turn north,
	That he could end the war in a few days
	By driving eastwards. I am now out of
	Telephone communication with Bradley.
	And the Germans are not finished by any means.
	I have isolated myself to perfect the art
	Of field command from the front, keeping TAC HQ
	Separate from Main, and I see with military
	Eyes, not political or national antennae.
Brooke.	We are seeing the rise as a great power
	Of the United States, to whom events now pass.
	I fear we shall see the decline of the British Empire.
Montgomery	(*depressed*). War happens when nations' interests conflict.
	Either through misunderstanding or aggressive greed,
	Which must be checked; and rightness is settled
	By a challenge of strength as in a tournament
	Two knights jousted with lances while kings watched
	And territory was ceded by the fallen
	Giant in armour. So jousted Rommel and I.
	Such a contest is primitive, and unless
	Providence is with the winner, not always just.
	Councils and conferences are better, but
	Words must be enforced. If national interests are
	Behind war, it is better that there should be
	Large regional blocs or a world government.
	And I dream of a world in harmony,
	In which my battlefield skills are not required,

In which men and women go about their lives
Without seeing their homes and families knocked to bits
By tanks and heavy bombers and artillery.
I deploy fire-power, but the great need is
For a new system of international law
And universal harmony under
A benevolent, benign authority,
And a single, decent, humane, good World Lord
Who represents all regions of the world.
Then greed and territorial dispute
And racial or historical aspiration
Can be sorted out without recourse to all this
Planned carnage, chaos and destruction
Which when I stop and think fills me with disgust.

Brooke.　　　　　It doesn't do to stop and think like that.

Montgomery.　　Right now, I can see into the depth of things
And I am filled with horror and despair.
I know that all the wars and leaders' plans
And all the territorial gains they made
Are not worth one sentence of a philosopher
Who has seen truth and reflects the hidden One,
Or one memorable line of an epic poet
That reveals how the universe really is,
And all my skill in battles is as worthless
As tantrum fisticuffs in a school playground.

Brooke.　　　　　You need a good night's sleep. You'll look on things
Differently in the morning when you're less tired.

*(30 August. Churchill's underground HQ. CHURCHILL in bed in blue and yellow
dressing-gown. BROOKE.)*

Churchill.　　　　I've got a temperature of a hundred and three.
Pneumonia.　Did you see Monty?

Brooke.　　　　　　　　　　　　　　　　　　I did.
He's bearing up, but pretty devastated.

Churchill.　　　　I want to make him a Field Marshal on

110

September the first, to mark the approval
Of the British people for his leadership.

(*31 August. Same scene.* CHURCHILL *in bed and* GEORGE VI.)

Churchill.   I have the submission ready, sir. Could you
Sign it now, using my pillow as a table.

(*The* KING *signs.*)

It is the highest rank in the British Army.
It puts him on a par with Wellington,
Haig, Kitchener – and Brooke. He is paying
The penalty for being unable to
Communicate with his superiors.

(*1 September, evening. Dangu, Montgomery's new HQ.* MONTGOMERY *sitting alone on a canvas chair, being painted by* JAMES GUNN. *They are observed by* HENDERSON.)

Henderson.   He looks like a medieval English king
Surveying his lands at Crécy or Agincourt.

(*The session is over.* MONTGOMERY *rises and goes into his caravan.*)

Montgomery.   Demoted. Elevated to Field Marshal
But demoted as Commander, from Land Forces
To Twenty-first Army Group. And by a man
Who had not seen a shot fired in his life
Before Overlord, does not understand strategy,
Has failed to impose a clear strategic plan
On the battlefield, squandering all our gains,
And is therefore useless as a field commander.
He's completely and utterly useless.
Demoted after the greatest invasion ever
And a three-month battle resulted in victory,
And me, across the Seine, heading for Brussels.
Where is the justice in that? What is the meaning?
(*Praying.*) O Lord, I asked for your help for Overlord.
You gave it, and we were victorious,
But the task is only half-done, and now the command
Is in the hands of a man who will lengthen the war.

Is this what you want? Is this part of your purpose?
If it is, I am content, though I cannot see
The benefit to the Allies, the troops, or
The German people of prolonging the war.
Is it time for America's Grand Design?
Is it time for the British to hand over
Their imperial rule and their world role?
O Lord of Light, I accept my demotion
If it is a part of your greater plan.
We warlords tussle for power but over all,
Our Overlord, is your Providential Light
Which knows the whole tapestry of history,
The past, the future, why events happen,
When one power rises and another declines,
Why one General rises and another is demoted.
What is baffling in nineteen forty-four
May be clear fifty years later, part of a pattern.
Shine into my soul, for I do not understand.

SCENE 5.

ARNHEM

(*3 September. Lailly, near Amiens, Dempsey's HQ.* DEMPSEY, BRADLEY, HODGES, MONTGOMERY.)

Bradley.

It's a pity General Eisenhower can't be here.
The American commanders met yesterday –
Ike, Patton, Hodges and me, it was going on
When you rang me, Monty, to fix this council –
And he flew back to Granville yesterday in high winds
And injured his knee trying to pull his plane
To safety. What emerged from our meeting was,
That the main American effort will be to Frankfurt
Through Metz and Nancy. Monty, we strongly felt
That Hodges' 5 US Corps should be switched
From you to cover Patton's left flank as
He thrusts into Saar south of the Ardennes. We felt

You don't need help with your effort north of the Ruhr
As you won't find much opposition up there,
And that the First US Army on your flank
Should be depleted. The Americans don't
Need British help with an airborne drop near Liège,
But thank you for offering.

Montgomery   (*thinly*).   We are getting away
From the original plan of one big thrust
Of forty divisions who need fear nothing.
I have not seen General Eisenhower for nearly
Two weeks, and have had no orders from him, so
I am drawing up plans to advance to the Ruhr
And I need your help, Brad. Brussels is falling,
The Canadians are stuck on the Seine and the Somme,
Now Dempsey has to approach Antwerp and attack
The whole of the Ruhr without significant
American help, and Hodges is going east.
It isn't going to work.

Bradley.   I'll tell you what.
I will make two simultaneous thrusts to the Rhine,
One south, one north of the Ardennes. That will help
You, Monty, in place of Hodges. There can be
A pincer attack on the Ruhr.

Montgomery.   The British must still cross
The Meuse and Rhine. We will need an airborne drop
To secure the bridges ahead of my thrust.
Given the withdrawal of American support,
And that I have no orders, an airborne drop
Seems essential in the region of Arnhem.

(*4 September. Granville, Eisenhower's Forward HQ. Meeting with* BEDELL SMITH, FREDDY
MORGAN, HUMPHREY GALE, STRONG, JOCK WHITELEY. *Bedell Smith is talking as he is
handed a telegram.*)

Bedell Smith.   The German army is retreating along the coast.
Antwerp has fallen, but not the approaches
To Antwerp harbour from the North Sea. Should you
Give the order for these to be taken?

(*Reading telegram.*) Telegram from Montgomery. He says
One thrust to Berlin can now end the war,
And it should go through the Ruhr rather than Saar
As the American plan states. I'll pass it round.
He wants to meet you, sir. He wants a decision
By tomorrow.

Eisenhower   (*sighing in exasperation*). He hasn't spoken to me
For nearly three weeks, and now he wants a decision
By yesterday. No, I've got too much on:
My broadcast to the peoples of North West Europe,
Linking the Italian campaign with *Overlord*,
A conference with General Devers on control
Of the Franco-American forces. And there's Greece.
He's four hundred miles away, and my knee....
What should we do?

Strong.   Speaking for Intelligence,
I vote for one strong thrust through Belgium to
The Rhine.

(EISENHOWER *looks at* STRONG.)

Eisenhower.   Can we go outside?

(*They go out,* EISENHOWER *limping, in pain.*)

                              Read this telegram.
It's from Stimson, our Secretary of State for War,
Urging me to take control. What can I do
In the face of this? I have to take account
Of the political ramifications. If I put
Monty in charge of the British and Americans,
Stimson will be angry, besides Brad and Patton.
There must be two thrusts, for political
If not military reasons.

(*They return to the meeting.*)

(*To Bedell Smith.*) Draft a written reply
To Montgomery. Say I like his idea

Of a powerful and full-bloodied thrust towards
Berlin, but that I do not agree it should be
Initiated at this time to the exclusion
Of all other manoeuvres. There can be
No question of a thrust to Berlin until
Le Havre and Antwerp harbours are operating.
The Allies will advance to both the Ruhr
And the Saar. I believe Montgomery's thrust
To the Ruhr will be via Aachen, and this can be tied
To Patton's thrust via Metz.

Strong.   Sir, shouldn't you
                    Meet Montgomery?

Eisenhower.   And be insulted by
                    The new Field Marshal? No, the telegram will do.

(*4 September. Rastenburg. Hitler's HQ.* HITLER *is in bed with jaundice.* HITLER *and*
GOEBBELS.)

Hitler.   Why have my Generals withdrawn from France
                    In defiance of my orders that they fight on?
                    My telegram to the German HQ in Paris
                    Said: "Paris must only fall into the hands
                    Of the enemy as a field of rubble."
                    Although the Eiffel Tower, the Elysée Palace
                    And forty-five bridges were wired with charges
                    That would cause a firestorm and burn the city down,
                    Choltitz did not act, and the Allies are in Paris
                    And all its cultural treasures are intact.
                    I do not trust the officer corps. They withdraw.
                    I want more party men who will observe
                    My orders to the letter.

Goebbels.   My *Führer* you are
                    A thousand miles away from the action,
                    And cannot appreciate that the German force
                    Is short of fuel and ammunition.
                    The British and Canadians under Montgomery
                    Have covered two hundred miles in four days
                    And are in Belgium, have taken Brussels

And Antwerp. Hodges has moved as far
And is in South-East Belgium, and has Liège,
Patton has reached the Moselle and has linked
With the French American Army from the Riviera.
We need to prepare the defence of the Fatherland.
The Siegfried Line is largely unmanned,
The West Wall, and many guns have been stripped.
The British and Americans are four hundred miles
From Berlin. The Russians a mere three hundred.
In three months since D-Day we have lost
A million and a quarter men, dead, wounded,
Missing - fifty divisions in the east,
Twenty-eight in the west. We have no guns,
Tanks, lorries, our allies have deserted us.
Germany now stands alone. The Allies have
Two million men in Europe, the Soviets have
Five hundred and fifty-five divisions.
We need a defensive plan. I will raise
A new army of a million men, and all
German industry will produce the arms
And equipment we need to repulse our enemies.

Hitler.   No withdrawal. We must keep on fighting
Until, as Frederick the Great said, one
Of our enemies tires and gives up.

Goebbels   (aside). Hitler's very name is terror, he is seen
As a wolf who has gobbled up the countries round him,
But somehow he's acting that part, calling
His headquarters "the Wolf's Lair", for the man within
Is really quite gentle, awkward, hesitant
Even, and watching him fumble his way
To his decisions I marvel that so uncertain
A man should have thousands of helmets, planes,
Tanks, ships hanging on his slightest word.
Of course he is not now, since Stauffenberg's bomb,
As he was before, when his hand did not tremble
And he rode, standing in his car, his right arm out,
Through hundreds of thousands of soldiers in miles of ranks
On both sides of Berlin's East-West Boulevard,
On his fiftieth birthday, in the most awesome

Display of power mankind has ever seen,
But even then in his quieter moments he
Was not the tyrant the world dreads. But he
Is able to open to a current of energy,
Which fills him and radiates conviction, faith.
It is not a good energy, it cannot be
Seeing where it has led him and his people.
He thinks it's a demonic energy,
An evil power that has come from Lucifer.
But he's not possessed by this for much of the time.
When he is possessed by it, even I fear him.
But the more vulnerable he becomes, the more
I know I must follow him to the end.

(*5 September. Granville, Eisenhower's HQ.* EISENHOWER *alone.*)

Eisenhower.   Stalin has personal rivalries to endure.
Zhukov and Koniev hate each other, I have heard
And Rokossovsky is not easy. How is it
That when he sets them to compete, they do,
Whereas when I do the same, Monty, Patton
And Bradley demand priority over each other?
Monty is the worst. He thinks he is a better
Commander in the field and planner than me.
His overweening egotism and self-esteem,
His vanity and brashness and arrogance
Make him insubordinate. He writes,
"One really powerful and full-blooded thrust
Towards Berlin is likely to get there and thus
End the German war." He demands all the
Fuel and transport, and says Bradley
Can do the best he can with what is left.
I know I try to keep everyone happy
And tend to compromise, but I bristle
When he weighs the Ruhr and Saar and writes, "If we
Attempt a compromise solution and split
Our maintenance resources so that neither
Thrust is full-blooded we will prolong the war."
I shall repeat that a thrust to Berlin
Should not be initiated at this moment
To the exclusion of all other manoeuvres.

There will have to be a compromise: a broad front,
Resources split between Monty and Bradley.
We must take the ports of Antwerp and Le Havre
Before we go to Berlin. All SHAEF agrees.

(*9 September. Everberg, Montgomery's HQ.* MONTGOMERY *and* DAWNAY.)

Montgomery   (*angrily*). I have received Ike's reply in two parts,
                      The second part two days *before* the first part.
                      Now, four days after my message, signal:
                      "Providing we can have the ports of Dieppe,
                      Boulogne, Dunkirk and Calais, and in addition
                      Three thousand tons per day through Le Havre
                      We can advance to Berlin." Tell Ike I
                      Must see him in Brussels tomorrow, please
                      After my 9 a.m. conference with Dempsey.

(*10 September. Brussels airport. Eisenhower's aeroplane.* EISENHOWER, TEDDER,
MONTGOMERY *in the cabin with others.*)

Eisenhower.   I hurt my knee last week when we landed
                      On a beach in a high wind, and we had to push
                      The plane away from the sea. I can't move. It's
                      Been as much as I can do to fly to Brussels.

Montgomery.   I want everyone to leave the cabin including
                      Tedder.

                      (EISENHOWER *gestures, all leave.* TEDDER *is still in the plane but out
                      of earshot.*)

                      Ike, I have your signal here.
                      It arrived in two parts, the second part first,
                      The first part two days later, so I didn't get
                      The drift till yesterday. How can we run
                      A war if we can't communicate where we're
                      Going? I had no orders from you for a fortnight.
                      There's no communication apart from telegrams
                      Written four hundred miles away from the front line.
                      There's no plan, we in the field don't know what we're
                      Doing, we're making it up as we go along.

It seems that Patton, not you, is running the war.
The double thrust will end in certain failure.
You've dispersed the Allied war effort, there's no
Field command or grip –

(EISENHOWER *puts his hand on* MONTGOMERY's *knee.*)

Eisenhower.   Steady Monty. You can't
Talk to me like that. I'm your boss.

Montgomery (*humbly*).   I'm sorry, Ike.
A new weapon hit London yesterday,
The V-2 rocket, which is silent and
Arrives without warning. It came from Holland.
We need to go through Holland to capture the sites.
The British Government wants me to find and destroy
The V-2 sites near Rotterdam and Utrecht
And that means I need to get to Arnhem.
If I can do that I must have priority
Of supplies over Patton and command in the north
Over American supplies and troops. I think you're wrong,
But I'm not insisting on a thrust to Berlin.
Arnhem is the gateway to the Ruhr as well
As to the V-2s, and after that Berlin.
But I need fuel and tanks. Give me these now
And I can get there.

Eisenhower.   Monty, you must understand
There are certain things that I cannot change.
The Allied armies must be kept separate;
You cannot command American troops in the north;
Your Ruhr thrust cannot have priority
Over Patton's Saar thrust as regards supplies.
I am now running the war, and that's my view.
And as I said in my signal, we cannot start
A thrust to Berlin now. But we can look
At your bold plan for a bridgehead over the Rhine
At Arnhem, which I wholeheartedly support.
If you can achieve that, you can cut off the Ruhr
And advance into northern Germany.
There can be a combined Anglo-American

Airborne drop. I'll wire you. Now if you'll call
Tedder, my knee is hurting.

Montgomery   (*aside*).   This man is no
                     Commander. He's a genial fellow,
                     He talks to everyone and is popular
                     And then works out a compromise all like
                     That pleases everyone. He has no plan.
                     He finds out what his subordinates think,
                     Collects their ideas and then reconciles them.
                     He visibly flinches from bold moves, he is
                     Timid and fearful in the teeth of pain, like a boy
                     Who winces at the whine of a dentist's drill.
                     He holds conferences in order to liaise,
                     I to give orders.

(*11 September, Granville, Eisenhower's HQ. EISENHOWER and BEDELL SMITH. KAY
SUMMERSBY, going.*)

Bedell Smith.   There are now three armies, and the Germans,
                     Fighting on three fronts, are far from beaten.
                     The way to the Saar is blocked by good divisions.
                     I can see a drop to seize Walcheren would
                     Control the approach to Antwerp the Navy want,
                     And help open the port. Montgomery's
                     Arnhem thrust would secure a Rhine bridgehead
                     And be most useful to our present cause.

Eisenhower   (*aside*). I am torn this way and that. It is not easy
                     To be a Supreme and a Land Commander.

                     (SMITH *receives a paper.*)

Bedell Smith.   A signal from Montgomery. He has postponed
                     The Allied airborne drop across the Rhine
                     For twelve days, because he lacks supplies.

                     (EISENHOWER *buries his head in his hands.*)

Eisenhower.   Do I accept it? Or do I keep the drop?

Bedell Smith.   It will be useful.

Eisenhower.   Go and see Monty,
And give him all he needs. We will stop the thrust
To Saar in view of the German opposition.
Give priority to the Ruhr and the Arnhem drop:
Operation Market Garden on the seventeenth.
(*Aside.*) I am giving Montgomery what he has urged.
I hope I am not making a strategic blunder.
If Arnhem fails, I should have said No.

(15 September. Granville, Eisenhower's HQ. EISENHOWER and BEDELL SMITH.)

Eisenhower.   A signal to Monty: "Berlin is the main prize,
In defense of which the enemy is likely
To concentrate the bulk of his forces.
There is no doubt whatsoever in my mind
That we should concentrate all our energies
On a rapid thrust to Berlin. But this should
Not be concentrated but spread across
The whole front, with combined US-British forces."

(15 September. Rundstedt's HQ. RUNDSTEDT and his Chief of Staff, General GUNTHER BLUMENTRITT.)

Blumentritt.   Why have the Allies not gone for Berlin?
There were no German forces behind the Rhine
At the end of August, the front was wide open.
Berlin was the Allies' target, Germany's strength
Is in the north. Berlin and Prague were there
For the taking. Why did the Allies not take them?

(15 September. SPEER listening to radio.)

Goebbels' voice. Germans, you know my total mobilisation
Is to find a million men for our war effort.
I warn you what to expect if we lose this war.
Roosevelt and Churchill, meeting in Quebec,
Have discussed the US Treasury's plan, which
Secretary Morgenthau has drawn up. Germany
Will be dismembered, our heavy industry

Destroyed, much of our territory will be transferred
To Poland, the Soviet Union, Denmark, France.
Germans, we will be a pastoral economy
Existing at subsistence level under this plan.
You must strengthen your will, work with the *Führer*
And repulse the enemy before these things happen.

Speer.   He did not say that Churchill opposed the plan,
And that the plan is dead. Propaganda,
And taking my skilled men from my industry.

(*27 September, 11 a.m. Eindhoven, Montgomery's HQ.* MONTGOMERY, *depressed and deep in thought.* WILLIAMS.)

Williams.   You were very close to victory at Arnhem.
The largest airborne landing in history,
And the road for our troops was wide open.
There's an *Ultra* message from the German
Commander-in-Chief on the twenty-fourth, asking
Hitler for permission to withdraw all forces
In Holland to the Meuse (or Maas) and Waal.
Hitler refused and ordered von Rundstedt
To counter-attack. It's been suggested
Market Garden was betrayed by Bernhard,
That ex-SS man who took refuge in London.
He knew the plan.

Montgomery   (*philosophically*). The target was not Arnhem,
But the Ruhr. Urquhart was to threaten to seize Arnhem
While O'Connor's 8 Corps turned eastwards towards
The Ruhr. We have advanced our Ruhr campaign.
Here we are now in Eindhoven, we have
A bridgehead across the Waal at Nijmegen,
Enough life was lost across the Neder Rijn.
We did the best we could, given the lack
Of American support, which made it
A British effort; given that Eisenhower
Reinstated the Saar's equal priority.
There are many ifs – those two German armoured
Divisions, the rain – but we must put a brave face
On Arnhem, and consider what we gained.

(*Enter* GENERAL URQUHART, *exhausted and downcast, with* HENDERSON.)

(*Gently.*) My good fellow.

Urquhart. I'm sorry. I failed.

Montgomery. You're
Worn out, you've had no sleep, you're exhausted,
You'll spend tonight in my caravan. I only move out
For Winston Churchill and the King, but tonight it's yours.
Tomorrow I'll ask you what went wrong at Arnhem,
But tonight, you sleep in there. Where's my batman?

(*Exit* MONTGOMERY, *looking for his batman.*)

Urquhart (*to Henderson*). I'm overwhelmed. Such a gentle reception.

Henderson. He calls "A" Mess here his family, and he's like
A caring father concerned for his children.

(*5 October. Versailles, Bradley's HQ.* EISENHOWER, MONTGOMERY, BROOKE, RAMSAY, BRADLEY, PATTON, DEMPSEY, CRERAR, HODGES. *A conference for all commanders.*)

Ramsay. We are an Allied force, as for *Overlord*,
I don't defend operations on national grounds.
Arnhem was a British undertaking. Perhaps
There could have been more American support,
But the plan was Field Marshal Montgomery's
And any criticism he should accept.
I am concerned that he didn't choose to secure
The approaches and port of Antwerp, rather than
Undertake this risky drop behind enemy lines.

Montgomery (*thinly*). There were no orders from the Supreme Commander
To take the approaches and port of Antwerp.
What does the CIGS think?

Brooke. I have to say
I feel that for once Field Marshal Montgomery's
Strategy was at fault. Instead of advancing

On Arnhem, he should have made certain of Antwerp.
I have been a supporter of the Field Marshal,
Who won a brilliant victory in Normandy,
But on Arnhem I have to agree with
Admiral Ramsay. The port of Antwerp first.

Eisenhower.   To conclude, we have had a reverse at Arnhem.
For this the blame is entirely mine as I
Approved Field Marshal Montgomery's plea
To operate an airborne drop at Arnhem.
Any blame belongs to me alone and is
My responsibility, and no one else's.
Now we need to get on with the war, and our thrusts
Into the Ruhr and the Saar against an enemy
That is not as defeated as we thought a month ago.

(*The conference breaks up into talking groups.* BROOKE *and* RAMSAY
stand together. MONTGOMERY *stands alone, isolated.*)

Ramsay.   That was spoken like a military statesman.

Brooke.   Whatever his shortcomings as a battlefield
Commander, he has great personal stature.

Ramsay.   He has a nobility that I admire.
And Montgomery has now been marginalised.

Brooke   (*sadly*). He has been the victim of an American *coup*,
But he has also contributed to his undoing
And has to some extent marginalised himself.
After Arnhem, and with only a quarter of
The Allied troops, Britain has a junior role.

(*6 October. Eindhoven, Montgomery's TAC HQ.* MONTGOMERY *alone.*)

Montgomery.   I am in gloom. I know I could have ended
The war in three weeks from my Normandy victory,
Which left me invincible in the German mind
If not in SHAEF's. And now, in this vacuum,
Without my single thrust I have been defeated
By the Germans at Arnhem, and the Americans.

I will open the port of Antwerp, but
I am full of scorn at the useless Eisenhower
And Bradley, who want to show the world the power
Of American might, and blunder in their decisions,
Dispersing the Allied effort on too wide a front.
And I am powerless to alter the course
Of the shambles they have created, and so the war
Will last through winter till next spring. My men
Visit mistresses in Brussels. I turn a blind
Eye. Not much happens. It's cold and damp.

(*Enter* DAWNAY.)

                          Oh Kit.
I am sending you to England, to Phyllis Reynolds.
You will take my summer wear – vests, pants and shirts –
And bring me my winter clothes: thick vests and pants,
Woollen pyjamas and my dressing-gown.
You wouldn't have had to do this if I'd been in charge.

(*About 6 October. Stalin's office in the Kremlin.* ZHUKOV *standing by a map on a table with green baize in front of Stalin's desk.* ROKOSSOVSKY, MOLOTOV *and* ANTONOV. STALIN *pacing, smoking his pipe.*)

Zhukov.   My site meeting with Rokossovsky confirms,
The Forty-Seventh Army has many casualties.
The Seventeenth Army is in a bad way.
Supply lines are affected by our Russian winter.
The First Belorussian Front is worn out.
It needs time to recover and reinforce.

          (STALIN *has looked at the map, and has then resumed pacing. He puts down his pipe.*)

Molotov.   Germany is virtually defeated.
It is mad to ease up now.

Zhukov.   The Red Army
Has suffered huge losses, if we do not have time
The situation on the Vistula will deteriorate.

Stalin.   Do you agree with Zhukov?

Rokossovsky.   I do.

Stalin.   Both of you,
          Go out to the ante-room with your maps
          And think a little more.

(*8 October. Eindhoven, Montgomery's HQ.* MONTGOMERY *and Gen.* MARSHALL, BRADLEY *and* HODGES.)

Bradley.   General Marshall, Chief of Staff of the US
                Army.

Montgomery.   General, could you spare me a few moments
                In my office caravan? Would you mind Generals?

                (MARSHALL *looks at* BRADLEY *and* HODGES, *shrugs and follows* MONTGOMERY *into his caravan.*)

                I feel you should know that since the Supreme Commander
                Took personal command of the land battle
                As well as forces on the sea and in the air,
                The armies have become separated
                Nationally, not geographically.
                There is a lack of grip, of operational
                Direction and control. Our operations
                Have become ragged, disjointed, and we
                Have now got ourselves into a real mess.

Marshall.   Field Marshal, I have listened.

Montgomery.   And?

Marshall.   There is
                More than one view in such complex matters.

Montgomery.   I can see that you entirely disagree.

Marshall.   There has to be a balance of national effort.
                General Eisenhower is the Supreme Commander.

(*Silence.*)

(*12 October. Eindhoven, Montgomery's HQ.* MONTGOMERY *and* DAWNAY.)

Dawnay.   A reply from Eisenhower. He's threatening you
With dismissal.

(MONTGOMERY *reads the signal.*)

Montgomery.   On October the ninth
He urged me to take Antwerp or Allied
Operations would reach a standstill. I
Replied reminding him that at Versailles
He had made the attack in Holland the main effort.
He replied it was now Antwerp, and Beetle Smith
Rang and demanded when there would be action
And threatened through Morgan I would lose my supplies.
I wrote back blaming the failure at Arnhem
On lack of co-ordination between Bradley's troops
And mine, and I asked to be given sole control
Of the land battle. Now he threatens to go
To the CCS, and he will win. I have pushed
Him as far as I can and must now promise
A hundred per cent support, and give Antwerp
Top priority, when I can wind down Holland.

(*13 October. Rastenburg, Hitler's HQ.* HITLER *and* BORMANN.)

Bormann.   My *Führer*, I have a report on Rommel.
You recall, Speidel testified on October the fourth
He knew of the plot against you from Hofacker
And passed the information on to Rommel.
You arranged for Keitel to summon him here.
Rommel pleaded his head injury. He
Has recovered from the crash, the *Gestapo* report
He goes for walks "leaning on his son", and I have
Reports from local party officials who say
He is still making mutinous remarks.
He should be told to see you if he's innocent,
Or behave like a Prussian officer
And gentleman, or face the People's Court.

| Hitler. | Send Burgdorf and his chief law officer |
| | To Rommel's villa with such a request. |

(*14 October, lunchtime. Rommel's villa near Ulm.* ROMMEL *in the main living-room and voices.* LUCY.)

| Lucy | (*nervously*). Two men to see you. They're from the *Führer.* |

(*Exit.*)

(*Gen.* BURGDORF *and Gen.* ERNST MAISEL *appear.*)

| Burgdorf. | Field Marshal. A letter from the *Führer.* |

(ROMMEL *reads it.*)

| Rommel. | Does Hitler know about the two statements, |
| | By Speidel and Hofacker? |

Burgdorf.	Yes, he does.
	If you don't go to Rastenburg to contest
	The evidence of Speidel and Hofacker,
	The choice is the People's Court and execution –

| Maisel. | Sequestration of your house – |

| Rommel. | Or? |

Burgdorf.	Poison,
	Not pistol, and a State funeral with full
	Honours, your reputation still intact.
	No one will know. You will have died of your injuries.
	And there will be a guarantee of safety
	For your family, which will be revoked
	If you choose the other way, the People's Court.

| Rommel. | It is "die now" and save my family |
| | Or "die later" and put them both at risk. |

(BURGDORF *nods.*)

I need time to think.

Burgdorf.   We'll wait in the garden.
We will leave in the staff car. You will say
Goodbye to all who wait downstairs, then go.

Rommel.   Send up my wife.

(*Exeunt* BURGDORF *and* MAISEL.)

                    The moment I have expected,
For three months has arrived. There is no choice.
Disgrace and poverty for my family,
Or this, oblivion, and my family keep
This house and all I have mustered for them.
I knew of the plot, was shocked and would not join,
But I wanted our surrender and an honourable peace.
Speidel's testimony has done for me.
He was trying to save himself. I am innocent,
But cannot disprove the evidence, and I
Will not stoop to plead or beg for mercy.
There is no choice. Just the furtherance of
A legend. Montgomery, you wanted my end
But you never dreamt it would be at Hitler's command.
I think you will be sorry. And I hope
That one day, there can be reconciliation.
Perhaps our sons will be friends.

(*Enter* LUCY. *He holds her.*)

                    My dearest Lucy,
You must be strong and look after Manfred.
I have to say goodbye.

(*He gives her the letter.*)

Lucy.   But it's not true,
What Speidel has said. You can deny it, and prove –

Rommel.   No, it will be execution, and you will lose
Everything and Manfred.

| Lucy. | There's no other way? |

| Rommel. | The choice is clear. They are waiting for my cap,
My Field Marshal's cap and baton. |

(*Enter* MANFRED.)

| Manfred. | Papa. |

(ROMMEL *hugs* MANFRED.)

| Rommel. | You must be very strong. I have to say goodbye. |

| Manfred. | Those men? |

| Rommel | (*nodding*). I have to go with them. It is for the best.
My first thoughts are of you, and of the life you will have.
Remember me as an honourable officer
Who fought well but couldn't stand the casualties,
Who when he knew we had lost the war, sought peace,
And pulled the front line further and further back.
I love you both very much. |

| Manfred. | You're going
With those two men? |

| Rommel. | Yes. They are waiting for me.
I will be going in a staff car. But you
Will remember. |

| Manfred. | Yes, Papa. |

| Rommel. | I love you both.
Now, goodbye. Be strong. |

(ROMMEL *embraces both.* LUCY *escorts* MANFRED *out.* ROMMEL *is briefly alone. He puts on his greatcoat and cap and picks up his baton.*)

Montgomery, a Prussian officer's salute.

(BURGDORF *and* MAISEL *return.*)

Rommel.	Where?

Burgdorf   (*holding a packet*). On the back seat of the staff car. You
Died from your injuries. There will be no pain.
Believe me, this is the best way. I am sick
At what has happened to our culture. (*Exeunt.*)

(*Later in October. Goebbels' office. GOEBBELS and SPEER.*)

Goebbels.   Germany is now under siege. Last month
The *Führer* announced a scorched earth policy.
Any land conquered must be reduced to a desert.
No German wheat must feed the invaders,
All industrial plant and food supplies must be
Blown up. I am now cutting food rations.
The youth are digging trenches, and today
Himmler has set up the People's Storm, so each
Male of active years can be drafted to defend
The Fatherland. The *Führer* has ordered
The building of a bombproof bunker beneath
The Chancellery, and when it is ready
He will move back to Berlin. The company that
Are building it are Hochtief.

SCENE 6.

THE ARDENNES

(*Later in October. Rastenburg. HITLER and his GENERALS. RUNDSTEDT, MODEL, GÖRING.*)

Hitler.   While I was in bed with jaundice in September
And recovering from the bungling Stauffenberg's bomb,
I studied maps and have found the weak point
In the American front line. The Ardennes!
Where Manstein and I struck in May 1940.
The Americans have three weak divisions there,
If all goes well, my offensive can annihilate
Twenty or thirty divisions, and drive them back.

I shall amass twenty-eight divisions.
My Panzers will cross the Meuse and take Antwerp,
Drive a wedge between the British and Canadians,
And the Americans. It will be another Dunkirk.

(*The* GENERALS *protest.*)

Hitler.   No, I will have no objections. I have drawn up my plans
With Jodl, and I have given Rundstedt instructions
That they must not be altered. The British
Are worn out, the Americans will collapse. We can defeat
Them in the west and then turn our forces to the east
And attack the Red Army on the Vistula.

(*The* GENERALS *protest.*)

Generals.   But sir –

Hitler.   I will hear no more. I have two Panzer
Armies, six hundred thousand men. I shall wait
For bad weather when Allied planes cannot fly.

(End of October. Churchill's underground HQ. CHURCHILL *and* BROOKE.)

Churchill.   I am exhausted. I have been twice to Moscow,
Travelling like a wandering minstrel
In the cause of Allied unity, and of the Poles.
They are unspeakable. I told Stalin
I reaffirmed the Curzon Line as Russia's
Eastern frontier, as we agreed at Teheran.
I raised the Balkans, I told him Britain
Has an interest in Greece, but Romania
Is a Russian affair. He said he didn't want
To use the phrase "dividing into spheres" because
"The Americans might be shocked". I wrote
Some percentages on a piece of paper,
Suggesting proportional interest in five countries:
Romania, Greece, Yugoslavia, Hungary
And Bulgaria. He studied the list and ticked
It with a blue pencil and gave it back.
There was a silence, he said I should keep it.

I wrote Stalin a letter saying no ideology
Should be imposed on any state. I showed it
To Harriman, the US Ambassador. He said
He was certain Roosevelt would repudiate it
So I did not send it. That evening the Free Poles
From London joined us. They refused to accept
The Curzon Line as it gave Eastern Galicia
And Lvov to the Soviet Union. Stalin said
They must accept the Curzon Line without conditions.
I had a further talk with the Poles the next day,
And proposed to Stalin that they would accept
The Curzon Line in return for fifty-fifty participation
In the new government. Stalin agreed -
But the Poles stuck out for Lvov. I lost my temper
With them, told them, "I will have nothing more to do with you,
I don't care where you go, you deserve to be
In your Pripet Marshes." Then I offered
To appeal to Stalin to throw in Lvov.
But they still wouldn't accept the Curzon Line.
Eden proposed we saw the Curzon Line
As a demarcation line, not a frontier.
Stalin refused to accept anything less than a frontier
And stayed with the Lublin Communist Poles.
I made one more appeal to the Poles.
They said No. I've had the Poles, they're the end.

(*12 November, evening. Nancy, Patton's HQ. MARLENE DIETRICH sings 'Lily Marlene' for
PATTON, who wears his pearl-handled pistols, on his 59th birthday, and his "niece" JEAN
GORDON. A notice says 59.*)

Patton   (*drunk*). Thank you Marlene, and thank you everyone
                          For wishing me a happy thirty-ninth birthday.

                          (*A chorus of "Thirty-ninth?"*)

                          Now we Americans are showing how
                          To win this war, and if you look at my headquarters
                          Here, you'll understand why we still haven't reached the Saar,
                          And with gals like Marlene around, and my niece Jean,

                          (*A chorus of "Niece?"*)

You'll understand why we ain't too worried about that
And why we think this is a better way
Of running the war than Montgomery's way,
Cooped up in his poky little caravans.
Bring me the maps of the Saar.

(*Burlesque map is produced: a pair of knickers.*)

Dietrich   (*suggestively*).   Did you say S.A.?

(PATTON *draws his pearl-handled pistols, fires them in the air, and collapses back, paralytically drunk.*)

(*Mid-November Moscow. Stalin's Kremlin office.* STALIN *and* ROKOSSOVSKY.)

Stalin.   The Soviet general staff have now drawn up
               A plan for the greatest campaign in history,
               An offensive that will take the Red Army
               Forty-five days, and start between the fifteenth
               And twentieth of January. It will cover
               The entire eastern front from Barents
               To the Black Sea, eight countries, and its aim
               Is the lair of the Fascist beast, Berlin.
               There will be three fronts to Operation Berlin,
               It is vital that you, Rokossovsky,
               Zhukov and Koniev should put aside
               Rivalries and work together, co-ordinate.
               Your three fronts will end the war in the west.
               If you and Koniev don't advance, Zhukov
               Will not either. You will approach from the north,
               Koniev from the south, Zhukov from the east.
               I attach such importance to the drive
               That I will direct it, not my Supreme
               Command staff, the Stavka, or army general
               Staff – I will co-ordinate the three fronts,
               First and Second Belorussian and First
               Ukrainian and a fourth front, the Third
               Belorussian, which will help the northern flank.
               The commander in the field will be Marshal Zhukov,
               Who stopped the Germans at Moscow and then
               Defeated them at Stalingrad and Kursk.

He will spearhead the offensive, and take Berlin.
I want no arguments, no defiance.
You were sentenced to death seven years ago,
Though still under sentence I made you a Marshal.
And I look to you to co-operate
In our great undertaking as we kill the beast.

(*7 December. Maastricht. Conference of commanders.* BRADLEY *and others.* MONTGOMERY.)

Montgomery.   First Army is struggling forward, but there are no reserves,
Everybody is attacking everywhere,
With no reserves anywhere. I propose Patton's
Third Army should be moved north for the Ruhr
Offensive, and that Brad should be Commander-
In-Chief of Land Forces, as General Eisenhower
Is simply not doing the job. Or at the least,
That Brad should command all Allied forces north
Of the Ardennes, so that the Allies can fight
With one effort, under one unified command.

Bradley.   That is not a good idea. There should be separate
National armies, with me as Commander
Of the American forces, and they should fight
In separate places.

Montgomery.   Then how do we deal
With the Sixth SS Panzer Army, which is now
Strengthening German lines according to reports?

Bradley.   Those Panzers are to plug holes that will be made
When Hodges and Patton attack the Ruhr and Saar.
Patton's new drive will start December nineteen.

Montgomery.   So although the present plan has failed, we must
Consider it has not failed and stick with it?

(*Mid-December. Rastenburg.* HITLER *and* BURGDORF.)

Hitler.   What is the weather in the Ardennes?

Burgdorf.   Sir, misty. The clouds are in the treetops.

Hitler.   Treetop cloud? Good. I have prayed for such weather
Since September. The sun always shines for my parades
But now I want mist, Providence gives me mist.
The time has come to strike without warning!

*(*16 December, 8 a.m. Luxembourg, Bradley's HQ.* BRADLEY *having breakfast with his aide*
Major HANSEN, *who takes a call.*)

Hansen.   Sir, Hodges on the line.

Bradley.   An attack at dawn
On 8 Corps? A spoiling attack, I agree.
Can you handle it, I'm about to leave for Paris
To meet the Supreme Commander.

(*16 December, 11.30 a.m.* HITLER *has woken up.* BURGDORF *has a report from* MODEL.)

Hitler.   What is the news from the Ardennes? The Allies?

Burgdorf.   Taken totally by surprise. An artillery
Bombardment rained down on the American line,
So fast it seemed it hailed mortars and shells.
Then came the tanks out of mist over forty miles.
The American First and Ninth Armies were
Driven back.

Hitler.   Providence be praised!

*(*16 December, morning, Eindhoven. Golf course.* WILLIAMS *arrives.*)

Williams.   Field Marshal Montgomery? Is he here?

Club Official.   He is playing golf with Dai Rees over there.

(MONTGOMERY *and* DAI REES.)

Montgomery.   Ah, Bill. Have you met Broadhurst's driver?

Williams.   Who's winning?

Dai Rees.   The Field Marshal.

Montgomery.	Oh, I'm having a lesson.
	Trouble? Excuse me.

Williams	(*to Montgomery*). Sir, the Germans have attacked
	Hodges' First Army in the Ardennes, in force.

Montgomery.	This is no ordinary move. LOs must scout.
	(*To Dai Rees*.) I'm afraid I must fly back to Zonhoven.

(*16 December Zonhoven, Montgomery's HQ. MONTGOMERY and HENDERSON.*)

Montgomery.	Signal to General Eisenhower's *deputy*
	Chief of Staff that we have no reserves to block
	Enemy penetration, that we have no plan,
	That our attacks are unco-ordinated,
	That the Supreme Commander's last directive
	Was on the twenty-eighth of October, eight weeks ago.
	Unless he makes up his mind and issues orders
	We will drift into difficulties with the enemy.

(*16 December, 6p.m. Versailles, Hotel Trianon Palace, Eisenhower's HQ. EISENHOWER playing bridge with BRADLEY, BEDELL SMITH and his friend EVERETT HUGHES. KAY. Champagne. Bradley's aide CHESTER HANSEN, leaving.*)

Eisenhower.	Yes, von Rundstedt lived here until recently.
	A staff wedding, and my fifth star, come on,
	Stay and celebrate with us.

Kay.	Yes, we don't want
	Anyone to go. Stay and have something to eat.

Hansen.	Brad and I had a huge lunch at the Ritz,
	I couldn't. Besides, Ernest Hemingway's waiting
	For me at the Lido –

Kay.	That's where bare-breasted girls
	Do the hootchy-kootchie most of the night. Stay here.

Bedell Smith.	Sir, a call for General Bradley from Hodges
	In the Ardennes. He says it's more than a spoiling attack.

Bradley	(*more interested in his cards*). I stand by what I told Strong: it's a spoiler.
Bedell Smith.	Strong did say there's German radio silence.
Bradley.	Tell him the two most senior American Commanders, having discussed infantry Replacement, can't be disturbed till they've finished Five rubbers of bridge.
Eisenhower	(*looking at cards*). It'll be a spoiling attack.
Bedell Smith.	You ought to take the call, sir.
Bradley.	Oh, very well. Yes. Yes. Listen, you can have the Seventh Armoured Division of the Ninth Army, and the Tenth Armoured Division of the Third Army.

(*He rings off.*)

Eisenhower.	Everything all right?
Bradley.	A captured enemy document speaks of A pincer attack on Aachen, in the Ninth Army Area. Hodges has it under control.
Hansen.	Sir, do you need me? Hemingway –
Bradley.	Go and meet him.

(HUGHES *opens his Highland Piper Scotch.*)

Tell him we're drinking a bottle of Scotch
And playing cards in Louis the Sixteenth's palace,
As Louis the Sixteenth did with his courtiers.

Eisenhower	(*looking at cards*). Tell him it's like Drake's bowls, we must finish Our game before we beat off the German Armada.

(*Laughter. The champagne and Scotch are flowing.*)

(*17 December, early morning. Same setting.* BRADLEY *and* HANSEN.)

Bradley.   I didn't sleep well. I was thinking
About the German attack. The main thrust
Is at Liège, our supply line, and the diversion
Is at Luxembourg. I'm sure that von Rundstedt
Is trying to delay Patton's drive to the Saar.
But he's struck where we have not got many troops.

Hansen.   I don't like to say it, General, but it's
What Montgomery warned Ike about,
And you replied he should mind his own business.
If it is a big attack, Montgomery will say
"I told you so."

Bradley.   And I will have been away
From my post, like Rommel.

Hansen.   I hope it's minor.

(*The phone rings.*)

Sir, it's the Commander of 4th Infantry Division

Bradley.   Yes? We might have to evacuate our HQ
At Luxembourg? Never. I will never
Move backwards with a headquarters.

(*17 December. Zonhoven, Montgomery's HQ.* MONTGOMERY, DAWNAY *and* POSTON.)

Poston.   The enemy gained surprise. The Americans
Have all their troops in the front line and have no
Reserves. The Ninth Army are sending two
Divisions, the First: one. The First Army
Has no idea what to do.

Montgomery.   Twenty-eight
German divisions and I argued for forty
In my single thrust. (*Shaking his head.*) I foresaw all this.
We are now in danger. (*To Dawnay.*) Send three British Divisions –
The 43rd, 53rd and Guards Armoured –

Towards the Meuse to protect our southern flank.
And signal General Whiteley at SHAEF that
The Americans are transferring troops from their
Northern flank, which will set back the crossing
Of the Rhine by months; and that they should draw instead
On their southern flank and cancel Patton's thrust.

(18 December, evening. Spa, Hodges' HQ. HODGES and GEN. KEAN, his Chief of Staff. Breakfast is laid, there is a Christmas tree.)

Hodges.   Three German armies are approaching us.
Panzers are in Stavelot and heading here,
Our headquarters are manning a roadblock,
It's only a matter of time before we are overrun,
The Chief of Intelligence wants us to fly out
In the Cub plane that's waiting. There are four
Million gallons of petrol here, which will fuel
The Germans to Antwerp. We have spoken
Six times with Bradley today, and we're still not sure
If he appreciates the seriousness of
Our position. He's still talking about Patton's
Thrust from Metz to Saar which has weakened us.
Montgomery has urged him to cancel
That thrust, and therefore, out of pride, he won't.
He wants us to survive without weakening Patton.
He's met Patton and there may be token help,
But it is likely to be too late for us.
Bradley isn't interested in coming here.
What should we do?

Kean.   We have no alternative
But to move HQ.

Hodges.   I agree. We will burn our secret files,
Abandon these buildings for Chaudfontaine.

(18 December. Verdun. Eisenhower's conference. EISENHOWER, BRADLEY, PATTON. Not MONTGOMERY or HODGES.)

Eisenhower.   I'm very worried about the German offensive.
I've reinforced Bastogne to hold the line.

I'm tempted to take field command myself
But am turning to George. Can you go to Luxembourg
And counter-attack with at least six divisions
In three days' time? You will have to turn your
Entire army from eastwards to northwards.

Patton.   Sure, I can do it. But three of the six
                             Divisions Have been overrun.

Eisenhower.   Oh, yes.

Patton.   I've only three divisions.

Eisenhower.   So you will abandon the thrust to Saar.

Patton.   That's no problem.

Eisenhower   (aside).   He spoke so bitterly
                             Against Monty's single thrust in August,
                             Yet he is happy now to support it
                             Because he has a star role.
                             (Aloud.)   I will issue
                             A directive ordering Devers to
                             Cease his offensive in the south and relieve
                             Patton's Third Army so it can move north.
                             Once this German offensive has been blocked
                             Bradley's Twelfth Army will mount a single offensive
                             To the north.

Bradley   (tensely).   That is what Montgomery proposed
                             At Maastricht, and I opposed.

(19 December, after lunch. Churchill's Cabinet War Room. CHURCHILL, having had several
sherries, marks a map; with BROOKE.)

Churchill.   There's no information corning out of SHAEF.
                             The War Office, Roosevelt and the Combined
                             Chiefs of Staff all find the same. The only
                             Person who knows what's going on is Monty.
                             I'm using his personal signals to you
                             To mark the Cabinet map. And I can see

A British counterstroke, in the tradition
Of my great warrior ancestor, Marlborough.
I want to order Monty to hurl Horrocks'
30 Corps at the Germans.

Brooke.   Prime Minister,
Only Eisenhower can order Monty,
And no one in London can tell a Field Marshal
In the Ardennes how he should act.

Churchill.   Oh, well. What can I do to help?

Brooke.   Telephone
Eisenhower and say that the northern front
Should be under the command of one General:
Monty.

(*19 December, 5 p.m. Zonhoven, Montgomery's HQ.* MONTGOMERY *on the telephone to Dempsey.*)

Montgomery.   There is no doubt about it, my Liaison Officer
To Bradley, Tom Bigland, went to Hodges' HQ
This morning, and found no one. Breakfast was laid,
The Christmas tree decorated. A German woman
Said they went down the road at 3 a.m. –
Without telling anybody. I have heard nothing
From General Eisenhower, the Commander-in-Chief
In the field, from Versailles; and Bradley's
Out of telephone communication in Luxembourg.
So I have arranged for you to have four divisions
From dawn, to stop the Germans from crossing the Meuse.
My LOs report there are no Americans
Garrisoning the Meuse bridges, so I have sent
Tank patrols fifty miles into the American sectors
Under cover of darkness. I shall tell Mather
To find Hodges and "order" him to block
The Meuse bridges with farm carts. We're ready for Rundstedt –
Despite the confusion, lack of information
And faulty command we have to operate in,
I have told Whiteley at SHAEF, and Brooke, that I
Should be in operational charge of the northern front.

The question is: will someone now compel
General Eisenhower to accept, three months too late,
What he should have accepted three months ago?

(*20 December, 3 a.m. Versailles, Hotel Trianon Palace, Eisenhower's HQ.* BEDELL SMITH *in
bed in his quarters next to his office.* MAJOR-GEN. STRONG *and* GEN. WHITELEY, *two British
SHAEF officers, knock and wake him up.*)

Bedell Smith.   For Christ's sake it's three in the morning. Well?

Strong.   German forces are beyond Bastogne and near
The Meuse. We know there has been no contact
Between General Bradley and First Army
HQ, Hodges', for two days, and a report
Suggests confusion and disorganisation.
We feel that Monty should command all troops
In the Allies' northern sector.

Bedell Smith.   I'll phone Bradley.

(*He rings.*)

Oh, it's Beetle here, sir. Sorry to wake you.
I have Major-General Strong and General Whiteley
Here, they say the Germans are on the Meuse,
That you've lost contact with Hodges, and suggest
That Monty takes over the whole of your front
North of Bastogne. Would you object? Huh huh.
You doubt the situation is serious enough
To warrant such a fundamental change of command,
Especially considering the effect it might have
On opinion in America. Thank you sir, good night.

(*He rings off.*)

You sons of bitches and limey bastards, you've
Put me in the position of questioning
General Bradley's competence, you're sacked.
Because of the view you've taken of the situation
You can no longer be accepted as
Staff officers to General Eisenhower.

You will receive instructions tomorrow
And return to England.

(*20 December, early morning. Versailles, Eisenhower's HQ.* EISENHOWER *and* BEDELL SMITH.)

Bedell Smith.　　　Sir, this report that German paratroops
Dressed in Allied uniform are out to kill
You, General Bradley and other Allied commanders,
And that the murderous Skorzeny is on his way
To Paris with sixty men to kill you – sir,
Your senior staff members feel you should stay
In your office and not go home at all.

Eisenhower.　　　Are you sure it's necessary?

Bedell Smith.　　　　　　　　　　Quite sure.
And you shouldn't go out at all, no conferences,
No visits to any Generals or to the front.

Eisenhower.　　　Very well. I'll remain here in the Trianon Palace.
Tell Kay we're living here now.

(*20 December, 9.55 a.m. Versailles, SHAEF Chiefs of Staff conference.* STRONG *and* WHITE-LEY, BEDELL SMITH, EISENHOWER.)

Strong.　　　　I agree with Colonel Lash. The two armoured
Thrusts may now have joined up, and Panzer divisions
Are being pulled back from Italy and Russia
To aid the offensive, and they have captured fuel.
So that concludes my briefing of the enemy
Situation. We're now going to see
General Eisenhower.

(STRONG *and* WHITELEY *leave.* BEDELL SMITH *takes their arm.*)

Bedell Smith.　　　　　　Listen, I've been thinking.
I'll put your proposals to him as my own.
I'll recommend putting Montgomery
In charge of the north, but you must keep silent.
It's better coming from an American.

You wait here. He'll call you in.

(BEDELL SMITH *knocks on Eisenhower's door.* EISENHOWER *calls in Bedell Smith.* STRONG *and* WHITELEY *wait outside.*)

(*To Eisenhower.*) I am concerned at the situation in the Ardennes.
The Germans are on the Meuse with many divisions,
Two thrusts may have linked up, and General Bradley
Has lost contact with Hodges, who seems to have left
His HQ. All the details are in this report.
Montgomery is on the spot. Bearing
In mind you can't go out because of the paratroops,
I reluctantly recommend that he is given
Command of the northern forces, two of Bradley's
Three armies.

Eisenhower   (*astonished*). I can't go along with that.
The American press would never accept it.

Bedell Smith.   The press doesn't know how serious the situation
In the Ardennes is. And there's wartime censorship.
And I remind you again, you and General Bradley
Are targets for Skorzeny's assassins.
If Montgomery takes over, they'll switch to him.

Eisenhower.   I'm shocked. I need to question General Strong
And General Whiteley about the latest picture,
And their intelligence and operational reports.

(*Later.*)

Eisenhower.   I suppose I'll have to go along with it.
I don't like it, but I've no alternative.
I'll telephone Bradley and Montgomery.

(*Later.* BEDELL SMITH *emerges from Eisenhower's room.* STRONG *and* WHITELEY *are waiting.*)

Bedell Smith.   It's done. I'm sorry about last night. You're not sacked.
What made me really mad was I knew you were right.
He's told Bradley, he's phoning Monty now.

Strong.	How did Bradley take the news?

Bedell Smith.	Not at all well.
	He objected, but was overruled by Ike
	Who said "Well Brad, those are my orders" and
	Put down the phone. He's hurt. Thank you, fellows.

(*Exeunt* STRONG *and* WHITELEY.)

(*Aside*.) I thought Bradley could handle the armies.
I flared up at the suggestion that he couldn't.
But I've solved the situation well for Ike.
The American Generals shouldn't go out until
The assassins have been caught or killed. Till then,
Let British Generals risk assassination,
The most prominent being: Montgomery.

(*20 December, 10.30 a.m. Zonhoven, Montgomery's HQ.* MONTGOMERY. DAWNAY, *Montgomery's* MILITARY ASSISTANT, *answers the phone.*)

Dawnay.	It's General Eisenhower.

Montgomery.	Hello? Yes. Yes.
	You're speaking very fast and it's difficult
	To understand what you're talking about. (*To Dawnay*.) I don't know
	What he's saying, he's very excited.
	(*To Eisenhower*.) It seems we now have two fronts? And I am
	To assume command of the northern front.
	That's all I want to know. (*Shouting*.) I can't hear you
	Properly. I shall take command straightaway.

(*He puts down the phone.*)

He's still talking wildly about other things.
I want the largest Union Jack that will go
On the car bonnet and eight motor-cycle outriders.

Dawnay	(*quietly*). Congratulations, sir. (*Exit*.)

Montgomery	(*aside*). Field Commanders
	Are least important to governments when they sense

Victory, most when they start to smell defeat.
I have control, albeit temporarily,
Of Allied forces north of the Ardennes,
Of Hodges' First Army and Simpson's Ninth
North of Bastogne, and Coningham commands
All supporting American air forces.
While the Supreme Commander cowers in his Hotel
And Bradley vacates his bedroom, fearing attack
From Skorzeny's assassination squad,
I will show a commander has no fear,
I will boost the morale and self-confidence
Of the American commanders in the field.
Let them call me a showman. It will work.

(*21 December, 11 a.m. Zonhoven, Montgomery's HQ. MONTGOMERY. DEMPSEY and* CRERAR. *Conference for British and Canadian commanders.*)

Montgomery.   My strategy is not to attack the Germans –
The thick forests and hills of the Ardennes
Are easy to defend, hard to attack –
But to outflank the Germans and take the Ruhr.
We should hold the Germans with American troops,
And give American ground if necessary,
And thrust to the Ruhr with British and Canadians.

(*21 December. Versailles, Eisenhower's HQ. EISENHOWER and* BEDELL SMITH.)

Eisenhower.   This Montgomery crows like a rooster,
I have had to give him command, there's no one else
Up there. But the man is impossible.
I have just received this message: "In a press
Statement Monty is claiming his new command
As a personal vindication." He seems to forget
Who is fighting this war. Tell General Marshall
That either Monty or I will have to go.

(*21 December. Verviers. MONTGOMERY arrives, Union Jack on the bonnet of his Rolls Royce, and gets out with HENDERSON. HODGES and SIMPSON greet him.*)

Henderson   (*aside*). He's like Christ come to cleanse the temple.

Hodges.   We're sure glad to see you, Commander. We've
                Not seen Bradley or any of his staff since
                This battle began. We just want someone to
                Give us some firm orders.

Montgomery.   We'll soon have
                A properly organised set-up for command,
                The battle will soon be under control.
                We're going to win, we're going to push the Germans
                Back where they came from.

(*22 December. Zonhoven, Montgomery's HQ.* MONTGOMERY *and* HODGES.)

Montgomery.   No, you must withdraw, don't think what Bradley will say.
                Bradley and Patton think of counter-attack,
                But there are now twice as many German troops
                In the Ardennes as we landed on D-Day –
                Three hundred and thirty-five thousand – and more
                Than nine hundred tanks in the ice and snow,
                And Bradley, in his Luxembourg Hotel,
                And Eisenhower, locked and shuttered inside
                His Versailles Palace, and swashbuckling Patton
                Talk of counter-offensives, and do not know
                The picture I have from my LOs. They wage
                Their war by telephone, I mine by scouts
                Who each day visit the entire front line
                And bring back sightings of enemy movements.
                Bradley underestimates German strength,
                And so, therefore, in Versailles does Eisenhower,
                And optimistically thinks that Patton
                Is about to finish the Germans off completely.
                Bradley draws lines on maps with a brown crayon
                Which indicate advances to be made
                But does not know where the men are who will make them.
                Let him call me over-cautious, but I honour
                The fighting man, and I say "Hodges' troops" are
                Tired, have been under strain and should now withdraw
                And become reserves, which will be most useful.
                No more American lives should be lost
                Than is necessary.

Hodges.   I agree to be overruled.
                    I will order the withdrawal.

(*25 December. Zonhoven, Montgomery's HQ.* MONTGOMERY *in full battledress, Christmas cards.*)

Montgomery.   Inside the Bulge Hundred-and-First Airborne,
                   Encircled at Bastogne, were asked to surrender, their
                   Commander said "Nuts" and beat the Germans back.
                   Skies cleared and Allied planes strafed the Germans
                   And Patton began his thrust towards Bastogne
                   To lift the siege. And now, having been out of touch
                   Since December the seventh, almost three weeks,
                   Bradley has come out of his Hotel, has braved
                   The assassins, and is flying up here to be briefed.
                   I have not sent a car.

                   (*Enter* BRADLEY, *in an old combat jacket, looking tired.*)

                              Brad, you found the way.

Bradley.   In a staff car provided by General Hodges.

Montgomery.   I haven't seen you since Maastricht, when I
                   Proposed one unified command, and you
                   Preferred to command the American army.
                   Come up to my study, and I'll brief you.
                   I know what's going on in the American sector.

(*Later.*)

Montgomery.   So the Germans have given the Americans a bloody nose.
                   And the Americans deserve this counter-attack,
                   It's entirely their own fault for trying two thrusts
                   At the same time, neither being strong enough.
                   If there'd been a single thrust, none of this
                   Would have happened. Now we are in a muddle.
                   I always advised against the right going so far.
                   You advised in favour of it and General
                   Eisenhower took your advice. So we must withdraw.
                   If Patton's counter-attack is not strong enough

Then I'll have to deal unaided with Fifth and Sixth
Panzer armies, in which case General Eisenhower
Will have to give me more American troops.
Do you agree with my summary?

Bradley   (*uncomfortably*).   I do.

Montgomery.   Then what does General Eisenhower propose to do?
He hasn't spoken to me since giving me command
Of the main battle in the Ardennes. The Supreme
Commander has given no orders. So I ask
You, what does he propose to do?

Bradley.   I don't know.

Montgomery.   Don't know? Don't know? A commander has to know.

Bradley   (*uncomfortably*). I have not seen Eisenhower recently.

Montgomery.   But you and he agreed a better way
Than a unified command at Maastricht.
Surely he has been in touch?

Bradley.   Skorzeny
And his paratroops in Allied uniform
Are trying to kill him and me –

Montgomery.   And I have been
Riding round the front line in a Rolls Royce
With a large Union Jack, and I haven't seen them.

Bradley.   The security problem has hindered communication,
And my telephone lines were cut.

Montgomery.   Because you went
Too far, and in too weak a second thrust.

Bradley   (*aside*). He is humiliating me, shaming
Me like a Headmaster shaming a naughty boy.
I shall not forgive him for this. I shall demand
That Ike returns the First and Ninth Armies

To my command.

(*27 December, 8 a.m., Versailles, SHAEF conference.* EISENHOWER, TEDDER *and* STRONG.)

Eisenhower.　　　I believe the German divisions in the Bulge
　　　　　　　　Are understrength and pummelled, and that their
　　　　　　　　Supply lines are poor. I want to hit them
　　　　　　　　Hard and quickly. The Allies are running late
　　　　　　　　In their counter-attack.

Tedder.　　　　　　　　　　　　The good weather
　　　　　　　　Will not last much longer, and we must attack
　　　　　　　　While our planes can still fly.

　　　　　　　　(*A message is received.*)

Strong.　　　　　　　　　　　Montgomery
　　　　　　　　Has a new plan for attack, involving two corps,
　　　　　　　　Seventh US and 30th British.
　　　　　　　　A northern counter-attack, Twenty-first say.

Eisenhower.　　　Praise God from whom all blessings flow.

(*27 December. Zonhoven. Montgomery's HQ.* MONTGOMERY *and* DAWNAY.)

Montgomery.　　　I have no idea where Ike is. I ask Bradley,
　　　　　　　　He doesn't know. Freddie de Guingand asks
　　　　　　　　Bedell Smith, who says Ike's locked up, whatever
　　　　　　　　That means. Perhaps Bedell is fed up with
　　　　　　　　His indecision and has locked him up
　　　　　　　　To leave it all to me and Bradley. And then
　　　　　　　　We hear he's sending Tedder and Bull to Stalin,
　　　　　　　　To discuss Russian offensive plans. He can't
　　　　　　　　Get anyone to the Ardennes, but he can to Moscow.
　　　　　　　　And the visit will be seen as desperate begging.
　　　　　　　　He's more concerned with the Russians than the Ardennes.
　　　　　　　　Now we hear he's trying to fly to see me,
　　　　　　　　And now he's coming by train. I can't wait
　　　　　　　　Any longer, so I have come up with my
　　　　　　　　Strategic plan, which I'll put to Hodges,

Dempsey, Crerar and Simpson tomorrow
At our conference. *Ultra* shows the Germans
Will attack, we must lure them onto our positions.
Collins will feint, and we'll strike at the Ruhr.

(*28 December, early afternoon. A carriage on Hasselt station. Eisenhower's train has arrived. Machine-gunners leap out to guard the carriage.* MONTGOMERY, DE GUINGAND *and* WILLIAMS. *Subzero temperature.*)

Montgomery   (*to Eisenhower*). Having arrived in a mere armoured car,
                    I feel naked before assassins.

                    (*He greets* EISENHOWER *on the train.*)

Eisenhower   (*uncomfortably*).   In due course
                    There will be an enquiry on the need for all this.

Montgomery.   Ike, this meeting I want without any staff
                    Present. You haven't brought Bedell Smith or
                    Tedder. De Guingand and Williams can wait
                    Outside in the corridor.

Eisenhower.   Come to my study.
                    Now, I've heard that your northern counter-attack
                    Will use two corps in an offensive role.
                    Bradley came to Versailles yesterday afternoon
                    And is strengthening the southern flank and then
                    Attacking. I want to hit the Germans hard.
                    How soon can you attack?

Montgomery.   I can't discuss
                    Timing. You must understand, we are fighting
                    A defensive operation in the Ardennes.
                    You can't attack in thick forests and hills.
                    Germany will make one last big attack
                    On the northern shoulder of the Bulge. We must
                    Receive the attack, and then counter at the tip
                    Of the Bulge, drive the Germans back to the West Wall.

Eisenhower.   The tip? We need to attack their flank and
                    Cut them off. We can't wait or Rundstedt will

	Withdraw from the Bulge or put up infantry divisions,
	Pull his tanks back in reserve. You must attack quickly.

Montgomery.   But first we must receive the German attack.

Eisenhower.   There will be no attack. What if there is no attack
                Today or tomorrow? Would you counter-attack
                On January the first?

Montgomery.   I suppose I'd have to.
                But once we've held the Germans here, we can
                Invade Germany, take the Ruhr. I have
                A master plan for the future conduct
                Of the war. It is vital to decide on this
                So present action accords with the future plan.
                It means allotting all offensive power
                To the northern front under one man's command.
                Bradley has made a mess of the situation.

Eisenhower.   Bradley, Patton and Devers all wanted
                The Frankfurt thrust, and I gave way to them.
                There are difficulties about the unified command.
                I've explained about American public opinion.

Montgomery.   I think you will find it difficult to explain
                That the true reason for the bloody nose
                You have just received from the Germans was
                Your division of the unified command.

Eisenhower.   You still don't understand that Americans
                Cannot be commanded by British as they
                Are supplying three quarters of all troops.

Montgomery.   I say it again, I will serve under Bradley
                If that will see a unified command.

Eisenhower   (*aside*). He doesn't understand political
                Realities.

(*30 December. Versailles, SHAEF HQ. EISENHOWER, BEDELL SMITH and DE GUINGAND.*)

De Guingand.	Montgomery will not attack until January the fourth.

Eisenhower.	The fourth? He told me the first.

De Guingand.   You must have misunderstood.
He would not have said that.

Bedell Smith.   What makes me so mad
Is that Monty won't talk in the presence of
Anyone else.

Eisenhower.   Damn it, he agreed. He's lied
To me, he's trying to lead me by the nose.
We have a great opportunity in the Ardennes
Which he is squandering by slowness,
Wanting the optimum conditions for his attack.
The time has come to break with Montgomery.

Bedell Smith.   We're all in rebellion at how he's carried on.
You should dictate a letter to him.

Eisenhower.   Tell him
That if he doesn't live up to his promises,
He will be sacked.

De Guingand.   Please do not send it yet.
I will talk to Monty and straighten things out.

Eisenhower   (*aside*). He is an affable man, in contrast to his boss.
I like him, and he may secure an attack.
(*Aloud*.) Very well, I'll hold it back till you've seen him.

(*31 December. Versailles, SHAEF HQ.* EISENHOWER, BEDELL SMITH *and* STAFF, DE GUINGAND.)

De Guingand.   I've spoken with Montgomery, and he confirms
That the proper strategy is to let the Germans
Exhaust themselves with one final attack
Before an offensive.

Eisenhower   (*angrily*).   But he definitely

	Promised to attack on January the first. Tomorrow.
De Guingand.	You must have misunderstood.
Eisenhower.	And Bradley's attacked In the belief that Montgomery is attacking then. If he doesn't, the Germans will move Panzer divisions From the north to the south. We want an attack now. Montgomery's timing in military Operations is seriously flawed. He's unable to see things from SHAEF's viewpoint. He's welched.
De Guingand.	He's written you a personal letter.

(DE GUINGAND *hands over the letter.* EISENHOWER *reads it.*)

| Eisenhower. | He says my policies are wrong and demands
Control of the land battle. He says there must be
A single thrust to the north to seize the Ruhr,
With Patton held, or else the Allies will fail.
He sends a directive along those lines
For me to sign. |

(*General indignation and outrage. "O-o-h."*)

(*Aside.*) I've lost control of him.
But he's gone too far. My credibility
Is at stake. He is insubordinate. I must
Keep my staff together.

Tedder.	It's outrageous, It makes me seethe. Sack him.
Eisenhower.	Bedell, cable General Marshall and the Combined Chiefs of Staff, Saying it's Monty or me. And if it's me, Then I want Alexander.
Tedder.	I'll help you find Some appropriate words.

(BEDELL SMITH *receives a signal.*)

Bedell Smith.   A signal from General
                            Marshall, Chairman of the Combined Chiefs of Staff.
                            It says you have their complete confidence,
                            That you're doing a grand job, and are not to pay
                            Attention to British press reports that call
                            For a British Deputy Commander – Monty? –
                            To lighten your task as this would be resented
                            Back home.

                            (*He hands* EISENHOWER *a paper.*)

De Guingand   (*aside*).   If Ike sends his cable, Monty will go.
                            (*Aloud to Eisenhower.*) Please don't send your cable for a few hours,
                            Until I've spoken with Monty in Zonhoven.

Eisenhower.   All right. But I'm now issuing my directive
                            Which contradicts Montgomery's on every point.
                            First Army is back in Bradley's control,
                            There must be a double thrust into Germany.
                            We must seize the initiative at once,
                            We must act quickly, with speed and energy
                            Before the Germans move in more Panzers.
                            Now draft a covering letter to Montgomery.
                            I do not agree there should be a single ground
                            Commander. I don't want to hear any more
                            About putting Bradley under his command.
                            I have planned an advance to the Rhine
                            On a broad front, and will no longer tolerate
                            Any debate. Say I don't want to take
                            Our differences to the CCS, but if necessary I will
                            Even though it damages the goodwill between
                            The Allies.

(*31 December, 3 p.m. Zonhoven, Montgomery's HQ.* DE GUINGAND *is drinking tea with* MONTGOMERY *in "A" Mess.*)

De Guingand.   The fog is really thick.

                            (MONTGOMERY *rises.*)

156

Montgomery.	I'm going upstairs to my office.
	Please come up when you've finished your tea.

(They go up to Montgomery's study.)

Well?

De Guingand.	The feeling against you at SHAEF is very strong.
	Eisenhower has drafted a signal to Marshall
	Saying it's him or you. He's set to resign.
	Marshall has cabled the CCS's support.
	Smith's very worried. They think you'll have to go.

Montgomery.	It can't be that serious?

(DE GUINGAND hands over Eisenhower's letter and directive.)

De Guingand.	The Americans
	Now have three-quarters of the war effort.
	If the CCS sack you, there is little
	That Churchill can now do.

Montgomery.	Who would replace me?

De Guingand.	Alexander. His name is in the draft signal.

Montgomery.	Alexander? He's a weak commander
	Who knows nothing about field operations
	And is unable to give firm and clear decisions.
	He's ineffective in Italy, he'd be a disaster.
	What a team: Eisenhower, Bradley and Alexander.
	The Germans would push them back to Normandy.

De Guingand.	He's in the signal.

Montgomery.	What shall I do, Freddie?
	What shall I do?

(DE GUINGAND pulls out a letter from his battledress pocket.)

Sign this. It's a letter

Of apology to Eisenhower. It says
There are many factors "beyond anything I realise",
That he can rely on you "one hundred per cent",
And that you're "very distressed" your letter
Upset him, and that he should tear it up –
The one about you having sole command.

(MONTGOMERY *signs the letter.*)

Montgomery   (*aside*). I humiliated Bradley in this room
And Eisenhower on his train, but now it's me.
I've had to swallow my pride and humble pie
To keep my job.
(*Aloud.*)   I shall begin my attack
Twenty-four hours early, at dawn on the third.

De Guingand.   I'll take this straight back to SHAEF. Good-bye, sir.
(*Aside.*) He looks nonplussed and so terribly lonely,
I feel sorry for him. He knows he's lost.

(*Exit* DE GUINGAND.)

Montgomery.   And yet it hurts my principles to recant.
The single thrust, the sole command, were right.
Marshall and Roosevelt behind him have clipped my wings
Just when the eagle was soaring again.
I will not accept this American interference
Which has taken away my command just when I have
Defeated the Germans in the finest
Defensive Allied battle of the war,
The second time they've removed my command
At the height of victory, four months after
I defeated the Germans in the finest
Offensive Allied battle of the war.
(*Defiantly.*) I will hold a press conference about how I won
The Battle of the Bulge.

(*5 January 1945. Zonhoven, Montgomery's HQ. His study.* CHURCHILL *arrives with* BROOKE.
MONTGOMERY.)

Churchill.   We've been travelling on Eisenhower's train,

	The *Alive*. Your battle seems to be going well.
Montgomery.	In three feet of snow in places, which makes It hard for tanks to advance, and the Germans won't Withdraw. Collins is fighting hard, but we May not have the strength to push the Germans out Of the penetration area. We are fighting A defensive, not an offensive, battle No matter how they present it in SHAEF.
Brooke.	And the business with Eisenhower was sorted out.
Montgomery.	Ike has abandoned the American advance To Frankfurt via the Saar, and the main effort Is to be north of the Ruhr, with the US Ninth Army under my command, in Twenty-first. I have "power of decision" to plan for the Ruhr, And Bradley has to move his headquarters To be nearer to mine. I have most of what I asked. And Ike has given me a new Dakota As mine was destroyed in the New Year's Day air raid.
Churchill.	But Bradley's not pleased. He's driven to Etain Airfield to protest to Ike.
Brooke.	On the switch to the north.
Montgomery.	Bradley wants the Ninth Army back, but Ike Knows he's been the cause of an American defeat.
Brooke.	And the American public will soon know As SHAEF have held a press conference today. For the first time, Americans will know That you have fought the battle of the Ardennes, Not Bradley.
Churchill.	The Anglo-American Alliance is still strong?
Montgomery.	Yes. I am giving Hodges two hundred British tanks. We're closely knit.

The German breakthrough would have been most serious
But for the unity of the Anglo-American Army.
But we need more fighting troops if we're to advance.

Churchill. I will cable President Roosevelt tonight.
There is a campaign in the British press
To cast doubt on Eisenhower's fitness
To command the Allied Armies in Europe.
Eisenhower has had difficulties with de Gaulle,
He's had to help the French defend Strasbourg
With troops who should be reserves for the Ardennes.
I'm concerned to preserve Allied solidarity.

Montgomery. Could I help Eisenhower and set things straight
By talking frankly to the press? I would
Tell the story of the battle of the Ardennes,
Explain how we have stopped the Germans in
A joint effort, stress the great friendship between
Myself and Ike, and call for more Allied
Solidarity and team spirit.

Churchill.   That would be
Invaluable.

SCENE 7.

STALIN'S OFFENSIVE

(*6 January.* STALIN *and Gen.* ANTONOV.)

Stalin. Churchill has written asking for a Soviet attack
In the east to prevent German troops being switched
To the western front. He wants an attack
Across the Vistula in January. Reply we will attack
Not later than the second half of January. Now phone
The four Marshals involved to start at once for Berlin
Regardless of the bad weather. Koniev first,
He must use artillery without air cover.

One day later, Chernyakhovsky, and one day later
Zhukov and Rokossovsky. Tell them they are all
In a race for glory - Western competition!

(*7 January. The Adlerhorst, or Eagle's Nest, Hitler's western field HQ near Bad Nauheim, in the
Taunus mountains outside Frankfurt.* HITLER, *with his* GENERALS.)

Hitler.   The offensive has ended, you say, and we
                 Must protect our forces. Very well. I will
                 Allow a withdrawal from the Ardennes,
                 But only a limited one.

                 (GUDERIAN *waves a paper in* HITLER*'s face.*)

Guderian.   I have
                 An intelligence report, there will be
                 A massive Soviet offensive in the east
                 At any time now. We must withdraw
                 Troops from the west and send them to the east –

Hitler   (*raging*). The report is incorrect. Who is responsible
                 For it? He must be mad, he should be locked up
                 In a lunatic asylum –

Guderian.   General Gehlen
                 Is my intelligence officer in the east,
                 And if he is mad, then I should be certified
                 As well –

Hitler.   The eastern front has never been
                 Stronger. It is a concrete wall of men over
                 Seven hundred and fifty miles in length.
                 Our reserves have never been greater in the east.

Guderian.   The eastern front reserve are twelve divisions.
                 One breakthrough and the whole front will collapse.

Hitler.   What do you think, Himmler?

Himmler.   The Russians are
                 Bluffing, my *Führer*.

(HITLER *smiles*.)

(7 January. Zonhoven. Montgomery's press conference. MONTGOMERY *in a red Airborne Corps beret with two badges.* WILLIAMS *next to him.)*

Montgomery (*jauntily*). As soon as I saw what was happening,
I took certain steps myself to ensure
That if the Germans got to the Meuse they would
Certainly not get over the river.
And I carried out certain movements to meet
The threatened danger, i.e. I was thinking ahead.
Soon General Eisenhower put me in command
Of the northern flank, and I then brought the British
Into the fight and saved the Americans.
And the Germans never reached the Meuse or Antwerp.
You have thus the picture of British troops fighting
On both sides of American forces who
Have suffered a hard blow. This is a fine
Allied picture. It has been a very interesting
Battle, rather like El Alamein. Indeed,
I think it's possibly one of the most
Interesting and tricky battles I have ever handled.
GIs make great fighting men when they are
Given proper leadership.

Williams (*aside*).   It's coming across
As if he rescued the Americans,
As if the British won the Battle of the Bulge
When the Americans stopped the Germans
Before he came on the scene. It's appalling,
He's preening himself like a cock on a dunghill.
The Americans will be furious.

(7 January. PATTON *and press.)*

Patton. Hardly any British forces were even engaged
In the Bulge and Montgomery didn't direct
The victory but got in everyone's way and botched
The counter-attack so we missed bagging
The whole German army. I wish Ike were
More of a gambler, but he's a lion compared

162

To Montgomery, and Bradley is better than Ike
As far as nerve is concerned. Monty is a tired
Little fart. War requires the taking of risks.
And he won't take them.

(*8 January. Zonhoven, Montgomery's HQ.* MONTGOMERY *and* HENDERSON.)

Montgomery. Goebbels has broadcast an edited version.
And Churchill has heard from Marshall and wants
Me to eat humble pie, and in public I must.
But the truth is, the Germans have given
The Allies a bloody nose. Eighty thousand
American casualties in the battle
Of the Ardennes. This need not have happened.
It would not have happened if we had fought
The campaign properly after our great victory
In Normandy. Now the war will drag on
Another six weeks. And hundreds of thousands
More will die in extermination camps.

(*8 January. London, underground war rooms.* CHURCHILL *and* COLVILLE.)

Churchill. We must not offend the Americans.
They have borne great losses in the Battle
Of the Bulge, under Monty's leadership. I
Will say there was only a minor British involvement
In the greatest American battle of the war,
A famous American victory.
We need American resolve and troops,
And Monty for reasons of personal vanity
Delights in irritating Eisenhower.
Monty may be a great General, but he is
Still in the kindergarten in diplomacy.

(*8 January, evening.* BRADLEY *and* HANSEN.)

Bradley. SHAEF have given me a direct order
Not to make an unauthorised statement
To the press. I can't do it.

Hansen.   The staff's morale

Is breaking. Montgomery is the symbol
Of the British, you of the American effort.
Ike has to straddle the two, it's for you to speak
To correct the British press and the BBC
Who are saying there was an increase in
Montgomery's command.

Bradley.   I'll do it. But
Although I am pleased my Ardennes plans are passed,
Ike still pursues the northern thrust to the Ruhr
And I am still upset that the Ninth Army
Stays with Montgomery. At bottom he's
A British General whose plans have one aim:
To further his own aggrandizement.

(*8 January. Bad Nauheim*. HITLER, GÖRING, RUNDSTEDT, BORMANN.)

Rundstedt.   *North Wind* has failed. The enemy nearly
Evacuated Strasbourg, but sidestepped.
Montgomery's new offensive in the north
And Patton in the south are attacking the Bulge.
We have destroyed one thousand two hundred tanks
And taken twenty-four thousand American prisoners,
But it is now time to cut our losses. Model
Has requested we pull back on our western flank
The 47th Panzer Corps. I ask you
To authorise this move.

Hitler.   And also the south
Panzer Army, which should now be in reserve.

Rundstedt   (*aside*). He has indirectly admitted that
He has lost his Ardennes gamble.

(*Hitler withdraws.* BORMANN *follows him.*)

Bormann.   The war is not lost because we are pulling back.

Hitler   (*depressed*). The war was lost two years ago.
But still the killing must go on. It is a crusade
Which must take precedence over everything,

Including the war effort, so that there are no Jews
Left to worship the Satanic Jehovah,
The demiurge who created the evil world.
So that a New Order can prevail for
The Aryan Sixth Root race, a race of Supermen.
Jodl did not understand this. He said
That in Warsaw the SS were proud of
Their killing, "their murder expedition",
But he did not understand that genocide
Is how we cleanse the earth, change the world.
Genocide can transform the world for good.

(*10 January. Berlin, a courtroom in the Prussian Court of Appeal.* FREISLER *is trying* VON
MOLTKE, DELP *and* SPERR.)

Moltke.   This Court's proceedings are secret, I must object.
                 The others are innocent.

Freisler   (*banging the table*).   I will not stand
                 For that sort of thing, I will not listen. They all
                 Plotted against the *Führer*, we have heard the evidence.
                 What do you say about the evidence against you?

                 (MOLTKE *is silent.*)

                 You will speak when the Court speaks to you. The Court
                 Is now interested in your guilt, as leader
                 Of the Kreisau Circle of Prussian plotters.

Moltke.   My great-great grandfather was the Field Marshal
                 Who crushed France in 1870 so
                 Bismarck could unite Germany under
                 Prussian rule. My grandfather was chief justice
                 Of South Africa. I am Prussian and
                 I was brought up with a sense of justice
                 And I tell you, the six other accused
                 Are innocent.

Freisler.   Enough. I will have no more
                 Of this.

(*He puts on a black cap.*)

The Court sentences Count Helmuth
James von Moltke, Jesuit Father Alfred
Delp and ex-Colonel Franz Sperr to death by hanging.
Sentence to be carried out in Plotzensee prison.

(*21 January.* EVA BRAUN *and her sister* ILSE *are dining in the Chancellery library, white-gloved* SERVANTS *serving from silver dishes.*)

Eva.	The *Führer* left the Adlerhorst nearly
	A week ago. He came into Berlin
	Early in the morning with the blinds pulled down
	The car windows, because the bomb damage
	Upsets him. He was shocked to see how badly
	The Chancellery was damaged. Every window
	Broken, the west wing with our private apartments
	Collapsed. General Rattenhuber of the
	SS advised him to move his office
	And our residence into the bunker
	Under the garden outside. This was his study,
	Where he holds his conferences. He has his SS
	Guards round him all the time following the
	Wicked attempt on his life in July.
	Even though we cannot put you up here,
	We can still give you dinner in the Chancellery,
	And you will find the Adlon Hotel very comfortable.
Ilse.	I cannot believe the luxury in Berlin,
	When in the countryside, the snowy roads are lined
	With fleeing refugees who have nothing.
	There was one train at the station, and several
	Froze in open wagons, waiting for it to leave.
	People are trudging south or west through snow.
	I was three nights without sleep travelling here.
Eva.	I shall join you in Breslau in two weeks' time.
Ilse.	Breslau is lost. Do you not understand?
	The Russians have taken Silesia, Germany
	Is finished. As I travelled here I saw

	Columns of hungry refugees and the Russians

Columns of hungry refugees and the Russians
Are burning and plundering and raping all.
Your *Führer* is responsible for the invasion.
He's destroying our country, and you, and us.

Eva.   You're mad. Crazy. How can you say such things
About the *Führer* who is so generous?
He's invited you to stay at his house at Obersalzberg.
You should be shot.

Ilse.   You need to open your eyes.

(*Enter* HITLER *briefly. He is a wreck, his left hand trembles, his left side shakes, he stoops, hunchbacked, with a pot belly. He shuffles.* BORMANN *is with him.*)

Eva.   My sister will gladly stay at your house.

Hitler   (*nodding, to Bormann*).   I want
Eva to follow her. She is a distraction here.

Bormann.   *Jawohl, mein Führer.*

(*Fade on* EVA *and* ILSE.)

Hitler   (*to Bormann*).   I have decided,
In view of the failures of my Generals
In the Ardennes, that every General should inform me
In advance of every movement in his unit,
In time for me to intervene in their decisions
If I think fit, and for my counter-orders
To reach the front-line troops.

(HITLER *goes to* Führer *bunker. Below, conference room or map room and Hitler's office or study/living room in which is Anton Graff's life-sized portrait of Frederick the Great. Hitler sits by dim candlelight and stares at the painting.*)

(*Alone.*) Frederick the Great, you expanded Prussia,
You fought Russia and Austria and France
And your luck turned when Tsarina Elizabeth died.

You are called "Great" because of what you endured.
Your spirit is with me, help me, help me.

(*He lights another candle and performs an occult incantation.*)

O power that I first contacted when Dietrich
Eckart opened my higher centres, power
Whose Will has carried me from the Munich
Beer-cellars to the highest point in the world,
Power which has filled me with an electric current
Of dynamic energy when I needed it,
Power which I have summoned through ritual magic,
And human sacrifice as Eckart taught,
Power you knew, Frederick, in your illumined search,
Do not desert me in my hour of need.
I have done your Will, I have speared Jehovah,
Whom there will soon be no Jews left to worship.
I am the chosen spear of the Antichrist,
The man chosen to wield Longinus' spear
Which I took from the Vienna Hofburg
And hid in sacred safety in Nuremberg,
And, inspired by Lucifer, to conquer the world
And lead the Aryan race to glory as
A race of Supermen – do not abandon me,
Your foremost Superman, *your* Overlord,
Fill me with your power, but more importantly
Strike down my enemies, give me a sign
That you are still supporting my world rule.
Strike dead Stalin or Roosevelt, my Overlord.

(*A knock on the door. Enter* BURGDORF *and* GUDERIAN.)

Burgdorf.   Sir, The Chief of the General Staff, Heinz
                 Guderian, who you summoned.

Hitler.   Ah yes.
                 My Generals continue to defy my orders.
                 General Hossbach has withdrawn his Fourth Army
                 From East Prussia after it was overrun
                 By Rokossovky. Did you know this?

Guderian.	No sir, but I know Hossbach wants to save As many men as possible, and keep a corridor open For the East Prussians –
Hitler.	Pah! The man is a traitor.
Guderian.	He cleared the withdrawal with Colonel-General Reinhardt –
Hitler.	Commander of Army Group North, But not with you – or me. I demand that You now dismiss Hossbach and Reinhardt and Their treacherous staffs, and court-martial them.
Guderian.	Sir, I'm an East Prussian, born on the Vistula, And I do not consider these men traitors.
Hitler.	I will dismiss Reinhardt immediately. Replace Reinhardt with Colonel-General Rendulic, He is a National Socialist.
Guderian.	But sir –
Hitler.	And Army Group Centre is now in the command Of Colonel-General Schörner.

(GUDERIAN *leaves and meets* RIBBENTROP *in the corridor.*)

Guderian.	Foreign Minister, the war is lost. I urge You to negotiate an armistice in the west And transfer troops to face the Russians.

(RIBBENTROP *enters Hitler's office or living room,* GUDERIAN *waits. Then* HITLER *appears.*)

Hitler	(*shouting*). Anyone who tells anyone that the war is lost Will be treated as a traitor, with consequences For himself and his family. I will take action Regardless of rank and reputation.
Guderian.	My *Führer*, I do not mean that the war is lost,

Only that it *will* be lost unless we transfer more troops.

Hitler.   No.

Guderian.   My *Führer*, we need a new emergency
Army group to support Army Groups North
And Centre and stop Zhukov's advance.

Hitler   (*calming*).   Yes,
That is good.

(*24 January. The row of eight meat hooks on a girder. VON MOLTKE, DELP and SPERR are hanged under film lights. The nooses are of rope and are in figure of eight shape.*)

(*24 January. Berlin, the* Führer *bunker. The conference room.* HITLER *and* GUDERIAN.)

Guderian.   I recommend Field Marshal von Weichs as
This commander.

Hitler   (*thinking*).   No, I have decided.
The new reserve army will be known as
Army Group Vistula. It should be commanded
By Himmler.

Guderian   (*exploding*). But Himmler has had no previous
Military experience, except as an
Army cadet.

(BORMANN *has appeared.*)

Bormann.   SS leader Himmler is a great
Organiser and a good administrator,
And he is the only man who can immediately
Form such a force.

Himmler   (*appearing, enthusiastically*). My *Führer*, I will be
Honoured to raise a reserve army for
The eastern front, and I will go to Danzig.

Guderian   (*alone*). So Bormann is envious of my rapport
With the *Führer*, and has just clipped my wings.

But the *Führer* now believes in a non-existent
Force.

(27 January. Moscow, Stalin's office in the Kremlin. STALIN *and* ANTONOV.)

Stalin.   My Generals have now submitted reports and plans.
                 Where do they all stand? Start with Koniev.

Antonov.   Koniev's First Ukrainian Front broke through
                 The German defences in snow with non-stop shells
                 And advanced along a two hundred mile line,
                 And with the sun glistening on snow, took Lodz
                 And the same day Krakow, the capital
                 Of Poland's kings and of the Nazi "General
                 Government", in the rear. The Germans fled
                 And Hans Frank's city fell without damage.
                 Koniev has pushed on and taken Silesia
                 And has crossed the Oder.

Stalin.   And Zhukov?

Antonov.   Zhukov's
                 First Belorussian Front, led into battle
                 By Chuikov, the hero of Stalingrad, bombarded
                 The Germans and advanced south of Warsaw,
                 And cut the city off from the west, then
                 With another artillery barrage, tanks smashed through
                 The Germans in the south while the 47th
                 Army crossed the Vistula to the north
                 And surrounded the city. The Germans destroyed
                 Warsaw, shooting, hanging and burning thousands
                 Of Poles, and evacuated the city.
                 And Posen is now surrounded. Zhukov
                 Is crossing the Oder.

Stalin.   And the defiant Rokossovsky?

Antonov.   Rokossovsky's advance to the north of Zhukov
                 Has been slower because of the Masurian lakes,
                 And the ice of the River Narcis was not thick
                 Enough to bear tanks. The Imperial

Russian Army was defeated in that terrain
In the First World War, at Tannenberg.
Even so Rokossovsky is near the Baltic, he has
Advanced along the Vistula towards Danzig
And has cut off Germans in the Baltic
And East Prussia, and forced them to dig up
The remains of Hindenberg and his wife
Who were buried at Tannenberg.

Stalin.   Good. But
Rokossovsky has not advanced as fast
As the others who cover fifteen, eighteen,
Twenty-five miles a day. Tell him to turn
Towards East Prussia and support Zhukov.
He will not go down in history as
The Soviet General who took Berlin.
What is Zhukov's plan?

Antonov.   In February, a new
Non-stop offensive, smashing across the Oder
And into Berlin with one gigantic thrust.

Stalin.   And Koniev's plan?

Antonov.   Destroy the German forces
At Breslau, and reach the Elbe, then join Zhukov
And capture Berlin.

Stalin.   Both men seek to become
The "conqueror of Berlin". Let them race each other.
The one will spur the other.

(*A message comes in.*)

Antonov.   News just arrived. This morning a Soviet scout
In a snowstorm, entered a camp with wooden buildings
At Monowitz near Katowice in
Upper Silesia, and found a slave labour
Factory belonging to I.G. Farben.
Half an hour later, the Hundredth Division
Found six hundred sick, emaciated people

And a pile of corpses. This afternoon
Our men took Oswiecim, Auschwitz-Birkenau
As the camp is known, and found a gas chamber
And crematorium the Germans left
Eleven days ago when they blew up
The barracks with prisoners inside. They have
Found an extermination camp for Jews.

Stalin.   The Final Solution Heydrich announced.
For three years we have known they were doing this.

(*27 January. Berlin, the* Führer *bunker. The conference room.* HITLER *and* GUDERIAN.)

Guderian.   Himmler's defensive line of reserves should be
From north to south. It is from east to west,
From the northern Vistula to the Oder.
It does not protect Berlin, and Zhukov has ignored it.
He has passed it on the south and has reached the Oder.
The eastern front has crumbled.

Hitler.   I tell you,
The British and Americans are wary of the Russians.
They will join the Germans to fight in the east.

Guderian.   A fantasy –

Hitler.   No, there have been reports.

Burgdorf.   Sir, Colonel-General Schörner of Army Group Centre.
He has ordered the evacuation of Silesia.
Hitler.   But I forbade retreat on pain of death.

Schörner   (*on phone*). These troops in Silesia have fought hard
For two weeks and are finished. If we don't relieve
Them, we will lose the Seventeenth Army
And Bavaria. We are moving back to the Oder.

Hitler   (*wearily*). Yes. Schörner, if you think that it is right,
I will have to agree.

*(*30 January.* BURGDORF *to* HITLER. *He hands Hitler a paper.*)

Burgdorf.	Sir, a message from Speer: "The war is lost,
	Now Upper Silesia is lost and with it our coal
	For sixty per cent of our coal is from Silesia."

Hitler.   The war is not lost, Speer is completely wrong.
            I am taking afternoon tea with the Goebbels
            At their home in Schwanenwerder. Fetch me
            A flask of tea and a bag of cakes.

Burgdorf.   The Goebbels
            Are surely trustworthy, sir?

Hitler.   I trust no one. (*Fade on* HITLER.)

Burgdorf   (to *a colleague*). A message from Neukölln. Women have charged
            A truck of potatoes, police have fired
            And killed several. And the *Führer* is eating cakes.

(*30 January, later.*)

Hitler's voice   Berliners, keep up your morale. Berlin
on radio.   Is fully armed. Like a vast porcupine
                  With steel quills it will pierce the heart
                  Of any attacker or turn him back.
                  My new secret weapons will soon expel
                  The enemy from our Fatherland. I
                  Am with you in this crisis, this emergency,
                  And our Great German *Reich* will emerge
                  Stronger, defending Europe against the east.
                  Germany will never surrender, will
                  Fight to the very end. I am with you.

(*Late January. Versailles, Eisenhower's HQ.* EISENHOWER *thinking aloud, to* BEDELL SMITH.)

Eisenhower.   All our armies are fighting towards the Rhine.
               Monty will cross north of the Ruhr, Hodges
               And Patton to the south. With Monty coming
               Down from the north and Bradley coming up from the south,
               The two Army Groups can encircle the Ruhr.
               How did Hannibal encircle the Romans
               At Cannae? Can you find me a book? We can then

Fan out and overrun Germany. I know
Monty and Brooke favour a thrust to Berlin,
But we want it done quickly, so the main effort
Should be given to Brad. Monty would take six months
To prepare. Marshall's happy with that plan,
But Patton wants a larger role, and Brad
Is not happy that Monty has any role.
But that's the plan.

Bedell Smith.   That's right.

Eisenhower.   But we're not getting
There. American casualties in the Ardennes
Are almost as many as in the entire
Normandy battle. And for what? Brad has Hodges'
First Army, but won't give Simpson's Ninth the
Division he needs for Monty's pincer plan,
Because the Ninth is Monty's and Hitler
Is transferring his Sixth Panzers to Hungary.
We're not making an impact on the Germans.

Bedell Smith.   So what do we do?

Eisenhower.   End the Ardennes offensive,
Shut down Brad's operations and transfer him
To Monty's flank in the north to capture
The Roer dams.

Bedell Smith.   Brad won't like that.

Eisenhower.   But it's right.

Bedell Smith.   It also smacks of what Monty's been saying.

Eisenhower.   It's the way forward to the plan. I've decided
To end the Ardennes offensive. I'll clear it
With the CCS and then ring Brad.

(*3 February. Chorus of* BERLINERS.)

Chorus.   The American bombers have filled the sky.

For two hours the ground reverberated.
Craters, fallen trees, roads filled with rubble,
Fragments of walls, no lights or water.
Hitler was unharmed in his bunker,
Freisler the judge was killed by shrapnel.
We queue at standpipes to fill saucepans, pails.
We now have one loaf a week and most shops
Are ruined or boarded up, and money is worthless.
After each air-raid we just carry on
Alas, what will become of us? Alas!

(*5 February, early evening. Yalta, the conference.* CHURCHILL, EDEN, STALIN *and* ROOSEVELT.)

Stalin.   Germany should be dismembered into five
                          Separate states, as Roosevelt proposed in Teheran.
                          We then agreed Poland's borders would be
                          Between the Oder and the Curzon Line
                          And that Prussia should be isolated
                          And we have now agreed the zones the four
                          Allied powers, including France, will occupy.
                          We should now dismember occupied Germany.

Churchill   (*to Eden*). The only bond of the victors is their common
                          Hate. To make Britain safe in the future
                          She must become responsible for the safety
                          Of a cluster of feeble states.
                          (*To Stalin.*)   I advise caution,
                          There should not be a too-rapid dismemberment
                          Of Germany. We must remember the mistakes
                          Made after the First World War. Twenty-five million
                          Troops hang on our words.

                          (STALIN *reacts with chagrin.*)

                          (*Aside.*)   I can tell he's disgruntled.
                          I've thwarted him, and I must now watch out
                          That he does not dismember Germany
                          In practice with his army or by some other way.
                          Roosevelt's powers are failing, he is frail,
                          He could not get out of his car and he

	Doesn't say anything and does what his adviser, Alger Hiss, says, which is generally to Stalin's liking. I must be doubly vigilant.
Stalin.	Well, can we at least reaffirm our policy Of unconditional surrender. We Will not make any separate peace with the enemy, Who therefore cannot divide our unity.
	(CHURCHILL *looks at* ROOSEVELT, *who looks at* ALGER HISS. *Hiss nods. Roosevelt nods.*)
Churchill	(*to Eden*). We can't object to that? (*Aloud.*) Yes, we agree.
Stalin.	(*impassively*). And to help our eastern front, we request A heavy Allied air attack on all German communications in the Berlin- Leipzig-Dresden region. The bombing of These cities is now a matter of urgency.
	(CHURCHILL *looks at* ROOSEVELT, *who looks at* HISS. *Hiss nods. Roosevelt nods.*)
Churchill.	We agree.
Stalin	(*aside*). They fell for it. They resisted Dismemberment, and conceded what I Was really after, unconditional Surrender, in other words: the assistance And time for me to conquer eastern Europe And then dismember Germany through my strength.

(*6 February. Zhukov with his* FIVE ARMY COMMANDERS *and his Chief of Staff,* GENERAL MALININ.)

Zhukov.	If we are to take Berlin in ten day's time, We must have new bridgeheads across the Oder And forward airfields for the Red Air Force Within four days and all tanks and heavy guns Must have had their refit and be ready. It is asking a lot.

Chuikov.	But it must be done.
	One knock-out punch and the war will be over.

Zhukov.	You speak like Montgomery. But if the Germans
	Attack us from the north on our right flank
	Which Rokossovsky has not yet protected
	We will be cut off.

(*The phone rings.*)

Malinin.	Comrade, Stalin from
	Yalta.

Stalin	(*on phone*). Where are you? What are you doing?

Zhukov.	At Kolpakchi's headquarters, with the army
	Commanders, planning to reach Berlin.

Stalin.	You are wasting your time. Consolidate
	On the Oder, then join Rokossovsky
	And smash the enemy's Army Group Vistula.

(ZHUKOV *puts down the phone and rises, saying nothing.*)

Chuikov.	Berlin is postponed?

Zhukov	(*bitterly*). Because Rokossovsky is slow.

(*A few seconds later.* STALIN *in Yalta, with* MOLOTOV *and* ANTONOV.)

Stalin	(*putting down phone*). My Generals are in a hurry.

Molotov.	Was that wise?

Stalin.	I can now tell you, Churchill and Roosevelt
	Have confirmed to me that they will not accept
	Anything less than unconditional surrender –
	No separate peace that transfers troops to the east.
	We can take our time, we need not take risks now.
	We can build up our forces for the final attack.

Molotov	(*enthusiastically*). You have done well.

Stalin.   One good conversation
Is better than a month of ten armies.
And now I need to dictate a memo.
Your wife, please.

Molotov.   Yes, of course.

(*Exit* MOLOTOV.)

Stalin   (*aside*).   I can delay
Taking Berlin until I have overrun
All eastern Europe and unconditional
Surrender gives me the time.

(PAULINA MOLOTOV *appears*.)

(*Gently.*)   Come here, my dear.
I have had a trying day outwitting Churchill
And Roosevelt. Lock the door.

(PAULINA *locks the door, then sits on his desk.*)

Paulina.   You are so clever.

*(6 February. HITLER *dictating his memoirs to* BORMANN.)

Hitler.   A desperate fight is a shining example.
Leonidas and his three hundred Spartans
Did not accept their desperate situation.
Frederick the Great was in great difficulties
During the Seven Years' War, then the Tsarina died
And the situation was reversed. If Churchill
Were to disappear, everything could change.
We can still snatch victory at the eleventh hour!
Providence will give us a miracle yet.

*(8 February. MONTGOMERY *and* 21st *Army Group* LEADERS .)

Montgomery.   Winter is now over, and four million Russians

Are only fifty miles from Berlin, thanks
To Hitler's rashness in taking troops from
The east to attack us in the Ardennes.
Now it is our turn. I have agreed with Ike
That we will break through the Siegfried line
Of Hitler's western frontier, and cross the Rhine
To Wesel and the flat country north of the Ruhr.
In Veritable the First Canadian Army
And British Second Army will drive for the Meuse,
While in Grenade, Simpson's U.S. Ninth Army,
Which is under my command for this operation,
Will advance between Venlo and Julich and
Join the British and Canadians on the Rhine.
I wish you good hunting in Germany!

(*11 February, noon. Yalta. The Big Three:* STALIN, CHURCHILL *and* ROOSEVELT, *who is very sick.*)

Churchill.   So here we are at the end of our Yalta talks
To sign a Declaration on Liberated
Europe, which "upholds the right of all peoples
To choose the form of government under which they will live"
And pledges "the restoration of sovereign rights
And self-government to those peoples who have been
Forcibly deprived of them by the aggressor nations".
The Big Three will jointly assist in the holding
Of free elections as soon as possible.
Let us all now sign this Declaration.

(*They sign.*)

Then there is a *communiqué* on Poland,
That free elections will be held to establish
A Polish Provisional Government of National Unity.
The Lublin government will be reorganised
On a broader democratic basis, with the inclusion
Of democratic leaders from Poland and Poles abroad.
The London Poles are relegated to "Poles abroad"
And I do warn Marshal Stalin again that I
Will be strongly criticised for this at home as
We have yielded completely to the Russian view.

	We went to war for Poland and we expect
	A democratic and independent Poland now.

Stalin.   But Soviet troops are masters of Warsaw
And stand on the banks of the Oder, and that
Is the reality.

Churchill.   Let us sign the *communiqué*.

*(*11 February. Yalta.* STALIN, MOLOTOV *and* ANTONOV.)

Molotov.   Koniev has broken out west of the Oder
And smashed a hole in the German defences
Forty miles deep and ninety miles wide,
Surrounding Glogau and Breslau, and he
Is now on the Neisse, the Germans in flight.

Stalin.   He must stay there until Rokossovsky
Advances to Zhukov, and blocks an attack
From the north.

Antonov.   Rokossovsky has been slowed down
By mud, rain, sleet and snow. His men sink knee-deep.
Roads are like quagmires.

Stalin.   The Germans may counter-attack.
We must wait for the gap to the north to close.

(*13 February. Berlin, the Chancellery.* GUDERIAN, *with his Chief of Staff* WENCK, *his adjutant* LORINGHOVEN *and* ADC BOLDT. *They surrender their weapons to* SS OFFICERS *and* GUARDS *outside the ante-room, or refreshment room, to Hitler's office or study. The guards examine their briefcases.*)

Guderian.   I am Chief of General Staff, and with me are
My Chief of Staff, adjutant and ADC
Am I not above suspicion?

SS guard   (*shrugging*).   No one is here.

Guderian   (*left alone, to Wenck*). Remember, we are staking everything,
Your head and mine, to obtain a counter-attack.

Troops must be moved from Italy, Norway,
The Balkans, East Russia.

Wenck.   The last two rows
You had with Hitler were awesome. If we
Had not pulled you back, Hitler would have hit you;
But he would not pull troops from the south,
And sent our best Panzers into Hungary.

Guderian.   This time I must argue more strongly.

Wenck.   No please –

(*The* SS GUARD *returns. The four go into the ante-room, or refreshment
room, where a group are having coffee and sandwiches:* BURGDORF,
BORMANN, KEITEL, JODL, DÖNITZ, HIMMLER, FEGELEIN,
KALTENBRUNNER, GÖRING. *Burgdorf, Hitler's adjutant, goes into Hitler's
study and returns.*)

Burgdorf.   The *Führer* would like you all to come in.

(*All enter in strict order of rank:* GÖRING *first.* HITLER, *head and limp left
arm trembling, shakes each with a trembling hand. Hitler sits. They all sit.*)

Jodl.   Under the leadership of our *Führer*,
The situation is excellent on all fronts.
On the east our defensive line is holding
Thanks to SS *Reichsführer* Himmler's
Army Group Vistula. On the west, likewise.

Hitler.   Guderian, what do you think?

Guderian.   I disagree.
The Russians on the east are tired, we must
Counter-attack them in two days, strike hard.

Himmler   (*stammering, taking off his pince-nez and polishing them*).
I-It can't be done. The front line needs more fuel,
More ammunition.

Guderian   (*shouting*).   We can't wait for

	The last can of petrol and the last shell, The Russians will be too strong.
Hitler.	I will not allow You to accuse me of procrastination.
Guderian.	I am not accusing you of anything, But there is no sense in waiting for supplies And losing the most favourable moment To attack.
Hitler.	I have just told you, I will not allow You to accuse me of procrastinating.
Guderian.	I want General Wenck as Chief of Staff At Army Group Vistula or the attack will fail. Himmler can't attack without help. Look at him.
Hitler	(*rising*). The *Reichsführer* is man enough to lead The attack without help.
Guderian.	He does not have The experience or the staff. He needs General Wenck.
Hitler.	How dare you criticise the *Reichsführer*! I won't have you criticise him!
Guderian.	I insist, General Wenck must join Army Group Vistula To lead the attack.

(*The others have quietly slipped away into the ante-room, leaving* HITLER, HIMMLER, GUDERIAN, WENCK *and their* ADJUTANTS. *Hitler explodes with rage, his fists raised, trembling, strutting up and down the carpet, stopping to scream accusations.*)

You come in here and accuse me of delay,
And the *Reichsführer* of inadequacy –
I will not take any more of your arrogance,
I will not have you criticise us, when
We are the ones who are defending Berlin

Against the Russians. You say there must be
A counter-attack, but....

(*Two hours later.*)

Hitler.   Himmler is well able to lead the attack.

Guderian.   It must be General Wenck, or it will fail.

Hitler   (*suddenly giving up*). Well Himmler, General Wenck will go tonight
                 To Army Group Vistula as Chief of Staff.
                 (*To Guderian.*) Now let us continue with the conference.
                 Today, Colonel-General, the general staff
                 Has won a battle. Call the others in.

                 (GUDERIAN *and* WENCK *go to the ante-room.*)

Keitel.   How dare you upset the *Führer*.

Others.   That was not right.

                 (GUDERIAN *looks at them contemptuously.*)

Guderian.   Wenck, give orders for a counter-attack
                 In two days' time.

(*13 February, night. Chorus of* DRESDENERS.)

Chorus.   Alas! Dresden is flattened. The Allies
                 Rained bombs from the night, first the British with
                 Eight hundred bombers, setting the city on fire
                 With high explosive bombs and incendiaries,
                 And then a wave of American bombers when
                 We were fleeing the firestorm, heading west.
                 Refugees choked the roads, German reinforcements
                 Could not get through the burning city to
                 The eastern front, as Stalin no doubt wanted,
                 But at what cost! Sixty thousand of us,
                 Sixty thousand civilians have been killed,
                 And all to choke the roads and slow down
                 The German reinforcements, to the Red Army's

Advantage. Alas, we are homeless, widowed, orphaned.
Alas, Dresden is no more, and we've nowhere to go.

(*16 February.* ZHUKOV, *and his aide,* MALININ.)

Malinin.   News of Wenck.

Zhukov.   Ah yes, of the counter-attack.

Malinin.   Wenck's troops captured Pyritz and pressed against us,
He drove to Berlin and briefed Hitler all night.
At dawn his driver was sleepy, so Wenck took
The wheel of his staff car – and fell asleep.
The car crashed into the side of a railway bridge,
And burst into flames. Wenck was pulled out
But he has fractured his skull and five ribs,
And the counter-attack is finished.

Zhukov.   We are in luck!

*(1 March. Moscow. Stalin's Kremlin office.)

Stalin   (*on the phone*). Zhukov. I'm glad you're there. Rokossovsky
Has thrust at the Baltic coast and has holed
The German defences near Stettin, cut off
Their forces in Danzig and Gdynia.
He is at the mouth of the Oder, and can
Attack Berlin from the north. Join him there.
Bombard the Germans and when your tanks are ready
And the Germans think you are heading for Berlin,
Go northwards, take Stargard and link up with
Rokossovsky. I want our entire force
On the Oder.

* (*Early March. Versailles, Eisenhower's HQ.* EISENHOWER *and* BEDELL SMITH.)

Eisenhower.   It's March, and a month of fighting through thaws
Has ended in triumph. Monty's two pincer movements,
Veritable and *Grenade*, have reached the Rhine
Under one plan and a single commander,
The Allies have taken a hundred thousand prisoners.

Simpson's Ninth US Army is on the Rhine,
And now we're preparing to cross: *Operation Plunder.*
I intend to move Bradley north, and give
Him command of Ninth and First US Armies
Alongside Monty's Second British and First
Canadian Armies. Do you think they can work together?

(*8 March. Reims.* EISENHOWER *in his HQ.*)

Eisenhower   (*alone*). My broad front in the west is now ready.
                    Monty has smashed nineteen German divisions
                    And ninety thousand men, and has occupied
                    The west bank of the Rhine from Nijmegen
                    To Düsseldorf. From there Bradley has cleared
                    Eighty miles on the west bank down to Koblenz,
                    Southwards, and Hodges has captured Cologne,
                    And taken out forty-nine thousand men
                    And has also crossed the Rhine at Remagen
                    And established a bridgehead several miles deep.
                    Patton has reached the Rhine from Moselle.
                    We are all in place to advance into Germany.
                    The Ruhr is now within the Allies' reach.
                    I have told Marshall and Roosevelt, the Red Army
                    Is fifty miles from Berlin, while we are
                    Two hundred and eighty-five miles away.
                    I have asked: do they want us to take Berlin?

(*9 March. Berlin, the* Führer *bunker.* HITLER *and* BORMANN.)

Bormann.   Sir, a message. The US Third Army
                    Has reached the Rhine and joined the First Army.

                    (*Silence.*)

Hitler.   Cowards! The German soldiers are cowards.
                    How can my generals allow this to happen?
                    I am betrayed by my Commander-in-Chief.
                    Sack von Rundstedt, replace him with Kesselring.
                    He has more fight in him, that will remove
                    Him from negotiating surrender in Italy.
                    And I issue a decree against cowardice:

Anyone captured without being wounded
Or having fought has forfeited his honour.
I will have executions for cowardice.

(*13 March. Berlin, Defence Council building near Brandenburg Gate. Lieutenant-General*
REYMANN *and* GOEBBELS.)

Reymann.   The first I knew of any of this was
                  After the firebombing of my Dresden.
                  Burgdorf rang me and said, "The *Führer* has
                  Appointed you military commander of Dresden."
                  I said, "Tell him there is only rubble here."
                  An hour later he rang again. "The *Führer* has
                  Appointed you military commander of Berlin."
                  I was astonished, then I found my sick
                  Predecessor von Havenschild had done
                  Nothing to protect the civilians here
                  Or evacuate children or the elderly.
                  And now this thirty-three page document
                  Which I have never seen bears my signature:
                  "Order for the defence of the *Reich* capital."
                  It details three rings, outer, second and inner.
                  Did you write it?

Goebbels.   I did, and you are wrong
                  To criticise the lack of evacuation.
                  There is enough canned milk to last three months,
                  Enough men, weapons, food and coal to last
                  For eight weeks under siege.

Reymann.   I am a trained soldier
                  And I can see a lack of ammunition,
                  And where is the military equipment apparently
                  Stored in railway sidings? I need men
                  And materials to build defences. I need
                  Two hundred thousand men.

Goebbels.   You speak like a bourgeois General,
                  And I remind you of Hübner's court martial
                  Which executed the General who did not
                  Blow up the bridge at Remagen, and seven

Senior officers. And that General Fromm,
Executioner of that traitor von Stauffenberg,
Was shot on the ninth for cowardice. Generals
Are not exempted if they are incompetent.
You can have thirty thousand men, there are no more.

(*14 March*. Dr. MORELL, *Hitler's doctor, is visited by* MAGDA GOEBBELS.)

Dr. Morell   (*concerned*). I hear the Ministry of Propaganda
Was destroyed in last night's heavy air raid.

Magda.   It is completely destroyed. When my husband
Heard it had been hit, he drove at once
To the Wilhelmstrasse to see for himself.
It was still blazing, and he was afraid
Five hundred Panzerfaust missiles in the basement
Might explode. That beautiful old palace
Which he restored. At home he was melancholy.
He still says we can win the war, but I know
The end may come soon. When I raise such matters,
He says I should take our six children and
Go westwards, find safety with the British, but I
Cannot leave him. I have not told him I am here.
I must not weaken his will to resist.

Dr. Morell.   What would you like me to do?

Magda.   For nine years now,
I know, you have given the *Führer* pills,
And kept him going with amphetamine
Injections I believe. My children....
I see the future, I know in a few weeks' time
I may have to kill them. They are so innocent.
I wonder how I shall do it. I cannot talk
To my husband, undermine his resolve,
And so I turn to you.

Dr. Morell   (*giving her two bottles and a syringe*). I will be happy
To give you what you need to end their lives.
This is a sleeping draught, you inject their
Chocolates, and these are cyanide capsules.

You make them bite when they are asleep.
And I hope you will not have to use them.

Magda.   I am full of grief but thank you, thank you.

(*18 March. Berlin, the* Führer *bunker,* SPEER *waiting in the corridor ante-room or reception room.* BURGDORF.)

Burgdorf.   The *Führer* rose at midday, he is on the phone.

                           (*Enter* HITLER.)

Hitler.   To Goebbels about the daylight air raid.

Speer.   Two thousand American planes filled the air,
                           Glinting in the sunny Sunday morning,
                           There was some opposition, our Messerschmitts
                           Shot some down, but the *Luftwaffe* is short of fuel,
                           Aircraft and pilots, and the bombs thundered down,
                           Everywhere now there are fires, and the people suffer.

Hitler.   The Allies' air raids are assisting our
                           Scorched earth policy. The Soviets will have nothing.
                           They will find rubble, as they found Warsaw.
                           I will destroy Berlin and the whole country –
                           Its industrial plant, power stations, water and gas works,
                           All stores, bridges, public buildings, ships, trains –
                           Rather than hand them over to the Soviets.

Speer.   I built your new Berlin and your Third *Reich*
                           To last a thousand years, I beg you, please
                           Do not do this. I have brought a report.
                           The economy will last one month or two,
                           Then the war must stop. Please think of the people.
                           They need electricity, gas, water and bridges
                           To continue their food supply so they survive.
                           Führer, on human grounds, do not raze Berlin.

Hitler   (*contemptuously*). If the war is lost, the nation will perish.
                           And the nation will not be the good ones, who will have been killed.
                           But inferior ones and cowards who did not die.

If the war is lost, Germans do not deserve
To have the essential services, and they will not.
Tomorrow I issue my Nero Order
To destroy all installations and services.

Speer   (*quietly*). Nero burned Rome and is now considered mad.
               I tell you, German civilians will fight
               Kesselring's men as they implement your will.
               (*Wearily.*) But Allied air raids will accomplish all
               Your order seeks. You and the Allies will leave
               A pile of rubble for the advancing Soviet tanks,
               The rubble of what I built, of my life's work.

(*19 March. Himmler's pillared HQ at Birkenhain,* GUDERIAN *with SS Brigadier General*
LAMMERDING, *Himmler's Chief of Staff.*)

Guderian.   The *Reichsführer*?

Lammerding.   He is not here. Can I help?
               I am his Chief of Staff.

Guderian.   Since Wenck's car crash
               The general staff have not received one report
               From Himmler. We have a huge Soviet build-up
               Around our bridgehead at Küstrin and Frankfurt.
               We can't wait any longer, we must have news.
               On the west we have Kesselring, a soldier
               And we have the Weser and Elbe as barriers.
               On the east we have Himmler and only fifty miles.

Lammerding.   Sir, can't you rid us of our commander?

Guderian.   That is a matter for the SS. Where is he?

Lammerding.   At a clinic twenty miles away. He has flu.

(*19 March. Hohenlychen.* GUDERIAN *and* HIMMLER.)

Himmler.   I have a slight cold in my head, that's all.

Guderian.   My sympathy. Perhaps you've been overworking.

	As well as commander of Army Group Vistula,
	You are leader of the SS, chief of police
	And the *Gestapo*, Minister of the Interior,
	And commander of the Reserve Army.
	It's enough to burden anyone. Why not
	Give up one job, such as Army Group Vistula?

Himmler   (*eagerly*). It is true, I have too many positions
                   For my health, but how can I tell the *Führer*?
                   He would not like it if I said that.

Guderian.   Will you
                   Authorise me to say it for you?

Himmler   (*nodding*).   Thank you.

Guderian.   There is a need for an immediate armistice.

Himmler.   I will not be drawn on matters such as that.

(*19 March. Berlin,* Führer *bunker.* HITLER *and* GUDERIAN.)

Guderian.   The *Reichsführer* is overworked and wants
                   To be relieved.

Hitler.   It is very inconvenient.
                   This is the wrong time to make a change on the east.
                   Himmler has knowledge, who can replace him?

Guderian.   Colonel-General Heinrici, First Panzer.

Hitler.   He is a cousin of von Rundstedt, whom I sacked.

Guderian.   He is in eastern Czechoslovakia,
                   He knows the Russians, they haven't broken through him.

Hitler   (*sighing*). Oh very well.

(*20 March. Berlin, the Chancellery.* HITLER *walking with* HIMMLER. *Enter* GUDERIAN,)

Guderian.   Can I speak with the *Reichsführer* a minute.

(HITLER *gestures*.)

(*To Himmler*.) The war cannot now be won, the bombing must end.
You and Ribbentrop alone have contacts
In neutral countries, to arrange an armistice.
Ribbentrop will not approach Hitler, so you
Must go with me to ask him for an armistice.

Himmler.   I share your concern, but cannot support you.
                Hitler would have me shot for such a proposal.

(*That evening. Berlin, Führer bunker.* GUDERIAN *and* HITLER *after the daily conference.* BOR-
MANN *is present in the background.*)

Hitler.   Guderian, Himmler has spoken to me.
                I understand your heart condition is worse.
                You should go to a spa for a cure at once.

Guderian   (*taken aback*). My deputy General Krebs has been wounded
                In an air raid. I cannot leave my post.
                Until I find a replacement. Then I'll go on leave.

(*21 March. Straelen, Montgomery's HQ.* MONTGOMERY *and* GENERAL JOCK WHITELEY.)

Montgomery.   I've been explaining *Plunder* to the senior
                Officers of my three armies, Jock. Now
                Eisenhower wants me to share command in the north
                With Bradley, once the Allies are across the Rhine.
                I have a better plan. Gerow should hold
                A defensive front across the western Ruhr.
                Bradley should stay south and pincer-attack
                From Remagen, join me and encircle the Ruhr.

Whiteley.   That sounds a very good idea to me.

Montgomery.   One man must be in general command
                North of the Ruhr, and that man should not be Bradley.
                Can you dress this up as a SHAEF proposal
                So it can be put to Ike in Maastricht?

(*21 March. Cannes.* EISENHOWER *and* BRADLEY *in conference.* KAY *and* THREE WAC

GIRLS *playing bridge.* EVERETT HUGHES *and* TEX LEE.)

Hughes.
Ike's back to himself today. He's slept two days.
Yesterday Kay suggested bridge. He said
"I can't keep my mind on cards at present,
All I want to do is sit here and not think."

Lee.
The stress of great men's jobs and lives.

Hughes.
You share
An office with Kay. Do you think Ike sleeps with her?

Lee.
No, I don't. He's always writing to Mamie.
He's cooling towards Kay. She's fun to be with,
Someone he can talk privately with. That's all.
He knows there's no place for Kay in his life.

Hughes.
I disagree. I think he does. But one thing's sure,
There is nothing we can do about it.

(*Fade on* HUGHES *and* LEE.)

Bradley.
You ask me about the risks of taking Berlin.
Even if Monty reaches the Elbe before
The Red Army reaches the Oder, fifty
Miles of Lowlands, with lakes, streams and canals
Would still lie between the Elbe and Berlin.
It would cost us a hundred thousand casualties.
For a prestige objective, then we'd have to fall back
Because Yalta gave a large part of Berlin to the Russians.

Eisenhower.
Brad, you were my friend and classmate at West Point.
I want you to lead the final victorious assault
Against Hitler. A SHAEF directive will
Instruct you to send Third Army over the Rhine
Near Mainz-Frankfurt and advance to Kassel.
Hodges will push east from Remagen and link
First and Third Armies, encircle the Ruhr.
I shall take the Ninth Army from Monty's command,
Remove it from Twenty-first and give it to you,
And shift the main thrust from the north to the centre.

I have decided not to take Berlin
But to leave it entirely to the Russians
And go for Dresden and Leipzig instead.
This is for your ears only at this stage.
We all have our masters, mine are Marshall
And Roosevelt, who agreed at Teheran
And Yalta to draw a line down the map of Europe
And place part of Berlin on the Russian side.
In the prevailing political climate
Of Yalta, and of those who control
Our President and Stalin, it is wise
To leave Berlin to the Russians. But Brad,
Political considerations aside,
I have been coming round to this view on my own
For military reasons I find sound.
Since January I've wanted to strengthen your front.
I first saw your front as a diversion, then
As a secondary thrust to help Monty,
Then as a major thrust if he gets bogged down
As he did near Caen. But now I see it as
The main thrust, and Monty's as secondary.
I have decided, I will not be lectured
Or dictated to by Monty any more.
He has been so personal, denying the Americans
And me credit, that I have stopped talking to him.
I know Monty wants to lead the armies
Into Berlin, and I know I should explain
This change of strategy to Churchill.
But I shall follow my masters and keep silent.

(*He rises and moves away. Fade on all except* EISENHOWER.)

(*Aside.*) General Marshall has pointed out again,
Berlin's in the Russian occupation zone
As agreed at Yalta, and we should not interfere.
Berlin is in the Russian sphere of influence.
There will be a problem if we take Berlin
At a cost of a hundred thousand Allied lives
And then withdraw under the Yalta terms,
Hand part over to the Russians. At home
They'll say, "Why were so many Americans killed

To hand Berlin over to Russian occupation?
Was this what we voted for four months ago?
Let the Russians take the casualties, not us."
I'll secure Marshall's approval to cable
Stalin and suggest the Americans meet up
With the Russians at Dresden, well away from Berlin,
A token meeting-place this side of the Elbe
That will justify the bombing Stalin sought.

(*22 March. Zossen.* HEINRICI, *a short stocky man with a moustache, with* GUDERIAN.)

Heinrici.   I am shocked at how weak we are on the Oder,
                 How little information Himmler has given.
                 I have two armies.

Guderian.   Manteuffel's and Busse's.
                 And Busse will soon attack the Russians round Küstrin.
                 Hitler has ordered five Panzer divisions
                 To cross the single bridge at Frankfurt where
                 They will be under Russian artillery fire.

Heinrici.   Our troops will be driven back to the Oder.
                 It will be a disaster.

Guderian   (*looking at his watch*). It is time to leave
                 For the *Führer's* daily conference. It makes me wild
                 The way they run this war, their idiocies.
                 The *Führer* is surrounded by incompetents,
                 Hangers-on, flatterers, featherers of their own nest.
                 Hitler will discuss the Küstrin. attack. Come.

Heinrici.   No, I am still uninformed, I must stay
                 With my Army Group. Hitler can wait a few days.

(*22 March, later. Berlin.* HIMMLER *and* HEINRICI. *A* STENOGRAPHER *records the conversation.*)

Himmler.   And I tell you, my policy was right,
                 The Army Group Vistula has held back
                 The Russian attack at each of its strong points.

Heinrici.	You have spoken for forty-five minutes And I still know nothing of the forces I command, or of the situation.

(*The phone rings.* HIMMLER *answers.*)

Himmler.	It is Busse. You are the new commander Of Army Group Vistula. You take this call.
Heinrici.	Busse says that the Russians have broken through And enlarged the bridgehead near Küstrin.
Himmler.	You are the commander. Give the right orders.
Heinrici.	I do not know a thing about the Army Group, What troops I have, or who is where or when.

(HIMMLER *is silent.*)

(*On phone.*) What do you propose? I agree, counter-attack.
I will join you, we'll inspect the front line.

Himmler.	My policies, then, have been proved right, and I –
Heinrici.	It is imperative that I have your assessment Of the Küstrin. situation and our war aims.

(HIMMLER *leads* HEINRICI *to a couch out of the* STENOGRAPHER'*s
earshot.*)

Himmler.	I want to tell you something in confidence. I am negotiating peace with the West.
Heinrici.	Fine. Through?
Himmler.	Through a neutral country. Well now You are in charge, I have to go. I am glad I will not be in charge if the eastern front breaks.

* (*23 March, evening. The eastern front.* HEINRICI *and* BUSSE.)

Heinrici.   Today I've driven behind the entire front line,
                 Looking at the terrain. The Russians will strike
                 Between Frankfurt and Küstrin.. Our defensive line
                 Will therefore be along the Seelow Heights.
                 And I will open the sluice gates of the lake,
                 Empty the Ottmachau into the Oder
                 And flood the Oderbruck as an obstacle
                 For Chuikov. Now attack Küstrin again.

(23 March. Namur, Bradley's HQ. BRADLEY is on the phone to EISENHOWER.)

Bradley.   A new SHAEF plan? I wouldn't wait until
                 Mid-April to command the First and Ninth
                 North of the Ruhr, I'd have immediate
                 Command of the First and Third and push south of
                 The Ruhr into Germany. Whiteley's plan.
                 And then drive on towards Frankfurt, do you say?
                 I'm very pleased with it. It keeps me apart
                 From Montgomery. What was that Marshall said?
                 "The overdose of Montgomery which is now
                 Coming into the country." (Laughing.) He's right on.
                 So you've approved this plan and you want me
                 To hold a press conference now about
                 Twelfth US Army Group operations.
                 The Ruhr, north and south, it is. I just wonder.
                 You don't think Montgomery wants to finish
                 The war himself, and leave Devers and me
                 With subordinate roles? Or is he being possessive?
                 Does he want to command as many American troops
                 As possible, including the Ninth Army?
                 You'll come and see me tomorrow? That's good.

(23 March, just before 9.30p.m. Straelen, Montgomery's HQ. MONTGOMERY, CHURCHILL and
BROOKE leave Montgomery's caravan in moonlight near the Rhine. Churchill is in the uniform
of 4th Hussars. Sound of artillery barrage.)

Brooke.   It's good news that Eisenhower has approved
                 The Whiteley plan that will put you north of the Ruhr
                 And Bradley south. You'll be in a good position.

Churchill.   That was a good dinner, and now we have

Studied the maps, all that remains is to watch
The boats and pontoons drift to the other side,
Which is, what, five hundred yards, would you say,
As we put a quarter of a million men
Across the Rhine, the first military crossing
Since Napoleon, the first time British troops
Have fought on German soil since the battle
Of Leipzig in 1813, against the French.

Montgomery.   Have you seen my message to the troops?

Churchill   (*reading*). "Over the Rhine then let us go. And good hunting
To you all on the other side. May 'The Lord
Mighty in battle' give us the victory
In this our latest undertaking as He has done
In all our battles since we landed in
Normandy on D-Day." Very eloquent.

Montgomery.   There go the first commandos across the river.
Do you see their green berets?

Churchill   (*excited*).   Yes.

Montgomery.   Through the night there will be landings along
A twenty-mile front, in ten places, two
Airborne divisions –

Brooke.   They've started.

(DAWNAY *approaches*.)

Dawnay.   Sir, Patton
Is across.

Montgomery.   What?

Dawnay   (*handing him a message*). We've just heard, the Americans
Crossed near Mainz at ten last night. Bradley gave
Patton permission to cross in assault boats
By stealth – no barrage or paratroop drops –
And has put ten divisions into the new bridgehead.

	He has given Hodges ten divisions to break out.
	The US Twelfth Army Group plan to race
	Your Twenty-First Army Group into the *Reich*.
	Patton has said, "I want the world to know
	Third Army made it before Monty starts across."

(*Silence. Exit* DAWNAY.)

Montgomery. Ike is behind it.

Churchill.   And Roosevelt behind Ike.

Montgomery. Even now the Americans are fighting their own war.
      But for them, we would be in Berlin now.
      It is time I retired to bed.

Churchill.   You can't leave this.

Montgomery. Nothing disturbs my routine. Well, good night.

      (*Exit to caravan.*)

Churchill. How can he go to bed at such a time?
      Despite the ominous news about the Yanks
      I am exhilarated, let us walk
      In the moonlight and watch and talk until
      I return to my red boxes in my caravan.
      What do you think the Americans plan to do?

(*Fade on* CHURCHILL *and* BROOKE. MONTGOMERY *in his caravan, praying.*)

Montgomery. O Lord, who helps the righteous in peace and war,
      O Lord of Love and Light, O mighty Lord,
      I have flung a quarter of a million men
      Across the Rhine to thrust towards Berlin
      And root out the Nazi evil around Hitler's power.
      O Lord of Light, fill me with your wisdom,
      O God of Light, come into me now, come.
      Purify my thinking, so my decisions are right,
      Exonerate me from the deaths I cause.
      I submit to you the power I have over men.

Guide me with your power, you ah! bright Light,
Guide me with your Providence. Thy Will, not mine,
Be done. If it is Thy will, let me have
The victory, let the Germans surrender to me
As your chosen instrument doing your will.
Not to the Americans, but to me.
Let me cleanse the earth with the Light you give me.
And after its moral cleansing may the soil
Return to your beauty, devoid of tanks
And guns and shells, the machines of war
Which so disfigure your simple paradise.

THE WARLORDS

PART TWO

SCENE 1.

CROSSING THE RHINE: BERLIN OR DRESDEN?

(24 March. Straelen, near the bank of the Rhine. CHURCHILL and BROOKE sitting with a hamper near an armoured car, watching the airborne operation and crossing.)

Churchill   *(excitedly).* Monty's missing a treat, he ought to be here,
                     Not discussing the new plan with Eisenhower
                     And General Simpson at Rheinberg Castle.
                     Two thousand aircraft, paratroops in the sky
                     Assault craft ferrying men, guns and, tanks.
                     Before our grandstand.

Brooke.   You are like a small boy!

Churchill.   You know, I have long held an ambition
                     To urinate in the Rhine. Will you join me?

                     (CHURCHILL and BROOKE stand on the bank of the Rhine with their backs to the audience.)

                     The British Prime Minister and the Chief
                     Of the Imperial General Staff, Field Marshal Brooke,
                     Will now express their opinion of Hitler,
                     Of the Third *Reich* and the Nazi movement,
                     And of American underhandedness.

                     (They urinate in the Rhine. Enter JOCK COLVILLE, Churchill's private secretary, covered in blood. He stares in disbelief.)

Churchill.	Jock, what has happened?
Colville	(*proudly*). I crossed the river. German shells fell round us, and our driver Was hit by shrapnel. This is his blood, not mine.
Churchill.	What a lark.
Montgomery	(*entering, angrily to* COLVILLE). You had no permission to cross. You exposed yourself to danger without my permission.
Churchill.	I would like to have crossed, I envy him. Talking of exposing ourselves, we made a gesture. (*He points to the Rhine.*)
Montgomery	(*understanding*). You didn't.
Churchill, Brooke.	We did.
Churchill	(*sadly*). But there were no press Photographers to record the occasion For posterity. Come on, Monty, your turn.

(*24 March, evening.* MONTGOMERY *questions his last* LIAISON OFFICER, *who is then replaced by* DE GUINGAND. CHURCHILL *sits outside with* BROOKE.)

Churchill.	I've been watching Monty and working out How he conducts a battle on this gigantic scale. He's questioned his young officers for two hours now. Each one has been to a different part of the front With power to question anybody. Each one's At least a Major, and some have travelled Hundreds of miles by jeep or plane. Monty Listens to their reports, then questions each Searchingly. At the end he gives directions To de Guingand, which go into the staff Machine. His Liaison Officers are based On Wellington, but it was my ancestor, The Duke of Marlborough, who first stationed look-outs, Lieutenant-generals, to watch the battle.

We won the war because we broke Hitler's codes.
He's never fathomed that, he blames his Generals.
Wherever he puts his Generals, we are there
And we have told the Russians, until now.
We won the war because a Polish genius, Rejewski,
Cracked the *Enigma* code, and another
Genius, Turing, invented the world's first
Electronic programmable computer,
The Colossus machine at Bletchley Park,
Which meant we knew Hitler's orders before
They had even reached his Generals. But you know,
If we hadn't broken his codes, I reckon Monty
Would still have beaten him through his LOs.

(*Exit* DE GUINGAND.)

Montgomery.   That's it for tonight. I didn't tell you,
At Rheinberg I discussed with Eisenhower
Enveloping the Ruhr from the north and south,
The new plan, and then racing on to the Elbe
And I drew on a map the boundary I would like
Between Bradley and me, and Ike said Magdeburg
Should be on Bradley's side. No other comment
Was made, and I'm wondering if he has approved
My drive to the Elbe and thence to Berlin.

(*25 March.* CHURCHILL, MONTGOMERY *and* BROOKE *sitting with* EISENHOWER, BRADLEY *and* SIMPSON, *at Rheinberg Castle, Simpson's Ninth Army HQ overlooking the Rhine.*)

Churchill.   We have come from a Palm Sunday Service.

Eisenhower.   I rested in Cannes, then flew to Wesel
And watched Simpson's Ninth Army cross the Rhine
Virtually unopposed. The plan's going well,
Under Monty's leadership.

(*He exchanges pointed glances with* BRADLEY.)

(*To Brooke.*)   Do you agree
With the new plan, with going north and south
Of the Ruhr, and in the south, pushing for Frankfurt

And Kassel?

Brooke.   I see no danger in it.
                   The Germans are crumbling and we should push
                   Them wherever they crumble.

Churchill   (*showing a note*). Ike, read this.
                   I received this note last night from Molotov.
                   He accuses Britain and America
                   Of lying, of going "behind the back
                   Of the Soviet Union, which is bearing
                   The brunt of the war against Germany," by
                   Opening negotiations for a separate peace
                   In Switzerland and in Italy. The accord
                   Between the three powers at Yalta is strained.

Eisenhower.   These are unjust and unfounded charges
                   About our good faith. They make me angry.
                   We will accept surrenders in the field
                   When they are offered. In political matters
                   We will consult the heads of governments.

Churchill.   I think the Allied Expeditionary Force
                   Should beat the Russians to Berlin and hold
                   As much of east Germany as possible, until
                   My doubts about Russia's intention have been cleared away.

                   (EISENHOWER *exchanges glances with* BRADLEY.)

Eisenhower.   The truth is, we're five times as far from Berlin
                   As the Russians are. You want me to think
                   Less about the Germans than the Russians,
                   But I don't believe the *Wehrmacht* is finished
                   Until it has surrendered unconditionally.
                   It can set up Headquarters in the Austrian Alps,
                   With Hitler as its guerilla leader.
                   I want a quick end to the war. That means
                   Capturing the Alps, moving towards the south:
                   The Alps are a more important objective
                   Than Berlin, or racing the Russians there.

(*There is a silence with exchanged glances.*)

Churchill.   The Kremlin has stressed the importance of the Alps
                  To divert our attention from their goal of Berlin.

Montgomery.   But the main thing is, the objective is still Berlin.

Eisenhower.   These are political considerations
                  But our assessment is primarily military.

Churchill.   Berlin is our priority objective.
                  It is a political centre and if we can
                  Beat the Russians to it, the post-war years
                  Will be easier for us. We must look ahead.

(*There is a silence with exchanged glances.*)

Bradley.   Political considerations can complicate the war
                  With political foresight and non-military objectives.

Eisenhower.   The Ruhr should be surrounded and mopped up
                  Before any advance to the east begins.

(*25 March.* CHURCHILL, MONTGOMERY, EISENHOWER *and* SIMPSON *on the riverbank with others.*)

Churchill   (*cigar in mouth*). I would like to get in that boat and cross.

Eisenhower.   No, Mr. Prime Minister. You might be killed.
                  I'm the Supreme Commander, I refuse to allow it.
                  Now I am due at my next appointment. Good-bye. (*Exit.*)

Churchill   (*to Montgomery*). You see that small US Navy launch, there?
                  Why don't we go across and look at the other side?

Montgomery.   Why not?

Simpson.   Are you sure?

Montgomery.   I'm in charge now Ike's gone,
                  And the US Navy's under me, including

That tank landing craft just there.

Churchill   (*excitedly*).   Wesel,
Where the fighting is, let's go down to Wesel.

(*Later.*)

Simpson.   I was so worried, to spite Ike Monty
Drove the PM in his jeep to the Wesel railway bridge.
Churchill scrambled among the wrecked iron girders.
He was under fire from snipers, shells and mortars.
They were landing all round him, he was thrilled,
There were plumes of white spray in the river.
We could not get him away. He was like a boy.

(*28 March, late morning. Reims, Eisenhower's Forward Headquarters.* BUTCHER *and* BEDELL SMITH.)

Bedell Smith.   He really needed his holiday in Cannes.
He had flu, his back hurt where the cyst was cut out,
His knee was badly swollen, he had bags under
His eyes, his blood pressure was high, I said
To him, "You can hardly walk across the room."
He slept most of the time for a couple of days.
He was really run down, physically. Since Cannes
He's been travelling: to Namur to see Brad,
Then he crossed the Rhine at Remagen with Brad,
Hodges and Patton, then back here to Reims
Yesterday, then to Paris with you. He's got new zest.

Butcher.   His press conference in Paris was a peach,
And then he had some R and R: a preview
Of a D-Day film in the Champs Elysées,
And don't tell anyone, but he spent the night
With Kay at the Raphael Hotel incognito –
I booked them in myself – and I think you'll find
He wasn't impotent for once, he's got
Untired, he's bodily fit. And now back here.

(*Enter* EISENHOWER.)

Bedell Smith.	Sir, a signal from Montgomery. You're not
	Going to like it sir. He has ordered
	His army commanders to go for the River Elbe
	"With all possible speed and drive", and then Berlin.
	He says he feels SHAEF will be "delighted".
	Your Rheinberg directive of yesterday
	Laid down that the Ruhr was to be surrounded
	And mopped up before any advance to the east.

Eisenhower	(*stunned, reading*). He's ordered his British Second Army
	And Simpson's US Ninth to Magdeburg.
	He ends: "My TAC HQ moves to the north west
	Of Bonninghardt on Thursday 29th March.
	Thereafter my HQ will move to Wesel,
	Munster, Wiedenbruck, Herford, Hanover –
	And thence by *autobahn* to Berlin, I hope."
	(Blowing up.) It's open-defiance of my orders.
	He thinks he's Supreme Commander, not me.
	Of all the imperious and tactless things he's done,
	This tops the lot. My reply will show my anger.
	My message will be clear and uncompromising.
	I will think it out while I lunch with Brad.

(*Later.* EISENHOWER *and* BEDELL SMITH.)

Eisenhower.	Brad says again that capturing Berlin
	Would cost us a hundred thousand casualties.
	If Brad were to the north, I might say Yes.
	But it's Monty, after his slowness in the Ardennes.
	The American armies are having great success.
	I am determined to do right by Brad
	Regardless of the British Chiefs of Staff,
	And give him back his three US armies.
	I've talked with Brad, it's time to block Monty.
	I will be decisive. Say, "There will be no drive
	For Berlin." Say, "Simpson's Ninth Army will
	Be under Bradley's control once it has joined
	With US First Army and encircled the Ruhr."
	Say, "Bradley will deliver his main thrust
	On the axis Erfurt-Leipzig-Dresden
	To join hands with the Russians." Dresden

Is the shortest route to the Red Army, it will
Cut the German forces in half. Say, "Bradley
Will swing well south of Berlin, the mission
Of your army will be to protect Bradley's
Northern flank." Say, "My present plans
Are co-ordinated with Stalin." Cable Stalin,
Tell him of my intentions, ask for Soviet plans
To harmonise the operations of our two armies
Which are advancing from east and west.
Make it a personal message to Stalin
Via the Allied Military Mission
In Moscow. Say I am encircling
The enemy in the Ruhr until late April,
That I'll then seek to divide the enemy
By joining hands with Russian forces on
The axis of Erfurt-Leipzig-Dresden,
The focus of my main effort, and later in
The Regensburg-Linz area to stop
All resistance in a southern redoubt.

(*Surprised,* BEDELL SMITH *hesitates.*)

Bedell Smith.　　Sir, are you sure –

Eisenhower.　　　　　　　　It's all right, I know what I'm doing.
Don't question me about this cable. Do it.

(*28 March. Moscow, the Kremlin. Stalin's office.* STALIN *and* ANTONOV.)

Stalin.　　　　I have just told the State Defence Committee
I am pleased with Eisenhower's signal
But I am suspicious that the Americans
Are trying to lull me into a false sense of security
And snatch Berlin from my grasp. Send a signal
To Marshall, complaining the information
About the German Sixth Panzer Army is false.
Suggest the Americans misled the Soviet Union.

(*Enter* ZHUKOV. STALIN *extends a hand.*)

Zhukov.　　　　Chuikov has taken Küstrin.

	Hitler and Guderian ordered Busse to break-out,
	Heinrici was against it. We massacred them,
	Then entered the fortress at two this afternoon.

Stalin   (*nodding*). The German front in the west has collapsed for good.
          The Hitlerites didn't want to halt the Allies.
          They are reinforcing the units facing us.
          I have a letter from "a foreign well-wisher"
          That warns the Germans may be doing a deal
          That gives the Allies a clear run to Berlin.
          How quickly can we start our Berlin offensive?

Zhukov.   In two weeks' time. Koniev will be ready then.
          But not Rokossovsky.

Stalin.   We shall have to begin without him.
          Antonov has the maps, sit with him now.

(*28 March. Berlin, the* Führer *bunker, the daily conference in Hitler's conference room.* HITLER;
BUSSE, *a large man with spectacles;* GUDERIAN; JODL, KEITEL, LORINGHOVEN *and*
THOMALE.)

Hitler   (*frostily*). You are here to give an account of yourself.

Busse.   All three counter-attacks on Küstrin. were doomed.
          The orders were impossible, given the strength –

Hitler   (*shouting*). Why did they fail? Because of incompetence
          And negligence. I am the Commander.
          I gave the orders you are questioning.
          The whole military command is incompetent.
          Busse, Guderian, Heinrici. There was not
          Sufficient artillery preparation.

Guderian. There was not enough ammunition for a barrage.

Hitler   (*shouting*). Then why did you not supply Busse with more?

Guderian (*shouting*). Yesterday I explained that General Busse
          Was not to blame for the failure of the Küstrin attack.
          He followed orders. He used the ammunition

Allotted to him. Look at the casualties.
The troops did their duty.

Hitler.   They failed, they failed.

Guderian.   You do not know what you are talking about.
You are an amateur meddling in
Military matters you do not understand.
We professional soldiers are operating within
A context of bungling amaterishism.
And interference and wrong-headedness.

(HITLER *has sunk lower in his chair. He jumps up, his face blotchy, his left side and arm trembling. He glares at* GUDERIAN.)

Hitler.   The whole of the general staff and officer corps
Are responsible for every failure
And disaster of the last few months. They are
Fools and fatheads, cowards, incompetents.
They have misled, misinformed and tricked me.
They are dominated by deceitful aristocrats.

Guderian   (*shouting*). The disasters in the Ardennes and the east,
In Hungary and the Baltic have been caused
By your incompetence, your misjudgement,
Your lack of skill as a military commander.
We desperately need divisions; you sent eighteen
To Latvia. When will you bring them back?

Hitler.   Never.

(LORINGHOVEN *dashes out to the corridor or reception room and phones Krebs.*)

Loringhoven.   Krebs, Guderian is shouting at the *Führer.*
Do something before he is taken out and shot.

(JODL *and* THOMALE *pull* GUDERIAN *away from* HITLER. BURGDORF *helps* HITLER *to his chair.*)

Krebs has an urgent message for you.

Guderian	(*shouting on phone*). Calm down? Calm down, you say. The man is a lunatic, We're ruled by an imbecile without military sense.

(*15 minutes later, Hitler's conference room, but all are calm.*)

Hitler.	Everyone leave except Guderian and Keitel. (*Coldly.*) Colonel-General Guderian, you are In a poor state of health, you will now take Six weeks' sick leave immediately.
Guderian	(*saluting*). I'll go.
Hitler.	Please wait until the conference is over.
Burgdorf.	Sir, the conference is finished.
Hitler	(*calling him back*). Guderian, Take good care of yourself. In six weeks' time The situation will be critical. I'll need you. Where will you go?
Keitel.	The spa at Bad Liebenstein?
Guderian	(*caustically*). It's in American hands. (*Leaving, to Loringhoven.*) It's safer not to say.

(28 March. Berlin, Defence Council building. GOEBBELS and REYMANN and his Chief of Staff, Col. REFIOR.)

Reymann.	I am worried about the defence of Berlin. Fourteen anti-aircraft batteries have been removed To the eastern front, and there is no plan To evacuate children. How will we feed babies? There is no milk.
Goebbels.	We will bring cows into Berlin.
Reymann.	Into a battle area where they can't be fed or milked? We must consider the immediate evacuation Of women and children before it is too late.

Goebbels.	If an evacuation becomes necessary,
	I will be the one to make the decision.
	But it will create panic if I order it now,
	There is plenty of time. Good evening gentlemen.

(Later.)

Refior.	Good news. Berlin has been placed under Heinrici,
	Whom you know well, and Army Group Vistula.

Reymann	*(gloomily)*. Heinrici is holding the Oder front. He will not
	Accept the hopeless task of defending Berlin.

(28 March, 9 p.m. Straelen, Montgomery's HQ. MONTGOMERY and DAWNAY, his senior staff officer.)

Montgomery	*(devastated)*. I am stunned by Eisenhower's cable.
	I am shocked. "My present plans being co-ordinated
	With Stalin." And no mention of Berlin.
	I am speechless. "The mission of your army group
	Will be to protect Bradley's northern flank."
	I am devastated, fuming at his folly.
	Why are they so hostile to me at SHAEF?
	Who are my enemies? Public opinion?
	Simpson's Ninth Army, taken away from me
	And reverting to Bradley to mop up the Ruhr.
	Bradley having the main role, and to Dresden.
	And nothing of this said to us at Rheinberg.
	And co-ordinating with Stalin, a Commander-in-Chief
	With a Head of State. And did Tedder know?
	Not going to Berlin, I can't believe it.
	Is he blind, does he realise what he's giving Stalin?
	The US and Russians must have made a deal.
	There is very dirty work behind the scenes.
	Until I know what Eisenhower is doing
	With Stalin, the wisest counsel is silence.

(He goes to his caravan.)

(Praying.) O Lord, I do not understand your ways,
But if it is your will that Stalin should have

Berlin, and control free elections there,
Then I'm happy to accept that Bradley should
Lead Simpson to Dresden. Thy will, not mine
Be done. But how, Lord of Light, how, how, how
Is your will served by Stalin having Berlin?
By Communism ruling eastern Europe?
By a regime as bad as Hitler's controlling Poland?
Please give me an answer, for I do not understand.

(*28 March. London, underground war rooms.* CHURCHILL *and* BROOKE.)

Brooke.   A wire from Monty: "I consider we
                 Are about to make a terrible mistake."
                 He hopes Eisenhower's order can be rescinded.

Churchill.   Ike did not consult his Deputy Supreme Commander,
                 Tedder, about his change of plan, nor did
                 He mention it to the Combined Chiefs of Staff.
                 He said nothing of this to us at Rheinberg,
                 And for a General to communicate directly
                 With a Head of State, and so untrustworthy a one
                 As Stalin, leaves me speechless. It signals
                 To Stalin that his troops can take great tracts
                 Of Germany, a danger I foresaw
                 In Yalta, and tried to prevent. I ask myself,
                 It must have been premeditated, he
                 Must have known this when we talked at Rheinberg?
                 And Stalin. He must have cleared it with Marshall.
                 Not even Monty would cable Stalin
                 With a change of plan without contacting us.
                 But given that he cleared it, the question is,
                 Did Ike act alone, or was he under orders
                 From higher up? Let us try to find out.

                 (*Exit* BROOKE.)

                 (*Aside.*) In every time there has been an eruption:
                 The French Revolution, the guillotine and
                 Napoleon, which came out of a suppressed
                 Bavarian movement; the Bolshevik
                 Revolution, Lenin and firing-squads,

213

Which have been funded by the Rothschilds' banks;
Now the Nazis, Hitler and extermination camps,
Which came out of Eckart, Rosenberg and the Thule
Society in Munich, Bavaria.
What if this seismic movement against government
And religion which kills in different times
Has one volcanic source which is behind
The hand of Robespierre, Napoleon, Lenin,
Stalin, Hitler - and Roosevelt? What if Eckart,
Lenin, Baruch and Marshall are all connected?
What if there is one single idea behind
All the warlords who have shaken our century?
It's a nightmare I prefer not to think about.

(29 March. Washington. Gen. MARSHALL, *US Chief of Staff with* AIDE.*)*

Aide.   A protest from the British to Roosevelt.

Marshall.   Now the President is sick I have taken charge
Of the conduct of the war. I will reply.
Ike is the most successful field Commander.
It is incredible that the British
Do not trust his military judgement now.
Churchill has phoned Ike at SHAEF to protest,
He's urged our forces to turn north, not east.
It is not clear whether he wants the Ninth
Army back, or the capture of Berlin.
Churchill says the fall of Berlin will send
A signal to the German people and will have
A psychological effect on German resistance.
Ike here denies he has changed his plans.
He says the British have called for one big thrust
Which he gave to Bradley; that his aim
Is to defeat the German forces, not turn aside
With many thousands of troops; that he has one thought:
The early winning of this war. It makes sense to me.
Only Ike is in a position to know
How to fight his battle, and exploit the changing situation.
Montgomery is slow, overcautious.
He wants to be sure before he attacks.
He'll mass hundreds of tanks when thirty will do.

He won't take risks. Eisenhower, for all his faults,
Is the best Commander the Allies have.

(*Exit* AIDE.)

(*Alone.*) The young American civilisation,
Like Rome after two Punic wars, is poised
For a world role: involved in Europe and
Controlling the older Russian civilisation
Financially, American money will
Undertake urban reconstruction and spread
American influence and use Moscow
To end the European empires before
Our coming world rule. I wanted to squeeze
Europe, contract it to the east.
I did not want the Allies to take Berlin.
And I made sure, through Ike, they did not, so
The post-war world is America's, not Europe's.
Baruch did well when he identified Ike
And promoted him as the instrument
For our larger long-term, global purpose.

(*31 March. Reims, Eisenhower's HQ.* EISENHOWER *and* BEDELL SMITH.)

Bedell Smith. Sir, a wire from Churchill: "Why should we not
Cross the Elbe and advance as far eastward
As possible?" He says the Russian Army
May take Vienna, that we must not give
The impression the Russians have done everything,
That we must avoid "the relegation
Of His Majesty's Forces to an unexpected
Restricted sphere". He says Britain is being
Relegated to an almost static role
In the north, and that the British cannot now enter
Berlin with the Americans. He says, "I do not
Consider that Berlin has yet lost its
Military and political significance."
He's very critical.

Eisenhower.   I am upset by that.
Say, I have not changed my plan. I still intend

To send Monty over the Elbe, but towards
Lübeck, not Berlin, to keep the Russians out
Of Denmark, an important objective.
Say I am disturbed and hurt that he should suggest
I have "relegated" his forces, or "restricted" them.

(*31 March. Reims. Eisenhower's HQ.* EISENHOWER *and* BEDELL SMITH.)

Eisenhower.   A further signal to Montgomery:
"You will note that in none of this do I mention Berlin.
That place has become, so far as I am concerned,
Nothing but a geographical location,
And I have never been interested in these. My purpose is
To destroy this enemy's forces and his power to resist."

(*1 April. The Kremlin, Stalin's study.* STALIN, ANTONOV *and* SHTEMENKO.)

Stalin.   Cable Eisenhower that Dresden is the best place
For the AEF and Red Army to meet.

(*He chuckles quietly.*)

Add, "Berlin has lost its former strategic significance,
The Red Army will allot secondary forces
To capture the German capital in
The second half of May." Do not add that
Berlin is our primary objective,
We have allotted a million and a quarter men
And aim to take it by mid-April; or that
I want it taken now in frantic haste.

(*Enter* MOLOTOV, BERIA, MALENKOV, MIKOYAN, BULGANIN,
KAGANOVICH *and* VOZNESENSKY *in no order of precedence. Also*
ZHUKOV *and* KONIEV. *They sit and form the State Defence Committee*
which runs the Soviet war.)

Stalin.   I have received information about the Allies' plans
Which are less than allied. The Little Allies
Intend to get to Berlin ahead of the Red Army.
(*To Shtemenko.*) Read the telegram from the Soviet mission
To Eisenhower's HQ.

Shtemenko.	"The Ruhr will be surrounded. The Allies will advance to Leipzig and Dresden. British and American forces under Montgomery Will attack north of the Ruhr and take Berlin Before the Soviet Army. This is Montgomery's plan."
Stalin.	Well, who will take Berlin? We, or the Allies?
Koniev.	We will take Berlin, and before the Allies.
Stalin.	So that's the sort of fellow you are! But how Will you do it? Your main forces are to the south.
Koniev.	Don't worry, comrade Stalin. We will organise them.
Stalin	(*nodding*). Zhukov.
Zhukov.	The men of the First Belorussian Front Are ready now. We are nearest to Berlin.
Stalin	(*smiling*). Very well. You will both stay in Moscow And prepare your plans. You will report them To the Stavka within forty-eight hours. We shall pay attention to your starting dates. (*Aside.*) He quotes Livy and Pushkin, this Koniev, But in February at Korsun, he massacred Thirty thousand trapped Germans, crushed their tanks While the Cossack cavalry slashed with sabres. He carries a library of classics But the mind of a brutal exterminator.

(*2 April. Brunen, Montgomery's HQ. MONTGOMERY and DAWNAY.*)

Montgomery.	There is nothing more to be done. The advance To the Elbe is off, we have to halt. I must Hand over the Ninth tomorrow, and without it I cannot advance to the Elbe between Hamburg And Magdeburg and must wait near the Ruhr. It's strange That Eisenhower, who has been impatient for Reckless advance, should halt us now when I could Be seizing Holland, Bremen and the North German

Ports, and keeping Denmark from the Russians. Churchill
Has had to accept that I am relegated
To a secondary role. To Roosevelt he
Has expressed his "complete confidence" in Ike,
And his "admiration for his great and shining quality,
Character and personality", adding that
He still feels the AEF should take Berlin.
He has sent Ike a copy of this message.
For the record, write that I consider
It useless to continue to argue with
The American Generals as they cannot see
My point of view, and that I have decided
To make no comments of any kind
On the American plan, and to adopt
A policy of complete silence. They are wrong!

(*3 April. The Kremlin, Stalin's study.* STALIN, ZHUKOV *and* KONIEV.)

Stalin.   I have heard you both, and your plans agree.
                 Zhukov's eight armies are along the Oder,
                 And on the Neisse from Guben to Schwedt
                 Koniev's five armies are along the Neisse.
                 Your two fronts will attack simultaneously.
                 The starting date, we agree, the sixteenth of April,
                 One month earlier than I told Eisenhower.
                 I expect Berlin to fall in twelve to fifteen days.

Koniev.   Where will my front boundary be? It affects
                 Whether I get to Potsdam or Berlin.

                 (STALIN *takes a coloured crayon and draws a line on the map.*)

Stalin.   The line goes as far as Lubben. If the Germans
                 Offer heavy resistance to the east of Berlin
                 And Zhukov is delayed, you can strike from the south.
                 Whoever breaks in first, let him take Berlin.

SCENE 2.

THE DEFENCE OF BERLIN

(4 April. Berlin, the Führer bunker. The conference room. HITLER with KREBS, Guderian's replacement.)

Hitler.　　　The Soviet preparations for an attack
　　　　　　On Berlin are simply a deception,
　　　　　　A secondary thrust. The main attack
　　　　　　Will come round Prague, which we must defend.

Krebs.　　　But *Führer* –

Hitler.　　　　　　　No, Schörner has written:
　　　　　　(Reading.) "Remember Bismarck's words 'Whoever holds
　　　　　　Prague holds Europe.'" Schörner is loyal to me,
　　　　　　He is facing Koniev, he has been hanging
　　　　　　Deserters from trees with placards round their necks.
　　　　　　I promote him to Field Marshal, and transfer
　　　　　　Four of Heinrici's divisions from the Oder
　　　　　　To defend the Reich in Czechoslovakia.

(5 April. Berlin, the Führer bunker. The conference room. HEINRICI with KREBS.)

Heinrici.　　Half my armour taken. Now twenty-five
　　　　　　Divisions face one hundred and ninety-two
　　　　　　Russian divisions on a hundred-mile front.

　　　　　　(KREBS *takes him in to* HITLER *who wears tinted green dark glasses,
　　　　　　shuffles and shakes his hand limply.* BORMANN *and Krebs sit behind him
　　　　　　on a bench,* HEINRICI *stands on Hitler's left,* EISMANN *stands on Hitler's
　　　　　　right.* KEITEL, HIMMLER *and* DÖNITZ *sit at the table.*)

Krebs.　　　You know Heinrici and Colonel Eismann,
　　　　　　His operations chief. They will now give
　　　　　　Their report on the Oder front, and then return
　　　　　　To their headquarters.

Heinrici.　　　　　　　*Führer,* gentlemen,

The Soviet armies are building for a huge attack.
The main thrust will be against Busse's Ninth Army.
I am doing everything to strengthen
Our defences there. I am taking troops from the left,
Manteuffel's Third Panzer Army, but they
Are of poor quality: Hungarians,
Russian ex-prisoners, young boys. We have no
Artillery or ammunition.

Krebs.   There will soon
Be a delivery of artillery.

Heinrici.   I need
More than promises. When the spring floods go down,
Rokossovsky, who is heading for Zhukov's right,
Will attack Manteuffel on our left.
We need to strengthen the Ninth Army round
Frankfurt, and I propose that the fortress there
Should be abandoned, releasing thirty thousand
Men who can help with our defence.

Hitler   (*harshly*). I refuse to accept this. It is like Küstrin..
I had this argument with Guderian.
There must be no withdrawals from fortresses.

Heinrici   (*patiently*). Sir, Eismann has the figures in a paper.

(EISMANN *lays a paper before* HITLER.)

My *Führer* I feel that it would be wise
To give up the defence of Frankfurt.

Hitler   (*nodding*). Krebs, the General is right. Prepare the order.

(*The other* GENERALS *are astonished.* HEINRICI *is impassive but
exchanges glances with* EISMANN. *Enter* GÖRING, *noisily. He shakes*
HITLER's *hand.*)

Göring.   I'm sorry I am late, I've been visiting
My *Luftwaffe* troops on Heinrici's front.

(GÖRING *sits between* DÖNITZ *and* KEITEL.)

I found everything ready, the men well-armed.

Hitler. No one is doing what I want. Fortresses
Are essential. In Posen and Breslau
We have tied up countless Russians. Fortresses
Should be defended to the last man. History
Has proved me right. The fortress at Frankfurt.
Must not be abandoned.

(HITLER *falls back, trembling in his chair.*)

Heinrici (*patiently*). My *Führer*, we need
Troops to strengthen Busse's position, we must
Withdraw troops from the fortress at Frankfurt

Hitler. Six battalions only, I will not allow
Any more.

Heinrici. My *Führer*, the Oder front
Cannot resist the Russian attack. The transfer
Of the Panzer divisions south has left us men
Without experience like the paratroops
Göring has just visited –

Göring. I will not listen
To scurrilous talk about my paratroops.

Heinrici. I am saying they are untrained. Experience
Has shown that untrained men are shocked by war.

Hitler. Then units must be trained. There is still time
To train them before the battle.

Heinrici. That can be done.
But we have no reserves. All troops must go
Straight to the front line. We will lose a division
Each week, we have no replacements. I need
A hundred thousand men, or in a few days
Our resistance will come to an end.

(There is a silence.)

Göring (*standing*).   My *Führer*,
I will give you a hundred thousand men
From the *Luftwaffe*.

Dönitz.   I will give you twelve thousand men
From the navy.

Himmler.   My *Führer*, the SS will give
Twenty-five thousand men for the Oder front.

Hitler (to *Krebs*). Bring in Buhle.

(Enter MAJOR-GENERAL BUHLE, *Reserve Army, from the ante-room in the corridor, or reception room.)*

How many men can you supply
For the Oder front?

Buhle (*drunk on brandy*). Thirteen thousand men.

Hitler. You have a hundred and fifty thousand men

Heinrici. I am grateful for this generosity,
But they are untrained and will be against
The most battle-hardened troops in the world.
They will be massacred.

Hitler.   These reserve troops
Can be in a second line eight kilometres
Behind the first. The front line will absorb
The shock, the second line will get used
To battle, and can fight if the Russians break through.

Heinrici. I must have my Panzers back.

Burgdorf (*whispering*).   Finish. No more.

Heinrici. My *Führer*, I must have my Panzers back.

Hitler.	I had to take them away. The Russian attack Will be against Prague, not Berlin, so Schörner Needs them more than you. You will have to face A secondary attack.
Heinrici	(*staring in amazement*). In that case, I cannot guarantee To fight off the Soviet drive towards Berlin.
Hitler	(*shouting*).You must have faith, you must believe in success. You must fill every commander with confidence. You must radiate faith and inspire your troops.
Heinrici.	My *Führer*, faith alone will not defeat The Russians.
Hitler.	Colonel-General, if you believe This battle can be won, it will be won. If your troops believe it, you will have victory. Miracles can happen to those who believe the most.

(HEINRICI *looks at them all, then leaves.* KREBS *stops Heinrici in the ante-room or reception room.*)

Krebs.	Don't count on more than thirty thousand men.

(*5 April, evening. Berlin, the Führer bunker.* GOEBBELS *to* HITLER *in his office or study.*)

Goebbels.	I have brought Carlyle's *History of Frederick the Great.*
Hitler.	My favourite book,
Goebbels.	I want you to read the turning-point In the Seven Years War of 1762. Prussia was at war with Russia, Austria and France. Frederick said he would commit suicide If there was no improvement by February 15th. His greatest enemy, Tsarina Elizabeth, died. Her successor made peace and became an ally, Prussia went on to victory.
Hitler	(*listening*). Wonderful.

Goebbels.	The story told by a British writer, is
	Prophetic and it agrees with the horoscope
	That was cast the day you became Chancellor.
	In the second half of April, all difficulties cease,
	And Germany will begin to rise again.
	It is in the horoscope.

| Hitler | (*nodding*).   Yes, I believe it. |

Goebbels.	I have issued this proclamation to the troops:
	"The *Führer* has declared that there will be
	A change of fortune in this very year.
	The true quality of genius is its awareness
	And its certain knowledge of approaching change.
	The *Führer* knows the exact hour of its arrival.
	He has been sent to us by destiny,
	So that we... shall testify to the miracle."
	Good night, my *Führer*.

| Hitler. | You alone are loyal. |

(*Exit* GOEBBELS. HITLER *puts down the book and sits before his picture of Frederick the Great.*)

I am waiting for a miracle, like you,
Frederick. I believe it is coming.
But it is taking a long time, and I feel
The pressure of my February 15th.
Help my will to manipulate the power.

(*8 April. Schönberg.* BONHOEFFER *dressed as pastor with* VASSILIEV KOKORIN *and* EX-PRISONERS.)

| Kokorin. | That was a wonderful service. I now believe |
| | The war is over, and there will be no more trials. |

| Bonhoeffer | (*smiling*). I am still trying to believe that I |
| | Have been learning Russian from the nephew of Molotov. |

| Ex-prisoner. | Bad news. Dohnanyi was tried on Friday |
| | At Sachsenhausen, lying on a stretcher, |

Only semi-conscious. He was then executed.

(BONHOEFFER *is silent. He makes the sign of the cross. Two* SS MEN *appear.*)

SS Man.   Dietrich Bonhoeffer?

Bonhoeffer.   Yes?

SS Man.   Please come with us.

Bonhoeffer.   Where to?

SS Man.   To Flossenbürg, to join your friends.
                Canaris, Oster, Sack, Strünck, Gehre.

Bonhoeffer.   A trial?

SS Man   (*nodding*). All conspirators have to be dealt with
                Before the Red Army reaches Berlin.

Bonhoeffer.   I submit myself to the will of God.

(*8 April. Hanover, the outskirts.* EISENHOWER *and* BRADLEY.)

Bradley.   We encircled the Ruhr a week ago,
                And when the Ninth Army was removed from
                Monty's control, Simpson's advance units
                Were across the Weser. I told him to proceed
                East to Magdeburg, seize a bridgehead over the Elbe
                And go down the *autobahn* towards Berlin.
                I want to draw off resisting Germans
                From east of Berlin, to help the Russians.
                I am merely seeking to establish
                A diversionary threat, and then go no farther.
                I want to keep Hitler out of the Alps,
                But Simpson has one thought: to take Berlin.

Eisenhower   (*nodding*). I wrote to Marshall yesterday, that we should
                Capture Berlin if it is feasible
                As we proceed on the general plan,

But that it is militarily unsound
To make Berlin a major objective
As it's only thirty-five miles from the Russian lines.
Marshall approves this strategy,
And has not discussed Berlin with the Chiefs of Staff.

(*Enter Major-General* BOLLING.)

Alex, when you have taken Hanover,
Which you will easily now you have a map
Of the city's defences from a captured German,
Where are you going next?

Bolling.   General we are
                   Going to push on ahead to Berlin, and nothing
                   Can stop us.

Eisenhower   (*holding his arm*). Alex, keep going. I wish
                   You all the luck in the world. Don't let anyone stop you.

(*9 April, 5.30 p.m. Flossenburg.* BONHOEFFER *kneels and prays. He rises and takes off his prison garb, and a* GUARD *leads him, naked, to a gallows with steps. He again prays, then climbs the steps, composed, and is hanged by* ANOTHER GUARD. *The first guard takes down the body and picks up his possessions.*)

Guard   (*dragging Bonhoeffer's body*). He's to be burned with all his possessions
                   Same as Canaris and the other bomb-plotters.

(*9 April, 5.30 p.m. Rheine, Montgomery's HQ.* MONTGOMERY *with* DAWNAY.)

Montgomery.   Write to Ike: "It is quite clear what you want.
                   I will crack along on the northern flank.
                   One hundred per cent, and will do all I can
                   To draw the enemy forces away
                   From the main effort being made by Bradley."

Dawnay.   Right, sir.

Montgomery.   We are moving fast, and as we move
                   I am shocked at the scenes of destruction I see.
                   Civilisation reduced to rubble, ruin.

At Munster, tank tracks crunched the carved faces
And limbs of medieval stone statues.
Here at Rheine, bombed shells of houses
And a pervading stench of decay and death.
We are driving through a Hell, and though I am pleased
We are liberating the wretched, I feel sad
That American mistakes have prolonged it all,
That we are not now in Berlin, and at the end.

(*Silence. Exit* DAWNAY.)

(*Aside*.) A civilisation is a gathering
Round an idea that can be found in its new religion.
It grows and expands, it has a style or art
And architecture, maintains an ordered life
In cities, an economy, fine manners.
Civilisation is the highest aspirations
Of the finest minds in a civilisation.
Barbarism is the lowest expression
Of the sickest minds in a civilisation.
Something went wrong in this one. All this rubble.
We caught the illness of barbarism.
A disease had to be cured, and at what cost.
Is the price of civilisation to purge
A civilisation from time to time?
Is the idea it grew round still here, your Church?
O Lord, your cathedrals round which Europe grew?

(*13 April, just after midnight. Berlin, Ministry of Propaganda.* GOEBBELS *returning to his office.*)

Goebbels.	Ribbentrop has asked diplomats to leave Berlin.
	I have visited Busse near Küstrin, and I told
	The officers of the miracle that saved
	Frederick the Great, and urged them to believe in fate.
	What are those fires?
Staff 1.	The Adlon Hotel, and
	The Chancellery, both hit in the evening raids.
Staff 2	(*calling out*). *Herr Reichsminister*, Roosevelt is dead. It is true.

(*Enter Goebbels' press officer,* RUDOLF SEMMLER.)

Semmler.   It is confirmed. Truman is the new President
            Of the United States.

Goebbels.   This is the turning-point.
            Is it really true? Open the best champagne.
            I must telephone the *Führer*. (*On phone.*) My *Führer*,
            I congratulate you. Roosevelt is dead.
            You recall the horoscope. The stars proclaim
            That the second half of April will be our turning-point.
            Providence has struck down your greatest enemy
            On Friday the thirteenth, it is like the death
            Of Tsarina Elizabeth for Frederick the Great.
            (*Putting down phone.*) The *Führer* is overjoyed. It's the miracle.

(*13 April. Berlin, the* Führer *bunker. The conference room.* HITLER *at his daily conference with his Generals, who include* JODL *and* KEITEL. RIBBENTROP *is leaving.* KREBS *has escorted him to the door.*)

Ribbentrop.   The *Führer* is in the seventh heaven.

            (*Exit from ante-room or reception room.* KREBS *accepts two messages and returns.*)

Krebs.   The US Ninth Army now have two bridgeheads
            Across the Elbe near Magdeburg.

Hitler.   The situation is under control, as
            The new German Twelfth Army, commanded by
            General Wenck is ready to counter-attack.

Krebs.   My *Führer*, there is also a message
            That Vienna has fallen to the Red Army.

Hitler.   That is of no consequence. The war will be won
            In Berlin. When Zhukov's diversionary attack
            Begins, our units will fall back from the Oder
            And form a magnet that will draw the Soviets
            To it. German armies will then attack
            From around it and destroy the enemy

	In a decisive battle. I will remain
	In Berlin to inspire the victory.
Jodl.	But, Berlin is not safe.
Keitel.	You should leave the city,
	My *Führer*, as you can inspire our forces,
	Should you not be in the safety of Berchtesgaden?
Hitler.	I will not consider it. I will remain with the troops.

(*14 April. Reims, Eisenhower's HQ.* EISENHOWER, *sombre, with* BEDELL SMITH.)

Bedell Smith.	Sir, General Bradley on the phone for you. (*Exit.*)
Eisenhower.	Brad, how are you? I'm still recovering.
	From that concentration camp near Gotha
	We went to yesterday with Patton. I've
	Never experienced an equal sense of shock.
	What? The bridging operation's a success?
	I'm glad to hear that. Brad, what do you think
	It might cost us to break out from the Elbe
	And take Berlin? You could take it fairly easily.
	But once there lose a hundred thousand men?
	Say that again? A high price to pay
	For a prestige objective and then fall back
	To let the Russians take over? That's what I think.
	But Simpson thinks he can beat the Red Army there.
	Huh-huh. Bye Brad.

(*He puts down phone.*)

Kay.	Can I join you, General?
Eisenhower.	Not just now Kay. I have a decision to make.
Kay.	You always have a decision to make.
Eisenhower.	But this
	Is some decision. If I get it wrong,
	It will return to haunt me. Send Beetle in.

(*Exit* KAY.)

I am in agony, for I must make a choice
That will have a universal application,
Affect all mankind, and men still unborn,
Shape history, and if I become President,
Tie my wrists with the rope of my own decision.
Should Berlin be American or Russian?
Militarily, I have only fifty thousand men
Who have advanced two hundred and fifty miles
In two weeks, and have already stretched
Their lines of communication. Racing them
Are two and a half million men, who are fresh,
Who have prepared two months, and are twenty miles
Away, and who must surely get there first.
To try and lose is worse than not to try.
Politically, if I win, I present Truman,
A new President, with the choice of rescinding
The Yalta agreement, that Berlin is part-Soviet,
And, worse, I raise doubts in Stalin's mind
About American good faith over Yalta.
He is anyway quick to say we are misleading him.
Then a hostile Soviet army, like a tidal wave,
Two and a half million men against our small force,
May keep going into Normandy, to the Atlantic
And sweep over all that we have won from Hitler.
It is better not to anger the Russians.
It is wiser to stick to our agreement
And not risk what our hard-won efforts have gained.
Politically, I know, since the First World War,
There have been men in Washington, and London,
Who seek to promote Communist world rule,
Who would dearly love Stalin to have Berlin.
They follow their own agenda, not SHAEF's.
I have my suspicions about some men, including
Two who promoted me from nowhere to
This pinnacle from Lieutenant-Colonel
To Supreme Commander within three years,
Two years nine months. My career progressed
When, like Churchill, I wrote to Barney Baruch.
Now I must choose on military grounds,

As the voice of SHAEF, and shut out all interests.
I am in anguish as I must decide
A course I know to be politically wrong,
But militarily right. Judgement is like love,
You weigh everything up, and then choose heart
Or head. I must choose head, but my heart yearns.
Berlin, Kay. A leader reviews, decides,
Communicates, inspires, and then defends,
And I will have a lot of defending to do.

(*Enter* BEDELL SMITH.)

Bedell Smith.   You sent for me, sir?

Eisenhower.   Telegraph the Combined
Chiefs of Staff. I intend to hold a firm front
On the Elbe; to undertake operations
To the Baltic at Lübeck, and to Denmark;
And to thrust in the Danube Valley to join with
The Russians and break up the southern redoubt
So Hitler can't continue the war in the Alps.
As the thrust on Berlin must await the success
Of these three operations, I do not include
It as part of my present plan, the essence of which
Is to stop on the Elbe and clean up my flanks.

(*15 April. Wiesbaden, Bradley's HQ. BRADLEY and SIMPSON, who has just stepped off a plane.*)

Simpson   (*shaking hands*). You have received my plan to take Berlin?

Bradley.   Simp, I have to tell you right now. You have to stop
Right where you are on the Elbe. You are not
To advance any further towards Berlin.

Simpson.   I could be in Berlin in twenty-four hours.
Where did this come from?

Bradley.   From Ike. My orders
Are to defend the line of the Elbe. The supply
Columns are being attacked with German tanks

And assault guns, round Hanover and elsewhere.
We hold the bridgehead as a *threat* to Berlin.

Simpson   *(depressed)*. So this is the end of the war for us. This is
As far as we go. We're not going to Berlin.

(15 April. The Oder front. HEINRICI *and* EISMANN, *his operations chief.)*

Heinrici.   Waiting, waiting for the Russians to attack.
The tension is in the atmosphere and every limb.
When will the attack come? Now? Tomorrow?
We are outnumbered ten to one, and no
Intelligence reports contain hard facts.
I can only speculate, among possibilities.
I must imagine that I am Zhukov.
I plan to pull my troops back from the first barrage
So the shells fall on empty trenches and –

Eismann.   Sir, Speer is here. *(Exit.)*

Heinrici.   I cannot be distracted now.

(Enter SPEER *with* TWO CHIEFS, *of roads and state railways.)*

You come when I am deep in thought. The attack.

Speer.   I want your support. Hitler has ordered
A scorched earth policy: industrial plant,
Bridges, power stations to be destroyed. Why should
They be destroyed when Germany is already defeated?

Heinrici.   I will do what I can to stop the blowing up.

(Re-enter EISMANN.)

Eismann.   Sir, Reymann is here.

Heinrici.   Ah Reymann, thanks for coming.
You know these gentlemen? I wanted to explain,
Army Group Vistula cannot take Berlin
Under its command.

Reymann.	I cannot defend Berlin.

My position is hopeless.

Heinrici.   If the Russians break through,
I will withdraw to the north or south, there will be
No battle within Berlin. Do not count on
Units I may be ordered to send in.

Speer.   The *Führer* has ordered you to destroy
Most of the nine hundred and fifty bridges
Across our waterways, which carry water
Gas or electricity. If you do, Berlin
Will be paralysed for a year and millions
Will catch disease and starve. Do not obey
The *Führer's* orders, I implore you.

Reymann.   In that case
I will be shot.

Heinrici.   On this map, I will mark
Bridges that carry no services and can be blown.

(*Later.* HEINRICI, *alone again.*)

Heinrici   (*concentrating*). When will it come? What would I do if I
Were Zhukov? (*Suddenly.*) Tomorrow, in the early hours,
Of course. Chief of Staff, an order to Busse.
Move back to the second line of defence.

(*16 April. Chuikov's command post on a hill overlooking Reitwein on the Oder's west bank.*
ZHUKOV, CHUIKOV *and officers leave their dugout for observation post. Three red flares.*)

Zhukov   (*quietly*). Now, comrades, now.

(A *bombardment.*)

Chuikov.   No answer from German guns.

(*Soviet searchlights.*)

Zhukov.   Out of the trenches, throw yourselves at the river.

Chuikov.	They are launching pontoons. See the assault boats.
Zhukov.	Your infantry men are silhouetted.
Chuikov.	Dust. I can't see. Visibility zero.
Zhukov.	Radio telephones. Where are the messengers?

(He receives a message.)

(*Irate*.) Tank detachments and guns falling behind.
The bridges across the Old Oder and canal
Have been blown. Reports of quagmires and mines.
No air support because of the dust clouds.

(Silence. Sound of guns.)

Heinrici's drawn us into a dust trap.
Gunners are opening fire from the Seelow Heights.

Soldier.	We have a bridge.
Chuikov	(to *Zhukov*). Our troops are pinned down.
Zhukov.	What the hell do you mean?

(16 April, 1 p.m. Moscow, the Kremlin. Stalin's study. The phone rings.)

Stalin.   Zhukov. You expect to take the Seelow Heights
This evening? Tanks? I would use bombers as well.
Oh, Koniev is doing well. He has crossed the Neisse
And is pressing forward without too much resistance.

(He chuckles as he rings off.)

(16 April, towards midnight. Moscow. Stalin's study still. Again the phone rings.)

Stalin.   Zhukov. You haven't taken the Heights yet?
Three houses on the edge? That's not a breakthrough.
You should not have departed from the plan.
You should have sent in the First Tank Army

Where General Headquarters ordered. What do you mean,
The slower now, the quicker you'll take Berlin?
It's easier to crush the enemy on a battlefield
Than in a city?

(PAULINA *appears.* STALIN *loses patience.*)

We have been thinking
Of ordering Koniev to take his tank armies
From the south towards Berlin, and Rokossovsky
To cross the river and attack from the north. Good night.

(17 April, morning. Moscow. Stalin's study. The phone rings.)

Stalin.   Koniev. Where are your headquarters? An old castle
Near Cottbus. Your tanks are rolling forward. Good.
Koniev, Zhukov has not yet broken through.
You can turn your tank armies towards Berlin
At Zossen? What map are you using? The one
To two hundred thousand.

(STALIN *searches his map.*)

You know the German
General Staff Headquarters is at Zossen?
Very good. Turn your tank armies towards Berlin.

(18 April, morning. Zhukov's HQ. ZHUKOV and his Chief of Staff, POPIEL.)

Zhukov.   All commanders are to go for the front line
And speed things up. Koniev is heading for Berlin.
I want the Heights taken, whatever the cost.
Then full speed to Berlin. (*Exit.*)

Popiel.   He is roaring like a lion.

(18 April, evening. Moscow. Stalin's study.)

Stalin.   Zhukov. Chuikov has the Heights and has broken
The Germans' first line of defence? Good, good.
The cost, thirty thousand men? They gave their lives

For their motherland.

(*He puts down the phone.*)

Thirty thousand,
That's war. Hitler attacks me with Barbarossa,
Seeking to eradicate all Soviet Jews.
And fifty million die in repelling him.
Thirty thousand to drive towards Berlin.
This blood will achieve territory, our rule.
I took over from Lenin a divided land,
I killed six million to unify it,
Reshape its borders, rule a vast expanse
From the Baltic to the Pacific from a strong centre,
A union that will now expand westwards,
As far west as the Allies allow my troops.
If they weaken, I am ready to push on
Till the whole continent, from the Atlantic to the Pacific,
All Euro-Asia, will be under Red rule.
The Byzantine Russian civilisation
Is in its greatest extent under my Tsardom.

(*He stands before a picture of Ivan the Terrible.*)

Ivan the Terrible, I look to you.
You approve of everything that I have done.
You know our Byzantine Russia must expand
At the expense of the Holy Roman Empire
And the Habsburgs, and their successors,
And the British Empire, the non-Orthodox faiths.
You know Russia's Byzantine destiny
To rule the world through a creed that captures minds.
Autocracy, through Communism, is our way.
I keep the tradition of the Russian Tsars,
I unite our lands and cultures with the glue of power,
And keep it stuck together by repelling force.
Thirty thousand is a small price to pay.
A human life is material which the State
Can remould into a peasant or a soldier.
It *is* while it is alive and then, is nothing.
Death is like a curtain drawn across a window.

It is nothing, it has no significance.
It is the end of life, as evil is the end of good.
There is no sacredness, men have bodies
That can be used like shell cases. There is nothing
Sacred about life, no good. Ivan you knew.
We have millions of material units
To sacrifice, to expand our empire.

(*20 April, just after 12 noon. Berlin, the* Führer *bunker. The refreshment room outside Hitler's office.* HITLER *in greatcoat and peaked cap with* BORMANN, GOEBBELS, RIBBENTROP, SPEER, HIMMLER *and* JODL, *all in uniform.* GÖRING *arrives in plain olive uniform.*)

Burgdorf.   The *Führer* rose at eleven and is greeting
                   Well-wishers on his fifty-sixth birthday.

Göring.   My *Führer*, congratulations on your birthday.
                   I passed Goebbels' banners on my way here.
                   One, stretched across a ruined building, says
                   "We thank our *Führer* for everything."

Speer.   I was just saying to the *Führer*, there are posters
                   On doors, walls, windows, saying "Should Berlin
                   Share the fate of Aachen and Cologne? No!"
                   The early morning shelling of Berlin has brought
                   Out resistance. What news of the air raid?

Göring.   A thousand American bombers, silver
                   Planes glistening in the blue sky, too high for flak.
                   We have no German fighters to attack them.
                   They had a clear run and have knocked out
                   The city's water, gas, electricity and sewage
                   Supply. There is no power. The bombardment
                   Ten minutes ago was from Zhukov's long-range guns.
                   The Allies' "Happy birthday" to our *Führer*.

Goebbels   (*taking message*). My *Führer*, the news is bad. Weidling, Heinrici
                   And Busse have been overrun, as you know.
                   Reymann says it is no longer possible to defend
                   The capital. All possible troops must be
                   Dispatched to the front.

(HITLER *nods tiredly.*)

Göring.   My *Führer*, you should leave Berlin.
You should fly south and go to Berchtesgaden.

Speer.   *Führer*, he is right, you should leave today.

Hitler.   No, I will remain. I must inspect the parade.

(*He climbs the stairs to the wrecked Chancellery garden with* BURGDORF,
AXMANN, KREBS, FEGELEIN *and the others.* GÖRING *goes to a phone.*
SPEER *returns.*)

Speer   (*to Göring*). I can remember when, for his birthday parade,
Forty thousand men and hundreds of tanks
Took three hours to salute him while he stood
On a dais. On his fiftieth birthday
I rode with him in his car as he stood,
Arm raised in salute; slowly we passed hundreds
Of thousands of soldiers standing silently.
He was like Tamberlaine in a chariot.
The Army had increased sevenfold in four years,
The Rhineland, Austria, Sudeten and Czech lands
Behind, Danzig, East Prussia and the Polish
Corridor ahead, and who could stop him?
Each man had sworn an oath to his Napoleon.
He was magnificent. I knew then it was war.
When he spoke the world trembled, and we were all proud
To follow him. Now a few SS men and
A few boys from the Hitler Youth. He's trembling
Fumbling for their hands, patting their cheeks, pinning
Iron Crosses on those Axmann points out,
He's staggering unsteadily, saying
The enemy will be destroyed outside Berlin.
It's pathetic. I couldn't bear to watch any more.
I know Stauffenberg's bomb began the decline,
And Dr. Morell's syringe has played a part,
But I can't help feeling power festers in the flesh
And infects the blood till the health corrupts.
I've seen it in other leaders. Power ruins
Like a drug an athlete takes to enhance

Performance; soon the body craves for more
And is addicted, and the doses must be increased,
And his health is past its peak. So it is with him.
Amid the trappings of power, he is impotent.
He was the mightiest in the world, and now
He looks like a drug addict who's terminally ill.

Göring.   It's finished, you are right. I am leaving Berlin.
This morning I learned that Rokossovsky is
Twelve miles from my estate in north-east Berlin,
Karinhall. I have packed my possessions –
Things I brought back from countries we conquered,
Souvenirs, you might say – into twenty-four lorries
And blown up the building. I could hardly bring
Myself to press the plunger, but I did.
That beautiful castle is now rubble.

Speer.   And the lorries?

Göring.   Parked at the *Luftwaffe* game park
Near Potsdam. I'm joining them now. We will drive
In convoy to my house at Obersalzberg.
Do not be trapped in Berlin.

Speer.   I certainly won't.

(HITLER *returns down the steps. The* Führer's *conference begins in the
conference room.*)

Krebs.   The overall picture shows Berlin is
Half encircled. In the north, Rokossovsky
Has cut Manteuffel from the rest of the army.
Zhukov is in the north-east suburbs and
Will attack to the north-west. On the Oder,
Busse is encircled – but not Weidling's Panzers –
And Koniev has cut it off from the south.
Koniev is attacking the north and at Zossen,
In the south. Four hundred aircraft have been destroyed.
The Americans have trapped Model in the Ruhr pocket
With over three hundred thousand troops, while
Montgomery is attacking Bremen and the Elbe.

The Americans have taken Leipzig and Nuremberg,
The French Stuttgart and the Poles Rothenburg.
Berlin can only survive if Busse's Ninth Army
Is pulled back from the Oder.

Hitler.   No withdrawal.
I refuse to allow any withdrawal.

Krebs.   Heinrici
Reports that all along the line, men are retreating,
On foot and in vehicles. He is trying
To prevent them, but he now needs more troops.

Hitler.   Send the Müller Brigade from Wenck's Twelfth Army.

Krebs.   *Führer*, without transport will they arrive in time?

Hitler.   Heinrici must take Reymann and Berlin
Under his command.

Göring.   My *Führer*, I am now convinced
You must leave Berlin. Planes are standing by
At Tempelhof to fly out you, Keitel
And Jodl.

Hitler.   If the Russians and Americans
Cut Germany in two, the northern half
Will be under General Admiral Dönitz, and I
Transfer the command to him now. The southern half
Will be under Kesselring, but I retain
The command in case we fight on from the Alps.

(*Silence. The* GENERALS *all talk among themselves. The conference
is over.*)

Jodl.

Jodl   (*surprised*). Yes, my *Führer*?

Hitler.   You have been a good
OKW operations chief. I shall fight

As long as the loyal fight beside me,
And then I shall shoot myself.

Göring.   Good bye, *Führer.*

Hitler.   Good bye.

               (*Exit* GÖRING.)

Speer.   Where are you going, Himmler?

Himmler.   To meet Schellenberg
               At Ziethen. And you?

Speer.   To Hamburg, for a radio speech.

Himmler.   We are on the same side. You will call on
               The people to stop fighting. I know. While I,
               Let me say I am preparing peace.

               (*All leave except* HITLER. *Enter four secretaries,* TRAUDL JUNGE, GERDA
               CHRISTIAN, CHRISTA SCHRÖDER *and* JOHANNA WOLF *with schnapps.*
               They toast him in the ante-room or refreshment room outside his office
               or study.)

Secretaries.   Happy birthday.

               (*Enter* EVA BRAUN. *She sits beside him. Silence.*)

Eva.   Happy birthday.

Hitler.   Who else would have come back
               To Berlin when they could have gone to the Berghof?

Junge.   Can I ask you something, as it's your birthday?

Hitler.   Go on.

Junge.   We're all wondering, will you leave Berlin?

Secretaries.   Yes tell us.

Hitler.	I can't leave. Why I would feel Like a lama turning an empty prayer-wheel.

(*All laugh.*)

I must resolve this war here in Berlin
Or go under. I must stay and see it through.

(*Silence.* HITLER *and* EVA *rise and go to his office or study.*)

Christian.	He believes the war is lost.
Schröder.	That's clear.
Wolf.	She knows it.
Junge.	She defied his orders five days ago. She chose the room next to his bedroom, she made Soldiers carry down her bed and dressing-table.
Christian.	She's here for the end.
Wolf.	And we?
Junge.	Our clothes are dirty. We have nowhere to wash, we stink.

(EVA *returns.*)

Eva.	Come on, We're going upstairs to the old Chancellery To our private apartment.

(*They go up the stairs with* BORMANN *and* DR. MORELL *who carry champagne and a gramophone which is put on the one circular table.* HITLER *joins them. Outside Soviet guns.*)

Let's drink and dance.

Bormann.	We only have one record.

(He plays 'Red Roses Bring You Happiness'. He and MORELL *dance with two of the secretaries.* HITLER *and* EVA *dance, he tiredly, she radiantly.* BORMANN *plays it again, 'Red Roses'. A terrific crash.)*

A Red shell.

(A telephone rings. BORMANN *answers. Another crash. All return to the* Führer *bunker rapidly, leaving the glasses.)*

(21 April, 9 a.m. Zossen HQ. KREBS *takes a phone call, with* BOLDT.)

Krebs.   Yes Krankel. Your attack on Koniev has failed?
          Heavy losses? We must evacuate.

(He phones the Führer *bunker.)*

                    Burgdorf.
          It's Krebs, from Zossen. The counter-attack has failed.
          Koniev's tanks are advancing, we must evacuate
          Headquarters. Please ask the *Führer* for permission.

(He waits.)

(To Boldt.) The answer is no.

(11 a.m. KREBS *again with phone.* KRANKEL *stands before him, covered in mud. Tank sound above.)*

Krebs.   Burgdorf. It's Krebs again.
          Krankel is here, the Russians have taken Baruth.
          A Russian tank is passing overhead now.
          We again request permission to move out.

(He waits.)

(To Boldt.) The answer is again no.

Boldt.   A Russian camp for us.

(1 p.m. KREBS *again on the phone.)*

Krebs.   Burgdorf. It's Krebs again. There is a line
                        Of Russian tanks, unopposed. If we do not move out
                        There will be no one to direct the war.
                        Everyone is out of contact – Busse, Weidling.

                        (*He waits.*)

                        All OKW operations staff are to go
                        To the army barracks at Krampnitz. The *Führer*
                        Wants me at his daily conference, half an hour
                        Earlier than usual, at 2.30? And Loringhoven?
                        We must leave at once.

                        (KREBS *puts down the phone, shaking his head in disbelief.*)

(*Chorus of* BERLINERS.)

Chorus.   We have extra rations for Hitler's birthday:
                        A pound of meat, half a pound of rice and beans.
                        We leave our shelters and queue outside food shops,
                        At every water pump or standpipe.
                        The Russian guns are shelling our city.
                        We live in cellars and come out for food.
                        When will our misery end? When will Hitler give up?

(*21 April. Soltau, Montgomery's new TAC HQ.* MONTGOMERY *and* EARLE.)

Montgomery.   Dempsey fears he can't cross the Elbe until
                        May the first after he takes Bremen.
                        I want you to go forward to Lüneburg
                        And visit General Barker and obtain his plan
                        For crossing the Elbe with 53rd Division.
                        But be careful, there are enemy troops
                        On the edge of Lüneburg Forest.

Earle.   I'll take
                        The shortest route north of the Forest, I'll
                        Take John with me, we'll be back by nightfall.

(*21 April, 3 p.m. Berlin, the* Führer *bunker. The conference room.* BURGDORF *and* WENCK.
KEITEL *nearby.*)

Burgdorf.	The *Führer* is in good spirits now. He was shocked To learn how close the Soviet guns have reached, And by the Russian occupation of Zossen And its underground rooms. It was bad news that Model has shot himself in the Ruhr. But Schörner Has counter-attacked Koniev and held him up – And has been made Field Marshal. And Dr. Morell Has given the *Führer* an amphetamine injection And the *Führer's* valet Linge has given him eye drops, Five times the normal dose. They contain cocaine.
Wenck	(*to Hitler*). *Führer*, I am about to counter-attack American forces in the Harz Mountains And on the Elbe.
Hitler.	That's excellent. My maps. Tell Koller at Werder to send jets from Prague And attack Soviet forces south of Berlin.

(BURGDORF *attempts to ring Prague*.)

I will pull back the 56th Panzer Corps
To the edge of the city. They can then link
With Steiner's SS German Panzer Corps.

Burgdorf.	*Führer*, we have no communications with Prague And anyway, jets cannot fly as the Russians Control the skies. And 56th Panzer Corps Are already on the edge of Berlin.
Hitler	(*transfixed*). Steiner will be the saviour of Berlin. Every available man is to be given To Army Detachment Steiner, to push south And cut off Zhukov's advance, while Busse goes north. It's a bold plan which cannot fail to succeed. Get Steiner.

(BURGDORF *dials and hands* HITLER *the phone*.)

(*Excitedly*.) Steiner, all your SS troops
Are to be disbanded at once and sent into battle,

Every man between Berlin and the Baltic
Must join the attack I have ordered.

(*He puts down the phone.*)

We will mobilise thousands of new troops
And send them against the Russians, while Wenck attacks.

(*The phone rings.*)

Burgdorf.   Steiner? What do you mean, you don't know what's going on?
The *Führer* has just explained. You have no troops
Or weapons?

Hitler.   Let me speak to him. Steiner?
The Russians will suffer their greatest defeat
Before the gates of Berlin, thanks to you.
Officers who do not comply will be shot.
You are answerable with your own head.
The fate of the *Reich* capital depends on your success.

(*He puts down the phone. The phone rings.*)

Burgdorf.   Koller? You want to know where to send the men
You have raised?

Hitler.   Let me speak to him. Are you still
Questioning my orders? I thought I had made myself clear.
All *Luftwaffe* personnel are to join Steiner
For a ground attack. Any officer who
Keeps back men will forfeit his life within
Five hours. Your own head is answerable.

(*The phone rings.*)

Burgdorf.   Heinrici? Steiner must mount his attack.
You cannot reject the order, it has come from the *Führer*.

(*He rings off.*)

Hitler.   Heinrici is a good General, but can be defeatist.

I will give him a new Chief of Staff, a Nazi,
General Trotha. He will see Heinrici complies.
Reymann is also defeatist. I will replace him
With Kaether of the Waffen SS, Reymann
Will take over the defence of Potsdam.

(*Enter* EVA *with* JUNGE *and* CHRISTIAN, *the two secretaries.*)

Get changed and fly south, all of you.

Eva   (*taking both his hands*).   But you know
I am going to stay here with you.

(HITLER *kisses her lightly on her lips.*)

Christian.   We will stay here.

Hitler.   I wish my Generals were as brave as you.

(*21 April, 6p.m.* EARLE *and* POSTON *in jeep, Earle driving.*)

Earle.   This route is nearer the Forest, we'll be back by dark.

(*Shooting.* POSTON *fires back with a sten.*)

Poston.   I'm out of ammunition.

(EARLE *drives the jeep at the machine-gunner, killing him.* POSTON *and
Earle are thrown out of the jeep and are surrounded by boys in German
uniform. Earle tries to wipe a location map and is shot in the back and falls
three yards from* POSTON, *who is lying unarmed, hands above his head.*)

N-no. Stop - stop.

(POSTON *is bayoneted above the heart and is killed. The German boys
remove a watch and valuables and go.* EARLE *is still alive and is found by
a farmer.*)

(*22 April, morning. Berlin, Führer bunker.* HITLER *and* DR. MORELL.)

Hitler.   I feel ill, not as I did yesterday.

Dr. Morell.	I gave you a huge dose of amphetamine. Shall I give you an injection of morphine?

Hitler.	You want to put me to sleep so I can be Flown out of Berlin to Berchtesgaden. As my Generals want. You are plotting with them.

Dr. Morell.	My *Führer*, no.

Hitler.	You will move out of your room at once. I will give it to the Goebbels, who are loyal. Goebbels knows I will stay in Berlin.

(*22 April. Soltau.* MONTGOMERY *by his caravan.* DAWNAY.)

Dawnay.	Sir, a signal from Peter Earle.

Montgomery.	Ah, he hasn't been captured.

Dawnay.	Sir, it's bad news. Earle is alive, but Poston. (*Reading.*) "Regret to report John Poston killed at Eighteen hundred hrs Saturday twenty-one April." Earle's in 212 Field Ambulance Station. Poston was last seen in a ditch. I'm sorry, sir.

Montgomery.	Kit, send my physician, Hunter, to check Earle's condition, and then Recover Poston's body.

(MONTGOMERY *turns on his heel and goes into his caravan.*)

(*Later. Meadow by trees. Poston's funeral.* MONTGOMERY *weeps by Poston's grave.* TINDALE, *a Scottish Presbyterian padre.* HENDERSON *talks with* HUNTER, *the doctor, away from mourners.*)

Henderson.	There was a touching message from Churchill. He's like a father weeping for a son. John was Monty's youngest LO, and had been With him longest. Twenty-five, and he had A Military Cross and bar. Did you know he

	Fell in love with a girl in London, and asked
	Monty what he should do, as there was competition
	And he needed some leave to propose,
	And Monty said "Take my plane, fly to London
	And keep the plane there till the girl says Yes."

Hunter.

He was a vivid fellow with a current
Of energy. He was always up to something.
Monty was very devoted to him, I think
He represented something Monty couldn't be
Because he's so disciplined, on a tight rein.
A meadow on the forest edge, with full
Military honours....

Henderson.

He's still weeping openly.

Hunter.

It's a kind of breakdown. He's been inconsolable.
He's suffered so many blows and disappointments –
His command being taken away, then given back,
Then taken away again – and he's no family,
And for a long time he's suppressed his hurt feelings
And carried on and let some out in prayer.
"A" Mess has been his family, and I'm sure
You're right, he's looked on Poston as a son,
And his death has brought out what should have come up
Months ago. It's cleansing, healthy, cathartic,
It's good. I predict he'll snap out of it now.

Montgomery

(*to the padre*). He would certainly have sailed with Drake.

(*Later.* HENDERSON *and* DAWNAY. DE GUINGAND.)

Dawnay.

It's SHAEF at Reims on the phone. What do I do?

(MONTGOMERY *appears at his caravan door. He has "snapped out of it".*)

Montgomery.

SHAEF? I'll take it. Yes, yes. Of course I realise
The need to get to Lübeck before the Russians.

(*He rings off.*)

(*Expostulating*.) This is adding insult to injury.
Freddie, get on to Whiteley and inform him
I've always been well aware of the urgent
Need to reach and cross the Elbe quickly, that
It was SHAEF that stopped this plan a month ago,
And removed the Ninth Army, weakening and
Slowing down Twenty-First Army Group, and
If the Russians get to Lübeck and Denmark
Before we do, SHAEF should accept full blame.

(*Later.* MONTGOMERY *and* DAWNAY.)

Dawnay.   Sir, a cable from General Eisenhower.
It reminds you of the importance of
Lübeck and the Danish Peninsula,
And says SHAEF will do anything to ensure
The speed and success of your operation.

Montgomery (*quietly*). Justifying themselves, that's all they're doing.
They've sent seven armies to cut off Hitler's
Last stand in the Alps, when he isn't there, leaving
Two armies to clear Holland, North Germany
And the North Sea ports, and secure Denmark from
The Russians who are now on the Oder.
Two armies out of nine, and they want more speed!
It's the planning of nincompoops.

(*22 April, 3 p.m. Berlin,* Führer *bunker. The conference room. The daily conference.* HITLER,
BORMANN, KREBS, KEITEL *and* JODL *in the ante-room or reception room.*)

Keitel.   The *Führer's* face is yellow and expressionless.

Jodl.   He's sacked his doctor and has withdrawal symptoms.
He can't concentrate. He needs amphetamine.

       (*In the conference,* HITLER *twice gets up and goes to his private office and
returns, abstracted.*)

Krebs.   The situation is grim – Koniev has taken
Our main munitions depot, Busse's army
Is trapped. Weidling has retreated to the Olympic village.

We are trying to arrest him.

Hitler   (*not listening*).   Where is Steiner?
                Steiner's Army Detachment. How is his attack?

Krebs.   *Führer*, Steiner has not yet given the order
                For an attack.

(*Silence.*)

Hitler.   Everyone is to leave the room
                Except Keitel, Jodl, Burgdorf, Bormann
                And you Krebs.

(*The others leave.* HITLER *then raves, trembling.*)

                        I ordered Steiner to attack.
                Why has this not happened? I am surrounded
                By cowards, traitors, incompetents and Generals
                Who are insubordinate and disloyal.
                Even the SS cannot be trusted, and tell lies.
                Everything is collapsing. The war is lost.
                I will stay here and lead the final battle.
                I shall not fall into the hands of the enemy.
                When the last moment comes, I will shoot myself.

(*He crumples into a chair.*)

(*Sobbing.*) It's over. The war is lost. I shall shoot myself.

(*Silence. All are embarrassed.*)

Bormann.   There is still hope. You must remain in charge.
                But you should move to Berchtesgaden, and
                Continue the war from there.

Hitler.   You can all leave
                Berlin. I will stay and go down with my troops.
                I have taken my decision.

Keitel.   This is madness.

You must fly to Berchtesgaden tonight
So there is continuity of command
Which can no longer be guaranteed in Berlin.

Hitler.   You go. I order you to go. I stay.
East Prussia held while I was at Rastenburg,
It collapsed when I moved back to Berlin.

Keitel.   I will stay with you.

Jodl.   And so will I.

Hitler.   I want
Keitel, as Commander of the armed forces,
Göring, my deputy, and Bormann to fly
Down south tonight.

Keitel, Bormann.   We refuse.

Hitler.   If
There is negotiating to be done,
Göring is better at that than I am.
I told Schörner, my death may now remove
The last obstacle that prevents the Allies
From making common cause with Germany
Against the Russians. Either I fight and win
Here, or I die here. That is my final
And irrevocable decision.

(*22 April, evening. Berlin,* Führer *bunker. Hitler's office.* GOEBBELS, MAGDA *and* HITLER.)

Goebbels.   All afternoon the telephone has been ringing.
And voices have implored you to leave Berlin:
Dönitz, Ribbentrop, Himmler, a visit from Speer.
But I have moved into Morell's room to stay
With you.

Hitler   (*quietly*). I know, that's why you have Morell's room.

Goebbels.   I will die in Berlin. I told Speer,
My wife and children are not to survive me.

	The Americans would brainwash them
	And turn them against me and my memory.
	They would make propaganda from my death.

Hitler.   Speer told me you felt this. You are loyal.
           You are the only one I can really trust.

Goebbels. I am honoured that we have a room so near to yours.
           Magda has told the children they will soon
           Be given chocolates so they will not be sick.

Hitler.   I have now sorted my documents. Those not burned
           Up in the garden, to be kept for posterity,
           Are being flown to Munich tonight in ten aircraft.

Goebbels   (*quietly*). In the coming days, know that I am with you.

           (*They clasp hands.*)

(*22 April, night. Berlin, Invalidenstrasse, waste ground. It is raining, there is a glow from fires. Sixteen discharged PRISONERS under SS GUARDS in two groups. The first group consists of Bonhoeffer's two brothers-in-law, KLAUS BONHOEFFER and RÜDIGER SCHLEICHER, and the poet ALBRECHT HAUSHOFER. They carry bags with their personal possessions. HERBERT KOSNEY is nearby.*)

Haushofer.   Why are we leaving the Invalidenstrasse?

SS Officer. We're taking you to a new prison, there is
             A short cut through here. From the Lehrterstrasse
             Prison, through here.

Bonhoeffer.   This is the ruined Ulap
             Exhibition hall.

SS Officer.   Wait for the others. If
             You try to escape, we shoot.

Bonhoeffer.   Look at those fires.

           (HAUSHOFER *puts down his bag.*)

Haushofer.	I'm working on a sonnet. It's just bright

Haushofer.   I'm working on a sonnet. It's just bright
              Enough to read the opening lines. Listen.
              Your brother-in-law Dietrich would say yes to this.
              "There are times when only madness reigns, and then
              It is the best that hang."

              (*The other 13 prisoners have caught up. The* SS MEN *push them all
              forward.*)

SS Officer.   Stand against the wall.

Bonhoeffer.   They're going to shoot us.

SS Officer.   Faces towards the wall.

              (*All sixteen are shot in the back of the neck and fall. One,* HERBERT
              KOSNEY, *is only wounded in his neck. The SS guards go.* KOSNEY *raises
              his head.* HAUSHOFER's *hand still clutches his poems.*)

(*22 April, evening. Lübeck, the Swedish consulate.* HIMMLER *and* SCHELLENBERG *with*
COUNT BERNADOTTE.)

Himmler.   The *Führer*'s great life is drawing to a close.
              I feel released from my oath of loyalty.
              I expect to be the new *Führer*, the Overlord
              Of the German peoples, and I authorise you
              To convey my offer of surrender to
              The Western Allies and General Eisenhower.
              The German Army will continue to fight the Soviets
              Till the Allies advance and relieve us.

Bernadotte.   I will leave
              For Stockholm at once.

(*23 April, morning. Wenck's HQ in the Wiesenburg forest near Magdeburg.* WENCK. KEITEL
arrives.)

Keitel.   The *Führer* orders you to drive east and
              Save Berlin and the *Führer*.

Wenck.   Very well.

I will dictate an order to the Army now.

(*He goes and returns with a document.*)

Your copy to take back to Berlin.

Keitel.   Thank you. (*Exit.*)

Wenck   (*to aide*). Call my staff to the next room.

(*He stands and, just visible, talks off stage.*)

                                                              Keitel has left
With my order to you to go to Berlin,
Which has been requested by the *Führer*. I
Have no intention of leading you to Berlin.
We will hold our position on the Elbe
As an escape to the west, and we will drive
Close to Berlin and get out as many men
As we can.

(*23 April, 3.30 p.m. Berlin, the* Führer *bunker. The conference room.* HITLER *and* KEITEL *at the end of their conference.*)

Keitel.   *Führer*, can I persuade you now to leave Berlin?

Hitler.   No.

Keitel.   You may find yourself cut off. I need
To know of any peace negotiations.

Hitler.   It is too early to talk of surrender.
It is better to negotiate after
A local victory, such as the battle for Berlin.

Keitel.   I am not satisfied with that answer.

Hitler   (*tiredly*). I have approached Britain through Italy
And Ribbentrop is coming here on this.
I will not lose my nerve, you can rest assured.

(KEITEL *and* JODL *leave the ante-room.*)

Keitel.   He will die here.

Jodl.   Göring is the only hope.
I have sent Roller to Berchtesgaden
To tell Göring of Hitler's collapse and tears
And to ask him to intervene.

(*23 April, 6p.m. Berlin, the* Führer *bunker.* KREBS *and* BURGDORF *receive* WEIDLING *and his intelligence officer,* CAPT. KAFURKE.)

Weidling.   Why has the *Führer* ordered my execution?

Krebs   (*coldly*). For deserting your position and moving to
The Olympic village.

Weidling.   I can prove I have been
Within a mile of the front line for days.
And nowhere near the Olympic village. What
Is going on?

Burgdorf.   There has been a misunderstanding.
You will see the *Führer* now. What is your position?

Weidling.   Busse has ordered me to withdraw as Soviet
Tanks are advancing.

Krebs.   The order is cancelled.
You will defend Berlin.

Weidling.   Kafurke will phone Dufving
And reverse the order.

Krebs.   We will speak to the *Führer*.

(KREBS *and* BURGDORF *leave.*)

Weidling.   It was irresponsible to relieve me
Of my command.

Krebs.   The order will be revoked.
                    Hitler will speak with you.

                    (*At the door* WEIDLING*'s revolver and holster are removed. He goes into*
                    the ante-room or refreshment room past RIBBENTROP *and on into the*
                    office or study, HITLER *rises from a table of maps. His face is bloated, his*
                    eyes look feverish, his hands and left leg tremble. He grins.)

Hitler.   Have we met before?

Weidling.   You decorated me, oak leaves on my
                    Knight's Cross.

Hitler.   I recall the name, but not the face.
                    Now your position.

                    (WEIDLING *points it out on the map.*)

                           You will stay in Berlin
                    And take over the southern and eastern sectors.
                    Wenck is coming from the west, Busse from the south-east,
                    Steiner's army detachment from the north.

                    (WEIDLING *leaves* HITLER. *To* KREBS *outside.*)

Weidling.   Berlin is a graveyard.

                    (*Fade on* WEIDLING.)

(*23 April, later. The* Führer *bunker, Hitler's office.* HITLER *and* BORMANN.)

Bormann.   A cable from Göring. (*Reads.*) "My *Führer*, in view
                    Of your decision to remain in the fortress
                    Of Berlin, do you agree that I take over
                    The total leadership of the *Reich*,
                    With full freedom of action at home and abroad,
                    As your deputy, in accordance with your decree
                    Of 29th June 1941?
                    If no reply is received by twenty-two hundred hours
                    I shall take it for granted that you have lost
                    Your freedom of action, and shall consider

The conditions of your decree as fulfilled,
And shall act in the best interests of our country...."

(*He hands the cable to* HITLER.)

Hitler   (*stunned*). What do you think of this?

Bormann   (*softly*).   It is treasonous.

Hitler.   Göring?

Bormann.   *Führer,* I have a radio message
                From Göring to Ribbentrop, ordering him
                To go to Berchtesgaden if nothing
                Is heard from you by midnight. Göring wants
                To start peace talks at once.

Hitler   (*devastated, incredulously*). Göring, Göring?
                (*Pulling himself together.*) Tell the SS to arrest him. Strip him
                Of all offices and titles. Göring. A traitor.

                (BORMANN's *eyes gleam as he leaves* HITLER. *Fade on* HITLER.)

Bormann   (*alone*). A word here, a raised eyebrow there, no more.
                I do not have to suggest my rivals come down.
                Kluge, Rommel, Rundstedt, Model, I've seen them fall.
                Göring, Himmler, I have had them in my sights
                For months, no years. And others too. Burgdorf,
                Guderian, Krebs, Jodl, Keitel, Goebbels.
                I remember things and bide my time, put on
                An oafish air so they do not suspect
                My cunning, my deviousness. The way
                Of advancement is to be at hand, of use,
                To flatter the confidence of a great man,
                And knock out the others one by one, secure
                Their confidence by taking their side, suggest
                A course of action here, an indiscretion,
                Then undermine them by subtle reports
                Which parade the misdeed unobtrusively,
                Then arrange for them to have a disaster,
                Then bring it, reluctantly, to the great man's eyes,

And then dispatch them on his authority,
Until in the end all have gone save you and him.
But what if I have to flee before the prize?
And flee I shall. There will be no trace of me
If the Russians put an end to my grand schemes.

(*24 April, 10.45 a.m. Berlin, the* Führer *bunker. The reception room.* KREBS, *his adjutant* LORINGHOVEN, *and* BOLDT, *his ADC.*)

Loringhoven.   I am not pleased to have moved here last night.

Boldt.   Nor me. It is a doomed place. But what
Can we do? We are professional soldiers.

Loringhoven.   Hourly reports. You on Berlin, me Germany.
What can we say? The war is finished.

Boldt.   The upper bunker doesn't look very secure.
The concrete roof has fallen in, the floor
Is ankle deep in water with wobbly planks,
The air is unhealthy. I don't like it here.

Krebs.   Come in, you two.

(*They move into Hitler's office or study.* HITLER *is with* GOEBBELS *and* BORMANN.)

Führer, *our hourly reports.*

(*He lays two papers before* HITLER *who reads them and looks at his map.*)

Hitler   (*shouting at Krebs*). The Oder is a natural barrier.
The Russian success can only be put down
To the incompetence of Manteuffel
And the other army Generals.

Krebs.   Their men are untrained,
And reserves have been transferred
For the attack to the north of Berlin.

Hitler.   It must take place

Tomorrow, no later. Pass that on now.

(KREBS *signals to* LORINGHOVEN, *who leaves the room.*)

Krebs.   Steiner will lead the attack.

Hitler.   The *Waffen* SS
                    Are arrogant and incompetent. I will not have
                    Steiner in command there. Weidling is the man.

Krebs.   We nearly had him shot.

Hitler.   He will save Berlin.
                    Appoint him commandant of the Berlin
                    Defence Region, responsible to me.

(*25 April. Chorus of* BERLINERS.)

Chorus.   Germany is cut in two, Koniev and Hodges
                    Have met on the Elbe. At dawn this morning
                    As we cowered in cellars, the Russian attack began.
                    A barrage of artillery, pounding
                    Our houses into rubble, starting fires,
                    Raining shells onto our squares and gardens.
                    Then the tanks, crushing barricades, blowing
                    Apart any building which had a sniper.
                    Then the infantry, not down open streets
                    But under cover of ruins, creeping
                    To cellar doors with grenades and flame-throwers.
                    Half a million Russian troops, and hundreds
                    Of tanks against sixty thousand of us,
                    Pounding our city to a pile of rubble,
                    And a thousand fires and columns of thick smoke.
                    We are frightened of what the Russians will do to us.

(*25 April, afternoon. Berlin, the* Führer *bunker, which receives a direct hit from a shell. Bits of concrete fall from the ceiling.*)

Krebs   (*coughing*). Turn off the ventilators, they are sucking
                    In fumes and smoke and dust instead of fresh air.

Loringhoven.   The telephone's not working.

Boldt.   We are cut off.
To the north Steiner attacked and advanced for miles,
But has been forced back.

Hitler   (*tiredly*).   Under Steiner's leadership
The attack was bound to fail.

(*25 April, 10 p.m. Berlin, the* Führer *bunker. The conference room.* WEIDLING *arrives for a conference.* HITLER *with* GOEBBELS, BORMANN, KREBS *and* BURGDORF. *Also* MOHNKE *and* AXMANN. *Weidling shows a map with a ring on it.*)

Weidling.   This is the Soviet ring. We are being forced
Inwards to the centre of Berlin.

Hitler.   Berlin
Must be defended to the end.

Goebbels.   Yes.

Bormann.   Yes.

Hitler.   The East-West road can be a landing strip.
Axmann, five thousand boys on bicycles
Can hold the bridges.

Weidling   (*disgusted*). Yes, *Führer*.

Hitler.   Jodl,
Speed up relief. Steiner must attack south-west.
Busse must link up with Schörner and with Wenck.

(*26 April, evening. Berlin, the* Führer *bunker. The conference room. The daily conference.*)

Krebs.   We had some good news yesterday, the disunity
Between the Americans and Soviets
About the sectors to be occupied.
And now Wenck has launched his attack
And Busse is fighting towards him.

(HITLER *is holding a torn map.*)

Hitler.   And Steiner?

Krebs.   He has not started his attack.

Hitler.   He is useless.

Krebs.   And there is a report that Soviet troops
                Are using the U- and S- Bahn tunnels.

Hitler   (*in a rage*). The tunnels must be flooded immediately.

Krebs.   But *Führer*, our own troops use them, and trains
                Take the sick and wounded to hospitals,
                And thousands of refugees –

Hitler.   Blow up what keeps
                Out the Landwehr canal and flood the tunnels.

Krebs.   It will be a human disaster. A wall of water
                Will pour through the tunnels, many will be killed.

Hitler.   Flood the tunnels. They do not deserve to live.

(*Chorus of* BERLINERS.)

Chorus.   Misery, there is no end to it. We crouched
                In our underground command posts in the stations,
                A cascade of water swept through, people fought
                Round the ladders, many were trampled. The
                Torrent rose a metre, then dropped. Many had drowned.
                There were floating bodies, screams, cries in the dark.
                Where can we shelter if not underground?
                Who has done this to us? Who flooded us?

(*27 April, evening. Berlin, the* Führer *bunker. Hitler's office.* EVA BRAUN *and* HITLER.)

Eva.   You were looking for Hermann.

Hitler.   Fegelein. He

	Cannot be found. Besides being your brother-in-law
	He is Himmler's representative here.

Eva.
                    He has rung me this evening. He said that you
                    Must leave Berlin, and that if you will not,
                    I must leave alone.

Hitler.
                                    What did you reply?

Eva.
                                                        I said
                    He should not antagonise you, and that Gretl
                    Is about to give birth to his child in Bavaria.

Hitler.
                    He has an apartment.

Eva.
                                        Off the Kurfürstendamm.
                    At 10 to 11 Bleibtreustrasse.

(*27 April, later that night. Berlin, the* Führer *bunker. The social room next to the adjutants' room.*
BORMANN, KREBS *and* BURGDORF*, drunk.*)

Burgdorf.
                    I tried to bring the army and party
                    Closer, but my officer friends despise me,
                    And say I am a traitor to the officer code,
                    That my idealism is wrong.

Krebs.
                                        May I remind you,
                    We are with Bormann.

Burgdorf.
                                        The party leaders have sent
                    Hundreds of thousands of young officers
                    To their deaths, not for the Fatherland but for
                    Their own megalomania and high living.
                    You have trampled our ideals in the dirt,
                    Our morality, our souls. Human beings
                    To you are nothing but uses for your power.
                    Our culture goes back hundreds of years.
                    You have destroyed it, and the German people.
                    That is your guilt.

Krebs.
                                        Remember who you are with.

| Bormann. | There's no need to be personal. Others |
| | Have got rich, but not me, I swear. |

| Burgdorf. | What about |
| | Your estates? Your, your.... |

(*He passes out.* BORMANN *laughs and pours himself another drink.*)

(*28 April, 5.30 a.m. Berlin, the* Führer *bunker. Hitler's office. Bombardment in progress.* HITLER *and* BOLDT. BORMANN, KREBS *and* BURGDORF *slumped asleep.*)

| Boldt. | The ventilation system has been off too long. |
| | I have a headache and am short of breath. |

(*A crash brings part of the ceiling down.* HITLER *puts a hand on* BOLDT'*s arm.*)

| Hitler. | What gun was that? Could it penetrate here? |

Boldt.	A hundred and seventy-five millimetre
	Heavy artillery. In my view, it
	Cannot destroy this bunker.

(HITLER *is relieved.*)

There is no telephone.
Reports are brought by runners braving shells.

*(*28 April, 6.30 a.m. Crossroads near Neu Brandenburg.* KEITEL *with* HEINRICI *and* MANTEUFFEL.)

Keitel.	You did not tell me yesterday that Manteuffel's
	Units would retreat, contrary to Hitler's
	Orders, and mine.

Heinrici.	I cannot hold the Oder,
	And I do not intend to sacrifice the lives
	Of my soldiers.

| Manteuffel. | I shall withdraw further |
| | Unless I have reinforcements. |

264

Keitel.	There aren't any.

The *Führer*'s order is you will hold your positions.

Heinrici.	I shall not give that order.

Manteuffel.	My army

Only takes orders from me.

Keitel.	It is outrageous

That you should defy the *Führer*'s orders,
And mine. You will have to bear responsibility
For your defiance before history.

Manteuffel.	The Manteuffels

Have served Prussia for over two hundred years,
And have always accepted responsibility
For their actions.

Keitel	(*to Heinrici*). If you shoot a few thousand men,

There will be no retreat.

Heinrici.	Look, thousands of exhausted men.

Why don't you shoot them. Go on.

Keitel.	From now on

Follow OKW orders.

Heinrici.	How can I follow your orders

When you are out of touch with the situation?

Keitel.	You will hear more of this. (*Exit*.)

(*Manteuffel's* MEN *emerge from behind trees with machine pistols. They had* KEITEL *covered.*)

(*28 April, 7p.m. Berlin, the* Führer *bunker. The conference room.* HITLER *and* KREBS.)

Krebs.	The Russians have appointed a commandant

Of Berlin. Orders by Berzarin have
Appeared in Alexanderplatz. The Russians
Have started raping German women.

(BORMANN *ushers in* LORENZ, *press officer. Enter* GOEBBELS.)

Bormann.   *Führer,*
Something that you should know.

Lorenz.   The BBC
Have reported that Himmler has offered the Allies
An unconditional surrender in
The name of all our troops.

Hitler.   Himmler? *Himmler?*
Can it be? First Göring, and now Himmler?
I always thought him trustworthy and loyal.
Has he gone behind my back on so important
A matter? It is the most shameful betrayal
In history. Bormann, Goebbels, come with me.

(HITLER *takes* BORMANN *and* GOEBBELS *to his conference room, leaving*
KREBS *and* LORENZ *in the ante-room or reception room.*)

Bormann.   *Führer,* we have Himmler's representative,
Fegelein. We found him with his mistress
In his apartment, drunk. He has betrayed
Eva's sister, and his master has betrayed you.

Goebbels.   Bring Fegelein.

(BORMANN *snaps his fingers in the reception room. Enter* FEGELEIN
under guard.)

                     Did you know Himmler would offer
The Allies unconditional surrender?
This gathering is now a court martial.

Fegelein.   No, I swear I didn't.

Bormann   (*wheedling*).   Someone must pay.
For Himmler's treachery.

Hitler.   You are close to him.
You knew.

Fegelein.	No, *Führer*, I implore you, as The husband of Eva's sister.
Hitler.	Shoot him.
Fegelein.	No.
Hitler.	Take him upstairs into the garden And shoot him.
Fegelein.	No, please. I am innocent.

(*He is taken away, protesting his innocence. A shot is heard. Then another.* HITLER *goes out to the sickroom, where* GREIM *sits.*)

Hitler.	Greim, you are to leave for Plön and arrest Himmler. A traitor must not succeed me as *Führer*. You will take letters with you.

SCENE 3.

THE FALL OF HITLER

(*29 April 3.30 a.m. Berlin, the* Führer *bunker. The conference room.* TRAUDL JUNGE, *who has been asleep for an hour, goes to* HITLER *with her secretary's dictation pad.* BURGDORF *is outside.*)

Burgdorf	(*to Junge*). He's been sitting in his private quarters, Not moving, his face quite expressionless. He's thinking about Himmler's betrayal.

(*The table in his study has a white cloth with AH on it.*
Silver dinner service, eight champagne glasses.)

Hitler	(*alone*). I made European civilisation Replace its weak, impure, democratic way With a stronger, purer stance. But Churchill and Montgomery stopped me, calling in two

Outside civilisations like starving wolves –
America and Russia - to feed on
The sides of Europe's dying carcass. Both
Have torn off lumps of flesh: Paris, Warsaw.
Europe will now be weak, and as she bleeds
Her wounds will be impure, perhaps gangrenous.

(*Enter* JUNGE. HITLER *winks at her. He stands at the map table.*)

Hitler.　　　　I will now dictate my last political testament.
More than thirty years have passed since I made
My modest contribution as a volunteer
In the First World War, which was forced upon the *Reich*.
In these three decades, love and loyalty
To my people alone guided me in all my thoughts,
Actions and life. I never wanted war,
But it was forced upon the world by the machinations
Of international Jewry. The sole responsibility
For all the subsequent death and horror, including
The death of many Jews, lies with the Jews themselves.
But now the end has come I have decided
To remain in Berlin. I die with a joyful heart
In the knowledge of the immeasurable deeds
And achievements of our peasants and workers
And of a contribution unique in history
By our youth which bears my name.
I cannot, however, speak admiringly
Of the German officer corps which unlike me,
Has failed to set a shining example
Of faithful devotion to duty, till death.
Two of my most trusted Generals have let me down.
I expel Göring and Himmler from the party
And strip them of all office. They have brought
Irreparable shame on the whole nation
By negotiating with the enemy
Without my knowledge and against my will.
When I am dead, Grand Admiral Dönitz
Will be President of the *Reich*, and Supreme Commander
Of the *Wehrmacht*. Goebbels will be *Reich* Chancellor.
Bormann party Chancellor.

(*He hands* JUNGE *a paper.*)

> Traudl, I have written
> Who will hold the other offices of state.
> I urge my successors to uphold the racial laws
> To the limit and to resist mercilessly
> The poisoner of all nations, international Jewry.
> During the years of conflict, I was unable
> To commit myself to a contract of marriage
> So I have decided the day before the end
> Of my earthly life to take as my wife the young
> Woman who, after many years of faithful friendship,
> Has of her own free will come to the besieged capital
> To link her fate with my own. She will, according
> To her wishes, go to her death as my wife.
> For us, this will take the place of all that was
> Denied us by my devotion to the service
> Of my people. My wife and I choose to die
> To escape the shame of flight or capitulation.
> It is our wish that our bodies be burned at once,
> Here, where I have performed the greater part
> Of my daily work during the twelve years I
> Served my people. That is all. Now type it, please.

(JUNGE *looks at him, rises and goes through to her office and starts typing. Enter* GOEBBELS, *tears running down his cheeks.*)

Goebbels.   (*to Junge*). Hitler has ordered me to leave Berlin
But I don't want to leave the *Führer*. My place
Is here, if he dies my life has no meaning.
He said to me, "Goebbels, I didn't expect
You to refuse to obey my last order."
I want to dictate my own will, which should
Be attached to Hitler's as an appendix.

(*29 April, later. Berlin, the* Führer *bunker. The conference room.* HITLER *and* GOEBBELS.)

Goebbels.   No one in the bunker is legally
Empowered to hold a marriage ceremony.

Hitler.   I must have a legal authority. I have been

Married to Germany. She is not worthy
Of me, she has failed me, and so I have divorced
Her, and by marrying Eva I will demonstrate
That I have rejected Germany for good.

Goebbels.   I know a registrar who is in Berlin.
His name is Wagner.

Hitler.   That is appropriate
We are approaching the *Götterdämmerung*.

Goebbels.   I will send SS men to find Wagner.

(*29 April, later. Berlin, the* Führer *bunker. In the conference room, or map room,* EVA *in a long black silk dress;* HITLER *in uniform;* WAGNER, BORMANN, GOEBBELS; GERDA CHRISTIAN, *now senior secretary;* CONSTANZE MANZIARLY, *Hitler's vegetarian dietician;* KREBS, BURGDORF, AXMANN.)

Wagner.   I shall not ask the usual questions about
Aryan origins and hereditary disease.

Goebbels   (*impatiently*). That's quite all right.

Wagner.   And after the ceremony,
Two witnesses must sign.

Goebbels.   Bormann and me.

Wagner   (*nodding*). Do you, Adolf Hitler, take Eva Braun,
To be your wife?

Hitler.   I do.

Wagner.   Do you, Eva Braun,
Take Adolf Hitler to be your husband?

Eva.   I do.

Wagner.   I have the pleasure to pronounce you at law
Man and wife. Please sign the wedding contract.

(HITLER *and* EVA *sign, followed by* BORMANN *and* GOEBBELS. *Arm in arm, Hitler and Eva go to the refreshment room before the office or study and offer the guests champagne and sandwiches.*)

Eva   (*chatting happily*). It's so good of you to witness our marriage.
I am so honoured to be the *Führer*'s wife,
And so pleased that our long association
Has ended like this, I am so happy my *Führer*.
O look, Bormann has the gramophone.
I am afraid there is only one record, you know it.

(*The gramophone plays 'Red Roses'.*)

I must go outside to greet the others who
Have not been invited to our private party.

(*She appears in the corridor outside, or reception room, and greets* JUNGE, WOLF, SCHRÖDER, BOLDT, LORINGHOVEN *and others who say "Congratulations".*)

(*29 April, 8 a.m. Berlin, the* Führer *bunker. The reception room.* BURGDORF *and* JOHANNMEIER.)

Burgdorf.   You will now undertake a very important
Secret mission. You will take the *Führer*'s
Last will and political testament out of Berlin
And give it to Field Marshal Schörner, who
Is now Commander-in-Chief of the army.
Zander, Bormann's personal assistant, will take
A copy to Dönitz, the new Head of State,
And Lorenz will take a copy to Munich,
Where National Socialism was born.

(29 April, 12 noon. Berlin, the Führer *bunker. The conference room. The bombardment stops. Silence. Conference conducted by* KREBS. BOLDT, LORINGHOVEN, WEISS *and* BORMANN.)

Boldt.   Soviet tanks are heading towards the Wilhelmplatz.
And have stopped five hundred yards from the Chancellery.
Wenck is out of contact at Werder.

Loringhoven.   It

Would make sense if Boldt and I go to Wenck
And brief him direct.

Krebs.   The *Führer* might not like that.

Bormann.   I think it is a good idea.

Burgdorf.   So do I.

Weiss.   I'll go with them.

Krebs.   I'll ask the *Führer*.

(*He goes into* HITLER.)

Führer, three officers
Want to break out of Berlin to brief Wenck about
The situation round the Chancellery.

(HITLER *stares at his map.*)

Hitler.   Who are these officers?

(*The three step forward.*)

How will you leave Berlin?

Loringhoven.   By boat down the Havel, at night.

Hitler.   Yes, that is
The best way. I know where there is a boat
With an electric motor.

Loringhoven.   We can find a boat.

(HITLER *nods, rises and shakes hands with each.*)

Hitler.   Give my regards to Wenck. Tell him to hurry,
Or it will be too late.

(*Outside the door the three men smile.*)

Loringhoven.   We have escaped.

(*29 April, afternoon. Belsen.* MONTGOMERY. HENDERSON *and* ERNIE, *a private.*)

Henderson.   The Chief's upset. He ordered cameramen
                  To record "German bestiality" and he's made
                  The people in the neighbouring villages
                  Parade through the camp so they can see what was done
                  By their own countrymen.

Ernie.   Yesterday we saw
                  Some Canadians so incensed that they took
                  The women guards to the edge of the camp where there
                  Are supple trees, they pulled two down and tied
                  A woman's legs to each and then let go
                  So she flew into the air and was torn apart.
                  They did several. I cocked my Browning, but
                  My commanding officer said, "Don't interfere
                  Or they'll turn on us."

                  (*Enter* MONTGOMERY. ERNIE *withdraws saluting.* HENDERSON *is at
                  hand.*)

Montgomery.   I don't like to see
                  The realities of war, the blood and bone.
                  It upsets me. I avoid seeing wounds.
                  A commander deals in fit soldiers, and this
                  Makes me ashamed to be European.

                  (THREE BELSEN FIGURES *have tottered near him.*)

                  We knew the Final Solution was happening,
                  Ever since D-Day we've hurried the best we can.
                  But this was worse than I ever imagined.
                  If I had had sole command, the war would have
                  Been over last September, and those corpses would be
                  Alive. Their deaths are a German responsibility,
                  Of course, but if Eisenhower, Bradley and SHAEF
                  Had made better decisions, hundreds of thousands
                  Who are now dead would now be fully alive.

(*Exit* HENDERSON. MORE BELSEN FIGURES *gather.*)

(*Aside.*) War is the Devil's game. He inflates egos,
Urges land-grabbing, feeds envy and hate,
Delighting in the ruin that follows,
The destruction and sense of injustice
Smiling at a Paradise on earth destroyed,
At rubble and these puny, thin-armed men
Who resemble walking skeletons in Hell,
More cadaverous skulls with sunken eyes than what
I think of as starving human beings.
The Devil's onslaughts must be repelled, rebuffed
And my skills do this, but my skills, such as they are,
Are of a diabolical order, and for that
I feel self-disgust. The only cleanness
Is in my caravan after nine o'clock,
When I can be pure, and open my self, my heart
And be filled with the health-giving Light of God
And I do not know how it can help you now.
Poor wretch, you tear my heart with your cupped hand.

(*The Belsen men kneel at his feet.*)

(*Aloud.*) Get up.

Belsen man.   Thank you, Montgomery, thank you.

Belsen men.   Montgomery, thank you, Montgomery.

(MONTGOMERY *turns away, his eyes filled with tears.*)

Montgomery   (*aside, moved*). Not a cupped hand, he's blessing me. He wants
Nothing, only to give his thanks – and I,
Six months late, am not worthy of his gratitude.
I would like to embrace him to demonstrate to all
Our common humanity, but a commander can't.
He is isolated from his fellow men
By the barrier of his command and decorum.

(*Re-enter* HENDERSON *holding a jug and a chipped mug. He offers it to*
MONTGOMERY.)

(*Aloud.*) Give each of these men a drink.

(*29 April, later. Berlin, the* Führer *bunker.* HITLER *fondles his* SHEEP DOG.)

Hitler.   Haase, Himmler has given me cyanide capsules.
He is not to be trusted, I want to know
If they work, or if they are to drug me
So he can hand me over to the Bolsheviks, alive.
Take Blondi, with Tornov. In the toilet. Now.

(HITLER *fondles* BLONDI. HAASE *and* TORNOV *take Blondi. Off stage a dog's whimpering is heard. Hitler winces. Haase returns.*)

Haase   (*quietly*). Instantly, my *Führer.*

(*Hitler goes out to look. He returns and encounters* TRAUDL JUNGE *and* GERDA CHRISTIAN.)

Hitler   (*handing them cyanide capsules*). I am sorry to reward your loyalty
And courage with such a parting gift.

(*29 April, 7 p.m. Berlin, the* Führer *bunker.* BAUER, *Hitler's pilot at Hitler's office.*)

Bauer.   My *Führer*, you can still escape. I can
Fly you out. In a Junkers bomber with
A range of six thousand miles. I can fly
You to the Middle East or South America.

Hitler   (*shaking his head*). You have carried Frederick the Great to all
My headquarters, now he is yours. Take him.

Bauer   (*stunned*). Thank you, my *Führer.*

Hitler.   I want my epitaph to be:
"He was the victim of his Generals."

(*29 April, evening. Berlin, the* Führer *bunker. The* conference *room. Hitler's last conference.*)

Burgdorf.   My *Führer*, a report. Mussolini and his mistress –

Hitler.   Dead?

Burgdorf.	Shot by Italian partisans.
Hitler	(*sombre after a silence*). How?
Burgdorf.	He bared his chest and said, "Shoot me here." They were left for dead, then hanged upside down.
Hitler	(*after a silence*). No one will hang Eva or me upside down. Weidling, tell me, what hope can you offer?
Weidling.	Sir, there is no more ammunition, there are No tanks, no Panzerfausts and no repairs, Nothing. Everything must finish tomorrow.

(*A long silence.*)

Hitler	(*tiredly*). Mohnke, what do you think?
Mohnke.	I agree with Weidling.
Hitler.	Krebs.

(HITLER and KREBS *confer.*)

    Troops may attempt to break out, but I
Absolutely forbid the surrender of Berlin.

(*29 April, evening. Berlin, the* Führer *bunker.* HITLER *alone with his Lorenz coding machine.*)

Hitler.	Keitel, where are the advance units of Wenck, Busse and Holste?

(*30 April, 1 a.m.*)

Burgdorf.	Sir, Keitel's reply.
Hitler	(*eagerly*). Yes, go on, go on.
Burgdorf.	Wenck's Twelfth Army cannot attack Berlin, Busse's North Army is encircled, and To the north Holste is on the defensive.

Hitler   (*after a silence*). The end. I shall not be hanged upside down.

(*30 April, 3 a.m. Eva's sitting-room/bedroom.* HITLER *sitting alone on the settee,* EVA *asleep on her bed.*)

Hitler.   In 1940 I offered the British peace
        On generous terms. I ruled from Norway to Spain.
        I still don't understand why the British
        Used up their imperial resources
        By fighting a power that did not threaten them.
        I said in July, only the US and Japan
        Would profit from the end of the British Empire.
        I was depressed when Japan took Singapore.
        As we approached defeat, I became more
        Ruthless, to make our soldiers fight harder.
        Someone sitting watching me now, as if
        I were talking in a doctor's waiting-room,
        Must think I am pitiless, without remorse,
        But Britain made me snarl like a wolf at bay,
        That intransigent Churchill who threw away
        The British Empire to corner me, when I
        Did not want to threaten the British Isles
        For which I, as a German, have a deep respect.
        What did Britain do mostly in the war?
        Killed Italians in North Africa and
        Bombed German civilians. Why? I know why.
        Bankers were behind us all, Churchill, Roosevelt,
        Stalin and me, and wanted our cities destroyed
        So they could lend their billions to rebuild.
        Bankers and Zionists rejected my peace.

Eva   (*stirring*). Adolf, my husband, my lord, my Overlord,
        I love you very much. I adore you.

(HITLER *embraces her.*)

(*30 April, 5 a.m.* HITLER *sitting,* EVA *sleeping.*)

        It is the Feast of Beltane, the thirtieth,
        Walpurgisnacht, when witches meet on the Brocken
        And revel with the Devil, the pagan day

Most suited to favourable reincarnation.
And now I must face my own fate. It was
Not supposed to end like this. Many times
I stood in the Hofburg Treasury and gazed
At the spear of Longinus, which pierced the side of Christ,
And called me to war and to rule the world,
And when I took Vienna, I went there
With Himmler, and held it in my hand, certain
That my destiny was to rule the world;
And to be crowned Kaiser Adolf the First,
Of a Third *Reich* that would last a thousand years;
And to destroy Jehovah by liquidating
The Jewish millions who worship him, so that
The power I serve could fill the vacuum.
It seems only yesterday that Eckart
And I discussed the Final Solution,
How we'd be on the side of divine good
Against the Jewish Satan, the demiurge
Jehovah who is responsible for all
The ills in the world, how we'd be
On the side of a power that opposes
The Jewish Satan and its Christian mask,
And do its work in this impure, tainted world.
My work's incomplete, three million more must die.
But the power that has vitalised my great will
And made me more feared than Napoleon
Is still abroad and still possesses me
And rejoices in universal destruction.
In Vienna I read Nietzsche and Schopenhauer,
And I have tried to bring in the Superman.
My will to power has dominated the will
Of my people and has possessed them all,
And I have left mankind more pure through it.
My power, I know, is a power of darkness, which
Has pierced Christendom and Jewry with its spear.
Lord of Darkness, I am ready for you.

Eva   (*stirring*). Adolf, I love you, adore you, my husband.
Come to bed now, you have shed your burden.
You can be virile now you've put down your cares.
Now you have been released from your bond with

Germany, by the betrayal of your Generals,
You can love me without any sense of betrayal.

(30 April, 3 p.m. Hitler has finished lunching with his secretaries in the bunker's refreshment room.)

Traudl Junge   (*smoking*). Look what Eva has given me. This coat.

Gerda Christian   (*smoking*). Her silver fox coat with four-leaf clover
Entwined with her initials, E.B. It's beautiful.

Günsche.   The *Führer* wants to say goodbye to all his staff.

(JUNGE *and* CHRISTIAN *put down the coat. In the corridor, or reception room, outside the refreshment room* HITLER *walks down the line and murmurs a few inaudible words to each.*
EVA *is with him, her hair done up and in black with pink roses on either side of a square neckline.*)

Eva.   Traudl, try to get out of here, you might
Make it. Give my love to Bavaria.

(HITLER *and* EVA *go through the refreshment room into Hitler's office.* GÜNSCHE *stands outside the door.* HITLER *sits on the left of the settee, picks up his gun and cyanide capsule and stares into space. He speaks more to himself than to Eva, who is more concerned about the practical business of dying.*)

Hitler   (*aside*). And yet, and yet, now that the time has come,
Now that the time has come for me to die,
To release the vapour some call the soul,
What if I find, on the other side, millions
I have put before a wall, waiting to judge me?
I blew up Warsaw – only two houses
Remained standing – and so many places,
And all the extermination camps. Auschwitz-Birkenau,
In one month alone two hundred thousand Jews
From Hungary, one month alone.... The vision I had
In the First World War, of eliminating Jews –
And five out of eight million are now dead,
European Jews, that is, not the world's;

What if Jews too have an immortal *soul*
That comes from a divine web, a *good* whole?
Was I wrong? Will history judge me adversely?
For thirty years, I believed in power over men,
The Thule Society, Ariosophy.
I saw men as unclean souls, to be crushed
So that the world could be cleansed and transformed
For the pure souls who will channel the power.
And now that I must die, I wonder if
When I am the vaporous body in this flesh
I must pay for all I have done on this lower plane.
Why did I not think more about these things
When I heard the applause echo my words
In the Munich beer-cellar, the Hofbrauhaus,
As I first announced the name "National Socialism",
When my mentor Dietrich Eckart urged me
To give myself to the occult for power?
Lord, fill me now with your power. Nothing.

Eva   (*summoning him back to the situation*). Adolf.

Hitler   (*aside*).   I had a vision of a new Europe
               Led by Germany, and in every state free peoples
               Going about their business, living free.
               There had to be a transitional phase –
               Extermination camps and the rule of the gun –
               But at the end, under one Overlord,
               A great *union* of free democratic peoples
               Who are anti-Communist, with a strong centre.
               This may still come to pass, people may come to see
               That even though my racial ideas are
               Repudiated, I brought it into being,
               It came out of my anti-Communist vision.
               Every leader must keep things developing,
               Must have something ahead to aim for, some goal,
               To keep the support of his followers. If
               There is nothing ahead, or a contradiction,
               Then he is lost. My death is necessary
               To release all German soldiers from their oath to me,
               And so that Dönitz can negotiate a peace
               And win the Allies over to oppose the Russians.

By this sacrifice, I will make possible
A German-Allied front against the Bolsheviks.
My sacrifice will turn the war around,
Will save Germany, wrest victory from defeat.
I had a vision and I improvised. Nothing ahead.
Nothing.

Eva   (*holding him*). What are you thinking?

Hitler.   I am remembering
How clean the air is in Berchtesgaden
And you reclining like a beauty queen
On the stone veranda in the sun, knee up,
Your bikini on, the mountains behind you,
Smiling above the green slopes while I loll,
My head on a cushion, and gaze at Paradise,
And there is nothing you could not make me do.
I, the master of the world, am bewitched by you,
I am your obedient and devoted slave.

Eva.   You will do as I say, you will be my slave.
I will bite to commit suttee like an Indian's wife.
Then you will bite and fire. We will be together.

(EVA *embraces* HITLER. *Fade on* HITLER *and* EVA. *Outside* MAGDA
GOEBBELS *rushes down the corridor into the refreshment room and
pushes past* GÜNSCHE *into Hitler's office.*)

Magda.   Please leave Berlin, I don't want my children
To die beside me in this bunker.

Hitler.   No.
Leave us.

Magda   (*weeping*). He will not speak to me.

Günsche.   Too late.

Junge.   Have your children had lunch? No? I will make
Some sandwiches. There's fruit. Cherries.

(*A shot is heard.* GÜNSCHE *waits and enters, arm raised in the Nazi salute.* HITLER *is on the sofa, left, leaning over the arm, his head hung down, blood dripping on the carpet. He has shot himself in the right temple with his 7.65 mm.* EVA *is curled up on the sofa, right, her unused revolver lying on the table next to her pink chiffon scarf.*)

Günsche.   Cyanide.
He shot himself in the mouth to make sure.

Magda   (*picking up a capsule like a tube, to Günsche, of Eva*) Cyanide.

(GÜNSCHE *picks up a knocked-over vase of flowers. He examines* HITLER *and* EVA *quickly.*)

Günsche   (*shouting*).   Orderly, Linge, Bormann.

(BORMANN, GOEBBELS *and* AXMANN *enter, arms raised in the Nazi salute, and view* HITLER.)

Goebbels.   My *Führer* is dead. I want to go out on
Wilhelmplatz and stay there until I am hit.

(GOEBBELS, BORMANN *and* AXMANN *follow as an orderly,* GÜNSCHE, *and Hitler's valet,* HEINZ LINGE, *wrap the bodies in blankets and carry them out.* MAGDA *stands and stares until Günsche returns.*)

Magda.   So. Our world has ended. Well?

Günsche.   We carried them
Up the stairs and out to the park above,
And laid them in a shallow trench. Then Kempka,
Hitler's chauffeur, came with three soldiers,
And sprinkled petrol on them from jerry cans.
Shells were falling round them, some very close.
And they tried to set fire to it, but it would not light.
Kempka made a spill from paper and set it alight
And threw it into the trench, and up it blazed
And black smoke rose above the funeral pyre.
We put out arms in a Nazi salute,
Then ran back inside. It's not safe up there.

Magda.	So died the man who would be Overlord
	Of the whole world, feeling betrayed
	By all he had trusted, doubting Göring and Himmler,
	Save the noble woman who died at his side
	And instead of a State funeral through Berlin
	This Napoleon received a hurried bonfire
	On a patch of waste ground under exploding shells.
	A pitiful end.

(*Fade on* MAGDA. KREBS *and* BURGDORF *have appeared at opposite ends of the bunker.*)

Krebs	(*alone*). He was a chancer. He restored German pride
	After the humiliation of the First World War.
	He took power by fairly constitutional means.
	He did not plan war with Britain and the U.S.,
	It somehow happened as a consequence of what he did.
	His name is terror, under him there was terror
	But at the centre was a fumbling man
	Who lived from event to event, reacting mostly,
	Blaming his Generals for the inadequacy of his plans.
	His name is terror, he was responsible
	For terror on a colossal scale, but
	For all the amphetamine injections there was
	Something indecisive at the heart of his vision.

Burgdorf	(*alone, scathingly*). So ended the life of a man who shamed
	Germany, and its noble Prussian tradition,
	Who dabbled in the occult, mixed weird ideas
	From the drunkard drug addict "poet" Eckart,
	The crazy anti-Semitic Rosenberg
	And the "root race" nonsense of Theosophy,
	And thought his foul butchery was doing good.
	He never grasped that as all are from the One,
	Souls are droplets from the divine thundercloud
	Which veils the radiant often-hidden sun,
	And return to it as raindrops evaporate.
	His racist philosophy conflicts with the One
	And how the universe in practice works,
	And can now be reduced to ashes, like himself.
	I speak from a noble German tradition,

I think all Fascists and racists are to be pitied
For they are separated from the One
And therefore have a false view of the world,
Which they infect with their odious inadequacy.
I despise myself for having joined the army
And been caught up in such a foul episode,
And I am filled with self-disgust that I
Did not join Stauffenberg's plot and rid the earth
Of a creature who was a disgrace to humanity.

(*Chorus of* BERLINERS.)

Chorus.   We have heard the good news. Our trials are over.
                       The dictator is dead, by his own hand,
                       Leaving a ruined Germany, ruined buildings,
                       Smashed plant and services, a heap of rubble.
                       We are overjoyed, the Russians and Allies
                       Will liberate us from all senseless war.
                       The Jews are safe, no more the killing wall.
                       Gone the extermination camp, gas chambers
                       And chimneys. We are free once more.
                       We can come out of our cellars and breathe the air.

(*30 April, 11.30 p.m. Berlin.* CHUIKOV *is finishing supper with music and army guests.*)

Glazunov.   Sir, a German Lieutenant-Colonel Seifert
                       Has crossed the Landwehr Canal suspension bridge
                       With a white flag and news that General Krebs
                       Chief of German Staff, a senior officer,
                       Wants to talk to senior Red Army officers.
                       Sir, he may surrender Berlin to you.

Chuikov   (*calmly*). We are ready to receive the envoys.
                       Cease all firing around the suspension bridge.

(*1 May, 3.50 a.m. Berlin, Chuikov's HQ.* KREBS, DUFVING, *Weidling's Chief of Staff, and* NAI-LANDIS, *a Russian interpreter, with* CHUIKOV *and* KLEBER, *a Jewish German interpreter.*)

Krebs.   I will tell you something secret. You are
                       The first foreigners to know, Hitler has
                       Committed suicide.

Chuikov	(*hiding surprise*). We know. But when?

Krebs	(*handing over documents*). Around 15.30 hours, yesterday.

In his testament he left all his power
To Dönitz, Goebbels and Bormann,
Who has empowered Goebbels to contact Marshal Stalin,
Leader of the Russian troops. I represent
The German Army and now seek peace talks.

Chuikov.   Do these documents relate to Berlin or
To the whole of Germany?

Krebs.   Goebbels has empowered
Me to speak in the name of the whole German army.

Chuikov.   You are here to surrender, or for peace talks,
Not both. Goebbels and you must now lay down
Your arms. I will telephone Zhukov. Wait here.

(*He phones.*)

Krebs   (*to Dufving and Nailandis*). I am buying time, so Bormann and Dönitz
Can open talks with the Allies, who mistrust Stalin.

(*1 May, 4 a.m. Kuntsevo, near Moscow. Stalin's dacha. STALIN in bed takes a call from Zhukov. His telephone system allows him to hear the caller as he lies in bed.*)

Stalin.   Zhukov, I was asleep, it's four o'clock.

Zhukov's voice. The Red Flag is flying over the Reichstag.
We cannot clear Berlin by the May Day parade,
But Hitler is dead. Suicide.

Stalin.   So that's the end
Of the bastard. Too bad we could not take
Him alive! But where is Hitler's body?

Zhukov's voice.   Burnt.

Stalin.   Hmm. You have Krebs, you say, at Chuikov's place.
Relay this to Krebs. Ask him directly now,

Is your mission to achieve a surrender?

Zhukov's voice.   The interpreter will interpret Krebs' reply.

Interpreter.   No, there are other possibilities.
                   Permit us to form a new government
                   In accordance with the *Führer*'s will, and
                   We will decide everything to your advantage.

Stalin   (*angry*). There can be no negotiations, only
                   Unconditional surrender. No talks with Krebs
                   Or any Hitlerites.

(*1 May, 5 a.m. Chuikov's HQ.*)

Chuikov.   General, we are waiting for you to surrender.
                   Unconditionally.

Krebs.   No, we shall then
                   Cease to exist as a legal government.

Chuikov.   You insist on an armistice and want
                   Peace talks, but your troops are surrendering
                   Everywhere. Our men are now advancing.

                   (*He picks up a Russian newspaper.*)

                   Listen. "Himmler offers peace to the Allies."
                   "Göring seeks a separate peace with the West."

Krebs.   I can do nothing more without direct orders
                   From Goebbels.

                   (SOKOLOVSKY *arrives.*)

Sokolovsky   (*after conferring*). I will lay a telephone
                   Line from Chuikov's military HQ
                   To the *Führer* bunker. (*Points to Dufving.*) This officer
                   Will lay it across no-man's-land. I will
                   Speak to Goebbels. Take him to Prinz-Albrechtstrasse,
                   To the *Gestapo* HQ. (*Exit Dufving.*) Comrades, come

For tea and sandwiches.

(KREBS, SOKOLOVSKY *and others follow.*)

(*1 May, 9 a.m. The* Führer *bunker.* DUFVING *arrives after being under fire.* GOEBBELS, BOR-MANN, WEIDLING.)

Dufving.   The Russians are demanding unconditional surrender.

Goebbels.   I shall never, never agree to that.
                   Is it possible still to break out of Berlin?

Dufving.   Only singly and in civilian clothes.

Goebbels.   I will speak to Krebs.

(*A few hours later.*)

Krebs' voice.   I have been talking to Chuikov, the Russians
                       Are demanding unconditional surrender.

Goebbels.   The *Führer* forbade capitulation.

Bormann.   We must reject it.

Weidling.   But the *Führer* is dead.

Goebbels.   The *Führer* insisted we continue the struggle
                   To the end. I don't want to surrender.

Weidling.   It is too late now for further resistance.
                   Are you coming with me, Krebs?

Krebs' voice.   I shall stay
                   Till the end, then put a bullet through my brain.

(*1 May, 6.15 p.m.* MAGDA GOEBBELS *has got five of her six children into bed.* HEIDI *is the youngest.*)

Heidi.   They are all in bed, mama. I have a sore throat.

| Magda. | I will put a scarf round your throat. There, there.
And now I will brush all my darlings' hair
And give you a chocolate, for you are going
To Berchtesgaden, with Uncle Adolf.
And you will not be air sick if you have your chocolate.
(*Aside.*) A sleeping potion and then a capsule
Of poison, a gentle and painless death.
Finodin to make them drowsy, then cyanide. |

| Heidi. | (*seeing Sgt. Misch, laughing*). Misch, Misch, you are a fish! |

(MAGDA *goes into the bedroom. Silence from the room, then sounds of a struggle.*)

| Magda's voice. | Your chocolate. |

| Helga's voice. | No, no, no. |

| Magda's voice. | Helga, have your chocolate. |

(MAGDA *comes out and sits in Goebbels' study and plays solitaire. She is pale and smokes. Fade.*)

(*1 May, 7.15 p.m. Light on* GOEBBELS *and* MAGDA *sitting in the conference room with others. Enter* ARTUR AXMANN.)

| Axmann. | I have come to say goodbye. |

| Goebbels. | We had good times
In Wedding, fighting in the streets, punching
Communists and socialists, converting workers
To National Socialism. I remember our *Führer*
Speaking in a Munich beer-cellar one
August, on how the enemy was the Jews. |

(*1 May, 8.15 p.m.* GOEBBELS *and the* SS GUARDS, *who include Sgt.* MISCH.)

| Misch. | Up there is yellow dust and smoke, yet it
Is better than down here. *Reich* Chancellor,
How long must I operate the switchboard?
I would like to be away before the Red Army come. |

Goebbels.	Try and break out to the west with Rauch's men.

(*Pause.*)

(*Aside.*) I am sick at heart. My darlings all dead.
And she, a Medea, without asking me.
And yet, it was my intention all along
That it should be this way, so I should be relieved.

(*Pause.*)

(*To the guard.*) My wife and I will commit suicide
The same way as the *Führer*, with cyanide
And my Walther P-38 revolver,
But out in the garden, in the open air.
Not down here in this airless bunker. You
Will not have to carry our bodies upstairs.

(GOEBBELS *puts on his hat, scarf, uniform greatcoat and kid gloves, and offers his arm to* HIS WIFE. *Arm in arm they mount the stairs, watched by* BORMANN. *Fade. Two shots are heard. Light on* KREBS *as* BORMANN *returns.*)

Krebs.	Well?

Bormann	Outside they stood together. Magda

Bit her capsule and slumped to the ground.
Goebbels shot her in the back of her head
As she knelt, then fell on the pitted earth.
Then he bit his capsule and put his gun
To his temple and fired. The SS guards
Have sprinkled petrol on their bodies. They
Are now on fire.

(BORMANN, WEIDLING, *others make haste to leave.* JUNGE *appears*)

Junge.	Gerda and I will reach

Wenck's troops with Günsche and Mohnke. Will you come?

Krebs.	No, I will shoot myself with Burgdorf and Schädle.

Bormann.   I shall vanish, no one will know if I
Am alive or dead.
(*Aside*.)   But I have planned my escape
And have a fortune on the plane that will
Fly me out.

SCENE 4.

UNCONDITIONAL SURRENDER

(*1 May, 10.20 p.m.* CHUIKOV *tries to sleep with a blanket over his head. Distant noise of merriment. An officer, Lt. Col.* MATUSOV,*enters.*)

Matusov.   Sir, a message received by 79th Guards division
In Russian language.

Chuikov   (*sitting up*). What are they doing up there?

Matusov.   Roasting an ox,
And dancing, the poet Dolmatovsky
Is reciting patriotic verse.

Chuikov   (*scoffing*).   Dolmatovsky!
Poets meddle in wars and use their horrors
To scan their lines as Homer did. But how
Did poets change the world? It is Generals who
Change it by smashing armies.

Matusov.   Poems outlast
Empires, and poets understand their Age
And fix it in the pattern of history
And the universe, and make the world aware
For all time, in all places, universally
Of the horrors of wars, so men think twice
Before starting what we've finished.

Chuikov.   Pah! There are
Always wars.

Matusov	(*sadly*). The world does not listen to poets,
	And resists being changed. Sir, the message.
	(*Handing it over.*) German envoys are on their way to
	Potsdamer Bridge.

| Chuikov. | Ceasefire around Potsdamer Bridge. |

(*2 May, 12.50 a.m. A cellar. KISELYOV is waiting to attack.*)

| Kiselyov | (*shouting into the darkness*). Who is asking for a Soviet officer? |

Voice.	Truce envoys. We have a statement of the
	Berlin garrison commander, addressed to
	Marshal Zhukov.

| Kiselyov. | Come over with your hands up. |

(*Germans appear under a white truce flag, holding a brown folder, with a Hitler Youth boy in a steel helmet. ABYZOV covers them with submachine guns. KISELYOV takes out two papers.*)

| German. | One is in German, the other is in Russian. |

| Kiselyov. | The light is too dim. |

(*He hands the Russian text to his comrade.*)

Abyzov	(*reading, choking with emotion*). The German command
	Is prepared to negotiate an immediate
	Ceasefire. Weidling.

(*Silence. KISELYOV puts the papers back in the folder. A Young Communist League organiser arrives.*)

| Kiselyov. | Take the envoys at once |
| | To Potsdamer Bridge. |

(*They leave.*)

| Abyzov. | I can smell lilacs. |

(2 May, 5.50 a.m. CHUIKOV *is still trying to sleep.)*

Matusov.   There has been a call from Dr. Goebbels.

(CHUIKOV *jumps up and splashes his face with cold water.* THREE
DELEGATES *appear, one with a pink folder.)*

Heinersdorf.   I am Senior Executive Officer Heinersdorf
                  Of the Ministry of Propaganda.
                  This letter is from the Director, Dr. Frische.

Chuikov   *(reading).* "Former *Reichsmarschall* Göring cannot be reached.
                  Dr. Goebbels is no longer alive.
                  As one of the few remaining alive, I request
                  You to take Berlin under your protection."

                  (The phone rings.)

                  Yes, yes, I see. Weidling has just surrendered
                  In person. Berlin has fallen to the forces
                  Of Marshal Zhukov. Our war is over!

(3 May, 8 a.m. Luneburg Heath, Montgomery's last TAC HQ. Flagpole without a flag.
MONTGOMERY *and* HENDERSON *before breakfast.)*

Montgomery   *(with satisfaction).* We beat the Russians to Lübeck by twelve hours
                  And sealed off the Schleswig peninsula and Denmark.
                  I was just thinking, TAC HQ has done well
                  As the nerve centre of four Allied armies
                  In Normandy, and then three, and now two.
                  Yet we've doubled in size: from twenty-seven
                  Officers to fifty, from a hundred and fifty
                  Other ranks to six hundred, and two hundred
                  Vehicles. We're not so much gypsy nomads now
                  As an army within an army.

                  (Enter DAWNAY.)

Dawnay.   A phone call
                  From Colonel Murphy, Dempsey's Intelligence Officer.
                  He's received four German officers who wish

292

To negotiate surrender terms.

Montgomery.   Tell Dempsey to send
Them here, then report back.

(*Exit* DAWNAY. MONTGOMERY *pushes a buzzer in his caravan.*)

(*Aside.*)   If they come to seek
Unconditional surrender, they must be made
To believe in my personal authority
And command, and my determination
To fight the war relentlessly to the end
Unless they obey me. I must be on a pedestal.
They must see me as the Montgomery who
Took on Rommel in the Egyptian sands
Near the pyramids that marked the limit of
Napoleon's power, and fought him to Tripoli,
Invaded Sicily and southern Italy,
Threatening Rome, and then, as Overlord,
Swept through Normandy, France, Belgium, Holland
And Germany, to the Baltic and the Elbe
Without losing a battle. I must be
The invincible Montgomery they fear,
A man as awesome as Napoleon.
I must be Overlord.

(*Enter* TRUMBELL WARREN *with* DAWNAY.)

                          Four German officers
Are coming and may have power to surrender.
I want you to get the Union Jack up,
And when they arrive, line them up under it, facing
The office caravan. Get everyone else
Out of sight, get your side arms and stand at ease
To the side about here and don't move till I say.
Get Colonel Ewart and his interpreter.

(DAWNAY *and* WARREN *raise the Union flag, and, with rifles, escort in*
FOUR GERMAN OFFICERS, *two from the Navy in long black leather*
greatcoats, and two from the Army in grey greatcoats, one - a General - with
red lapels. From right to left: General Admiral VON FRIEDEBURG,

Commander-in-Chief of the Fleet; Gen. KINZEL, Chief of Staff of the German Army, North, who is in his late forties, 6 foot 5 inches and wears a monocle; Rear Admiral WAGNER, Flag Officer to the Admiral of the Fleet; Major FRIEDL, Gestapo, 6 foot 2 inches, 28, with a very cruel face. They represent Dönitz and Keitel. They wait a long time facing closed doors of the three caravans. They are uncomfortably hot in their greatcoats. The door of the centre caravan opens and MONTGOMERY appears, dressed in battledress and black beret. The four Germans immediately salute, Friedl keeping his arm down until Montgomery has finished his salute, which takes a long time. Friedl is then nonchalant and casual.)

Montgomery   *(bellowing austerely)*. Who are you?

Friedeburg.   General Admiral von Friedeburg, Commander-in-Chief the German Navy, sir.

Montgomery.   I have never heard of you. Who are you?

Kinzel.   General Kinzel, Chief of Staff of the German Army, North, sir.

Montgomery.   Who are you?

Wagner.   Rear Admiral Wagner, Flag Officer to the Admiral of the Fleet, sir.

Montgomery.   Who are you?

Friedl.   Major Friedl.

Montgomery.   Major? How dare you bring A major into my Headquarters.

Warren   *(whispering)*.   The Chief's putting on A pretty good act.

Dawnay.   He's rehearsed this all his life.

Montgomery   *(barking)*. What do you want?

Friedeburg.	We have come from Field Marshal Busch,
	Commander-in-Chief, North, to offer the surrender
	Of the three German armies facing the Russians
	In Mecklenburg, withdrawing between Rostock
	And Berlin.

(COL. EWART *interprets Montgomery's words into German.*)

Montgomery.	Certainly not. The armies concerned
	Are fighting the Russians. If they surrender
	To anybody, it must be to the Russians.
	Nothing to do with me. But I will naturally
	Take prisoner all German soldiers who come
	Into my area with their hands up.
	I demand that you and Field Marshal Busch
	Surrender to me all German forces on
	My western and northern flanks, from Holland to
	Denmark.

Friedeburg.	We refuse to agree as we are anxious
	About the civil population there.
	We wish to reach an agreement to look after it.
	Then we can withdraw our forces as you advance.

Montgomery.	You talk about your concern for civilian life.
	Six years ago you bombed Coventry and
	Wiped out women, children, old men. Your women
	And children get no sympathy from me,
	You should have thought of them six years ago
	Before you Nazis blitzkrieged England. You
	Have mistreated your own civilians appallingly.
	Near here in Belsen there are Germans like skeletons.
	You caused their suffering. There are concentration camps
	All over Germany, you have systematically
	Killed millions of Jews who were civilians.
	Don't talk to me about your Nazi concern
	For your German civil population.
	I reject any agreement regarding civilians.
	Unless you surrender unconditionally
	Now, I will order the fighting and the bombing
	To continue, and German civilians will die.

(MONTGOMERY *turns his back on them. The Germans salute. Montgomery goes to* DAWNAY.)

Montgomery. They need to reflect on what I've said. Put on
The best possible lunch in the Visitors' Mess
And supply all the drink they want.

(*Later. "A" Mess dining-marquee. Two mess tables together. Army blankets over tables. Two maps. The four Germans are led in by* DAWNAY *and* WARREN. *They sit on four chairs at the end of the table while Dawnay and Warren sit on either side.* MONTGOMERY *comes in and sits at the other end of the table, wearing his Field Marshal's tunic. Col.* EWART *interprets.*)

Montgomery (*abruptly, quietly*). First. You must surrender all forces to me
Unconditionally. Second. When I have these
I'll discuss with you the best way of occupying
The area and dealing with civilians.
Third. If you refuse to agree I will go on
Fighting, and a great many soldiers and civilians
Will be killed. This map shows the western front.
Your front line is marked in blue, ours in red.
We have tremendous strength pouring into Germany
On the ground, and sufficient aircraft to have
Ten thousand bombers in the air, day and night.

(*The Germans study the maps.*)

(*Aside.*) The strength is untrue, we have no more troops
Or bombers, but they have believed me. They
Have no idea of the front lines. One look
At the maps, and they are giving in.

Friedeburg.   We have no power
To agree with your demands. We came about
The civilians. I am prepared to recommend
To Dönitz and to Field Marshal Keitel,
The Chief of Staff at OKW, that they
Offer you unconditional surrender in the north
To save further loss of life. I will go
To them now with Friedl, and return in forty-eight hours.

Montgomery. Twenty-four, and there will be day-and-night

Allied bombing if there is no surrender.
And ask Keitel about the surrender of
Other areas, for example Norway.
I can send you on to SHAEF. I will draw up
An account of this meeting which you will sign
And take a copy to Keitel.

(4 May. Mürwik, near Flensburg. The conference room in the Cadet School. DÖNITZ *and* VON
FRIEDEBURG.)

Dönitz.   Now that Hitler is dead, the last obstacle
                 Has been removed for an Allied-German alliance
                 Against the Soviet Union. The Allies may
                 Now regard Germany as a bulwark against
                 Communism in Europe and may choose
                 A new policy of an East-West split,
                 Which will also split the Alliance. Truman's terms are
                 Unconditional surrender of all German armies
                 To the Big Three. Eisenhower and Churchill
                 Support this. They say they will not accept
                 A general surrender in the West
                 Only. While we pursue an Allied-German
                 Alliance, our policy should be piecemeal
                 Surrender to the Western Allies, to SHAEF,
                 While fighting on in the East, and resisting
                 Capture by the Red Army, which is to be feared;
                 And delaying surrenders as long as possible
                 So our troops in the East can escape to the West.
                 You have done well with Montgomery. Delay
                 Him this afternoon, and then go to SHAEF,
                 To Eisenhower, and seek to surrender
                 The remaining German forces in the West.

(4 May, 5p.m. Luneburg Heath. MONTGOMERY *in his caravan.)*

Montgomery.   Warlords expand into their neighbours' land
                 As pain expands into a healthy limb,
                 Sending waves of troops like bacteria.
                 They unify their civilisations through hurt,
                 Or defend them against a spreading sore

Like inoculations that control disease.
Warlords are aggressors or defenders,
Attackers of civilisations or preservers
Like germs or antibodies which cause pain
Or bring relief. I cauterised the wound,
I acted to preserve the whole body.
Civilisation swells into barbarism
As a healthy body erupts into a boil
That infects the circulation of the blood
And turns septic with putrefying matter,
The squeezing out of which restores its health
So the limb can move as freely as before.
Is not all mankind one body with many limbs?
Warlords, stern men whose authority controls
Front lines on wall-maps without pity, and moves
Armies and orders thousands to their death,
Embody their nation's ego in their own,
Harangue the people forward to their whim
Or just defence. The worst poison the whole
Until they are lanced by the best. I, a jousting
Knight and preserver, have pierced the German boil
And now squeeze out the puss that oozes from
The inflamed mound, plaster it back to health,
Immunise the diseased flesh so it's free from germs.

(*Enter the four Germans with a fifth,* COL. POLLOK. *Escorted,* VON
FRIEDEBURG *climbs the steps and enters the caravan.*)

Montgomery.   Will you sign the full surrender terms as
I demanded?

Friedeburg.   Yes.

Montgomery.   In that case, come with me.

(*They go into a newly erected surrender tent where there are* ALLIED
PHOTOGRAPHERS, SOLDIERS *and war* CORRESPONDENTS, *all very
excited. A trestle table covered with an army blanket, an inkpot and army
pen. Two BBC microphones. The* GERMAN DELEGATION *salute*
MONTGOMERY, *who salutes back.*)

I shall now read the *Instrument of Surrender*.

(*He puts on tortoiseshell-rimmed reading spectacles.*)

"The German Command agrees to the surrender
Of all German armed forces in Holland,
In Northwest Germany including the
Frisian Islands and Heligoland, and all
Other islands, in Schleswig-Holstein, and
In Denmark, to the C-in-C 21 Army Group."
Unless the German delegation sign
The document in front of me, I will order
Hostilities to resume at once.

(*Col.* EWART *translates. The German delegates nod.*)

(*Rising.*) The German officers will sign in order
Of seniority.

(VON FRIEDEBURG, KINZEL, WAGNER, *then* POLLOK *sign.*)

And Major Friedl
Will sign last. (*Pause.*) Now I will sign on behalf of
The Supreme Allied Commander, General
Eisenhower. That concludes the surrender.
(*Aside.*) The war is over, and they surrendered to me.
I have appeared a ruthless commander
Who will not be disobeyed. I took a million
Prisoners in April, making three million since D-Day,
And I have just saved two million civilians in
Schleswig-Holstein from starvation, while Bradley,
In Wiesbaden, has said we may be fighting
A year from now. I have just saved millions
From suffering and have ended the war
And I bluffed to further your will, O Lord.

(*5 May, later. Reims, SHAEF's HQ.* BEDELL SMITH, STRONG *who interprets, and* VON FRIEDEBURG.)

Bedell Smith.   General Eisenhower insists that there must be
A general surrender on eastern

And western fronts simultaneously.
General Eisenhower will not see any
German officers until the document
Of unconditional surrender has been signed.
No bargaining, sign it now.

Friedeburg.   I have no power
To sign.

Bedell Smith.   I insist. Look at these maps. The might
Of the AEF makes your position hopeless.

Friedeburg.   I will cable Dönitz.

(*6 May, evening. Reims. JODL, a Prussian with a monocle, is with* SMITH *and* STRONG.)

Jodl.   General Jodl, the German Chief of Staff.

Bedell Smith.   We've been waiting for von Friedeburg for two days.

Jodl.   Admiral Dönitz did not give von Friedeburg.
Permission to sign. He is willing to surrender
To the Allies, but not to the Red Army.
He will order a ceasefire on the western front
No matter what SHAEF do about the surrender.

Bedell Smith.   The surrender has to be a general one
To all the Allies.

Jodl.   I'll need forty-eight hours
To get the instructions to outlying units.

Bedell Smith.   That's impossible. I'll ask General Eisenhower.

(*He knocks and goes into Eisenhower's room next door.*)

Eisenhower.   I heard it. I think he's trying to gain time
So Germans can escape across the Elbe
From the Russians. Tell Jodl I'll break off
All negotiations and seal the western front,
Preventing any westward movement by

German soldiers and civilians, unless he signs.
But I can grant a forty-eight hour delay
Before announcing the surrender, as he requests.

(SMITH *returns to* JODL *who is with* STRONG.)

(*7 May, 1 a.m. Mürwick, near Flensburg. The conference room.* DÖNITZ.)

Dönitz   (*angrily*). Eisenhower's demands are sheer extortion.
I will have to accept them, and at least
Many troops can escape from the Russians
During the forty-eight hour delay. Cable
Jodl: "Full power to sign in accordance
With conditions."

(*7 May, 2.41 a.m. Reims, SHAEF. Eisenhower's office.* STRONG *enters with* JODL, VON
FRIEDEBURG *and an* AIDE. EISENHOWER *sits behind his desk, Jodl bows and then stands
to attention.*)

Strong.   All the signatures are here. Jodl, Friedeburg.

Eisenhower.   Do you understand the terms? Are you ready to
Execute them?

Jodl.   Yes.

Eisenhower.   If the terms are violated
You will be held personally responsible.

(JODL *bows and leaves with* VON FRIEDEBURG *and the* AIDE.)

I'm dead beat.

(*He rises and goes outside.* PHOTOGRAPHERS *appear. Newsreel
camera.*)

(*Later.*)

Eisenhower.   Message to the CCS. "The mission of
This Allied force was fulfilled at 02.41
May 7 1945."

(*Champagne is opened.*)

I haven't been
To sleep for three days. The war's ended.

(*Everyone cheers and shouts "Hurrah".*)

(*7 May, 8 a.m. Luneburg Heath, TAC HQ. DAWNAY to* MONTGOMERY.)

Dawnay.   The surrender to Eisenhower has been signed at Reims.
The Russian one will be signed in Berlin
Tomorrow by Jodl and Keitel.

Montgomery.   Not before time.
If Eisenhower had seen the emissaries,
And not left Bedell Smith to negotiate
While he waited in the next room, three days
Would not have slipped by, allowing German units
Facing the Russians to escape westwards.
True to the end in his incompetence.

SCENE 5.

VICTORY IN EUROPE

(*8 May, V.E. Day. Chorus of* LONDONERS.)

Chorus.   Victory in Europe Day. Huge crowds in New
York, where ticker-tape and confetti snowed
Through the air; in Paris, where citizens cheered
From their balconies as Allied planes flew past;
And in Moscow where crowds hoisted Russian soldiers
High above their heads. And here in London,
Standing, leaning from windows, hanging from lampposts,
Crowds filled the streets waiting for the expected news,
Silent as the official announcement came.
In London we heard Churchill speak at three:
"The German war is therefore at an end."

There was a gasp as he spoke of "the evil-doers
Who are now prostrate before us".
The war against Japan has yet to be won
But Japan is far away, the threat is over,
No more will V-ls and V-2s rain down
From the skies, bringing death and destruction to our cities.
We heard the words, he ended "Advance Britannia,
Long live the cause of freedom. God save the King."
We cheered with relief and hope of renewal.
We massed in front of Buckingham Palace and sang
"We want the King" and he came out with the Queen
And his two daughters and we waved and sang
"For he's a jolly good fellow", and they waved back.
Churchill came out with the King and Queen;
The King, bare-headed in naval uniform,
Churchill in a civilian, parliamentary suit.
We cheered and waved, and crushed into Whitehall
And Churchill came out on the balcony
Of the Ministry of Health and we all sang
"Land of Hope and Glory", he too. Then he spoke.
"This is your victory," he told us. "No, it's yours,"
We roared back. He said, "In all our long history,
We have never seen a greater day than this."
He gave the V-sign, and that night we danced
In the streets and drank and embraced strangers,
London was floodlit, searchlight beams played
In the sky, ships' sirens sounded from the Thames,
There were bonfires, fireworks, and we drank and laughed,
We revelled and sang and danced and cheered till late,
We were joyful, for danger had passed, we had
Survived the Blitz and the flying rocket bombs.
Europe was free from Nazi tyranny,
There was a great hope, a new world had been born!

(5 June. Berlin. EISENHOWER, ZHUKOV, DE TASSIGNY and MONTGOMERY at the riverside
club which is the Soviet delegation's HQ.)

Eisenhower.   I'm worried about Churchill. In his first election
               Broadcast he said a Labour government
               "Would have to fall back on some form of Gestapo
               No doubt very humanely directed

In the first place." He's said Socialism is
"Interwoven with Totalitarianism
And the abject worship of the State".
He's presenting Labour – Attlee – as Nazi.

Montgomery   (*shrugging*). He's overexcitable and larger than life,
                    He must have been carried away when he said it.

                    (EISENHOWER *turns to* ZHUKOV.)

                    (*Aside*). Here I am in Berlin to divide it into four zones,
                    And to divide Germany into four zones too,
                    And I, a soldier, will command the British
                    Sector of Berlin and of occupied Germany,
                    Military Governor of a quarter of each.
                    If I'd got here in November, Yalta
                    Would not have happened, I would have dictated zones,
                    I would have told the Russians where they stopped.
                    Instead the Soviet army controls Poland.
                    My TAC family's broken up. Sweeney
                    And Ewart dead like Poston, Warren in the law,
                    Dawnay and Henderson in the City,
                    Williams a don, BonDurant US Army.
                    Many of us have been together since Alamein.
                    I shall live alone at Ostenwalde and rule
                    Sectors of Germany, like a Viceroy,
                    Without any sense of revenge at all
                    And now that the war is over, sink into
                    Lassitude, boredom, disillusionment.
                    I have little interest in the occupation.
                    I am a man of action and contemplation,
                    Not a man of administration and red tape.

(*21 July. Berlin, Charlottenburger Chausee. Victory parade, the British saluting base.*
CHURCHILL *and* MONTGOMERY *beside* ALEXANDER, EDEN, ATTLEE.)

Churchill.   You must have felt strange, acting for the King
                    And investing Zhukov and Rokossovsky
                    With the Order of the Bath under the Brandenburg Gate
                    For conquering Berlin.

Montgomery.   The Berliners cheered.

Churchill.   The day after I arrived and you greeted me
                  I visited the ruins of Hitler's
                  Chancellery, went down into the bunker
                  With Eden and Sarah, saw the settee,
                  And when I came out a crowd of Germans gathered
                  And they all began to cheer, except for one old man
                  Who shook his head. Berliners regard us as
                  Their liberators. My hate died with the surrender.
                  The next day at Potsdam I lunched with Truman
                  And Stimson put a piece of paper in front
                  Of me saying "Babies satisfactorily born".
                  I didn't know what he meant. He explained:
                  The test in the American desert has worked.
                  The atomic bomb is a reality.
                  Next day I told Truman I wanted to continue
                  The reciprocal relationship between
                  Britain and the US. The reply came back,
                  Eventually, that the US Chiefs of Staff
                  Will be willing to consult with their British
                  Opposite numbers, but in the event of
                  Disagreement the final decision
                  On the action to be taken will lie with
                  The US Chiefs of Staff. And Britain will
                  Have to accept American strategic
                  Direction in the war against Japan.
                  We're in a new era, Monty. The US
                  Is a superpower above the rest. Stalin
                  Doesn't know yet. I had dinner with Stalin,
                  He was very friendly, told me I would have
                  A majority of eighty. He assured
                  Me he is "against Sovietisation" of
                  The eastern European countries, which "will have
                  Free elections". The question is, is he lying?
                  And if so will the atomic bomb make him back down?
                  Oh look, here comes the Victory parade.

(24 July. Potsdam, the Cecilienhof Castle. End of plenary session of the Potsdam conference. Round table. TRUMAN, STALIN and CHURCHILL.)

Churchill.   Mr President, we British went to war
                          To stop Hitler from having the atomic
                          Bomb before anyone else and using it
                          To wipe out every Jew, till none were left.
                          Two German scientists got the formula,
                          Niels Bohr confirmed the equations with Einstein.
                          Admiral Canaris confirmed it all to us.
                          If Hitler had got nuclear weapons first,
                          He would have ruled the world. Roosevelt and I
                          Rebuffed Bohr when he tried to persuade us
                          To hand nuclear knowledge to Stalin.
                          Is it really wise to tell him now he rules
                          Eastern Europe?

Truman.   But Stalin has to know.
                          In view of what we propose to do in Japan.
                          I must tell him, I'm going to tell him now
                          In a way he will not wholly understand.

                          (TRUMAN and STALIN talk.)

Churchill   (to Eden). Can you see what Stalin's saying? "A new bomb?
                          Of extraordinary power? Probably decisive
                          On the whole Japanese war. What a bit of luck!"
                          Now Stalin knows about the atomic bomb,
                          As he had to, he will want one for himself.
                          I have an ominous feeling that we
                          Are facing a new order that is insecure,
                          That we'll need to strengthen the United Nations
                          In the coming post-war world.

(27 July. Downing Street. BROOKE and Capt. PIM.)

Pim.   Outwardly he's taken it on the chin
                          Without flinching. I brought him the early returns
                          Yesterday morning, the loss of ten seats.
                          He was in his bath. He appeared surprised, asked me
                          To get him a towel. He spent all day in his
                          Blue siren suit in the Map Room, when it was clear
                          There would be a Labour landslide. After all
                          He's done for them.

(PIM *shakes his head in disbelief*).

Brooke.   He has been wrongly advised.
He said that Labour would need "a *Gestapo*"
To rule, a comment so obviously untrue
It suggested to the electorate
He is out of touch.

(*Enter* CHURCHILL.)

Churchill.   I'm saying goodbye to my
Chiefs of Staff. We've been through a lot, you and I.
We came through, to be shot down not by Hitler
But by the British people.

Brooke.   I'm so dreadfully –

(*He chokes back tears and cannot speak.*)

Churchill.   They are perfectly entitled to vote as they please.
This is democracy, this is what we've been fighting for.
Attlee's flown to Potsdam this morning. He asked
If I'd continue there as he's inexperienced,
But I said No, the British people want you,
You go and deal with Stalin on their behalf
And make sure he keeps his word and holds elections
In Poland and the Eastern European countries.
You and Stalin are both socialists, you go
And sort out Russia's misinterpretation
Of the Yalta decisions. The Potsdam meeting
Grew out of what I told Truman on May the twelfth,
That an iron curtain is drawn on the Russian front
From Lübeck to Trieste, including Poland,
And we don't know what is going on behind it.
Still, it's not my problem now. But it grieves me,
Because of Roosevelt's illness and death, and now this
Popular hankering for a form of social reform
We can't afford in our post-war bankruptcy,
Two inexperienced men who were not at Yalta,
Truman and Attlee, will give Stalin what he wants,
He will get away with a military empire.

The Victory in Europe was a partial victory.
In eastern Europe we've all been defeated.
What galls me most is, I have been denied
The power to shape the future of the post-war world.
It's like Monty. You give them victory and
They demote you. They are as fickle as
A woman with several lovers. In May
They shout "It's *your* victory", in July you're out,
They depose you.

(BROOKE *places a reassuring hand on his shoulder.* PIM *and*
BROOKE *leave.*)

(*Slumping, alone.*) Hitler offered me peace, I rejected it.
I was not chosen to follow Chamberlain's line.
We went to war to stop Hitler's research
So he would not explode an atomic bomb over London.
Two German scientists had discovered
Uranium fission in Berlin in
December thirty-eight. Hahn and Strassmann.
Frisch and Meitner confirmed it that February,
When Bohr isolated isotope 235
Before he and Fermi went to Washington.
On August 2nd Einstein wrote to
Roosevelt about the military implications
Of atomic energy, and the same day
Roosevelt appointed a three-man Advisory
Committee on Uranium, and though U.S.
Atomic weapons development did not begin
Until October forty-one, that is when
We knew we had to fight Hitler, for he
Could threaten London with an atomic bomb
If Heisenberg were to build it fast enough,
And all Jews in the world could be put in
One territory and wiped out in a flash.
The high curve of my Prime Ministership
Was to stand alone against the evil might
Of the barbarous Nazis. I advanced the stature
Of my nation by measuring it against a giant,
I took it on and beat it before an admiring
World. Like Bismarck. I showed that the British Empire

Was the main great power and could not be challenged
By a German rule that threatened her interests.
I acted to perpetuate the strength
Of the British Empire, I drew on our reserves,
Confident that we would get them back by
Advancing our position, securing goodwill
Contracts and trade. Instead, our American allies
Ensured that Stalin took our position;
An ungrateful nation replaced me with socialism,
Which will not cash in the goodwill, and will
Bankrupt us; and now, looking back I wonder,
Should I have staked our empire when I could
Have reached an accommodation with Hitler
As Chamberlain tried? I sometimes think politics
Is persuading people to believe fantasies,
And that politicians are convincing preachers
Of dreams the public would like to believe.

(*Silence.*)

Now that I am in the wilderness again
I ponder that had I remained Prime Minister
I would have persuaded the Americans to use
Their new power, which is drawn from victory and
The atomic bomb, to confront Stalin,
To make him behave decently in Europe;
And I cannot help wondering, Truman has been weak
Towards Stalin, was this deliberate,
Has Marshall an understanding with him,
Is that why Eisenhower sent Stalin that cable?
I am better placed to judge than most,
And I see the hand of Zionism in the war.
At Yalta Roosevelt told Stalin he was a Zionist
And Stalin said he was one "in principle".
The Jews will have a new state in Palestine
For which I spoke in 1939,
In accordance with the Balfour Declaration
Which was made in exchange for Rothschild's guarantee
He'd bring America into the First World War
On the British side and save us from defeat.
So America entered the First World War

In return for Balfour's promise to a Rothschild
That there would be a homeland for the Jews
In the British mandate of Palestine,
And now the German Jewish Rothschild family
Have seen the Nazis fall and will have their state,
And if I were suspicious I might think
That Hitler was lured into war with Zionist money
Through House, Baruch, Schacht, Wall Street and I. G. Farben,
Vast sums that reached the Nazis through Warburg banks
So that Nazis could massacre Jews and swing
International opinion behind this new state.
But I cannot be suspicious. That way madness lies.
That way history is not what it seems, and leaders
Who appear to do their best for their nations
In fact work to another agenda, luring
The unsuspecting into catastrophic wars
That suit their own interests that remain hidden
From view. And what the history books describe
Is wrong, for history is what a cabal intrigued.
I do not want to believe that, I prefer
The view that leaders do their best for their peoples
Without pressures they know nothing of.

(*Silence.*)

I want to believe that Eisenhower chose
On military grounds not to go to Berlin –
Not that there has since Lenin been
A Zionist-American-Communist joint front
Which engineered the rise of Roosevelt
And, also, the succession of Stalin,
And that Eisenhower was under orders
To make sure that Russia's post-war position
In Europe will be the dominant one,
That he therefore had a political objective
In making sure that Stalin was first to Berlin
By vetoing my wish to attack the soft
Underbelly of the Reich, and then Monty.
I rose after writing to Baruch in thirty-nine,
And after speaking in the House of Commons
In favour of setting up a Zionist state

In Palestine. I fell at the hands of
Public opinion, which can be manipulated.
I do not want to think I fell through a plot,
Because I tried to stand up to Stalin
And was felt to thwart a hidden alliance
Between Zionists, Americans and Russians
Who influenced public opinion against me.
I prefer not to believe that Zionism
Was behind my rise and engineered my fall.
I want to accept the surface of history
And not stir the muddy depths which cloud the reflection.
I prefer not to know about "groups" that would run the world.
I stood up to the two most terrible tyrants
Mankind has ever suffered; and I fell.
I am full of questions that will echo
To the end of this century and beyond,
As we regroup in a United States of Europe
And eventually in a United States of the World.

(End of July. Potsdam. STALIN *speaks through an* INTERPRETER *at the conference.)*

Stalin.   You were not at Teheran where we agreed
That I would co-ordinate my offensive
With *Overlord* in return for a new
Western Soviet frontier that will make sure
Germany can never again invade Russia,
A defensive barricade; and at Yalta
We agreed that the Oder-Neisse line should be
The western boundary of Poland and that all
East German territory to the western side
Of the Neisse should be under provisional
Polish administration, which will organise
Free elections, as I discussed with Churchill
Before he left for England.

Truman.   I think Poland's
Western boundary should be deferred to another
Conference.

Stalin   *(casually).* The rest is acceptable?

(TRUMAN *and* ATTLEE *look at each other uncertainly and nod.*)

(*6 August. The cruiser* Augusta *returning from Potsdam.* TRUMAN *and* AIDE.)

Aide.   I have an eye-witness report from Hiroshima.
The uranium bomb was two thousand times the blast
Of the heaviest bomb ever used before.

Truman.   Describe what happened.

Aide.   A flash and with a roar
A yellow and orange fireball rolled and shot
Eight thousand feet into the sunny air
And turned into a ten-mile high column
Of black smoke, a mushroom cloud rose and hung,
And as the great wind dropped, on the ground
A flat desert where there had been a city,
The roads like tracks across endless waste ground:
Hiroshima has disappeared, and in its place
Rubble, ruins, twisted metal and people
Horribly burned, lying still, stirring or
Groaning and crawling or just sitting dazed.
Over ten square miles a thousand fires blazed,
And a hundred thousand may have died at once.
Birds had burnt up in mid-air, and people's brains,
Eyes, intestines burst, their skin peeled, and some
Burned to cinders as they stood. Others had
The print of their clothes burnt onto their naked backs.
It was awesome. Sir, this new weapon which
Makes a thousand-bomber firebomb raid look
Insignificant, has in one blast outmoded
Six years of war, which must now be strikes like this
That can wipe out half a country without warning.
A new terror has arrived, that makes one yearn
For the sort of world war we have just seen
Where hatred has a limited radius,
That of a conventional high explosive bomb.

Truman   (*with awe*). This is the greatest thing in history. We had
To drop the bomb, I had a report that
Half a million Americans would be killed

If we were to invade Japan. General
Marshall and I are quite clear it will stop
The Pacific war before the Russians reach
Japan, which we can occupy alone.
We have learned from Berlin, where the Russians
Occupy half to our quarter. The hope is that
This bomb will abolish war because no one will
Invade another's territory and risk its use.

Aide.   So long as Stalin doesn't steal it from us.

(*Silence. They exchange glances.*)

(*6 August. Moscow, the Kremlin.* STALIN, ZHUKOV *and* EISENHOWER, *with the US
Ambassador to Moscow,* AVERELL HARRIMAN. INTERPRETER. *Stalin speaks in Russian.*)

Stalin.   Have you and Zhukov had a good time in Moscow?

Eisenhower.   Very good, thank you.

Stalin.   Tomorrow there is a Sports
               Parade in Red Square. You will stand with me
               On Lenin's Tomb.

Harriman.   A unique honour for
               A non-Communist.

Stalin.   And I wish to apologise
               For the actions of the Red Army in April.
               I told you it would advance towards Dresden,
               The place you proposed in your cable to me.
               There was a last-minute change to Berlin,
               I would like to explain the military reasons
               In detail later. You have the right to accuse
               Me of lack of frankness, and I would not want
               You to believe this of me.

Eisenhower.   We were expecting Dresden
               But what's done is done. I appreciate your apology
               And your frankness.

Stalin.   The Soviet Union needs
                      American help to recover from the war;
                      Not just money but technicians and science.
                      (*To Harriman*.) General Eisenhower is a very great man
                      Not only because of his military accomplishments
                      But because of his human, friendly, kind and frank
                      Nature. He is not a coarse man like most military.

Eisenhower.   Marshal Stalin impresses me as benign
                      And fatherly. There's a genuine atmosphere
                      Of hospitality.

Stalin   (*laughing*). Eh, Zhukov.

Eisenhower.   And,
                      I see nothing in the future that would prevent
                      Russia and the United States from being the closest
                      Possible friends.

                      (*A message has arrived which* STALIN *reads.*)

Stalin   (*to Eisenhower*). Your Government has dropped
                      An atomic bomb on Japan, at Hiroshima.
                      The city is devastated, hundreds
                      Of thousands are dead.

                      (*Silence.*)

Eisenhower.   Before this, I could see
                      No danger to friendly relations between our countries.
                      Now I am not so sure. I had hoped that
                      This bomb would not figure in this war. People
                      Will feel insecure again.

Stalin   (*laughing*).   The Soviet Union
                      Can now declare war on Japan as I promised
                      At Yalta.

(*15 August. Washington, The White House.* TRUMAN *and Gen.* MARSHALL.)

Marshall.   Now that Japan has surrendered, the post-war

Arrangements need to be made. For four years
We have supplied the British with food imports
Without any cash payment: Lend-Lease should stop.
The British people have voted out Churchill
For a crowd that want Beveridge's Welfare State
With universal health care we haven't got here.
They're financing something they can't afford
On the back of our subsidy, which should now be stopped.

Truman.   They've virtually bankrupted their Empire fighting the war.
There will be austerity if we cancel our aid.

Marshall.   There should be no consultation, just cancel it.
If they want to give things to their people that ours
Haven't got, fine, but not on our subsidy.
Let them do it out of their Empire or
Their own wealth-creation, as we do here.
We should not be paying for their socialism.

Truman.   Cancel it. It was a war-time arrangement,
And the Japanese war has come to an end.

(*November. Frankfurt, the office of I. G. Farben. EISENHOWER alone. He studies a tea-mug.*)

Eisenhower.   This mug has all life on it. A town at war,
At peace; bodies, lovers; a ruin, a church;
A storm, sun; disease, health; a wolf, a dove;
Fields, tanks. It's a work of art, and it holds my tea.

(*He puts down his mug.*)

America won the war and rules the world
As the only power to have the atomic bomb,
Having fought in Europe and the Pacific.
I led America to victory and
Like Octavius see greater things ahead.
As Commander I found life exciting,
I had an appetite for each day's news.
I find administering Germany tedious,
Here in the office of I. G. Farben.
Marshall is going to China to sort out

The civil war, the Communist threat to Peking,
And I can succeed him as Chief of Staff
And judging from the cheering as I rode
In triumph in an open car, and waved,
I could then become Augustus in the White House.
I long for the States. But what do I do about Kay?
In June I wanted to divorce Mamie,
But Marshall told me it would ruin my career
And refused permission, and I now want to live
With Mamie and not with Kay. Away from war
And exhausting hours and tension, I can be myself,
Vital, virile again, with my natural flow,
Which power has blocked, restored. Kay feels alone
And deserted. And I know I've failed her.
I've got her a job in Berlin with General Clay.
Now I will dictate a business-like letter
Explaining she cannot work for me any more,
And go to Paris at once, and then the States.

(*He picks up the mug.*)

I do not want to visit the ruins
Of our relationship, like a smashed city,
And wander in the rubble of its streets
Where once there were avenues and green parks,
And say goodbye amid broken memories
Of when it was sunlit and magical,
I would rather slip away without despair.
There is a waste in my heart, a devastation.
I am as shattered as this Germany.

(*November. Stalin's Kremlin HQ.* STALIN *and* BERIA.)

Beria.   Our agents Vasilevsky and Terletsky
                Received answers to their questions from Niels Bohr
                At two meetings with him in Copenhagen
                On the fourteenth and sixteenth of November.
                The twenty-two questions were put by Kurchatov.
                Bohr had the blessing of the Americans
                Oppenheimer, Fermi and Szilard for
                This leak of the American atom bomb.

He said there must be international control
Over atomic weapons, hence their leak.
Kurchatov, Khariton and Sakharov
Are now confident that there will be a
Soviet uranium and plutonium bomb.

Stalin.   Good. We want our well-wishers in the US
And Britain to find out the technology
To make comrade Sakharov's task easier.

(*Exit* BERIA. STALIN *is alone.*)

(*Satisfied.*) I did it. All along I had my own agenda
To transform the Soviet Union from a nation
Of backward peasants with horses and carts
Into a major world power all would fear.
I terrified them into the twentieth century,
Then I allied with Hitler to carve up part
Of Poland. I made overtures to Britain to
Keep pressure on Hitler from the western side.
I counted on Hitler to attack me.
He fell into my trap, he readily obliged.
Then my main thought was a Soviet empire
In eastern Europe and the Balkans. I delayed
Taking Berlin until I had overrun
Eastern Europe. At Yalta, I used their fear
Of Hitler, who was already finished, to redraw
Occupation zones and Poland's borders,
Knowing my stooges would seize power, invite
Russian troops in and give me indirect control.
The Allies were too trusting, they believed my words.
I made them honour their mistake, and took
Berlin. If I were Montgomery I would feel
Aggrieved, but imperial diplomacy
Is about power and achieving your interests.
The Russian civilisation is in a stage
Of union, of reunifying its own lands.
It has expanded to control its parts,
All its territories. It has always claimed
Poland and Eastern Europe, there has been no conquest
Of the European civilisation, which is younger than ours,

Merely a readjustment of our borders.
I secured the Soviet Union's interests –
I needed less than a week to invade
Japanese-held China and secure our
Interests at Port Arthur and at Dairen –
And will go down in history as the ruler
Who, like Ivan the Terrible, held the union
Together and expanded it to its greatest extent.
I have been a Genghis Khan, a Tamburlaine
Over a greater area than they conquered.
Berlin was the key, for with it came Poland,
Czechoslovakia, Hungary, and all the rest.
Occupation is nine points of the law.
And now, thanks to Niels Bohr, though he barely
Knows it, I am about to have the atomic bomb.
I shall challenge America and spread
Soviet influence throughout the rest of the world.
Man is material, which can be raised
Like clay a potter shapes on a turning wheel.

(*December. Lüneburg Heath.* MONTGOMERY *standing alone on the heath.*)

Montgomery.   So many times during the last eight months
I have longed to feel this heather under my feet.
Travelling around Germany on my train,
Which I captured from Hitler, I longed to see
Lüneburg Heath again, the place where I
Ended my long campaign from the Egyptian sands
And my command of the Americans
By receiving the German surrender.

(*He falls silent and looks around.*)

Marginalised, I was marginalised,
And with me Britain, and as a result
It's an American-Russian world now.
Did the Americans do it deliberately
To advance their power, or were they just blind?
In not going to Berlin, was Eisenhower
Just being fair, too trusting and naive?
Or honouring a deal that Roosevelt made

At Teheran with Stalin, to secure
A Russian offensive that would coincide
With my *Overlord*: Berlin in return for attack?
If I had led the Allies into Berlin
Before Churchill met Stalin at Yalta,
I could have held back the Communist tide,
All Europe would be Anglo-American.
Now the Soviet Union surrounds Berlin
And controls Poland. If my way had prevailed,
This would not be so. Does it matter now?
Yes, for many millions will not be free.
Or is there a stability I don't know about,
Is there now a secret east-west accord?
I can't believe that. Once again, I have been proved right.

(*Silence.*)

I sometimes question what my battles were for.
Was the world a better place for what I did?
Yes. I pushed back Fascism in North Africa
And Italy and North Europe. But as fast
As I rolled it back, Communism took its place.
Hitler was Overlord of Europe till
I invaded Normandy. Who's Overlord now?
Not Eisenhower; not Churchill, nor me, we
Were marginalised. Europe is now divided
Between Truman, all-powerful with his new bomb,
And Stalin, whose huge Red Army has occupied
The east and who cannot be dislodged by
An atomic bomb. Stalin is Overlord –
Apparently, for the real Overlord is you,
My guiding, Providential, loving Light
Without whom Hitler would have won this war.

(*Silence.*)

Now America is an atomic power
Thanks to German scientific insight,
And Russia will soon be one too, warfare
As I have known it is of the past, finished:
Operating from mobile caravans through scouts

Close to the battle front, like Marlborough
Or Wellington or Napoleon. War
Is now a distant nuclear missile threat.
And where does that leave Great Britain? Not great.
The body of our European civilisation
Has suffered a malignant cancer, which has been cut out
With our consent by the surgery of two other
Civilisations: the American and the Russian.
Now, after our civil war, we are convalescing
And our health will be restored.
But no more have we the energy for empire,
No more is our role in Africa or Asia.
Empire is at an end. We have ended
An imperial phase in our long history.
If that had to happen, then the civil war had to too.
Now the British Empire will collapse for we've
Bankrupted ourselves to recover from Hitler,
And a new Europe will grow out of this ruin.
I, who rule a quarter of Germany, consent
That German people should be in our new Europe
In which Britain, an island, will be different.

(*Silence.*)

Now, hearing the birds, watching the butterflies,
I know Nature's content. Rabbits, flowers, bees,
Birds, fish, grass, leafy trees, the universe
Just grows despite titanic wars like storms,
Which wreak havoc and uproot. After a storm
The air is so sweet, the earth is so pure,
Unsullied by the blot of tanks and guns.
I love the earth, the trees, the sky, the sun,
And you, my Overlord, who manifests
Into bud and blossom and lambs in the spring
And copper leaves, hips, haws, berries in the autumn.
I love the clear blue sky, the vast seas
The green hills and forests and mountain streams
And valleys and pure rivers. Your storms
Serve a purpose, they shake what is dead,
Blow off crinkled leaves, smash down the old
To prepare for the new. Lord, may there be

No more war. But I know, there must always be
Renewing storms. I would gladly live
In my caravan to be near your world,
At one with your will, in union with Oneness.

(*Silence.*)

Civilisations go through seasons, we are
In a new season now, a season of winter,
A bleakness and clearing up of devastation,
And then a new growth. I can feel it ahead.
A cold time as we recover, and then,
Though I may not live to see it, spring.
I accept your universe, with its storms and growth.
Through contradictions harmony prevails.
Life is an endless gush of opposites.
A tussle between darkness and light,
Pain and joy, hate and love, and war and peace.
All are manifestations of the One Light
You are, which I know at nine each night,
Which guided me to this point. And now I see
That evil swells like a dark thundercloud
That must grow darker for the rain to burst,
But it is always temporary in your scheme.
Hitler laid waste like a great hurricane;
Now Stalin is gathering like a tornado.
Of his own accord he will blow himself out.

(*Silence.*)

I see I was not meant to reach Berlin.
That was the will of the one Great Harmony,
And, Providence, with Ike as its instrument
(And Patton and his "niece", who are both now dead),
Blocked me, and in my self-will, egotism,
Vanity and national pique, I did not see this,
And complained, not understanding. But now I see.
The earth is made leprous by volcanic wars,
Happy is the place that does not erupt,
Where opposites live at peace, in harmony,
Which is not disfigured by the disorder of war.

Lord, your ways are magnificently strange,
And the loving spirit in your universe
Endlessly brings new shoots from desolation
And reconciles all diverging views in
A latent harmony that is often obscured.

(*He pauses.*)

I said goodbye to the other kind of love
When an insect bite took my wife from me.
I sat with her, she looked so calm, peaceful.
I rose and gently kissed her serene face.
Then the men came in and screwed down the coffin lid.
Since then I've had no use for that kind of love.
I've preferred the cheering of crowds, as when I rode
In an open horse-drawn State landau, and waved.
As a German bomb had destroyed my flat.
I asked the King for a grace and favour home,
But gratitude did not extend that far.
And so I must live in a "borrowed" home, alone.

(*Silence.*)

For over a year I implemented a plan.
Now there is no need for it any more
I feel slightly lost, a warlord without a war.
I must live again without a plan, I must find
My meaning in God's world, beneath reason.
I must look for the plan in the universe,
Rather than Rommel's, and there is as much
Deception and subterfuge, God is a General
Who guards his secrets from his troops' eyes.

(*Silence.*)

Under the atomic bomb the world will draw together.
There is a need for a new philosophy
Which embraces all mankind, all religions,
A metaphysic for the United Nations.
The only way I can live without a plan
Is to piece the potsherds of the universe

Into the tessellated urn from which they came
And, like an archaeologist, know its pattern
In the fresh air of the universal sunshine.

(*He pauses.*)

I understand that Brooke and I will be
Made peers in the New Year Honours, and I will be
Viscount Montgomery of Alamein.
But I have moved beyond war and conflict,
I look for opposites being reconciled.
I hope my son and Rommel's become friends.
And I ask of future generations
Not glorification or triumphalism,
But sober assessment, and credit where due.
More than Lawrence of Arabia, like the moon I drew
Tides of men, and flung them like a stormy sea
Up the beaches across the Channel, towards here.
Like Marlborough, I never lost a battle.
I stood for a Britain that had greatness.
I was a potsherd in the larger pattern,
A fragment, an episode, a chain of events
In the unfolding process of our history;
But I am proud of what our deeds achieved,
How our courage transformed our time, our Age,
And in the stillness of the trees, round this heather,
In the ghostly moaning of the winter wind
Which sounds as if the dead are gathering,
I hear the million men of *Overlord*
Roar their approval for a job well done.

THE TRAGEDY

OF

PRINCE TUDOR

or

A PRINCE WITHOUT A KINGDOM,

A record of seditious events, authenticated and published by the
Minister of World Culture in 2100.

(A Nightmare)

"Dodi is the man who will take me out of one world into another."
Princess Diana, quoted in the *Washington Post*, in August 1997.

"The world has to be really naïve to believe that the crash which happened two days ago was accidental."
Muammar al-Gaddafi, President of Libya.

*

"Democracy passes into despotism."
Plato, *Republic*, pt 4, bk 8. 562

"The time is out of joint. O cursed spite,
That ever I was born to set it right!"
Shakespeare, *Hamlet*, I v 189-90

"This land of such dear souls, this dear dear land,
Dear for her reputation through the world,
Is now leas'd out – I die pronouncing it –
Like to a tenement or pelting farm.
England, bound in with the triumphant sea,
Whose rocky shore beats back the envious siege
Of wat'ry Neptune, is now bound in with shame,
With inky blots and rotten parchment bonds;
That England, that was wont to conquer others,
Hath made a shameful conquest of itself."
Shakespeare, *Richard II*, II i 57-66

"We must recollect...what it is we have at stake, what it is we have to contend for. It is for our property, it is for our liberty, it is for our independence, nay, for our existence as a nation; it is for our character, it is for our very name as Englishmen, it is for everything dear and valuable to man on this side of the grave."
William Pitt,
Speech, House of Commons, 22 July 1803

"The play's the thing
Wherein I'll catch the conscience of the King."
Shakespeare, *Hamlet*. II ii 600-1

DRAMATIS PERSONAE

MAIN CHARACTERS

The Queen of England
The Duke, her consort
Prince, the heir to the throne
Princess, his estranged wife
Prince's Heir, their son

William Thorn, Stage name for a Goon
    jokingly appointed the Prince's Fool
Lord Horace Green, the Prince's confidant
Sir William Hawkes, Lord Chamberlain

The English Prime Minister (Olympian)
Wormwood, his media adviser, a Minister
Mr Rockefeller,
    World Government leader (Olympian)
Mr Rothschild,
    World Government leader (Olympian)
Chairman of Olympians
An Iraqi dictator
Dictator's double
An Egyptian financier
His son

An Israeli leader 1 (ally of Rockefeller)

An Israeli leader 2 (ally of Rothschild)
Ambassador for Iraq
Mrs R, a clairvoyant
The President of the United States
His First Lady

MINOR CHARACTERS

Minister of World Culture
Jenkins, a journalist
Harrison, a journalist
President of EC
UN Secretary-General
Aides
Nurse 1
Nurse 2
Philosopher
Physicist
Neo-Darwinist
Poet
Painter

Composer
Murderer 1
Murderer 2

Psychiatrist
Presenter
Five technicians
Studio Manager
Production manager
Doctor
Newscaster

LOCATIONS

The Royal Palace, London
The Prince's principal estate
A Hotel near Atlanta, Georgia

A suite in a Jerusalem hotel
The Oval Office, the White
House,Washington

Manhattan

The Great Hall, Rothschild's English estate

Mrs R's house, Central England

A square in Jerusalem, Israel

The deck of the financier's ship

A hotel foyer, Paris

A hospital mortuary, Paris

A royal palace in the English countryside

An enormous suite in a London hotel

A square in Baghdad, Iraq

A palace in Baghdad, Iraq

The financier's house, London

A suite in a Senegal hotel

A hotel at Turnberry, Scotland

A mental hospital, London

A television studio, London

Windsor Castle, London

SCENES

Recommended Interval: At the end of Act 3.

PREFACE TO THE 1999 EDITION OF THE TRAGEDY OF PRINCE TUDOR

I have long held the view that there should be a revival of verse drama to create a new unnaturalistic contemporary theatre. Naturalism is limiting with its realistic settings, and conveys a social view of people in naturalistic, mundane language. The unnaturalistic verse drama of Sophocles or Shakespeare is liberating in its settings and heightened language: a dramatist can set a scene literally anywhere (on the Falaise battlefield or Luneburg Heath, as I discovered in my last two-part verse drama about General Montgomery, *The Warlords*) and can use imaginative language with verbal pictures, evocative comparisons and Marlovian rodomontade. Soliloquies carry the audience behind the social surface deep within the soul of the characters, who reveal a universal dimension as we become party to their inner thoughts. Unnaturalistic verse drama on a contemporary historical theme is Universalist as characters can be connected through their inner life to the central force of the universe, as Sophocles' Oedipus is to Fate and Shakespeare's sovereign Henry V, who championed the autonomy of the soul, is to God.

A new unnaturalistic verse drama looks back to the plays of Sophocles, Shakespeare and Marlowe, and to the plays of Ben Jonson, Webster and Middleton, which flourished before c1640. The Civil War closed the theatres and when they opened Restoration comedy was in vogue. The only unnaturalistic verse plays in the Shakespearian tradition since c1640 are Dryden's *All for Love* (1677) and Eliot's *Murder in the Cathedral* (1935). I exclude the plays of Shelley, Byron, Yeats and Auden, which are more poetic than dramatic; and the plays of Christopher Fry, who has recently acknowledged that he did not write true verse. (The realistic plays Eliot wrote after *Murder in the Cathedral* must also be disqualified.) A contemporary verse drama embodying the Elizabethan tradition of eschewing realistic sets can be as topical today as was the drama of Shakespeare and his contemporaries, who were "modern" in their day.

The idea for *Prince Tudor* came to me during the spring of 1998, when a number of events – in Britain, Europe, the US and the Middle East – impinged themselves on my consciousness simultaneously and I saw that they were all interconnected and could not be understood in isolation (a Universalist view of contemporary history). Events involving Britain in particular raised the question of the relationship between national sovereignty and the coming world government, a preoccupation in *The Warlords*. Shakespeare wrote some of his greatest plays as acts of political will – to warn Elizabeth I against the manoeuvrings, machinations and plots of the Cecils, who consequently made life difficult for him (if we accept one reading *of Hamlet*). At one level *Prince Tudor* is a warning against the impending break-up of the United Kingdom by hostile international forces. By showing the Prince as a man who grasps the danger and refuses to collaborate with the modernisers who seek to bring about the break-up on behalf of the world government, the play elevates the Prince into a national hero and presents his reaction to the national predicament in heroic terms. The Prince's own predicament and dilemma echo Hamlet's, and like Hamlet he feigns madness – to preserve British sovereignty.

Sovereignty exists on different levels. There is the sovereignty of a nation (in the sense that a nation's independence guarantees power over its own destiny without interference from other nations); there is the sovereignty of the monarch (in the sense that the monarch has supreme power within the nation without interference from subjects within the realm), which is traditionally derived from God by the divine right of kings; and there is the sovereignty of the soul (in the sense that the soul has autonomy and self-governing independence without interference from the State or any of its bodies). All three sovereignties are under attack today. The United Kingdom may not be a nation-state much longer, but may be split into four states within the European Union, one of which (England) may be fragmented into nine Euro-regions. The United Kingdom may therefore become twelve mini-states. The Crown may lose its constitutional power to dismiss a government. And when its existence is not denied, the soul is disregarded by shallow governments which erode people's individual choice and the private control they exercise over their lives. Not since the Civil War has there been a more urgent time in our history to focus on the threefold, interconnected concept of sovereignty.

In our time the advantages and disadvantages of world government need to be aired. A benevolent world government can abolish war, starvation and much disease. A malevolent world government using Stalin's or Hitler's concentration-camp methods would be a nightmare. The Western and Pacific countries are seeking to establish a world government, but at present it is divided. We hear little about it as it operates in the shadows through its proxies, the Presidents and Prime Ministers who, it is said, owe their appointments to their willingness to go along with its transnational aims. Never since Augustus's world rule has there been a more urgent time in Western history to focus on the quality and attitudes of the world government that is being mooted.

Some of English Literature's best works have contained allusions to contemporary events. Shakespeare's *Hamlet,* for example, contains no fewer than 81 topical allusions out of the 593 allusions in 25 Shakespeare plays listed by Admiral Holland in *Shakespeare, Oxford and Elizabethan Times.* When specific names are referred to in plays they date quickly, as in John Osborne's *Look Back in Anger.* When the allusions are incorporated into the imaginative framework of a play, they do not date in the same way. The 81 topical allusions have not dated *Hamlet* but have served to give a universal theme added resonance.

An artist is a maker of an artefact, a work of beauty, regardless of whether he makes a picture, sculpture, symphony, poem, short story or play. As an artist I am a weaver of dreams, and *Prince Tudor* is intended to stand outside our mercantile time as does an intricately woven silk tapestry of a unicorn – or like Eliot's Chinese jar or Keats' Grecian urn. I have woven a pattern, and we follow a Prince concerned about the impending dwindling of the Kingdom he expected he would one day rule, and we see how the paradigm of the inexorably divided American-European world government works, and how Presidents and Prime Ministers have apparently acted as its pawns. His wife is a victim of its machinations, and there are references to events in the US and Iraq. But any topical allusions are as incidental to the imaginative universal theme as are the 81 topical allusions in *Hamlet*.

16 July 1998

PREFACE TO THE 2007 EDITION OF
THE TRAGEDY OF PRINCE TUDOR

This play was written in 1998, when I first learned that Britain was being split into 12 regions, each of which would have tax-raising powers, within what can only be described as a coming United States of Europe. About this time an official in a certain County Council leaked to me a secret document issued when John Major was British Prime Minister, which proved this. When the play first came out in 1999 it was too close to the painful events surrounding   Princess Diana's death in 1997 to give characters their original names. And so I used other names to obfuscate. As a result the play had the appearance of being a *roman-* (or drama-) *à-clef* ("a novel in which real persons or events appear with invented names"), and the serious message of the play was obscured.

Now we are at some distance from the events leading up to 1997, and I have since published *The Syndicate* about the plan for a world government (which includes regionalization), and its companion volume *The Secret History of the West*, both of which focus on the Rockefellers and Rothschilds and supply numerous sources. I feel it is now time to restore these two original names, and to remove most of the obfuscating names so that the message can come through more clearly, and to include the original subtitle, *A Prince without a Kingdom*. The obfuscating names can be found in the 1999 edition of the play.

The abolition of England is now a very real possibility. The new European constitution has to be ratified by the end of October 2006. If 20 out of the 25 members of the European Union vote for ratification (i.e. four-fifths), then the European Council of heads of government are empowered by the constitution document itself to recommend the adoption of the constitution, which would impose a superstate on all member nations, including England, and turn them into states. (The actual wording in the document is: "If, two years after the signature of the Treaty establishing a Constitution for Europe, four fifths of the Member States have ratified it and one or more Member States have encountered difficulties in proceeeding with ratification, the matter will be referred to the European Council", 'Declarations', 30.) The UK would fragment into 12 Euro-regions: Scotland, Wales, Ireland, London and eight English regions. This process, which I confirmed through the leak of the County-Council document, has progressed. *The Syndicate* gives full details, and more recently Lindsay Jenkins' *Disappearing Britain* lays out further evidence. This play is now very much a creature of its times.

The leaders of the two Syndicate factions are composite characters and are not based on particular individuals; rather they embody a particular emphasis of commercial pattern – an emphasis within the ethos and outlook on life of the Syndicate rather than the influence of specific individuals. Both represent the commercial drives of conglomerates of companies or corporations with a shared common interest in the Syndicate, and I make no imputation against the specific behaviour of any individual, family, company or corporation.

The courtiers remain imaginary and have composite, multiple inspiration. Sir William Hawkes has no connection with (the then) Sir Robert Fellowes or Sir Robin Janvrin (who did not become Private Secretary to the Queen until 1999, *after* the events in the play). Lord Green is not based on Sir Stephen Lamport, Mark Bolland or Sir Michael Peat (all of whom have done stints as Private Secretary at St James's Palace), and any resemblance is coincidental; I was not thinking of any particular courtier. The politician Wormwood is not based on Peter Mandelson, dubbed in the popular press "the Prince of Darkness"; it must be borne in mind that in recent times although he has attended the Bilderberg Group Mandelson has been a close adviser to the Rothschilds rather than a Rockefellers' hatchet man. Mrs R was probably based on a newspaper account of a highly publicised visit Princess Diana and Dodi al-Fayed made to clairvoyant Rita Rogers at her Central-England home in Chesterfield a few weeks before their deaths; my obfuscation allowed me to exercise some dramatic licence with the timing and content of the consultation, as it did with the manner of Rabin's killing. The Fool – the Goon jokingly appointed Fool – may have echoes of Spike Milligan, but again he is a composite character who is much more akin to Shakespeare's Tudor Fools than our modern Goons. (It is significant that on 3 July 1998 I had lunch with John Southworth, author of *Fools and Jesters at the English Court* and an expert on Shakespeare's Fools, whom we discussed for most of that afternoon.)

It goes without saying that the Prince is also a composite character. No Prince of our realm has gatecrashed a Bilderberg Group conference and denounced the world government. Nor has one been murdered and replaced by a double.

Finally, I should point out that it is the Minister of World Culture, in 2100, not me, who accepts his scholars' view that the Prince was murdered and replaced by a double to perpetuate the Windsor line. It must not be ruled out that the Minister of World Culture in 2100 has slipped the idea of the murder and the double into the text for spin and propaganda purposes – to discredit the ex-regime that preceded his world-government superstate. To put it more strongly, his claim that the Prince was assassinated for seditiously opposing the world government and replaced by a pretender who had no title to the throne is outrageous black propaganda on the part of the world government, and is patently absurd and in no way credible. His claim reveals much about the Utopia of 2100 towards which we are creeping.

16 January, 2 February 2006

THE TRAGEDY OF PRINCE TUDOR

PROLOGUE

(United Nations building, New York, AD 2100. Enter the MINISTER of WORLD CULTURE *for the United States of the World. He speaks in an American accent.)*

Min. of World Culture.	Friends of Europe's most northern isles, good folk
	From regions dear to Brussels and New York,
	Citizens of our great World Government,
	As the Minister of World Culture, I
	Invite you to leave your enlightened time
	And make an imaginative journey
	Not to a distant age or place – not Rome
	Or Abyssinia – but to an era
	In Europe's recent past when there was still
	A nation-state called England, far advanced
	In its death-throes like a convulsing lion,
	That kept subservient in hegemony
	Three other regions – Scotland, Wales, Ireland –
	And its own muttering English people
	In a hated Union, suppressed by
	An archaic electoral system that
	Ignored proportional representation
	And kept in power an oppressive Commons
	And Crown remote from subjects in unrest;
	An unfamiliar Age of Kings and Queens
	Guarded by an unelected Chamber,
	The feudal House of Lords, that cared about
	Quaint notions: sovereignty, independence,
	The purity of transient currency,
	The pound which is now a collector's piece.
	In our reformed, federal republic
	We unveil this newly discovered work
	As an example of the paradigm
	Under which the oppressed English suffered
	As Anglo-American heroes like
	An English PM, US President
	Struggled to create our New World Order

Which is the epitome of world rule
And sets an example to all mankind,
The four billion the earth's food can sustain,
Who've earned their right by work to be alive
And not be classified "useless eaters".
This social document from a passed Age
Catches the moment when it ceased to be
And our Order was born and monarchies
Lost sovereignty and sanctity, and passed
To our republican World Government
Like baubled jewels left in a codicil.
Go back to the end of the Windsor line
When crown and pageantry spoke for London –
Hanover, rather, for they were German
Until the First World War when they disguised
Their Germanness and took their castle's name –
And to the untold tale of how the last
Of the line came to be an impostor,
Pretender with no title to the throne
As Perkin Warbeck impersonated
One of the princes murdered in the Tower
To claim the throne from Henry the Seventh;
"Prince Tudor" posing as King George the Seventh.
Good people, leave our secular time for
One when a sunburst meant more than the sun,
And though our tale stops just short of the time
When quaint England abolished itself for
Eight regions within polyglot Europe
That include Picardy and Normandy;
And though it tells of narrow-minded men,
Leave our time of correct attitudes and
Be amazed at the struggle to resist
Our first movers' visionary exploits;
Applaud our Founding Fathers' brave efforts
And the leadership of Rockefeller
And Rothschild who pioneered – despite huge
Odds – our vast United States of the World
Which towers like a mountain, superhuman
Olympus above mankind's tiny towns.

ACT ONE

SCENE 1

(*The* PRINCE *and* LORD HORACE GREEN *are inside the Royal Palace, London.*)

Prince.   Some Olympians have undermined the Crown,
                   I know, and others have defended it.
                   I can't believe the Lord Chamberlain will
                   Upbraid my estranged wife in the palace.

Lord Green.   The plan is that he will do it just here.

Prince.   It does not bode well for the coming weeks.
                   He is a harbinger of gloomy times
                   As is an owl that hoots in creeping dusk
                   And sends a shiver of impending night.
                   He knows what's ahead and it's bad for us.

Lord Green.   They're approaching. Press back and observe them.

                   (*They hide. Enter* SIR WILLIAM HAWKES *and the* PRINCESS.)

Princess.   I don't understand why we're over here.
                   Why couldn't we talk in my drawing-room?

Hawkes.   Because I don't want your servants to hear.
                   It's not easy for for me to say this, but
                   It's said you are upstaging your husband.
                   I'm sure you're not aware of this, but – with
                   The greatest respect, not to give offence,
                   And having your best interests at heart as
                   I do, it's being said your profile's too
                   High, you're pushing yourself into his place,
                   "Hogging" the limelight that's meant to be his,
                   Photo opportunities that are his –

Princess.   How dare you say such things. You have no right –

Hawkes.	I don't want to offend, ma'am. It's not I
	But others in high places who say that
	If you don't take a step backwards, and shun
	Publicity instead of courting it,
	There can only be grave consequences.
	I am just the messenger, I have heard
	A message you need to be aware of
	To help the smooth running of the palace.

Princess.   You're just a bureaucrat. Who are you to
Run the palace, who are you speaking for?

Hawkes.   People in high places – oh dear, you put
Me in a very awkward position –
Who have your husband's best interests at heart,
People in another palace – er, place –
And experienced courtiers, who say
If you won't co-operate, then perhaps
There will be slow progress in resolving
Your divorce settlement –

Princess.   *You* threaten *me?*

Hawkes.   Not I, ma'am, not threaten, merely advise
For your own good. I would not like to see
You send out signals that could give offence
And be misinterpreted in the Court
And lead to problems over custody
Or even where you reside in future.

(*These last words have been whispered. The* PRINCE *and* LORD GREEN
do not hear them. The PRINCESS *shrieks and collapses into tears. Exit* SIR
WILLIAM HAWKES. *The* PRINCE *emerges*)

Prince.   What's wrong? You look as if you've seen a ghost.

Princess.   I have – the unscrupulous face behind
Your threats. Don't touch me.

(*She runs out crying.*)

| Prince. | What threats? I'm aghast. |
| | Did you hear what he said? |

Lord Green.   No, but it was
                   A veiled threat.

Prince.   She thinks I am behind it.
                   Sir William's in the Rothschilds' faction, he
                   Toyed with her like a cat that has just pounced.
                   He's doing this as he supports the Crown.
                   I do not want support of such a kind
                   That makes her think I am behind such threats.
                   I'm stupefied, it confirms my worst fears.
                   Pro-Olympian bureaucrats threaten us.
                   I feel so impotent. What can I do?
                   I fear all is not well in our Kingdom.

Lord Green.   I'm glad you have heard him with your own ears.
                   Now you will believe me and my reports.

Prince.   I know the Olympians are meeting now.
                   I know industrialists and bankers who
                   Are on the guest list. Their lips will be sealed.

Lord Green.   I have a journalist who will get in.

SCENE 2

(*A hotel near Atlanta, USA. A* GUARD *with a mobile phone shakes his head and points. A journalist,* HARRISON, *turns and walks towards another* JOURNALIST *nearby.*)

Jenkins.   What did he say? Can I gain admittance?
                   Can I attend the globalists' debate?

Harrison.   The gate to Lake Lanier island is sealed.
                   The last guest left the Hotel Wednesday noon,
                   Guards intercept enquiries and ring through,

And admit only those on the guest list.
They've turned away a hundred journalists.
The Hilton is a fortress under siege,
There is a news blackout, and editors
Will decline to print what reporters file.
It's pointless waiting here, I'm going home.

Jenkins.   The globalists' control is absolute.
                  Presidents, Premiers, press barons, monarchs
                  Dance on strings, their puppetmasters dictate
                  The next crises, events that suit their ends,
                  Who's in, who's out, who has to change his ways.
                  The NSA at Maryland's Fort Meade
                  Monitor Europe's communications
                  Via radio dishes at Menwith Hill,
                  Their listening post on the North Yorkshire moors,
                  And every phone call, fax and e-mail flies
                  Into their information net as flocks
                  Of migrating swifts cross their radar beams.
                  Their satellites snoop on what we're saying.
                  It's frightening. We're not free. I'll stay on.

SCENE 3

(*Inside the hotel.* ROCKEFELLER *addresses the Bilderberg Group's conference. He is an old man. He speaks monotonously in an American drawl.*)

Rockefeller.   Olympians, we are the gods who control
                  Human events from this Mount Olympus,
                  Decide the fates of leaders and dispose
                  As Zeus and the immortals did on crags
                  Where eagles nest and swoop, peaks streaked with snow.
                  We are apart and look down on the world
                  Whose lands resemble wastes of parched desert,
                  Chaotic rocks and tranches of wasteland,
                  And our lofty concerns order its mess
                  As unhooded falcons hunt for quarry.
                  From our great height, omniscient eminence,
                  Hawk-eyed observation, omnipotence,

We see an overpopulated earth
Riven with borders like rivers. Our cure,
Malthusian local wars, famines and plagues,
Disasters delivering quotas of dead,
Will stop our six billion rising to ten,
And checking of libido, this restraint
Has a new ally, WMDs
Iraq has stockpiled, which can kill all men
Twice over. Olympians, this last year we
Have made progress in not resisting culls
Among multiplying useless eaters
By allowing natural disasters scope.
Since Bosnia, the New World Order rules.
NATO has become the UN army,
Globalism's triumphed, WMDs
Offer new options for good management.
And, Olympians, we have made some progress
In dissolving borders like dried rivers,
In merging differences like currencies
And monarchies, so everywhere's the same,
A multi-cultural global unity
Of egalitarian republics.
We welcome our new English leader's vision
In loosening the United Kingdom
So Scotland, Wales, Ireland and London rule
Themselves and leave the English Crown weakened,
Its sovereignty reduced (the Dutch model),
Set to give up its currency, the pound.
England will have eight self-governed regions.
He'll deliver the monetary union
His predecessor was unwilling to.
We welcome our new Israeli Premier,
Who is set to withdraw from the West Bank,
Leave Palestine, Gaza, the Golan Heights,
And live in harmony with the Arabs –

(ROTHSCHILD *stands. He is generally silky-tongued but is now angry.*)

Rothschild.   No! Enough! You and I are allies here
But I insist that Israel must retain
The lands she conquered when she was attacked

By Arabs who still deny she exists
And do not want peaceful co-existence.
The West Bank is Judaea, and the word
"Jew" comes from "Judaea". Jews have a right
To live in Judaea, and no Premier
Planted by your faction to do your will
Can undo what England pledged my forebear
And cancel the Balfour Declaration.
I have not consented to a U-turn
On our policy towards Israel – or
The English monarchy. Our global pact
Embraces monarchs besides presidents
And respects crowns as well as republics.

Rockefeller.   We admire spirited rodomontade.
Emotional outbursts are regrettable,
They spoil our genial atmosphere with bile.
Be rational! There must be a concession
If Hamas is to end terrorist acts.
The Arabs will make peace if you withdraw –

Rothschild.   Surrender, you mean. Never! If we leave
The lands we occupied, what will happen?
Hostile Arabs will surround and encroach
On our "national home", try to wipe us out.
They do not want Israel in Palestine.
We will never withdraw from Judaea,
Which has been our homeland since Moses' time.
I will resist your intrigues to reduce
Our sovereignty in our homeland and that in
The homeland of our staunch English ally,
The English Crown, which you would undermine
Through negative press articles and books
That promote republican views. Like Zeus
You preach harmony and fling thunderbolts,
Loud lies that destroy calm and ignite war.
You have gone too far this time. I resist!

(ROTHSCHILD *walks out with his entourage. He stops and listens to*
ROCKEFELLER.)

Rockefeller.	Olympians, Our world rule needs harmony
	In each place of conflict – Northern Ireland,
	Palestine, Hong Kong – and if one of us,
	Who stands for our Anglo-Israeli wing,
	Withdraws from Olympus in dudgeon, we
	Must continue our policy of hope
	And reconciliation everywhere.
	There can be no change in our settled course.
	All must subordinate their interests to
	The greater good, the universal whole.
	We will occupy lowlands like cornfields
	As crows squat among cornstooks, pecking grain.

Rothschild.	The American eagle, resembling
	A hideous vulture, circles above
	The noble, imperial English lion,
	Erstwhile king of the beasts and now made lame,
	And would swoop and devour it with hooked bill.

(*Exit* ROTHSCHILD *and his entourage. The* AMERICAN PRESIDENT *steps forward with the* PRESIDENT OF THE EUROPEAN COMMISSION.)

President of EC.	What's your reaction, Mr President?

US President.	Alas, an earthquake has shattered our peace
	And split our mountain range into two peaks,
	Each separate with a different perspective,
	One republican and one monarchist,
	One against nation-states, the other for,
	One for dissolving borders, one against.
	Our global monolith, long cracked, has sheered.
	And our world rule has fractured, and now
	Two hostile rivals are at civil war.
	Rothschilds are mourning their heir's "suicide".
	He was found hanged, kneeling by a towel rail,
	And I think he suspects it was murder
	And that's coloured the attitude we've heard.
	You'll guess who he thinks ordered their heir's death.
	Gone are the days when two allies agreed.
	Alas! How can division run the world?

SCENE 4

(*The Royal Palace, London.* PRINCE *and* LORD GREEN.)

Lord Green.   Your parents request your attendance, sir.

Prince.   Do you know why?

Lord Green.   Prime Minister's coming.

Prince.   He's Prime Minister in name, not deed. He's
Like a peacock who struts and is aloof.
He has little contact with Ministers.
Last week he didn't even recognize
A junior Minister at a launch.
Cabinet meetings aren't on politics.
Committees meet infrequently, business
Is done in informal groups or through young
Messengers from his Policy Unit.
In his court, this King has his advisers
And a small group of Ministers, whose chance
Remarks make or break those who work for him,
And patrons protect duds. He just attends
The Commons for a few hours on Wednesdays,
Never supports his team on the front bench
Or opens a debate. He leaves reforms
To the Lord Chancellor or a stand-in.
He sees fragments and has no overview.
Policy is set via the media.
He's quite detached from his own government
As if he'd delegated all worries
And kept to himself just what makes him smile.
He has eyes everywhere that spy for him,
And spreads his fantail with two dozen eyes.

Lord Green.   They are waiting, it's best you go at once.

(*The* PRINCE *enters and bows to the* QUEEN *and the* DUKE.)

Queen.   Please be seated. Can I pour you some tea?

344

Prince.	Where are our staff?
Duke.	Pruned in the latest cuts.
Prince.	They're snicking out where they don't understand From envy and malice. They have no sense. They're like a blundering gardener who has Deadheaded fine blooms with his secateurs And justifies his error as fairness, For is it fair to weeds that roses grow?
Duke.	And now they're breaking up our Kingdom by Giving the Scots and Welsh their parliaments, Which will just serve to whet their appetites So they are hungry for independence.
Queen.	Our new Premier said the change would strengthen The unity of our Kingdom, and now We find it has weakened it, as we knew.
Duke.	Each change is for the worse, hastens decay. I fear for *your* crown.
Queen.	*The* Crown must survive. Like the mortar in a four-walled garden That holds all bricks in place, or glue that sticks Seat, back and two arms of a model throne The Crown bonds our four-state constitution.
Duke.	Distance and decorum unify states, Not earnest hugs and tearful sighs and sobs Played towards the *paparazzi's* cameras Between glances at a Muslim escort.
Queen.	We have report of the Olympian Group. The American, republican wing Demands the weakening of the British Crown, Some of our sovereignty given to Brussels. The Anglo-Israeli wing is opposed, But most of our new Cabinet agree With America's onslaught on the Crown,

	And our new Prime Minister is still green And will support both sides to offend none.
Duke.	If one were cynical one could now say He comes to do the Olympians' bidding. By tradition the Prime Minister sides With the Anglo-Israeli Rothschilds' view But this one seems closer to policies The republican Rockefellers want – Palestine; and his wife's republican And won't bend her knee in curtsey to us. He is ambivalent in his support.
Prince.	He grins, is vague and has no policies. Is he the sort of dummy who would sit On an Olympian ventriloquist's knee?
	(*Enter* LORD GREEN.)
Lord Green.	Your Majesty, the Prime Minister's here.
	(*Enter the* PRIME MINISTER, *with* SIR WILLIAM HAWKES. *Sir William Hawkes takes notes.*)
Prime Minister.	Ma'am, sir, sir, I've come on just one issue. We are a modernizing government And the people demand a new approach To the State opening of Parliament. To be popular is to be perceived As being of the people, one of us. The people want you to be one of them. No pageantry, no glittering, no crown. They want to see you as more ordinary. Just come in a dress and read out my speech. That is the way to make you popular. Of course it will only be surface change. Perception is all, old can seem quite new If it is perceived so. We are not now A country in decline but coming back, Progressing, dynamic, energetic. The monarch can seem full of energy

If wearing modern dress and slickly shown.
Just as truth can seem a lie to liars
A lie can seem truth if properly dressed.
A monarch will seem popular if shown
As a mirror-image of the people.
I recommend we do the people's will.

Queen   (*icily*). And how have "the people" expressed this will?

Prime Minister.   Why, through the mandate they bestowed on me.

Queen.   And did they know they were expressing it?

Prime Minister.   Why, yes, we said we'd reform Parliament.

Queen.   And did they understand what "reform" meant?

Prime Minister.   I'm their elected leader, I can do
Whatever I wish if there's a mandate.

Duke.   The Queen is Head of State, not you. Not you.

Prime Minister.   The people admire the Princess and want
A monarchy modelled on her, want change.

Queen.   We are adaptable, and will adapt
If it is felt appropriate. We will
Study the matter. Will such modern dress
Strengthen or weaken the Crown, do you think?

Prime Minister.   Oh strengthen, without doubt, for the Crown will
Be perceived as relevant, of today;
Not an anachronism from the past.

Duke.   You said that Scottish and Welsh Parliaments
Would strengthen the Crown but they will weaken
Our Kingdom if they bring independence.

Prime Minister.   Oh no, the perception is quite different.
People will have their say and want to stay
Within a Kingdom they will have strengthened.

A modernised monarchy will be strong.
People will find you more like them, and will
Vote for retaining you in great numbers.
If you are perceived as being remote,
Aloof, distant, they will vote for a change.

Prince.　　　　　You think the way to save the monarchy
　　　　　　　　Is for us to adapt, become modern?

Prime Minister.　I do, and I recommend compromise.
　　　　　　　　Change and the Crown's secure. Don't and it's not.

(*The* PRIME MINISTER *bows and comes to the front of the stage.*)

(*Aside.*) Like a chameleon who takes the colour
Of his surroundings so he is not prey,
I take on the personality and
Opinions of others to be all things
To all men, whose "Proime Min'star" I appear,
At ease with golfers, pop singers and film stars,
One of the lads sipping a pint of beer,
Having a laugh, not thinking seriously
About interest rates or atomic bombs,
In tune with all men, criticized by none,
With high approval ratings from voters,
Able to be natural with royalty.
I appear vacuous. Vacuity's
My secret weapon – public's vacuous.
I tune to their wavelength to win their votes,
Act a calculating vacuousness.
I am a good actor, can play a part,
Now firm, now hesitant, now near-tearful.
I agree with all men – bosses, workers,
Eurosceptics and pro-Europeans,
Liberals and hardliners, I love them all,
And include their opinions in my own.
Republicans and ardent royalists,
Conservatives and clause-four socialists,
Scottish, Welsh, Irish or just plain English –
Inclusiveness means adopting their views
And changing my colour for camouflage.

I support both sides of the Olympians.
All views blend in newness, modernity.

(*Exit the* PRIME MINISTER. SIR WILLIAM HAWKES *remains.*)

Hawkes.　　　That was outrageous, inexcusable.

Duke.　　　What cheek! He talks as if *he's* Head of State.
He invokes "the people", he does not know
"The people's" will. He tells us what to do.
His line is American-Olympian,
It can't be by design, he's too naive.
He can't be an Olympian salesman
Though like the President he was a Rhodes
Scholar, and Rothschild picked both of them out.

Prince.　　　I'm shocked, taken aback. He's interfered
In how we run ourselves, in our domain.
(*Pointedly*.) No politician or bureaucrat should.
Power must have gone to his head. He smiles,
Uses opaque language that means all things
To all, reassures with inclusiveness,
Manages our responses with slickness,
Blurs our perception of his agenda.
He's a cuckoo who's seized a songbird's nest.
He is a new man at war with the old,
He forces his enemies to be friends
And stabs with a simper, a dimpling grin
That woos the female voters while he thrusts.
His request that we should all "modernise"
Is unacceptable. He does not know.
He's a con man who's tricked the people with
Promises he can't deliver. He's conned
The warring Irish parties with his fudge
Which means opposite things to either side.
He's sitting on his predecessor's boom
Like a cuckoo who's occupied a nest,
And when the economy turns down, as
It will, he'll be seen for the rogue he is.
He's all image. A hundred articles
Bear his name, but all were written by hacks,

Not one's by him. He's a demagogue who
Has duped the mob. He's all impression – fake.
But how we reject him matters. We can't
Simply be offhand, we must use his terms.
We live in a time when the finest words
Are weapons of State and used against us.
We must adopt a posture and language
If we are to head off this smiling threat
To the Crown's continued independence.

(SIR WILLIAM HAWKES *whispers to the* QUEEN, *who nods, and then to
the* DUKE, *who nods. He then leaves.*)

Queen.   I was telling you before he arrived
Of a report on the Olympian Group.
There is more in the report than you've heard.
The other half of the coalition,
Rockefeller, 's been promoting your wife,
Involving her in prominent causes.
She'll campaign for the needy and her style
Will be contrasted favourably to ours.
An informer says *you* will be approached –
We don't know by whom, just that you will be –
As they associate you with your wife.
They want to win you over, divide us,
And ask you to support "reform", which they
Call "modernizing" –

Duke.   They mean "wresting power"
Or supporting Olympian campaigns.
I've no time for that Olympian clan.
World-rule Freemasons are nice to our face,
Behind our backs they want to close our Firm.
When I asked for your mother's hand, the King
Made me pledge I would become a Mason.
I left it six years, when he died I felt
Duty-bound to honour my word, but.... But
Once in I did no more and snubbed them all.
I feel the same about the Olympians.

Queen.   Your father hopes you will discourage them.

Duke.	I have made no secret of what I think
	About your wife's conduct. She has not grasped
	Her royal role, the duty it requires.
	She's held the hands of the sick and dying,
	The poor and downtrodden. She's exposed us
	To this round of "divide and rule". They praise
	Her style and expect it of us. They say
	She has the grace of a roe hind. I have
	To say, you have not helped by your public
	Wrangle with her, which has sent a confused
	Message to the public and to the world.
	You have rejected her, and she has won
	Public sympathy for a "hands-on" style
	She calls reform, but which is defiance.

| Queen. | She has lost her title but can still harm. |

Duke.	She flaunts her Muslim escort to the press,
	Tarring us with vulgar commerce and wealth.
	And now they seek to weaken us through you.
	It's like that American hussy they
	Inflicted on the King, hoping that when
	He abdicated the monarchy would
	Be in a dunderhead's hands and collapse.
	I do not say this lightly, we have thought
	Long and hard, your mother and I. Could you....
	If she is not controlled, you won't be King.
	For you to be King, she must be controlled.
	If the Olympians control her, you won't
	Be King. For you to be King she must be
	Prised from her controllers, not forcibly.
	It would be good if you were reconciled
	To her so you could pinion and prevent
	Her flights of saintliness when cameras click,
	And so ease Olympian pressure on us.
	You can see who you like when reconciled.

Queen.	What she has done will make it difficult
	To ask, but your boys will be pleased. We all
	Need a united front when foxes prowl.

Prince.

I know you've been exasperated by
My wife and with good reason, but your staff
Have not helped by entrenched statements and leaks
That have enraged rather than dampened down.
I want the survival of our Kingdom
And of the Crown, but not mindless reform.
I will do as you request on one count.
I won't support reform when they urge me.
On the other count, I need time to think.
I cannot bring myself to look at her,
Let alone approach her on your behalf
And beg her for reconciliation.
And if I could steel myself to do it
I could not promise success; she's a law
Unto herself, a very loose cannon.
I lost control of her long, long ago.
I understand your thought. I must ponder.

(PRINCE *bows and leaves.*)

SCENE 5

(MRS R*'s house in Central England. Mrs R. has just greeted the* PRINCESS *and* FINANCIER'S
SON*. She leads them towards a table.*)

Princess.

Your bonfire guided our helicopter.

Mrs R.

I am so pleased for both of you. I've heard
So much about you, young man.

Financier's Son.

And I, too,
Have heard much about your clairvoyant powers.
You've seen the Princess shrouded in white light.
We want to know what the future holds, if
There's a message from the spirit world.

Princess.

I
Can't wait to learn what the spirits will say.
The first reading you did for me you said

They said I'd meet a man and fall in love
And that we'd be together on a boat.

Mrs R.   Sit there, young man, please.

Princess.   I will sit outside,
          Claire.

(*Exit* PRINCESS. MRS. R. *sits and contemplates with her eyes closed.*)

Mrs R.   The clouds are parting. I see you both
          On water, smiling, deeply in love, now
          Standing in a speedboat, its nose raised.
          As you speed up a river. It's the Seine.
          I feel you won't have another girlfriend.

Financier's Son. I've been waiting for a special person,
          And this summer I have at last found her.
          I'm very much in love, I admire her.
          I respect her and want to protect her.

Mrs R.   And now I'm looking at Hebrew writing.
          Am I in Israel? Ah! You're in a car,
          I see a black car, a voice is saying....
          It....

Financier's Son.   Yes?

(MRS.R. *is silent.*)
                    Tell me what you can hear.

(MRS.R. *is silent.*)

                                    What's there?
          I'm dying to know.

Mrs R.   I can feel danger.
          A voice is saying "Black saloon". I see
          A tunnel, water. You must not visit
          France. You must not go to Paris or ride
          In a black saloon there. Right?

Financier's Son.   I will be
                 Careful. She's very precious. We've no plans
                 To go to France.

                 (*Re-enter* PRINCESS.)

Princess.   What have you seen? Tell us
                 What the spirit world knows.

Mrs R.   It's gone cloudy.
                 There are no pictures now. You must not go
                 To Paris or ride in a black saloon
                 There. I have a feeling of danger, and
                 I heard a voice saying "Black saloon". That's
                 All.

Princess.   We must be careful. The spirits did
                 Not speak for long. Last time they spoke or sent
                 Images for a good half hour.

Mrs R   (*evasively*).   Sometimes
                 It goes cloudy again very quickly.
                 I am a medium. I channel but can't
                 Control events or what I see coming.
                 I'm sorry I can't be more forthcoming.

                 (*She shakes hands with* PRINCESS *and* FINANCIER'S SON, *who leave.*)

                 Sometimes I see too clearly. Now I am
                 Appalled at what I've seen, and I'm aghast
                 And full of foreboding. The future has
                 Already happened on another plane,
                 In spirit where curved space bends two events
                 Like emblems far apart on flat paper
                 Which come together when the ends are joined
                 So past and future are both in the now,
                 And can both be known in the same instant.
                 In this strange dimension, future events
                 Are one with present potentialities.
                 Freewill is real, but the future reflects
                 On the curved surface of a tranquil mind,

And when I see something reflected there
I tremble, for I know it will happen.
Alas young lovers, your young love is doomed.

ACT TWO

SCENE 1

(*The* PRINCE *in the garden of his principal estate and country house, holding a hoe.*)

Prince.   The Crown rises to a point, divine Light
Whose rays descend and enfold a King's head,
Infusing wisdom and guidance so touch
Can heal the maimed, remove a leper's scars.
The divine steals towards my garden peace
Like sunlight spreading across clouded grass.
The Crown is shaped like the Light pouring round
A King's judgement, which heals a nation's soul
As does the power that channels through a priest.
A King's High Priest of the Church of England.
I would that I lived in the Tudor time
When a King had direct contact with all
Like a priest at communion, blessing each,
Not through the barrier of the alien State.
The King is the spirit of his nation
And channels divine Fire to its leaders.
I had a wife who usurped holiness
And held the sick and touched the poor as if
The divine right of Kings were hers, not mine.
I rejected the world's most stunning face
Spurning the senses for celibate life
As befits Plato's Philosopher-King.
I could not compromise my destiny,
And even my mother reproaches me.
She has cuckolded me with a Muslim,
Made me a laughing-stock with my people,
And now I must act in my own charade
And stoop on bended knee and ask her back

To protect my mother from dark reform,
Huge compromise of my integrity.
The Crown on my head is the divine Light,
And my Kingdom will be like this garden,
I plead for its soil to be organic,
Pure, uncontaminated by science,
Free from all pesticides and nitrogens
That destroy health and stimulate cancers
As much as nuclear waste. This garden's earth
Is like this Kingdom's culture, for it blooms
Self-controlled flowers and waste, profligate weeds.
The King, like a gardener, nurtures the earth.
The King must purify the soil with Light,
So from its metaphysical ferment
Grow herbs, roses, herbaceous borders
That reveal the perfection of the One
In individual forms, God's Universe.
The King is God's anointed, crowned with Light,
And his Kingdom nurtures the finest growths
Which riot colour like a spring hedgerow.
This garden is a miniature landscape,
A Kingdom where organic souls unfold.
The Sovereign guarantees sovereignty in
The nation and in souls, both soil and flowers,
And loss of sovereignty is spiritual loss.
A nation without sovereignty becomes
A cultural desert that knows no Light
Or tangled undergrowth of thistly weeds
Without order, morality or soul.
True aristocracy is in spirit,
True Kingship is illumined consciousness.
I will be the Defender of the Faiths.
I stand for the Tudor time, old England,
When Kingship was mystic and understood.
I'm rooted in the Tudors though German.
And so have nicknamed myself Prince Tudor.
I'm opposed to our anti-English time.
I must inform my people of this threat
From the Olympian Group. I must and will
Mobilize the nation to save the Crown,
Defend the monarchy so it survives.

To be Sovereign I must control my wife.
I must oppose all threats to sovereignty
And beg her stubborn frown to return home.

(*Enter his* HEIR, *a boy of 14.*)

Prince's Heir.   Father, I have been feeding the five geese.
Have you been hoeing?

Prince.   Hoeing and thinking.
I've been thinking about your mother. I
Am going to ask her to live with us.

Prince's Heir.   For the good of the Crown, the throne or me?

Prince.   All those, my clever heir. Especially you.
The Crown needs a united family.
Grandmother's throne will be stronger for it.

Prince's Heir.   I love Mummy, but am sad she's hurt you.
I want you to know that I understand
And thank you for trying for my sake now.

(*Exit* PRINCE'S HEIR.)

Prince.   Like bellbind, my flaw, strangling, chokes my soul,
The restless blood that made me turn elsewhere.
No one mentions that I have caused his pain.
I looked elsewhere for female company,
On my level, not her vacuity,
And found a depth that fills me with remorse.
My soul-companion is my paramour.
Liaisons suit Princes above the law.
But I've now withdrawn from carnal desires,
Renounced the flesh, purged and prepared my soul
To be enlightened by a spiritual crown
While I wait to inherit its temporal
Shadow, symbol of God's illumined power.
I am farther on my moral journey,
But am responsible for what I did,
And so I must now make amends and do

What I do not want but what duty should.
I've given my life to duty just as
A player gives his evenings to the stage.
I am an actor who has to perform:
Being a bland Prince from the royal train,
Stopping at stations, being cheered by crowds
And waving back, walking up muddy fields
In boots, discussing the countryside with
Farmers (who're in suicidal despair)
In seventeen-hour days with little food
And not much sitting down, keeping to their
Tight schedule, shaking hands, meeting people
Who toil in difficult, unrecognized
Lives, over whom I will soon reign as King.
It's a gruelling round of hard work, and I
Do it without complaining and I now
Must beg that preening flibbertigibbet
Who trumpets charity and loves to hear
The adoration of the mob, to live
With my sons (and me), out of duty. I
Long for the peace of this garden where I
Do not have to impersonate myself,
Where duty is a morning with a hoe.
I am apart from my people, who glint
From a great distance with their chilly smiles
As on a crisp evening a host of stars
Wink and twinkle in frosty, friendless air.
I am alone, am solitary in crowds
As a timid tree sparrow on a roof
Looks nervously around and then flies off,
But I am ruled by duty to the Crown.
My son, I should have made a sacrifice
For you that year my blood sang in my ears.

SCENE 2

(*The* PRINCE *at the Royal Palace, London. Enter* LORD GREEN.)

Lord Green   Why didn't you speak with me before you
                  Agreed to a reconciliation
                  With the Princess? Your attempt (for which she
                  Is typically an hour late) will be doomed.
                  The idea came from Rothschild's aide, through Hawkes.
                  He fed the idea to the Queen, he fears
                  The Princess is too close to Rockefeller,
                  Who's close to her new friend and his father
                  Along with the PM, who's on her side
                  And is encouraging her to become
                  An Ambassadress for his work abroad,
                  Which is mere image and can be conveyed
                  By her image-conscious presentation.
                  Hawkes does not want you reconciled for you
                  Or her, but to reduce Rockefeller's power.
                  I would have told you to refuse the Queen.

Prince.   It's easier to try and fail and say
                  I tried than to refuse and anger her.
                  Hawkes is a sinister…, like the PM.

Lord Green.   Much less sinister than their controllers,
                  And her new friend's financier father,
                  Who brought the last government down by gifts.
                  He intrigued to change the government and
                  Weaken your family, causing a storm
                  Of public opinion to turn against
                  Some blundering Ministers so Rockefeller
                  Could install his PM at the helm of
                  The nation to promote his policies
                  Of weakening the Crown and the Kingdom.
                  You'd think the Princess would avoid his yacht.
                  I have to tell you she's been seen aboard,
                  Sunbathing and familiar with his dad
                  While waiting for her new friend, ever since
                  We saw her rush from Hawkes in tears. She is
                  On her way to her rendezvous with you
                  From his dad's ship.

Prince.   She has been seen, you say?

Lord Green.	Photographed for tomorrow's newspapers.
Prince.	It's a public relations disaster –
Lord Green.	Not for Rockefellers, or tipped-off press.
Prince.	For her, for me, for the Queen. It now seems She's serious about this Muslim, or is She just defiant?
Lord Green.	Hawkes drove her aboard, But she chose to go.
Prince.	Any fool can see It's crazy to accept the financier's Hospitality on his yacht. She must Be being defiant.
Lord Green.	Or else under The sway of his great charm as he holds out The bait of his son, and thus she's fallen Under the sway of Rockefeller, as Both Rothschild and Hawkes fear. Hence his request For you to be reconciled.
Prince.	She may be Naively in love with this young man Just as she was with that fey army man. Where does that leave this chat?
Lord Green.	Doomed, in ruins.
Prince.	I must still try. I can then say I tried. (*Aside.*) A thunderstorm has spread dark wings across The sky like a huge cruel hook-billed eagle.

(*Enter* SIR WILLIAM HAWKES. *He looks askance at* LORD GREEN.)

Hawkes	(*aside*). This struggle in my soul fills me with gloom. I wanted to serve the Queen and Rothschild. Rockefeller discovered my secret

And I am now beholden to his will
And must perform whatever he requires.
I must report on the Princess's words
And I am filled with a disturbed feeling.
(*Aloud.*) Sir, the Princess is here. I will stay and –

Prince.   Take notes for the Queen?

Hawkes.   Make sure all is well.

Prince.   I'd rather meet her on my own, thank you.

Hawkes.   Sir, you put me in a most difficult
Position. It would be most unwise if
You saw the Princess without a witness
Who can confirm in future what you say
Should there be any dispute. The Queen has
Expressly requested this. I'm afraid
I must be present.

(*Enter* PRINCESS.)

Princess.   What's he doing here?
I left to escape him and his veiled threats.
I shall leave if he stays.

Prince.   Please leave. And you.
I know you've been requested, I'll take care.
(*Slowly* HAWKES *leaves, followed by* LORD GREEN. *They listen from
the side.*)

Even now I'm spellbound by your beauty.
You have the freshness of the bashful maid
I took as my bride near apple blossom,
And you have now matured in confidence.
Your grace, your poise, your deportment all draw
Me to you as I see the girl within
Ripened into a peach-cheeked lady's face
That now smiles from a thousand magazines'
Front covers and is widely held to be
The most beautiful in the world, and I

Am tongue-tied like a schoolboy by your power.
To think, you are my wife. You're still precious.
I think about you with such tenderness.
Even after so much, I'm sick with love
For you who once were meant to be my Queen.

Princess   (*harshly*). Why have you called me back, interrupted
My vacation?

Prince.   On Arab credit – with
The entire nation via tomorrow's press.
How could you when his father's vilified
Stay with a man of his reputation?
(*Controlling himself.*) But I did not ask you here to quarrel.
I have been talking with our elder son.
He misses you as I do. Can we put
The past behind us? Can we make it up?

Princess.   I don't believe I'm hearing this. Guy Fawkes
Must be behind this. You said I disgust
You, remember? You asked me to leave. You.
I cried a week at your cruelty. Now
You want to pretend that nothing's happened,
That there's no change. It has, there is. I love
My new man, and I want to bear his child.

Prince.   You what? A half-caste? A Muslim brother
Or sister for our son? What will the Queen
Say?

Princess.   Frankly, I don't care.

Prince.   A Muslim in
Our family? It's awful, I'm aghast.
And our son will head the Church of England.

Princess.   And his mother will be Muslim. So what?

Prince.   How can the mother of the Church's Head
Be a Muslim? The divine right of kings
Enfolds a King with power from the beyond.

A *Muslim*!

Princess.   I thought that would spike your guns.

Prince.   You've done this deliberately, I know.
                Your silence confirms that you've defied us.
                A Muslim. The word conjures Saladin
                And the Crusaders, the Lionheart's roar.
                A Muslim! My blood cries out against it.
                O please, please, say you were having me on.

Princess.   I love my new man and I'll marry him –

Prince.   Muslim stepfather to the future King?

Princess.   And honeymoon upon his father's boat,
                And sun myself in Southern France's ports.
                This palace is a prison. Do you think
                I can stay here, to be threatened by Hawkes
                Who spies on me and tells tales to the Queen?

Prince.   Not to the Queen –

Princess.   I want my happiness,
                I want to feel close to someone who cares.
                Someone *does* care for me, his father too.
                You don't care, you've turned to your paramour.
                Your family are cold and lack feeling,
                Their staff are cruel and unpleasant and old.
                Did you really believe I could return
                To you after you asked me to leave and
                Your family and staff insulted me,
                Made me a victim of their cold disdain?
                I love our sons and am taking your "heir"
                To see a film, remember – of my choice.
                The film's about Irish freedom-fighters.

Prince.   Not the one that sides with the terrorists?

Princess.   It's my choice and you can't do anything.

(Re-enter HAWKES, followed by LORD GREEN.)

Kindly excuse me, I am due elsewhere.

(Exit PRINCESS.)

Hawkes.
We heard it all, she did not lower her voice.
I am stunned and appalled, for you, the Queen.
I will report what I have heard to her.

Prince.
We don't know that she was telling the truth.
She's impetuous, wants to shock the world.

Hawkes.
We will find out.

(Exit HAWKES.)

Lord Green.
It is worse than I thought.

Prince.
I did my duty. I am still alone.
O Horace, I am sick at heart. My "heir"
Was hoping I would mend the jagged tear
Down the sheet of my marriage-bed. I loved
Her once, and part of me still does, despite
The hostility she shows me which is
As fierce as a goose's, its neck stuck out.
Marry a Muslim and then bear his child.
A Muslim in her royal womb. I have
Often proclaimed that all mankind follows
One religion – that Christians, Muslims, Jews
Are one with Hindus and Buddhists in Light –
But I also know the Church of England's
The best way to reveal the common Light
Which rises in all places of worship
Like water-table springs in ancient wells.
I'm a sovereign of the world, but first I
Must be Sovereign of the English nation,
And though I see the Fire of the *Koran*
And admire Muslim culture, may sympathise
With Muslims, I, who have been born to rule
England, abhor a Muslim in our blood,

Half-Arab half-brother of my own heir,
Who will be near the throne when he is Head
Of the Church of England and guided by
Fire that descends from Heaven, shaped like a crown.
O Horace, I have the world in my soul,
But a Muslim. A Muslim. It's awful.

Lord Green.   It's been a shock and you are exhausted.
It's best to lie down and maintain your health.

(*Exit* PRINCE. SIR WILLIAM HAWKES *appears*.)

Hawkes.   This is catastrophic. A Muslim child,
A half-caste Muslim near the English throne.
To her face we receive her ambition
With deference, but now judge it with contempt.
This will break the Queen's heart, unless we can
Solve the problem.

(*Exit* SIR WILLIAM HAWKES.)

Lord Green.   He must have bugged this room.
If Sir William Hawkes knows, then Rothschild will.
He is condescending to the Prince and
The Princess and treats them like small children.
What did he mean, "Solve the problem"? I fear
That something terrible will soon happen.

SCENE 3

(*The Royal Palace, London. Sir* WILLIAM HAWKES, *the* QUEEN *and the* DUKE)

Hawkes.   Ma'am, she won't hear of it. She's adamant.
The Prince tried, but to no avail. She is
Exceptionally strong-willed. And so we
Still have a problem. She is now back on
His father's ship off Rockefeller's port.

Queen.   I am saddened by her intransigence,

And disappointed by her defiance.

Duke.   She's like a child in a minefield, without
Understanding of the danger she's in.
And we are in a quagmire, our feet stuck.

Hawkes.   I will control the news around the boat.
I will throw a ring of silence round it.
Mr Rockefeller wants more pictures
But our launches will keep *paparazzi*
At a distance. We will frustrate their plan.

(*Sir* WILLIAM HAWKES *bows and withdraws.* AN AIDE *enters.*)

Aide.   Sir, Mr Rothschild's here.

Hawkes.   Please, show him in.

(ROTHSCHILD *enters.*)

My dear friend, thank you for visiting us.
Before you see the Queen I must ask you –
We have a small problem with the Princess.
She's now back on his father's ship, the press
Are circling my exclusion zone. Can you –

Rothschild.   Your information was invaluable,
And your control is appreciated.
Rockefeller's waged war on the Queen and
The territorial integrity
Of Israel, and I'm just not having it.
This tiresome girl does not deserve the Prince.
He should take a new bride who can be Queen.
My dear William, leave everything to me.

SCENE 4

(*A square in Jerusalem, Israel. The Israeli* LEADER, *ally of Rockefeller, is speaking in English.*)

Leader 1.	Fellow Israelis, I now say to you,
	It is time to make peace with all Arabs.
	We have been at war now for fifty years,
	Our State bristling with barbed wire like a camp.
	If we withdraw from neighbouring territories
	And co-exist with open borders, we
	Will live at peace, and trade as globalists –

(*From among the audience a lone assassin fires shots. The* LEADER *falls back dead. Some of the audience scream.*)

SCENE 5

(*A square in Jerusalem, later. The new Israeli* LEADER, *an ally of Rothschild, enters from the back of the theatre with his* ENTOURAGE *and stands in the audience and makes a statement for selected* JOURNALISTS.)

Leader 2.	Now that I've succeeded (*aside*) that wimp (*aloud*) hero
	Who was murdered by a lone assassin
	Appalled at new concessions by Israel,
	The peace process is at an end. Israel
	Will remain within her borders and build
	A settlement in east Jerusalem,
	Permanent homes for Jews on Jewish soil –

(*A* PALESTINIAN *shouts out.*)

| Palestinian. | East Jerusalem's part of Palestine. |

| Leader 2. | Arrest that man. |

(*The* PALESTINIAN *is arrested and taken away, struggling and kicking.*)

	East Jerusalem has
	Always been part of Israel, and will be.
	No more questions.

(LEADER 2 *fights his way onto the stage, where* ROTHSCHILD *appears.*)

Rothschild.	Bloody, but for the best.
	He had to go, he jeopardized our State.
	Congratulations, an excellent start.

Leader 2.   Thank you, very much. Our Israel is safe.
I've reversed Rockefeller's peace process.
The American President will baulk –

Rothschild.   We're dealing with the Vice-President now.

Leader 2.   But the process is reversed in Israel.
What's next on your agenda?

Rothschild.   It concerns
The English Crown, Israel's faithful ally.
I want to reverse Rockefeller's plan
To hole and sink the monarchy, using
The Princess as unwitting Exocet.

(LEADER 2 *nods. Exeunt.*)

SCENE 6

(PRINCESS *in swimsuit and the* FINANCIER'S SON *are sunbathing on the deck of the financier's boat. Enter* FINANCIER *to one side.*)

Financier   (*aside*). All my life I aimed to be near the Queen.
Ever since my friends who're in high places
Arranged for me to leave the Middle East –
Where I was a Bedouin camel trader
Who lived in desert tents before I moved
To Alexandria's poorest district –
And come to England, and put me in touch
With bankers whose loans started me in trade
So I now own a great department store,
Castles and palaces, huge country homes,
Ships like floating hotels and private planes,
I dreamed of being royal by marriage.

I wanted a passport and when those fools
In that tired government rejected me
I brought them down with my brown envelopes.
But I had only respect for the Queen,
Donated to the Princess's charities
And heaped her sons with electronic gifts,
My managers have often rung her staff,
And now I have the prize within my grasp
As I listen to my own son, my boy,
Propose to the Princess, make me royal and
Win me longed-for citizenship while I
Hobnob with the royals as family
And impress Egypt and the Syndicate.

(*The* FINANCIER *hides and eavesdrops on* PRINCESS *and his* SON.)

Financier's Son.   I am so happy, I wish this moment,
This sun, sparkling sea and cloudless blue sky,
And you in the centre, between them all,
Could last forever. My heart's full of love.
You are everything to me, and I dread
The ending of this trance-like ecstasy.
My love, I would be glad to die to keep
Alive forever this serenity,
Our breaths in unison, our beings tied
To each other, the world outside a haze.
My love is as deep as the ocean bed
And aspires to the height of mountain peaks.
But no, not even the whole universe
Could include all my love, if it could be
Shaped into a receptacle for it.
I love you, *you*, now and forever, none
Other, and I want you to bear our child.
I have here a large diamond of great worth.
I tremble as I offer it to you,
My goddess, in the hope that it will soon
Be followed by our marriage when you are
Ready to declare that you will be mine.

Princess.   It's a beautiful diamond. Oh, thank you.
It will always remind me of this sea

In which a million diamonds flash and fade.
My love, I too am happy, ecstatic.
I want to be with you and no other.
But first I must return to England and
Talk to my sons, explain our future life.

Financier's Son.　You can live with me in Los Angeles.
We can be US citizens, it's been
Agreed, and your sons can live with us there
And still attend boarding-school in England.
We are flying early this afternoon
From this sunshine to Paris –

Princess.　　　　　　　　　　　　　　Not Paris.

Financier's Son.　It's the only flight that can transport us
In time to reach England tomorrow. Oh,
You're thinking of Mrs R? Yes?

Princess.　　　　　　　　　　　　　　I am.

Financier's Son.　We'll only be in Paris a few hours.
I have to pick up an important ring.
We'll fly to England tomorrow morning.
Paparazzi. In the helicopter.
Run for cover. We can't stay here now.

SCENE 7

(*A hotel foyer in Paris. The* PRINCESS *and* FINANCIER'S SON.)

Financier's Son.　The Hotel's besieged with photographers.
We're going to leave by the rear entrance.

Princess.　　　　　I do not understand why so many
Paris agency photographers met
Our plane at the airport. Who tipped them off?

Financier's Son.　Someone had information, and tracked us.

The *paparazzi* have been camped outside
For several hours now, someone's after us.

Princess.   They're after me, not you. They want us both.

Financier's Son.   I see you in the speedboat on the Seine.
This afternoon we stood together, spray
Whipping beside us, cool wind in our hair,
And no photographers could match our speed.

Princess.   The speedboat's nose was up, wind blew our hair.
You steered the wheel, we were just one motion,
One forward surge that dashed a haze of spray
And left photographers standing on banks.
Time stopped and I had a premonition:
We were two angels speeding towards Heaven.

Financier's Son.   Come on, our driver's waiting. Run for it.

Princess.   Oh no, a black saloon. It's black, it's black.

SCENE 8

(*At The Prince's Estate. The* PRINCE *asleep, and* LORD GREEN.)

Lord Green.   Sir, please wake up. Something awful's happened.

Prince.   What is it?

Lord Green.   Sir, the Princess has been killed.

(*The* PRINCE *sits bolt upright.*)

He too. They left their hotel soon after
Midnight in a large black car with tinted
Windows so no photos could be taken.
The French driver drove fast, they were pursued
By speeding helmeted motorcyclists.
They came to a tunnel at too great speed.

Somehow their black car swerved and collided
With a central reservation pillar,
Ripping off a mirror, shattering glass
And crunching it into a battered wreck.
Both the driver and he were killed outright.
The Princess was tended at the scene by
A doctor. The French police cordoned off
The car, and yet a crucial hour elapsed
Before she was driven to hospital,
Where she was pronounced dead two hours later.
No seat-belts, which would have saved them, were worn.
All CCTV cameras on their route
Had been switched off, no one is quite sure why.
It's a very suspicious accident.

Prince.   I am devastated. I am distraught.
I loved her, Horace, more than I can say.
I do not know whether her death was caused
By human or divine hand. Please leave me.

(*Exit* LORD GREEN. THE PRINCE *sobs.*)

Dead. Killed in a car accident with *him*,
The woman I once loved, my sons' mother,
The woman who should have become my Queen.
I see her in a formal garden, on
A moor, in a field of wild flowers, before
She defied me and vied for my people.
Dead, with him and the driver. His father
Has lost his son while I have lost a wife
Who laughed in my face as she turned to him;
And my sons have lost their dear mother. Dead.
Dead, and now she can't marry a Muslim
Or bear a Muslim child who could then be
My sons' half-brother, swarthy Muslim child
Who would bring impure blood into our line
And would be near the throne, bring his father
Into my extended family. Who
Is that man? Why did he ask her to stay?
Dead. Now neither *he* nor his father can
Worm their way into my sons' waiting years.

Dead in an accident, or can it be
That both were murdered by Olympians?
If so I suspect Hawkes' Israeli side,
And I am now afraid the Palace is
A dangerous place, where staff spy on us,
And I cannot be sure whom I can trust.
She doubted everyone and is now dead,
And I must now be canny to survive.

SCENE 9

(*A hospital mortuary, Paris.* TWO FRENCH NURSES.)

Nurse 1.   The Prince has come to take the Princess home.

Nurse 2.   He's asked to see her first, he's with her now.

(*The* PRINCE *is disclosed, standing affected beside the body of the* PRINCESS.)

Prince.   Alas, alas, that after all my love
It should have come to this. You look so pale
And peaceful, your proud beauty torments me.
I brought you to this, and now feel remorse.
I would I had stayed with you and my sons.
And yet, you turned away from me and would
Not return when I asked you to. You said
You had been threatened, and I did nothing,
Thinking that you thought I was behind it.
And look at you now. I will not forget
How disdainful you look and how you came
To be here, who might have done this to you.
If this was no accident but design,
There can be no forgiveness for this deed
And I will take revenge on all those who
Did this to you and will not rest till I
Have exposed those who drove you to your death,
Planned for your car to smash into the post,
And caused these ghastly injuries that stain

Your broken body. I now trust no one,
And must work secretly to guard the Crown.
I am in mysteries like a child alone
In a dark castle, who imagines sounds
He's soon convinced are ghosts or murderers.
As in a crenellated rampart seized,
I must protect myself from ruthless foes
Who rule the Palace and lurk within each
Nook and cranny, and plot for their own ends,
Courteous and fawning enemies within.
It would be easy to fall ill and be
Paranoiac about their total power.
If, if this is no mishap but intent,
I will not exact blood revenge – I scorn
To stoop that low – but public exposure.
As I expose them and take my revenge
I must not show my true feelings, I must
Hide my real thoughts behind a grinning mask.
I cannot champion "modernizing"
But I can pretend to be deluded,
The victim of a dark conspiracy.
If this is no chance but a planned event,
I will protect myself by adopting
A deranged Prince's persona, speak out
And rail against what's rotten in the land,
Be dissident against the Syndicate.
I'll put aside my thoughts for more extreme
Opinions that may seem a little mad
So courtiers say that I am crazed with grief
For you, my love, and have changed my beliefs
And had the pattern of my mind disturbed.
I will now challenge the Olympian plan,
Rockefeller's and Rothschild's dark plottings.
I will oppose both sides and expose them.
I swear this on your heart, my faithless wife.
And now I'll take you home for burial.

ACT THREE

SCENE 1

(The Great Hall at Rothschild's English estate. Enter ROTHSCHILD and an AIDE.)

Rothschild.   I warned Rockefeller I would resist.
I will not tolerate his encroachments
(Which happen stealthily, without warning,
Via proxies) – Presidents or financiers –
On Israel and her ally, England's Crown.
Now the danger to the throne's been removed,
Her whose soft heart embarrassed the monarch,
Rockefeller is rethinking his plans.
Gone's his window of opportunity
To kidnap and influence the Prince's sons,
Using her young friend like a terrorist,
And hijack Britain's Royal Family
By stealth to undermine our alliance
And then, by-passing my known objections,
Create a *republican* world empire
And run the world from New York, all nations
States in a United States of the World.
The New World Order's still a compromise,
A power-sharing between his views and mine,
Europe and America in balance.
I knew the Princess well and much regret
That it should come to this, but given the course
She most unwisely chose, it's for the best.
I suspect the PM will be sent as
Rockefeller's next envoy, to encroach
With plans to "modernise" the monarchy.
I know Rockefeller would abolish
The Queen's constitutional powers so that
She can't dismiss the British government
When (having abolished the House of Lords
After hereditary peers' voting rights,
Including Rothschilds', her husband's and sons')
It breaks the Kingdom up into twelve states
And slides each fragment to mighty Europe.

I fear Rockefeller's asked the PM
To camouflage, with calls to "modernise",
This plan and secure royal assent. I've warned
The Queen, but go now and alert Lord Green.
A united, nation-state land's the best
Defence against this Rockefeller's drive
To fragment all countries and "Yankeeize"
The bits as states in *his* World Government.

SCENE 2

(*The Royal Palace, London. The* PRINCE *alone.* LORD GREEN *enters.*)

Lord Green.　　　　Sir, the Prime Minister's here.

Prince.　　　　　　　　　　　　Send him in.
But listen, for he's like a bird of prey,
A kestrel hovering upon the wind,
Now still, now flapping wings, but motionless,
Benign, benevolent, harmonious,
Eyes intent on a rustle in the grass,
Who swoops when he sees field mice he can hunt,
Whose apparent calm hides murderous intent.

(*Exit* LORD GREEN. *Enter the* PRIME MINISTER.)

Prime Minister.　　Sir, I have come to consult you as we
Prepare to mourn for our people's Princess.
Across our states and regions there has been
An upsurge of popular grief, and we
Must catch the mood of the people during
Her funeral service in our packed Abbey.
Our preparations have broken new ground.
Her family should give the eulogy.
I will read the lesson. We thought a song
Would be more popular than a poem
From the Poet Laureate, which will perplex,
And we have chosen a pop singer whose
Chords are sentimental and will secure

A high approval rating for his song.
We want the people to show their feelings
And such a service will release sorrow
And show our regions united in grief.
Will you approve our radical approach?

Prince   (*aside*). He's breaking up my Kingdom, and he wants
To convey through the funeral an image
Of a whole nation united in grief.
He needs this for *his* approval ratings.
(*Aloud.*) It's both modernised and modernising.

Prime Minister.   Exactly. While we are on that subject,
I wonder if we have your full support
For our modernizing reforms? You are
Sympathetic to the causes that were
Dear to the Princess's heart – poverty,
Comforting the underprivileged and
Homeless, finding jobs for the unemployed –
And can see that, through no fault of her own,
Because her advisers have not kept up
With the times, the Queen has a staid image
That needs changing. Would you help me change it?
Will you oppose the wasteful pageantry
Of the State Opening of Parliament?
Can I call on you to support reform?
You know the House of Lords blocks change, will you
Support me in removing voting rights
For hereditary peers, who are perceived
By the people as leeches who do not
Contribute to society? Would you
Speak to the Queen and recommend ending
The voting rights of *élite* parasites
On my behalf, for the popular good?

Prince   (*aside*). This is the approach my mother warned me
Rockefeller would make. I'm shocked that it
Has come from my mother's Prime Minister
Who's supposed to be within Rothschild's camp.
He seems ambivalent in his support.
I promised her not to support reform

Which would weaken the Kingdom's unity
And my family. And if I agree
I will be in danger like the Princess.
I must prevaricate and dissemble.
(*Aloud.*) Prime Minister, I am in no fit state
To think clearly about anything now.
I am exhausted from the shock we all
Felt when we heard the dreadful news, and from
The journey to recover her body.
I keep seeing her pale face in the morgue
And my sons' crying after I told them.
I am not well, I'm somewhat feverish.
I need to go and lie down. We will talk
Another time when I am thinking straight.

Prime Minister.　　We'll speak again. My way's the only way
To save the monarchy in this dark time.
If you won't support me, you may find you
Have no throne or Kingdom to inherit.

(*The* PRIME MINISTER *bows and leaves. Enter* LORD GREEN.)

Prince.　　You heard?

Lord Green.　　　　Yes, sir.

Prince.　　　　　　　　If I won't seek reform
"The people" will destroy the monarchy.

Lord Green.　　That argument goes back to Cromwell's time,
Cook used it at the trial of Charles the First
And it's in the US Constitution.
The PM's echoing Rockefeller
Who's drawn on those two ancient precedents.
You answered well. Now wait for his response.

SCENE 3

(*Next morning at the Royal Palace, London. The* PRINCE. *Enter* LORD GREEN.)

Lord Green.	The papers all carry the same story:
	The Queen has not come to London to grieve
	And therefore has given the impression
	She does not care about the Princess. She
	Has not even flown the Royal Standard
	At half mast. That's protocol, of course, but
	It's suggested she's old and out of touch
	And the monarchy must be modernised.
	It's pressure on you to agree to that
	And pressure on your entire family.

| Prince. | Pressure from whom? The Prime Minister or |
| | Olympians? |

| Lord Green. | Both. |

| Prince. | Hmm. |

Lord Green.	The world government
	Wants to cut the monarchy down to size,
	Which means reducing its traditional role.
	They have three press barons who do their will.
	They own the quality and gutter press.

Prince.	I am appalled the press has such stories.
	I'm equally appalled at our image
	Of being out of touch. It's misleading.
	The government's manipulating us.
	I'm going to see my mother to ask
	Her to revolt against all sinister
	Politicians and devious bureaucrats.

SCENE 4

(*A Royal Palace in the English countryside. A screen. The* QUEEN *and the* DUKE *are watching the Prime Minister on television.*)

| Prime Minister. | They grieve with us. They feel our pain. The press |
| | Has got it wrong. They care and are of us. |

(*The* PRINCE *enters with* SIR WILLIAM HAWKES, *who turns and leaves. The* DUKE *switches off the screen with a remote.*)

Duke.

He's got a nerve. *We* feel *his* pain! Who does
He think he is? Whose family's bereaved?
It makes my blood boil to hear him hijack
Her in the name of our "people" and plead
For us as if we were heartless strangers.
Why, he's adopted a cockney accent
And dropped his aitches and descends into
Estuary English – " 'as go' i' wrong".
He's dumbed down his accent to be a man
Of the people, "demo'ic" and caring.
His glottal stop's a deliberate ploy.
His reverse elocution lessons say,
"I'm one of you, slovenly. Vote for me."
He drops his dignity with his dropped "t"s.

Prince.

Father, mother. The country's in uproar.
He's stirred the people up, his pleading has
Made us all seem remote and cold-hearted,
Germanic and almost misanthropic,
As if we had disowned a relative
Who was my wife and mother of my child.
I won't have it. I won't put up with it.
You told me, mother, I would be approached
And asked to side with reform against you.
It's happened as you said. *He* approached me –

(*Enter* SIR WILLIAM HAWKES, *having overheard.*)

Queen.

I think you must have been mistaken. He
Wanted your support for his Party's views.

Hawkes

(*aside*). I must speak up for Rockefeller's faction,
Yet the Prince makes me feel uncomfortable.
(*Aloud.*) With great respect, sir, Her Majesty's right.
You must have misconstrued something he said.
He is not an Olympian.

Prince.

But –

380

Duke.
                              He is
              Supportive of our monarchy, and what
              We need to do to guard our ancient throne.

Prince.
              Just now you had no time for him. And now
              You're using his language.

Hawkes.
                              With great respect,
              Your parents are both right, for they have seen
              If we make some cosmetic changes, we
              Will outmanoeuvre what is being said.
              It has been decided by consensus,
              We're leaving for London tonight, and we'll
              Fly the Royal Standard at half mast. We'll
              Show we're not out of touch.

Prince.
                              And you, father?

Duke.
              It's been decided that we must respond
              To public disquiet to neutralize it.
              I personally am not happy that
              We who embody the best old values
              Should be dictated to by this small man
              Who would be President and his new code.
              But I defer to the Queen and consent
              To adopt a modern posture for now
              And spin new popularity for us.

Prince
              (*aside*). They're pretending to champion his views
              And welcome modernizing and profess
              He's not an Olympian. Something's happened.
              (*Aloud*.) I never thought to hear my proud father
              Speak so submissively, compliantly.

Hawkes.
              And you, sir? Do you support your parents
              In their wish to bring themselves up to date?

Prince.
              I do of course, which is to say I don't
              Enjoy departing from our ancient past,
              The sacral kingship that brings sacredness
              And meaning to British institutions –

But the demands of the present come first
And I will consent to bring in a time
When we are but pale shadows of the kings
Whose faces still send shivers down the spines
Of people who gaze at the old monarchs
And feel the awe so many used to feel.

Hawkes.   On your way out, sir, may I have a word?

(*The* PRINCE *looks at his parents and follows* SIR WILLIAM HAWKES.)

It's not easy for me to say this, but
I must. The monarchy is doomed unless
The Queen moves with the times, adapts, presents
Herself as being modern. She sees this,
And so does the Duke, and it is unwise
To destabilize them now with your doubts.
The Queen's advisers are all of one mind
And it would be comforting to them if
You pulled in the same direction as them.
The Princess wouldn't, look what befell her.
I mean, she went her way, cause had effect.
It would be a relief to all concerned
If you now support modernization.

Prince.   You spoke in such a tone to the Princess.
Who do you think you are? You do our will –

Hawkes.   You put me in an awkward position,
But out of respect I must correct you.
No, *not your* will. My masters' will.

Prince.   And who
Are your masters? (*Aside.*) I think he means Rothschild
But he must say.

Hawkes.   They are running the world,
And we are pawns in their profound chess moves.
I was appointed to serve them, and you.
They have your best interests at heart, but know
You're of the old world of blind nation-states,

They're of the new world of global vision.
I think we'll leave it at that for now, sir.
But just remember, there's a monarchy
Only because it suits my masters. And
The Queen's role is precisely what they wish.
In view of that it would be wiser if
You did not mention this conversation
To her. I have your best interests at heart,
I'm still perturbed at what struck the PM's
Labour predecessor – now at a sink
By a window, then suddenly no more,
And replaced by a stronger globalist.
It would be very wise if you did not
Attempt to see your parents for a while.
Till they've adjusted to their new role – till
The funeral service for your late Princess.
It would be wise to stay on your estate
And not see anybody for a month.

(*Enter* LORD GREEN, *who hovers.*)

Oh, Lord Green's been seconded to Scotland.

(*Exit* SIR WILLIAM HAWKES. *Enter* LORD GREEN, *who whispers.*)

Lord Green.   The clampdown has happened. We can't talk here.
It's unwise to talk within this Palace.
I have to leave at once and must now pack.

(*Exit* LORD GREEN.)

Prince.   What has happened? There's been a Palace *coup.*
My uncle advised me not to become
A Mason, and my father wasn't keen,
My grandmother opposed. They were all right.
I won't join a secret society.
And so I've opposed the Olympians –
And so I am now a target they scorn.
I can't talk to my parents now, but must
Appear supportive of a *coup* I loathe.
I am alone, I do not understand

What's happened, who's in charge – Rockefeller,
Rothschild – but I now know I must conceal
My resistance under a cloak of mirth,
Geniality, bonhomie and rapport.
I am maddened at the turn of events,
And I must act as if I am half-mad
And bide my time and expose the tyrants.

SCENE 5

(*The Royal Palace, London. A Goon, the Prince's jokingly appointed* FOOL, *is waiting. Enter* LORD GREEN.)

Lord Green.   What are you doing here?

Fool.   Everyone's got
To be somewhere. I'm here.

Lord Green.   You're not supposed
To be here today. Nor am I. I'm just
Collecting something I left behind, then
I'm off to Scotland.

Fool.   And Scotland will be
Off from you.

Lord Green.   Not off me?

Fool.   No, drifting like
An oil rig with no anchor, pirate flag
Crossbones, no skull.

Lord Green.   Saint Andrew's cross?

Fool.   Correct,
Mastermind. Your nationhood's piracy.
Cutting your rig adrift, out with the plank.
You'll be in the water, Scotland will be
Off from you, and you'll be a banished skull.

And that reminds me, I don't watch TV.
Tell me what happened at the funeral.

Lord Green.   It was a sunny day. The sad Prince walked
With his two sons behind the gun carriage
That drew the Princess's coffin through streets
So thick with crowds it seemed war had ended.
Many people were in tears, many threw
Flowers into the road so the progress was
Fragrant and slow on a carpet of flowers.
The Prince looked straight ahead, very composed,
And glanced at where the half-mast Standard flew.
He reached the twin-towered, many-turreted
Abbey, left the sunshine for steepling gloom
And took his place by his sons and the Queen.
The eulogy was on loudspeakers in
The streets, the Princess's brother spoke out
And called the royal family heartless
And cold in their dealings with the Princess –
He meant he still had a mature mistress
When he proposed to the innocent girl,
It's true they've never lost their Hanovers'
Coldness – and spontaneously the people
Began clapping, and the applause swept down
The Mall and, hearing it, those at the back
In the Abbey took it up and it spread
Down to the front. The Prince sat po-faced but
His parents' faces showed pain and rage. Our
PM read unctuously, a pop star sang.
The august architecture of the gilt
Abbey became a backdrop for a gig.
She left by hearse. The driver drove slowly
And throughout its long, solemn, slow progress
People threw flowers that strewed the road and heaped
On the windscreen. The driver could not see.
Many wept openly in a display
Of national grief that has not been known since
The funeral after Kitchener drowned – no,
The funeral of the Duke of Wellington.
People have queued twelve hours to sign books of
Condolence at a hundred different towns.

	The outpouring has been phenomenal.
	The Princess has united the nation
	Against the globalists and their new world.

Fool.
I think the people threw flowers because she
Treated them as persons with souls, not as
Statistics like the Olympians, who see
"Useless eaters" to be liquidated.
She was sweet-smelling, the Olympians stink.
His face was like a chamber-pot because
He knew that.

Lord Green.   "Po-faced"?

Fool.
                         "Po-faced" means "pot-faced".
The Prince must have felt really peed on at
The clapping of the wife who so vexed him.
The media which destroyed her have now made
An icon of her, a secular saint.
The people have contrasted her caring –
And here I must speak with a Fool's licence –
With what they call the "righteous" family
She married into, which "treated her ill",
Condoned his crumpled mistress. Why does he
Need a dowdy wench more than a fresh bride?
That's how the people see it, not the Fool.
I think the people should be in the Tower,
Along with their tribunes and demagogues.
The Prince needs a lid put on his po-face,
And cheering up. When will he arrive here?

Lord Green.
He won't be here tonight, he's with his sons
On his estate. You're wasting your time here.

Fool.
I came on the off-chance. My whole life's been
On an off-chance. I'm off to his estate.

SCENE 6

(*The Prince's Estate.* SIR WILLIAM HAWKES *and* ROTHSCHILD.)

Hawkes.   Lord Green has been banished to the Highlands.
                The Prince is putting his two sons to bed.

Rothschild.   Good, Sir William. You have done well.
                Tragic accidents can have good results.
                The Prince is now under our control, and
                We can plan the guest list for his weekend.

                (*Voices off.* HAWKES *goes to see. Enter* WORMWOOD. *He confronts*
                ROTHSCHILD.)

Wormwood.   You're the man I've been sent to castigate.

Hawkes.   Oh dear, this is most unseemly. Not here,
                The time and place are inappropriate.
                Not now, you're an uninvited caller –

Wormwood.   I'm not going till I've told Mr Rothschild
                What Mr Rockefeller wants me to say.

                (*Enter* PRINCE *unobserved in his dressing-gown. He has heard the uproar.*)

Wormwood.   You lot killed her, Rockefeller's furious.

Rothschild.   We deny all responsibility.

Wormwood.   We're *both* running the world. You can't take out
                People without agreeing it with us.

Rothschild.   This isn't the place to discuss these things,
                Nor the time. Just remember where you are.

Wormwood.   We know you did it via intelligence
                And with encouragement from the Duke of –

Rothschild.   Complete and utter rubbish –

Wormwood.	Who said, "Such
	An affair's racially and morally
	Repugnant and no son of a Bedouin
	Camel trader is fit for the mother
	Of a future King."

Rothschild.	He's entitled to
	His opinion, you have no evidence.

Wormwood.	You asked the US President for help.
	He turned you down as he had just agreed
	To give them both US citizenship
	So they could raise her sons in Los Angeles
	During the school holiday access times
	In the house of his Arab stepfather –

Rothschild.	"*He agreed* "? You mean it was *your* order –

Wormwood.	A lie. You feared for the whole dynasty.
	You told Mossad to steal one of *his* new
	Limos, remove the electronics and
	Rebuild the car so that it could respond
	To external radio controls –

Rothschild.	Rubbish.

Wormwood.	The French driver had worked for many years
	For the French Secret Service and received
	Four thousand pounds a month in his account.
	You told him his route through the Seine tunnel.
	You told him to taunt the *paparazzi*.
	The poor unsuspecting driver lured them
	To provide cover for your agent who
	Was helmeted. Your motorcyclist roared
	Alongside him in the tunnel and shone
	A laser pen into the driver's face.
	Men in your white car sent a radio
	Signal that caused the black car to veer left
	And swerve into the central concrete posts.
	And then you switched blood samples in the morgue
	To claim that the driver had drunk too much –

Rothschild.	This fantasy suggests *you've* drunk too much. If there were external radio controls Why would we need a laser? It's rubbish.
Wormwood.	Though three bar staff and other bodyguards Say he did not drink at all that evening. You hit her and blamed Rockefeller's spies And he's livid and will retaliate –
Rothschild.	Calm down. If we had wanted to kill them, No way would we have chosen a high-speed Car crash. This was a banal accident.
Wormwood.	You chose that way to conceal your traces. You've removed yourself from our alliance –
Rothschild.	You were running *him*, you can't now complain. Just because you effected the transfer Of power from the last Prime Minister to This one by manipulating voters – By running a third man to split his vote.
Wormwood.	Rockefeller will sever all contact Unless you deliver at once to him His view of the monarchy like the head Of John the Baptist on a silver dish, Or rather, Louis Seize in a basket: Modernised, without a crown, taxed and not Above us, cut down to size. The Queen must Broadcast tomorrow saying that mistakes Have been made and will be remedied. You, Sir William, will ask this. Rockefeller Will be watching in his London hotel. You will submit the speech for me to read And make corrections – otherwise they stop, The dynasty will end, they'll be has-beens, The Queen, the Prince, his sons and the whole line Will be defunct if I don't read this speech. Either they modernise or abdicate, And if they won't, we're Cromwellians who Will take them out as you take people out.

If they're stubborn, they're dead.

Hawkes.   How distressing –

Wormwood.   You will submit a second speech that strips
                More than twenty HRH titles from
                The horde of grace-and-favour hangers-on.
                Secondly, the next dinner you host for
                The Queen or Prince must include me as we
                Can't trust you any more. We *both* now rule
                England, and we *both* shape their brand image.
                They're our prisoners as much as they are yours.
                I have two guest lists in my pocket here.
                Rockefeller wants these guests invited
                For the days on the top of the paper.

                (WORMWOOD *hands over two lists.*)

Rothschild.   The President of Europe's Commission,
                The UN Secretary-General. Will they
                Be in London on these dates?

Wormwood.   Yes, they will.

Hawkes.   We need to sit and scour these names. This way,
                We will discuss this further sitting down.

                (*Exit* SIR WILLIAM HAWKES, ROTHSCHILD *and* WORMWOOD.)

Prince.   We are their "prisoners", we do not count now.
                They choose what my mother will say and who
                Sits at my table. They want me – on pain
                Of death to the Queen, me, my sons – to be
                A compliant, complaisant puppet, their
                Ventriloquist's dummy, like their PM.
                Dark Wormwood put him in power and now works
                His smile, speaks from the corner of his mouth,
                Feeds Rockefeller's words into his lips.
                And they believe they are pulling my wires
                And, trapped in ceremonial events,

I cannot flee except to my garden.
They rule the world, there is no safe refuge;
Only my garden where I hoe and think
And can be my true self, not the "image"
They have already hung around my neck
Like a placard saying "I am for them" –
"I have no being beyond their wishes,
Support them and will deceive the public".
I will not accept such an existence.
And I am shocked. For what I overheard
Confirms my secret suspicions that she
Was not the victim of bad driving or
Reckless motorcyclists, but of murder.
The Princess murdered. That's what Wormwood thinks.
By intelligence. Though this is denied
And I have no objective evidence,
It is wisest to assume it is so,
It is safest to conclude that's the case.
The monarchy's a battleground between
Two factions of the world government. One
Seeks to abolish the Crown, hand England
To Europe as one of its many states;
The other would defend the royal line,
And this faction, using intelligence
Agents which it, this same faction, controls
(Though all think that British intelligence
Is under British government control),
Was too zealous in defending the Queen
From a threat to introduce Muslim blood
Into a line that's pure since George the First's
Hanoverian bough branched from Alfred's trunk
Like a limb on a great English oak's bole.
Royalists loyal to the monarchy
Defending the Crown I will one day wear
Have bereaved me and orphaned my children.
O misguided support that's laid me waste.
I must follow my hunch, which resonates,
And act as if she was in fact murdered.
Act how? Do what? Take my revenge on them?
If she was indeed murdered as I fear,
They doubtless thought that they were helping me.

Take revenge on those who, misguidedly,
Thought they were salvaging my family
From her headstrong liaison with Muslims?
Anglo-Israelis would not want the Queen
Soiled by a sullied Muslim connection.
The most telling revenge is exposure.
If our side's lieutenants ordered her death
They want to hide their deed from my people,
And I resolve to inform my people.
I don't want allies who do such things.
I must conceal my path, not leave footprints,
Work under cover of a false "image",
One that wrongfoots them. It is still allowed
To grieve, and to be left alone to grieve,
And I will appear grief-stricken – aloof,
Abrupt, intolerant when they're around,
Or their henchmen and spies. I will excuse
Myself as withdrawn into private grief.
I am their prisoner in the outer world
Whose full extent they rule – the whole globe's filled
With bugs and spies and beams they monitor –
But they cannot reach my inner world. I
Will withdraw into the sovereign Kingdom
Of my enclosed mind as I steal away
And hide within the walls of my garden.
From now the world is in disharmony
And the only order is in my mind
Within my herbaceous borders, my flowers
And the organic exchange between us
When mind and bloom are one, knower and known,
Within the Cosmic Order that sends rays
Deep into souls and pistils, vital force
Of Fire that strengthens faces and petals.
From now I will appear reclusive and
Detached from the hurrying, plotting world
Which is out of kilter with tranquil soul –
I will seem an intolerant recluse
Who is deemed mad by men who think they're sane
But whose violent deeds are far crazier.
I will withdraw from insane globalists
Into the sovereign peace of mere madness

And be as free as, in a prison cell,
A prisoner watching birds peck garden worms.
Oh dreadful world that defines freedom so!

SCENE 7

(*A suite in a London hotel. A television is on showing the Queen on an outside balcony.*)

Queen's voice.   Mistakes have been made. We will learn from them.
We will move closer to the people. We
Did not fly our London Royal Standard
At half-mast as we were not in London,
But we have now corrected this. Our flag
Flies at half-mast. We will learn the lessons.

(AIDE *appears.* ROCKEFELLER *turns off the television.*)

Aide.   That publisher's turned down the book that we
Commissioned on the Queen.

Rockefeller.   Does he realise
What he's got?

Aide.   No, sir.

Rockefeller.   That I asked?

Aide.   Yes, sir.

Rockefeller.   Send his shares into nosedive. Bankrupt him.

Aide.   The Ambassador for Iraq.

Rockefeller.   Come in.

(*Enter the* AMBASSADOR FOR IRAQ. *Exit* AIDE.)

Ambassador.   The Middle East is full of stories that

The Princess was murdered. Some say Western
Intelligence services, some Israel.
Iraq's President thinks it was Israel.

Rockefeller   (*nodding*). He thinks right, my friend. I would like to see
Israel repaid for her aggression. You –
The President and Iraq – both know well
What measures can be undertaken now.

Ambassador.   We obstruct the UN Inspection Team?

Rockefeller.   Throw them out. Don't obstruct them, throw them out.
But there are other measures you may take.
The Anglo-Israelis and rash Rothschild
Must learn that their acts have consequences,
And that when they attack a financier,
Who has been a good friend to the Arabs,
Killing his son and his son's future bride,
And when they kill Israel's Leader, who worked
For peace, they're threatened by Iraq's missiles.

SCENE 8

(*The* PRINCE *in the garden at his estate.*)

Prince   (*aside*). After the tempest I feel a strange calm.
It's like the cool after a thunderstorm.
The lashing rain seems like a mist and then
The stifling heat has gone, and there's relief,
And all Nature's as fresh as yellow gorse,
Or blood-red poppies splashed on a wheatfield.

(*Enter his* HEIR.)

Prince's Heir.   I thought I'd find you here in your retreat.
I thought you had some scientists?

Prince.   They've not

Arrived yet. My boy, we must speak alone
For it will be hard to talk alone now.
My boy, you've been so brave the last few days.
I was so proud of you at the service.
I don't want to say anything that will
Worry you at the present time. I must
Tell you things are not right in our Kingdom.
You know the world's run by Olympians
And that there are two factions – groups – at war
With each other, one for us, one against.

Prince's Heir.   Rothschild is for, Rockefeller against.

Prince.   Just so. Our government supports Rothschild
But knows it's controlled by Rockefeller.
At least that's how it seems. Brown envelopes
Manipulated the electorate
And made it vote to change Prime Ministers.
Some men thought that your mother was now with
Rockefeller, that your mother's new friend
Had somehow prised your mother from the Crown.
They feared she might weaken what we're doing.
I'm going to tell you something I've found out.
Rockefeller's men are sure that it's true.
This is a secret, you must never tell
A single living soul. They killed Mama.
It was not an accident. They killed her.

Prince's Heir.   You mean...?

Prince.   Yes.

Prince's Heir.   Are you sure?

Prince.   I overheard
Wormwood, who's with Rockefeller, accuse
The other camp. Your mother was murdered
By the world government, and they now want
To take the Crown away so I, and you,
Will not be King. I won't let that happen.
I am going to keep Britain sovereign.

I'm going to tell the English nation
What has happened. They will be on our side.
But I can't talk inside the Palace now.
They're listening. We mustn't talk inside,
Only here in my walled garden. And I
Must be clever and act like my Fool, so
They don't suspect what I'm doing. So if
I behave strangely, don't say anything,
And don't be worried. We will see this through.
If anything happens to me, you will
Carry on the fight for me, and Mama.
Together we will oppose the bad men
Who killed your mother and would take our Crown.
Will you be strong and brave and stand by me?

(PRINCE'S HEIR *clutches his father's hand and clasps him. They stand together holding each other.*)

Prince's Heir.   Poor Mummy. I wish she had never met....

Prince.   Someone's coming. Go now, out of that gate.

(*Exit* PRINCE'S HEIR, *running. Enter the* FOOL.)

Fool.   How now, nuncle. Your Fool to cheer you up.

Prince.   You haven't changed.

Fool.   My underpants, I have.
But you've changed, or your situation has,
Even though you were estranged from the Princess.

Prince.   No I'm just the same, solitary in crowds.
A little sadder, perhaps. I am still
Trying to make sense of the universe,
A Philosopher-King brooding on death.
I was deep in thought. Not too cheerful thought.

Fool.   Ah, a nihilistic thought, nothing thought,
A thought about nothing, a no-soul thought.
I have often been in just such a thought,

A little melancholy, black-biled, when
Care weighs. A Fool has more cares than most men.
Elizabeth the First had a Fool – not
Richard Tarlton, her official Fool, or
Will Somer, on whom Yorick was based. This
Was an unofficial Fool, a crackbrained
Italian who lived about Court and thought
All ships that came into port were his – named
Monarcho, who called himself "the Monarch
Of the World" and sometimes "Supreme Ruler
Of the universe". He was hugely weighed
Down by care. A serious Fool like him
Is a "philisipher", he's filled up, he
Takes all creatures into his soul and cares
How hedgehogs live and squirrels bury nuts.
Your peacocks are eating your flowers. They are
"Flosedacious", my neo-Euphuist
Neologism for "flower-devouring".
And the Supreme Ruler cares for earwigs.
The Sovereign of the World's loaded with care.
Only a Supreme Fool cares so widely.

Prince   (*laughing*). You've cheered me up. My care is a small care.
                Your "pavonism" tickles my fancy.

Fool.   Pavonism? What's that?

Prince.   Peacock-ism.
                My new word for a neologism
                That displays its feathers too wantonly.
                Like "flosedacious". Your fantail is up!

                (*Enter* SIR WILLIAM HAWKES.)

Hawkes.   Your guests are waiting.

                (*Exit* SIR WILLIAM HAWKES.)

Prince.   Bores from the sad world,
                Materialists, humanists and sceptics
                Who gnaw at surfaces on narrow leaves,

	Caterpillars, bright flosedacious bugs
	Who devour beauty, sting intelligence,
	Invited by Hawkes or by the PM.
	Thorn, all your good work's been undone. I feel
	A huge dismay at greeting such half-wits.
Fool.	They have no wits, not even quarter-wits.
	A mad linguistic philosopher, daft
	Atheist neo-Darwinist, hunchbacked
	Crazed Theory-of-Everything physicist –
	I wouldn't have your job for all the world.
Prince.	Creeping, Cheeping and Leaping, they're enough
	To make a distraught Prince appear half-mad.
	Stand back and observe, and we'll have some fun.
	Regard the effect on Sir William Hawkes.

(*Enter a* THIN MAN, *a* FAT MAN *and a* HUNCHBACK *with* SIR WILLIAM HAWKES.)

	Welcome to my garden. Sit on that seat.
	The Lord Chamberlain will no doubt listen.
	I'm sure he won't mind standing. I have been
	Listening to my Fool talking about
	The Ruler of the universe. I am
	A philosopher and pursue wisdom.
	He's a philisipher and probes folly.
	As philosopher and scientists, tell
	Me what existed here an hour before
	The Big Bang.
Philosopher.	Sir, there was no time before
	The Big Bang, so there was no hour before.
Prince.	So was there nothing before the Big Bang?
Physicist.	Sir, our mathematics go back to one
	Second before the Big Bang, no farther.
Prince.	But that one second could not be there if
	There was no time as you maintain, could it?

Physicist.	Our mathematics are notional, sir.
Prince.	I'm not interested in notions. I want To know how the universe came to form, From timelessness, eternity, to time. If you can't tell me that, then your science And your philosophy are flawed, and I Prefer mine, which are metaphysical. I say there was an infinite movement In the One, from which regular movement Created a spiral, squeezed out a point That was a vacuum of Non-Being From which unfolded existence, or form. Can you explain it in physical terms?
Philosopher.	Sir, one can't speak of timelessness. It's not A meaning we acknowledge. Only time.
Prince.	But I've used the concept, it *has* meaning.
Philosopher.	No, sir.
Prince.	I say Yes.
Physicist.	The world of physics Excludes metaphysics.
Prince.	But Einstein said Physics soon leads to metaphysics.
Physicist.	He Was wrong –
Prince.	But right on relativity. Spaceships voyage the cosmos through slingshot. His physical ideas work, why should not His metaphysical ideas also? Do you Believe life has order and purpose, or That it's an accident?
Neo-Darwinist.	An accident.

The universe is like a heap of dung.
Evolution began as a blind chance.

Prince.   You don't believe there is an after-life?
                           For you? For that ant? That stag-beetle there?
                           What has a soul? Do you? Or are your thoughts
                           Controlled by an outside force as if
                           You were dummies?

                (*The* PHILOSOPHER *and* SCIENTISTS *turn to* SIR WILLIAM HAWKES)

Neo-Darwinist.   I think it's best we go.

Philosopher.   There is no reasoning with His Highness.

Hawkes   (*almost whispering*). He speaks foolishly, I fear he's deranged.

Fool.   No, nor is he de-distanced, de-regioned,
                           De-ovened, de-targeted or de-rowed.
                           No, he is just overwhelmed by his grief.

Prince.   Goon, what do you think of this logician
                           And these scientists who see no meaning?

Fool.   Do they dribble words from their own mouths or
                           Do they spout others' thoughts like church gargoyles?

Prince.   You're a philisipher studying folly,
                           What is the meaning of this trio's pith?

Fool.   A spongy, rindy, marrowy meaning.
                           The logician and scientists cannot
                           Say how the universe emerged from God.
                           They are foolish for thinking that they can
                           And for channelling a rocker fellow's words.
                           I who know that they can't am less foolish.
                           He who thinks you are mad's a bigger fool.
                           But the Supreme Fool of the universe
                           Has taken leave of his reason and knows
                           He's a Ruler of irrational silence
                           As Monarcho did and as you do now.

The Sovereign of the World defends all things,
All creatures, plants and faiths, and plays God's role.
I bow to your vision, Monarcho.
You are a mad Ruler, I a sane Goon.

(*The* FOOL *takes his cap and bells off and puts it on the* PRINCE'S *head.*)

Prince.

A Fool has faith in life despite reason.
You're right, Goon, God's the biggest Fool of all.
I, Sovereign of the World, wear this for him.

Hawkes

(*hastily*). It's time to be off, thank you for coming.

(*Exeunt the* PHILOSOPHER *and* SCIENTISTS.)

Sir, I think it's time you came in for bed.
(*To the Fool.*) You should be ashamed of yourself, this cap
And bells mock His Highness's dignity.
You know he is beside himself with grief.

Fool.

Dignity is most mocked by deference
Which conceals a scathing, lying contempt.
I am Spike the Fool. On the radio
I entertain with jests, here wear a cloak
Of motley to tell truths to men who lie
And like an actor lie to tell the truth.

Prince.

Fool, entertain, enlighten and provoke
And stir with truths these serious new men.

(*The* FOOL *ambles forlornly away. The* PRINCE *addresses* SIR WILLIAM
HAWKES.)

The Fool is old. He's made the nation laugh
Like a caged hamster in a turning wheel
Who scampers nose up and goes nowhere fast.
But now he's stuck in the past, hates the world,
Thinks of his childhood, music hall parents,
His youth in India's burning white sun,
His wartime memories, battle fatigue.
He was born into the British Empire,

He's seen the nation dwindle while he mocked.
Like Yorick he's had tables on a roar,
He's spent a lifetime lapping up applause,
But now he's rather sad and you must make
Allowances and not be so severe.
(*Exit* SIR WILLIAM HAWKES.)
Dwindled, from an estate to a garden.
My Kingdom's overgrown and in decline.
This England is at best a jewelled isle,
Apart from Europe, set in a blue sea
Like a precious diamond set in turquoise
Or the central knot in my herb garden.
She has a special destiny, to bring
All men to a perception of the truth,
The infinite, reality, spirit.
Those born in England had their consciousness
Raised by her culture to a high level.
Sovereignty gave them sovereignty over
Themselves – evolutionary advancement.
The Cecils dispersed this with their profane
Imperialism (which meant genocide
For brave Ireland), made the Queen their puppet
From the year of the Spanish Armada
And Dudley's decease, looked beyond these shores
Towards America and India
(Both of which were run from Smythe's London house)
And took to stealing others' property
Like Falstaff cutting purses, occupied
Islands, regressed from angels' souls to beasts.
Now our Cecils are globalists who strut
On a world stage and colonize this globe,
And this England is the last colony
Of a vanished Empire, whose purse they cut,
A new challenge to English sovereignty.
Yet England still has her proud destiny.
Her sovereignty is like a golden coach
Drawn by horses which give it motive power.
So do the people give it vital force,
As praying men give God motive *élan*
And keep the divine power moving through minds.
A monarch embodies Truth and the Light

Like Phoebus in his flaming chariot,
And service to the Truth-bearing monarch
Keeps mystic sovereignty shining in souls
As service to the Truth keeps Light alight.
Our sovereignty is our great destiny
And is led by people's willing service
As four horses draw Plato's chariot
And are held in place by the charioteer.
England's the world's spiritual centre,
Having sloughed off two empires to become
The Light of the cosmopolitan World.
Here all the world's citizens can arrive
And learn to conquer their base natures and
Aspire to visions of profound things like
The philosopher's stone, spiritual gold,
And I will be the universal Crown,
Symbol of crown *chakra* opened in bliss,
Serene eyes, mental calm and tranquil mood.
I will look to tradition's mystic way
As Raleigh and Oxford looked to Bruno
And Dee's occult Neoplatonism
To flee the dangers of the Protestant-
Catholic conflict, beheadings and burnings –
I will be crowned with a spiritual crown.
I will lead my Kingdom back from what's soiled
To the rich soil of our English garden,
Back from town filth and corrupt ways, from deep
Decline and disintegration (its four
Quarters all sundered to fragments) to this
Rural, pastoral idyll, to this peace
Which could be lifted from the Tudor time.
I am head of a spiritual nation,
I will regenerate the English soul
And oppose foreign tongues with English speech
And draw on the medieval values
That preceded the time of the Cecils
And champion the truthful vision as
A patriot of old English culture –
When I have exposed the world government.

ACT FOUR

SCENE 1

(*A suite in a Jerusalem hotel, Israel.* LEADER 2 *and* ROTHSCHILD.)

Leader 2.   Ever since he lost his estranged Princess,
I've heard worrying things about the Prince.
His behaviour is quite bizarre. He tells
People he does not want to see them, and
Openly says they are boring, tiresome.
Our Ambassador thinks he's going mad.

Rothschild.   He's still distressed at the Princess's death.
He was much closer to her than was thought.

Leader 2.   Now Iraq's ruler's turned hostile, blames us
For the Princess's death and threatens us
With chemical and germ warfare weapons.
We know he's many WMDs
Which the UN Inspection Team has missed.
We've asked the American President
To act, but he dithers. We want him out
And his Vice-President to take his place.
He is a friend of Israel and will bomb.

Rothschild.   You've asked for this before, and it's our plan:
The President impeached for his scandals –
His corrupt property dealings, of course,
But we reckon his sexual outrages
Offer the best chance. The name of one dame
He propositioned is on every lip
But there are others. So many women
Will testify to what he did to them.
There's one woman who is willing to speak.
A Jewish lady has researched her case
And now controls her friend who's taped her words.
They're incriminating, I can tell you.

Leader 2.   Can we agree that he will be removed?

| Rothschild. | Yes. He's all image and no substance, we |
| | Already ignore him for his Vice-President. |

SCENE 2

(*The Oval Office in the White House, Washington. The* PRESIDENT *and his* FIRST LADY. *On the television screen a lady is shown, and another. Then the independent prosecutor.*)

Prosecutor.	I want to bring my inquiry into
	Property dealings and alleged affairs
	To a swift conclusion, and I may name
	The President as perjuring himself.

(*The* PRESIDENT *turns off the screen.*)

US President.	Can you believe that prat? He's crazy, he's
	A zealot, he'll do anything to hang
	Me. How long can I brush legal lynching
	Aside and seem untroubled in public?

First Lady.	If you hadn't propositioned that tramp
	And lowered your – exposed yourself to her,
	And had that trollop come in this office
	Right here to hug your knees because you think
	Casuistically the mouth keeps marriage vows,
	And carelessly stained her dress with your – urghh!
	So after she walked out past all the guards
	The manipulative bitch could boast that
	She had evidence of your sordid act,
	Then we would not have half this problem now,
	And we'd be concentrating our efforts
	On blocking the trumped-up property charge.
	You're an addict, you're compulsively weak,
	You can't help yourself, you have no willpower
	On evenings when a flunkey invites you
	To sign her lips like an autograph book.
	Well that's all right, that's part of our deal, but

You were always going to be discreet,
And you've, stupidly, taken risks and been
Selfishly thoughtless, thrown caution aside,
You've not behaved like a true President.
As usual I will have to bail you out.
You will deny it, using words I'll write.
I'll scour dictionaries and judges' judgements
For definitions that skirt what you did,
So you can deny "sexual relations".
I'll find a formula whose semantics
Deny without lying, so if that dress
Comes back to haunt us you won't be impeached.
I will give an interview and go out
Across our land, from east coast to the west,
Stating your innocence, and accusing
Right-wing conspirators of hounding you.
We know that's true: Rothschild is after you
Because you're urging Israel to withdraw
From Palestine. He wants you out and your
Vice-President in: he will support them
And oppose all Israeli withdrawal.
Rothschild's friend Israel has paid that trollop
And the mercenary who taped her complaints.
So you must appear to take Rothschild's side.
Have nothing more to do with withdrawal,
Transfer that role to the naive PM,
Who'll love to take it on for the kudos.
Let England and the EU press Rothschild
For Rockefeller, that's why he's given *him*
And all those pompous Europeans jobs.
Subcontract urging, distance us from it.
Then square up to Iraq. *His* weapons threat
Gives you a chance. The UN Inspection
Team's finding nothing – say you'll bomb Iraq.
Send an aircraft carrier, no send two
To the Mid East to protect Israel and
Threaten Iraq with a cruise missile strike.
Israel will be delighted and will stop
Plying you with tarts, knowing you are soft
And weak and cannot help yourself and will
Easily fall for plots so transparent

And obvious a child could fathom them.

US President.   You say I'm soft, yet I've already signed
                    An order to nuke Iraq if its boss
                    Does not back down and admit the UN
                    Inspectors to his palaces.

First Lady.   Mossad
                    Showed you "evidence" you believed.
                    They know you're gullible. You have to be
                    Ahead of events, not puffing behind.
                    You did the right thing for the wrong reason.
                    You signed the order because you believed
                    Mossad, who always lie, and not because
                    You were picking your way through the minefield
                    Of Rockefeller's and Rothschild's landmines.

US President.   You are a formidable First Lady.
                    Can you, do you think you can turn them round,
                    The American people? And make out
                    She's lying if she testifies on oath
                    To things she said she did with me?

First Lady.   I can.
                    But I need help. When the PM comes here,
                    I need him to say in public that you
                    Have integrity. You yourself once said
                    A lie can seem truth if properly dressed.
                    The perception of you is all that counts,
                    What the public perceives the truth to be.

US President.   I'll be indebted to you, and I won't
                    Forget this rescue. I will play my part.

                    (*Exit the* PRESIDENT.)

First Lady.   My poor husband. He's helpless in their hands.
                    For all our separate lives, I love him still.
                    He's like a child and needs my staying hand.
                    He lacks self-restraint and must be restrained.
                    He does not see Rockefeller will do
                    Anything to stop the Vice-President

From succeeding him for Rothschild's faction,
Would prefer a Rockefeller to him,
That if he falls they will be asking me
To take over the reins and steer the world
From the Oval Office in the White House.
He's only in the coachman's seat as long
As I protect him and allow him there.

SCENE 3

(*The* PRINCE *in his garden at his estate, reading a report. Enter* LORD GREEN.)

Prince.   Horace.

Lord Green.   It's my day off. I have slipped in
Without being seen. No one knows I'm here.
I have not telephoned, your phone is bugged.
The news from Scotland is not good. Iraq
Has threatened to attack. Its ruler has
Sent anthrax here which agents will release
Into our air, spores small as motes of dust.
It drifts like pollen on a summer wind,
Only whoever breathes one grain will die
Unless we find it first and make it safe.
Our customs have sealed off each port and search
The bags of all who land by sea or air.
Iraq has threatened to attack Israel
With anthrax missiles. Both moves emanate
From Rockefeller, who's using his men
To threaten royal England and Rothschild.
I know the PM is due here shortly.
Iraq has enough anthrax to kill off
The whole world's population twice over.
Please ask him to urge that Rockefeller
Should withdraw these deadly germs which make all
Right-thinking men shudder and cross themselves.

Prince.   I'll do as you suggest. But there is worse.
Your journalist sent me this report. Look,

Rockefeller has a "management" plan
To reduce the world population from
Six billion – ten billion in ten years' time –
To four billion by wars, disease, famine,
Refugees, epidemics, crop-failure.
The first stage was approved by the US
President over eighteen years ago.
It's called *The Global Two Thousand Report*.
It "forecast", just a way of saying "planned",
One hundred and seventy million deaths
From disease and famine in the Third World
From among what it calls "useless eaters"
Who eat food but produce nothing of worth.
Some nations have to deliver quotas
Of so-called "natural deaths" by "natural means".
Cambodia was an experiment.
Rwanda's massacres are a quota.
Iraq's anthrax is part of a programme
Of deliberate Malthusian reduction.
There's a conspiracy of huge extent.
It covers the whole world, slaughters millions,
And controls its loyal servants without
Ever letting the world know it exists.
The System's hard-hearted and uncaring,
As ruthless as an executioner's frown.
A stand must be made against such evil.
I declare a revolution against
The world government, which would slice and carve
My Kingdom into four quarters, then one
Into nine, and change its coinage –
And kill its citizens with anthrax spores -
And I rage and pour scorn and fulminate
Against our disintegrating culture
Which reflects the world government's values,
Three of whose representatives are now
On their way to bore me with their botched works.

Lord Green.   Someone's coming. I must make myself scarce.

(LORD GREEN *hides. Enter* SIR WILLIAM HAWKES.)

Hawkes.	The cultural deputation's here, sir.
	I know their works are not quite to your taste
	But please try to be nice to them and show
	An interest in their work and in their art –
	In literature, painting and music. I
	Want an exchange of views, not quarrelling.
	(*Exit* HAWKES. THE PRINCE *addresses* LORD GREEN.)

Prince. These caterpillars and aphids gnaw through
Our leafy State and leave ragged roses.

(*The* PRINCE *picks up a book. Enter a* POET, PAINTER *and* COMPOSER.
The PRINCE *ignores them.*)

Poet. What you reading, sir?

Prince.   A play on the war.
It's on sovereignty and world government.
The author's something of a dissident.
Such works are walled with silence to wither
Without reviews like plants without water.
He writes in metric blank verse, not rhythmic
Free verse with random stresses, cut-up prose.
Such discipline is not admired these days,
He will never be Poet Laureate.
Truth-tellers are considered fools, weirdos.
Do you also write about sovereignty,
And think it's the main issue of our time?

Poet. No, I write about everyday things like
Having a cup of tea in a café.
And memories of when I was a child.
I write as it comes, in uneven lines.

Prince. And that is art?

Poet.   We call it the new art.
You dwell on my phrases and share my thoughts.
In literature, painting and music some
Observe the rules of composition, some
Break them. We break the rules and then we break

What we have broken, then break those again.
We're known as technical iconoclasts.
We have been called the "novel nomoclasts".
Novelty, newness, is our aim.

Prince.   But don't
You have something to say? For can't you say
Something better if you observe the rules?

Poet.   Oh no, true artists have nothing to say.
They give you a feeling. They do not say
"He fell asleep", they say what it feels like
To fall asleep.

Prince.   But isn't that boring?
I mean, why should people want to read more
Than they need to, to understand the work?

Poet.   No one's ever bored by what we create.
It's more chatty if you just write your thoughts
Without worrying about form or rhyme.

Prince.   From Chaucer to Hopkins, five hundred years,
Poets wrote in set forms with rhymes –

Poet.   Old hat.
We do it better.

Painter.   It's the same with paint.
I don't show scenes like Constable's but squares
With a splodge near the centre, and a blob.

Prince.   Does that take me to Truth?

Painter.   Oh no, it shows
The chaos in the outside world.

Prince.   And if
I look at art to find order?

Painter.   There is

No order in the universe. I paint
The mess I see, and so it looks a mess.
The Rubens-Gainsborough line is out of date.

Prince.   And in music?

Composer.   The same. I do not write
Music like Beethoven or Brahms, but like
The sound you hear in a factory or shop.
Discordant noises blending together.

Prince.   It sounds as if you write, paint and compose
In blots and smudges, blotches and screeches
To catch the disorder in our dull time.

All.   Exactly, sir.

Prince.   I don't want chaos and
Disintegration, but beauty and truth,
Order and harmony. I do not read
For ordinary settings and memories
But for the main issue of our time, which
As much as in the warlords' Germany
And Augustus's new Roman Empire
Is universal rule, world government
Which fascinated Virgil, fazed Einstein –
And its downside of genocide. Could you
Be inspired by the suffering in Auschwitz?

Poet.   I wouldn't know how to begin.

Prince.   Your work
Is not for me. I would gladly sentence
All artists who offer trivial themes
And shy away from all the serious ones
To be detained for weeks to read the giants
Of the Renaissance time, learn their grand themes
And how to state them in pentameters.
I'd execute all those who did not change.
I call for a Revolution against
All culture that avoids the central Truth

	Which is metaphysical and global,
	And whose standards are lower than the past's –
	Because the artists are breaking its rules.

Painter. You'd have to execute all the artists.

Prince. No, change their subjects so that they reflect
The universalist ganging up of
The world's people against the genocides.

(*Re-enter* SIR WILLIAM HAWKES, *unobserved*)

Poet. I can't follow you, sir.

Composer. You've lost me, too.

Prince. You're unaware of how the world is run.
A poet, like a paraglider, soars
Among the clouds, beneath blue sky, looks down
From the One that's behind his fluffy verse.
An artist understands what the Whole is
And reveals Truth to universal man.
You can't do that, you don't see the whole plot.
You haven't heard of the world government.

Composer. There's no need to be abusive –

Painter. I think –

Poet. We'll end it there.

(SIR WILLIAM HAWKES *steps forward.*)

Hawkes. We'll have to end it there.
His Highness is unwell and out of sorts.

Poet (*aside*). He only speaks of some world government.

Hawkes (*aside*). He is not himself today, gentlemen.
He is still shocked by the Princess's death.
The Prime Minister's here to see you, sir.

(*Exeunt the* THREE ARTISTS, *the* POET *shaking his head.*)

With all due deference, sir, I did request
That you should appear interested in them.
I would not like it said at Court that you
Are behaving bizarrely. Be polite,
All visitors are worthy of respect.
Now please come in. Prime Minister's waiting.

Prince.   Let him come out. I'll see him here, alone.

Hawkes.   No, you come in.

Prince.   I'll only see him out.

(*Exit* HAWKES *with bad grace. Re-enter* LORD GREEN.)

Lord Green.   I could cut the atmosphere with a knife.
                     If the Prime Minister's at all aware,
                     He'll detect it at once and tread with care.

Prince.   I'll lambast the spying creep with my tongue.
                     He's in with Rockefeller and anthrax,
                     But he's also in with "royal" Rothschild.
                     He will be smarmy, unctuous and shocked.

Lord Green.   Go easy on him, and, please, not too long.
                     I'm getting cramp crouching behind this bush.

(*Exit* LORD GREEN. *Enter* SIR WILLIAM HAWKES *and the*
PRIME MINISTER.)

Hawkes.   The Prime Minister, sir.

Prince.   I trust that your
                     Modernizing programme is going well.

(HAWKES *sits on a seat with a pad and takes notes*)

Prime Minister.   Very much so, sir, yes. I've seen the Queen
                     And want to keep you informed. I shall soon

Visit Israel and urge the new leader
To withdraw from Palestinian lands
As the US President's peacemaker.
To help this process we are now taking
A tough line against Iraq's vile ruler.
He's a dictator who kills his people,
Gassing rebellious mountain villagers
And dropping chemical bombs from the air.
He has used genocide and will again.
If he doesn't admit our UN team
Within three days, we will cruise-bomb Baghdad.
We mean to confiscate all his anthrax
And other weapons of mass destruction
Which are hidden within his palaces.

Prince.   And how will bombing help to serve that cause
                   Save killing thousands of Iraq's children?

Prime Minister.   He will not want our cruise missiles flying
                   Round street corners, exploding his weapons.

Prince.   But if they do they'll send a cloud of spores
                   Up in the sky to kill Iraq's people.

Prime Minister.   He will hand over his anthrax to us
                   Before that happens. That's our assessment.

Prince.   And if your assessment is wrong, what then?
                   The population of Iraq will be
                   Wiped out –

Prime Minister.   There would be a cull, certainly –

Prince.   As in Cambodia and Rwanda.
                   You will have genocided half Iraq.

Hawkes.   I have to intervene, I must object.
                   This questioning is inappropriate.

Prime Minister.   No, let him speak. Worries should be declared.
                   He will have brought it on himself, by not

Handing over his germ warfare weapons.

Prince.   But if you are minded to have a cull
                           That is a way to genocide Iraq.
                           And as Iraq has sent agents here with
                           Suitcases of anthrax, which they'll open,
                           Releasing spores into our atmosphere,
                           You'll then have genocided half England.

Hawkes.   I must protest in the gravest of terms.
                           Your suggestions are unacceptable.

Prime Minister.   Really, sir, you seem to suggest that I
                           Want to genocide Iraq and England –

Prince.   There may be men who might urge the US
                           President to welcome such genocide.

Prime Minister.   Oh no, he wants peace and safety for all.

Prince.   And who are his masters, and who are yours?

Prime Minister.   I don't follow you, sir.

                           (HAWKES *moves over to the* PRINCE.)

Hawkes.   Sir, respect's due
                           For the Prime Minister. I am distressed
                           At the turn of your questioning, which is
                           Quite unacceptable and distasteful.

Prince.   I thought you were on Rothschild's side and would
                           Be pleased that I'm probing Rockefeller.

Hawkes.   Leave my side out of it.

Prince.   Prime Minister,
                           If you have masters, urge them to give up
                           Such horrible weapons.

Prime Minister.   No, I'll answer.

416

	The President and I have no masters.

The President and I have no masters.
What you see is what you get. We are both
Sincere, honest men of integrity.
We care about improving people's lot –

Prince.　　　　And you are not implementing any
Agenda for meetings of globalists?
(*Silence.*)

Hawkes.　　　　Really, sir, your questioning's gone too far.

Prime Minister.　　You are mistaken. You must take me at
Face value. I am transparent, sincere.
I will be open with you as I don't
Want suspicion to cloud the work we do.
The President and I have supreme power.
No one pulls our strings. My policy's mine.
I believe in devolving power and in
Uniting with Europe. And I believe
In modernizing our institutions
And in presenting them in a good light,
And in showing we care and have feelings
And want people to feel good about us.
My England is Arcadian, and we
Care about all and express our concern.
I also want newness and reform of
The constitution. If you're not with me
There will be calls to abolish the Crown
For an elected President who will
Rule with support from Cromwellians who want
England to be a republic again.
(*To Sir William Hawkes.*) I have kept His Royal Highness informed.
I must return to running the country.

Hawkes.　　　　He is still confused by his bereavement.
Please do not take what he has said to heart.
(*To the Prince.*) We'll speak later, this has been ill-advised.

(*The* PRIME MINISTER *bows and leaves with* SIR WILLIAM HAWKES.
LORD GREEN *re-enters.*)

Prince.	His Arcadian England's an illusion
	To disguise what he plans for our country.
	He says the new Europe's the most peaceful,
	Prosperous union since the *Pax Romana*,
	But Brussels rule's hostile to English law,
	Culture, language, Parliament, nation-state.
	He is a traitor to old sovereignty.
	If these were Tudor times, I'd have his head.

SCENE 4

(*The Oval Office, the White House, Washington. The* PRESIDENT *and his* FIRST LADY.)

First Lady.	That tramp, that whore, parades your sexual act
	(And innuendos about her stained dress)
	Through studios, editors, committees,
	And what have you done? Nothing. Sweet FA.
	For goodness' sake, stop dithering and act.
	You have to bomb Iraq to save our skin.
	You got us into this mess, get us out.
	Act swiftly and decisively, and blow
	Baghdad to bits and silence Israel, please
	Rothschild, then explain to Rockefeller.

US President.	No, I've found a better scenario.
	We threaten Baghdad, yes, but play the game
	So Rockefeller triumphs over Rothschild.
	Rockefeller supports Iraq, so I....

SCENE 5

(*A square in Baghdad, Iraq. The* DICTATOR *on a dais by the Tigris.*)

Dictator.	Iraqis, we mourn fifty-two children
	Of our dear country, who must be buried,
	And we know who is responsible for
	This genocide: those who imposed sanctions

And so deprived us of medicine, causing
These children to die from disease – Britain
And America, who have sent their ships
To threaten us from maritime Israel,
And frighten us, in vain! To whom we say,
There will be grave consequences unless
Economic sanctions are lifted. We
Will not permit UN Inspectors to
Accuse us of having chemical and
Biological weapons and ransack
Our country on a wild-goose chase for them,
Excuse for spies to spy on our systems.
I warn Britain and America, ships
Or no ships, we are undeterred, we, *I*
Will unleash germ warfare weapons against
Israel, who has pressed America and
Britain to perpetrate their genocide.
Genocide against Iraq will rebound
Against Israel, who'll suffer genocide.
I will release the deadliest black cloud
Of germs ever assembled in warfare
Into the lower atmosphere and kill
All Israelis, and, if an east wind blows,
All personnel in the invasion fleet,
Most Europeans and Anglo-Saxons –
If sanctions are not lifted by Israel.
At this funeral I say, we'll be revenged
On Israel and Europe that caused these babes
To die of lack of medicine in Iraq.
We are not afraid of cruise-bearing ships
And aircraft carriers, the Western fleet.
No UN inspections in our heartland!
Attack Israel with anthrax if we must.
Support me as I use our great weapon
To restore the glory of Iraq to
That of Nebuchadnezzar's Babylon!

(*There is a roar of applause, which the* DICTATOR *acknowledges with waves. An* AIDE *steps forward.*)

Sir, the UN Secretary-General will

Come to Baghdad to resolve the crisis.

(*The* DICTATOR *smiles.*)

Dictator   (*aside*). Good. Rockefeller's keeping his promise.
He needs me to threaten Rothschild from where
I stand by the brown Tigris before hordes
Of chanting, ululating volunteers
Who will be proud to die for me if I
Call on them to sacrifice themselves in
A holy war, *Jihad*. I am supreme.
Each day I execute thousands to clear
The prisons for new prisoners who might kill
Me, and to intimidate my people
Into cowed submission on occasions
Such as this when some take their places in
The midst of a throng of secret police.
They are still cheering, one in nine is mine.
I am quite safe, the rest are too frightened.
Now I am building the world's largest mosque
On an old airfield in central Baghdad.
It will stand in an artificial lake
Fed by the waters of the brown Tigris,
Shaped like the Arab world. Its dome will stand
Four hundred feet high and will house a huge
Digital statue of myself facing
Towards Mecca. Four minarets will soar
Nine hundred and twenty-five feet skywards,
Bigger than the pyramids in Egypt,
The tallest towers since Nebuchadnezzar,
The highest in the world so that they are
Closer to God than any other. I
Am the voice of God in the Arab world.
Self-glorification is what life's for.
You seize power and then build a monument,
Colossus that will last as long as Time.
A great man's measured by his worldly power,
And he should dedicate it all to God.
(*Aloud.*) Inform my double he will act for me.

SCENE 6

(*A palace in Baghdad, Iraq. The* UN SECRETARY-GENERAL *and the* DICTATOR'S DOUBLE. ATTENDANTS.)

UN Sec-Gen.	Mr President, I am delighted Our talks here in Baghdad have succeeded. Mr Rockefeller will be well pleased.
Dictator's Double.	My Deputy will sign on my behalf.
UN Sec-Gen.	I would be more comfortable if you signed.
Dictator's Double.	One moment, please.

(DICTATOR'S DOUBLE *confers with his officials. The* REAL DICTATOR *is disclosed among the audience with* ROCKEFELLER. *He speaks into a microphone.*)

Dictator.	Don't sign. My Deputy Will sign, not me, as intermediary.
Dictator's Double.	My Deputy has been our go-between. It is appropriate that he should sign.

(DICTATOR'S DOUBLE *shakes hands with the* UN SECRETARY-GENERAL *and leaves. Taken aback, the* UN SECRETARY-GENERAL *and the* DEPUTY *sign.* DICTATOR *speaks from among the audience.*)

Dictator	(*aside*). I won. I've signed nothing. I'm told we've moved The anthrax out of all the palaces. They will find empty rooms, no furniture, Nothing – and no anthrax, which is hidden Near missiles that target Rothschild's Israel. I have Scud missiles whose warheads are filled, Some with anthrax, some with VX nerve gas Tested at Al-Muthanna, which I'll use To spread germs and gas as in the Gulf War. I won. I tweaked the lion's tail and checked Uncle Sam and defied his threatening fleet.

I'll be feted throughout the Arab world.
And now I'll provoke a further crisis
And force them into a missile attack
And then I'll forbid all inspections and
I'll aim nuclear missiles at Eilat.
I will force the UN to lift sanctions.

Rockefeller.   Congratulations, Mr President.

Dictator   (*aside*). Rockefeller's pleased, he'll review sanctions
And I am now the Middle East's great power.

SCENE 7

(*A suite in a Hotel in Jerusalem, Israel.* LEADER 2 *and* ROTHSCHILD.)

Rothschild.   The President's not carried through his threat
To topple from power Iraq's dictator.
He's weak, and is playing a double game,
Saying what we want to hear but doing
What Rockefeller, his protector, orders.
Rockefeller's won. The Pres. is too strong
For us to force him out for sexual crimes,
Though we'll keep trying to get him impeached.
We can't promote his Vice-President yet.
Israel was on the verge of wiping out
Our arch-enemy Iraq with US
Missiles, but now there's an anticlimax.
We're disappointed. Nothing is resolved.
Iraq's chemical bombs still threaten us.

Leader 2.   We must retaliate against someone.
If not Iraq as its top man's guarded
And has doubles, then against Rockefeller.

Rothschild.   That Egyptian is saying the Princess
Was killed in an Anglo-Israeli plot.
Time to send Rockefeller a message.

SCENE 8

(The Financier's house, London. The FINANCIER alone.)

Financier   *(aside).* My life's dream of becoming royal is now
In tatters. The Queen will not speak to me.
The royals ignore me because I dare
To say my son was murdered in a plot,
That they could not have a Muslim Arab
As the stepfather of the future King
And Arab blood mixed with their royal blood.
They blame me for her death and not themselves.
They gave their order to intelligence
Who sent a motorbike *paparazzo*
To shine a light into the driver's eyes,
A strobe flash-gun planned for Milosevic,
And crash the car and then switch blood samples.
If there were ostracism I would be
Banished as the least loved public figure.
The royals turn away and will not speak
Words of comfort. They look down on me as
A Bedouin camel trader who moved to
Alexandria's poorest district and
They have now ended all contact with me.
As if I'd been Colonel Nasser's agent
And this was the year that he seized Suez.
They all snub me, and don't see the castles,
Palaces, homes, ships and shops I've amassed
As my own enterprise and just reward.
They think I've made it from intelligence.
They say I'm naff, that I have no breeding
And that I have more money than sense. They
Belittle me as a jumped-up "Gypo"
While I who lost my son because of them,
Because of the Syndicate's civil war,
Secrete bitterness like a poisonous toad.
Whoever's grateful for intelligence,
I'd like to work exclusively for him.

(A noise.)

(*Aloud.*) Who's there? Who's there? Security, where are
My armed guards? Who is it?

(*Enter* TWO MASKED MEN *with a rope.*)

You look like two
Angels of Death.

Murderer 1.   We've come to escort you.

Murderer 2.   It's payment time, you nasty piece of work.

Financier.   Who are you? Who sent you?

Murderer 1.   I've a message.
If you hadn't invited the Princess
Onto your boat, she'd be alive and so
Would your son, so would you. What sealed your death
Was your talk of a royal conspiracy.

Financier.   Ah, you are from Israel.

Murderer 2.   Enough. Confess.

Financier.   I regret my deeds but I stand by them.
My conscience is clear. I've no appetite
To live a life in which murderous factions
War like the Mafia that's under us.
I'm not afraid to die.

Murderer 2.   Now write your note.
You've been depressed, you were wrong to allege
That there's been a conspiracy. That was
A fantasy on your part, an untruth.

Murderer 1.   Write it.

(*The* FINANCIER *writes.* MURDERER 2 *throws his noosed rope across a
beam and secures it. The* MURDERERS *read the note.* MURDERER 1
screws it up.)

Murderer 1.	You're messing us around.

        (MURDERER 1 *and* MURDERER 2 *belabour him with open palms.*)

Put in

"Depressed", "no conspiracy", "fantasy"
Or else *this* will be your last note. Read it.

        (MURDERER 1 *thrusts a paper at him.*)

Financier.	No, no.

        (MURDERER 1 *offers him a new sheet of paper. The* FINANCIER *writes again.*)

Murderer 2.	That will do. Head inside the noose.
Financier.	If I refuse?

        (*The two men hustle him into the noose and pull him up. He dances and is hanged.*)

Murderer 1.	Let this be a warning.

This noose can pay you for the harm you did.
Your link with powerful men did you no good.

SCENE 9

(*A suite in a hotel in Senegal, Africa. The* US PRESIDENT *is holding a guitar near a drum. Enter an* AIDE.)

Aide.	Mr President, you are in the clear.

A judge has thrown out the main case against
You for sexual harassment. You've been cleared.

US President.	That's really true? There's no mistake?
Aide.	It's been

Confirmed. She's left the court in tears. You've won.

US President.   Thank you.

(*Exit* AIDE.)

(*Aside.*) I've won. It worked, to deny it
And tough it out and feint to bomb Baghdad,
Then escape adverse publicity by
Coming out to Africa to surround
Myself with leaders of integrity.
Image is all. Convey an impression
And the truth, which I would rather forget,
Is lost. Innocent. Well, I seemed blameless.
The judge was a student of mine. She owed
Me one for the high mark I gave her in
Her final exam when her work was lost.
Thank you, babe, thank you, thank you very much.

(*The* PRESIDENT *sits and twangs his guitar. He puts the guitar down and beats the drum in a bongo rhythm with his hands.*)

I won! I – won! I'm clear. I toughed it out!

SCENE 10

(*The* PRINCE *in his garden on his estate, alone.*)

Prince.   There is a moral murkiness abroad.
President acquitted by female judge.
That man near hanged, intimidating thugs.
No solution in Baghdad, nothing changed.
I do not like the world I now live in.
It is as shallow as clouds reflected
In a puddle left on a garden path.
The American President's a wolf,
A sexual predator. His counterpart
In Russia is a drunken buffoon. Both
Are easy prey for the Olympians,
As is the PM who believes nothing.
There's no political philosophy,

Design, his mind's a blank videotape
On which they record their foul messages.
He's ideal to be manipulated.
He's post-modern, he has no vision save
Newness and only stands for common sense,
Which is nothing more than common daftness.
He's a spivvy con man who has expelled
Hereditary peers from the Lords to make
Spaces his cronies sell to fund his power,
General elections, and install Yes-men
Who'll soon vote to abolish my Kingdom
When his European cronies impose
A constitution that ends the UK.
I wonder what thank-yous are given for that?
President of Europe? Or a fortune?
Cash sent from Zurich to a Belize bank?
Or cash sent from New York to offshore funds?
Zurich suggests hero, New York traitor.
The difference is of Syndicate profiles.
I do not like the world in which I must
Fight for sovereignty and become a King.

(*Enter the* FOOL.)

Fool.   Aching? Head, heart, feet? It's the times, nuncle.
                   A letter to cheer you up. Sent via me.

(*The* PRINCE *opens the letter.*)

Prince.   It's from Horace. The world government meets
                   In Scotland.

Fool.   I told him Scotland's adrift.
                   It's floating off and will be our Cuba,
                   No our Ireland, more hardline than Iran
                   And full of dreams of unification.
                   He sent it to me as it's not safe here.
                   This is a prison camp these days, a place
                   Where your enemies – the world government
                   And their jumped-up and bossy functionary,
                   The Prime Minister – monitor your phone,

Keep your movements under surveillance and
Record your words and thoughts on sovereignty.
You are a prisoner in your own palace.
Even your mistress creeps through gates unseen.
Lord Green knows that and so does your old Fool.
I don't trust the hawkish beak, nor his worm.
Both will devour you in their different ways.
This garden is the one place you are free.
Lord Green knows he can trust your Fool with news.

Prince.   He tells me that they meet. Why should I care?

Fool.   I see that in your eyes. You'll permit me?

Prince.   Why?

Fool.   You already know, sir.

Prince.   I'm confused –

Fool.   No, weary under the profound burden
Of carrying knowledge that's so secret
And which must not remain secret much more.
You could not talk about it with the Queen.
No, don't protest. I see it in your eyes.
I know what it is to keep one's counsel,
As my solicitor said to the judge.

          (*The* PRINCE *aims a mock blow at the* FOOL.)

Prince.   And what, pray, is the secret knowledge I
Keep bottled up?

Fool.   I've seen it in your eyes,
What you're thinking and why you must travel
To Scotland.

Prince.   Why?

Fool.   To address their meeting.
You must label them as the Pope does us.

You must berate them with their own misdeeds.
I mirror what's uppermost in your thoughts.
You feel that we're not told the real news.

Prince.   Our balance of payments deficit is
Three billion pounds, four times what sank a stale
Government back in nineteen sixty-three,
But it is not even mentioned. England
Is to be broken into nine regions.
It's as if this garden were quartered twice,
And the south-eastern part is to be linked
With Normandy and Picardy, as if
That bed were linked with two beyond that wall.
This is not mentioned. Our decline's censored
As if reports of rife weeds were suppressed.
There's a new censorship. We are only
Told phoney good news – control of schools, drugs,
Health, paedophiles, abuse, AIDS, starvation,
Like control of thistles and dandelions,
Things that are supposed to make us feel good
But which demoralize the discerning
For there is never progress in such things
And only unheroic times probe them.

Fool.   Our time has no heroes save prancing fools
Who strut across a stage or football pitch.
I see it in your eyes, I reflect right.
We are being run by a President –

Prince.   Who seeks perpetual power and would replace
Our constitution, which has given us
Three hundred years of stability, with
One that emasculates the Commons and
Upper House (takes its independence and
Removes its hereditary principle),
Civil service and backbench discipline,
And manipulates the media, breaks up
Our Kingdom for devolved "regions", brings in
Proportional representation so
The electorate will not turf him out,
Gets bureaucrats to scold his elected

Ministers and compel them to obey,
Intimidate them into agreement.
The English – I omit the Scottish and
Welsh, and the Irish (who are being given
Unity by consent) – the English are
Being dismantled by a President –

Fool.
Who would become a fawning dictator
Who uses anodyne and soothing words
And warm feeling in place of argument.
I am a Fool, and so I am not soothed.
If you don't see this, you're a bigger Fool.
Your eyes tell me that I have read them right.

Prince.
You've read me like a book, *and* my disquiet.
Rockefeller's ordered him to break up
Our Kingdom and dump the pound, and so he
Must get devolution through the Commons –
Where his majority's huge, and where
The Leader of the Opposition's now
An Olympian and in cahoots with him,
So their exchanges across the dispatch-
Box are shadow boxing, a sham, an act –
And he must fix things so the Lords cannot
Veto his programme, so he's removing
The voting rights of hereditary peers.
The Leader of the Opposition in
The Lords was at last year's Olympian Group.
It's terrible, since the Middle Ages
The Lords have been like our unconscious mind
In which the conscious Commons is rooted.
Abolishing their wisdom is folly.
I don't know why there isn't an outcry.
It's not that *he* doesn't grasp what he's done,
He knows too clearly, that's the trouble, and
If he has his way, I'll lose three-quarters
Of my crown before I attain the throne.
Someone should exile, *banish* the traitor
Before he wrecks the nation. I would cheer
If the Army seized power and locked him up
Before he does what Hitler failed to do

And legislates our nation into bits
Without a second chamber's staying hand.
You know I must inform my people that
He's encouraging disintegration.
I am the sovereign –

Fool.   Monarcho –

Prince.   – to-be.
And I must hold together my Kingdom
Which is being dismantled, like my mind,
By men who do not wish me well at all,
Before my very eyes. Yet I'll endure.
Somehow I will hold it all together.
Even though death-watch beetle's everywhere.
I feel so isolated. You are right,
The burden of carrying this knowledge
Alone has weighed heavily. Am I mad?
Can a King-to-be be a dissident?
I wonder if I'm having a breakdown,
I wonder if solitude's unhinged me.
I wonder if I've changed places with you.

Fool.   You're like a Tudor ruin in a moat
Whose front door leans inwards, gusted by wind,
Lonely, near-derelict, but still noble,
Your tall chimneys and gables a proud sight.

Prince.   I don't like our broken society
Whose fragments I must rule like an old Mound,
A Castle in medieval times, now
A once-occupied hill strewn with potsherds,
Vestiges of a fractured way of life.

ACT FIVE

SCENE 1

(A hotel at Turnberry, near Glasgow. The annual Olympian Bilderberg Group meeting. ROCKE-

FELLER *faces the delegates which include* ROTHSCHILD *and the* PRIME MINISTER.)

Chairman.   Our President, Mr Rockefeller, will
                        Summarize our progress during the year.

Rockefeller.   Olympians, another year has passed
                        And from our god-like vantage-point on high
                        Our over-populated earth seems ripe
                        For our impending global rule. We have
                        Resolved the divisions which have racked us.
                        Israel will give up land to Palestine,
                        The question is, how much? Northern Ireland
                        Is moving towards union with the south
                        Thanks to the implementing of our plan
                        By the PM, who has courageously
                        Released bombers and killers from jails so
                        They can fight on. Our coalition's firm,
                        And we will progress through the euro and
                        Economic and monetary union
                        In Europe, which must be speeded up, to
                        One global currency, so long our dream.
                        The world is now grouped in zones and regions
                        That can be garnered into our great blocs.
                        Our administrative work's nearly done.
                        The UN army exists and has teeth.
                        No state will dare take arms against our will.
                        We have outlawed guns in restless countries.
                        Most cities have a by-pass or tank-route
                        So we can blockade rebellious peoples.
                        We can dispose of all insurgents who
                        Challenge our authority, in the camps
                        We have secretly set up, and we have
                        Perfected surveillance on citizens
                        Through the guise of traffic-control cameras.
                        We will soon introduce in Britain
                        Cameras mounted on bridges that will take
                        Photos of all cars' number plates and so
                        Monitor the population's movements.
                        The most satisfying *coup* has been seen
                        In Britain, where, after decades of work
                        Against the world-wide British Empire, we

Have split its Kingdom into four countries,
Three of which will be states in New Europe
And the fourth, England, is now nine regions
Or Euro-administrative units.
The Titans among us have long pressed for
The survival of sterling, but they (our
Anglo-Israelis) have now conceded
That a millennium's currency will be
Replaced to expedite global control
And we pay tribute and thank them for this.
This change is due to the leads of PM
And his predecessor, who puffed our cause,
And it is with great joy I now present,
Just flown up here to join us at Turnberry
From the G8 meeting at Birmingham,
Soon to be joined by US President,
Our "moderniser" of Britain, the PM.

(*Applause. The* PRIME MINISTER *appears and grins.*)

Prime Minister.   Olympians, I'm now wearing your hat
And, speaking among friends within these walls,
I can say openly that we are all
Opposed to national sovereignty and are
Committed to transcend the nation-state
For a union of federal states that will
Start in Europe and end with global rule.
As our host has just said, the hard part's done.
We are modernisers, we sweep away
The past and emphasize a popular
Present. PR perception's everything
In today's world, the image and soundbyte.
So that our iconoclasm can be
Perceived we are eclipsing royal power
And we have cancelled bowing to royals
And curtsying to the Queen. We attack
The mystique of royalty, so we show
The Queen at ceremonies formerly
Private, admit cameras where they've been banned,
To garden parties and investitures,
And show her as an ordinary person –

Running, laughing – and so reduce her power.
We promote popular culture – pop songs,
Fashion, rock music – not highbrow culture
(Elitist Shakespeare and opera) which is
Of the past and lacks popular appeal.
This will be the culture of New Europe.
We want pop music at the Albert Hall,
Rock lyrics at poetry readings in pubs,
And blockbuster writers at Festivals.
Olympians, we are preparing for
A devolved Britain of quite separate states
To be ruled by Brussels and Strasbourg, with
The euro as the currency of each.
I am proceeding as fast as I can
But nationalism is slowing me up.
We're doing all we can to introduce
A United States of the World formed of
The United and European states
And all the global regions and their blocs:
South America, Africa, Asia,
China, Oceania and the Russian states.
That is our truly international aim –
Dream of Rockefeller's Olympians!

(*There is loud applause, a standing ovation. The* PRIME MINISTER *waves. The* PRINCE *emerges from nowhere and takes the podium. There is a stunned silence.*)

Prince.	I thank you for inviting me to speak To you today –
Rockefeller.	Sir, you're not on our list.
Rothschild.	No, let him speak. Sir, you are welcome here.
Prince.	I am grateful for Mr Rothschild's plea That I should join your deliberations. I'm sorry if I've taken you aback. I know you don't officially exist And so there can be no reports of my Presence here. I want to appeal to you

To end the war between your two factions
Which lurks behind the loss of my Princess
And which foments unrest throughout the world.
One's led by the richest American,
Whose trillions are unquantifiable,
Who owns half the oil, Russia and China,
Controls the UN, the most powerful man
Ever. The other's led by the richest
European, whose banking family
Had more wealth than the crown heads of Europe
And controlled the US reserve system,
Israel and most of the remaining oil.
If the two of you could co-operate,
Work together without scheming conflicts,
If you could be humane towards mankind
Then you could abolish war, famine, plague
And bring in a Golden Age for mankind.
An age of peace, plenty and health in which
Genocide, hunger and disease aren't known.
But as it is, you're both Malthusians,
Your trillions are used to maim and destroy,
To starve and waste with man-made germs like AIDS –
One of forty-eight strains of viruses
That kill, that were discovered in US
Laboratories – and anthrax. As it is,
You plan to cut the world's population
From six to four billion by massacres,
Planned crop-failures and epidemics and
Contaminate the pure earth God gave us
With blood and bones, two billion skeletons,
Far worse a crime than Hitler, Stalin, Mao
Perpetrated with two hundred million
Murders between them, crimes that rank you both
In history as Satanic Antichrists.
Sovereignty in nations under their law
Is better than union and genocide.
The sovereignty of the soul is supreme,
The sanctity of life must be upheld.
I appeal to you both, for mankind's sake,
Abolish your genocide plans and your
Plans for world government that will approve

Such dreadful things. Abolish yourselves.
Abolish this sullied Bilderberg Group!

(*There has been mounting muttering and protests from the participants of the meeting, who are the audience.*)

Rockefeller.   Escort this gatecrasher from this building
And dump his fantasies outside the door
Like suitcases bulging with calumnies.

Rothschild.   Throw out the deluded intruder who
Voices such disgraceful allegations.

(SECURITY GUARDS *seize the* PRINCE *and begin to frogmarch him roughly to the door.*)

Prime Minister.   No, wait. I understand such an extreme
Reaction, but please recognize that he
Is not himself. Since the Princess's death
He has become quite sick, and delusions
Of conspiracies are merely symptoms
Of his disorder. Deal gently with him.
Take him outside, drive him to the airport.
I'll have him met in London, he needs help.
I'll be personally responsible
For seeing he receives the loving care
That all our people are entitled to.

(*The* SECURITY GUARDS *escort the* PRINCE *out in a more deferential manner.*)

I apologise to all delegates
For this unseemly scene. His great grief at
The Princess's death has unhinged the door
Of his reason. His madness needs treatment.

(ROCKEFELLER *and* ROTHSCHILD *whisper together.*)

Rockefeller.   I have a bone to pick with you.
I have to pay you back for *her* friend's death –

436

Rothschild.	I'm not admitting we're responsible.
Rockefeller.	But first we must make common cause on this. There's only one end for public figures Who speak against us at a Group meeting. Before he violates our news blackout.
Rothschild.	Agreed. On this we must make common cause.

SCENE 2

(*A mental hospital, London. The* PRINCE *sitting in a dressing-gown beside his bed, and* PSY-CHIATRIST.)

Psychiatrist.	So you agree, there's no conspiracy? Only a delusion within your mind?
Prince.	Will you release me if I say Yes?
Psychiatrist.	Yes.
Prince.	Yes. Can I go now?
Psychiatrist.	"Admits delusion." You are no threat now you have admitted There never was any conspiracy, That your wife died in a freak accident. I will discharge you but you must remain In this mental hospital one more week Under observation.

(*A* NURSE *enters and confers with the* PSYCHIATRIST.)

Prince.	And what will you observe? My mind? Where is the deluded mind you Will observe? Is it dependent on brain?

(*The* NURSE *leaves.*)

Psychiatrist.	It's brain function. The mind is brain function.
Prince.	There's no evidence for that. It may be That mind is transmissive and uses brain, Hovering outside brain with lightning strikes Like a thunderstorm, leaving it at death.
Psychiatrist.	That's another delusion.

Prince.

A Nobel

Prizewinner was deluded, then – I got
That view from him. Yours is materialist.
You see the mind as matter, do you not?
Materialism is a delusion.
I think it's you who needs observation.
(*Aside*.) I feel frustrated and marginalized.
The Crown should have a spiritual impact
On the multicultural mishmash I'll rule
In which materialism is rife
Like a rank weed in a Tudor garden.
I want my reign to be universal
But I feel distaste for the attitudes
That strangle my land like tangled bellbind.

(*Enter* HOSPITAL ATTENDANT)

Psychiatrist.	Your son has come to see you. Bring him in. I think it must be all right if he's here. There may be trouble if we turn him back. (*To the Prince*.) I'm supposed to be here. I won't intrude.

(*Enter the* PRINCE'S HEIR. *Exit* PSYCHIATRIST.)

Prince's Heir.	Father, why are you in this dreadful place? I think the Olympians who took Mummy Put you here so they can remove our Crown.
Prince.	My clever boy, my clever, clever boy. I told the Olympians that they must change. Nobody knows I'm here except for them And Sir William.

Prince's Heir.	He doesn't know I'm here.
	Your Fool brought me in his old car. He said
	I must tell no one. He's waiting outside.
	He said you had told the Olympians off.
Prince.	Sir William Hawkes told you that I'm unwell?
	(*The* PRINCE'S HEIR *nods*)

I'm not unwell. But if you tell the truth
They say you are unwell and put you here
So you can "get better", which means "keep quiet".
They won't let me speak to the nation now.
But the nation must be told what they're like.
I must warn our people they want to take
The Crown and British sovereignty away.
My son, my strong, brave, clever, clever boy,
Will you do something for me? Will you say
To Sir William you'll give an interview
To this presenter whose name I've written?
Will you ring him at this number and set
Up a live interview and audience?
He won't ask questions, he'll do as you say.
Sir William must clear it with the PM,
And there'll be no problem if he says you
Will talk about your feeling for Mama.
He's sentimental, he's sure to say Yes.
If you can set up a time and place for
An interview and let me know by phone
I will escape from here and take over,
You won't have to speak, I will say it all.
Will you tell Sir William you want to speak
About how you're coping without Mama,
And say this presenter contacted you,
And ask him to clear him with the PM?
Will you do this for me, my clever boy?

Prince's Heir.	For you, Mummy, England and our Kingdom.
	Especially for you, dear, kind Papa.
	Here, I've brought you my cassette-recorder.
	In case you want to dictate messages.
	Have my mobile phone so I can ring you.

I'll give you details of the interview.

(*The* PRINCE *is touched. He clasps* HIS SON.)

My thoughtful boy. Speak as if walls have ears.
Have you seen the Queen?

Prince's Heir.	No, Sir William said
	She's in Scotland. They're keeping us apart.
Prince.	She's just as much their prisoner as I am.
Prince's Heir.	I'll change places with your Fool now, he wants
	To see you. He blames himself for this pass.

(*Exit* PRINCE'S HEIR. *Enter the* FOOL. *He looks at the* PRINCE *and taps his own forehead with his finger.*)

Fool.	Oh Monarcho, too much care's made you mad,
	And your universe is a padded cell
	You think you rule but which is measured by
	Demented men in white who tuck you up.
	How often have I said that you're the Fool
	And I am sane?

(*The* FOOL *turns his finger backwards and forwards by his forehead and sadly points at the* PRINCE.)

Those jests were prophetic!
It wasn't hard to get the future right,
The world government's mad and therefore so's
Our government, and with such barminess
Around us like a high pollen level
It was just a question of time before
You started sneezing and were diagnosed
As catching a hay fever of the mind.
The way to stay sane's – keep apart from them,
Have nothing to do with conspirators.
Wear a motley cap and bells as a badge
Of solitude and shun their lunacy
As if they were lepers who think they're cured.

Prince.	Fool, as always you've made me feel better. Thank you for bringing my son to see me. You ran a risk, as we both know you knew.
Fool.	This new regime's a No, say all wise men. When wise men denounce fools, the fools reply By calling them mad and locking them up In a House for the Insane like this jail, Imprisoning them with no irksome trial. I chide myself for not pointing this out When I encouraged you to denounce them.
Prince.	I knew the risks, I've no complaints. I spoke.
Fool.	And I rim myself for the hub you wheeled. I've heard you had them in a great panic. Fear breeds and aborts. Beware, Monarcho, for Sometimes ruthless and nasty men are not Content with walling dissidents inside Mental hospitals as the Russians did (Rockefeller's flunkeys). Beware, Monarcho, Look what happened to the Princess. Look out.
Prince.	You must leave before you are discovered. Thank you again for bringing my son here.
Fool.	Thank *you* for giving me three minutes' work. I am a poor sad Fool on a pension, I need your salary as a top-up. Bringing the Prince was a supreme folly. Only a Fool would act so stupidly. And only the Supreme Fool, Monarcho, Could be grateful for such a foolish act.

(*Re-enter the* PSYCHIATRIST.)

Psychiatrist.	The Prime Minister's arrived to see you. You'll have to leave, don't say I let you in.

(*Exit the* FOOL *hastily. Enter the* PRIME MINISTER, *with* WORMWOOD. *They push past the* PSYCHIATRIST *who hovers and then leaves.*)

Prince   (*aside*). That Wormwood's as alert and menacing
                As a heron above a golden orfe.
                (*Aloud.*) This is an unexpected pleasure –

Wormwood.   Cut
                The waffle. The important thing is, you've
                Admitted you're deluded, and that there's
                No conspiracy. We have that on tape.
                What were you playing at in Turnberry?
                You're meddlesome, your place is to shut up.
                We only tolerate kings who're silent.

Prime Minister. You tried to subvert the Olympians.

Prince.   They are a conspiracy. You can shout
                As loud as you like but it won't change that.

Wormwood.   Of course *we're* a conspiracy, you prat.
                We have been since my grandfather joined it,
                And long before that – seventeen seventy-six,
                When the Illuminati were founded,
                And Dee's circle at Elizabeth's court.
                We do all the things you said at Turnberry.
                We do. *You* don't say it, that's the point. *We*
                Say it, *not you*. And we say privately.
                You go public like that once more and you
                Are dead. I mean it, I don't prat about.

Prime Minister. You will remain here until your treatment's
                Complete. In our England we care for all,
                And we will smooth away the delusion
                Of conspiracy in your brain just as
                The gentle waves on a beach smooth the sand
                And knock down the bucket-and-spade castle
                A child has made to honour sovereignty.
                The gentle waves of global oceans will
                Wash your symbols of sovereignty away.

Prince.   It sounds like brainwashing.

Prime Minister.   More loving care,

It has the same effect as brainwashing.
The main thing is, you will now toe our line.
As will all the people of England. We
Have seized power like Cromwell the Roundhead, and
Have set up a caring dictatorship
That will last twenty years, twice Cromwell's time.
We rule by high approval ratings, which
Draw on our caring, feeling posture that
Cries out for England to be modernised.
We demand wheelchair ramps in all buildings.
We will change you out of compassion, and
We will change England by modernising
England's institutions, dumping the wigs
Of the Lord Chancellor and his lawyers,
And showing that we care for glossy looks.

Prince.   Your glossy England fills me with distaste.
I am a King in waiting and I see
Institutions that have lost their meaning
In false, caring language and compassion;
Schools where children are not educated
With discipline and judgement of what's good
But indulged with warm praise, play and high marks;
A welfare system that serves dependence,
Not self-respect, responsibility,
And a health service ruled by sentiment;
Churches empty of doctrine, tradition
And rules that seek cosy self-esteem in
Modern services of banal words through
Happy-clappy, touchy-feely smiling,
Hugging neighbours, not confronting dread God –
Hence church attendance halved in fifty years.
Our Foreign Office trumpets ethical
Policies yet still arms dictatorships;
Our Agriculture Ministry proclaims
That eating meat is safer than it was
When nothing's changed except your caring smile.
I want real institutions in my land,
Not fakes that look good and are images
Of caring, niceness and popular smiles;
Real policies, not gesture politics.

I lambast your fake society and
Its fake institutions. I want what's real,
What includes reason, bears grief with restraint,
Is moral rather than sentimental.
Something is rotten in this dear green land.

Wormwood.   That's a scurrilous piece of defiance.

Prime Minister.   Your jaded view is dangerous to our cause.

Wormwood.   You're in no position to say such things.
The clampdown has happened. It has gone well.
Your mother, the Queen, is our puppet. You
Will soon abdicate in favour of Prince....
Your son. Our dictatorship is in place,
Though we call it "increased democracy".
It has the world government's approval,
The UN will accept it. You – shut up.

Prince.   You intimidate like a hunting owl
That hoots before it swoops upon a mouse.
Your bird-of-prey instincts threaten terror.
Shouting and abusing cannot convert
What's wrong into what's right. When I am King
I will be King until I die. But you
Are just in power till the next election.

Prime Minister.   You say you have distaste for our England.
You're of the past – deluded, out of date.
We will by-pass you. Our futurist dream
Has no place for royals in new England.
We are against history as that is past.
We are for the future and the people.
What you call conspiracy's our future.

Prince.   The present is what has flowed from the past.
The future's what will flow from the present.
It's all one river and you've built a dam
Against the current. You will be submerged.
You cannot dam the current of history.

Wormwood.	It's not a river, it's a state of mind
	And how we are perceived in people's minds.
	You are irrelevant – *élite* and past.
	We will know every movement that you make,
	So don't try anything, or you will pay.

(*The* PRIME MINISTER *and* WORMWOOD *leave. They encounter the* PSYCHIATRIST.)

He is not to be let out of your sight.
No visitors, he's on suicide watch.

(*Exeunt The* PRIME MINISTER *and* WORMWOOD. *The* PRINCE *removes the cassette-recorder from his bed and rewinds. He plays.*)

Prime Minister's voice.
Your mother, the Queen, is our puppet. You
Will soon abdicate in favour of Prince....
Your son. Our dictatorship is in place.

(*The* PRINCE *presses "Fast Forward".*)

We will by-pass you. Our futurist dream
Has no place for royals in new England.

(*The* PRINCE *stops the cassette-recorder.*)

Prince.	I have the evidence that I have lacked.
	Now I must bring it to the public ear.
	This PM and Wormwood are deceptive,
	The're like summer days that conceal showers,
	Hide black thunder within their warm sunshine.
	They smile and smile but their lightning can kill.
	I should expose them, they are dangerous.
	Yet if I do I know I'll risk my life.
	Rockefeller'll try hard to silence me
	But I must not let fear affect my course.
	I must stand up for what I know is right
	And not flinch when the counter-attack comes.
	Olympians worship false gods – money, power –
	And indulge mind and body. As vicar

Of the True God, Defender of all Faiths,
I stand for the spirit which controls mind.
My metaphysical idea threatens
Their materialism. I challenge it.
I am not driven by Fate like Oedipus
Or by a vicious mole in my nature
But by virtue which triumphs over vice
And all evil which destroys human good.
I choose for good against global evil.
My choice is universal though made here
In this mental hospital, at this time.
To some I am tilting at a windmill,
But I know I am that windmill, towering
Above my people's small houses, sails driven
Round by an invisible wind, which blows
Spiritual life in energetic gusts.
The Invisible turns my creaking soul
And grinds words from the millstones of my mind
Whose grained Truth nourishes my people's bones.
I receive Holy Light which fills my crown
And guides my judgement. I have asked the Light
What I should do and heard a voice within
Say, "Wear the Crown whose bright Light bears
    the Truth."
I must speak out, the Truth must out, I can't
Live under this dictatorship of lies
Without warning my people of their plight.
They live under evil but do not know
That what they approve is malevolent,
Tyrannical, seeking perpetual power,
Devoted to halving humanity.
Killing half of mankind – the words fall short.
It is a shocking, outrageous concept
Wrapped in anodyne words that state the facts
But do not show their full enormity,
Like poison in transparent sweetpaper.
Familiar language conceals true meaning.
How can I speak out and be understood
If ordinary, familiar words hide Truth?

(*The* PRINCE *holds his head in his hands.*)

I despise those two phoney hypocrites.
The G8 leaders giggled, hugged and kissed,
Embraced, tickled each other's ribs, swapped ties
And trivialized all the serious issues.
The PM's a presentational genius,
And his media-manipulating team
Is the best in the world. He has the style
Of a President. His minders keep him
Among adorers, away from hecklers.
He's naff and creepy, he's looted fifteen
Billion in taxes, and is photographed
Praying in a pew, he's a posturer.
He poses to prepared applause. Wormwood
Is slimy and mendacious, slippery
As a grass snake, a reptilian brute
Who's smarmy-sanctimonious as he bites.
Just looking at the creeps makes me shudder.
But I will have the measure of Wormwood.
For through a go-between's off-shore account
That conveys funds from New York to London
Like the flow in a urinal's runnel
He's had a small fortune in gratitude
For putting the PM in charge, breaking
My Kingdom into twelve Euro-regions
(For which more funds leave Zurich for Belize),
And there's documentary evidence
That will bring him down – when news is released,
When our side gives word that the press should know.
Wormwood stinks like a half-drowned sewer-rat.

(*Enter* SIR WILLIAM HAWKES.)

You have the look of an undertaker.

Hawkes.   I bear sad news from the Prime Minister.
Lord Horace Green has died by his own hand.

Prince.   How? How?

Hawkes.   He hanged himself – allegedly

| Prince. | He would never have hanged himself. Never. |

| Hawkes. | The balance of his mind had been disturbed. |

Prince.	By questioning what our new rulers plan,
	Just as *my* mind's "disturbed", a different shade
	Of meaning from your own.

Hawkes.	He left a note.
	He said he was distressed at the slow pace
	Of changes to the monarchy.

| Prince. | He would |
| | Never have said such a thing. |

Hawkes.	I now need
	A tribute from you, an *encomium*,
	An epitaph, about your deceased friend.

(*Exit* HAWKES.)

Prince.	Horace. "Died by his own hand." That's a lie.
	Murdered for holding inconvenient views.
	Alas, poor Horace, my only true friend.
	So long as you were there, I still had hope.
	My despair rises like an evening fog.
	The nightmare deepens. They're picking us off
	One by one, and I'm powerless to stop it.
	Princess, and now Horace. I am resolved,
	I will vanquish the globalist plotters.

(*The* PRINCE's *mobile phone rings.*)

Yes. Yes. Good, my boy, good. You have done well.

SCENE 3

(*An enormous suite in a London hotel.* ROCKEFELLER, ROTHSCHILD, *the* PRESIDENT *of the* EUROPEAN *Commission and an audience, which is the audience.*)

Rockefeller.   Olympians, the day has come at last.
We will impose our regime on the world.
This evening we will place the globe under
A Global Council that will run mankind
And put into effect our Global Plan
For controlling the numbers eating food.
There will be no announcement, it's secret.
We shall impose a global currency
And parliament, a reform package.
Rothschild has made concessions in return
For guarantees on issues dear to him.
Israel will give up land, the British Crown
Will soon be abolished, the puppet Queen
Will abdicate and England will become
A republic, PM as President.
The monarchy did not heed our warnings,
It's slow to change and we have lost patience.
All this will be imposed at eight o'clock.
We've had to bring the timetable forward
As the nation-state servant Lord Green learned
Details and was caught red-handed sending
Them on to the Prince, who then tried to wreck
Our Turnberry meeting which voted in our
Scheme. I have to report Green's "hanged himself ".

Rothschild.   I'm sorry to interrupt momentous
Announcements that culminate our life's work,
But I have just received intelligence,
An intercepted call by a scanner,
Of a plan to abduct the sick Prince from
His hospital bedroom and take him to
A television studio. I have
No more details, but it is happening now.

Rockefeller.   I told PM, keep him isolated
And incommunicado. I shall be
Livid if he's blundered and bungled this.
Do you know what studio?

Rothschild.   Not yet.

Rockefeller.   Find out
                    And get our "ushers" there to deal with him.

SCENE 4

(The mental hospital, London. The PRINCE *and the* FOOL, *who whispers.)*

Fool.   I've come to drive you there in my old car.

Prince.   Thank you, my loyal Fool. I'll come at once.

Fool.   You won't be recognized. A letter from
                    Lord Green. The envelope's addressed to me.

Prince.   Lord Green?

                    (The PRINCE *scans the letter.)*

                            I know now why they murdered him.
                    This is a copy; they confiscated
                    The original in an envelope
                    Addressed to me. He defied them and sent
                    Me this copy he'd made, to inform me
                    They're imposing their Global Plan tonight.
                    They've a plan to make the Queen abdicate.
                    They caught my brave Horace letting me know.

Fool.   I'll check the route we are going to take.
                    We must not be observed as we escape.

                    (Exit the FOOL.)

Prince.   Now I have no illusions on *my* route.
                    They killed Horace, fearing he would release
                    Their Global Plan, which I will now reveal.
                    I have chosen a path that once seemed safe
                    But like a climber, eye on the summit,
                    I find I must ascend a ridge that's sheer
                    With precipitous drops to left and right,

And I must go on up to reach the peak
And remove the alien flag planted there
On my Kingdom's Ben Nevis, in Scotland,
And plant the Union Jack for all to see,
Claiming my birthright, staying on my feet
Despite the sickening chasm at my back.
Long live the Tudors and our Golden Age!
I have chosen a perilous ascent
That's fraught with danger, whose outcome's unknown.
It could soon prove the way of martyrdom
For the cause of national sovereignty.
I risk following Horace to the grave
To save the Queen and my sons from *their* wiles,
And to preserve England's integrity.
I must choose for myself but also for
My people and all mankind everywhere,
For whom sovereignty is a sacred right.
It is a tragic choice and I must play
A noble hero, quaking in my shoes,
As I challenge the most cruel and powerful
Men in the world who will stop at nothing,
And, defenceless, risk being struck down. I,
Hesitant, diffident Prince Tudor, who
Am happiest in my garden, my estate
(Who would be a symbol of sovereignty,
Heraldic emblem of quiet harmony
That reconciles opposites – rampant lion
And mystic unicorn – as if I were
The Tudor rose of red encircling white
That united both Lancaster and York)
Feel pity and terror for that climber –
There but for the grace of God go I – and
As in a nightmare find that I am he;
And, despite having a terror of heights,
That I, who know my limitations and
Have more self-knowledge than most thinking men,
Must clear-headedly, with no blatant flaw –
Except perhaps a little arrogance
Towards the flawed leaders of my flawed land,
And perhaps Romantic self-indulgence,
Preferring my own world in my garden -

Decline to stoop to personal revenge;
Preferring to educate or "lead out"
My unaware nation to awareness,
Will myself on a path of destruction
Out of my own choice, not for my own good,
But to benefit universal man.
I hope I shall survive. If it turns out
I must be martyred, warts and all, to save
My people from Olympian clutches,
I accept my fate and offer my soul
To God as did my ancestor King Charles
As he laid his frail head upon the block.
I, a descendant of King George the First
Of Hanover, who could not speak a word
Of English, a German, am English now
And defend England against German might,
German-led Europe and the Syndicate,
Men whose names still have a strong German ring.
I walk in history as I scuffle leaves
On the dry walks of my estate's garden
And I walk to the future as I leave
Footprints behind me on new-fallen snow.
I've enjoyed life. I go with heavy heart.

(*Re-enter the* FOOL)

Fool.   The way is clear. Nobody is about.
               Come quickly, now, before they find us here.

SCENE 5

(*A television studio, London. An audience, which is the audience. A* PRESENTER. TECHNI-
CIANS *are seen joining the audience.*)

Presenter.   And now we come to our live interview.
               Since his mother was tragically killed
               In an accident, her eldest son's coped
               With a maturity beyond his years.
               Tonight, for the first time, he talks about

His feelings during this difficult time.
Please welcome ....

(*Applause. The* PRINCE *appears.*)
It's not ....

Prince.   My son's asked me to stand in for him so
                 I can explain how his mother was killed.

(*The* STUDIO MANAGER *and* PRODUCTION MANAGER *are standing.*)

Studio Manager. Cut.

Production Man.   Keep rolling.

Studio Manager.   Loss of transmission sign.

Prince.   By globalists who want world government.
                 They are split into two factions. One is
                 American-led, Rockefeller's; and one
                 Led from Europe and Anglo-Israeli,
                 Rothschild's. Rockefeller wants one global state,
                 And will impose it this evening at eight.
                 Behind the scenes, with a well-hidden hand.
                 He wants Israel to yield to Palestine
                 And give up land. He's against nation-states
                 And wants a United States of Europe.
                 Rothschild wants Anglo-American rule.
                 The two have reached an understanding and
                 Will set in motion a veiled *coup d'état*
                 Tonight, that will abolish the Crown and
                 Declare England a republic. Scotland,
                 Wales and Ireland will be independent.
                 They've made the Queen their prisoner and have forced
                 Her to agree to abdicate at once.
                 I have a letter written by Lord Green
                 Of the Royal Household before he died,
                 Before they murdered him to keep this quiet.

Studio Manager. I said cut. Cut.

Production Man.	Presenter, keep talking.
Prince.	The Prime Minister's party to the plot. I'll play you a tape in which he says there'll Be dictatorship for twenty years.

(*The* PRINCE *plays the cassette-recorder.*)

PM 's voice.	We Have seized power like Cromwell the Roundhead, and Have set up a caring dictatorship That will last twenty years, twice Cromwell's time.

(*The* PRINCE *switches off the cassette-recorder.*)

Prince.	Rockefeller wants the government and press To bring down the monarchy so England Is a mere state in Europe and the world. Someone asked an Egyptian to invite The Princess to his ship, hoping he would Entrammel her with his son and destroy The monarchy by mingling Muslim blood With its pure Anglo-Saxon royal blood. Another globalist faction knew this And they arranged for his new limousine To be stolen and tinkered with so its Steering would respond to radio control. Their *paparazzo* on a motorbike Drove her car at speed till a white car sent A radio signal that caused it to swerve And veer into a post. Their French police Delayed calling an ambulance until They were sure death was inevitable.
Studio Manager.	For Christ's sake, pull the bloody plug. Cut.
Production Man.	Ask a question.
Presenter.	So someone murdered her?

(*A* TECHNICIAN *gives a signal.* FIVE TECHNICIANS *start moving towards the stage.*)

Prince.   Yes. But Rockefeller is the power behind
The world government, and picks presidents
And prime ministers, who do his bidding.
What a distasteful world we now live in.
He controls what the nation's leaders say,
He has made puppets of the Royals here.
We're controlled by the PM and Wormwood.
They're controlled by Rockefeller, who rules
The Olympian Group that manages the world.
The Crown opposes them. Our sovereignty
Is drawn from its enfolding mystic Light.
Stand on your nationhood and we will win.
If I survive this attempted *coup*, I
Will embody as the heir to the Crown
The sovereignty of the nation's soul which
Opposes the Olympian usurpers.
They think the world has too many humans,
They want to kill two billion to save food
And so they've unleashed diseases, famines
And genocides – Cambodia, Rwanda –
Which seem accidents but are planned –

(*The* TECHNICIANS *surround him. From the entrance passage, the*
PRINCE'S HEIR *watches. The* FOOL *is beside him.*)

Technician.   Like this.

(*The* TECHNICIANS *stab the* PRINCE. *The audience barely sees the*
knives. The PRINCE *gasps and drops the cassette-recorder.*
A TECHNICIAN *throws a blanket over his blood-stained chest.*)

Prince.   Stand up if you'll oppose the globalists.

(*The* PRINCE *collapses back, holding his blanket-covered chest.*)

Prince's Heir.   Papa!

(The PRINCE'S HEIR *rushes to the* PRINCE *and throws his body over him*
to protect him. The TECHNICIANS *back off. The* STUDIO MANAGER

appears and addresses the audience as a DOCTOR, *urged on by the* FOOL, *appears and examines the* PRINCE. JENKINS *the journalist picks up the cassette-recorder and backs away.*)

Studio Manager.   Ladies and gentlemen, sadly
His Royal Highness has been taken ill.
We are calling an ambulance. We're not
On camera now. Due to technical faults
Sound failed just before His Royal Highness
Began talking. Vision continued but
We had no sound. Our doctor will speak now.

Doctor   (*to the studio audience*). His Royal Highness has been under stress
His mind is in a whirl, he spoke nonsense.

Studio Manager.   Please disregard everything you have heard.

(*The* FOOL *looks at the* PRINCE'S HEIR, *who stands up.*)

Prince's Heir   (*in the studio audience*). No, listen. He spoke the truth. All you here
Heard the truth about the world government.
Never ever forget what you have heard.

(TWO PARAMEDICS *arrive with a stretcher. They carefully lay the* PRINCE *on their stretcher and carry him out. The* FOOL *goes with him.*)

He spoke the truth. He's been martyred
For speaking out when silence is the rule.

(*The* PRINCE'S HEIR *points at the audience.*)

You – you are in complicity. Keep quiet
And you're accessories to this foul deed
And to the world government's usurping.
Go out and spread the word and make it stop.
Truth nourishes a nation's sovereign power.
Speak freely and you oppose conquerors.
Serve our nation by standing up for Truth.
Stand up if you oppose the globalists.
Come on, stand up for British sovereignty!

(*On the screen appears a* NEWSCASTER. *The* PRINCE'S HEIR *watches.*)

Newscaster.   Our main story, the Prince is taken ill

(*We see the* PRINCE *after the attack, labouring for breath.*)

An eye-witness said he appeared confused
Concerned technicians gathered round the Prince
He's now being treated in hospital
Where he's expected to stay overnight.

(*The* PRINCE'S HEIR *turns away in tears. The* FOOL *returns. Together they walk off very slowly.*)

SCENE 6

(ROCKEFELLER'S *enormous suite in a London hotel.* ROCKEFELLER *turns off the television screen. He addresses* ROTHSCHILD.)

Rockefeller.   We can't impose our Global Plan tonight.
By all accounts, enough people heard him
To cause us problems if we go ahead.
I've received a copy of a cassette,
Threatening remarks by the bungling PM.
The New World Order can't start in scandal.
We need to put distance between his death
And our announcement of the Crown's demise.
We announce nothing, and the Prince's words
Will seem deranged tomorrow, obsessive,
Unduly concerned with conspiracies,
Paranoiac, bizarre. In a word, mad.
He has a double who is much more bland,
Who'll be passed off as the Prince – mark my words.
To guarantee the Crown the family
Would have an actor to play the Queen's heir.
We need to give them time to launch the oaf.
We want the people to believe the heir
Is mad, when the Queen at last abdicates.
We'd better put off our preconceived Plan

For at least six months, till people forget.
We'll deal with the man who sent us the tape
And seize and destroy the original.

Rothschild   (*quietly*). He won. He saved the Crown and sovereignty
For his son by seeking this martyrdom.
I concurred in his fall, I was outraged
That he denounced us at a Group meeting.
But my position is well known and as
A monarchist I'm not sorry he won
Or that the Crown will endure for a while
Although it must never impede our Plan.
You turned the tables on me through Wormwood.
It seems the tables have been turned on you.

Rockefeller.   He's only won a temporary stay
Of execution. There'll soon be no Crown.
Our Plan demands it go, as you accept.
And when we do impose our Global Plan
There will be no sovereignty anywhere.
We're as inexorable as gathering night.
Nothing can stay our coming global rule.

SCENE 7

(*Windsor Castle, London. The Prince's private funeral service. The* PRIME MINISTER *gives the eulogy from the pulpit.*)

Prime Minister.   The untimely death of our much loved Prince
From a brain haemorrhage has shocked us all.
We all feel devastated that the heir
To the throne should be taken from us, and
We haven't had a chance to say goodbye.
We felt for him the day the Princess died,
How bravely he walked behind her coffin.
And now we feel for his two sons, who are
So brave at this dreadful, so dreadful time.
The Prince had so many fine qualities.
But most of all he had great strength. He was

A rampart, tower of strength to those of us
Who want to modernise institutions
And bring the monarchy more up to date.
He welcomed our new Britain, and for that
We are grateful to him. He longed to see
A new England take her place in Europe
As a new state that is forward-looking.
We bow our heads in farewell to the Prince
And welcome his stand-in who'll play the role
So the institution can be stable,
But will of course depart before he's crowned.

(He greets a look-alike of the Prince.)

SCENE 8

(Windsor Castle. SIR WILLIAM HAWKES *stands near* ROCKEFELLER *and* ROTHSCHILD *after the departure of the Prince's coffin. The* PRINCE'S HEIR *stands nearby with the* FOOL. *The* QUEEN *and the* DUKE *are nearby, with the* CHIEF OF POLICE, *the* US PRESIDENT, *the* PRIME MINISTER *and* WORMWOOD. ROTHSCHILD *is talking exclusively to* ROCKEFELLER.)

Rothschild.   The prisoners-of-war have turned their backs on
The Japanese Emperor along the Mall.
They booed and called the PM a traitor.

Rockefeller.   They are stuck in the past, the nation-state,
And have not seen the world with global eyes.
I've no time for them. Or for that Irish
Bigot who says the Queen is our parrot.
We know she parrots our global ideas –
We feed them to bring down the monarchy –
But *he sees* Ireland as a nation-state
And not in terms of global unity.

Rothschild.   My emphasis differs, as you well know.
I'm all for nation-states so long as they
Do not impede our global strategy.
We can't have him blurting. I'll deal with him.

	The journalist who sent you that cassette
	Was called Jenkins.

Rockefeller.   Was?

Rothschild.   He fell down some stairs
Last night and broke his neck.

Rockefeller.   And the cassette?

Rothschild.   We found the original. It's destroyed.

Rockefeller.   There may be another copy somewhere.
We'll still lie low for at least six more months.

(SIR WILLIAM HAWKES *moves to the* PRINCE'S HEIR.)

Hawkes.   You'll speak to Mr Rockefeller now
And to Mr Rothschild, and then we'll leave

Prince's Heir.   Mr Rockefeller and Mr Rothschild,
Please, come here. Grandmama, Grandpapa, sir,
Prime Minister and Mr Wormwood, I have
Something to say which will affect you all.
First, I want my grandparents to return
To London to be near me as I come
To terms with the loss of my dear father.

Duke.   We will return, if that's acceptable.

Prince's Heir.   Secondly, I want the Chief of Police
To investigate my dear father's death,
And the death of my mother. My father
Did not die from a haemorrhage. That is
Untrue.

Prime Minister.   With respect, that's not right –

Prince's Heir.   I saw
It with these eyes and will give evidence.
Please be sensitive to *my* feelings now.

Chief of Police.   I will investigate if we're agreed.

(*The* QUEEN *nods. Exit the* CHIEF OF POLICE *after a bow.*)

Prince's Heir.   Thirdly, I want a change in the Household.
                  Sir William's served us with distinction but
                  It's time for a fresh start. He should retire –

Hawkes.   I am not ready to retire just yet.

Prince's Heir.   And I want Mr Thorn Lord Chamberlain,
                  And grandmama, I want him knighted for
                  Loyal service to my father – and you.

Wormwood.   He can't be Lord Chamberlain, he won't know
                  What to do –

Rockefeller.   Sir William knows protocol –

Rothschild.   You're quick to intercede on his behalf.

Prince's Heir.   I want Sir William Thorn Lord Chamberlain.

Prime Minister.   We all want what's best for the young Prince, but –

Duke.   I think the Prince's idea's excellent.
                  Mr Thorn counselled my son with wisdom.

Queen.   We're grateful for all Sir William has done.
                  Is Mr Thorn prepared to play this role?

Fool.   I am, ma'am. Sir, I thank you most humbly.

Hawkes.   I may have grounds for unfair dismissal.

Rothschild.   I have questions about your loyalty.

Fool.   The Queen will accept your resignation
                  In accordance with Palace protocol.

Prince's Heir.   And lastly, I want Mr Rockefeller

	And Mr Rothschild kept away from us Till I've probed the deaths of both my parents –
Hawkes.	This has gone too far –
Prime Minister.	That must be withdrawn –
Prince's Heir.	*And* Lord Horace Green, who was good and kind.
Wormwood.	Control your grandson, ma'am.
Fool.	The Prince is right. My first duty in my new appointment Will be to assist the Chief of Police In how the Prince's parents met their ends, And what part these two men played in their deaths. Until the outcome's known, you'd both be wise To stay away from England, and the Queen.
Rockefeller.	You haven't been appointed yet. (*Aside.*) You squirm.
Duke.	I think I can say for the Queen, he has.
Rothschild.	The Royal Family takes *our* advice –
Prince's Heir.	Not any more. We don't need advice now.
Rockefeller.	You are under a misapprehension. I want to consider your feelings but *You* can't change how the world is run. You're young And will learn how positions are allowed And how some who hold them would abdicate Or find their positions taken away, Titles abolished, if they *weren't* allowed.
Prince's Heir.	We ground our position on sovereignty.
	(ROCKEFELLER *turns away with* ROTHSCHILD.)
Rockefeller.	We will make common cause to work against The British nation and British Empire,

	Which must be transformed expeditiously.
Rothschild.	We're allies within the New World Order
	And overtly we both co-operate
	And our common cause guarantees world peace,
	But covertly we're in opposition
	And fundamentally we still differ.
	Palestine's my main concern. I've agreed
	To make concessions on Britain, although
	I want America to be part of
	A British-led world government. And you
	Want Britain to be part of a US-
	Led world government. Can we co-exist?
	Can we be at peace over Palestine?
	You drop requests for land, we drop armed raids?
Rockefeller.	We'll bring forward our Global Plan. PM.
Prime Minister.	Coming, Mr Rockefeller.

(ROCKEFELLER, ROTHSCHILD *and the* PRIME MINISTER *gather. They
are followed by* SIR WILLIAM HAWKES. *The* US PRESIDENT *steps
towards* ROCKEFELLER.)

US President.	Not so fast,
	Mr Rockefeller. I need a quiet word.
	Pakistan's tested five nuclear bombs
	On the border with terrorist Iran.
Rockefeller.	Now both India and Pakistan have gone
	Nuclear – my thanks for "encouraging" them
	And urging Rothschild to take India's side
	And for your protests and talk of sanctions
	And your admission of your impotence –
	We need to use the heightened tension to
	Urge fast global union on the world,
	Say that these bombs threaten to devastate
	Parts of India, Pakistan and China
	And wipe out one billion "useless eaters".
US President.	That ain't that easy, Mr Rockefeller.

Rothschild.	Do it. Or else that tart will testify.
US President.	Anything you say, Mr Rockefeller, If you agree what Mr Rothschild's just said.
Rothschild	(*to Rockefeller*). It won't be long before Iraq tests one And threatens Israel with a Muslim bomb. I want Pakistan tied up before that. (ROCKEFELLER *nods*.)
Rockefeller	(*aside*). I'll make sure Iraq receives Muslim help And threatens Israel and odious Britain With nuclear, not just anthrax, missiles. Régime-change Iraq and it will be said The balance of power's tilted to Iran For Iraq's Sunnis will cease to offset Her Shias, who'll look to Iran's Shias. We should tolerate Iraq's dictators Or else we'll have a nuclear Iran. I controlled the Shah for oil, now Rothschild Controls post-Shah Iran, also for oil. I'll re-turn the tables on this Rothschild.
US President.	Very good, Mr Rockefeller. I'll Raise UN sanctions on both sides, send up A smokescreen of international talk. (*The* PRIME MINISTER *approaches as* ROCKEFELLER *begins to move away*.)
Prime Minister.	Thank you for coming, Mr President.
US President.	We two are the hope of the Western world. What shall we do, Mr Prime Minister? Shall we tell Iraq to nuke Israel and Get Rothschild off our backs, or shall we just Strum our guitars and forget about power?
Prime Minister	(*grinning*). Anything you say, Mr President. You can come and sunbathe in my garden.

US President.	I wouldn't mind a swim right now, a glass –
Rockefeller.	I'm going, PM. Got to see someone.

(ROCKEFELLER *moves away.*)

Prime Minister.	Oh Mr Rockefeller, wait for me.

(*Exeunt* ROCKEFELLER, ROTHSCHILD, *the* PRIME MINISTER *and* SIR
WILLIAM HAWKES.)

Duke.	I've just seen what I never thought I'd see.
Wormwood.	Now you listen to –
Prince's Heir.	Please ask him to leave.
Duke.	You can see it's the Queen's will. Please leave us.
Wormwood.	This won't be the last you hear about this.
	You can't get away with this outrageous
	Show of independence just because we're
	Standing in your private Windsor Castle.
	I shan't make a scene now. But you just wait.

(*Exit* WORMWOOD, *who follows the* PRIME MINISTER.)

Queen.	My heir, you were truly magnificent.
	The Crown will be in good hands when it's yours.
	And you, Sir William Thorn, will make a good
	Adviser to our future King. Good has
	Come into darkness like a faint light.
	I mourn my son, this boy's father, and yet
	In my sorrow there gleams a distant hope.
Duke.	It is a consequence of his broadcast.
	The Prince sacrificed his life so that
	A Revolution could take place against
	The Olympians, in the short term at least.
	He's bought us breathing-space. We must use it.
	He stood for the old world of sovereignty

Against the new world's dark conspiracies.
He would have been a marvellous King, he was
A deeply perceptive spirit who knew
The meaning of the divine right of kings.
(*The* QUEEN *and* DUKE *move away. The* FOOL *is alone with the*
PRINCE'S HEIR.)

Fool.
What a surprise. Poacher turned gamekeeper.
It's a topsy-turvy world, all upside down.
The Wheel of Fortune's turned, some things have changed.
My predecessors were free to say things
And comment humorously and make jests
On the courtiers' competition for power,
But they never ever achieved office.
It's the apotheosis of the Fool.
I bequeathe my old role to versifiers.
You won't regret the wisdom of your choice.
I thank you from the bottom of my heart.
I've scraped by in my old car and pension
But now I've gone up in the world. The Fool
Advise the King. Your father would be pleased.

Prince's Heir.
I know.

Fool.
You were magnificent. You took
Them all by storm.

Prince's Heir.
Just as you told me to.

Fool.
It worked. The counter-revolution worked.

Prince's Heir.
You master-minded a minor defeat
For the Olympians. You're a wise old Fool.

Fool.
And somewhere up there your father's cheering.

Prince's Heir.
Can you see where?

Fool.
Yes, on that balcony,
High up, your father and your mother stand
Shrouded in white light, royal presences

As if in a masque, married in Heaven,
A higher union under Providence.
They're surrounded in Light, together now,
United in death, at peace in white Light,
In harmony in a Temple in Heaven,
And radiant happiness shines from each face.
Nothing comes between them, they're done with time.
They're eternally guarding the nation.
Can you see them?

Prince's Heir.   Yes, yes. I can see them.
Horace is with them, father's delighted.
Goon, I have high hopes for this land of ours.

(*Exit the* PRINCE'S HEIR. *The* FOOL *advances to the front of the stage.*)

Fool.   This is the moment the Prince should appear
To let us know he faked his death – to win.
But there's no happy ending to this rule.
He made a tragic choice, and that is that.
And I've had to work with a look-alike
(And that's just me, for I can't play the fool
These days, though once a Fool, always a Fool...).
Isn't life dying to be born anew?
The philosophic death makes all new men,
Aren't we all different from our yesterday?
We're in the new time now, hey-ho, hey-ho.
I've not forgotten you, my friends. You bear
The burden of this new knowledge. It's you
Who must act to stop them. Our little play
Has been no mere entertainment, nor yet
A nightmare vision. What you have seen is
A reflection, as in a true mirror
Held up to Nature, of how the world works.
Your nation's being hung, drawn and quartered.
This Kingdom ruled a quarter of the world.
Now this England's been carved to a quarter.
It's smaller now than in the Tudor Age.
Hey-ho, we all live in a dwindling time.
You've all been warned. Now's the time to respond.
You are responsible. I'm just a Fool,

A quirky, zany, quibbling simpleton
Who earns a living by telling the truth
In jests which laugh at wrong and applaud right
(Which laugh at – no, applaud! – Lord Chamberlains),
A simple-minded fellow who believes
That good sometimes triumphs over evil,
That evil men are sometimes stopped by good.
I solicit virtue and berate vice,
But you are witnesses to treachery
And must stand and defend our nationhood.
Rise up in the name of your sovereignty!

EPILOGUE

(United Nations building, New York, AD 2100. Re-enter the MINISTER OF WORLD CULTURE *for the United States of the World. He walks across behind the* FOOL, *shaking his head.)*

Min. of World Culture.	And so our recently discovered tale Written by an anonymous playwright In the nineteen nineties as a protest To demonise Rockefeller, Rothschild Actually shows their heroism; and To present the Prince as a martyr shows The moral bankruptcy of the Prince's court Which sought to undermine our noble sway. Our scholars hold this version of events More accurate than old-world history books Which conceal the Prince's defiant death And his replacement by a bland double, Pretender who claimed to be George the Seventh, And took the Prince's paramour for Queen, Deceiving to perpetuate the Crown At the corrupt ex-monarchy's behest. It's clear he had no title to the throne, This double, and was justly swept aside. And so we've shown what really happened, how The Crown became remote from the people And opposed our glorious world government; How the Prince spoke out against our world rule.

And so our retrieved, near-lost manuscript
Written before our New World Order's birth
Ends in narrow, insular attitudes
Which typify what we must all expunge.
If any of you recognize such views –
Admiration for sovereign monarchies
Or praise for frail, fragmenting nation-states,
Reactionary hankerings for past times –
In any of your neighbours, denounce them!
Rise up and point a finger at them now!
Stern guardians of our World Order, arrest
All world citizens who have been denounced.
Take them from their seats to the waiting trucks!
And as good citizens of our regime,
Defend the United States of the World!
Keep it untainted and unpolluted
By national or feudal revisionists,
Keep it republican and transnational,
Population barely four billion as
My great-great-grandfather, Rockefeller,
Once dreamt before we halved the world's eaters!
I believe in the triumph of virtue
Which covers decadence like fallen snow.
As earth now covers Tudor streets and stones
And all on progress with the Virgin Queen,
History has buried sovereign nationhood.
The earth that interred sovereignty is just!
Applaud our Founding Fathers' levelling!
And the leadership of Rockefeller
And Rothschild who gave us this Paradise,
This mountain peak which towers above all lands
That wear the uniformity of snow,
This eyrie that presses against the clouds
From which all humans seem like tiny ants;
Applaud those who rule like Olympian gods!
Rise up and cheer the brave World Government!

OVID BANISHED

A Tale of Transformation

"And for matters of state, the story of Titus Livius, though it extolled that part which Pompey held, was not therefore suppressed by Octavius Caesar of the other faction. But that Naso was by him banished in his old age, for the wanton poems of his youth, was but a mere covert of state over some secret cause: and besides, the books were neither banished nor called in. From hence we shall meet with little else but tyranny in the Roman empire."

John Milton, *Areopagitica*, 1644

DRAMATIS PERSONAE

MAIN CHARACTERS

Augustus
Livia, his wife
Tiberius, Livia's son by Tiberius Claudius Nero and third husband of the elder Julia
Julia (Senior), Augustus's daughter by Scribonia
Julia (Junior), her daughter by Agrippa and Augustus's granddaughter
Lucius Aemilius Paullus, her husband
Iunius Silanus, her lover

Paullus Fabius Maximus, a friend of Augustus
Marcia, his wife
Messalla Corvinus, Rome's leading literary patron
Cotta Maximus, his younger son
Ovid, the poet
Ovid's wife
Propertius, the poet
Ibis, a spy in the pay of Livia

Governor of Tomis
Constantia, Ovid's secretary in Tomis
Priest of Apollo, her brother
Claudius and Flavius, Ovid's servants

MINOR CHARACTERS

Plautius Rufus, Audasius, Epicadus, Telephus, Clemens: pro-Julian conspirators
Iullus Antonius
Official
Slave-girl
Slave
Guard
Messenger
Executioners 1 and 2
Soldiers 1 and 2
Praetorian Guard
Ovid's friends
Tomitan natives

Ship's crew

LOCATIONS

Rome
Messalla's House
Augustus's House
Ovid's House
Julia Junior's House
The Praetorian Barracks
Livia's House
Tiberius's Palace
A Salon

Other
Ovid's Family Villa, Sulmo
Cotta's Villa, Elba
On Board Ship
Nola, Augustus's Sick-Room
Ovid's Hut, Tomis
Temple of Apollo, Tomis

Recommended Interval: after Act 3, Scene 5

PREFACE TO
OVID BANISHED

This play is about freedom of speech particularly in relation to a world government. It is clear that Ovid, the artist, has offended Augustus, and (as the epigraph from Milton's *Areopagitica* indicates) not because of his sexually-frank *Ars Amatoria*, which mocked the fashionable *genre* of didactic poetry. For a reason never disclosed be was banished to the Pontus, where he died. He refused to say what his offence was.

In *Tristia*, "Sad Poems" (also "Sorrows"), II, 207 ff, he addresses Augustus: "Though two crimes, a poem and a blunder (*carmen et error*), have brought me ruin, of my fault in the one (i.e. the blunder) I must keep silent, for my worth is not such that I may reopen your wounds, O Caesar: it is more than enough that you should have been pained once. The other remains: the charge that by an obscene poem I have taught foul adultery." Elsewhere he makes it clear that his "offence" (*offensus*) wounded Augustus. It was something he saw: "Why did I see anything? Why did I make my eyes guilty? Why was I so thoughtless as to harbour the knowledge of a fault? Unwitting was Actaeon when he beheld Diana unclothed..." (II, 103-5). What he saw happened by chance: "It is not a brief tale or safe to say what chance made my eyes witness a baleful evil. My mind shrinks in dread from that time.... Nothing then will I say except that I have sinned, but by that sin sought no reward; folly is the proper name for my crime, if you wish to give the true title to the deed" (III, vi, 27ff). He took his secret to the grave.

Ovid Banished narrates a set of events which have baffled historians. It draws on new historical research. The "mistake" (Latin *error*) for which Ovid is banished has been a subject of speculation in many articles and books over the years. What had Ovid done that deserved banishment for the rest of his life by Augustus personally, with no pardon contemplated by any of the imperial family, not even Augustus's son Tiberius when he succeeded his stepfather? It cannot have been a sexual peccadillo alone, for perpetual banishment would have been too extreme a punishment for its time for such a misdemeanour.

I have researched the background to the banishment and follow Peter Green in *Classical*

Bearings, who believes that Ovid stumbled across a Julian conspiracy. The Julian line was descended from Julius Caesar and included the line through Augustus's first wife Scribonia, by whom Augustus had a daughter Julia, who in turn had a daughter (his grand-daughter) also called Julia. The Claudian line was through Augustus's second wife Livia, who had had a son Tiberius by her first husband: Tiberius Claudius Nero, who gave his name to the Claudian line. Her son Tiberius was Augustus's stepson. The Julian line was plotting to succeed Augustus. The strong Livia was determined that her son Tiberius would be the next Emperor, and she achieved this outcome. It seems that Ovid stumbled across Julian plotters and that his crime was not to inform Augustus. He knew too much for his own good, and had to be removed from Rome.

Analysts now agree that Ovid inadvertently discovered and was suspected of being involved in a plot to restore the Julian imperial line (the two Julias) in place of the Claudian line (Tiberius). Such a plot would have struck at the very basis of the *imperium*, Augustus's "new" world order.

I have been faithful to the history of the time. There is considerable evidence that Ovid opposed Augustus's *imperium*, Rome's world empire or new world order which pacified barbarian tribes by military massacres. Ovid was a dissident in relation to Augustus's world government, and this must have been a factor in his banishment. The two men shown being executed after the two conspiracies – Iullus after the first, Paulus after the second – were actually executed. Paulus's crime, *laesa maiestas*, high treason (i.e. plotting against the State), may well have been Ovid's crime. News of Silanus's escape from execution can be found in Tacitus, *The Annals of Imperial Rome*, 3.24. There is some evidence to suggest that Livia finally poisoned Augustus, and I have gone with this interpretation.

The details of Ovid's voyage to the Black Sea and his exile I have taken from his *Tristia* and his *Epistulae Ex Ponto* ("Black Sea Letters"), both of which include letters to his wife. Both are full of autobiographical detail. A literal translation can be found in the Loeb *Tristia Ex Ponti* and a verse translation in Penguin's Ovid, *The Poems of Exile*.

My view of the reason for Ovid's banishment is historically based and is not a mere fancy. Ovid is thus a universal victim of the excesses of world government. I have used more poetic licence in interpreting Ovid's transformation in Tomis on the Black Sea, where his complaining, self-absorbed, self-pitying letters (*Tristia* and *Epistulae Ex Ponto*) give way in the end to dignified acceptance and silence. There is nevertheless considerable historical evidence for seeing Ovid as transforming himself into a mystic in his relative solitude away from the cultural desert of Rome.

The artist living in a time of world government – like Virgil, Horace and Ovid, who lived when Rome ruled the known world through Augustus – has a duty to tell the truth. He is at risk, and if he is banished for the remainder of his life, he only has his pride and his personal growth with which to occupy and console himself. My Ovid ends as a mystic who comes to see the shallowness of Rome. The barrenness of Tomis, so bleak when contrasted with Rome's opulence at the beginning of his exile, finally appears desirable as it lies outside the materialism of metropolitan Rome.

I have always been fascinated and appalled at the knowledge Ovid came by, a knowledge it would have been safer for him not to have had. The plight of the dissident who knows more than is good for him is a universal one. It was Solzhenitsyn's plight in the Communist USSR. The spurned artist can embody true values to which the all-powerful but shallow world government of his day cannot aspire.

A Universalist play, besides relating its story to a global theme and perspective and to the Light, seeks echoes in all civilisations and times. Shakespeare drew on the Roman time, and I have found focusing on Rome at its most powerful liberating. The Universalism of the play should not blind the reader to the fact that *Ovid Banished* is fundamentally a play about our own time, in which State censorship, though more subtle than in Augustus's Rome, is still a hazardous weapon of government.

This play continues the revival of verse drama I began with *The Warlords* and *Prince Tudor*, and later developed with *The Rise of Oliver Cromwell*. It is written in tight blank verse, with fewer characters than appear in my other historical verse plays, which are of epic scale and scope. But first and foremost it is a play that sides with freedom of speech against the self-interested immorality (or amorality) of the most powerful government there had ever been.

27 October 2000; revised 17 January, 2 February 2006

SUMMARY OF OVID BANISHED

ACT 1

Sc.1. Rome, Messalla's House

Messalla's literary salon: launch party for *Ars Amatoria*. Ovid meets his third wife and is proposi-
tioned by the Emperor's daughter, Julia Sr. Ibis overhears.

Sc.2. Rome, Augustus's House

Livia urges the Emperor to banish Scribonia's line. Augustus soliloquizes on the succession.
Julia Sr is banished to Pandateria for breaking the *Lex Julia,* though the real reason is sedition.
Iullus Antonius is condemned to death and executed.

Sc.3. Rome, Ovid's House

Ovid and Messalla discuss Ovid's work in the context of Julia's banishment. The latter urges a
change of course – no more dissident art. "You must awaken from erotic dream,/Channel your
senses into ancient myths."

Sc.4. Sulmo, Ovid's Family Villa

Ovid proposes to his third wife. She accepts.

ACT 2

Sc.1. Rome, Augustus's House

Livia is shown as the Emperor's chief of staff, directing policy. She demands that Augustus raise
up her son Tiberius as his successor and that he banish his last remaining grandson, Agrippa
Postumus. In a soliloquy, Augustus talks of his ailing condition.

Sc.2. Rome, Messalla's House

Messalla's salon: launch party for *Metamorphoses.* Julia Jr propositions Ovid, like her mother
before her, and openly criticises the *imperium.* Ovid says, "It's Rome that counts, not the *imperi-
um.*" Once again, Ibis eavesdrops.

Sc.3. Rome, Julia JR's House

Julia greets Ovid naked and desires to be vanquished. Ovid witnesses the blood bond of the
Julian conspirators and flees.

Sc.4. Rome, Augustus's House

Augustus soliloquizes again about the succession and whether or not he should banish Julia Jr.
Ibis names the conspirators and points to Ovid's complicity. Paullus (Julia's husband) and her
lover Iunius Silanus are condemned to death and Julia to banishment. Livia is behind
Augustus's decisions. Silanus is in fact exiled.

Sc.5. Rome, The Praetorian Barracks

The execution of Paullus is carried out.

Sc.6. Rome, Augustus's House

Julia Jr is banished to Timerus, and like her mother before her, adultery is the pretext. She too
has broken the *Lex Julia.* Augustus decides to use Ovid as a scapegoat.

Sc.7. Elba, Cotta's Villa

Ovid and Cotta are discussing Ovid's works. Ovid is putting the finishing touches to *Metamorphoses* and feels a new self emerging ("a consciousness as boundless as that sea"). Soldiers arrive to take Ovid to the Emperor.

Sc.8. Rome, Augustus's House
Ovid's interview with Augustus. Livia is present. Ovid stands up for his sovereign independence as a writer and tells Augustus that the *imperium* is a killing machine. Ovid is relegated to Tomis for high treason and his works are banned from Rome's libraries.

ACT 3

Sc.1. Rome, Ovid's House
Ovid's wife guesses the reason for his banishment and marvels he could have been so foolish. She will ask Fabius (whose wife Marcia is a friend) to intercede with Livia.

Sc.2. Rome, Livia's House
Fabius intercedes unsuccessfully on behalf of Ovid.

Sc.3. Rome, Ovid's House
Ovid is with friends, among them Messalla. He inveighs bitterly against Augustus for his hypocrisy, in particular his own breaches of the *Lex Julia*. Messalla urges him to write letters in verse from exile.

Sc.4. Rome, Augustus's House
Messalla intervenes on behalf of Ovid. He defends *Metamorphoses* as pro-Rome and says the work has been misinterpreted. Augustus says he cannot afford to be magnanimous until he has created a United States of the World.

Sc.5. Rome, Ovid's House
Ovid's farewell. His wife wants to accompany him into exile, but he asks her to stay and work for his recall.

SUGGESTED INTERVAL

Sc.6. Rome, Livia's House
A messenger informs Livia of Ovid's departure. In the soliloquy which follows the Emperor's wife reveals her true colours ("I've had Ovid in my sights for years").

Sc.7. On Board Ship
Ovid is writing on deck during a storm. His purse is stolen by Claudius, one of his appointed servants.

Sc.8. Tomis.
Ovid arrives in Tomis. The Governor escorts him to his house, a draughty hut. Ovid is appalled and thinks he has arrived in Hades.

ACT 4

Sc.1. Tomis, Ovid's Hut
Ovid laments his fate. Claudius, who stole his purse, has escaped back to Rome. Flavius

remains to share his master's fate and introduces him to Constantia, a local woman who will act as secretary. A hail of arrows hits the roof; they all run to repel the attack.

Sc.2. Tomis, Ovid's Hut

Ovid dictates to Constantia. He rants against Augustus's rule. Constantia, who is in love with Ovid, tells him to turn his back on Rome, for now he has her.

Sc.3. Rome, Livia's House

Ovid's wife and Fabius's wife go to Livia to intercede for Ovid in the wake of Messalla's death. Livia is not moved.

Sc.4. Tomis, Ovid's Hut

Ovid laments the death of Messalla. (He is reading his wife's letter.) He is deeply depressed: "I sit in solitude,/A Roman spectacle, like a panda/In a zoo viewed by curious Getic folk." Constantia introduces her brother, a priest of the Temple of Apollo. The priest gives Ovid an ear of wheat, Eleusinian symbol of rebirth.

Sc.5. Tomis, Ovid's Hut

Ovid receives a letter which gives him hope again (Augustus has visited Agrippa Postumus), but it is clear that Constantia wants him to stay.

Sc.6. Rome, Livia's House

Livia gives Augustus the news that a son has been born to Julia on Trimerus. He says it must be exposed to die. Fabius comes to intercede once again on Ovid's behalf, but is peremptorily refused. Augustus: "I never liked the poetry of Ovid."

Sc.7. Tomis, Temple of Apollo

The priest of Apollo, Constantia's brother, helps Ovid contact the Light. Ovid sees the face of Apollo.

Sc.8. Nola, Augustus's Sick-Room

Livia has summoned her son Tiberius to Augustus's death-bed. Tiberius realises that Livia has poisoned him. Prompted by Livia, he orders the death of Agrippa Postumus. With his dying words, Augustus says that Ovid was right and that he has built his vast empire on sand. He also realises that Livia has poisoned him.

Sc.9. Tomis, Ovid's Hut

News is brought of Augustus's death and deification, but Ovid is not moved with new hopes of return. He has rejected Rome. Constantia, realizing her prize is within reach, kisses him and draws him to her breast.

ACT 5

Sc.1. Tomis, Ovid's Hut

The Governor comes to see Ovid's shrine to Augustus. Ovid's prayer shows his new Universalist awareness. The Governor says he will report the news to the new Emperor, Tiberius.

Sc.2. Tomis, Temple of Apollo

Ovid addresses the Tomitans on his new spiritual insight. He is now a syncretist, a Universalist, who urges them to worship the new god, Augustus-Apollo. He also predicts that they, the Getic peoples and other barbarians, will inherit the Empire: "My Getic friends, the future will be yours./Rome will decline and fall. Your descendants/Will pour through its walls and inherit Rome."

Sc.3. Rome, Tiberius's Palace

Ovid's wife pleads for the final time with Tiberius for Ovid's return, but to no avail. Livia is, as ever, there to prompt him, telling him to be pitiless like the Roman eagle. Tiberius: "He will die in Tomis."

Sc.4. Tomis, Ovid's Hut

The Getae, goaded by the Governor, come to complain about Ovid's description of them and their land. Ovid sets the record straight and once again attacks the *imperium.* He succumbs to a fit of coughing, and Constantia sends for the priest.

Sc.5. Tomis, Ovid's Hut

The priest comforts Ovid, who tells him he has stood for sovereignty against imperialism. They bring down the Light together, and Ovid has a final vision of the One – his orchard at Sulmo bathed in light – before dying.

Sc.6. Rome, A Salon

Cotta, Messalla's son, announces Ovid's death to a social gathering in Rome. He says the Golden Age of Roman Literature has passed. But the people are indifferent, and it is Ibis who has the last word: the Golden Age, which will be an age of World Government, has yet to come.

OVID BANISHED

ACT ONE

SCENE 1

(2/1BC. Marcus Valerius Messalla Corvinus's house in Rome. A literary salon. OVID, in his early forties, is in the foreground among friends. The poet PROPERTIUS. A hubbub.)

Propertius.   Pray silence for Messalla Corvinus,
Right-hand man to the Emperor Augustus,
Statesman, general orator and patron
Of the finest literary circle
Of poets since our majestic Virgil,
Of Tibullus, Gallus, the great Horace,
Aemilius Macer, Pontius, Bassus,
Of me, Propertius, and our brightest star
Who shines like the bright Venus at twilight,
The appearance of whose most recent work
We have gathered to celebrate – Ovid!

(A round of applause. OVID bows. PROPERTIUS waves an inviting hand at MESSALA.)

Messalla.   Some poets in my circle have followed
Alexandrian models – Callimachus,
Nicander, Parthenius – and parody.
Ovid is a neo-Alexandrian.
The *Ars Amatoria* has already
Taken Rome by storm. It is recited
On streets, in bath-houses and in bedrooms.

(There is laughter.)

These skilful measures teach with peerless wit
The art of seduction and follow on
From the *Amores* and confirm Ovid's
Our foremost poet of erotic love.
He is unequalled in polished verses
Which, it must be said, are of moral worth –

Are satire, not a manual of love.

(*There is applause.* OVID *bows. Messalla's younger son* COTTA MAXIMUS *approaches.*)

Cotta.   You are a rebel and you mock old ways.
Caesar has his spies in this very room
Who may regard your verse as subversive.
My father is uneasy, watch his face.
He fought with Caesar against Antony
At Actium, he's for the *imperium*.
It would be wise to praise the *imperium*.

Ovid.   An artist tells the truth and must not lie.
The truth, dear Cotta, closest friend, is that
I don't give a fig for the *imperium*.
Our rulers are blind and lack true vision.
Augustus sends our legions against tribes
As a boy moves toy soldiers in his play,
And busies himself with world government.
I live for art and love, not puerile wars.

Cotta.   Be careful not to offend the Emperor.
He may not take kindly to your verses.
He takes the *imperium* seriously
And his *Lex Julia* even more so,
His moral outlook that defends marriage.
Say you want an end to adultery.
He wants to reform women and marriage –

Ovid   (*scornfully*). He can't even reform his own daughter.
Look at Julia flirting. When he stops her
Adulteries together with his own,
Then I will take his laws seriously and
Pay attention to his moral reforms.

(PROPERTIUS *waves his arms.*)

Propertius.   Pray silence for our cynosure – Ovid!

(*There is loud applause.*)

Ovid.	I thank you, Messalla, for your support
	For your circle of versifiers where
	Propertius outshines all like a full moon,
	And for holding this serious reception
	In your magnificent and sumptuous house.
	And thank you all for attending this night
	To hear more amatory lines from Ovid.
	I can see some distinguished faces here –
	Your two sons, Messalinus and Cotta,
	And Fabius Maximus, Caesar's great friend
	And his wife Marcia. Thank you for coming.
	And I am especially honoured that
	Caesar's own daughter Julia is with us.

(*There is a prolonged burst of sycophantic applause.*)

Italy's thrust up poets like fruit-trees
Whose images, like olives in the sun,
Gleam as if they hang in a ripe orchard
That has been planted in our fertile soil.
Soon you will listen, I hope patiently,
To my verses, which I wrote to help boys
Seduce ex-slave-girls, not married women.
I support the *Lex Julia* on marriage.

(*There is nervous laughter. The speeches over, JULIA sweeps into a side-room and sits on a throne-like chair attended by a SLAVE-GIRL who fills her goblet with wine. Julia whispers to her. The slave-girl returns to the gathering and fills OVID's goblet from her jug.*)

Slave-girl.	Your verses will seduce me any time.
	My mistress wants to speak with you. This way.

(OVID *follows holding his goblet.* JULIA *waves the* SLAVE-GIRL *away. She indicates that Ovid should sit near her.* IBIS, *one of the guests, stands near the doorway, surreptitiously trying to listen but unable to see.*)

Julia.	Was that last statement not ironical?
	Your poetry's for all, not just callow boys.
	I think you were being satirical
	In keeping with your verses' languid tone.

I love your elegies. My favourite lines
Are: "Having located the spot where she
Likes to be touched, don't be shy to touch it."

(JULIA *stands and half-disrobes*.)

What, Ovid bashful? Ovid really shy?

Ovid.   I hesitate for fear I give offence
           To Caesar's daughter.

Julia   (*taunting*).   I am astounded.
           The *Art* is blatant in its bold advice.
           For all his swagger Ovid is timid.
           He urges boys to touch but shrinks himself.

Ovid.   My poetry must remain ambiguous.
           It is unwise, no dangerous, to flout
           The *Lex Julia* with Caesar's own daughter.
           Actaeon saw Diana's nakedness.
           I don't want hounds tearing me to pieces.

(JULIA *re-robes*.)

Julia.   Your love poetry is universal, for
           Everyone has secret erotic thoughts.

Ovid.   You were my model for my Corinna,
           Intellectual, sexual sophisticate.
           To long for love's a universal heat.
           The remedy for love's *Lex Julia*.

(JULIA *laughs*.)

Julia.   Ever witty. You have an elegant
           Turn of phrase. I like embarrassing you.
           I've made you blush, and now I'll challenge you.
           Tiberius is disgraced. Now is the time
           To perpetrate a pro-Julian *coup*
           With Iullus Antonius, son of Mark
           Antony, friend of Julius Caesar,

Who now supports our cause and is out there,
And other nobles who are now our friends.
I too look back to Julius Caesar.
My father, his grand-nephew, was his heir
And adoptive son so in a sense I
Am Julius Caesar's granddaughter. I
Remain loyal to him and now despise
His son, my father, Augustus Caesar,
Who has dispersed a king's power and restored
The Republic with himself as *Princeps*.
It's no longer "Rome first" as immigrants
From all nations crowd to our Capitol
And taint the purity of Roman blood.
Our Rome's become a whore to all comers.
On the day of my birth he divorced my
Mother Scribonia, and married Livia,
The bully who will not rest content till
Her son Tiberius is named Caesar.

Ovid.   You are outrageous. I admire free speech.

Julia.   Now you're unmarried for the second time
                 You're free to visit me at my 'At Homes'.

                 (*The* SLAVE-GIRL *returns.* OVID *bows and leaves.* PAULLUS FABIUS
                 MAXIMUS *approaches him with his wife* MARCIA *and a* YOUNG GIRL.)

Fabius.   Brilliant verses.

Marcia.   Another triumph.

Ovid.   Thanks.

Fabius.   You haven't met this beautiful young girl
                 Who lives in my household and helps my wife.

                 (OVID *bows. The* YOUNG GIRL *smiles dazzlingly and extends a hand.*)

                 Ovid wrote the song for our wedding. He
                 Will write a good song if you marry him.

486

(*There is laughter.*)

Young girl.	He knows too much about seducing girls.
	He's too familiar with Corinna's likes.
	I'm sure he has very many girlfriends.
	Marriage with him would be a massive risk.

(OVID *is clearly taken by the* YOUNG GIRL.)

Ovid.	Oh no, I just write erotic verses.
	My life's not like that. I'm a simple man.
	I write things on paper I would not do.
	We Roman poets are like new-born lambs.
	As a sheep in spring grazes while her lambs,
	Five frisky young, leap and run to her side
	And nuzzle under her for milk while she,
	Head down on grass, does not seem to notice
	And yet is fully aware where each is,
	So my Muse suckles me and four others
	And I –

Young girl.	You are a very frisky lamb!

(*All laugh.*)

But you have many girlfriends? Julia?

Ovid.	Julia has many boyfriends. I'm not one.
	As speckled hens crowd by a poultry fence
	To greet a farmer who might throw them grain
	And cock their heads and peer and blink and cluck
	And nuzzle to each other to stand out
	Like scrawny puritans with piercing eyes,
	So my fans gather and I pass them by.

(MESSALLA *approaches* OVID.)

Messalla.	Come this way, I invite you to begin
	Your reading of your remarkable work.
	(*Aloud.*) This way, my friends, into the audience room.

(Exeunt, OVID *clutching a scroll he has produced from under his tunic.)*

SCENE 2

(Augustus's house on the Palatine. The Room of the Masks. AUGUSTUS, *who has just turned 60, is with* LIVIA, *his Empress.)*

Livia.　　　　　Julia has just arrived. You must be strong
　　　　　　　And cover up your paternal feelings
　　　　　　　Like the masks that stare at us from the wall.
　　　　　　　For the good of the Principate you must
　　　　　　　Banish Scribonia's line, who would return
　　　　　　　Your Rome to the time of Julius Caesar.

Augustus.　　As lambs canter among a flock of sheep
　　　　　　　Grazing on a green hill, excitedly
　　　　　　　Exploring the green world they've come into,
　　　　　　　Yet each returns to its own mother's side,
　　　　　　　Each knows its mother in the grazing flock,
　　　　　　　So Roman children bond with their parents
　　　　　　　And expect help from them, not banishment.

Livia.　　　　　You must be strong. Act for the good of Rome.
　　　　　　　Consider the best interests of the State.

Augustus.　　I have brought peace to a divided world.
　　　　　　　Julius Caesar chose me to succeed him
　　　　　　　When he was felling a wood near Munda
　　　　　　　In Spain to make a camp. He spared a palm,
　　　　　　　Which put out a new shoot that outgrew it,
　　　　　　　And a flock of doves nested in the fronds
　　　　　　　Though doves dislike their spiky feel. My palm
　　　　　　　Of State has put out an aesthetic shoot
　　　　　　　In which the finest poets nest. Julius
　　　　　　　Caesar saw me as a portent of peace,
　　　　　　　Just as he did when at the age of twelve
　　　　　　　I gave the funeral oration beside
　　　　　　　His sister's, my grandmother Julia's, pyre.
　　　　　　　Long after, my only authority

Came from Caesar's will, which named me his heir.
His head and mine were on my earliest coins,
And I retained the association.
I, *divi filius*, son of a god,
Became *divus Augustus* but I kept
Julius Caesar on public buildings like
The Pantheon and Mars Ultor temple.
I wear his mantle on Prima Porta.
I am called Caesar by all, as he was.
And yet, and yet, I've charted my own course.
My way's different from Julius Caesar's.
He usurped power to end the Republic
And rule as king, dictator, dread monarch.
After the civil wars and Actium
I restored the Republic as *Princeps*
And gave Rome back the freedom she had lost.
The Julians would revive dictatorship
And civil wars would break the peace I brought.
The Claudians must continue my way,
Maintain the meaning I have restored to
The *Res Publica*, free from oppression.
I welcome all mankind to our city.
I keep the peace of the *Pax Augusta*.
My heir will preserve the Principate's peace.

Livia.   Caesar, you have stated with clarity
                        The context for today's special hearing
                        Which I will attend as we cannot trust
                        Our general secretariat not to leak.
                        This is a sensitive issue, we must
                        Accomplish our aim confidentially.
                        You must be strong and banish Julia.

                        (*Exit* LIVIA.)

Augustus   (*alone*). The succession has always troubled me.
                        The Principate is not an office that
                        Can automatically be handed on.
                        Like a proud gardener the *Princeps* must will
                        His lands to the child among his children
                        Who has the greenest fingers, most loves growth.

When I was near death twenty-one years back
And troubled by the succession – Julia
Unmarried, my stepsons Tiberius
And Drusus boys – I gave my signet ring
To Agrippa, victor of Actium.
When I recovered I appointed him
Proconsul over all the imperial
Provinces, sign that he would be the next
Emperor. That very same year I arranged
For Julia to marry Marcellus, my
Nephew, son of my sister Octavia.
And Julia was now therefore next in line.
Marcellus died, and Julia remarried
Agrippa on his return from the east.
Agrippa now became my co-regent,
And I adopted their two eldest sons
As Gaius and Lucius Caesar. But then
Agrippa died, and now my two stepsons,
Offspring of Livia's Claudian line
By Tiberius Claudius Nero,
Her first husband whom I made her divorce,
Tiberius and Drusus, led armies.
I made Tiberius renounce his wife,
Agrippa's daughter by his first marriage,
And become Julia's third husband. Drusus
Married my niece Antonia, daughter
Of Antony and Octavia – then died.
Tiberius was now heir-apparent,
But when I favoured Agrippa's two sons,
Julians Gaius and Lucius, he retired
To Rhodes in sullen protest, accusing
Julia of adulteries, leaving them
At the forefront of Roman public life.
I have favoured Julia, and I have made
Her five children by Agrippa my heirs.
Yet Livia wants Tiberius, her son,
A Claudian, to be my successor.
She urges me to banish Julia so
It's five Julians versus her Claudian,
And I must choose my beneficiary,
The one to whom I leave my lands, the one

Who can best cultivate our soil, and not
Alienate my wife or the Julians.
How burdensome to hold the supreme power!
(*Re-enter* LIVIA *holding a scroll, which she hands to* AUGUSTUS.)

Livia.   I've secured proofs of her adulteries.
You hold the evidence. It's all quite clear.

(AUGUSTUS *looks at the scroll.*)

Augustus.   It's hard to read, I am so myopic.
As a little black mouse skitters to squeeze
Under a door and vanish down a hole
Leaving a startled householder staring
At the floor and the blameless skirting-board,
So an Emperor is baffled when he tries
To catch a plotter that he knows is there.

(AUGUSTUS *looks at the scroll again and trembles with rage.*)

It fills me with fury that she can be
So inconsiderate of my feelings.
How could Caesar's daughter behave like this?
And with such people? I am ready to
Demand that she explains her vile conduct.

Livia.   Before that, I'd like you to hear Ibis.
Ibis reports that she's linked with Ovid.

Augustus.   Bring him in.

(*Enter* IBIS.)

Livia.   Tell Caesar what you told me.

Ibis.   Ovid's *Ars Amatoria*'s a treatise
On the art of seduction, tongue-in-cheek.
It undermines your programme of reforms.
It's subversive of the *Lex Julia*.
It encourages adultery, and mocks
The moral stance of Augustanism.

He's talking of a mock recantation.
Your daughter Julia attended the launch
At Messalla's house and told Ovid that
She admires his works, and quoted two lines.

Augustus.   That's all?

Ibis.   She invited him to her house.

(LIVIA *nods in the direction of the door. Exit* IBIS.)

Augustus.   This Ovid's a rebel who mocks our laws
And questions my world rule and the Empire.
He's an opponent, a dissident, yes,
But he's harmless and most of Rome likes him.
He's like a tiresome mosquito whose bite
Swells up and irritates an afternoon.

Livia.   You can regard him as an enemy
Of Rome and the *imperium*, of your plan
To make marriage the backbone of our State
And campaign against moral laxity.

Augustus.   He's Rome's leading love poet, I can't touch
Him without causing a public outcry.
But we're talking of an attempted *coup*
Led by my daughter with that snake Iullus.

Livia.   Julia flouts what you do and seems intent
On causing as much scandal as she can
To aggravate you. She can't be ignored.
She's been influenced by Ovid, she's been
Corrupted by his work.

Augustus.   But she rebelled
Before she had ever heard of Ovid.
We'll leave Ovid to one side – I have been
A patron to poets and permit Rome's
Best talents to express themselves freely.
Ovid once worked for us, and I expect
His undivided support in his works.

With heavy heart I know that I must now
Make an example of her, for Rome's good.
Bring Julia in for this cheerless duty.

(LIVIA *indicates. Enter* JULIA, *escorted by a* GUARD. *The guard retreats and stands at the door.*)

Julia.   Why is she here?

Livia.   Because it's sensitive.
What we're about to hear should be kept in
The family and not spread throughout Rome.

Augustus.   Your adultery with several lovers is
Well documented in reports to me,
Most recently with Iullus Antonius,
Son of my opponent Mark Antony,
Whom I defeated at Actium, and
Political intriguer. He will die.
How could you take up with Antony's son?

Julia.   You've been spying on your own daughter? Well!

Augustus.   Do you deny it?

Julia.   No. It's my business.

Augustus.   I have reports of four other lovers:
Quinctius Crispinus, Sempronius Gracchus,
Claudius Pulcher, Cornelius Scipio.
All my opponents – all will be banished.
You act the wanton, appear dissolute.
You know your behaviour causes us pain,
Anxiety and shame. Yet you persist.
You openly say you're provoking me,
Throw your affairs with my foes in my face.
Tiberius has washed his hands of you
And gone to Rhodes to escape the scandal,
Knowing that if, according to the law,
He denounced you as an adulteress
It would wound me, and he would not do that.

	Under my *Lex Julia*, under the law

Under my *Lex Julia*, under the law
The penalty for adultery is
Banishment to an island. Julia,
To save us further dishonour, you leave
With the guard who is standing by the door,
For the island of Pandateria,
Where your behaviour will not touch the court.
I banish you with a most heavy heart.

Julia.   You're banishing me. You, my own father!

Augustus.   The *Lex Julia* is the law, Julia.

Julia.   You made that law and you can unmake it.
So much for your paternal love! I'll go,
Glad to be far from you, no child of yours!

(JULIA *storms out but is apprehended at the door by the* GUARD. *Exit Julia with the guard.* AUGUSTUS *drops his head and wipes away a tear.*)

Augustus.   Why can't my family live by my rules?

Livia.   She has deserved her punishment, Caesar.
But you should now banish her accomplice,
Ovid, and silence him. Suppress his work.

Augustus.   I can't touch Ovid, there'd be street riots.

Livia.   Shall I despatch Iullus Antonius?
He's sitting outside.

Augustus.   Yes, despatch him now.

Livia.   Now it's visitors, then the Senate speech.

Augustus.   I refuse to see visitors or go
To the Senate. A *quaestor* can read this
To them. Julia is forbidden to drink
Wine or enjoy any luxury in
Her exile, and she is to be denied
All male company, freemen or servants.

494

I am in mourning, and will sit alone
While you do what must now be done with speed.

(Exit LIVIA.)
(*Alone.*) I've covered my true feelings with a mask.
I've denied my feelings and cannot see.

(AUGUSTUS *sits.* LIVIA *reappears outside the room with* TWO GUARDS.
They hold IULLUS, *whose hands are bound, and a sword. They makes*
Iullus kneel.)

Livia.   Bow your head to mighty Caesar, and give
Him the plot that's hidden within your skull.

(*One of the* GUARDs *strikes off* IULLUS's *head, which rolls.* AUGUSTUS
sits on. The OTHER GUARD *picks up the head. He gives it to* LIVIA, *who*
returns and shows it to Augustus, who nods. Enter a MESSENGER, *who*
hands over a message and then departs.)

Livia.   Phoebe, the freed woman Julia's talked to
Has hanged herself for shame. It's terrible.

Augustus.   I would that I'd been born Phoebe's father
Rather than the father of Julia.

Livia.   Government requires decisive action.
You have shown you can act. Rome will take note.
Your authority is enhanced, Caesar.

(*Exit* LIVIA, *still holding the head.*)

Augustus   (*alone*). As cherry blossom hangs over a pool,
Heady and white, and stuns with its beauty,
Then sheds its petals till it looks ragged
And an observer wonders at the joy
The same tree brought a month back, so Livia
Was once a perfect freshness I gasped at
And though she is now ragged and windblown
In my memory she is still stunning.
I recall how she was, while others see
Merely a time-weathered battling monster.

SCENE 3

(Ovid's house in Rome, near the Capitol. OVID is with MESSALLA.)

Ovid.   Relegated to Pandateria?

Messalla.   That's what I've heard. The Emperor's not pleased.
                       He holds your verses partly to blame. He
                       Is determined to reinstate the old
                       Morality. Now Julia's been banished,
                       It's serious your verses seem immoral.
                       You have written erotic elegies
                       Since you were sixteen. You should now recant
                       And undergo a transformation from
                       Love elegist to bard of ancient myths.
                       It is not wise to oppose or offend
                       Augustus at this most sensitive time.

Ovid.   I live for pleasure, also to amuse
                       The fashionable world of wives who peep
                       At others' husbands, who have roving eyes.
                       I've no time for religion or the gods,
                       Only to laugh. I am really shallow.
                       Rome's blinded me to all the deepest things.
                       I live from the rational, social ego,
                       For literary success, creature comforts.
                       I satirize, poke fun, play it for laughs.
                       I live where our secular people live
                       In surface sunlight, not the darker depths.
                       I am the norm. I am their consciousness,
                       A raconteur and wit with epithets.
                       I plead guilty to frivolity – though
                       My frivolity is just a mask – and
                       Levity, the Italian *levitas*,
                       In contrast to old Roman *gravitas*,
                       And to new mock-didactic parody,
                       But not to being seriously engaged
                       Or political towards Augustus.
                       I tell truths about human nature but
                       Do not oppose the *imperium* with deeds.

496

| Messalla. | For several months I've been uneasy at |
| | The collision course your work has taken. |

Messalla.   For several months I've been uneasy at
                   The collision course your work has taken.
                   Augustus is *Pontifex Maximus*.
                   He wants to revive the State religion,
                   Discourage luxury, self-indulgence,
                   Promote patriotism, plain living
                   And agriculture, the rustic virtues.
                   The great Virgil did that in his *Georgics*.
                   Great poets paint the countryside in verse
                   And show a garden on a Sabine farm
                   Like Horace's villa's, set in cool hills.
                   I have to co-exist with Augustus,
                   No patron can support subversive work.
                   You have to undergo transformation.
                   You must awaken from erotic dream,
                   Channel your senses into ancient myths,
                   Which are full of amorous encounters
                   But also patriotic, plain living
                   And the delights of pastoral countryside.
                   Augustus put scenes from Roman myths round
                   His great *Ara Pacis*, Altar of Peace.
                   Deepen your work into the human heart,
                   New ground that's safer than dissident art.

Ovid.   I don't like the civilised life of Rome,
                   Its pleasure-seeking, hedonistic smile
                   Which I have to flatter to get across
                   My poems – otherwise I'd be silent.
                   My mask is of frivolity and mirth
                   So I can draw an audience, who bore me.
                   I would gladly forego my audience
                   And live for real behind this mocking smirk.
                   A poet, like a singing bird – tit, finch –
                   Flies to a patron's bird-table and swings
                   On hung nuts, pecks, then peers through a window
                   To thank the helping hand that put them there.
                   Poets are best when countryside creatures.
                   As a green woodpecker squats on pasture
                   Near the galleries of a deep ants' nest
                   And catches prey with its long sticky tongue
                   Until, startled, it shyly flies off, so

A poet feeds on Imagination,
Which is as universal as turfed loam,
And extracts images like crawling things.
I'll heed your words and attempt to transform
As ploughed earth's transformed into a wheatfield.
I'll begin by proposing to a girl.
Just as a plain, unprepossessing herb –
Sage, hyssop, thyme, spiked rosemary, wormwood –
When pinched, leaves a fragrance on the fingers
That lingers and is revived with each sniff
Of the nostrils at forefinger and thumb,
So her fresh cheek, which I jokingly pinched,
And her pert charm's left traces on my mind
Which I revive when I recall the scene.
She'd be a good countryside influence.
I've had two wives; one was unworthy, one
Blameless. It's time I settled down again.

SCENE 4

(*Sulmo, Ovid's family villa 90 miles east of Rome. OVID is with the YOUNG GIRL from the Fabii.*)

Ovid.   My father dead, and now I inherit
            My patrimony, his equestrian rank,
            This house at Sulmo where my brother lived.
            He was a year older than me, Lucius,
            And studied oratory at Rome, and died
            When he was just twenty. I feel their ghosts.
            My father said Homer left no fortune.
            He meant there was no money in poetry.
            There was a time I'd love to have lived here
            In this valley under towering mountains,
            Among cool streams, vineyards, laden fruit trees.
            These fields where I spent my boyhood are like
            A vast garden, a wondrous Paradise
            Full of abundance where lush Nature gushed,
            A *cornucopia*, horn of plenty
            That poured out seeds and leaves and fruit as my

Can you feel the kiss in this summer breeze?
But now it's ninety miles from Rome and my
House near the Capitol. The journey is
Too far to do in comfort, and I've seen
A country villa at the junction of
Via Clodia and Via Flaminia.
It has an orchard, is available
And would suit my writing better than here.
If I exchange this house for that villa,
Would you, could you bring yourself to become
My wife and live with me in Rome and there?

(OVID *goes down on one knee.*)

Would you marry me, as Fabius proposed?

Young Girl. Oh, yes. I would be honoured – if Marcia
And Livia, the Empress, both approve.

Ovid. And be my wife no matter what life brings?
In sickness? In health? Riches? Poverty?

Young Girl. I will be true to you whatever should
Befall us – even if like Julia.....

(OVID *takes her in his arms and kisses her.*)

ACT TWO

SCENE 1

(*AD 4. Augustus's house on the Palatine.* AUGUSTUS.)

Augustus (*alone*). First Lucius killed on his way to Spain,
Now Gaius from a wound on his way back
From Armenia. Two of three grandsons dead,
And I suspect Livia intrigued this
To clear the way for her son. I loved her
But now fear her ambition and her will.

(*Enter* LIVIA.)

There's public criticism of how I
Banished Julia to Pandateria,
A harsh island. And so I will move her
To Rhegium, a less rigorous place.

Livia.　　　She does not deserve such an improvement.
But you must now adopt Tiberius
And nurture his great tribunician power,
Make him adopt his nephew Drusus and
Your last grandson Agrippa Postumus.
You must sever Agrippa legally
From the *gens Julia* by "abdication",
And banish him to Surrentum. Make it
Permanent, under military guard, his
Property forfeit to the Treasury.

Augustus　　(*sighing*). As always I do what the Empress bids.

Livia.　　　Thank you, wise Caesar. Your judgement is sound.

(*Exit* LIVIA.)

Augustus　　(*alone*). I'm ill, I am not well enough to oppose
Livia, who's too strong for a wreck like me.
I may have been considered handsome but
My body is covered with blemishes.
My seven birthmarks on my chest and stomach
Form a constellation like the Great Bear.
I have hard dry patches of skin that itch
Because I scraped them too hard at the baths.
It may be ringworm; they look like fungi.
I have a weakness in my left hip-bone
And almost limp. My forefingers go numb
When it is cold. I suffer bladder pains.
In spring my diaphragm tightens, and when
The sirocco blows I'm filled with catarrh.
It's a struggle to keep my body warm.
In winter I can wear four tunics and
A woollen gown above my undershirt

And a wool chest-protector, underpants
And woollen gaiters. I can't bear sunlight
Even in winter, and travel at night
By litter, with a broad-brimmed hat.
I don't bath often, prefer an oil rub.
My teeth are decayed, my left eye's part blind.
I can't see clearly, I've clouded vision,
But that doesn't matter – Romans believe
My eyes shine with a bright divine radiance.
I am a god, I'm worshipped as a god.
I'm shown as Apollo, god of order,
As befits a good administrator,
Whereas Antony aped Dionysus,
Eastern god of riot and drunkenness.
This god's falling apart, but worst of all
I have three boils on my sore soul. They are:
Julia; Julia; Agrippa Postumus.
And the worst of them all is young Julia.

SCENE 2

(*AD 7. Messalla's house. MESSALLA, OVID. Many of the same people who appeared in Act 1 Scene 1, only they are nine years older. JULIA, Augustus's granddaughter, is present along with IBIS.*)

Messalla.   Tonight we are honoured as Ovid will
                 Tell us about the work he's laboured on
                 For seven years in epic hexameters.

                 (*There is applause.*)

Ovid.   Thank you Messalla. My new work is called
                 Metamorphoses, or "transformations".
                 Parthenius, tutor to both Virgil and
                 Tiberius, has a work of that name.
                 Mine is very different. It collects myths
                 Found in Homer and the Greek dramatists
                 Into one volume, some two hundred and
                 Fifty tales woven in one tapestry

In fifteen different books of epic length,
All on one theme: Protean transformation.
It still awaits its final polish but
I will later read some finished excerpts.

(*There is applause. JULIA approaches. IBIS hovers nearby within earshot,
pretending he is looking elsewhere.*)

Julia.   What does it say about the *imperium*?

Ovid.   Nothing, Julia. It's a volume of myths.

Julia.   Oh come, it must suggest that there's a need
For transformation in my grandfather's
World rule? Don't you suggest that there should be
A transformation of Principate Rome
Back to the old Republican virtues?

Ovid.   You're inviting me into dangerous
Territory, and I'd rather not comment.
I secretly admire your grandfather.
I saw your mother banished, and I don't
Want a second Julia to go her way.

Julia.   That's the official line. Now tell the truth
As artists, you say, are supposed to do.
You can trust me, I loathe my grandfather –
For banishing my mother, for his rule.
My mother, Julius Caesar and I,
His great-granddaughter, look back to a time
When Rome was noble under his wise rule.
I believe in Julian dictatorship.
In *Metamorphoses* you show Caesar
As the god he became after his death,
As the fiery-tailed comet all gazed at;
And Augustus as the son of the god.
Five years ago you paid a tribute to
My poor brother Gaius, and I am pleased
That you have spoken for the Julian line.

(IBIS *is listening.*)

Ovid.	It's Rome that counts, not the *imperium*. Our culture's Roman, not *oikumene*.
Julia.	You're anti-militaristic like me. I feel it when I read your peaceful verse. Somewhere you say military vanquishing's Just a metaphor for sexual conquest.

(OVID *is silent.*)

I want to know your attitude. And if
You won't tell me now, tell me tomorrow.
Please would you sign my copy of your *Art*?
I'm free tomorrow afternoon at three,
Come to my house in a vanquishing mood.
I'll be alone and waiting for you. Then
When we've got to know each other better
You will trust me and answer my question.
Have you met Lucius Aemilius Paullus?

(*She beckons* PAULLUS, *who approaches and bows.* OVID *bows.*)

My husband, who supports the Julian
Rather than the Claudian succession.
He is my grandfather's chief opponent.

Paullus.	The flawed Republic ended when Julius Caesar's dictatorship began. He stood For a noble Rome-first ideal of Rome, Not the commercial world rule of his son.
Ovid.	I want that ideal back and I believe Caesar does too, and that he now deplores The brash, coarse Rome of the *imperium*.

(IBIS *has been listening.* OVID *realises and turns away.*)

(*Aside.*) I wear a comic mask like a player,
As a strategy to survive this time,
And appear naive to the foolish throng,
Gullible, innocent, easily duped.

In fact, I'm shrewd behind my buffoon's mask,
And ambitious for my own preferment.
If I visit the Julians tomorrow
And they succeed Augustus when he dies,
I will have advanced my fortune. If I
Don't go I'll lose an opportunity.
I have a quarrel within myself that
Enhances my art but hinders my life.
It's a risk but I have to take it for
Playing safe does not make for getting on.
I won't tell my wife. Julia's colourful
Reputation makes all wives defensive.
A fool knows best when folly makes him wise.

SCENE 3

(*The next day. Julia's house.* A SLAVE-GIRL *admits* OVID.)

Slave-girl.   My mistress is expecting you. In here.

         (OVID *follows the slave-girl. He stops.* JULIA *stands naked before him. She turns to show her body to him. Ovid is speechless.*)

Julia.   Ovid, welcome. My robe, please. I've just bathed.

         (OVID *walks round behind her and places the robe round her shoulders* JULIA *puts on her robe.*)

Ovid.   You are outrageous.

Julia.   We will talk in here.

         (OVID *follows her and is shocked to see* LUCIUS AEMILIUS PAULLUS *amid a group of conspirators.* IBIS *is among them. Ovid stands and watches, stunned.*)

Julia.   Dear friends, the celebrated Ovid's here.
He's come out of sympathy with our cause.
We are all very honoured. My mother

Would be so pleased that he can share our news.
A most reliable Palatine source
Informs us of a grave development.
My grandfather's chosen Tiberius
To succeed him as Roman Emperor,
And wants to banish my brother and me
To remote islands, worse than far-off towns,
So the succession's from Livia's line
And not Scribonia's or Agrippa's.
The imperial secret is out. We must
Prevent our banishment by striking first,
Release my mother, involve the army,
Overthrow Augustus, restore ourselves,
Prevent Tiberius from inheriting.
Who will depose my ailing grandfather
And install Julius Caesar's pristine line?
Who will release Julia from Rhegium,
Agrippa Postumus from Surrentum?
My mother championed the Julian line
As I do now, and all you who are here
Have said you'll help the Julians succeed
So the next Caesar is a Julian
Who looks back to Julius Caesar's Rome,
And not a Claudian of world empire
As is my grandfather, who has allowed
Livia to bully him into her view.
We will discuss our strategy for power.
But first we will mix blood as a proof that
We are in one group with a common aim.
Stand in a circle, each put out a hand
Over this bust of divine Augustus
And as the blood flows clasp right hands and place
Them on the head of my dumb grandfather.

(*The conspirators pierce their fingers with a knife* PAULLUS *has been
holding, pass it round, and stand in a circle.* IBIS *holds back.*)

Will you join us, Ovid? You encouraged
My mother, will you now encourage me?

(OVID *turns in confusion to leave. One of the conspirators,* CLEMENS, *intercepts him.*)

Clemens.   I am Agrippa's slave, Clemens. Don't you
              Think I look like my old master? Join us.
              The Julian faction still has wide support.

Ovid.   Imperial skullduggery's not for me.

Julia.   No, wait. I promised you could vanquish me.
              That's no problem, all here have been with me.
              Paullus does not mind, Paullus never minds.
              We'll trust each other better in the bath
              And exchange political attitudes.

              (OVID *is confused. He turns and leaves without a word.*)

SCENE 4

(*Augustus's house. The Room of the Masks.* AUGUSTUS *is alone.*)

Augustus.   Yet again the succession torments me.
              I am beset by wars and uprisings
              In Illyria and Pannonia;
              Taxation, famine and rebellions that
              Give cover for protests at Julia's
              Banishment and the lot of Agrippa.
              I must counter this bad publicity.
              After the banishment of Julia
              I made her two oldest brothers consul,
              First Gaius, then Lucius. Both have died,
              First Lucius, then two years later, Gaius,
              And I now wonder if they were murdered
              On Livia's instructions as she seeks
              To bring Tiberius back to public life.
              If I now banish their sister Julia,
              Who I married to Lucius Paullus,
              Only Agrippa Postumus will stand
              Between Tiberius and my Empire –
              And Agrippina, his younger sister.

If I banish him from Surrentum to
The harsh, bleak island of Planasia
As Livia wishes, then Tiberius
The Claudian will be my heir. Drusus'
Son (as I publicly call him, my own
Son by Livia, I think, before she was
Divorced by Tiberius Claudius Nero),
My Nero Claudius Drusus, has not come
Of age. He must marry Agrippina.
Worries! Thirty years of hesitation
Between Scribonia's and Livia's children,
My own blood and the blood of my own wife;
And now I stand at a crossroads. To choose
The Julians – not banish Julia or move
Agrippa Postumus; or Claudians –
Banish the pair and have Tiberius
As my sole heir. That's the choice I must make.
The Scribonians or the Livians – which?
I only married Scribonia because
She was related to my enemy
Sextus Pompeius, Pompey the Great's son.
We were completely incompatible.
I'm blown this way and that like shifting sand.
I sit among masks in this secret gloom.

(*Enter* LIVIA.)

Livia.	Ibis is waiting. Ready?
Augustus.	One moment.
Livia.	You need to tuck your tunic in, Caesar.
Augustus.	You treat me as if I'm a little boy.
Livia.	You couldn't be Caesar without my help.
Augustus	(*aside*). Livia's formidable, but she makes Things work when she's around, she helps me rule. Tiberius is of the Claudian house By birth, of the Julian by adoption.

He is the compromise that can please all.
But if I choose Tiberius I must
Have good reason to banish Julia.
I banished her mother on a pretext –
For sexual, not political reasons,
When her true crime was sedition. And now
I can banish *her* on the same pretext.
Ovid may play a part in my charade.
(*Aloud.*) We'll hear from Ibis about Julia's plot.

(LIVIA *turns and beckons.* A GUARD *appears and stands near the door.*)

Livia.   Ibis has named Julia's conspirators.

(AUGUSTUS *nods.* LIVIA *turns and beckons.* THE GUARD *turns and waves. Enter* IBIS.)

Who is in this foul plot against Caesar?

Ibis.   Lucius Aemilius Paullus, Julia's
Husband, leads it with Iunius Silanus,
Her open lover, Plautius Rufus,
Audasius, Epicadus, Telephus.
All plan to abduct your daughter Julia
And grandson Agrippa, fight your legions
And attack first the Senate and then you.
They want to kill you so the Emperor
Can be a Julian, not a Claudian.

Livia.   O foul, foul deed. You've seen the evidence,
Caesar, and have heard Ibis. Is that all?
Or do you wish to hear about Ovid?

(AUGUSTUS *nods.*)

Was Ovid among the conspirators?

Ibis.   He was. He arrived late and left early.

Livia.   And Ovid was at Messalla's salon?

(IBIS *nods.*)

What did you hear at Messalla's salon?

Ibis.   Caesar, his new book is about old myths,
And at the end he sees Julius Caesar's
Divinity as another old myth.
He's disrespectful and satirical
Towards the State religion you espouse,
Seeing it as a concoction of myths.
Your temples do not celebrate mere myths.
He is subversive and should offend you.

Livia.   He was not seeking to flatter Caesar?

Ibis.   No, great one. He pokes fun at all the gods,
Shows Jupiter as randy and debauched.
He is as irreverent about Caesar.
The end of *Metamorphoses* praises
Julius Caesar. It's a coded message
That the Julian line should have a *coup*.

Livia.   Did Julia say anything to him?

Ibis.   Caesar, I heard your granddaughter invite
Ovid to her house.

Livia.   For what? You must say.

Ibis.   She offered her favours and asked to know
If his new work supports the *imperium*.

Augustus.   What did he say?

Ibis.   He refused to comment.
But he did say he did not want Julia
To be banished like her mother, Caesar.
He saw me and would not say any more.

Livia.   And then this afternoon, at Julia's house?

Ibis.	I've found out as you requested, Empress. Julia asked the plotters to shed their blood And clasp hands. Ovid came.
Livia.	Did he join in?
Ibis.	My information is that he listened.
Augustus.	You're clear he was against the *imperium*?
Ibis.	Yes, Caesar. He was there, he must have been.
Augustus.	You've served us well. You have drawn attention To Ovid's more unacceptable verse, You've reported him and sued him for his Patrimony. Now you have denounced him. But I can't give you an informer's cut Of his property, as is normal when There's a charge of *maiestas minuta*. There's no informer's cut in Ovid's case.

(AUGUSTUS *nods.* IBIS *is escorted to the door by* LIVIA, *who gives him a purse. At the door Ibis confers with Livia and hands her a scroll; he points at a passage with his finger. Livia returns with the scroll.*)

Livia.	These are some lines from Ovid's latest work. Look as this *risqué* passage, which maintains That Rome is behind a dictatorship That will ruin rather than heal the world. He *is* implicated in Julia's plot.
Augustus.	I have to squint to read the simplest words. My own granddaughter.

(*He shakes his head.*)

	First my daughter, then Her daughter, my granddaughter. Two Julias. The direct Julian line, wanting me dead.
Livia.	They would certainly have tried to kill you.

Augustus.	What do you think I should do?

Livia.	Execute

The ringleaders, banish each accomplice.

Augustus.　　I married Julia to Lucius Paullus.
Just as rabbits play on a lawn at night
And bound into a walled garden and gnaw
The heads off cowslips, leaving severed stalks,
And sit and scamper, devour what they can
Till morning shows a bed of headless flowers,
So opponents of the *imperium*
Nibble the flowers of State and leave it worse.
They must be trapped and killed and like rabbits
Be thrown to magpies or scavenging crows.
Bring me a death warrant and then summon
Two Praetorian executioners.
Her husband and her lover must both die.
Despatch Paullus and Iunius Silanus.
No, Paullus must die, exile Silanus.
Silanus is deprived of my friendship.

(*Exit* LIVIA.)

(*Alone.*) I recall how at Actium I won
Victory over Antony and his bride,
Duplicitous Cleopatra, and then
Imposed the *Pax Augusta* that ended
Twenty years of civil war as Pompey,
Julius Caesar, Brutus and Antony
Vied for the sole rule which is now my own,
And how after hours of profoundest thought
I devised the Principate and restored
The old spirit of Rome that Caesar knew.
I am Rome, and cannot be blown aside
By a new breeze of moral laxity.
I need to stiffen Rome's resolve so that
Roman Italy wins her destiny
And this seven-hilled town by the brown Tiber
Is capital of the entire known world.
I am the Ruler of all provinces

In the vast, sprawling Empire of the World.
I must strike as hard as at Actium.

SCENE 5

(*The Praetorian barracks. Two executioners escort* LUCIUS AEMILIUS PAULLUS *and* D. IUNIUS SILANUS.)

Executioner 1.   Paullus, conspirator, it's payment time.
Kneel, pray to Jupiter for forgiveness.
Kneel and pray to the divine Augustus.
Have you any last words for Caesar's ears?

(PAULLUS *kneels*.)

Paullus.   I take full responsibility for
The plot to bring the Julians to power.
It was my idea. Julia knew nothing,
Nor did Silanus who shared her with me,
Nor did Ovid, who blundered in on us.
I stuck my neck out. It is stuck out now.

(*As* EXECUTIONER 2 *prods him in the back with his sword,*
EXECUTIONER *1 strikes off his head with his sword. The head rolls across the stage.*)

Executioner 2.   The husband's dead, now it's the lover's turn.
Will you say Paullus also knew nothing?

Silanus.   No, please, spare me. I'll give you my villa.

Executioner 1.   You're not as brave as the man you displaced.
Let's see some courage as we despatch you
Silanus.   No, no, please, I beg you, I'm not ready.
I need to go to the toilet. Please, please.

Executioner 1.   Don't wet your tunic as we despatch you.

(EXECUTIONER 1 *forces* SILANUS *to his knees.* EXECUTIONER 2 *now* has the sword. He prods Silanus in his back. Silanus cowers, looking apprehensively at PAULLUS's head.)

Executioner 2.   He isn't ready. Isn't that a shame.

(SILANUS *bursts into tears, pleading for his life.*)

Executioner 1.   He's not worth executing, this coward.

Executioner 2.   Take your snivellings off into exile.
Caesar has deprived you of his friendship.

(SILANUS *collapses in tears, then jumps up and runs off. Exeunt the* TWO EXECUTIONERS, *picking up Paullus's head and dragging his body.*)

SCENE 6

(*Augustus's house. The Room of the Masks.* AUGUSTUS *sits.* LIVIA *stands near* JULIA *who is under guard. An* OFFICIAL *is present.*)

Julia.   What has happened to Paullus?

Livia.   Beheaded.

(JULIA *collapses into tears.*)

But first he took the full blame on himself.

(JULIA *stops crying and stares at* AUGUSTUS.)

Caesar has decided your punishment.

Augustus.   I overlook your role in Paullus' plot.
You have committed adultery with
D. Iunius Silanus, and others.
You've taken after your wanton mother
And must share her fate. In accordance with
The *Lex Julia*, Julia, I banish you
To the barren island of Trimerus.

I have no daughter and no granddaughter.
The safety of the *imperium* is all.

(JULIA *is led away weeping.* THE OFFICIAL *remains.*)

Livia.   Caesar will now rule on Agrippa's fate.

Augustus.   By Senatorial decree Agrippa
                         Is moved from Surrentum to an island,
                         Planasia, near Elba, where he will
                         Live out his life in solitary exile.

(*Exit* THE OFFICIAL .)

Livia.   You have done well, Caesar. But there's one more
                         Decision you must take. Look at that wood.
                         As death-watch beetles enter wood and gnaw
                         For eighteen years and then emerge to die,
                         But perhaps fly into another beam,
                         And in due course riddle a roof which falls,
                         Some poets eat into the State's timbers
                         And threaten the protective roof of State.
                         They are noxious insects and must be sprayed.
                         They must be extracted. I will leave you
                         So you can think about what you must do.

(*Exit* LIVIA.)

Augustus   (*alone*). As a great-spotted woodpecker taps trees,
                         Drumming on decayed wood with rapid beak,
                         Pecking the crevices to extract grubs,
                         And dominates an early spring morning,
                         So an Emperor picks out harmful plotters
                         And rids the State of insects that make rot.
                         There's public sympathy for Julia
                         And her brother, scorn for the *imperium*.
                         I will stab all opposition. I need
                         A pretext for preferring Tiberius
                         To Julia. I banished her mother for
                         Political reasons, but gave the cause
                         As sexual. I must do the same again.

I need a public figure to take blame
For the banishment of young Julia.
A scapegoat whose banishment will silence
The public clamour and associate
Julia with erotic misdemeanours
And mute gossip about the succession.
Someone known for erotic love who will
Scamper like a chased fox away from Rome
And draw the baying public from the truth.
A known opponent of the *imperium*
Whose links with Julia will seem scandalous
And divert attention from Tiberius.
A dissident who's scandal-prone and *louche*,
Who opposes world government and who
Will leave the *imperium* healthier for
His ostracism and his banishment.
I bear him no ill will but need: Ovid!

(*Re-enter* LIVIA.)

Livia.   Caesar, you know what's next. I read your thoughts.

Augustus   (*aloud*). Now bring me Ovid, the *imperium*'s foe.

SCENE 7

(*AD 8. Cotta's villa on Elba.* COTTA *is busy.* OVID *is sunbathing.*)

Cotta.   I'm glad you've come. When I first heard from my
Father I could not believe you could have
Been so stupid as to offend Caesar.
How could you? I thought. Then I realised
You were set up and that we must limit
The damage. What has happened has happened.
Augustus can and must be placated.

Ovid.   I still don't know how I offended him.
Last time we spoke I got on well with him.
I sensed he likes me though he is the State.

No one's confronted me, it's just rumour.

Cotta.   If you don't know why he's taken umbrage,
           I certainly won't know. Be on your guard.

           (*There is a silence.*)

           This is a smoky island. The iron-mines
           Bring me some profit but there is a haze
           In the direction of Planasia
           Where poor Agrippa Postumus sits out
           His banishment there last year. Elba is
           The nearest point to it for news of him,
           Or a rescue attempt, if one were tried.

Ovid.   I love the blueness of the sparkling sea.
           How peaceful Elba seems in this March sun!
           I love the sunlight, it makes me see things.
           I am putting the finishing touches
           To *Metamorphoses*, 'transformations'.
           Your father said I had to undergo
           A transformation in my work to be
           Safe from Augustus. My work's been transformed,
           And looking at that calm, blue sea, I feel
           I may be transformed in myself, somehow,
           From the words of this social-villa world
           To the serenity of blue waters –
           As if my 'I' left this cliff-top villa –
           Its rational ego and its petty life –
           And blended with a self as wide and deep,
           A consciousness as boundless as that sea.

           (TWO ROMAN SOLDIERS *beat on the gate.*)

Cotta.   Yes? I am Cotta, son of Messalla.

Soldier 1. We have to take Ovid to the Emperor.

Cotta.   Ovid is here. How quickly must he leave?

Soldier 1. Immediately. The charge is high treason.

516

(OVID *has risen from his sun couch. He flinches.*)

Cotta. High treason? Why? What has he done?

Soldier 2 (*shrugging*).   Let's go.

Ovid. I'll gather my belongings. One minute.

Soldier 2. Be quick. Caesar is waiting to see you.

(COTTA *whispers to* OVID.)

Cotta. What have you done?

Ovid.   I don't know.

Cotta.   I'll find out.

(COTTA *goes to the* SOLDIERS *and produces a purse. He picks up a jug and pours them goblets of wine.*)

What's happened?

Soldier 1.   Plot against Caesar. Paullus
Has been beheaded, Julia banished.

Cotta. And Ovid?

Soldier 1.   Dunno. I'm bringing him in.

(COTTA *returns to* OVID, *who has gathered his possessions.*)

Cotta (*whispering*). What have you done?

Ovid.   Nothing. I don't know.
I....

Cotta.   What?

Ovid.   I came into some knowledge by chance.
It could be that. I won't say any more.

Cotta.	This could be serious. This could lead you on
	A path that will destroy all you have done.
	I'll get a message to father. He's not
	In the best of health, but he'll do his best.

SCENE 8

(*Augustus's house on the Palatine, Rome.* AUGUSTUS *presides over a private court in the* Room of the Masks.)

Augustus.	I sit among masks. My face is a mask.
	I must be inscrutable in this gloom.
	I can't see well. I peer myopically.
	It's as if I wore an ill-fitting mask
	And can't quite see through the slits of its eyes.
	(*Enter* LIVIA.)
Livia.	Caesar, Ovid is here, sitting outside.
	(AUGUSTUS *speaks regretfully*.)
Augustus.	We must deal with Ovid, who's not blameless
	This time. I turn a blind eye once. Not twice.
	Bring the prisoner in.
	(OVID *is brought in by a* GUARD.)
	(*Affectionately*.) Ovid, the last time
	We met we talked about the elegy.
Ovid.	And Literature's role in the Roman State.
	I still think fawning poets are like geese.
	As a gaggle of geese set up a cry,
	Like hungry seagulls' cawing, and then honk
	When they hear a farmer's footsteps pass near
	And then fall silent at the false alarm,
	So poets flatter an Emperor's triumphs.

Augustus	(*nodding*). Today is different. Please come nearer. I Can't see you clearly.
Livia	(*sharply*). Stand there, right hand raised. You were present at the Julian plot.
Ovid.	The one last year? The one whose outcome's left Paullus dead and young Julia banished?
Augustus.	Information has come to me, that you Were present when Julia, my granddaughter, Spoke to the plotters about killing me, And that you did not report this to me.
Ovid.	Caesar, I admit that I was present. But by accident, not by design. I Was invited by young Julia to sign A book. I blundered in at the wrong time. And nothing was said about *killing* you.
Augustus.	You knew my granddaughter Julia wanted To overthrow me for the Julian line. You "blundered" in on the conspirators But took no part. You blundered out again. I know. My spies have informed me. I know Julia invited you to talk with her. But you did not report what you stumbled On by accident. That was a mistake. Now some of those you blundered in on have Attempted to free both Julia and Agrippa Postumus from their islands. Enough is enough, I must sort you out.
Ovid.	I can't deny it. I will tell the truth. I admit it, I stumbled in on them By accident, as she'd invited me For what I thought would be…a private talk. I did not know the plotters would be there. I took no part in their Julian plot, And nothing was said about *killing* you.

Augustus.	Why did you not reveal this plot at once That you stumbled in on by accident?
	(OVID *glances round the room*.)
Ovid.	I will tell you the truth. I'll speak plainly. I greatly respect the stability That you have brought to Italy and Rome. The plotters worked for a new order that Could improve the world after your demise. I sympathized with their long-term goals, for I was born a year after Caesar died, I grew up in the Republic when Rome Was a metropolis for our nation, With Latin Italy's supreme language, Not a cosmopolitan melting-pot With a *lingua franca* of many tongues, A corrupt, impure, polyglot Babel. The mixing of peoples has weakened Rome's Beliefs and secularized Rome's culture. What was Roman's now multi-cultural – Diluted, contaminated, confused. You cannot be imperial and retain Rome's belief in traditional values, Rome's belief in itself, and so the seeds Of self-doubt, decline, disintegration And conquest by barbarians have been sown. I warn you that your Empire won't survive The *oikumene*. Inevitably Barbarians will enter the Roman home And destroy what greatness your conquests built. It is the law of imperial grandeur – That an *imperium* gets infected And can't resist those tribes it once suppressed. Your Empire is like a child's tower of bricks: One swipe from tiny fingers, down it comes – Or else it crashes when the balance goes. Rome will fall. I foretell the fall of Rome. My allegiance now's to you, Caesar. But My future support's for the Julians, Not for a militarist succession that

Would use conquest to build a World Empire.
I question a new world order which is
Enforced by Roman legions carrying
Statues of Roman gods, which they impose
On all parts of the imperial Empire.
I believe all parts of the Empire have
Their own cultures, which they should all retain.
I am opposed to massacres of tribes
And any calculated genocide
In the cause of brutal Roman conquest,
Torching towns in the Danube hinterland.
The *imperium* is a killing machine.
I write for all mankind, affirm the right
Of all to live at peace in their own way
In villages outside the *imperium*.
I am a writer, I work in Latin,
My attitudes are shaped by Literature.
I do not want the Roman culture mixed
With barbarian cultures in a world State.
I stumbled in on them and kept it quiet.
This is about my literary posture.

(*There is a stunned silence in the room.* OVID *has spoken too honestly for his own good.* AUGUSTUS *speaks very quietly, but he is shaking with rage.*)

Augustus.

This involves much more than mere Literature.
You have questioned the public policy
Of pacification of all regions.
I've been a peace-maker, a peace-bringer.
I've presided over the expansion
Of our Empire. I, who rode with Caesar
At his African triumph and served him
In Spain, in civil war conquered the West
(Italy, Sicily) and then the East,
Won Egypt from Antony and became
Master of the Roman World – to bring peace.
I defeated the hostile Alpine tribes,
Took Galatea in Asia Minor and
Mauretania in Africa, and then
Pacified Gaul and Spain and erected
My *Ara Pacis* to glorify peace.

I took Noricum so the frontier moved
From Italy to the upper Danube,
Then pacified Pannonia and crossed
The Rhine to invade Germany as far
As the Elbe, and took Bohemia, and
Judaea. Now much of Europe, Asia
And Africa are under my peaceful
Rule. Our legions imposed this peace. I've used
Troops to subjugate for the greater good
So there could be peace throughout the Empire.
I have continued Julius Caesar's Peace.

Ovid   (*quietly*). A lot of killing's gone into your Peace.
                        Pacification's something to be feared.

Livia.   How dare you speak so bluntly to Caesar!

Ovid.   There's a language of peace and one of war,
                        And poets use language to tell the truth
                        And speak of peace as peace and war as war
                        And not of war as peace and peace as war.
                        Literature cares about human beings.

                        (AUGUSTUS *is now cold and distant*.)

Augustus.   In Literature I look carefully for
                        Precepts and sound examples that will be
                        Salutary for the public. Literature
                        Should be didactic, "*prodesse*" (Horace) –

Ovid.   That's a utilitarian view of art.
                        Orpheus charmed birds from the trees with his lyre
                        Which also made flowers toss their heads and dance
                        As if in a sea-breeze. His verse revived
                        The parched gardens of Greece which weren't unlike
                        The arid Palatine and this garden.
                        Poets bedew the dessicated State –

Augustus.   You mock the old didactic view of life,
                        Lofty, high-minded Horace of wise saws.
                        You give us precepts of adultery,

	Examples of seduction. Your work is Worthless and insults the *imperium*.
Ovid.	I saw Virgil, heard Horace read his *Odes*. I have a new way of writing which you Do not appreciate or understand.
Livia.	This is outrageous and intolerable.
Augustus.	I understand more new writing than most. I have presided over the greatest Period in Latin literary history. After the Golden prose of Cicero I encouraged patrons (Maecenas and Messalla Corvinus) and polished verse On patriotic themes, love and Nature. In one decade I was presented with The greatest Roman works: Virgil's *Georgics* And *Aeneid*, Horace's *Odes* and his *Epistles*, Sextus Propertius's and Tibullus' elegies, Livy's history And Pollio's chronicle of events. I can't think you are in their league, surely? Is Ovid really in this Golden Age?
Ovid.	It's said I'm the last Golden Age poet.
Augustus.	I can't understand why, you're ordinary.
Ovid.	A poet of the ordinary life, As recognized by all your citizens. What it comes down to is, I learned by chance That you have chosen Tiberius as heir. You did not want the Julians to know this, And say I should have denounced them to you.
Livia.	He's both arrogant and impertinent. Enough of this defiance. Sentence him. He wants to live outside the *imperium*. Grant his wish. The place for him is Tomis.

(AUGUSTUS speaks with a quiet, cold fury.)

Augustus.   The charge against you is high treason, that
            You conspired with others against the State
            And opposed the world-wide *imperium*.
            I have examined all the evidence.
            We have witnesses who have denounced you.
            By your own admission you are guilty.
            You were implicated in my daughter
            Julia's intrigue which led to banishment.
            I spared you then. Now you're implicated
            In my granddaughter Julia's intrigue by
            Seeing treason and not reporting it.
            I will now proceed to my judgement. I
            Sentence you by imperial decree
            To banishment from Rome for ever. You
            Will be taken under guard to Tomis
            On the Pontus, beyond the *imperium*
            And you will live with the local people
            Outside the Roman Empire till you die.
            This is a *relegatio*, so your lands
            Are not confiscated. Your wife can stay.

(OVID *is deeply shocked.*)

Ovid.   Tomis. They don't speak Latin there, do they?

Augustus.   Greek and barbarian tongues, which you deplore
            But which will only be Latinised when
            Moesia's "pacified" by Roman legions.
            My *imperium*, world government, can bring
            Great boons to all mankind – peace, freedom from
            War, famine, plagues, disease and starvation.
            The *Pax Romana* is its greatest gift.
            Barbarians raid across the *limes*
            And have to be repelled to guard the whole.
            Local wars preserve the *Pax Romana*.
            They're a necessary evil, a means
            That is justified by the precious end.
            The writers of the Golden Age grasped this.
            They all understood Rome's world destiny.

You have opposed the *imperium* now;
See if you like life among barbarians.
You must depart by early December.
A guard will sail with you to dark Tomis.
Your *Ars Amatoria* will be banned
From Rome's three famous public libraries.
It has not been condemned by a decree
From the Senate, and so it can't be burned.

Ovid.   And my other writings?

Augustus.   They'll also be
Withdrawn from the libraries and you will
Have no audience in Tomis, your escorts
Will ensure that your writing's at an end.
Death by silence – we'll wall you in with quiet,
Cut off your audience so you are not heard.
That's our response to all who challenge us
And oppose our *Lex Julia*, and publish
Works that mislead the young, like my daughter.

Ovid.   This is a drastic form of censorship.

Augustus.   It defends moral reforms I'm proud of
And purges Rome of dubious verses.
Like Socrates you've corrupted the young.

(OVID, *still shocked, musters himself for a defiant exit.*)

Ovid.   What I've written will be circulated
In all times. My works will outlast my life
And will be read when your *imperium*'s gone.

Livia.   Take this insolent man back to his house.
Guard him while he packs for life-long exile.

ACT THREE

SCENE 1

(*Ovid's house.* OVID *and his* WIFE.)

Ovid's wife.   Banished. For ever. Because you went round
To Julia's last year and saw something bad
You did not report. It doesn't make sense.
Why did you go to Julia's when all knew
Her affairs were notorious round Rome?
And why did Caesar not act at the time?
Why's he waited a year? What did you see?

Ovid   (*tormented*). I mustn't say, I don't want you involved.

Ovid's wife.   I think Caesar's found out that Julia
And you had an affair –

Ovid.   No –

Ovid's wife.   I think you
Were the cause of Julia's banishment.

Ovid.   It wasn't like that, I swear. She wanted
Me to sign her copy of my poems.
I went to do that and blundered in on....

Ovid's wife.   What? What did you see?

Ovid.   I must not say more.

Ovid's wife.   Were there people there?

(OVID *says nothing.*)

                         Caesar is angry.
Oh, no. You disturbed a conspiracy
Against Caesar.

(OVID says nothing.)

And you're implicated
Because you did not alert Caesar.

Ovid.   He
                        Dislikes my *Art*. My error angered him
                        But I must not say more. I won't name names.

Ovid's wife   (*quietly*). I'll ask Fabius to visit Livia.

Ovid.   No, no. I don't want him implicated.

Ovid's wife.   He'll intercede and plead on your behalf.
                        You're too shrewd not to have seen the danger,
                        Which I, *I*, can see. You're not naive. How
                        Could you put yourself in that position?

Ovid   (*wretchedly*). I know how it must seem. I saw the risk
                        But hoped to turn it to our family's good.
                        It's wiser to avoid great men, who care
                        Nothing for us, just for their self-interest.

Ovid's wife.   How could you let yourself become Caesar's
                        Opponent, and subject to Caesar's wrath?

Ovid.   Just as a white swan builds a nest of reeds
                        And sits on it and flaps its wings, neck out,
                        And glowers at anyone who wanders near,
                        Then chases them with savage pecking nips,
                        So mighty Caesar pursues all who see
                        The eggless secret of his shallow home.

Ovid's wife.   What will become of us?

Ovid.   You can stay here.
                        Relegatio allows the wife to keep
                        The husband's property.

Ovid's wife.   That's small comfort.

SCENE 2

(Livia's house on the Palatine. Enter FABIUS, *shown in by a* SLAVE. LIVIA *nods.)*

Fabius.   Empress, I come as his wife's friend, to plead
On behalf of Ovid who's been banished –

Livia.   Caesar is adamant, Ovid must leave
For Tomis. There can be no compromise.

Fabius.   I realise he has done wrong, that he should
Have reported what he saw to Caesar –

Livia.   He should and did not, and has brought his fate
Upon himself. His wife can live in Rome,
His property's intact, Caesar has been
Lenient. His sentence could have been to die.

Fabius.   I realise Caesar's been very lenient.
Clearly Ovid must pay, but please review
The life-long banishment. Perhaps five years
And his punishment will be at an end?

Livia.   There can be no promises in this case.
He has committed a most grave offence
And offended Caesar, betrayed his trust.
His latest poem says Julius Caesar's
Divinity's a myth, equivalent
To the myth of Actaeon or Venus –

Fabius.   I'm sure Ovid did not intend to slight –

Livia.   I can't intercede with Caesar, nor beg
His sentence be reduced, not at this time.
Give my best wishes to your wife, Fabius.
It's turned a little colder, don't you think?
I can almost feel winter in the air.

(FABIUS *bows. Exit.*)

SCENE 3

(*Ovid's house*. OVID, MESSALLA *and* FRIENDS.)

Ovid.   Augustus is a hypocrite. He has
Done far worse things than I against his *Lex
Julia*. He divorced his first wife so he
Could marry Livia. He even forced
Livia's husband to hand her over
Although she was six months pregnant, and sent
The baby to its father. He seduced
Maecenas' wife Terentia, who then
Became his mistress. He took a consul's
Wife from a dinner-table, where she sat
Next to her husband, into a bedroom
And brought her back with dishevelled hair and
Red ears. He's written far less decent verse
Than mine – he's put six foul words in six lines.
The case against me is political.

Messalla.   I know how you must feel, but you'll only
Make things worse by intemperate language.

Ovid.   And as for that child-killing Medea –
Livia's now blaming *Metamorphoses*
For corrupting Julia's purity.
I wish I could disown that rotten work –
Reconfabulating classical myths
At your request to distance myself from
Erotic verse. My treatment's too witty.
I wanted to dignify Augustus,
Not slight his ancestry. A writer's lot
Is truly wretched. First he struggles and
Finds his work's not published, then when it is
It isn't read, then when he finds readers
He's misunderstood. *Metamorphoses* –
Transformations. It's sure transformed my life.
I understand how Virgil came to throw
His *Aeneid* on a fire. I've turned against
This shallow work. If it's offended *him*

Then burning's all it's fit for. Just like this.

(OVID *throws the manuscript of* Metamorphoses *on the fire.*)

Messalla   (*horrified*). Don't, you can't do that. Quick, help, snatch the work,
Stamp out the flames –

Ovid's wife.   Have you gone mad? That's eight
Years' work you've thrown on the fire. Are you ill?

Ovid.   It's not yet ready for publication.

(MESSALLA *has now rescued the work from the fire.*)

Messalla.   Other copies are in circulation.
Even so, this copy must not be destroyed.
Everyone leave. Thank you, good night. Good night.

(GUESTS *leave.*)

(*To Ovid's wife.*)   Leave Ovid to me. I will talk with him.

(*Exeunt* OVID'S WIFE *and* FRIENDS. OVID *and* MESSALLA *are alone.*)

Messalla.   Because Augustus has banished you, you
Must not lose heart, you must honour your work
And keep writing. You must avoid despair.

Ovid.   Avoid despair? Keep writing? In Tomis?
I can't work outside civilisation.
I need salons in great houses like yours,
Friends, urbane conversation, *bonhomie*
And cultured audiences who know Latin.
I need the glance and repartee of wit,
Banquets with friends, streets lined with shops and bars.
I need the buzz of city life and talk,
A *forum* agog with the latest news,
Gossip, chatter, prattle, easy laughter –
Not solitude amid barbarian tongues.
I will be leaving civilisation
For barbarism on an alien shore.

There's nothing there for me, no audience,
Not even my own language –

Messalla.   You must send
Letters in verse, and we will collect them
And some time soon Augustus will relent
And allow you to resume your career –

Ovid.   I don't think so. In the Garden of State
Caesar's an over-enthusiastic
Head Gardener who sprays insects with poison
And kills the redbreast poets that eat flies,
Swooping like skimming swallows on the wing,
To keep the garden healthy and alive.
His Garden is full of endless vistas
But nothing lives. His Rome's as dead as sand.
He's a dictator who wants State control
Of independent artists, and has made
Rome a cultural desert by his will.

Messalla.   You must live in hope and write to your friends.
Fabius has tried Livia, I will try
Caesar himself on your behalf. I'll do
My best to have your banishment reversed.

SCENE 4

(*Augustus's house. The Room of the Masks. Enter* AUGUSTUS, *his broad-brimmed hat pulled down.*)

Augustus.   The light is bright, I cannot see too well.
I prefer shadows like a hanging bat.

(Enter MESSALLA. AUGUSTUS waves that he should begin and listens.)

Messalla.   Caesar, between us Maecenas and I
Are patrons to the best poets of Rome:
Virgil, Tibullus, Propertius, Horace.
The works of such men will live for all time

And in so far as they glorify you,
You will live for all time through them. Virgil
Threw his *Aeneid* on a fire. Now saved,
It sees your rule as Rome's long destiny,
The climax of the years since Rome's founding.
Ovid, whose work I've also supported,
Is technically superb and for all time,
But his love elegies did not please me.
I edged him into myths, and now he has
Finished a compendium in which he too
Sees your rule as the acme of Rome's climb.
He culminates his book with praise of you
And refers to you as "Son of a god".
Unfortunately his good intention
Has been misinterpreted. It's been said
That he's seen you as equal to some gods
That are fanciful, not worshipped in rites.
That was not his intention, and, appalled
That he has displeased you, like Virgil he
Threw the work on his fire. I salvaged it.
Caesar, he is full of remorse and has
Not wanted to offend you. If you can
Find it in your heart to forgive him and
Revoke his relegation, I myself
Will undertake to read each line he writes
And excise any that may displease you.

Augustus.   You speak like an eloquent advocate.
You make your case well, have your point of view.
I do not disagree with what you've said.
However, what he did must be punished.
His *Art* poisoned my daughter against me –
No, let me finish. He has sided with
My granddaughter. There is evidence that
He sought to overthrow the *imperium*
Which he has always despised in his speech –
And with it me. Some have paid with their lives.
It's right that he should be relegated.
I understand your wish to plead for him
But with respect you were not at the trial
And do not know the facts laid before me.

The nature of his crime meant that the trial
Was in camera, at my private court.
The proceedings were secret, I cannot
Say more than I have said but feel I owe
It to you to give some explanation.
Charged with high treason, he was found guilty.
I encourage Literature, thus patrons.
I am indebted for all you have done.

Messalla.   Caesar, I thank you for your attention.
I do not excuse Ovid. But I know
That deep down he admires the *imperium*,
And if he sometimes professes not to,
Then, though the sentiment is culpable,
A Caesar as powerful as you may feel
Rightly indignant, yes, but with your famed
Noble magnanimity may still waive
Severe punishment, recognizing that
Literature is the temple of free speech,
Purified language that is handed down
From generation to generation,
Where all worship as if at your Altar,
Ara Pacis of the *Pax Augusta*,
Where high culture is guarded like a flame.
A Golden Age such as yours can withstand
A free proponent of the other side.
All opponents and dissidents can be
Accommodated in your greater State.
The Augustan virtues of tolerance,
Reason and sensibility must shrink
From censorship; rather they listen and
Put right a perceived wrong that's criticized.

Augustus.   The *imperium* has spread to all mankind.
I've built a United States of the World.
Very soon the Roman *denarius*
Will be the single Earth currency that
Embraces Parthia and the German tribes,
Pannonia and African Numidia,
Even India, which Alexander reached.
Once my world order is established, yes,

I can be generous to all my critics.
But until then the legions' action has
Precedence over urbane discussion.
I am a man of action. You're learnèd.
Action requires censorship that will shock
Learnèd scholars of Egyptian and Greek,
Persian and Roman knowledge and wisdom.
I am universal in my choices,
Which are made for the *imperium*'s good.
You are universal in your reading,
And take in all cultures and see all sides,
But your task is not like mine, to extend
The *imperium*, and if any of your
Client-poets blatantly undermine
The *imperium*, then they must be silenced.
I have to act decisively to keep
The world Roman and suppress all revolts.

Messalla.   You're quite right, Caesar, as in everything.
                     But is Ovid against the *imperium*?

Augustus.   Yes. I have evidence.

Messalla.   I see him as
                     A poker of fun who makes Literature,
                     Who does not know his political views.
                     He deals in situations and reflects
                     Philosophically in what he writes.
                     He is a man of letters who absorbs
                     History, mythology, philosophy
                     And displays them as a peacock displays
                     A many-eyed fantail to impress mates.
                     He's not a serious opponent of
                     Your *imperium* and what the legions do.
                     His way's the pen, it's not wielding the sword.

Augustus.   But the pen is as mighty as the sword.
                     It influences minds. Each book he writes
                     Is a political act that affects
                     The *imperium*. I do not like his work:
                     Pornographic advice, subversive myths

And provocative, jesting attitude.
Virgil's better – he wrote epic that can
Be compared to Homer, and pastoral verse.
But I fear him, for people look to him.
He cannot be ignored. He will be read.
I have walled him round with silence, and banned
His work from public libraries. He's ceased
To exist as a poet. I will not
Be deflected from crushing opponents
Of the world-wide *imperium*, my great work.
State power must swat ephemeral artists
Who whine and bite like maddening insects.

(*There is a silence.* AUGUSTUS *indicates that the discussion is over and that* MESSALLA *should leave. Exit Messalla after a bow.*)

SCENE 5

(*Ovid's house.* OVID *and his* WIFE. *Ovid's friends are gathered, including* MESSALLA *and* FABIUS.)

Ovid.   My friends, the light is fading, time's run out.
As today dawned, when by Caesar's decree
I must leave Italy's frontiers behind,
I still felt numb, listless. I had not packed
Or finished choosing from my wardrobe or
Fixed on my slaves and attendants. Sheer grief
Still dazed me, tears clouded my eyes. My wife
Embraced me, tears rivering her red cheeks.
Slaves lamented, everyone was in tears.
It was like the day of my own funeral.
I was sad that Perilla, my daughter,
Knew nothing of my plight in Libya,
Out there with her husband on desert sands.
I have procrastinated, in the hope
That news would come that Caesar's changed his mind.
You see, I have not shaved, my hair's uncombed.
I must not procrastinate any more.
I now appeal to the high gods of Rome

Who dwell in the citadel's temples I
Will see no more after today, that I
Should not be burdened by hate and that our
Little household gods, *Lares* of the hearth,
Should always remember that my exile
Was due to an error, my remissness,
And not to any crime. Dear friends I must
Now take leave of you, dear, staunch friends. I have
Bid you goodbye many times these past days,
But now for the last time, perhaps for good,
Goodbye. And goodbye to my loving wife.

(OVID'S WIFE, *sobbing, throws herself at him, her hair down.*)

Ovid's wife   (*sobbing*). I've entreated the gods within our shrine
To look after you. Don't want you to go.

(OVID hugs *his* WIFE and then *his* FRIENDS, kissing each of them.)

Messalla.   You must hurry.

Ovid.   Why? Think where you're rushing
Me to. Scythia! Think what I must leave:
My family, this home I'll see no more,
And Rome. One more glimpse, an extra half hour.....

Fabius.   The light is fading.

Messalla.   You've run out of time.
Caesar's guard is waiting for you to leave.
Caesar's messenger's waiting to take news
To him of your departure.

Ovid.   Let him wait.

(*To his wife.*) My dear wife I am being torn from you.

Ovid's wife   (*sobbing*). They can't tear me from you, I'll follow you
Into exile, we'll voyage together.
Your exile is caused by Caesar's wrath, mine
Will be caused by loyal love. There is room

	For me on ship, at the frontier station.
Ovid.	You must stay and work hard for my recall, And guard this property and my interests.

(TWO SERVANTS *appear carrying a box on four handles,*
Ovid's luggage.)

(*To all.*) I've been a writer for thirty-five years.
I leave behind all my works in a trunk
And take a pen and some parchment. Goodbye.

(OVID'S WIFE *lets out a moan and faints as* OVID *turns*
back.)

Messalla.	You'll have to go, it's getting dark.
Fabius.	We will Look after her and work for your recall.
Ovid.	Goodbye, everybody.
All.	Goodbye, Ovid.

(*All wave.*)

SCENE 6

(*Livia's house on the Palatine.* LIVIA *is alone. Enter* MESSENGER.)

Messenger.	Empress, Ovid's left Italy's borders On board a ship that's bound for Samothrace.
Livia.	You saw the ship depart, with him on board?
Messenger.	I did. He looked forlorn, a sorry sight.

(LIVIA *nods. Exit* MESSENGER.)

Livia   (*alone*). Good. I've had Ovid in my sights for years.
               He encouraged both Julias to believe
               They could intrigue a Julian succession
               And exclude – banish, kill – my Claudian line.
               I did not marry Caesar to witness
               The dashing of Tiberius' hopes, and mine,
               And the cruelty the two Julia tarts
               Would have shown us once they became Empress.
               Within an hour they'd both have despatched us.
               Now the opposition is on the run.
               Being humane, I've preferred banishment,
               But it will be necessary to despatch
               Agrippa Postumus as he's male line.
               I'll bide my time and strike when strike I must.
               Caesar is weak. He dithers and has doubts.
               I am the resolute one. I know when
               To make a decision and stick to it.
               I am like a cobra, I slither near
               And raise my neck above my coils, and strike!
               My aim's unerring and my bite's lethal.
               The Julians did not know their opponent.
               Nor did Ovid, that naive, fawning man.
               But I know naive men are dangerous
               As the impressionable believe them.
               I've struck. Ovid's writhing with a snake-bite
               And is on his way to the Underworld.
               Eurydice trod on a serpent and
               Died of its bite. Ovid trod unwisely.
               The Ovid of eight years ago has died,
               And now emissaries, like Orpheus,
               Will try to rescue him from Pluto's lair.
               They won't lead him back into Rome's sunlight.

SCENE 7

(*A ship in a storm.* OVID *is on board, writing. His two servants, the slaves* CLAUDIUS *and* FLAVIUS, *are nearby with the guard.* OVID *puts down his purse which has been getting in his way.*)

Ovid.   The day's black with storm-clouds, the sea is dark.

The wind-lashed rain beats into this shelter,
Soaking my parchment so it's hard to write,
Freezing my fingers as I scribble lines
And through this wintry tempest peer for coast,
Watch a barbarous shore slide by in mist.

(OVID *peers*. CLAUDIUS *creeps up behind him and steals his purse.*
FLAVIUS *and the* GUARD *have seen and say nothing.*)

December sea-voyage and a shaking hand.

Claudius. We're shipping water, come and help bail out.

Flavius. The waves are even higher than the ship.

Guard. The steersman's raised his hands high to heaven.

Claudius (*to Flavius*). He hasn't even missed the purse we took.

Ovid. I don't trust them with their swords. They'd rob me.
I am on earth to write, I won't bale out
Or join in their petty activities.
I'll carry on despite frozen fingers,
Mountainous seas, imperial anger –
Whatever obstacles Fate finds for me –
As we round the Isthmus of Corinth, head
For the Aegean, then to Samothrace,
Thence to Tempyra, then walk to Tomis.
I am like storm-tossed Odysseus, sailing
Past many islands towards dark Moesia
As I approach Tomis's Underworld.
Hey, where's my purse? Slaves, did you see my purse?
I put it on the deck.

(*The two* SERVANTS *look mystified and shake their heads. The* GUARD
looks away.)

Guard.   Perhaps it slid.

Claudius. Perhaps it's over here. This way, this way.

(Exeunt.)

SCENE 8

(Tomis. OVID *arrives with his* GUARD *and* TWO SERVANTS. *He is dishevelled after months of travelling.)*

Guard.   Wait here, I'll fetch the Governor of this town. *(Exit.)*

                    (OVID stands. A long-haired, fur-clad NATIVE *passes and jabbers at Ovid in Getic.)*

Ovid.   It's dreadful, far worse than I thought. Bleak, dark.
                    Flat, monotonous steppe, frozen grey sea.
                    No trees, no vines, no orchards. Nothing. Cold.
                    A wind that stabs at your rib-cage and howls.
                    I hope for Cicero's speedy recall.

                    (Re-enter GUARD *with* GOVERNOR.)

Governor.   I am the Governor of this town. Welcome.
                    We've been expecting you. Guard, I will sign
                    Your delivery sheet.

                    (The GOVERNOR *signs a paper. He starts walking.* OVID *follows. The* TWO SERVANTS *follow, carrying the luggage.)*

                          We have a house
                    For you, but you must understand, it's not
                    Much more than a wood hut. The wind gets in.
                    We're in a buffer zone against wild tribes –
                    Caesar's maintained Antony's policy
                    Of buffer towns in no man's land to hold
                    The barbarians back, so they don't press
                    On the *limes*, the *imperium*'s frontier.
                    We're a Greek colonial fortified town.
                    It's not safe outside the walls, the tribes shoot
                    Arrows at us but never breach our gates.

                    (He stops and shows OVID *a small shed-like bungalow. It has arrows*

sticking from the low tiled roof.)

You'll soon make your house quite comfortable, but
It'll be a bit of a shock at first.

Ovid.   A wood hut with gaps where the draughts whip in.
             It's more of a cart-shed, or cattle-shed,
             Than a house fit for Rome's most-read poet.

Governor.   It's better than a prison. You're here at
             Caesar's decree, not his invitation.
             This is exile beyond the *imperium*.
             You'll get used to it. The townsfolk will help.
             (*To the guard.*) Your papers must be signed and sent to
                 Rome.
             Then your escort duty will be over
             And you'll become his jailer. He must be
             Kept under strict house arrest. Come with me.

             (*Exit* GOVERNOR *and* GUARD. *The* TWO SERVANTS *gingerly go into the
             hut.* OVID *lingers, then goes inside. He sits down on the bare floor and
             sobs quietly.*)

Ovid.   The Black Sea's terrible. A wilderness.
             I've arrived in Hades. Everything's dead.

ACT FOUR

SCENE 1

(*AD 9. Ovid's hut in Tomis. The* GUARD *sits on the ground outside, playing dice by himself.
Inside* OVID *is alone, writing. He reads aloud.*)

Ovid.   This is a dark town on a rocky coast.
             Half-breed Greeks and full-bloodied barbarians
             Of Getic, Indo-European stock
             Mingle, dressed in skins. They wear their hair long,
             And beards. They carry arms. They're fine horsemen
             And good with bows, but they're all rude peasants

Who speak hybrid Greek, Getic, Sarmatian –
Not Latin. The country around the town
Is flat, treeless and marshy. Bad water
Makes us ill. It's so cold that wine freezes
In the jar and is served in pieces, and
The barbarians' long hair tinkles with ice.
The wild tribes ride from across the Danube
And fire poisoned arrows. The shepherds wear
Helmets as they tend their sheep. Everyone
Is kind-hearted but rough. I'm their prisoner.

(FLAVIUS *returns.*)

Ovid.   Where's friend Claudius?

Flavius.   He ran off in the night.
He's bought himself a passage back to Rome.

Ovid.   With the money in my purse, I've no doubt.

(FLAVIUS *is silent.*)

When does the ship leave?

Flavius.   She sailed out at dawn.
We won't be seeing any more of him.

Ovid.   What do you intend to do?

Flavius.   Stay with you.

Ovid.   I've no money till I get more from Rome.

Flavius.   I'll stay and share your hardship, and improve
Your lot where I can. We'll soon make this place
Comfortable, and I have already found
You a secretary, amanuensis.
She takes dictation, she can write Latin.

Ovid.   Are you serious? I've nothing to pay with.

Flavius.	She'll do it without payment for a while.
	It's enough that you're Rome's foremost poet.
	She's outside. Can I introduce her?
Ovid.	You're
	Incredible.
Flavius.	We'll make the best of things.

(FLAVIUS *leaves and returns with a* LOCAL GIRL. *She has long dark hair and is fur-clad.*)

Ovid.	What's your name?
Secretary.	In Latin, Constantia.
Ovid.	Welcome to my new home. You will help me?
Constantia.	Honoured to work for Roman nobleman.

(*Suddenly a hail of arrows falls round* OVID. *Two thud into the roof, which now bristles with arrows.*)

Barbarians. Quick.

(*The* SECRETARY *scurries outside.* FLAVIUS *peers out of a window, looking for arrows. The* SECRETARY *returns.*)

This way. We help repel.

(OVID *and* FLAVIUS *bend double and run after the* SECRETARY.)

SCENE 2

(*Ovid's hut in Tomis. The* GUARD *is sitting outside.* OVID *is with* CONSTANTIA, *who is taking dictation.*)

Ovid.	On my journey I wrote some "Sad Poems"
	And now I want to dictate another.

It's addressed to Caesar. First some ideas.
I am angry that I've been exiled here.
Caesar's thunderings are random, like Jove's
Whose lightning strikes a dead tree, then a vine
That droops with grapes – does not discriminate
Between a barren heart and an artist
As vibrant and as creative as me.
No less random are Caesar's flirtations,
Which are as many as his arch rainbows.
He takes his pleasure, then pontificates
Against verses on the art of pleasure,
Hypocrisy that cries out to be mocked.
He has corrupted the Roman ideal,
Turned the eagle into a cruel vulture,
Used the high gods to keep himself in power,
And fostered secular profanity.
As geese honk near a pond, heads in the air,
And a male scoots forward, its neck stretched out
To shovel off a foe that's after food,
So Caesar chases off all those he fears.
I resent what he's done to me. Avoid
Great men, live a quiet private life and thrive.
Why did he pick on me? I did not know
What they were doing when I blundered in.
An error and a book.... I don't make sense?
Write it down. He, the mightiest in the world,
Will stand up to all plotters who want change.
He stands for the blinkered world government
That wants all countries to be provinces
Within the great Roman Empire –

Constantia.   Ovid.

(OVID *stops dictating abruptly. He is shocked.*)

All that in past. I here now. I here now.

(CONSTANTIA *takes off her coat. She draws her chair next to* OVID*'s.*)

You have me. You not need to be lonely.
I look after you.

Ovid.	No. I have a wife.
Constantia.	In Rome. Not here in Tomis but in Rome.

(OVID *resumes dictating, but in a low voice so the* GUARD *outside will not hear.*)

Ovid.	I see the Emperor's Court as lusting gods.
	The Roman Empire's in decline, having
	Turned secular, unprincipled, greedy.
	The deification of Augustus
	Is secular humanism gone mad.
	I show him as vindictive Jupiter,
	Livia as manipulative Juno.
	I write of gods but they mask our rulers.

(OVID *breaks off.*)

We'll do a letter to my wife, asking
Her to plead with Livia on my behalf.

SCENE 3

(*Livia's house on the Palatine, Rome.* OVID'S WIFE *and* MARCIA, *wife of Fabius, wait outside.*)

Ovid's wife.	Messalla's death will hit my husband hard.
Marcia.	Your husband has lost his main protector.
	Had he been well, he'd have opposed Caesar
	Who'd have listened and revoked banishment.
	He did his best though terminally ill
	And a mere shadow of his former self.
	Caesar now understands how sick he was,
	And we must play on this with Livia.

(*Enter* SLAVE.)

Slave.	Livia can see you now. This way, please.

(*They enter Livia's house. Enter* LIVIA, *who greets* MARCIA *and ignores* OVID'S WIFE.)

Livia.   My good friend Marcia, good to see you.

Marcia.   Good to see *you*, Livia. Fabius
                Sends his greetings. I bring our relative,
                Ovid's wife –

Livia.   Ovid? Who's he?

Marcia.   The poet
                Who is unfortunately in Tomis.

Livia.   Oh yes, the plotter who planned to murder
                Caesar –

Marcia.   That was not how it was.

Livia.   He was
                Lucky not to have lost his head.

Marcia   I bring
                Ovid's wife, who, still distraught at her loss,
                Wishes to plead that you should intercede
                With mighty Caesar to review the case.

Ovid's wife.   Empress, if my husband has offended
                Caesar or you, I humbly beg pardon.
                I know he did not intend any harm.
                I know he wishes Caesar's good and was
                Horrified at the scene that met his eyes
                When he entered that room, expecting that
                He would be signing a book for Caesar's
                Granddaughter, which he deemed a great honour.
                He should have come straight to this door and told.
                He did wrong to keep the scene to himself,
                But he felt embarrassed, he thought I would
                Suspect Julia had propositioned him.
                His silence was to keep the scene from me,
                Not to compromise Caesar's safety. Please,

	Empress, ask great Caesar to think again.

Empress, ask great Caesar to think again.
Messalla tried but he was stricken by
His last illness, which sapped his energy.
The latest letter from my husband shows
He is unwell. Please be compassionate.

Livia. I understand how you must feel, but fear
I can't change Caesar's mind, which is set firm
Like an expression on a stone statue,
And cannot be relaxed with soothing words.
The crime they planned was very very bad.
Had they succeeded Caesar would be dead.
He's been deeply affected by their plot.
A less humane man would have despatched him.
What's done must be left as it is awhile.
I'm so sorry, but know you'll understand.

Marcia. Empress, thank you for listening to our plea.
I quite understand how Caesar must feel.
I'm sorry to have troubled you with this.
You have weightier things to discuss than us.

Livia (*agreeing*). Affairs of State, the management of Rome.

(*Exeunt* MARCIA and OVID'S WIFE.)

Ovid's wife. She wants him in Tomis, she's not sincere.
She's had them all banished so her son has
No rivals when he comes to claim the throne.
She wants them out of Rome – Ovid as well.
Now I have to write and lower his hopes.

Marcia. Your hopes have been temporarily dashed.
In a few months Fabius can try again,
Visit Caesar. A little time must pass.
Come back with me for lunch, I'll cheer you up.

SCENE 4

(OVID, *holding a letter, sits head bowed, depressed. The* GUARD *is sitting outside.*)

Ovid   (*alone*). Messalla dead. I have no protector,
No patron now. Octavian's General,
Who fought at Philippi and Actium,
Built aqueducts, roads and public buildings,
Wrote on the civil wars and pastoral
Poems in Greek and essays on grammar –
Dead! With his passing have perished my hopes.
Like Orpheus, whose verses made trees sing,
I've descended into the Underworld
To retrieve my art (like Eurydice)
From the courts of Hades where Augustus,
Lord of the Underworld, imprisoned her,
And bring her back to daylight and my Rome.
So far I'm empty-handed, and alone.

(OVID *shakes his head.*)

I have no patron, no circle of friends.
I do not choose to belong to a school.
As half a dozen fallow deer gather
In brambled shrubs on parkland and stand still,
Hiding, camouflaged in motionlessness,
Too shy to approach near the public that
Wants to feed them, so minor poets keep
Apart and together in a small herd.
A great poet roams alone, like a stag,
His many-branched antlers magnificent.
I am a stag and do not band with deer
Whose timid modesty I do despise.

(*Enter* CONSTANTIA, *who is intercepted by* FLAVIUS.)

Flavius.   He's had bad news from home. His wife's written.
Livia won't plead for his return to Rome.

Constantia.   I talk to him.

(*Exit* FLAVIUS.)

(*To Ovid.*)   You in Tomis, not Rome.

Ovid.   My mind's in Rome. My friends, my audience.
               Their wit, intelligence. There's nothing here.
               No one speaks my language. I miss my friends.
               I miss my home.

Constantia.   Your home now in Tomis.

Ovid.   I miss my Roman culture, Roman ways.

Constantia.   You write letters to Rome. Tomis your home.

Ovid.   It's cold, a waste. Barbarians attack.
               There's nothing to do except write poems.

Constantia.   Greek culture you like?

(OVID *nods.*)

                            I bring my brother.
               He priest of Apollo, know Greek culture.
               Soon we write letter, all about Tomis.

(*Exit* CONSTANTIA. OVID *sits.*)

Ovid.   I write carefully crafted poems. Why?
               No one will read them. No one understands
               My language here. I sit in solitude,
               A Roman spectacle, like a panda
               In a zoo viewed by curious Getic folk
               From time to time, alone with dreams of home.
               I who had Roman houses, wealth and friends
               Have nothing, no possessions save this trunk
               Which holds my writing papers and my pens.
               I'm an object of curiosity
               Like a barbarian prisoner roped behind
               A General's chariot at his triumph.
               I've been banished by the world government

Of Augustus Caesar's *imperium*
That seeks to silence me as an artist.
I won't be silenced, I'll protest with words
That will be read one day and resonate.
Writing poetry I cannot read aloud's
Like dancing in the dark. But it quickens
The vibrant soul in me that hankers for
The vineyards and wheatfields of Italy.
I'm mortified here in this treeless steppe
Among the wormwood shrubs of bleak Pontus.
I detest Tomis and scorn its people.
They're ignoramuses, illiterates,
Worthy folk but poor evening company
Once you have tasted Messalla's salons.
As ducks come waddling fast to the patter
Of flung corn on mud beside a green moat,
So come poets when a patron's hand's out.
Messalla dead. I have my memories,
But no more will he greet me at his door.
I had so much, but my self has been stripped
Of what I owned, and now I stand naked,
Alone, Ovid, body, creative mind
And memories in a Moesian waste land.
Who am I? Am I the Roman success
Or this scared whimpering man whipped by the wind
Under the stars of a huge Pontic sky
Wondering if death will end my consciousness?
Am I a social icon or a soul?

(*Re-enter* CONSTANTIA *with her* BROTHER, *a priest. The* GUARD *stands
up and checks his identity.*)

Constantia.   My brother from Temple of Apollo.

Ovid.   Greetings from Orpheus in the Underworld,
               Still waiting to take my art back to Rome.

Priest.   I know of your work, Ovid, and know of
               Your *Metamorphoses*, transformations.
               Apollo is the god of transforming,
               Who shines into cultures and private souls

With Light that inspires creativity.
You are well-known for what you have written.
Let Apollo speak through you and you'll grow.
Your stay here is an opportunity
For you to be transformed from old to new
As a silkworm larva spins a cocoon
From which it hatches as a flying moth.

Ovid.   Apollo guides your tongue like the Sibyl's
Or the Delphic oracle priestess's.
You speak my deepest thoughts in measured words.
You know me well, say what I must now do.

Priest.   I bring you a gift from our Mysteries.

(*The* PRIEST *carefully hands* OVID *a small container.*)

Ovid.   Why, it's an ear of wheat. At Eleusis
They show a reaped ear of corn at the end
Of the epoptic Mysteries.

Priest.   Contemplate
How Apollo's sunlight can ripen it
And how your soul is like an ear of corn.
If it abides by itself, it will die.
Plant it in fertile ground and it will grow.
The grain buried in earth brings forth new life
And represents the seed of Light in man.
Persephone, Earth-Mother, was carried
Off into the Underworld by Pluto
And returned each summer in harvest wheat.
In Rome....

Ovid.   Go on.

Priest.   In Rome you did not live,
Not from your deepest self Apollo knows.
You lived a social life like chaff, not grain.
Your life was recitals and flattery,
Falseness, ego. Now you can grow, ripen.
You must die from your old life to be born,

Reborn through redemption here in Tomis.
This solitude will improve your writings.
Isolation will benefit your works.

Ovid.　　　　　I do not know you, yet it seems that you
Know me better now than I know myself.
On the coins here the Emperor's face has lost
Its definition. The further one comes
From Rome the more the stamped face of Caesar's
Unrecognizable. So my own face
Now looks very strange to me, and the old
Pattern of my psyche is dissolving.
What do I have to do to be reborn?

Priest.　　　　Plant the corn in your garden and observe.
You are a mystic or you are nothing.
As a silkworm's entombed in a cocoon
And emerges as a silkmoth that flies
You must leave behind your erotic grub
And be transformed into a flying thing
That crawls up a window towards the moon.
Come to the Temple of Apollo, and learn.

(*Arrows thud into the roof. The* GUARD *leaps up.* FLAVIUS *appears.*)

Constantia.　　Barbarians. To the walls. We must repel.

(*Exit* OVID, *picking up a helmet, followed by the others.*)

SCENE 5

(*Ovid's hut in Tomis. Re-enter* CONSTANTIA *with a letter. She gives it to* OVID *and goes out to talk to the* GUARD. *Ovid reads.*)

Ovid.　　　　　I am emptied of hope, but each letter
Bubbles like a spring deep in an old well,
I feel hope trickling back and filling me.
Caesar has seen Agrippa Postumus,
He visited him on his island, he

May now be more kindly disposed to me.
Fabius will see Caesar on my behalf.
And so, just as I've let Rome go and lost
The craving to be there in my own home
With my dear wife and friends and hear them clap
As I finish reading, I am drawn back,
Separate no longer, now joined to Rome
As a well's one with its water-table.
But now I despise my expectations.
I hate my old poems, that dreadful *Art*,
More than I hate the oiks who walk the tracks –
The frozen mud with hoof-marks filled with ice –
Between these shacks. And yet, my friends, my friends!

(*Enter* CONSTANTIA.)

We will write to Fabius, urging him
To persuade Caesar to lift my sentence.

Constantia.   I no want you return to Rome, Ovid.

(OVID *turns away*.)

SCENE 6

(*Livia's house on the Palatine, Rome.* AUGUSTUS *and* LIVIA *are alone*.)

Livia.   She has borne a son on bleak Trimerus.

Augustus.   He must never be acknowledged or reared.
He must be exposed on a hot hillside,
Her "palace" – for that's what it is – must be
Razed to the ground. Her ashes must not be
Placed in my mausoleum. That's final.

(*Enter a* SLAVE.)

Slave.   Fabius is here.

Livia.   Send him in.

(*Exit* SLAVE.)

                              Don't listen.
You can't release Ovid while Julia
Is still defying you on Trimerus.
For all you know, Julia's son is Ovid's.

(*Enter* FABIUS. LIVIA *draws back but is present.*)

Fabius.   Caesar, I come for our relative's sake
As she mourns the loss of her beloved
Ovid, who all now know did wrong and who
Has paid for his error on the Pontus.

Augustus.   I've more important things to do than think
Of Ovid, who abused my patronage.

Fabius.   Words cannot express his profound regret
For inadvertently offending you.
But now it would be deemed magnanimous
If you pardoned him and allowed him back.
His gratitude would be so heartfelt that
I know his writings would not trouble you –

Livia.   The man offended Caesar twice and sought
To overthrow him for the Julians.
Why should Caesar pardon Ovid and risk
A further attempt to dethrone him?

Fabius.   I
Have heard that Caesar, most charitably,
Has visited Agrippa Postumus,
Signalling that he'd like to draw a line
Under the sad events that sickened all –

Augustus.   I have not drawn a line, my attitude
Is unchanged: plots are bad, both then and now.
I never liked the poetry of Ovid.
He has a poor view of the *imperium*,

554

Sets himself against the world government.
He despises the opulence of Rome
And is now living in a simple hut.
That is appropriate, given his beliefs.
I see no reason to end his exile.

(FABIUS *has been stopped in his tracks. He bows and leaves.*)

Livia.

Well spoken with Caesar's authority.
We won't be hearing from him for a while.
Ovid's a rallying point for malcontents.
It's best he stays outside the *imperium*.

Augustus.

I have had opponents. Yet he's the one
Who most irritates me, perhaps because
He's so pleased with himself, self-regarding.
Let us not think of him. He's marginal.

SCENE 7

(*The Temple of Apollo.* OVID *sits with the* PRIEST. *They are meditating. Both have closed eyes. They murmur to each other.*)

Ovid.

Just as a fantail dove leaves its dovecote,
Sits on a thatched roof, then flutters to grass
And explores its freedom before it flies
Back to the hole in its white-posted home,
So I have left the prison of my hut
To perch among your Temple's white columns
And savour the splendour of the sunlight.

Priest.

If you would see Apollo's midnight sun,
The Light that shines into darkness, you must
Remove yourself from this earth's attractions.
Cleanse your senses, purge yourself of desire,
Want nothing, rest content within your smile,
Live without attachment to worldly things,
Purify your inwardness, look within
At the images that will rise in you.

Apollo's Light will shine, and, illumined,
You will become a Shining One, a soul
That is enlightened and is most serene.
This is what the priests of Eleusis teach.

Ovid.

I do want to bask in Apollo's Light,
Like Prometheus steal the eternal Fire.
I have let go of Rome now I'm rebuffed.
I want nothing, I do not hope for Rome.
I've stripped myself of all acquisitions.
I have nothing and want to know the Light.

Priest.

Then let your rhythmic breathing deepen, close
Your eyes and see the Light break like the dawn
On shimmering water. Peer at the dark,
Peer into the darkness, and penetrate
Through to the Light concealed behind black cloud.

(A silence. Then OVID cries out.)

Ovid.

I can see it. A dawning in the night.
The sun's breaking. I can see its white rays.
The sun's emerging, it's so bright, ah! bright –

Priest.

The face of Apollo –

Ovid.

It's dazzling.
It's so intense. It's filling me. Ah! ah!
I'm filled with radiance of the inner sun.
It's so intense, it's –

(OVID swoons forward.)

Priest.

Apollo has healed
Your troubled mind, you are now whole, Ovid.

(He puts his hand on Ovid's head. OVID appears unconscious.)

SCENE 8

(*AD 14. Nola.* TIBERIUS *meets* LIVIA *outside Augustus's sick-room.*)

Tiberius.   I came as soon as I heard. How is he?
I was leaving for Illyricum and
Turned round when news came that he's gravely ill.

Livia.   The Emperor is sinking, Tiberius.
His incurable diarrhoea has turned worse.
He's weak from four days' feasting on Capri.
He had an inkling in April when he
Deposited his will and *Res Gestae*
In the House of the Vestals in Rome. He
Cannot last long. This morning he told me
Agrippa Postumus must die so that
You have no co-heir when you succeed him.

(TIBERIUS *turns to the Praetorian* GUARDS.)

Tiberius.   The Emperor wants Agrippa Postumus
Dead. See his order's promptly carried out.

(*One of the* GUARDS *nods. Exit the guards.*)

The Senate will soon enroll him among
The gods of the Roman State.

Livia.   And you as
The second Roman Emperor even though
The Principate can't be inherited.
Come in and see your father. Don't be shocked
By his appearance, he is sinking fast.

(TIBERIUS *looks at her.*)

Tiberius.   You haven't....?

Livia.   Shh. Don't ask questions. Accept.
It's your turn now. Don't question, just accept.

(TIBERIUS *enters the sick-room.* LIVIA *hovers behind him.* AUGUSTUS *is lying on a couch.*)

Tiberius.

Father, I came as soon as I was told.

Augustus.

Who's there? Is it Tiberius? I'm quite blind.
I'm glad you've come. You will be Caesar soon
And I can hand over the world to you
Like this orange. Excuse my lower jaw.
It has to be propped up by a pillow.
I've got worse very fast. I don't know why.
You see, I've had my hair combed. I am still
Ruler of the known world. Rumours of my
Illness may cause popular disturbance.
My father Octavius died in this room.
You must always remember, it's a play.
You are an actor with an audience.
Did I not play my part in life's farce well?
If I pleased you give me a warm good-bye.
I can't move my lower jaw. There will be
A lot of soldiers from Actium and
The battlefields that brought me into Rome,
Waiting for me. I have no regrets. One.
I wish I hadn't banished Julia,
Your sister. I loved her.

Livia.

                 Nonsense, Caesar.
She plotted to kill you with that Ovid.

Augustus.

I don't know, I don't know. Not with Ovid.
I think Ovid was blameless all along.
But he opposed the *imperium* and so
He had to be banished. I feel dreadful.
My mausoleum has long awaited me,
My deeds inscribed on the two bronze pillars
That flank the entrance doors – my *Res Gestae*,
And now I am ready to enter it
And dwell in gloom with the shades of Hades.
I, master of the Greco-Roman world,
Am mortal, and it is time I must die
And be cremated on a funeral pyre

In the Campus Martius and be scooped up
As two handfuls of powdery cinder-dust,
And, lord of riches in this Roman life,
Must sit with Pluto in the Underworld,
Twin umbrarchs of that dark sinister realm.
Leave me, I need to think about my life.

(LIVIA and TIBERIUS withdraw and keep an eye on AUGUSTUS from a distance.)

Livia.

(LIVIA and TIBERIUS return to AUGUSTUS's couch.)

It's as though I have been blind
And have opened my eyes for the first time,
And seen into an inner world of things
Beneath the surface of cause and effect,
And what I see disturbs me – my Empire
Crumbling like a house that is built on sand
Before the tide of history and slow time.
Ovid was right, my Empire will not last –

Livia. Nonsense, Caesar. Ovid was wrong, it will –

Augustus. The barbarians will enter Italy's
Cosmopolitan melting-pot and swamp
The integrity of the Roman State.
Ovid saw clearly that I have destroyed
Rome's survival with my imperial drive
By alienating those who will invade.
With your connivance I have sowed ruin.
I see my life's work has been meaningless,
A postponement of an incoming tide
That is inevitable. And I've left
As my successor an imperialist
Who will continue the ruin of Rome.
How could I settle the succession so?
A cuckoo's taken over my Empire
And pushed me from its nest – you intrigued this.
Have you poisoned me so your son can rule?

I have got worse and still do not know why.
The patches on my skin, the blemishes,
The sores and boils, my bladder pains, numbness –
Were they all symptoms of slow poisoning?

(*He falls silent.*)

Livia.   You're rambling, you don't know what you're saying.
His fever has made him delirious.

(*There is a silence.*)

Augustus.   Goodbye Livia, don't forget our marriage!
Forty young men are carrying me off!
I'm in a world of gloom. Darkness. Darkness.

(*He dies.*)

Livia.   He was speaking gibberish. His dying words
Were from a mind whose reason was a blur.
He was a great Emperor who carried Rome's
Influence throughout the world, but he was weak
And would not have done this without my help.
He needed my guidance at every turn.

(*Livia turns to* TIBERIUS.)

Hail, Caesar! I've waited years for this day.
All your opponents are banished or dead.
I am pleased to have helped in a small way.

SCENE 9

(FLAVIUS *stands by the* GUARD *outside Ovid's hut.*)

Guard.   I don't know who's more of a prisoner,
The man of letters or me, for while he
Is under house arrest, in my command,
He roams his room, chats to Constantia,

Walks to the Temple of Apollo while
I have to spy on him, can go nowhere
Without him, have to stay outside this door
So long as he's inside, as if I am
Chained to this door post like a tethered dog.
I throw my dice to while away the hours,
I'm bored and dream of Rome and envy him
His calm acceptance of his exile here,
His Stoic indifference to his own fate,
His scorn for what Caesar has done to him.
He knows that I report on him to Rome.
He puts on an act for me, he makes out
That he loves Caesar, but I see his scorn.
I have to salute Caesar, he is free
To rise above his lot with dignity.

(*There is a cry from the market-place. It is taken up.*)

Cry.   Caesar is dead! Caesar is dead!

Flavius.   You heard?

Guard.   I heard. If it is true, perhaps I'm free.
And you. Perhaps Tiberius will allow
Him to return to Rome, and us with him.

(*Enter* CONSTANTIA *hastily. She pushes past the* GUARD. OVID
appears within.)

Constantia.   Caesar dead. In market they say he dead.
He die quick. Livia hasten his end.

Ovid.   It will not make any difference to me.
The world government's a system, it's not
At the whim of a personality.
The system has a policy on me.
It's consistent, to keep me in Tomis.

Constantia.   Forty Praetorian Guards carry his
Body from Nola, where he die, to Rome.
Caesar a god. They say he now a god.

Ovid.	A god! The man who banished me a god
	Now ranked alongside Apollo's pure Light?
	That is the logic of humanism.
	Man equal to the one Creator god.
	When civilisations turn secular
	They die. Augustus' rule was secular,
	Secularisation's the death of Rome –
	Write that down please. Rome rose with the sacred
	And declined when it lost its true vision.
	The Rome I dreamed of has a worthless core.
	Now I understand, Rome was secular,
	A barbarous place of noise and raucous cries.
	This Tomis is more civilised for here
	There's a tradition of the deeper self
	Where all can locate their being's well-spring.
	In Tomis time is the season's progress,
	A natural rhythm of the days and nights.
	In Rome time wears a helmet and marches
	With shield and ruthless stride to world conquest.
	Imagine, Rome with all its fine togas
	And pillared temples, soaring aqueducts
	And marbled villa courtyards – barbarian!
	And Tomis with its hovels open to
	The wind and babblers in a foreign tongue –
	Civilised! Sound, silence. City, Nature.
	I, poet of sounds and warm city crowds,
	Prefer the solitude of silence and
	The steppes and skies and frosts of cold Nature.
	A metamorphosis that's surprised me!
	Now I see Rome was just a shallow place
	For all its glitter and bright elegance,
	And my frivolity there was a mask
	That blocked my own development and growth.
	If Caesar's dead, I don't want to return
	To Rome. I'm happy here, writing poems.

(*Quietly* CONSTANTIA *approaches* OVID *and kisses him.*)

Constantia.	And your wife? It's six year since you see her.
	She do nothing for you. You forget her?

Ovid.	I don't know, I don't know.
Constantia.	Ovid, come here.

(*Slowly* OVID *goes to her.*)

I love you.
(*She takes off her thick garments down to her waist.*)

Ovid.	I'm an old man, I'm grey-haired. I'm old enough to be your father. I....
Constantia.	What is matter?
Ovid.	I'm thinking of Caesar's Daughter and granddaughter.
Constantia.	Caesar is dead. You no think about them. Come here, come here.

(*She draws* OVID *to her.* OVID *nuzzles into her breast.*)

You think on me, not Caesar's family.
You like Tomis. You do not think on Rome.

Ovid.	I like the Tomitans, but not their land.

(*Exeunt.*)

ACT FIVE

SCENE 1

(*Tomis. Outside Ovid's hut. The* GOVERNOR *and the* GUARD.)

Governor.	Is it true that Ovid has built a shrine To Augustus in his sitting-room? There?
Guard.	It's true, sir. He invokes it several times

Each day. I've seen it with these very eyes
And heard him with these ears.

Governor.   Astonishing!
You'd think he'd hate Caesar, not worship him.
Is he sincere? Or is he hoping that
We'll report it so Tiberius will
Relent where his father was unmoved and
Revoke his exile?

Guard.   That was my first thought,
But now I believe that he's quite sincere.
He's made a turf-altar of his small hearth.
He's placed Caesar's statue on piled turf loam.
Look, you can judge for yourself. He's started.
Peep through this hole and you'll see what I've seen.

(*The* GOVERNOR *and the* GUARD *peep through a crack in Ovid's hut.
Inside* OVID *kneels before a small head-and-shoulders bust of Augustus on
a turf-altar.*)

Ovid.   O *Lares*, household gods of my poor hearth,
Tutelary presences who protect
Me in this humble abode, please revere
This newest god in Rome's dread pantheon,
Augustus, who is now an avatar
Of Apollo, and beams Apollo's Light
Down to us lesser mortals in these wastes.
In life he stood for his *imperium*,
And I rendered my tax to Caesar's law
And my spiritual calm to Apollo.
In death he is raised to Apollo's height.
His mortal imperfections, now perfect,
Like a magpie his black now rinsed in white,
Shed corruptible laurels for a wreath
Of incorruptible Light, reconcile
All opposites into one harmony.
O Augustus, image of glorious Light
With which we lowly men identify,
Divus Augustus, once my enemy,
The Light now shining behind your dark head,

Transcendent truth behind good government,
The universe's contradictions tamed,
Receive my prayers at this Altar of Peace,
My sacrifice and libation whose smoke
Rises to the gate of your Olympus.
Now I render to you the divine part
Of me that I withheld when you were still
Alive, and look to you to fill me with
The Light of Apollo, now your judgement
Has been cleansed by his wisdom. Look within
Your immortal spirit and send to me
The justice Jupiter expects of you,
For which I have vainly waited during
The time when you were a fallible man.
Caesar, your elevation to the gods
Brings divine faculties and a duty
To deal fairly where treatment was unfair.
O great Augustus, I revere the power,
The judgement you show as an Olympian
Who is now one with Lord Apollo's Light,
And rides in the chariot of the sun,
To me, a mere citizen of the world,
A cosmopolitan outside the sway
Of the Roman *imperium*'s world rule.

(OVID *bows to the bust and rises from his knees. Exit Ovid. The*
GOVERNOR *and the* GUARD *move away.*)

Governor.   It was hard to catch all he had to say
But certainly he seemed to praise Caesar
And seemed to be sincere. Who would have thought
Ovid's promoting the imperial cult?
He does this several times a day, you say?
I will report this to Tiberius.

SCENE 2

(*Tomis. The Temple of Apollo. The* PRIEST *addresses the audience.* OVID *stands beside him.*)

Priest.	A large audience has gathered, the Governor
	Has taken his seat, all to hear Ovid
	Hail Augustus as a god in Getic.
	Some of you will be surprised that a man
	Banished by Caesar can observe his rites.
	But I know he's seen all nations' gods as
	Manifestations of one divine power,
	Including all the Roman gods. Ovid.

(*There is applause.*)

Ovid.	I see all gods manifesting one power
	With the Stoics. After the Civil War
	We tired Romans looked to Hellenistic
	Philosophies rather than religion,
	Especially Epicureanism
	Which promised peace of mind and quiet pleasure –
	The hedonism of homely Horace –
	Yet went along with Caesar's revival
	Of religion, old temples and priesthoods.
	The Stoics like Virgil came to believe
	That all men have a spark of the divine
	That can transform – metamorphose – humans.
	The god-Emperor is lit with common Light
	That shines from Apollo, our Inner Sun.
	I reject polytheism and have
	A vision of one God for all nations
	Who manifests in many different forms.
	I, once an Epicurean, am now
	Metamorphosed into a syncretist
	Who sees all deities – even Caesar –
	As manifestations of a dark power,
	The One Light of the radiant Apollo,
	Himself a manifestation of Light,
	Of Zeus, Dyaeus Pitar, Jupiter,
	Interchangeable gods of three cultures.
	Dyaeus Pitar (Zeus or Jupiter) –
	The name in Sanskrit means "the Bright Heaven".
	Jupiter embodies the bright white Light
	In the universe, his manifestation
	Apollo reflects the Light in culture

And art, and his avatar Augustus,
Pontifex Maximus and now *divus*,
Reflects the Light in State ceremonies.
When I write "Jupiter" read Augustus –
They're one and the same at a deep level,
Though I abhorred his secular regime
That used religion to rule his subjects,
Falsely pretending it was religious.
I saw the breakdown of old Rome, I saw
Emperors will become grotesque monsters who
Are transformed into misusing their power.
As a Stoic, I invoke Augustus
And scorn his secular cult that has lost
Belief in itself and will surrender
The Roman *imperium* to "barbarians"
No different from you Getic Sarmatians,
You Goths from the Danube's cold hinterlands.
My Getic friends, the future will be yours.
Rome will decline and fall. Your descendants
Will pour through its walls and inherit Rome.
It is in that knowledge I now invoke
Augustus as a form of Apollo
Who has already ended Roman rule
Though the end will take centuries to unfold.
Your foe, my foe, is therefore our ally.
My foe now symbolizes the divine –
Each contradiction metamorphoses
Into a unity that contradicts.
We live in complexity, and yet I
Live with you in profound simplicity.
It is time to begin my reading now.

(OVID *moves forward and addresses the audience. He enters the audience
and advances through it.*)

Fellow Tomitans, all opposites are
Reconciled within the Great Harmony.
I sing Augustus, vengeful avatar
Of Jupiter, who banished me to dwell
Among you on your frozen steppe and taught
Me the warmth of your hearts amid your cold,

Despite the haughty frowns of Caesar's Rome.
Now Augustus has died, he is a god,
And should be worshipped as should all the gods,
But for his justice and his uprightness,
Qualities he fell short of in his life.
Augustus is now perfected as are
All who have died and merged with Apollo.
I pray to Augustus-Apollo that
You will approach divinity through him....

(Exit OVID.)

SCENE 3

(*Rome. Tiberius's palace.* LIVIA *and* TIBERIUS.)

Livia.	The Governor of Moesia now reports That Ovid's built a shrine to your father And publicly urges the imperial cult. I think he's putting on an act to win A pardon and a swift return to Rome. His wife's at the door, seeking clemency. He was a "friend" of Julia's, I still Suspect him of adultery with her. You must tell her he's exiled till he dies.

(TIBERIUS *nods.* LIVIA *turns and beckons. Enter* OVID's WIFE.)

Tiberius.	How many years ago was your husband Relegated?
Ovid's wife.	Eight years, Caesar.
Tiberius.	Eight years. Can you still remember what he looked like?
Ovid's wife.	I can as if he left just yesterday. I have reports that he has worshipped at The altar of the divine Augustus

And promoted the imperial cult.
His health has suffered in the harsh climate.
He is not well. Please pardon him.

Tiberius.   You know
We Claudians wouldn't dream of pardoning
Him after what he tried to do. You know
What I must say. He opposed my father
And the succession of the Claudian line.
There can be no forgiveness. He once made
His choice and must now bear the consequence.
He will die in Tomis. And you, my dear,
Would be advised to get on with your life.

Ovid's wife.   I hoped that Caesar's son might now relent
Where his father was obdurate, but now
I know how hard is the *imperium*'s heart,
I see that hope is at an end, and I
Must now abandon my poor husband to
His harsh life among barbarian arrows.

(Exit OVID's WIFE.)

Tiberius.   I almost feel sorry for her. She is
Not responsible for her husband's crime.

Livia.   Don't pity the plight of your enemies.
Strike them down and your rule will thrive through strength.
Be pitiless, like the Roman eagle.

SCENE 4

(*Ovid's hut.* OVID *is dictating to* CONSTANTIA. *The* GUARD *sits outside, throwing dice.*)

Ovid.   I sit as a pheasant squats in heathland,
Alone in a sea-like expanse of steppe.
I have stripped myself of all my comforts.
I have no desires, no cravings. I want
Nothing – not wine, not Rome, not wife, not friends.

I have freed myself from the distractions
Of superficial civilisation.
I despise Rome. I love Spartan Tomis.

(*Enter the* GOVERNOR *with angry* TOMITANS. *The* GUARD *stands and waves them towards the hut.*)

Constantia.   Something has happened.

(*The* GOVERNOR *enters the hut. The* TOMITANS *crowd and press behind him.*)

Ovid   (*surprised*).   Have I offended –

Governor.   The Tomitans know what you think of them.
They are indignant. They made you welcome
And you repaid their hospitality
By writing disparagingly about them.
They did not like some of the things you said
At the Temple of Apollo. They are
Angry, and you should now apologise.

Ovid.   I will speak in Getic. My friends, I am
A warm-blooded Italian who grew up
In the hot sun, in orchards and vineyards.
I can't pretend that your climate suits me.
I find it cold. That is no fault of yours.
But I like living among you. I find
You kind and caring, unlike my own Rome.
I've learned Getic, I defend our Tomis
Alongside you when raiders fire arrows,
I share your lives, I am now one of you.
I would not want to return now to Rome.
It would distress me greatly if you felt
Any animosity towards me.
You are my friends. I have no friends in Rome.
I am heartbroken if some words of mine
Have been misconstrued as criticism
Of you, your province or the life you lead.

(CONSTANTIA *nods her approval and adds words in Getic.*)

Constantia.	You heard the Roman, he loves being here.
	He's against Rome. He's been misunderstood.

(OVID *turns to the* GOVERNOR *and speaks quietly to him in Latin.*)

Ovid.	Who's set me up? Who's turned them against me?
	Was this an order you've had from Caesar?

Governor.	I will not dignify that last remark
	With a comment. Caesar's above reproach.
	(*To the Tomitans.*) My friends, Ovid has apologised if
	He's inadvertently offended you.
	(*To Ovid.*) You have a gift for offending people.

Ovid.	Only Emperors who want to crush the *plebs*
	As if they rode a chariot through a crowd.

Governor.	I will ignore that last remark. I did
	Not hear what you just said.

Ovid.	I speak the truth.
	The poet speaks the truth and Emperors quake
	For though they rule through lies, they cannot still
	The freedom of a poet's tongue. They may
	Ban all his books from public libraries,
	Make sure they're not reviewed and surround him
	With silence – place him among foreign tongues
	And under house arrest – as a danger
	For truth is dangerous, but poetry
	Is mightier than their guards and Governors' spies,
	A poet's words will outlast their regimes.
	My words will live for ever, I will be
	More famous than Tiberius Caesar
	In a thousand or two thousand years' time.
	And I say the *imperium* crushes
	Non-Roman peoples who've a right to live,
	I say military power's a blight on all
	Who live on the *imperium*'s borders.
	You bribe barbarians with luxuries
	And then crush all resistance to your rule.
	You make a desert and then call it peace.

Augustus Caesar sent me to witness
The policy that's already begun
To destroy the mighty Roman Empire.
I see Caesar's outlook is ruinous
And speak the truth, and he cannot stop me.

(*The* GOVERNOR *turns and leaves without a word. The* TOMITANS *follow him.* CONSTANTIA *stays behind with* OVID.)

Constantia. You speak too true for your own good, Ovid.

Ovid. I will not flatter Caesar. I invoke
Him as he should be, not as he falls short.
To me the imperial cult's how he *should*
Be. The best way to criticize Caesar
Is to speak of him as he ought to be,
Not of the awkward man he really is.

(OVID *is seized by an uncontrollable cough.*)

Constantia. You're ill. Again.

Ovid. Always fever, shivers,
Indigestion, insomnia. The snow
Does not suit me. It lies all winter and
The Danube and the sea are frozen hard,
And frosts and bitter cold attack my chest.
My hair tinkles with icicles when I
Bend down my head to write. I love the sun,
Warmth, heat, wine, friends, applause at turns of phrase.
Or rather, I loved those things. Now I've stripped
Myself of comforts, and my soul's naked.
But I am ill. My chest hurts when I breathe.
I've a pain here. I won't live much longer.

Constantia. You emaciated. You bad in lungs.

Ovid. I'm a bit frail, I agree. Don't tell Rome.
Rome brought me up to emulate great men.
Rome gave me noble qualities, but time
Has pocked and blotched my face like a statue.

Ahead's old age, creeping decrepitude.
I will be ready for Death when he creeps
Down our lane like a hooded peasant who's
Swinging a scythe through a swathe of long grass
And takes a wild rose with his sickle blade.
I am at peace with myself and my life.
I had to write, it was a compulsion,
An unstoppable force that made me sit
And scratch and fill wax tablets with verses.
My early work was poor stuff, but it took
Me into great men's salons, so I met
Caesar's daughter. That was my great mistake –
To catch the attention of a great man.
He did not like my work, it challenged him.
Poetry ruined me and brought me here.
And yet I am still a slave to my Muse.
For eight or nine years I have persevered.
I've destroyed much of what I wrote. The rest
Is one long lament, too monotonous
And full of rhetorical artifice
And barbarisms, for I've little chance
To speak in eloquent Latin save with
The Governor and my jailer, and they see
Me as an outcast who's better ignored.
I have no public and have been suppressed.
Yet still I write, for no one can control
My words, which now defeat the *imperium*
That put me in this Jove-foresaken spot.
I never thought, when Rome rose to my words,
I would be buried in a distant land
And lie in a grave in Sarmatian soil
Outside the city wall, far from the gate,
Trampled on by the thundering hooves of
The horses of barbarian bowmen
Who shoot arrows at huddling Getans.

(*He coughs again.*)

Constantia.   You lie down.

(*She helps* OVID *lie down on his mattress.*)

Now I bring my brother. He
Has good herbs for bad lungs in his Temple.

(*Exit* CONSTANTIA.)

SCENE 5

(*Dusk. Outside Ovid's hut the* GUARD *stops throwing dice and stands as the* PRIEST *approaches. The priest enters holding herbs and speaks to* OVID, *who is lying on his back, feeble and frail. He breathes heavily and breaks into a rasping cough.*)

Priest.   You are worse?

Ovid.   Worse.

Priest.   I've brought you herbs.

Ovid.   Too late.
Too late for herbs.

Priest.   The Tomitans decree
That you are exempt from all taxation.
This is your home, Ovid. They want you here.

(OVID *is gasping for breath.*)

Ovid.   It's come too late. I'm not long for the world.
The Underworld, where I, Orpheus, wait.

Priest.   To lead your art back to Roman daylight.

Ovid   (*nodding*). As I look back my writing seems worthless.
I wish I'd written epic, like Virgil.
I loved Erato, not Calliope.
I built my house on rock, like this old shack
On Moesia's rocky coast, this dark waste land,
This barren wilderness – I tried to be
True to my art and never compromised,
Even with Caesar, whom I told the truth,
Stood for the sovereignty of Italy

Against Caesar's imperialist principle.
But now my works seem slight, ephemeral.
I built them on rock but not big enough.
They're a mere hut like this, not a palace.
I wish I'd written epic, like Virgil.

Priest   (*sitting by Ovid*). But you're not dying of despair. You're calm.

Ovid.   Serene, and accepting of all that's been.
Reconciled to the weirdness of my life
And like Apollo gazing at its shape.
I see my life rising like a column
In your Temple, that supports the white roof
And pediment of Roman Literature.
And I sit in the initiate's dark
Chamber below the *telesterion*
In Eleusis, among the Mysteries,
A soul waiting to see Apollo's Light.

(OVID's *breathing is less troubled*.)

Priest   (*quietly*). Let's bring down Apollo's Light. Close your eyes,
Relax, let go your jaw, dispel tension
In your feet, knees, hips, elbows, fingers, neck,
Breathe deeply. Become your immortal eye
Behind your closed eyelids. Unveil your soul
And peer through thick clouds for the dawning sun.
Look for its shafts in the night sky. Open
Your being to its rays. Apollo's beams.
Breathe deeply, let the sun, like a lily,
Float on the dark waters within your mind.
Look for the sunrise, feel the Light's soothing
As it smoothes out the creases in your mist.
Look into all that veils the inner rose.

(OVID's *breathing becomes more peaceful*.)

Ovid.   Aah, aah!

Priest   (*breathing*). You can see the real now?

Ovid.	Bright Light, Aah! I'm flooded with sunshine. I'm standing....
Priest.	Where? Where are you standing?
Ovid.	Sulmo.
Priest.	Sulmo?
Ovid.	My family's villa outside Rome. I Am with my brother Lucius in Light. And now....
Priest.	Now what?
Ovid.	I'm with my new young wife. I'm in the valley. Streams. Vineyards. Mountains. I'm in a field of Light. Orchard. So bright. I'm walking into the Light. Apollo! It's like walking towards the sun, the One! My "I" has blended into boundless Light. I'm leaving the manifold universe, I'm leaving the many to be the One. I am the One, One Light.
Priest.	And your body?
Ovid.	Illusion. Clay. Ephemeral as leaves In autumn when they fall from trees and float On a stream's surface, drifting in the sky. I'm drifting in the sky, bathed in sunlight. I'm drifting, floating back towards the One. The stream includes what is on its surface. I am the One, Ovid drifted on me Like a white swan of immense elegance.
Priest	(softly). You've brought your art from gloom back to daylight. Your metamorphosis is now complete. You've been transformed from darkness into Light. You have become a reaped ear of ripe grain.

(OVID's *breathing is shallow. It stops.*)

Ovid. Ovid.
(*He prays.*)

 May Apollo take him
To the Underworld and look after him,
And shield him from the divine Augustus.

(*Enter* CONSTANTIA.)

Constantia. Ovid?
(*The* PRIEST *shakes his head. She cries out and kneels by* OVID.)

 Ovid!

(*The* GUARD *enters. And then* FLAVIUS. *They stand, transfixed.*)

 I loved you. Why you not
Love me?

(CONSTANTIA *bows her head and kisses his cheek.*)

 He always in Rome, not Tomis.

Priest. He's free now. No more trapped in time and place.
He lived on a level above others
As if he breathed rarefied mountain air,
And saw significance that others missed.
He was intense, single-minded, truthful.
He lived to mirror truth within his verse.

Guard (*to Flavius*). *We're* free now. We'll report to the Governor
And catch the next boat that's leaving for Rome.

SCENE 6

(*A Roman salon. Many people.* COTTA, *Messalla's son, claps his hands.*)

Cotta.   My friends, I have had news from Tomis that
              Ovid has died, and with his death has passed
              The Golden Age of Roman Literature.
              He was the last of a line of poets –
              Catullus, Virgil, Horace, Propertius –
              Who brought glory to Rome. We shall not see
              His like again. Lesser talents now walk
              Where once strode those who perfected the ode,
              The epic, the love elegy – all forms.

              (*Those listening turn back and resume their conversation. They are
              indifferent to the news of Ovid, and their own concerns have taken over.
              IBIS comes forward and addresses the audience.*)

Ibis.   He opposed the *imperium*, his work
              Was bad for Rome and for our world mission.
              He encouraged loose-living, undermined
              Marriage and poked fun at religious myths
              Which Caesar revived for the good of Rome.
              The *imperium* needs marriage and the gods.
              He had to be silenced. What a poet
              Writes is not important. What's important
              Is the spread of Rome's rule throughout the world.
              The Golden Age is when the world is one –
              Britain, Gaul, Judaea, Parthia, Egypt,
              India, China, any land mass that's found,
              All in one vast well-governed territory
              Where citizenship's cosmopolitan
              And, under the aegis of mighty Rome
              Which protects the known world with a hundred
              Bases for legions who with spear and shield
              Hold back barbarians massed on the frontiers,
              All nation-states suppressed for common good.
              Rome bombards barbarians near the Danube
              So Rome's *imperium* lasts a thousand years,
              A good sight longer than a poet's verse.
              My friends, the Golden Age is yet to come.

THE RISE OF
OLIVER CROMWELL

DRAMATIS PERSONAE

MAIN CHARACTERS

Oliver Cromwell
Mrs Elizabeth Cromwell, his wife
Elizabeth, his daughter
Henry Ireton, his brother-in-law
Sir Thomas Fairfax
Lady Fairfax, his wife
Sir Henry Vane
Earl of Manchester
Cornet Joyce
Speaker Sir John Finch
Speaker William Lenthall

Charles I
Henrietta Maria, his wife
Charles II his son
Henry and Elizabeth, his other children
Archbishop Laud
Prince Rupert, his nephew; Marquess of Newcastle: commanders in Charles I's army
Jane Whorwood,his mistress

Menasseh ben Israel, a Jewish Rabbi from Amsterdam
Don Antonio Fernandez de Carvajal, Jewish arms contractor
De Souza, Portuguese Ambassador
Manuel Martinez Dormido, a Jewish merchant
John Thurloe, Cromwell's envoy to Amsterdam

Arthur Hazelrig, John Hampden, John Desborough: Cromwell's relatives
John Pym, Denzil Holles, Edmund Ludlow, Bulstrode Whitelocke: Commons MPs
Col. John Lambert, Major-General Charles Fleetwood, George Monk: Cromwell's Army allies
Col. Whalley, Col. Whichcote, Col. Robert Hammond: Charles I's guarding officers,
Watson, Quartermaster-General of the Army; Hugh Peter, Independent minister
John Bradshaw, President of the court to try Charles I
John Cook, Solicitor for the Commonwealth, and Algernon Sidney, reluctant judge
Sir John Berkeley, John Ashburnham: confidantes of Charles I
Lord Digby, Col. Robert Gosnold, Earl of Lauderdale: Charles I's advisers
Richard Ingoldsby, Thomas Waite, John Downes, Col. Huncks: critics of Charles I's trial

Major Thomas Harrison, Col. Francis Hacker, Col. Thomlinson: Army guarding Charles I
Earl of Southampton, Bowtell: guards of Charles I's coffin
Capt. Thompson, Leveller; Major White, envoy
Col. Isaac Ewer, Sir John Hodgson: Cromwell's army commanders
Andrew Marvell, the poet

MINOR CHARACTERS

Commissioner
Constituent
Shepherds 1 and 2
Girl
Chairman of Committee of Both Kingdoms
Lord Chancellor
Scout, 4 messengers
Aide
Covenanter
3 rabbis
Blind man
Soldier
Leveller
Guards, Army officers, soldiers, Levellers
Army man 1 and 2
Saddle-bearer
Prosecutor
Clerk of the Court
Executioner and assistant (played by Cromwell and Ireton)
Scottish prelate and doctor
Scobell
Lord Mayor
An English Common Man
Clerk to the Council of State
Chairman of the Council of State
Council member

LOCATIONS

London
Cromwell's lodgings in Whitehall and Whitehall Palace
House of Commons, St Stephen's Chapel, Westminster
House of Lords

Palace of Westminster and Painted Chamber
Westminster Hall
Westminster, outside Commons
Room near Westminster Hall
Crown tavern
On board a ship on the Thames
Blue Boar Inn, Holborn
Covent Garden Piazza
Portuguese Ambassador's house
Fairfax's quarters
St James's Palace
Harrison's rooms
London street

Other

Flanders, a public place
Cromwell's houses in Hinchingbrooke, Huntingdon and Ely
Cambridge
Hampton Court
Christ Church, Oxford and elsewhere in Oxford
Nun Appleton House, Yorkshire
Raglan Castle, Wales
Lady Whortlewood's house, Holton
Scotland
Saffron Walden church
Holdenby Hall, Northants.
Kentford Heath
Childerley
Mulheim Synagogue and Amsterdam
Caversham
Windsor Castle
Carisbrooke Castle, Isle of Wight
Scone, Scotland and near Carlisle

Battlefields

Edgehill, York, Knaresborough, Marston Moor, Newbury, Lubenham, Naseby, Bristol, Preston, Knottingley, Burford in Oxon, Worcester
Drogheda and Wexford in Ireland
Dunbar in Scotland

Recommended Interval: at the end of Act 3.

PREFACE TO THE RISE OF OLIVER CROMWELL

This play puts the entire English Civil War on stage and therefore has an epic scope.

I knew very young that I would one day write a play on Cromwell. In 1961, while still at Oxford, I wrote to Jim Campbell, the history tutor at Worcester College, telling him I wanted to write a play on the Spanish Inquisition, to be called *The Holy Brotherhood,* and asking him for a reading list. He replied helpfully. Slowly the Holy Brotherhood turned in my mind into a play about Cromwell. I did not then know it would be a verse play. I wrote a poem on Cromwell while sitting on a boat travelling between Russia and Japan in 1966. It was a 'Moral Letter after Horace' entitled 'An Epistle to an Admirer of Oliver Cromwell', and was a preliminary covering of the ground. It raised questions that puzzled me, and it has taken forty years to discover the answers. I do not think that I had remembered that youthful title *Holy Brotherhood* when I began this play. (I also knew in 1961 that I would own a writing base in a Cornish harbour, and I am writing this overlooking the sea in the harbour I then visualized and later found, or was led to.)

Cromwell is fascinating because he overthrew the monarchy and achieved a revolution in England. I have always been interested in revolutions. I lived under the first Iraqi Revolution, and visited (and wrote poems about) the Russian and Chinese Revolutions. I was caught in the Libyan Revolution of 1969; I had driven to work and had to drive back through it with soldiers firing at every street corner. I researched Cromwell again in 1998, and interrupted this play to write a book on revolutions, *The Secret History of the West.* The reader can trace Cromwell's Rosicrucianism more fully in chapter 2 in that work, and in particular how two little-known letters involving the Mulheim Synagogue make it clear that Cromwell was offered funding for his New Model Army by Rosicrucian Jews in Amsterdam in return for killing Charles I and resettling the Jews in England. Cromwell, in fact, has to be understood in relation to Samuel Hartlib's Invisible College. The title *The Holy Brotherhood* could not be more appropriate. I have preferred *The Rise of Oliver Cromwell* as it focuses on the forces behind his rise rather than on the secret brotherhood of Rosicrucians that surrounded him.

Charles's final speech from the scaffold, relevant parts of which appear in *The Secret History of the West*, shows that he was aware he was being beheaded by international forces; he actually mentioned Alexander the Great and "conquests by forces of world imperialism", showing that he saw himself as the victim of internationalism. I have added Rosicrucian Freemasonry to his drift in the interests of clarity, but the spirit of what he says is unaffected. I have reviewed the evidence for Charles's executioner, and after reflecting on all the accounts have adopted the view that Cromwell, aided by Ireton, personally beheaded Charles: hence his non-appearance anywhere during the execution, and the executioners' disguise.

The Rise of Oliver Cromwell narrates a set of events which have baffled historians. It shows Cromwell's rise to power as being abetted by Dutch Jews. The full deal was that in return for additional funding of the New Model Army, Cromwell would kill Charles I and become King himself and (after a decent lapse of time) then allow the Jews to return to England, from which they had been expelled in 1290. At the same time Cromwell would return the monarchy from the Templars (who controlled the Stuarts) to the Rosicrucian Grand Master of the Priory of Sion, to whom the Dutch Jews were linked. In *The Secret History of the West* can be found details of the letter dated 16 June 1647 from Oliver Cromwell to the Mulheim Synagogue, and their reply on 12 July 1647 ordering Cromwell to allow Charles I to escape as "his recapture will make trial and execution possible". During the summer and autumn of 1653 Cromwell several times proposed an Anglo-Dutch union, and Menasseh ben Israel's visit to Cromwell in 1655 to negotiate the return of the Jews to England is well documented. I have followed this less well-known view of the Civil War, which focuses on Cromwell's links with Rosicrucian Freemasonry. Such an approach gives rise to an entirely new view of the Civil War and of the 17th century, in which Charles I is the victim of an internationalist conspiracy.

The Venetian Ambassador, who is a source for many events of the time, says (see *Venetian State Papers* 1655-6 collected by Edward, Earl of Clarendon, ed. by Scrope and Monkhouse, 1767-86, p160) – and Antonia Fraser in *Cromwell, Our Chief of Men* includes the story – in December 1655, after Menasseh's visit to London, that Cromwell had met Menasseh in his youth while travelling in Flanders. The evidence for this is not conclusive. However, I have adopted this view as it explains how the 1647 letters came to be written, and why Cromwell opposed the Council of State in championing the readmission of Jews into England.

There are contemporary echoes in what Cromwell set out to do. Cromwell has become a topical figure as a result of the constitutional changes in England since 1997. Cromwell abolished the monarchy and then the House of Lords, and attempted to change the English constitution fundamentally by splitting England into 12 administrative regions run by Major-Generals. Britain's "New Labour" government under the neo-Cromwellian Blair has abolished the voting rights of hereditary peers, thus fundamentally changing the composition of the House of Lords, which is now filled with his "yes-men" who rubber-stamp his Commons policies, and thus undermining and threatening the hereditary monarchy. He has split and devolved the United Kingdom into 12 administrative regions or Euro-regions: Scotland, Ireland, Wales, London and 8 English regions which are to have tax-raising powers and to form separate entities in the coming United States of Europe. All modern Cromwells achieve power through foreign help, and there is a parallel between the Dutch-funded Cromwell and the Dutch origin of the Bilderberg Group which backed the Blair government; indeed, the two are linked historically through their Rosicrucianism.

My Cromwell is in league with the Freemasons of the day, shadowy forces outside England who sought to make changes for their own benefit. Today the British Prime Minister operates within a context of similar pressure from the shadowy world government. At one level my study of Cromwell is about the betrayal of England. But of course it is not as simple as that. All revolutions begin with a noble spiritual Utopian vision which somehow goes wrong and degenerates into political and physical dictatorship and military rule. My Cromwell is the archetypal revolutionary, facets of whom can be found later in Washington, Napoleon and Stalin. In trying to preserve the revolutionary vision while compromising his principles due to the requirements of his own corrupting revolutionary government, my Cromwell is a universal revolutionary.

There is a historical basis for every situation and discussion in this play. There is evidence for every scene, and nothing has been invented. The evidence may be little known and the story may shock, but that is a different matter. I have endeavoured to be historically truthful. My derivation of Puritanism from Rosicrucianism is considered. (For a full account see chapter 2 of *The Secret History of the West*.) This is a view of the English Revolution which is faithful to the facts but conveys a new interpretation. T. S. Eliot remarked that the Civil War is still with us, and putting it on stage as a whole is worthwhile, despite its epic proportions (and cost implications). The English Revolution is an important part of our national heritage and it holds lessons that we need to learn today. I have no doubt that one day this play will be staged.

This play could not have been written in prose. Scale and scope of this order can only be tackled in the kind of verse play I revealed in *The Warlords* and *Prince Tudor*: the historical, Sophoclean-Shakespearean sceneryless, unnaturalistic play which uses words to evoke settings, a poetic drama not known since 1640 (or possibly Dryden's *All for Love*, 1677). Shakespeare characterized this drama in his Prologue to *King Henry the Fifth*:

> "Can this cockpit hold
> The vasty fields of France? Or may we cram
> Within this wooden O the very casques
> That did affright the air at Agincourt?
> O, pardon! since a crooked figure may
> Attest in little place a million;
> And let us, ciphers to this great accompt,
> On your imaginary forces work.
> Suppose within the girdle of these walls
> Are now confin'd two mighty monarchies,
> Whose high upreared and abutting fronts
> The perilous narrow ocean parts asunder.
> Piece out our imperfections with your thoughts:
> Into a thousand parts divide one man,
> And make imaginary *puissance*;

Think, when we talk of horses, that you see them
Printing their proud hoofs i' th' receiving earth;
For 'tis your thoughts that now must deck our kings."

So it is with the battlefields and armies in conflict in Cromwell's time in this play. Whereas *The Warlords* contained a number of metres, I have stuck to blank verse in this play just as I have in *Ovid Banished*.

I regard myself as the only man of letters, and therefore dramatist, operating today to have a full appreciation of the nature of the world government we are moving towards, which I have written about extensively elsewhere. I have also written about Universalism elsewhere. Besides being sensitive to the impact of the world government on national life and heroes like Cromwell who live by the Light, I have again adopted Universalism's own fluid method of narrative, which involves a structure of many dynamic scenes, some of which can be quite short, and an eye for the universality of the central figure. Montgomery, Prince Tudor and Ovid are all in a sense, Everyman. They could just as easily be Arjuna unsure whether it is right to kill his enemies in a coming battle in the *Bhagavad-gita*; Henry V regarding his State as a garden; and Solzhenitsyn being deported by the KGB-ruled USSR. Cromwell is also many of the revolutionaries who have conducted revolutions in different parts of the world (for example Gaddafi in Libya), but he is first and foremost an attitude found in British life today, which shows no respect for our history and tradition and believes that change is a good thing for its own sake. Cromwell is the archetypal moderniser.

27 October 2000; revised 17 January, 2 February 2006

PROLOGUE

(1662. London. Enter ARCHBISHOP JUXON, *who is aged eighty.)*

Juxon.

I'm Archbishop of Canterbury now
And I have reconstructed for the King
How Charles the First, his father, who gave me
This ring on the scaffold, a saintly man,
Could be beheaded – toppled like an oak
By a woodman's axe – on the warped orders
Of monstrous Cromwell. I have come up with
Answers that disturb me. Cromwell usurped
The royal power through a plot, having received
Financial backing from once Spanish Jews
Living in Amsterdam, who in return
Ordered that the King should be killed – most foul,
Sacrilegious treason and hewing of
The ancient, many-ringed hereditary
Lineage of England's State. I have found out
Cromwell did not act for himself alone
But on behalf of a foreign power that
Funded his new Model Army to end
The Stuart line in dark conspiracy
With Devil-worshipping Rosicrucians,
Who hid within Bacon's Freemasonry.
I have investigated Bacon's role
And I am not convinced that Bacon died
In 1626. I see his hand
In the events that destroyed Charles the First.
He sought to revive Solomon's Temple
As a symbol of internationalists.

I see him as head of a globalist
Conspiracy to reduce nationhood
And hand our England to Europe's Jewry
So our land passed under a foreign power –
The Jews of Holland who made war on us.
Thank heaven for the Restoration, which saved
Our nationhood, our Englishness, our land.

(JUXON kisses the ring.)
Which was guarded by this most holy ring.

ACT ONE

SCENE 1

(*1627. Flanders. A public place.* MENASSEH BEN ISRAEL, *holding two books, meets* DON ANTONIO FERNANDEZ DE CARVAJAL, *who sees the books and approaches.*)

Menasseh.   What is your sign?

Carvajal.   The Rosy Cross.

Menasseh.   Brother.

(*They shake hands.*)

You're Carvajal?

Carvajal.   I am. You're Menasseh?

Menasseh.   Yes, come from Amsterdam.

Carvajal.   Welcome, brother.
Jews are more welcome here in Flanders than
In my London, where I have to pretend
I'm Christian. Our synagogue's "an exchange".
Jews are no more welcome than when Edward
The First expelled them in 1290. We

	Need a brave champion. For a Rabbi
	You look extremely young.
Menasseh.	I'm twenty-three,
	And old enough to do the Priory's work.
	And teach the Kabbalah.
Carvajal.	And I have come
	From Robert Fludd to show you a new star
	Who we've identified as the leader
	Who'll bring the expelled Jews back to England.
	One day he should be in Amsterdam's pay.
Menasseh.	He's travelled to Flanders with you?
Carvajal.	No, with
	A friend at Cambridge University,
	Samuel Hartlib, who's watching him for me.
	He knows of your interest and is your link.
	He's nursing him into a place of power.
Menasseh.	What's the Messiah's name?
Carvajal.	Cromwell.
Menasseh.	The Jews
	Of Amsterdam, *Marranos* who have fled
	Where Jewry's allowed, await a Messiah
	Who'll lead them as into an overgrown
	Walled garden which they'll help him weed and clear,
	And look to England as the Promised Land,
	A new Paradise full of bee-hummed flowers,
	As a new Israel they will re-enter.
	They have waited three centuries to return.
Carvajal.	We will not disappoint them. The new King....?
Menasseh.	Must be dealt with. The Stuart line must go.
	They're Templars, and the Priory of Sion
	In the person of their wise Grand Master,
	Robert Fludd, will restore the lost kingdom

Of Jerusalem, the throne of our King.
Can Cromwell be King of Jerusalem
And lead a new world empire from England?

Carvajal.   That's how I see it if we control him.
Hartlib's working on him, and shaping him.
But look, they're coming. Shake hands on our pact.
Rosicrucian Freemasons are at one
With Kabbalistic Jews and Puritans.

(*They shake hands.*)

Menasseh.   And all are interchangeable – behind
All is Bacon's universal vision.
Carvajal. I must become an invisible spy.

(*Exit* CARVAJAL. *Enter* HARTLIB *and* CROMWELL. *Cromwell is about 28.
Hartlib greets* MENASSEH, *whom Cromwell acknowledges with a nod.
Hartlib is a Polish Jew who speaks with a German accent.*)

Hartlib.   Menasseh ben Israel of Amsterdam?
I've heard so much about your Kabbalah.
I want to talk philosophy with you,
But first I must present you to my friend
And inspiration, Oliver Cromwell.

Cromwell.   I am a Calvinist. I follow both
My schoolmaster and my Cambridge Master.
And though I believe in God's Chosen Ones,
The Elect who will have the Promised Land,
I believe God's Chosen include the Jews.
I am familiar with Jewish thinking
But believe there are two Kabbalahs – one
Which flows down from Moses, the patriarch,
A brimming brook which gushes downhill, clear,
Which is good; and the evil Kabbalah
Which branches off into a brackish ditch,
Whose bottom's full of past years' sodden leaves,
Writings that should not foul its limpid course,
In which the sacred tradition has been
Corrupted by the rabbis – no offence –

And their Talmudic interpretations
Just as the Catholic Church has corrupted
The purity of the one *Bible* source
With heretical interpretations.
I trust you keep the pure stream bubbling
And don't pollute it with human foulness?

Menasseh.   Very much so. I dig for the pure spring –

Cromwell.   Samuel's with Bacon and Comenius and
Does not believe in predestination.
But I have seen a course in which the Jews
Are destined – predestined, I hold – to be
Converted to Christianity when
The Papacy is overthrown. All my
Bible-reading makes me appreciate
The Jews as Chosen People, the Elect.
Holland's the place where churches are for saints
By dykes of Moses' pellucid spirit.
Protestant since the Netherlands' revolt
Against Spain and now called the United
Provinces, she's welcomed exiles who tired
Of waiting for reform of England's Church.
Separatists settled there to escape
Persecution some years ago, and from
Among them came the *Speedwell* pilgrims who
Joined the *Mayflower* Separatists to sail
To the New World. We must look to Holland.

Menasseh.   You speak like one who leads Gentiles and Jews.

Cromwell.   The Jews who fled from Spain are enemies
Of the Pope, who is the Calvinists' foe.
We can make common cause against his Rome.

Carvajal   (*to Cromwell*). Tell me, how many Jews live in Flanders?

(CROMWELL *senses that* HARTLIB *wants to talk to* MENASSEH.)

Cromwell.   I have to collect letters from a church.
I will see you at our rest-house, Samuel.

I'll leave you to discuss the Kabbalah.
Glad to have met you. Praise the Lord, my friends.

(*Exit* CROMWELL.)

Menasseh.   Tell me about this fiery Calvinist.

Hartlib.   He is a Unitarian, he sees
God as One, not a Catholic Trinity,
And he denies Christ had divinity.
His outlook's Deistic Freemasonry.
Of all my English friends he is the most
Visionary and ambitious. When a boy
He dreamed he would be King and I believe
That one day he'll be ruler of England.
He's strong enough, he has a woodman's gait.
He'll hunt prey like a hawk, swoop from a height.
He is your man. He has Jewish cousins:
His uncle's wife's first husband was the Jew
Palavicino who funded the Dutch
Rebels. They have their own lands in Holland.
He's come here to Flanders and I will go
On to Elbing alone, where Andreae
Patiently awaits me, while he returns
To England, tailed by discreet Carvajal.
Half of him wishes to seek employment
As a mercenary over here. He has
A military aptitude of great scope.

Menasseh.   And you have urged him into politics?
He will be a Member of Parliament?

Hartlib.   His mind's made up, he has to tell his wife.

Menasseh.   Pull away from him now and observe him
From a distance as a sparrowhawk floats
Eye-fixed on a vole in a green crop-field.
Stay on the wind but don't lose sight of him
Until I tell you to swoop for the kill.
Your quarry must go into Parliament
Before you pounce, snatch him in your talons

	And carry him to Rosy-Cross kingdom.
Hartlib.	He sees me as a Puritan, no more, Like others in my circle – John Milton. He does not know our Rosicrucian cause, That Bacon, Fludd, Maier and Andreae Brought paradise to the Palatinate Of Frederick the Fifth for a brief decade And that exiled survivors have hidden, Huddled in my circle of Puritans, Funded by Frederick and his English Queen, Disguised as black-clad English Israelites –
Menasseh.	As invisible as Dutch *Marranos*. Mmm. You have done well, and you have earned this. Thank you from all the Jews of Amsterdam.
	(MENASSEH *discreetly gives* HARTLIB *a bag of money, which he takes furtively.*)
Hartlib.	I've brought him here for the cause, not for gold. But this is very welcome. I thank you.

SCENE 2

(*1627. Hinchingbrooke.* OLIVER CROMWELL, *aged 28, and his wife* ELIZABETH.)

Cromwell.	The old family seat of the Cromwells, Sold to the Montagu family! This Nunnery my ancestor Thomas gave My great-grandfather after he'd dissolved And confiscated all the monasteries As King Henry the Eighth's chief minister Before he was beheaded on Tower Green On the command of the ungrateful King. For three generations we have lived here. My father and uncle welcomed King James Here on his progress to ascend the throne. We entertained him more times, but that day

I well remember standing as a boy –
The King sat there. I was just four and I
Bloodied the nose of Prince Charles Stuart, who
Was two years old. And where have those years gone?
And now this place of childhood safety – sold!
We gentry are in terminal decline.

Elizabeth.   Your father entertained the King, but you
Have nothing good to say about him now.

Cromwell.   No, he's a secret Catholic who likes Spain.
He went to Spain with Buckingham to woo
Philip the Third's daughter, but left when told
He should become a Roman Catholic,
Then pressed his father for war with Spain, then
Married the French King's Catholic sister,
Henrietta Maria. The Spanish war's
Turned out to be a thundering failure.
He has no appetite to defeat Spain.
I don't trust him. I don't trust Buckingham.
He ought to be impeached. And what's happened?
The King's dissolved Parliament to prevent
Impeachment! And now judges have declared
His act illegal, what's he gone and done?
He's sacked the Chief Justice! He's a tyrant!
He's put himself above the rule of law.
And now he's stuck for funds he's forced a loan –
He'll tax us gentry into deep decline.
Under this King, our State's like a garden
That's been put into shade by an oak-tree
Whose massive branches block the sunlight and
Prevent plants from growing. It must be felled.
This home of my uncle, Sir Oliver,
And his Dutch second wife Anne Hooftman – sold!
Sold to the Montagus because of tax.

Elizabeth.   I think your uncle spent his money on
Carousing with the King, giving him gifts –
A gold cup, horses, hounds and numerous hawks –

Cromwell.   And that bow window in the dining-room.

And what good did it do him? He carried
A herald's banner at the King's funeral!
Hospitality and tax did for him.
The King's guesting and tax bankrupted him!
I've had a thought.

Elizabeth.   Not one of your dark thoughts?

Cromwell.   I am in conflict, perpetual struggle,
I do admit. No, this one is a glimpse
Of Providence's path I should follow.
It's an idea Samuel Hartlib gave me.
I should be a Member of Parliament.
(*Excitedly.*) Think, I could represent Huntingdon, and
Oppose the King's taxation and Catholic
Manoeuvrings as the two men I respect
Most taught me – Doctor Beard of Huntingdon
Grammar School and Doctor Ward, Master of
My Cambridge college, both Calvinists who
Hold that men's sins are punished here on earth
While God guides the Elect through the spirit.
The English are now God's chosen people.
The Jews, who are among God's chosen ones,
Will want to join the English Elect who
Are now preferred by God despite their King!

Elizabeth.   Oppose the King's taxation. Is that wise?

SCENE 3

(*March 1628.* CROMWELL *in Parliament, where* CHARLES I *and* BUCKINGHAM *are seated.*)

Speaker.   The member for Borough of Huntingdon.

Cromwell.   I speak from personal experience.
Last year, Mr Speaker, due to the King
Six of my relatives were in prison
For not subscribing to the King's forced loan.
I know about the King's justice. It stinks.

And now I attack the King's rich bishops,
Who get between all Christians and their God.
Christians should have direct contact with God
Through prayer. The clergy should inspire lay folk
By preaching. Preachers bring men to the Light.
Bishops' rituals and authority are
In darkness, like the Bishop of Ely.
I support itinerant Protestant
Preachers from my pocket. Bishops line theirs.

Charles.   Who is that fiery Puritan?

Buckingham.   Cromwell.

Charles.   He speaks as if he's just stormed a pulpit.

Buckingham.   You will be hearing a lot from him, sir.
He's been appointed to a committee
To investigate all complaints against
The Bishop of Ely, whom he detests.

SCENE 4

(*March 1629. Parliament.* CHARLES I *is speaking. The Speaker, who is* SIR JOHN FINCH,
DENZIL HOLLES, BENJAMIN VALENTINE *and others, including* CROMWELL. *Charles is
addressing Parliament.*)

Charles   (*aside*). These MPs swarm like new-hatched flying ants.
I have a cauldron of scalding water
To throw on the lot of them, wipe them out.
(*Aloud.*) I won't tolerate your criticisms.
Ever since the Duke of Buckingham was
Assassinated in January, you've
Objected to "popish practices" in
My churches and my levies of tonnage
And poundage. I will govern without you.
I'll adjourn Parliament and rule alone.

(*There is uproar.*)

Speaker.	Order. Order.
	(*The* SPEAKER *is held down in his chair by* DENZIL HOLLES *and* BENJAMIN VALENTINE.)
Speaker.	Let me rise to adjourn. You're holding me down. I am the Speaker.
Holles.	God's wounds, you shall sit till we please to rise.
Cromwell.	Till Sir John Eliot's resolution Condemning popery is passed. Sit down While we read the resolution aloud.
Charles.	Parliamentary government's at an end. I have dissolved Parliament. You, go now. I shall rule without calling Parliament. Go back to your fields, forget Parliament.
	(*There is renewed uproar.* CROMWELL *speaks to his neighbour.*)
Cromwell.	I'll return to my fields at Huntingdon, But I have felt the nation's pulse and I Have heard it quicken towards liberty.

SCENE 5

(*Late 1628. Cromwell's house in Huntingdon.* CROMWELL *is on his knees, speaking in half-sobs.*)

Cromwell.	Oh God, I am not worthy. I'm worthless. I am of no more worth than a poor worm. I'm ruled by self, vanity and badness. I struggle against my inferior self. My mind's perplexed, it damages my health. I feel tense from inner self-division. My spiritual and psychological Struggle has coiled me like an unwound watch. I pray to you for Light but know darkness.

I speak in Parliament but feel I am
A miserable sinner, chief of sinners.
I cry out to you from this darkness. Lord!
Please enter me and fill me with your Light

(*There is a silence.*)

Ahhh! An explosion of Light, like a sun!
I'm filled with Light, and now I know for sure,
I'm one of God's Chosen, not a sinner.
I have a task, a destiny to work.
Providence has chosen me for its will.

(*Enter* HARTLIB.)

Hartlib.   Oliver. Oliver. Are you all right?

Cromwell.   I lived in and loved darkness, hated light.
The hammer and fire beat me into shape.
I was the chief of sinners. My soul is
With the Congregation of the First-born.
He gave me to see light in His Light, and
I am now one of God's Chosen, the few
Who have been saved by contact with the Light.
I've opened to sudden providences
And am a blunt instrument in the hands
Of a higher power. I must discover
The hidden purpose behind events or
What the mind of God is in all that chain
Of Providence. So I'll suspend judgement
And allow events to develop to
Get more light from the Light's dispensations.

SCENE 6

(*1631. Cromwell's house in Huntingdon. A* COMMISSIONER *knocks on* CROMWELL's *door.* ELIZABETH *answers.*)

Commissioner.   Are you the wife of Oliver Cromwell?

Elizabeth.	I am.
Commissioner.	I'd like to see your husband, please.
Elizabeth.	He's not here.
Commissioner.	Will I find him at St Ives?

(ELIZABETH *is silent*.)

You're both moving there. As tenant farmers,
Having sold this freehold Huntingdon house.
You will be farming cattle and chickens.

Elizabeth.	Who are you?
Commissioner.	A commissioner for fines.
Elizabeth.	Fines? For what?
Commissioner.	Six years ago your husband
Did not attend the King's coronation –

(*Enter* CROMWELL.)

Cromwell.	So what?
Commissioner.	Are you Oliver Cromwell, sir?
Cromwell.	I am. So what if I did not attend
King Charles' coronation? Not many did.
Commissioner.	Any freeholder whose estate was worth
More than forty pounds a year had to be
At the coronation and be knighted –
Cromwell.	An expensive honour I'll do without –
Commissioner.	Or be fined, and if blacklisting's ignored
Summoned before the Court of Exchequer
For contempt. You declined to make payment.

Cromwell.	I've ceased to be a freeholder –

Commissioner.	I know. You're leaving Huntingdon for St Ives, where You'll be a *tenant* farmer. Six years back You were a *freeholder*, you have a debt. I will now calculate how much you owe. Pay up and bend to the royal will, or Face the consequences before the Court.

Cromwell.	You may be a royal commissioner But unless you get out of my house now I'll break every bone in your frail body.

(*Exit the* COMMISSIONER, *nervously. He loiters by the door.*)

Elizabeth.	You must not threaten a commissioner. He can have the Court put you in prison. You must pay the fine.

Cromwell.	We can't afford it.

Elizabeth.	The family will pay it for us and We'll pay them back. Tell him before he goes.

Cromwell.	The King's rooking us with taxes and fines. We must stand up to him, not bow our knee.

Elizabeth.	When the wind blows it's best the reed should bend. When the wind drops, the reed straightens again.

Cromwell.	When the gale blows the oak tosses its head. When the gale stops the oak is undamaged.

(CROMWELL *thinks.*)

You're right.

(CROMWELL *calls in a soothing, pleasant voice.*)

Commissioner. Commissioner!

SCENE 7

(1638. London. Hartlib's lodgings. HARLIB *and* CROMWELL.)

Cromwell.   What are these books? *The Chemical Wedding*
                        Of Christian Rosenkreuz by Andreae.
                        And Robert Fludd's *Brief Apology for*
                        The Fraternity of the Rosy Cross.

Hartlib.   They've been sent to me by some friends of mine
                        Who live in Holland, on the Continent.
                        I thought you'd like to see them as they are
                        Similar to the Puritan vision.
                        They're Rosicrucian books, read at the guilds
                        Of Robert Fludd, who claimed he introduced
                        Rosicrucianism from Germany
                        To England as Rose-Cross Freemasonry.
                        Bacon and Fludd have turned their occult group
                        Into Rosicrucian Freemasonry
                        To oppose all Templar Freemasonry,
                        That of King James and of his son, the King

Cromwell.   Was the Rosicrucian Order founded
                        From Germany as Fludd claimed? Or before?

Hartlib.   The Rosicrucian Order was founded
                        In Egypt by Pharaoh Thothmes the Third
                        In the fifteenth century before Christ.
                        Its vision passed into Gnosticism.
                        It survived the pagan religions and
                        The rise of Christianity, and in
                        The ninth century Charlemagne established
                        A Rosicrucian lodge in Toulouse, where
                        Raymond, Count of Toulouse, was Grand Master.
                        A second French lodge rose in 898.
                        In 1000 heretical Catholic
                        Monks founded a Rosicrucian college
                        That flourished in secret among masons
                        Who built Gothic cathedrals' rose-windows.
                        The Priory of Sion's first Grand Master,

Jean de Gisors, founded the Rose-Croix with
A red cross as its emblem at the end
Of the twelfth century. The Rosicrucian
Order's Grand Masters included Dante,
Who wrote of Heaven's sempiternal rose;
Wolsey, first dissolver of monasteries;
Agrippa; Paracelsus; Dee; Bruno;
And Bacon, who formed Knights of the Helmet
Under Athena (who brandished a spear
And was called "*Engespallos*", "Spear-shaker" –
Bacon's arms show a spear, his friend de Vere
Was painted with a rose behind his ear)
And the Fra Rosi Crosse Society
Which existed by 1586.
It's rumoured that Andreae is Bacon.
His coat of arms is the St Albans arms.
It's possible that Bacon's still alive,
Now under Andreae's identity.
The Rosy-Cross tradition can be read
With profit, for it leads to Dante's rose.
We Rosicrucians hold that Heaven on earth's
Attainable, as Robert Fludd maintained.

Cromwell. I am perplexed, I seek for clarity.
There's a good Rosicrucian tradition
And one that's corrupted, turned secular,
Which honours Satan as bright Lucifer.

Hartlib. Some Rosicrucians see the Christian cross
And Rosicrucian rose that's twined round it
As a Christian-Dionysian union
That affirms a dualistic universe
And proclaims that Satan has just the same
Redemptive qualities as Jesus Christ
As the Demiurge who made our flawed world.
The Rose-Croix or snake-cross is the red snake
Of Satan, which blasphemes against Christ's cross.
Some Rosicrucians are firm dualists.

Cromwell. God, Christ. Satan. I am confused. What's right
Seems wrong, what wrong right. Unitarians,

Calvinists, First-born Congregationalists
And Puritans are all *against* Satan,
Yet Rosicrucian Freemasonry sees
Him as Lucifer, a bright star, as good.

Hartlib.   Lucifer is the bringer of the Light.

Cromwell.   No. I opened to the pure Light of God.

Hartlib.   No,the Light of the Rosy Cross, of dawn,
The universal Light of *Aurora*,
The Light of Lucifer's Freemasonry.

Cromwell.   No, I opened to the Light of the Lord.
(*Pause.*) I'm tempted to turn my back on Gothic
Rosicrucianism for the New World.
There everything's simple. Puritans see
The purity of the One Light in men
And not the opposites of the red cross.

Hartlib.   The Rosicrucian vision's the pure one.
It's the Pope and his Anglican ally
Who have confused what was once pure as Light.

Cromwell.   The Pope's teaching's impure, I do agree.
If you are right, the Puritan vision
Is Rosy Cross, and Lucifer is Christ.

(HARTLIB *looks at him for a long while.* CROMWELL *turns away in distress.*)

SCENE 8

(*1638. Cromwell's house at Ely.* ELIZABETH *and* CROMWELL.)

Elizabeth.   You've been deep in thought all day, Oliver.

Cromwell.   I've been thinking of our life in England,
The bad harvests and the King's dreadful laws –
Ship money to pay for the Royal Navy,

The new liturgy imposed on Scotland –
And though we've inherited my uncle's
Ely estate worth five hundred a year,
I look at the New World and long to go –

Elizabeth.   You want to emigrate when we have this?
You are a man of property and wealth.

Cromwell.   This is no country for Puritans, now.
The Puritan New World is full of hope.
The New Providence Company, begun
By the King's opponents, our relatives –
Like the Massachusetts Bay Company –
Has its own godly kingdom. The Elect
Can only look across the Atlantic
With amazement. Dearest Elizabeth,
Will you turn your back on English turmoil
And emigrate with me to the New World?
Will you do that?

Elizabeth   (*quietly*).   It's your spiritual state
Of mind, your inner crisis, your turmoil –
And confusion, disorder, that calls you.
The Light's directing you to remain here,
I'm sure of it, but I will follow you.
You belong in Ely, your destiny
Is here in England, not in the New World.
But Providence must send you that message.

Cromwell.   You'll go with me?

Elizabeth.   To the ends of the earth,
Even though I know your mission is here.

SCENE 9

(*1638. A ship lying in the Thames.* ATHUR HASELRIG *and* JOHN HAMPDEN, *Cromwell's relatives, stand with* CROMWELL *and his* WIFE.)

604

Hampden.	Come aboard. Don't hesitate, the New World's Better than this place of persecution.
Haselrig.	He should know, having been sent to prison For refusing to pay twenty shillings In ship money.
Hampden.	There's no tyranny there.
Cromwell.	It's a big step for me to turn my back On our house at Ely, on our estate. It's a bigger step for Elizabeth. She's happy in England. Though the Elect Have a Light-filled community across The ocean, I shall miss the timber-frames And the flat, isolated Fens I love.
Haselrig.	There is no time for backsliding. You've made Your decision to join the Elect. Forget Your doubts and look forward to the New World.

(*There is a silence.*)

Cromwell.	I entrust my soul to great Providence.

(*Enter the* CAPTAIN.)

Captain.	You three aren't sailing on this boat.
Haselrig.	Why not?
Captain.	The Council's not permitted you to leave.
Hamden.	The Council!
Haselrig.	Our opponents!
Cromwell.	Providence Has given me an answer. Disembark. (*To Elizabeth.*) We're walking down that gangplank and we're not Returning. We are staying in England.

605

You're right. Providence wants me to stay here.

SCENE 10

(1641. King Charles I's court. CHARLES *and* ARCHBISHOP LAUD.*)*

Charles.   I need to improve the English navy.
Parliament would not allow me the funds
To run the country as it should be run.
I would not borrow money from Jewish
Money-changers – money-lenders – to build
Up the navy. So I've imposed my own
Taxes, ship money, to update the fleet.
And I have built the *Sovereign of the Seas,*
England's first hundred-gun battleship, which
Will lay the foundations for naval power.
It has cost more than sixty thousand pounds.
I've governed without money, without Jews,
By levying my taxes. I don't need
Parliament. I despise all Parliaments.
I swat MPs like whining, biting gnats.

Laud.   Your Majesty, we are short of money.
The Scottish war is getting out of hand.
You need the support of your Parliament
Against the Scots. You need more revenue.
They must accept Anglican liturgy.
You must summon a new Parliament now.

Charles.   I've ruled eleven years without Parliament.
Strafford's coming with an Irish army.
He'll crush the Scots, and the English as well.

Laud.   Strafford wants you to summon Parliament
To raise money for a war with Scotland.

(There is a silence.)

Charles.   Strafford and Laud, both speaking with one voice.

Very well, summon a new Parliament.

SCENE 11

(*June 1641. Parliament.* CROMWELL *is speaking.*)

Cromwell.   Mr Speaker, what a year it has been!
What have we men of England just endured!
Parliament opposed renewing the war.
Pym called for a redress of grievances.
The King dissolved Parliament and was soon
Collecting ship money against the Scots.
We had the injustice of John Lilburne,
Who was whipped for distributing pamphlets,
Stood in a pillory, fined, imprisoned.
What way is that to run a country? Then
Scots crossed the border and defeated us,
And the Irish situation got worse
With Papists firmly entrenched in Dublin
And Strafford raising a Popish army.
Archbishop Laud and Strafford were impeached
And Strafford's been beheaded in the Tower,
Where Laud now moulders. And all England asks,
When not complaining of the monarchy,
How can such things happen without Members
Of Parliament meeting to oppose them?
The King must agree Parliament cannot
Be dissolved without Parliament's consent.

(*Cries of "Hear, hear".*)

And now the King is to visit Scotland.
We on this side of the House ask him: Why?
Why is his long journey necessary?
What is the occasion of his journey?
Is it to enlist Scots' support against
Parliament? And will he agree to full
Establishment of Presbyterianism?
If so, we oppose his journey, which is

Treasonous against the English people.

(LORD DIGBY *and* HAMPDEN *are near the front of the stage.*)

Digby.   Who is that untidy, slovenly man?

Hampden.   If (God forbid) we breach with the King he'll
                Be one of the greatest men in England.

                (CROMWELL *approaches* HAMPDEN.)

Cromwell.   Our Masonic Lodge meets at a tavern
                Called Crown. The Lodge is for the newly rich,
                The *élite* of Rosicrucian gentry.
                You should join us. The conversation's good.

SCENE 12

(*1641. London. The Crown, a tavern.* HARTLIB *and* CROMWELL, HAMPDEN *and others.*
Hartlib addresses all.)

Hartlib.   The way to power is through a brotherhood
                That meets secretly behind closed doors and
                Foments rebellion no one hears about.
                Rosicrucianism is an occult
                Grouping that by its very nature can't
                Have a great following. Its noble aim
                Is to see what is hidden in Nature,
                Reality, the One. Let's widen it
                Within the Freemasonry Bacon taught,
                Which he founded. Before Bacon's time men
                Believed the King's subjects should never search
                Into the gifts from God to kings. Bacon's
                Freemasonry made men free to reveal
                The secrets which God concealed in Nature.
                The Grand Architect of the universe
                Used his All-Seeing eye to create and
                Conceal his wisdom in the universe,
                And Bacon's lodge in 1586,

Based in London's Priory of St John of
Jerusalem, had two degrees, the Knights
Of the Helmet (named after Athena)
And the Fra Rosi Crosse Society.
(It's said he was the first Rosicrucian.)
He planned more degrees: Sons of Solomon;
The Society of Solomon's House.
Bacon concealed that his overt Order
Was in reality given to study,
A covert fraternity of learning
To seek hidden universal knowledge.
Freemasonry's established under Fludd,
Who has prepared Masonic workingmen
Guilds in England for Rosicrucian ends.
They're opposed to Spain and the Catholic Church,
Invisible circles of Puritans.

(HARTLIB *turns aside to* CROMWELL, *who speaks to him.*)

Cromwell   (*musing*). The way to power is through a brotherhood....
A Holy Brotherhood opposed to Spain
And the Catholic Church in Ireland and here,
A brotherhood whose aims are Puritan.
It needs organizing into degrees.
I'll do this, inserting the Rosy Cross,
So Rosicrucianism hides within,
Like a cuckoo nesting in a thicket,
A spreading network of secret lodges
Under cover of which we can combat
The King and subvert his tyrannous rule.
It won't be hard to do this – Andreae's
Imported German Rosicrucians here –
So we will elevate ourselves to power.

Hartlib.   I'm a metaphysical Freemason,
As a philosopher I look back to
The mystical idea that fed the Knights
Templar, Priory of Sion and Bacon.
You will secularise Freemasonry,
As a political reformer you
Look back to Cecil's imperialism,

Secret societies and confusion.
I'm metaphysical, you're secular.
I philosophise, you improve structures.
I conceptualise. You implement.

SCENE 13

(1 November 1641. Parliament, meeting in St Stephen's Chapel, Westminster. CROMWELL, PYM, LORD DIGBY and OTHERS.)

Cromwell. The Irish have risen and massacred
Fifty thousand English settlers. They act
In a barbarous manner, roasting alive
And eating men, pushing out leaking boats
Filled with women who drown, butchering small
Children, raping young girls and forcing all
Protestants to listen to their dark Mass.
The King is linked to the Irish Catholics.
A year ago he conspired to employ
Irish troops against his English subjects,
In Strafford's treasonous ill-fated plot.
Can such a man be trusted to suppress
The Irish rising? We have in our hands
The Grand Remonstrance which lists grievances
Against the King. Its two hundred clauses
Include one clause that demands that the King's
Choice of advisers must be approved by
Parliament. I give way.

Lord Digby.   That's a denial
Of the King's ancient rights.

Cromwell.   No, it isn't.
The King has no ancient right except what
Parliament has allowed him in the past.
And now he can't be trusted to subdue
The Irish, and may seek a new Strafford.
He should give up control of the Army.
He wants to retain bishops in the Church.

It's only prudent to ensure that his
Advisers are approved by Parliament.
I want the text of the Grand Remonstrance
To be published so the country can judge
For itself if the King's powers should be checked.

SCENE 14

(22 November 1641. Parliament meeting in St Stephen's Chapel. CROMWELL, PYM *and* OTHERS. *Mr* SPEAKER *Lenthall addresses the chamber.)*

Speaker.   Since the first medieval Parliament
It's been our practice to sit in daylight
And adjourn as soon as dusk starts to fall.
It's getting dark.

Cromwell   *(calling out).*   More candles! More candles!

(CROMWELL turns and speaks to PYM.)

The young Members are leaving for the town.
The older of us are thinking of bed.
We've got our chance. Let's force a vote at once
And get the Grand Remonstrance motion passed
While more candles are brought.

Pym.   We'll do just that.
(Calling out.) Vote! Vote! Vote! Vote!

Cromwell   *(to Pym).*   If this motion's not passed
And if we radicals don't beat the King,
I'll sell my lands and leave England for good.
The King's powers must be checked. All honest men
Must think the same, and I know many do.

SCENE 15

(4 January 1642. Parliament, meeting in St Stephen's Chapel. CROMWELL and OTHERS.)

Cromwell.   The King has promised reform of the Church
And he'll investigate the presence of
Bishops in the Lords, but he won't give up
His "natural liberty" to choose his own
Advisers, though we carried the motion
To pass the Grand Remonstrance. We suspect
The King will renege on the agreement
And raise an army against Parliament.
He fears we will impeach his Catholic Queen.
We fear he will use force against MPs.

(There is a commotion. Enter KING CHARLES with his nephew, the elector PALATINE. He sits in his chair, looking round. Mr Speaker LENTHALL bows and indicates by a gesture that he may speak.)

Charles   *(aside).* What squawking ducks flock round this tub of corn.
(Aloud.) I do not accept your Grand Remonstrance.
I have asked the Attorney General
To impeach five members for treason. I
Have four hundred men outside this building.
I seek the arrest of five ringleaders
Who'd remove my royal authority
By ending my control of the Army
And overthrow the monarchy: John Pym,
Hampden, Haselrig, Holles and Strode. I
Seek some sign of these absent Members, who,
No doubt forewarned, have fled like scared mallards.

Speaker.   May it pleasure your Majesty, I have
Neither eyes to see nor tongue to speak in
This place but as the House, whose servant I
Am here, is pleased to direct me.

Charles.   Then I
Shall depart from Parliament and London.
Negotiations will continue with

Parliament for the surrender of their
Five treasonous republican Members.

(*Exit the* KING.)

Cromwell.   The battle with the King has now commenced.

ACT TWO

SCENE 1

(*1642. The Crown, a tavern.* CROMWELL *and his Rosicrucian Masonic lodge.* CARVAJAL *and* HARTLIB *are present.*)

Hartlib   (*to Cromwell*). Call them to order now and state their task.

Cromwell.   Here at our Rosicrucian Masonic
Lodge at this tavern called the Crown, let us
Explore tonight how we regard the Crown.
Should it be absolute or should we hold
It accountable to all our people?
The Crown is a symbol of unity.
It has become a mark of tyranny.
What should be done to curtail the Crown's power?
Curtail the King and you curtail the Crown.
Now talk among yourselves, and later I –

(MENASSEH *has entered.* CROMWELL *half-recognises him and stops abruptly.* CARVAJAL *fades into the background, trying to be invisible.*)

Menasseh.   You look as if you have just seen a ghost.

Cromwell   (*quietly*). I've thought of you many times since Flanders.

(FAIRFAX *approaches.*)

Fairfax.   I know you. I met you in Amsterdam.

Hartlib   (*to Menasseh*). Sir Thomas Fairfax fought Spain with the Dutch.

(*To Fairfax.*) Menasseh ben Israel is from Holland.
We are in touch with Jews in Amsterdam –
Kabbalists like Menasseh ben Israel –
Who fled the Spanish Inquisition and
Settled in Holland, teach the Kabbalah
As rabbis in the Dutch metropolis
And believe a Messiah will return
To lead the Jews back to the Promised Land
When their Dispersal has been accomplished.

Menasseh.   Jews, Kabbalists, Rosicrucians, Masons
And Puritans are all parts of one tree.
From Kabbalistic trunk in Moses' time
Each Rosicrucian and Masonic branch
Put out Puritan leaves that thrive each spring.
We are a universal brotherhood.
Our roots are in Israel, our crown's the world.

Hartlib.   And all branches intersect in England,
The Promised Land, and radiate from there.

(MENASSEH *nods and takes* CROMWELL *aside.*)

Menasseh.   I have come specially from Amsterdam
Where there's support for you against the Crown.
Funders have been impressed by your proud stance
In Parliament, the country and this place.
Know that you have been chosen to foment
Revolution. I am to assist you.
Amsterdam Jews will fund a new army
So you can forcibly eject the King –
And when you take power, your new government.
There's unlimited funding – all you need.

Cromwell.   "Chosen"? By whom?

Menasseh.   By conscientious men
Who abhor what this selfish King has done,
And like you want to limit his great power,
Curtail it. If you comply, I promise
You will be ruler of England. Your rise

	Will be just as startling as Lucifer's.
Cromwell.	And what do they want in return?
Menasseh.	You know.
Cromwell.	The Temple of Solomon rebuilt in Our Freemasonry lodges and then in Jerusalem so they can visit it?
Menasseh.	More than that.
Cromwell.	Entry into England?
Menasseh.	More. The Jews were all expelled in 1290. They'll want to return and settle again. You must resettle the Jews in England. And to do that, you'll have to oust the King.
Cromwell.	Unlimited funding from Amsterdam For my Army, and in return I must Admit the Jews to England once again.

(CROMWELL *frowns and muses. He turns to the lodge and addresses everybody.*)

	Brothers, I propose that we all rebuild Solomon's Temple in this meeting-place And reveal the Great Architect's wisdom To our brethren in Amsterdam Jewry.

(*There is a hubbub.* CROMWELL *turns back to* MENASSEH.)

Menasseh.	You should join us.
Cromwell.	Your "conscientious men"? Who are they? Who do they revere? Under Whom do they serve?
Menasseh.	They serve our Grand Master –

Cromwell.	Who is your Grand Master?

Menasseh.	It's Andreae.
	I speak to you on Andreae's behalf.
	Both Andreae and I speak for Sion,
	Which protects the Merovingian bloodline.

Cromwell	(*aside*). Hartlib believes Andreae is Bacon.
	(*Aloud.*) What is Sion? And who does it protect?

Menasseh.	In 1090 Merovingians founded
	The Priory of Sion and fought crusades.
	They founded Knights Templar (in 1118)
	To protect the Merovingian throne
	In Jerusalem. That kingdom was lost.
	The Templars rebelled and were destroyed by
	Sion and the Merovingian French king.
	The Templars fled to Scotland and founded
	Templar Freemasonry, a secret cult,
	And vowed to destroy the Merovingian
	Throne of France. Now the Priory of Sion
	Works for a universal government
	Ruled by the secret Merovingian King
	Of Jerusalem, who reigns from a throne
	In Europe. The Grand Masters of Sion
	Have now moved from France to London to plot
	The downfall of the Stuart dynasty,
	Which turned Templar under King James the First.
	Your England's important – the Holy Grail,
	Brought here by Joseph of Arimathea,
	Is kept by our Grand Masters, who also
	Guard the lost treasure of Jerusalem's
	Temple, which will be returned to Israel
	When the time's right – when the secret King reigns
	From Jerusalem and governs the world.

Cromwell.	A Holy Grail bloodline to rule the world.
	And Sion founded Rosicrucianism.
	(*Aside.*) And Andreae is Sion's Grand Master.
	And Hartlib believes Andreae's Bacon.
	(*Aloud.*) Who will be your King of Jerusalem?

Menasseh.	You know. He who will end the Stuart line.

(CROMWELL *is stunned. Full realization dawns.*)

Cromwell.	King of England, and of Jerusalem?

(MENASSEH *nods.*)

(*Fervently.*) I am deeply inspired by what you've said.
Now I will organize Freemasonry,
Establish degrees for the Rosy Cross.
I am not primarily a Calvinist.
I am first and foremost a Freemason
With a thirst for universal knowledge,
And only incidentally from now
A Puritan and Unitarian.
When just a boy I dreamed I would be King,
I told my schoolmaster and was beaten.
I was often beaten – I scrumped apples,
Broke hedges, stole doves from dovecotes, for which
My parents and masters would chastise me.
Those beatings turned me into a rebel.
I drank in the High Street alehouses and
Led a dissolute life, ravished kisses
From decent young women, just like Tarquin.
St Augustine came to holiness late,
And so did I, I am ashamed to say.
But I have backbone and am determined.
I'll do it. I will oust this poxy King!

SCENE 2

(*Late August 1642. Cambridge.* CROMWELL *addresses his constituency.*)

Cromwell.	Men of Cambridge, most loyal Englishmen,
	After the King invaded Parliament
	He went up north to raise an army and
	The Queen went to Holland to raise funds by
	Pawning our crown jewels, as if they were hers.

The King tried to secure the Hull arsenal,
Settled in York and called on Royalists
To join him there. Parliament's sent Nineteen
Propositions – that Parliament control
The Army, support Ministers, decide
The future of the Church. The King has said
He runs a mixed government, that he's not
An autocrat, but he's prepared for war.
And now he has raised the royal standard
At Nottingham and fighting's breaking out
Throughout our Kingdom. I won permission
For Cambridge to defend itself with armed
Companies, and I've urged your colleges
To stop melting down plate to send the King.
I've enlisted a troop of cavalry
At Huntingdon. Now we must take up arms.
My motto is *Pax Quaeritur Bello*,
"Let peace be sought through war". Arm to keep peace!
Men of the people, arm yourselves and guard
Your Parliament from the King's tyranny!

Constituent   (*aside*). Alas! England's to be rent asunder
As if in a stricken, diseased body
The blood round the heart turned against the head
In a paroxysm, disordering stroke,
Or a cancerous tumour strangled its brain.
Division's now our lot as sons rebel
Against fathers, wives against their husbands.
Now all is rapine, English volunteers
Will storm our towns as foxes maul chickens,
And launch sallies as a graceful white swan
Devours a brood of newly-hatched ducklings.
We common men must endure civil war.
No good will come of it, only ruin
For our households and the crops we have sown,
And the cattle we pasture in our fields.

SCENE 3

(*23 October 1642. Edgehill.* TWO SHEPHERDS. *Sound of trumpet and drum.*)

Shepherd 1.	More sounds of war. Trumpet and drum. Our sheep Should be in fold, not out on this hillside.
Shepherd 2.	All we're trying to do is watch our flocks. I don't know what the country's coming to, What with armed men on horse rushing about Like swarms of bees and hornets with stings out.
Shepherd 1.	Soon the baas of our sheep will be mixed with The groans of dying men. What for? Madness. And they be ones read books. Should know better. Look, here comes that new Captain, off his horse.
Shepherd 2.	He fights under Essex. He's coming here!

(*Enter* CROMWELL *with his* ENTOURAGE. *They scan the battlefield in front of them from a ridge.*)

Cromwell.	Our men are beaten on all sides. It's not Been battle but execution. But now Prince Rupert's charged with his cavalry, he Can't rally them and take them up the slope. They've forfeited the advantage of the height. They've turned aside to loot Hampden's baggage. We'll counter-attack and secure a draw. If we don't charge them now, this was a rout. Nothing will stop King Charles reaching London. Charge! Onward into battle! Block the King! (*Exit.*)

(*The moaning of the badly wounded can be heard off stage. Enter* KING CHARLES *on foot with his entourage.*)

Charles.	The slaughter on this battlefield sickens. And the flies buzzing round the dead faces. I've told my troops that I am their cause and Their quarrel, and their captain. But it has Not won me my victory. We've fought a draw. That Captain Cromwell's denied us a win, That poacher who's brought thousands to our woods. Now both sides must pull apart and regroup. (*In a low voice.*) I never wanted to bring suffering

To my subjects on such a scale as this.

SCENE 4

(22 July 1643. Christ Church College, Oxford. CHARLES *greets* HENRIETTA MARIA.*)*

Henrietta.   I've sold some of my jewels in Holland and
Have bought you a shipload of arms. No more
Indecision! Delays have ruined you.
You must make a three-pronged attack against
London – from here in Oxford, from Yorkshire
And from the west. All three to combine strength.

Charles.   I'm glad of the shipload of arms. They will
Counter the forces of Colonel Cromwell,
Who're everywhere, like rats in the grainsacks
And flocks of black crows in the gold wheatfields.
Yorkshiremen and westerners won't leave their
Regions. They'll fight in Yorkshire or the west,
But they won't march on London. I know that.

Henrietta.   You must make them. They must obey the King.

Charles.   Colonel Gosnold.

(COLONEL ROBERT GOSNOLD *steps forward.*)

Can we attack London?
Or will we ourselves be under attack?

Gosnold.   We can try, but Colonel Cromwell intends
To counter-attack Yorkshire Royalists
So they don't penetrate eastern counties.
He'll have us under siege if he does well.

Charles.   Thank you, Colonel Gosnold.

(*He addresses* HENRIETTA MARIA.)

You see, my dear,

If we leave Oxford, Cromwell will storm in.
We need to stay here to block his progress.

SCENE 5

(1643 London. House of the Portuguese Ambassador, DE SOUZA, a Marrano or secret Jew. With De Souza are MENASSEH and CARVAJAL.)

De Souza.   Menasseh, Fernandez Carvajal is
              A financier and army contractor.
              Each year he imports gold bullion that's worth
              A hundred thousand pounds, I've heard it said.

Carvajal.   No comment from me, Your Excellency!

              (MENASSEH does not indicate that they have met.)

Menasseh.   I have heard of your work. England needs you.
              England is ideal for our Jewish needs.
              When Edward the First banished all Jews for
              "Grave offences that endangered his realm"
              (He claimed), and the King of France and other
              Rulers in Christian Europe followed suit,
              The Jews in Europe urgently appealed
              (Through Chemor, Rabbi of Arles in Provence)
              To Constantinople's Sanhedrin in
              January 1489, and in
              November the Prince of the Jews replied
              With practical advice, advising them
              To create a Trojan Horse in London,
              To make their sons Christian lawyers, doctors
              And priests and work to destroy the Christian
              Structure from within. In Spain, in the reign
              Of Ferdinand and Isabella, Jews
              Enrolled as Christians to destroy the Church
              In Spain. The Inquisition threw us out
              And we trekked across Europe to Holland
              And Switzerland and made the two centres
              Of Jewish intrigue. It then became clear

621

We Jews needed a seafaring nation
To which we could attach ourselves to trade.
We identified James the First's England,
A rising naval power whose ships sailed to
The four corners of the discovered world.
It was a Christian kingdom divided
Between Catholic and Protestant and we
Exploited this division, fanned hatreds
Between Christian communities. We sent
The French Cauin – Calvin – to Geneva
To bring revolutionary orators
To England and Scotland, revolution
Under the cloak of religious fervour.
He divided the English Protestants
Into Sabbath-observers and -breakers
And held the country in his power. We broke
The trusted circle round King James the First.
Buckingham's life was saved at the time of
The Kabbalist Gowrie Conspiracy.
We killed Buckingham and let it be thought
He'd died in mysterious circumstances.
We impeached meddling Strafford through the Earl
Of Bedford (whose family was founded
By a Jewish wine merchant named Roussel).
He was head of the faction that opposed
The King through Pym. We finished Strafford off.
After the King tried to arrest the five
Members of Parliament in January
Last year, and they fled London on the run,
We sent Calvinist "Operative" mobs
Into the City of London, all armed,
Chanting their cry, "To your tents, O Israel",
And led the five back, with arms and banners,
At least ten thousand, our militia
Of workers for insurgency. How well
They intimidated Parliament and
The Palace! And we've flooded London with
Thousands of revolutionary pamphlets
And leaflets from the new presses. And we'd
Hired Oliver Cromwell, our creature, to
Widen the split between the Protestants –

Anglicans and Puritans – for us Jews,
Hiding division under fervent prayer.
He'll kill King Charles and then others will split
England's most ancient traditions which bind
Monarchy, Church, State, nobles and people
In one solemn bond: Christianity.
I have paid him large sums of money so
His revolution succeeds, so he will
Be sole ruler and in a position
To invite the Jews back into England
And put us into trading positions
In England's burgeoning naval empire.
We hope England will become a powerful
Commercial empire under Cromwell, so
We international Jews can have influence
On world affairs through our own nominee.
I will be like Lord Burleigh to a new
Elizabeth – our Cromwell, our creation.
He needs a better army. You will be
Contractor of the New Model Army.

Carvajal.   I am most honoured, Your Excellency.
                   Funds will reach me....?

Menasseh.   From Amsterdam.

De Souza.   I want
                   All *Marranos* back here in England. I
                   Offer my services. Send the funds here.

Carvajal.   Most pleased to accept, Your Excellencies.

SCENE 6

(*September 1643. Nun Appleton House, Yorkshire. CROMWELL and FAIRFAX, who is black-haired and black-eyed. An AIDE is with them.*)

Aide.   The Parliamentary Commander himself,
                   Sir Thomas Fairfax, will now receive you.

Cromwell.	I've heard a lot about your sweet temper,
	Military steel and your reputation:
	Like Scipio Africanus you conquer
	The enemy but also ambition.
	I am honoured to serve alongside you.

(FAIRFAX *ruminates*.)

Fairfax.	You're twelve years older than me. I am pleased
	To have your great experience assist me.
	Come into the garden and meet my wife.
	She's a de Vere and still hankers to be
	In Castle Hedingham, at Kirby Hall.
	But she's getting used to Yorkshire – slowly.

| Cromwell. | There is some strategy I must discuss. |

SCENE 7

(*January 1644. House of Commons.* SIR HENRY VANE *the younger, who is now in effect leader of the Commons, and* CROMWELL.)

Vane.	Colonel Cromwell has won brilliant victories,
	At Gainsborough in Lincolnshire, where he stopped
	The Royalists on the day he was made
	Governor of the Isle of Ely, and then,
	Fighting with Sir Thomas Fairfax, our own
	Parliamentary General, at Winceby, he
	Blocked the Royalist counter-attack and
	Successfully besieged Newark in Notts.
	We are delighted with his victories,
	Especially after John Pym's sad demise.
	Some of us tried to make peace with the King
	At Oxford, but in vain, and so we have
	Allied with the Scottish covenanters.
	We have been reasonable, and now the news
	Is that a Scottish army has entered
	England on our side. The King has remained
	To hold his inner lines at Oxford. His

Nephew Prince Rupert makes cavalry raids
To harry us. We need a new Army.
I propose we should form a new Army
Under the Earl of Manchester's command.
Both Fairfax and Cromwell should be involved.

(*Cries of "Hear, hear". CROMWELL steps forward.*)

Cromwell.   If it's Parliament's will the new Army
Should be funded by a public levy
And be commanded by Lord Manchester,
I congratulate him, but I accuse
Some of his fellow officers, who are
Incompetent, profane, loose in conduct.

(*Shocked gasps of "Oh".*)

I offer myself as Lord Manchester's
Second-in-command to progress this war.

(*Cries of "Hear, hear".*)

Vane.   I propose Colonel Cromwell as Second
And Lieutenant General of the new force.
He should be on the Committee of Both
Kingdoms to talk with the Scots, and to be
Responsible for strategy, for all
Parliament's planning in this Civil War.

(MP*s receive this with great enthusiasm, and* CROMWELL *is appointed by
acclamation to chanting of his name,* "Cromwell, Cromwell".)

SCENE 8

(*1 July 1644. York. The* MARQUESS OF NEWCASTLE *embraces* PRINCE RUPERT.)

Rupert.   What a week! A twenty-two mile forced march
Through Knaresborough, then we crossed the Ouse, the Swale
And then the Ouse again, seizing the bridge

Of boats from a regiment of dragoons
To circle the Parliamentary forces
On Marston Moor – and here we are in York!

Newcastle.   You've raised the siege and I have nothing but
Thankfulness and obedience. The allies
Will quarrel among themselves now they have
Failed to keep York besieged and surrounded.
What now?

Rupert.   I fight the force on Marston Moor.
Manchester's Army stormed Lincoln in May
And's cock-a-hoop at joining with the Scots.
I have orders from King Charles to attack.

Newcastle.   I will obey you in all things.

Rupert.   We march
On the foe at four tomorrow morning.

(*Enter a* PRISONER *with a* GUARD.)

Who's this?

Guard.   This man has come from Marston Moor.

Rupert.   Is Cromwell there?

(*The* PRISONER *nods.*)

I'm going to beat him.

SCENE 9

(*Knaresborough. The top of a tower.* CROMWELL *locks the door, sinks to his knees and prays,* Bible *before him.*)

Cromwell.   Lord, if it is your will, please send England
And the Church of God a great victory

626

Tomorrow. Many young men will be killed.
Lord, our cause is just, please forgive their fate.
I don't want one Royalist to die, but
It will be necessary to kill some
To secure the end of this treasonous King
Who burrows up molehills on our State lawns.
Please fill me with your Light. I am open,
Please let your Light enter my soul, my heart.
Aaah! It's a sign that you are on my side.
I am filled with Light and your Providence.
I am the Light's instrument, and will cleanse
This Kingdom from its corrupt fief, the King.
Aaah! Explosions of Light like cannon fire.

(*A* LITTLE GIRL *appears and knocks on the door.*)

Girl.   Supper, Mr Cromwell. Supper's ready.

(CROMWELL *does not stir or reply.*)

Cromwell.   Lord, fill me with more Light so I may make
The right decisions on the battlefield
And kill where killing's right, spare where it's not.

(*Exit the* GIRL.)

SCENE 10

(*2 July 1644. Cromwell's Plump, Marston Moor.* FAIRFAX, CROMWELL *and* MANCHESTER
survey the battlefield from their command-post. It is early evening.)

Cromwell.   A battle-line a mile and a half long!
The battle will be the biggest ever
To be fought on British soil. Rain again!

Manchester.   It's been wet all summer. The green rye-fields
Are saturated. Both the armies will
Be soaked. Perhaps we should delay the fight.

Fairfax.   Look at their front line: Byron, Newcastle,
                  Tillier, Goring. Must be twenty thousand.
                  They're only a few hundred yards away.

                  (*Enter* MESSENGER, *who addresses* FAIRFAX.)

Messenger.   We have intelligence. It's Prince Rupert's
                  Belief there will be no battle tonight.
                  He's at supper. He'll attack tomorrow.

                  (FAIRFAX *nods. Exit* MESSENGER.)

Cromwell.   Newcastle's troops have been slow to arrive.
                  They're not fully ready. They're vulnerable.
                  We've the advantage of numbers and ground.
                  A surprise attack may put them to flight.

                  (*Thunder.*)

                  A storm's coming. Look, drenching rain. My men
                  Of the Eastern Association should
                  Make a short-reined charge at the trot. We will
                  Descend on the enemy like a cloud.

Manchester.   I don't fancy a cavalry charge in
                  Those bushes and scrub, but –

Fairfax.   We will attack.

SCENE 11

(*An hour later. Elsewhere on Marston Moor.* FAIRFAX, *panting, and* CROMWELL, *breathless.*)

Fairfax.   I was surrounded in those bushes. I
                  Escaped by tearing off the white favour
                  That marked me for Parliament and making
                  My way through enemy lines back to you.
                  What's happened to your neck?

Cromwell.	A pistol shot. I stopped at a cottage at Tockwith and Had the wound dressed. Prince Rupert leapt from meat And pressed us hard, but now we're routing him, His cavalry are in flight along by Wilstrop Road.
Fairfax.	You're not chasing them. You've pulled Your men up?
Cromwell.	They must stay together, not Lose their order. We're pressed hard on the right. Leven's fled to Leeds. Our pikemen have held. I'll charge Goring on the right. Newcastle's Whitecoats –
Fairfax.	Are now their winding-sheets. They've all Been slaughtered by Manchester's foot. I watched.
Cromwell.	I'll pursue Goring's horse to York. Rupert?
Fairfax.	He's hiding in a beanfield, finishing His disturbed supper: meat and runner beans!

(CROMWELL *laughs. He then turns sombre.*)

Cromwell.	The slaughter is appalling. Thousands dead. Three, four, five thousand Royalist young men. I ordered my men to take their revenge On Prince Rupert's cavalry, and they did. I had to give the order, yet I'm sad. We have made so many women widows. The Lord will comfort them and support them. I lost two sons, Albert and Oliver. The Lord supported me and took me through. I know the Lord will comfort their widows.

(*He turns away. Exit* FAIRFAX. CROMWELL *sinks to his knees.*)

(*Alone.*) O Lord, please send your Light into my heart
For I have had to slaughter fine young men,

Several thousand of them. I know it's wrong,
But our just cause required I ordered it.
The North of England is now Parliament's.
This could not be secured without slaughter.
The King has only ten thousand men left
In his army, and five with Prince Maurice.
If Manchester is quick, we will have won
This Civil War by the end of this year.
Do with me as you will. And Manchester –
Do you want me to take over from him?

SCENE 12

(*September 1644. Committee of Both Kingdoms, House of Commons.* CHAIRMAN *and*
CROMWELL.)

Chairman.   Please tell this Committee of Both Kingdoms
                   Your view on the Earl of Manchester's speed.

Cromwell.   He's slow. He's like a snail that drags his camp
                   Laboriously up a house wall all day,
                   Two horns poking in front, and is knocked off
                   By a clumsy boy thundering past him,
                   And has to start again. He does not reach
                   His goal. After Marston Moor he withdrew
                   Towards his own country and did not seek
                   More engagements. He would not take Belvoir
                   Castle in Lincolnshire or storm Newark,
                   The Royalist stronghold, or fight Rupert
                   At Chester. He's a sweet meek man who cares
                   About his men. After Marston Moor he
                   Spent hours with his men, sorting out their needs.
                   He's weak, he's willingly led by others.
                   He's a pleasant fellow but he is not
                   The sort of man who should be commander,
                   In charge of strategy. And now we have
                   Essex's defeat at Lostwithiel
                   In Cornwall, and the King has just captured
                   Eight thousand infantry. And my General's

Declined to march west to support Essex.
I've begged him at Ely and Peterborough
And at Huntingdon, but he won't listen.
He says he'll hang anyone who gives him
Any more advice. I suspect Major-
General Crawford's behind all his delays,
Which are deliberate, and his own choice.

Chairman.   The Earl of Manchester complains that you
Have filled the Army with Independents
And that the cavalry now call themselves
"The godly". Have you any comment, please?

Cromwell.   My cavalry triumphed at Marston Moor.
Without them the King would have beaten us.
They are fine men, and their belief in God
Has made them a formidable Army.
They lack leadership. Manchester must go.

(*A message is handed to the* CHAIRMAN.)

Chairman.   The Earl of Manchester is heading west.
Perhaps we can lay aside your complaint
For the time being? Let us now adjourn.

SCENE 13

(*27 October 1644, late afternoon. Newbury.* CROMWELL *and* MANCHESTER. *Sound of gunfire.*)

Cromwell   (*exasperated*). The King's in front of Donnington Castle.
His cavalry's left wing's on the river,
Protected by Shaw House, and his right is
At Newbury. Waller has taken the rear,
We've heard them chanting psalms. But you've delayed
Your assault on Shaw House because you can't
Hear Waller's gunfire. Now they've fought you off.
You've dithered and delayed, the two attacks
Should have been simultaneous and now
We're fighting by moonlight, the Royalists

Have left Shaw House and are advancing and
The King is winning. What are your orders?

Manchester. I don't accept your summary at all.
My orders are, that you should take your horse
And stop the Royalist advance at once.

Cromwell. My horses are exhausted. I refuse
To obey your orders. I did not make
This situation. If you had attacked
Shaw House when Waller took the rear, then we
Would have had the victory that's now the King's.
You must take the bitter consequences
Of your own muddle and delay: defeat.

SCENE 14

(*Early November 1644. London. Cromwell's house.* CROMWELL *alone.* CARVAJAL *is shown in.*)

Cromwell. Don Antonio Fernandez Carvajal.
Thanks for the intelligence you've gathered.
In return I have tolerated your
Secret synagogue in Cree Church Lane, off
Leadenhall Street near where you are living,
Where your "clerk" Moses Athias is rabbi.
I've liked what you have sent me, and now all
London's *Marranos* call you "the great Jew".
You ride fine horses and collect armour.

Carvajal. You are well informed, and I thank you for
Permitting our synagogue to function.
I've come from Menasseh, who has himself
Just come from Andreae. The time has come.
The Jewish Amsterdam money-lenders
Are displeased with the King. He's not allowed
Us Jews, expelled in 1290, back in
To England, and he's not borrowed money,
Which they would have lent him, to fight against

Parliament. In revenge for being expelled
And being ignored as money-lenders, they
Call on you to oust the King. In return
They will give you all the money you need
In addition to the public levy
To build up a New Model Army and
Defeat the King. I am the messenger
But also the conduit to bring you funds –

Cromwell.   For whom? Sion or these money-lenders?
Andreae, your mysterious Grand Master?

Carvajal.   All equally. They're interchangeable.

Cromwell.   Is Bacon Andreae? Did he endure
A philosophic death after disgrace
And seek revenge against the Stuart house?

(CARVAJAL *stares at him.*)

Carvajal.   Andreae's Andreae, Rosicrucian
Leader, Priory of Sion Grand Master.
I am not at liberty to say more.

(*He has a thought.*)

Both Bacon and Andreae fight for Sion
Against the Templar Stuart enemy.

Cromwell.   Fight? Bacon died in 1626.
Fought?

Carvajal.   The historic present can be used
Of historic people after they're dead.
What's important's the Rosicrucian cause
And how Bacon's ideas are spread today.
John Milton's a follower of Bacon
And owns Hermetic texts given him by Fludd,
Who was then his neighbour. Theodore Haak,
The German Rosicrucian's in his group.
His Cambridge college, Christ's, was a centre

For Kabbalistic studies; they've shaped him.
He's an invisible Rosicrucian
Who spreads Bacon's ideas as a Puritan.
I can fund you while you perform your role.

Cromwell.   You have come at an opportune moment.
Parliament's in desperate need of money
So we can wage war with the King.

Carvajal.   It's time.

Cromwell.   To oust the King? How? How?

Carvajal.   I will explain.
You must criticise Manchester and oust
Him as Commander of the Army, then
Propose a new Army you will control
(Though General Fairfax is the figurehead),
The "New Model Army". We will enflame
The populace so armed mobs agitate.
You will sit on the Committee of Both
Kingdoms and reorganize the Army.
You will drive out the King.

Cromwell.   And then?

Carvajal.   And then,
You will be sole ruler of all England.
And re-admit the Jews. We will ensure
That happens. You will then take orders from
Menasseh. If you want to write to him,
Send your letters to Mulheim Synagogue
Through Ebenezer Pratt, who'll convey them.
Just let me know there's a letter to send.

(*Exit* CARVAJAL.)

Cromwell   (*aside*). Sole Ruler of all England. It is what
I have considered in my darkest thoughts,
And never uttered to a soul. Why, I
Would do anything to be Sole Ruler,

I've always thought. I'd end the monarchy.
I can be monarch on behalf of God.
But would I do more? Would I kill the King
And re-admit the Jews into England?
I'm tempted by this figment of my thoughts,
This devil, but I must reflect and choose.
No, I must pray and leave the choice to God.

SCENE 15

(*25 November 1644. House of Commons*. CROMWELL, SPEAKER *and* MPs.)

Cromwell.   In short, Mr Speaker, the said Earl has
Always been slow and reluctant to fight,
To end the war by sword instead of peace
Which would disadvantage our Parliament.
I've listed charges in this *Narrative*,
A printed statement the public can read.

Speaker.   This complaint should pass to our committee

SCENE 16

(*28 November 1644. The House of Lords. The* EARL OF MANCHESTER, LORD
CHANCELLOR *and* NOBLEMEN.)

Manchester.   I accuse Cromwell of being against
The nobility and the House of Lords.
He hopes to see the day when there are no
Noblemen in England, and has told me
That all will not be well until I am
Plain Mr Montagu and not an Earl.
He was displeased when seventeen years ago
His old family seat of Hinchingbrooke
Was sold to my Montagu family.
He prefers those noblemen who don't like
The Lords, and hates those who venerate it.

(*Cries of rage from members of the House of Lords.*)

My Lords, I do not want to enrage you,
Only to help you understand this man.
I have issued this printed *Narrative*
In which I list Cromwell's many failings.
My Lords, I ask that Cromwell be impeached
As an incendiary who will destroy
The Lords and monarchy of this nation.
He's like a thrush thrashing a snailshell on
A stone so he can gobble up the snail.

Lord Chancellor.   This complaint should pass to our committee.

SCENE 17

(*December 1644. London. Cromwell's house.* CROMWELL *and* VANE.)

Cromwell   (*aside*). This Vane is gullible. He'll do my will –
God's will, I mean, for I'm doing God's work.
(*Aloud.*) The Jews of Europe are supporting us,
But they've lost confidence in Manchester.
They may send us donations if he goes.
To help advance the cause of Israel's Jews
I want you to propose in Parliament
This Self-Denying Ordinance we've discussed
Which is Puritan through and through. Will you?

Vane.   I will. But I do not understand why
A Puritan measure will help the Jews.
What is a Puritan, and why the Jews?

Cromwell.   I am a Puritan and men ask me
What a Puritan is. Can they not see
A Puritan has the Jewish outlook?
Our strict observance, our black garb and hat,
Keeping the Sabbath and drinking no wine,
Plain living close to the *Old Testament*,
All these are Jewish characteristics,

As is our cry, "To your tents, O Israel."

Vane. Puritans imitators of the Jews.
I had not realised our source is Jewish.

Cromwell. The Jews used to be settled in England.
If they think they've a chance of coming back
Their donations may be more generous.
We need to let them think we will support
The Jewish resettlement of England.
That would strengthen our Puritan ideals,
For with them would come Kabbalist ideas.
Onto the Jewish root I have grafted
The Rosicrucian Light of Bacon and
Freemasonry that is republican.
We need a new mix: Puritans as Jews!

SCENE 18

(*December 1644. House of Commons.* CROMWELL, SPEAKER, VANE *and* MPs.)

Cromwell. It's not for me to insist on complaints
Against any Commander-in-Chief or
On oversights of his. I am guilty
Of oversights, which can't be avoided
In military matters. Let us adopt –
I give way.

Vane. I propose a remedy.
The remedy: no members of this House
Or of the Lords will put their self-interest
Before the public good. They should practise
Self-denial. No member of this House
Or of the Lords should hold office within
The Army forty days from now, to stop
The quarrels his Commander picks with him.

Cromwell. I will deny myself an Army post,
So will the Earl of Manchester. A vote!

(*Cries of support from the Commons.*)

Speaker. The motion is carried. Mr Cromwell.

Cromwell. And I propose a new Army is formed
Under Sir Thomas Fairfax, who is not
Of either House and so's unaffected
By our Self-Denying Ordinance. He –
I give way.

Vane. Thank you. Mr Speaker, I
Propose that Oliver Cromwell should be
General Fairfax's Second-in-Command.
In view of his distinguished war record
An exception should be made. He's denied
Himself, but we should overrule him now.

(*Cries of "Hear, hear" from MPs.*)

Cromwell. No. I must be bound by the same Ordinance
That will now bind the Earl of Manchester.

Vane. General Fairfax must insist that he's made
Second-in-Command so we win this war.

(*Cries of "Hear, hear" from the Commons.*)

SCENE 19

(*Early June 1645. House of Commons. VANE, CROMWELL and SPEAKER.*)

Vane. Mr Speaker, now the King has Leicester
And has slaughtered many men and women
And plans to challenge the Scots from Chester
And General Fairfax, with no number two,
No Lieutenant of Horse close at his side,
Has petitioned that Oliver Cromwell
Should be his Second-in-Command, is it
Not time that he should cease to be bound by

	The Self-Denying Ordinance I proposed,
	Even if the Lords demur from loyalty
	To Lord Manchester, who is one of them?
Speaker.	Silence! Order! Mr Cromwell. Silence!
Cromwell.	Mr Speaker, as a subsidiary
	Of the Committee of Both Kingdoms, I
	Have organized the New Model Army
	Into ten regiments of horse, each with
	Six hundred men; twelve foot regiments of
	Twelve hundred men; and a thousand dragoons.
	We will soon have twenty-two thousand men
	At a cost of six thousand pounds a month.
	In January I proposed to this House
	That the new Army's Commander-in-Chief
	Should be Sir Thomas Fairfax, who's very
	Equal to the task and one of the few
	Generals who's not an MP. And then I
	Impressed some eight thousand additional men.
	The armies of Manchester, Essex and
	Waller have been remodelled so they have
	Now become an effective fighting-force.
	I did all this without all thought of gain,
	Observing self-denial with due care.
	But as Sir Thomas Fairfax now pays me
	The compliment of insisting that I
	Should now become his Second-in-Command
	And Sir Henry Vane endorses this view,
	I will consider myself no longer
	Bound by the Self-Denying Ordinance.

(*Cheering from some MPs.*)

Vane.	Sir Thomas Fairfax wants you to join him
	As soon as possible to fight the King.
Cromwell.	If this House grants the petition, I will
	Ride out at once to join the New Army.

(*More cheering.*)

SCENE 20

(*13 June 1645. Lubenham, near Market Harborough, Leicestershire.* KING CHARLES *and* RUPERT *with* ROYALISTS.)

Charles.   Now we have finished supper, who's for quoits?

                          (*Roar of approval.*)

Rupert.   The King should have the first throw.

Charles.   Very well.

                          (*He throws and misses. Sympathetic applause. Enter a* MESSENGER.)

Messenger.   Sir, your troops at Naseby have been captured.

                          (*A gasp round the court.*)

Charles.   At Naseby?

Messenger.   Yes, by Henry Ireton, sir.

                          (CHARLES *nods. Exit the* MESSENGER.)

Rupert.   This is unexpected. Bad news indeed.

Charles.   Ireton's seven miles south of Harborough. Should I
                          Continue my retreat to Leicester, which
                          May now seem more like flight, or turn and face
                          The New Model Army, that's quite untried?

Rupert.   I don't advise a fight.

Charles.   But we must fight.
                          If we can catch them with our cavalry
                          And wipe them out like new-hatched buzzing flies,
                          We can retrieve everything with one stroke.

SCENE 21

(*14 June 1645. Naseby battlefield.* CROMWELL *and* FAIRFAX *with* SCOUT. *It is cold and wet.*)

Cromwell.   The battlefield is between two ridges.
They are drawn up on the misty skyline.
It's as wet as Marston Moor. It's very
Boggy down there. Let's draw back to that hill
Which will encourage them to charge us as
They'll think we're retreating. If they do they'll
Be ruined.

Fairfax   (*to scout*). What hill is that?

Scout.   It's Red Hill.

Fairfax.   Come on, let's occupy Red Hill and wait.
Most of your horse should wait in that hollow.
They're out of sight of the Royalist gaze.

SCENE 22

(*14 June 1645. Naseby, elsewhere.* KING CHARLES *and* AIDE.)

Charles.   The Parliamentary foot are retreating
Before our pikes. Skippon's wounded. Only
Fairfax is standing firm. Look, there's Cromwell,
Charging down the slope with his horse. He's put
Our cavalry to flight. Now he has turned
And slammed into the left flank of our foot.
Where's Rupert?

Aide.   Sir, he's plundering baggage
Two miles away.

Charles.   Our infantry's routed.
Rally what's left of Langdale's horse.

| Aide. | Yes, sir. |

(*Exit* AIDE.)

| Charles. | They're fleeing. Oh no, the enemy's foot
Are at our wagons, plundering our baggage. |

(*He averts his eyes. Re-enter* AIDE.)

| Aide. | They're killing the camp followers hiding
Round our wagons. They're slashing the faces
Of women, claiming they are prostitutes.
They're doing what our troops did at Leicester
And calling out to God as they do it. |

SCENE 23

(*June 1645. House of Commons.*)

| Speaker. | At Naseby we wiped out five thousand foot
And captured rings and gems from Charles' baggage,
And papers granting the Irish Catholics
Concessions if an Irish army sails
For England to join foreign troops sent by
The Duke of Lorraine – treacherous intent.
I have a letter from Cromwell, which I
Will now read: "Sir, this victory we won
At Naseby was guided by none other
Than the hand of God. Sir Thomas Fairfax
Will also attribute this to the Lord."
There will be a banquet in Grocers' Hall
For both Houses, after which all will sing
The forty-sixth Psalm. And we will parade
Three thousand Royalist prisoners through the streets
So Londoners may rejoice with us and
Celebrate our victory over the King. |

SCENE 24

(July 1645. Raglan Castle, Wales. CHARLES *and the* MARQUESS OF WORCESTER.*)*

Charles. Why have so few Welsh troops joined my forces?
I am here at Raglan Castle for Wales.
The Welsh should guard me as their King, and fight.

(Enter MESSENGER.*)*

What news from Somerset?

Messenger. Not good news, sir.
Baron Goring held back until Fairfax
And Cromwell caught him at Long Sutton, near
Langport, and sent in Major Bethel with
A hundred and twenty men backed up by
Major Desborough and foot. A massacre.
Two thousand dead, your foot broken, thousands
Of men and horses captured. The fortress
Of Bridgewater fallen. A complete rout.
Sir, Cromwell says he's seen the face of God.
In London there is public thanksgiving.
Popish crucifixes and books are burnt
In our Cheapside to general rejoicing.
Sir, the war against Parliament's ended.

Charles. My last field army has now been destroyed.
All that remains is for the King to fly.
Naseby, and now Langport. I've lost the war.

ACT THREE

SCENE 1

(10 September 1645. FAIRFAX *and* CROMWELL *on top of Prior's Hill Fort, overlooking Bristol. Sound of bombardment.)*

Cromwell.	Look, Bristol spread below like a toytown.
	Rupert's Royalists are being pounded.
	My troops have been repulsed on one side, but
	The Gloucester side bombardment is working.
	Those puffs of smoke, so tiny, are deadly.
	From the top of this Fort you would not know
	That plague wafts through those streets on cannon smoke.

Fairfax.	God guards his own. Rupert's two thousand men
	Breathe in the plague for choosing the wrong side.
	Not one of Parliament's soldiers is ill.

(*Sound of the whine of a bullet.*)

That bullet just missed us, by two hands' breadth.

| Cromwell. | The God of Marston Moor and Naseby shields. |
| | Hey, look, those flames. Rupert's burning Bristol. |

| Fairfax. | He's withdrawing. With his army intact. |

SCENE 2

(*27 April 1646. Oxford.* CHARLES *and* RUPERT.)

Charles.	The situation is dreadful. Each day
	Brings news of the loss of a garrison.
	Cromwell thinks he can raise any siege since
	Devizes, Winchester and Basing House.
	Oxford is the last Royalist stronghold.
	Cromwell's been given two thousand five hundred
	A year from confiscated Royalist lands
	And had his commission renewed again.
	He's joining Fairfax here to break the siege.
	We are surrounded. Putting on disguise,
	I shall flee to Newark and join the Scots.
	Wales was useless, but Scotland will rally.
	I'll treat with the Army to save my rule.

SCENE 3

(15 June 1646. Cromwell's headquarters, Lady Whortlewood's house at Holton, just outside Oxford. CROMWELL and FAIRFAX.)

Cromwell.
    The tyrant's fled to Scotland, Oxford's ours.
    We'll come to terms with the covenanters
    They will hand back the treacherous English King
    When they surrender and the garrison
    Marches out. But this afternoon I have
    No thoughts but the wedding ceremony.
    Fancy, my daughter marrying Ireton!
    He's a fine man, though he's ten years older.
    She lives through her soul, he'll be her soulmate.

SCENE 4

(January 1647. Scotland. COVENANTERS and CHARLES.)

Covenanter.
    We've come to terms with the victorious
    English Parliament, and we're going home.
    Our troops have had enough of English war.

Charles.
    What about me?

(Enter TWO ENGLISH PARLIAMENTARY COMMISSIONERS.)

Covenanter.
    You're also going home.
    You've been ransomed. Four hundred thousand pounds.
    We're handing you over to the English
    Parliamentary commissioners. Good luck!

(CHARLES is taken prisoner by the two COMMISSIONERS.)

Charles
    (aside). Cromwell's swooped like a kestrel on a shrew.

SCENE 5

(*15 April 1647. Saffron Walden, outside the church, which has a steeple.* CROMWELL and FAIRFAX.)

Cromwell.   I have been ill, impostume in the head.
             So ill I nearly died.

Fairfax.   Thank God you're here.
             You've caught up with developments, I hope?
             Now the King has been captured, Parliament's
             Disbanded the Army, which is angry.

Cromwell.   I'm still convalescing, but am perturbed.
             The Army's restless now it's been placed for
             Twenty years under Parliament and been
             Disbanded. The soldiers have not been paid.
             Three hundred thousand pounds is owed the New
             Model Army in pay arrears. And once
             Soldiers are sacked they just receive a mere
             Six weeks' pay.

Fairfax.   You're not going to speak to them?

Cromwell.   I am. I'm on their side. I sympathise.

Fairfax.   And so do I. By hints, not direct speech.

Cromwell.   I shall tell them they have two more weeks' pay
             On Parliament's orders. It isn't much.
             These loyal men who fought at Marston Moor
             And Naseby may be unemployed for life.
             Eight weeks'pay is not much compensation.
             (Aside.) Now the Elector Palatine's asked me
             To win back his Rosicrucian kingdom.
             On my way to Germany I can go
             To Mulheim and discuss the Army's pay
             With Menasseh and his Dutch paymasters.

SCENE 6

(24 May 1647. Holdenby Hall, Northants. CHARLES and AIDE.)

Aide.	Sir, Sir Lewis Dyve's written from the Tower.
	Parliament's still at odds with the Army
	And Cromwell, who talks to both camps, has now
	Given up hope of bringing them together.
	The Independents are much more relaxed
	And mild towards you. Cromwell would serve you
	If he could feel secure from your vengeance.
	I've heard this from a bosom friend of his.
Charles.	That is very pleasing. I am obliged
	For Sir Lewis's good work in the Tower.
	(*Aside.*) Cromwell would serve me as a cormorant
	Reassures a whiting before it dives.

SCENE 7

(30 May 1647. London. Cromwell's house. CROMWELL and CORNET JOYCE.)

Cromwell.	You are cornet in General Fairfax's
	Regiment, I believe.
Joyce.	Sir, that's correct.
Cromwell.	Fairfax has called you an agitator.
Joyce.	Arch-agitator were his actual words.
Cromwell.	Your promotion need not depend on him
	If you do something for me.
Joyce.	I'll listen.
Cromwell.	This meeting is secret. I shall maintain
	It happened without my knowledge.

Joyce.   That's fine.

Cromwell.   You are to choose five hundred of the best
                   Revolutionary troops and descend on
                   Oxford and secure the magazine there,
                   Holdenby Hall and seize the King.

Joyce   (*stunned*).   The King?

Cromwell.   Colonel Graves plots to take him to London
                   To overthrow the Commonwealth.

Joyce.   Traitor!

Cromwell.   You must first arrest Colonel Graves, and then
                   Seize the King. New orders will then follow.

Joyce.   Me, seize the King. You did say "seize the King"?

Cromwell.   That's what I said. Is there a problem?

Joyce.   No.

Cromwell.   Then do it. But not a word. I'll deny
                   Having met you tonight. Even General-
                   In-chief Fairfax knows nothing of this plan.
                   It must remain that way. Just you and me.

Joyce.   I'll carry out your order sir. I won't
                   Breathe a word to anyone. Seize the King!

                   (*Exit* JOYCE.)

Cromwell   (*aside*). Good. Once I have the King, my masters will
                   Send me unlimited amounts of cash.
                   And I'll flood Parliament with Levellers
                   And Rationalists, egalitarians
                   Who'll help me purge it down to fifty men.
                   The foxy King's at bay from yelping hounds!

SCENE 8

(2 June 1647. Holdenby Hall. KING CHARLES *with an* AIDE. *Enter* CORNET JOYCE. *He bursts in with* ARMED MEN.)

Charles.   What is the meaning of this intrusion?

Joyce.   You're under arrest, sir. Please come with me.

Charles.   Who sent you? General Fairfax? No, Cromwell.

      (CORNET JOYCE *evades his look.*)

      Answer your King when he addresses you.

Joyce.   You are to come with me, sir. That is all.
I have authority from the Army
To seize Colonel Graves, officer in charge,
Who has plotted to take you to London.

Soldier.   Colonel Graves has escaped. Where do we go?

Joyce.   The Army will be giving instructions.
I'll take him to the Army headquarters
At Newmarket, and we'll go on from there.

SCENE 9

(4 June 1647. Kentford Heath. CROMWELL *and* FAIRFAX, *with* HUGH PETER.)

Cromwell.   We left London before dawn, for I learned
The Presbyterians have planned to arrest
Me at the House of Commons this morning.

Fairfax   (*drily*). You have thrown in your lot with the Army.
(*Sharply.*) Why did you give orders to move the King?

Peter.   He gave orders to secure him, because

I had intelligence that Colonel Graves
Was about to remove him to London.

Fairfax.   Cornet Joyce says you ordered that the King
Should be moved from prison at Holdenby.

Cromwell.   Cornet Joyce was ordered to keep him there
And seize Colonel Graves, who has run away.
If Joyce is saying that, he's mistaken.
If Major Huntington is saying that,
He's a hostile witness, he dislikes me.

Fairfax.   He was better secured at Holdenby
Than at Childerley. I am still annoyed.

Cromwell.   I will order Whalley to persuade him
To return to Holdenby very soon.

(FAIRFAX *nods. Exit* FAIRFAX.)

(*Aside.*) The King is the Army's prisoner, and mine.
My Dutch friends will be pleased, but I must seem
As if I never wanted Cornet Joyce
To take the King, must appear the King's friend.

SCENE 10

(*A few days later, June 1647. Childerley.* CHARLES, FAIRFAX, CROMWELL, IRETON *and*
SENIOR ARMY OFFICERS. FAIRFAX *advances and kisses the King's hand.*)

Charles.   General Fairfax, thank you for coming here.

Fairfax.   Sir, the Army at Newmarket's set up
An Army Council of Generals, senior
Officers and four representatives
From each regiment –

Charles   I've already heard.
The declaration was at Lieutenant-

General Cromwell's instigation.

Fairfax.   Correct.
The Army Council of Generals is here.

(CROMWELL *and* IRETON *merely bow their heads as other Generals kiss hands.* CHARLES *stares at them, hand extended to be kissed, and then lets his hand drop.*)

Charles.   And though Parliament has voted to pay
The Army its arrears, they've come too late
For the Army intend to overthrow
Presbyterianism.

Cromwell.   Also correct.
The Army wants liberty of conscience,
Which Presbyterianism quite denies.

Charles.   My own thoughts entirely. The Army's right.
I would like to be moved to Newmarket
To be closer to the Army. Are there
Any objections?

(FAIRFAX, CROMWELL *and* IRETON *exchange glances.*)

Cromwell.   Not from me.

Fairfax.   Nor me.

Charles.   Good. That's settled then. Sir, I have as good
An interest in the Army as you do.
London is in disorder, I have heard.
And what will happen if the Army now
Drawn up at Thriplow Heath will not disband?
You will need an arbitrator between
Parliament and the Army –

Ireton.   No, sir, no.
The Army is between Your Majesty
And Parliament, we're the arbitrators.
We'll purge Parliament and we will impeach

	Its Presbyterian members for plotting To disband the Army and start new war.
Charles.	I am with the Army. To Newmarket.
Cromwell	(*aside*). The King's crawled into my web like a fly. I did not have to persuade him at all. Whalley must not free him, nor oppose him. Now I will write to my Dutch friends. Their help Will enable me to seize power and rule. Foreign allies are better kingmakers Than friends at home too readily annoyed.

SCENE 11

(*16 June 1647. Mulheim Synagogue.* MENASSEH *and Ebenezer Pratt.* A RABBI.)

Rabbi.	A letter from Oliver Cromwell via Ebenezer Pratt, who was courier. It is addressed to Mulheim Synagogue.
Menasseh.	He's got the King. He's asking for our help.
Rabbi	(*reading*). He says he hoped to come here on his way To the Elector Palatine's army, But now he has the King he cannot leave.
Menasseh.	One Rosicrucian king helps another.
Rabbi	(*reading*). Cromwell says, "In return for financial Support I will advocate that the Jews Should be readmitted into England. That's impossible while King Charles is alive. Charles cannot be executed without A trial, for which there are no adequate Grounds at present. I therefore advise that Charles be assassinated. I will have Nothing to do with arrangements to find An assassin, but will help his escape."

Menasseh.	The King must not be assassinated
	While in Cromwell's care, so he must escape.
	We will approve Cromwell's request, which is
	A faithful implementing of our plan.

SCENE 12

(4 July 1647. Caversham, Lord Craven's house. CHARLES and CROMWELL. Charles extends a hand, Cromwell bows but does not kiss it. Charles lowers his hand.)

Cromwell.	General Fairfax sanctioned this interview.
	Three days ago ten Army men discussed
	The Army's broadside against Parliament
	With Parliamentary commissioners at
	The Katherine Wheele Inn at Uxbridge. And now
	The Army controls Parliament. MPs
	Are terrified. The Army headquarters
	Are now at Uxbridge, that is why you're here,
	Just across the river. That is why we
	Brought you here from Windsor. You have enjoyed
	Considerable freedom – hunting and bowls
	With courtiers and friends. The Army wants
	To reach a settlement with you within
	Two weeks.
Charles.	You must restore me to my throne.

Cromwell.	We will if terms can be agreed, and as
	A gesture of goodwill we will provide
	Access to chaplains and your young children.

(The KING is silent.)

| Charles. | And Roman Catholics? |

| Cromwell. | We'll tolerate them. |

| Charles. | You're pragmatic Puritans. |

| Cromwell. | We're realists. |

But they must not be under foreign rule.

Charles.   Rome.

Cromwell.   Correct. Just English jurisdiction.
                  I've heard that your Queen wants you to agree
                  To the Army's demands. Sir John Berkeley
                  Will tell you so.

Charles.   There is now a strong bond
                  Between the Independents and the King.

Cromwell.   Your three children are here. They have been brought
                  From Syon House just along the river
                  As a gesture of the Army's goodwill.

                  (CROMWELL *beckons. Enter the* THREE ROYAL CHILDREN. CHARLES
                  greets each silently. Not a word is spoken. Cromwell is visibly moved.)

Charles.   Thank you with all my heart.

Cromwell.   Thank the Army.

                  (*Exit* CHARLES, *ushering the three children.*)

Cromwell   (*aside*). Now I must restrain the Army, which must
                  Not march on London to restore the King.

SCENE 13

(*12 July 1647. Mulheim Synagogue.* MENASSEH *and* EBENEZER PRATT.)

Menasseh.   Send this reply to Oliver Cromwell.
                  "We will grant financial aid as soon as
                  Charles is removed and Jews are admitted.
                  Assassination is too dangerous. Charles
                  Should be given an opportunity
                  To escape. His recapture will then make
                  His trial and execution possible.

The support will be generous but it
Is useless to discuss terms till the trial
Commences." Ebenezer will take it.

SCENE 14

(*28 July 1647. Caversham.* CHARLES and JOHN MAITLAND, Earl of Lauderdale.)

Lauderdale.
Everything has gone wrong for the Army.
Agitators want to march on London.
Cromwell and Ireton have now lost control.
The Presbyterians have raised a huge mob.
Their mob has run amok through Parliament
And held Speaker Lenthall until he freed
The militia from his supervision.
Under mob duress, without a Speaker,
The Commons have recalled you to London.
The Scots are promising to fight for you.
It's chaos, and your position's strengthened.
You can reject the Army's proposals.

Charles.
I am quite clear about my strategy.
I'll keep negotiating and allow
The Army to hope for a settlement
And meanwhile bargain for fresh concessions.

(*Enter* IRETON *and officers. They bow.*)

Ireton.
Sir, we have come to reach a settlement.
Do you accept our constitutional change?

Charles.
The Army cannot survive without me.
I don't accept your constitutional change.
I reject your proposals. You need me!
You must come up with far more equal terms.
The Commons has recalled me to London.
The good Presbyterian minority
Has done well.

Ireton	(*sadly*).	Your words are like a cold shower
		And they freeze my feelings. They have undone
		All we have tried to do, all we've given.
		Your haughty confidence is much misplaced.
		You've challenged the Army. You'll regret it.
		The Army now has no alternative
		But to march on London and quell the riots,
		Sort out the Presbyterian disorder
		And save the nation from this anarchy.

SCENE 15

(*6 August 1647. London. A hospital for wounded Civil War soldiers. Cheering. A* BLIND MAN *stops a* WOUNDED SOLDIER *with one leg.*)

Blind man.   What's happened?

Soldier.   The Army's taken London.
Now England's under military rule.
The chaos is over. Order's restored.
At two in the morning, in bright moonlight.
Fairfax watched from a carriage with his wife
And Mrs Cromwell. He has been unwell.
It was a splendid sight, whole regiments
Pouring through the open gates of Southwark,
Each soldier wearing a sprig of laurel
In his hat as a symbol of conquest.
Cromwell rode before his own regiment.
The Lord Mayor met them in Hyde Park and spoke
A hasty welcome to the conquering troops.
The Common Council were at Charing Cross.
The Army took control of Parliament.
Cromwell restored the Speaker to his chair
And awarded the troops a whole month's pay.
In daylight eighteen thousand troops marched through
The City. Both the Tower and Parliament
Were guarded. Cromwell led the cavalry.
He looked splendid on horseback. I was there.
We've won a victory, these wounds that we got

Fighting for General Cromwell weren't in vain.

Blind man.   But they'ze fighting among themselves, you dolt.
Independents 'gainst Presbyterians.

SCENE 16

(*20 August 1647. Westminster, outside the House of Commons.* CROMWELL *and* EDMUND LUDLOW.)

Ludlow.   Our cavalry's drawn up in Hyde Park, and
You have ridden to Westminster here, yet
Parliament still refuses to repeal
All Presbyterian ordinances passed
When the Speaker was out, and to eject
The Presbyterian MPs – menaces!

Cromwell.   I say again, these men won't leave until
The Army pulls them out by their ears. I
Will ride into the Commons if need be.

(*Enter* TWO MPs.)

Look, Presbyterians making themselves scarce.

(*Enter* SIR HENRY VANE.)

Vane.   Sir, the Null and Void ordinance is passed.
The Commons are now down to a puny
Hundred and fifty.

Cromwell.   The Army Council
Is now clearly in charge.

Vane.   No sir, you are.

Cromwell   (*aside*). I've taken London and purged Parliament.
I must arrange for the King to escape.
(*Aloud.*) The King must be conveyed to Hampton Court.

SCENE 17

(*7 September 1647. Hampton Court.* CHARLES, CROMWELL *and* IRETON.)

Charles.
I feel at home in this royal palace.
Its largeness is what I'm accustomed to.
I hold Court here and have been pleased to feast
Your good ladies when they have visited.

Ireton.
Sir, you have been most kind, but the Army
Wants a settlement with you. There can be
No disbanding without a settlement.
The Army will insist that you accept
The Newcastle Propositions – which placed
The Army firmly under Parliament
For twenty years, and punished your allies –
Unless you accept *Heads of the Army
Proposals*, which have a Council of State
Controlling the Army.

Charles.
                    And who will be
The main grandees in this Council of State?

Cromwell.
Oliver St John and Sir Henry Vane.

Charles.
The Agitators will not like it, nor
The Levellers. Lilburne will detest it.

Cromwell.
He's in the Tower, he can't do anything.
He's very bitter towards Parliament.

Charles.
I will accept the *Heads of the Army
Proposals*. They are the best for England.

SCENE 18

(*18 October 1647. Windsor Castle. A* LEVELLER *at the head of other Levellers, and* FAIRFAX.)

Leveller.	I give you *The Case of the Army* as
	You're Commander-in-Chief.
Fairfax.	It says the House
	Must be purged and dissolved within a year.
	The mutinous manifesto of five
	Regiments –
Leveller.	That's what Cromwell has told you.
	He's had underhand dealings with the King –
Fairfax.	He's been upright and straight –
Leveller.	Don't give me that.
	Two Scottish commissioners have arrived
	In London and the King wishes to reach
	Agreement with the Scots. Cromwell's sold out.
	He supports Charles and the Scots, he's opposed
	To abolishing the Crown and the Lords –
Fairfax.	Nonsense! You don't know what you're saying, he
	Opposes anarchy – mutinies – and
	Wants to hold the middle ground –
Leveller.	Middle Hell!
	He wants to re-establish Charles as King –
Fairfax.	To hold the middle ground for the Army,
	To put an end to chaos as the Scots
	Invade our land –
Leveller.	Cromwell's a hypocrite!

(*Assenting cheer from his followers.*)

You defend Cromwell, we in the Army
See him as cosying with the King – too soft –
And if he's going to take supreme power
By killing him, as we hope, then his words
Are hypocritical. You should dismiss
Cromwell for he's both soft and insincere.

As I shall say in the Putney debates.
(*Exit*.)

Fairfax   (*aside*). I think I'll feel unwell when the Army
Debates the future of the Crown and Lords
In St Mary's, Putney – the wisest course!

SCENE 19

(*30 October 1647. Hampton Court, after dark.* CROMWELL *and* COLONEL WHALLEY.)

Whalley.   Cousin, I think the King wants to escape.

Cromwell.   He's given his parole that he will not.

Whalley.   The talk of monarchy as tyranny,
Of throwing out the King and House of Lords,
Has unsettled him. This morning he talked
Of fleeing to the Scots to start a war.
I know, I have guards inside the palace.
I have increased the guards to keep him here.

(*Enter* CHARLES.)

Charles   (*to Cromwell*). I must protest, the guards inside my Court
Are noisy. They've woken my daughter up,
The Princess Elizabeth. She's frightened.

Cromwell.   The guards have to be inside. I will ask
Them to be more considerate. Will you
Renew your parole, give an assurance
That you will not escape?

Charles.   Certainly not.

(*There is a silence.*)

On principle. I'm held against my will.
I won't give any help to my captors.

(*Exit* CHARLES.)

Whalley.   His reply doesn't inspire confidence.

Cromwell.   No, it doesn't. I'll keep an eye on him.

(*Exit* WHALLEY.)

The time has come for me to let him go.
My Dutch masters want it. His escape will
Seal his death warrant, put me in his place.
Like a spider that's woven a great web
I must let him fly to entangle him.
Then I will have what I have plotted for.
I'll write to Whalley with alarmist news
Then watch the King fly straight into my web.

SCENE 20

(*11 November 1647. Hampton Court.* CHARLES. *A* GUARD *stands within earshot. Enter* WHAL-LEY.)

Whalley.   I have received a letter from Cromwell.
He has intelligence of an attempt
By Levellers, extreme Agitators,
Upon your life. I have doubled the guard.

(*Exit* WHALLEY. *Enter* JANE WHORWOOD, *tall, red-haired in her 30s with a pock-marked face.*)

Charles.   Sweet Jane, come to me, I am reeling, for
Cromwell has written to his cousin Whalley
That there will be an attempt on my life.

Jane   (*whispering*). Sir, you must flee. Take this gold with my kiss.

(*They embrace.* CHARLES *fumblingly takes a bag of gold which she furtively produces from under her skirts.*)

Ashburnham says Colonel Robert Hammond,
Governor of the Isle of Wight is loyal.
It has been confirmed by Cromwell himself.
A boat awaits you by the river steps.
You will then be rowed across the river
To Thames Ditton, where I will be waiting
With Ashburnham, who's made the arrangements.

Charles   (*whispering*). I am resolved to flee. I'm loath to be
A prisoner under the pretence that I
Am being detained to secure my life.
I'm like a deer in a deerpark who hears
The huntsman's horn and knows it's time to go.
Go down the back stairs, take a boat and wait
For me with noble Ashburnham, my friend,
And with Berkeley and Legge. I will follow
You to the waterside. Look out for me.
(*Aloud*.) I'm safe here, the guards are guarding my life.

SCENE 21

(*Later in November 1647. Carisbrooke Castle, Isle of Wight.* BERKELEY, ASHBURNHAM and
Col. ROBERT HAMMOND.)

Berkeley.   The King is at Titchfield, Southampton's seat.
He's fled some Levellers who would kill him.
He requests your protection on this Isle.

Hammond   (*trembling*). Protection? Gentlemen, you've undone me.

Ashburnham.   But you met the King at Hampton Court when
You took up your appointment as Governor
Of the Isle of Wight, and described how you
Resigned your Army commission. We thought
You are a convert to the Royalist cause.

Hammond.   No! Don't you know? I am related to
Oliver Cromwell! One of John Hampden's
Daughters is my wife. I went to Hampton

Court to see Cromwell. You have been misled.

Ashburnham   (*thinly*). So what are you going to do?

Hammond.   I will
Escort the King from Titchfield and place him
Where he'll be safe from Levellers within
Carisbrooke Castle.

Ashburnham   (*relieved*).   He will be safe there.

Hammond   (*aside*). As a prisoner who is safe from the Scots,
Not as a guest who's free to come and go.

SCENE 22

(*November 1647. Windsor Castle.* ARMY COUNCIL and CROMWELL.)

Army Man.   The Army Council is now furious.
We are outraged that the King should have fled.
We've treated him with the utmost respect.
He's been given all a sovereign could want –
His Court, his friends, his chaplains and prayer book.
He has repaid us by breaking parole.
Why was he guarded so loosely that he
Could just walk down the back stairs and escape?

Cromwell   (*calmly*). It's the working of divine Providence.
He's now in the hands of the Army, and
Cut off from supporters and the Scots, in
Safe custody under my relative.
I cannot think what possessed Ashburnham
To assume that Hammond is Royalist.

SCENE 23

(*Carisbrooke Castle.* CHARLES, *holding a letter, and* ASHBURNHAM. HAMMOND, *hidden,   listens.*)

Charles.
I am a prisoner here, it was better
At Hampton Court. I've written to the Queen.
I've said the Scottish Presbyterians
And Army are bidding for me, and that
(*dropping his voice*) I should close with the Scots before the rest.
Sew this into the messenger's saddle.

SCENE 24

(*November 1647. Blue Boar Inn, Holborn. CROMWELL and IRETON put on disguise as troopers.*)

Cromwell.
Do I look a trooper?

Ireton.
                    More than I do.

Aide.
That's the horse. And that's the rider, bearing
His saddle on his head.

(CROMWELL *and* IRETON *rush on him with swords.*)

Cromwell.
                    Hand that over.

Saddle-bearer.
Sir, I'm just an ordinary fellow, I
Was told to bring my saddle in with me.
That's what I done. I'm sorry if I've given
You some offence.

Ireton.
                    Slit it open.

(CROMWELL *slits the saddle with his sword.*)

                              What's this?
Cromwell.
A letter. We'll have this.

Saddle-bearer.
                    I'll be for it.
I was told –

Ireton.
                    We're telling you, this is ours.

664

SCENE 25

(*28 November 1647. Carisbrooke Castle.* CHARLES and WATSON, *Quartermaster-General of the Army.*)

Charles.   Quartermaster-General, what's Cromwell said?

Watson.   Sir, the saddle letter has changed his view.
               He's told the Army Council you are not....

Charles.   What?

Watson.   I hesitate to say.

Charles.   Spit it out.

Watson.   You're not trustworthy, that it's Providence
               Saying there's no divine approval for
               Negotiations with you. It's been said....

Charles.   Yes? Come on, man.

Watson.   That you, sir, should be tried
               For your life as a criminal person.

Charles.   Why "criminal"? What do they mean?

Watson.   They mean
               That you have been consorting with the Scots.

Charles.   That I'm a traitor?

Watson.   Yes.

Charles.   They're the traitors.

Watson.   There is a surprising accord between
               Cromwell and the Levellers. Cromwell has
               Taken the Levellers' side against you, sir.

Charles.   Thank you for your information. You will
                  Be well rewarded. Jane.

                  (*Enter* JANE.)

                              Gold for this man.

Jane.   Very good, sir.

                  (*Exit* WATSON *and* JANE. *Re-enter* JANE.)

Charles.   No messages?

Jane.   No, sir.
                  Is there anything I can do for you?

Charles   (*tenderly*). You know I've missed you, sweet Jane.

Jane.   I've taken
                  Lodgings near here so I can see you more
                  And give such services as I'm able.

Charles   (*tenderly*). Hammond's given me a summerhouse, where I
                  Can escape this Castle's draughty chambers
                  And read Herbert's poems and Bacon, or
                  Gaze across Newport to the sun and hills
                  Of the mainland, England. We'll go there now.

Jane.   Will that guard want to come and chaperone?

Charles   (*tenderly*). I've reached an understanding with my guard,
                  Thanks to the gold you brought me yesterday.
                  Tell him we're going to the summerhouse.
                  Tell him you want to be alone with me.

                  (JANE *goes to the* GUARD, *who nods and disappears. Jane returns to*
                  CHARLES.)

Jane.   The moments we snatch are precious to me.

Charles.   Come this way. O, I've missed you, my sweet Jane.

666

We'll write to the Scottish commissioners,
Who want to restore me to my throne if
I accept Presbyterians in Scotland.
The people want me, troops will ride me back
To London, my legions will soon save me.

(*Exeunt.*)

SCENE 26

(*3 January 1648. House of Commons.* CROMWELL *and* MPs.)

Cromwell.   Members of Parliament, I say to you
The King has rejected your Four Bills, and
Again asked for a personal treaty.
I have received news from the Isle of Wight
That the King planned to escape to Jersey.

(*Indignation from* MPs.)

Governor Hammond has dismissed Ashburnham,
Berkeley and Legge from the Isle of Wight. No
More approaches should be made to the King.
He's obstinate and hypocritical.
We must negotiate with the Army
Without the King, their prisoner, even though
Parliament now faces another war.

SCENE 27

(*April 1648. Carisbrooke Castle.* CHARLES. *Enter* CROMWELL, *accompanied by* LORD SAYE.)

Cromwell.   I've done everything to preserve your throne.
I've prayed, argued with Levellers, gone out
On a limb for you, and now I've come here
To plead for peace, to persuade you to dump
Your Scottish alliance – though Parliament's

Decided not to approach you again.
I come in secret to prevent a war.
A Scottish army threatens England. We
Want to disband the Army, which guards us
Against Scots –

Charles.   And keeps me a prisoner here,
And prevents the public from sweeping me
Back into London as it wants to do.
No, I reject your overtures and I
Will offer no concessions. Principle
Rules my actions, not sly expediency.

(CROMWELL *shakes his head and withdraws. At the last moment he turns.*)

Cromwell.   You are responsible for what happens now.
The Lord is my judge, you have brought us to
A second Civil War and thousands dead.

ACT FOUR

SCENE 1

(*30 April 1648. Windsor Castle.* FAIRFAX and ARMY COUNCIL.)

Fairfax.   The news from Scotland fills us with despair.
A force is heading south to free the King
And restore him against the Army's will.

(*Enter* CROMWELL.)

Cromwell.   The situation's not of our choosing.
We have three options. A new model Church
And State, which the Levellers want; restore
The King but limit his powers; or depose
The King for Henry, Duke of Gloucester, which
Has my vote.

(*Mutters from the Army. Enter* MESSENGER.)

Fairfax.	Grave news from Wales. Adjutant- General Fleming's been killed by Royalists, Some of our troops have mutinied. (*Choking*.) The shock Will be great to you all. We loved Fleming.
Army Man.	And who's responsible? Charles Stuart is.
Fairfax.	My orders are: Colonel Lambert will march North; Sir Hardress Waller will proceed to Cornwall; and Lieutenant-General Cromwell Will march to South Wales with the biggest force.

SCENE 2

(*London. Covent Garden piazza. A* CROWD *waiting for an execution.* FAIRFAX *and a common* SOLDIER *who has not recognised him.*)

Fairfax.	You were in Wales. What were your impressions?
Soldier.	We marched to Gloucester. Cromwell made a speech, All regiments afore him. He urged us To fight with faithfulness. A great shout rose, We threw our caps in the air, pledged to die For him. This Colonel Poyer was our hate. I dunno, commander-in-chief for four Counties at the end of First Civil War, And now a turncoat leading unemployed Soldiers against Cromwell. Shooting's too good For him. And he was lippy with it. We Chased him round Wales, besieged Tenby Castle And then Pembroke Castle. Our camp was on The hills of Underdown. Cromwell had gout – Walking, fighting can't have done him much good. They had their water from a conduit pipe In Pembroke Castle. Fellow called Edmunds Showed us where to cut it, for a reward – Cromwell hanged him, he never got nothing. Then the three surrendered, Poyer, Laugharne And Powell. They was taken to the Tower,

669

Given death sentences. I've heard Fairfax said
Only one should be shot, they all drew lots.
Laugharne and Powell's said "Life given by God".
Poyer's paper was blank. Look, here he comes.
He was worst of the bunch. Justice was done.
He liked his drink. What good's drink to him now?

(POYER *is shot by firing-squad*.)

(*Shouting*.) Long live General Fairfax! Long live Cromwell!
Now go and shoot the Scottish invaders!

SCENE 3

(*18 August 1648. Preston.* CROMWELL *and* LAMBERT.)

Cromwell.   This rain's terrible. My men are all soaked,
Muddy, exhausted from marching twelve miles,
Not to mention trudging from south-west Wales
To the north of England, their shoes broken.
We desperately need more stockings and shoes.
They're wet and hungry, and wish they were camped
Somewhere more dry than this rain-sodden field.

Lambert.   We're outnumbered. The Scots must have twenty
Thousand or more, they picked up Royalists
On their way south, but they've no horses or
Guns and their troops are inexperienced,
Have not held pikes before, induced to fight
By promises of English land; and they've
Got lice.

Cromwell.   We won't let them sleep, or escape
Back north. Our two armies, now we have joined,
Have eight thousand six hundred men. We are
Outnumbered at least two to one, worst luck!
We need a quick decisive victory, for
Our men are all in, blisters on their feet,
Shattered by marching. We must stop the Scots.

We'll break them here in Preston, destroy them.

Lambert.   A messenger.

                  (*Enter* MESSENGER.)

Messenger.   Sir, we've engaged the Scots.

Cromwell.   The Lord be praised!

Messenger.   The Duke of Hamilton
And Langdale have fled into Cheshire.

Lambert.   Will
You pursue them? Or will you let them run?

Cromwell.   Our men are tired and so are our horses.
If I had five hundred fresh horse and men
I'd chase them back to Scotland, but we're tired.

Messenger.   Monro's army's retreating to Yorkshire.

Cromwell.   I'll cut it off as it heads for Scotland.

SCENE 4

(*October 1648. Carisbrooke Castle*. CHARLES and PARLIAMENTARY COMMISSIONERS
including the Presbyterian DENZIL HOLLES. GUARD *within earshot*.)

Holles.   Colchester has fallen, and Cromwell has
Entered Scotland and restored order there.
He has returned to Yorkshire and taken
Charge of the siege of Pontefract. This is
One final attempt to reach agreement
With you.

Charles.   I have not seen Cromwell for months.
Seven months. He's written to Hammond that I
Am not to be trusted, nor should there be
Any religious concessions. It will

	Be hard to reach agreement unless you
	Can change Cromwell's outlook. That will be hard
	For I know you loathe him.

Holles.   What are your terms?

Charles.   We should try Presbyterianism for
          Three years, as an experiment, and sects
          Should be tolerated up to a point.
          Parliament should control the militia
          For ten years.

Holles.   Parliament has already
          Rejected these proposals. Although we
          Presbyterians will agree.

Charles.   I'll think on.
          (*Softly*.) You may have to flee from the Army now
          It's turning against Presbyterians.

          (*Exeunt the* PARLIAMENTARY COMMISSIONERS. *Enter* JANE.)

Jane.   You made no concessions.

Charles   (*softly*).   I will escape.
          While we negotiate, I will escape.
          Come, we'll walk by the shores of the Solent.
          It is a little cold, you'll need a cloak.

SCENE 5

(*Early December 1648. Knottingley, near the siege of Pontefract.* CROMWELL. *Enter* MESSENGER.)

Messenger.   Sir, a private letter.

Cromwell   (*aside*).   It's from Ireton.
          "The House has sat all night and has carried
          The motion that the King's concessions are

Satisfactory to a settlement." Hmm.
The Stuart line must go, it is Templar.
The Priory of Sion must have the throne
Of England through me. I will be its King
Of Jerusalem and a world empire,
Fiefdoms held by the Mulheim Synagogue.
As King of Jerusalem I will be
King of the English Israelites as well.
That's why the Synagogue has funded me.
If the House reaches agreement with Charles,
I'll cease to be the Synagogue's agent.
(*Aloud.*) Wait while I write a reply.

(CROMWELL *takes paper and a pen and writes.*)

(*Reading aside.*)   "Son-in-law,
You know we have not fought this Civil War
To have the King reach an agreement that
Will be dangerous for us, when in the peace
He is released and has us arrested.
I want you to purge the House of Commons
This coming night. I want just fifty left.
A rump of Levellers and Rationalists
That will do as I say and will proclaim
Itself as the supreme authority.
Ask Colonel Pride to carry out this task.
Destroy this letter as soon as you can."

(CROMWELL seals the letter and turns to the MESSENGER.)

(*Aloud.*) This is private. Give this to Ireton. Let
No one else near this letter. Your reward.

(CROMWELL gives the MESSENGER a coin.)

Messenger.   Thank you, General, thank you, thank you indeed.

SCENE 6

(*4 December 1648. Windsor Castle.* ARMY COUNCIL, *including* IRETON.)

Ireton.   Fellow southern Army officers, we
Have a grave situation on our hands.
Last month we demanded the King be tried
As a Man of Blood, as our prayers confirmed.
First Parliament adjourned our remonstrance,
And we took the precaution of moving
The King to Hurst Castle where he will be
Well guarded by Colonel Ewer. Now, worse,
Parliament's rejected our remonstrance.
They say the King's concessions will bring peace.
The Army's camping in Hyde Park, and we
Are now ready to act – to purge the House
So it reaches the right decision now.
Fifty-eight voted for us, one hundred
And twenty-five against – they must be purged,
Culled like rats scampering round an old kitchen.

Army Man.   Where's Cromwell?

Fairfax.   I sent an express message
To Knottingley three days ago, asking
Him to hand the siege over and come here.
He should have come yesterday. He's not here.

Army Man.   He's sided with the King and doesn't want
To be part of the purge of Parliament.

Fairfax.   There's no evidence for that – the reverse.

Ireton.   We must proceed, we cannot wait for him.
Colonel Pride will purge Parliament. He fought
At Naseby and Preston and is loyal.
Lord Grey has listed those to be debarred.
We will surround the House at seven a.m.
With soldiers. All who resist will be held
In the tavern called Hell. There will then be

Eighty Members of Parliament, who will
Accept our remonstrance and try the King.
Are all agreed?

(*All slowly nod, some doubtfully.*)

Then let the purge commence.

SCENE 7

(*Wednesday 6 December 1648, evening. London.* CROMWELL, *dismounting from his horse, and* LUDLOW.)

Ludlow.   Hey there, take the General's horse.

Cromwell.   What's happened?

Ludlow.   Parliament's purged. The King is to be tried.

Cromwell   (*quietly*). I did not know of this design, but now
It's happened I am glad and support it.
It is clearly the will of Providence.

Ludlow.   My father would be proud. He was rebuked
By the Speaker for saying that the King
Is not worthy of his office.

Cromwell.   He would.
That was back in 1642?

Ludlow.   Yes.

Cromwell.   Parliament's not dissolved?

Ludlow.   No, purged. All who
Want to negotiate with the King are
Excluded, banned. It's Colonel Pride's doing.

(*Exit* LUDLOW.)

Cromwell	(*aside*). And Ireton behind Pride, I behind him.
	But I was not in London, no one can
	Connect this purge, which I ordered, with me –
	Nor with the Mulheim Synagogue, nor with
	Menasseh or Carvajal, who've placed me
	In innocence. A trial. I will pretend
	To be reluctant, will vote for the King
	At every turn. Sentence. Soon I will be
	King in his place, with funding. I'll admit
	The Jews, but by then I will have the whole
	Of England in the palm of my hand, like
	A juicy peach, a bag of gold, a crown.

SCENE 8

(*25 December 1648. Windsor Castle. Army Council chamber.*)

Army Man 1.	Did you hear Peter's sermon? He preached that
	The Army will root out the monarchy
	In England, France and other kingdoms too.
	He said the King is "this great Barabbas
	At Windsor".
Army Man 2.	Did you see him arrive here?
	Colonel Harrison brought him. He's now kept
	Apart from other prisoners, guarded by
	A company of foot. No one's to speak
	To him unless the guard can hear.
Army Man 1.	Cromwell
	Voted against that.
Army Man 2.	He's on the King's side.

(*Enter* ARMY COUNCIL, *including* IRETON *and* CROMWELL. *The* TWO SOLDIERS *stand to attention.*)

Ireton.	It's Christmas Day, when the Army should be
	In church thanking God for sending his son

To save mankind. But to us Puritans
Christmas Day is a normal working-day.
And some working-day! We have a grim task,
To discuss the trial of our enemy,
The King. For this we conquered England twice.

Cromwell.   I don't think we should take away his life.
If ever we are again pressed by Scots –
If there should be a third Civil War – then
We can bargain with the invaders, for
The King will be our stake. So long as we
Hold him alive we can buy off all war
And so preserve our peace – and our power.

Fairfax.   We will go into prayer on this matter.
We will adjourn to the Council chapel
And return when we've had an answer from
Divine Providence that answers all prayers.

(*Exeunt.*)

SCENE 9

(*Tuesday 26th December. House of Commons.* CROMWELL.)

Cromwell   (*aside*). "Swift transformation of society"
Sounds acceptable. "Violent change" does not
As blaring's harsh, while melody's in tune.
Does revolution differ from progress?
No, revolution delivers progress.
Rapid change yanks society forward
But's best presented as "evolution".
I'll be a "swift transformer". Providence
Is deemed to smile more on ameliorists –
Clean-shaven, bright-eyed improvers of things –
Than on armies that strew a battlefield
With the corpses of boys too young for beards
And blare out bloodshed like trumpet fanfares.
(*Aloud.*) We are debating whether to proceed

Capitally against the King. This is
Because Providence and necessity
Have brought us to this consideration.
Necessity, to keep public order;
Not to try him would bring disturbances.
Since God's Providence has brought us to this,
I must submit to Providence. I will
Accept the will of Providence when it
Reveals itself to my contemplative
Mind. I'll notify you of sudden Light.

SCENE 10

(*19 January 1649. Windsor Castle.* CHARLES.)

Charles   (*aside*). Carisbrooke, Hurst Castle and now Windsor.
The places evoke my doomed ancestors:
Edward the Second, butchered in Berkeley.
Richard the Second killed in Pontefract.
It would be convenient if I now died.
I am relieved to be here. All along
The muddy lanes – Hampshire, Surrey, Berkshire –
People waved, cheered and pressed to touch my hand
Despite the driving rain which soaked us all.
The women shouted insults at soldiers.
I have support, it will be hard for them
To kill me here, not privately, at least.
In the oak of State he seems a wise owl
But is a bird of prey, more crow or hawk
Than owl, while I, a gentle rabbit, sit
In shade, fearing an impending attack.
And now, what now? He cites the will of God.
What I did to Laud and Strafford was for
The common good, and he now thinks the same,
And I am in Laud's shoes and Strafford's clothes.
I knew what was best then, and he does now.

(*Enter Governor,* COLONEL WHICHCOTE.)

Whichcote.	You're now going to St James's Palace And then to the Palace of Westminster.
Charles.	A trial. There will be a trial. The climax Is near at hand, the martyr's *denouement*. Cromwell prowls like a cat stalking a finch.

SCENE 11

(*7 January 1649. Westminster Hall.* PROSECUTOR, ARMY COUNCIL *and* ALGERNON SIDNEY.)

Prosecutor.	All I know is, there's to be a new court. You're to be one of the judges. Look, your Name's here. There are dozens of names.
Sidney.	I don't Know anything about it. I won't serve. (*Enter* CROMWELL.)
Cromwell.	Yesterday the Commons passed an Act that Establishes the people as supreme Authority. Today they need a court. (CROMWELL *nods to the* PROSECUTOR.)
Prosecutor.	I now proclaim a High Court of Justice To try the King.
Sidney.	Two thirds of its members Are Levellers from the Army. It's rigged.
Cromwell.	Who said that? Come here. (ALGERNON SIDNEY *approaches*.) Now what is your point?

Sidney.	Sir, first the King can be tried by no court.
	Second, no man can be tried by this court.
Cromwell.	Nonsense. This is a people's court. It is
	Lawful. (*To Prosecutor*.) Have you found an English lawyer
	Who will draw up the charge?
Prosecutor.	No, sir. None will.
Cromwell.	None? (*Raging*.) One must be found.
Prosecutor.	Sir, there is only
	A Jewish lawyer, Isaac Dorislaus.
Cromwell	(*aside*). He knows Carvajal and Menasseh. They
	Have pushed him forward. (*Aloud*.) All right, he will do.

SCENE 12

(*20 January 1649. The Painted Chamber, Palace of Westminster*. CROMWELL at the window with JOHN BRADSHAW, Chief Justice of Cheshire; SIR HENRY MILDMAY; and SIR WILLIAM BRERETON.)

Cromwell.	The King has passed through the garden below.
	My masters, he's come. We're doing the great
	Work the whole nation will soon be full of.
	The first question he will ask us when he comes
	Before us will be: what authority
	Do we have to try him? We have to find
	An answer now so we are well prepared.
Bradshaw.	As President of the court, my answer's –
Cromwell.	The 6th-January Act, that the people
	In the Commons hold supreme power and that
	The King and Lords make no difference to that.
	We're a court that has to judge a tyrant.
	We're more tyrannicides than regicides.
	We represent the people, as a court.

We are against the monarch and the Lords.
We have to modernise England. That means
Ending the House of Lords and monarchy,
Empowering the people. We're populists.

SCENE 13

(*20 January 1649. Westminster Hall hung with Royalist colours. BRADSHAW sits at a table covered with a carpet. Many COMMISSIONERS. TROOPS. A MASKED LADY sits in the public gallery. CHARLES in black, holding a silver-tipped cane. Round his neck hang the Star of the Garter and the George and blue ribbon. He wears a hat.*)

Charles   (*aside*). Westminster Hall, three hundred feet long, built
By William Rufus, oak hammerbeamed roof
Added by Richard the Second who was
Deposed here. Here too Edward the Second
Abdicated. Here Charles the First's condemned
Under Royalist colours captured at
Marston Moor, Naseby and Preston, before
Fifty-two judges, all who have turned up
Out of a hundred and thirty-five men.
Bradshaw's a manly President, Fairfax
Looks uncomfortable. Who is that lady
Wearing a mask? Ah, there's Cromwell. He has
Waited a long while for this moment. He's
Like a carrion crow eying afar
A twitching rabbit broken by a trap,
Waiting to feed on its lifeless carcass,
Tear its flesh with its dagger-like bill. It's
An illegal court. Algernon Sidney,
Refusing to be judge, said "The King can
Be tried by no court, no man can be tried
By this court." To which Cromwell said, "We will
Cut off his head with the crown upon it."
It's a foregone conclusion. I will not
Remove my hat in deference to this court.

(BRADSHAW *raps on the table.*)

Bradshaw.   We are convened to try a tyrant King.
             The prisoner will remove his hat.

             (CHARLES *folds his arms and defies* BRADSHAW.)

Charles.   I won't.

Bradshaw   (*sighing*). Read out the charges.

             (JOHN COOK, Solicitor for the Commonwealth, stands up.)

Cook.   As Solicitor
             For the Commonwealth, deputising for
             The Attorney General who is unwell,
             I refer to the 6th-January Act
             Of Parliament which states that the people
             Are, under God, the source of all just power,
             That the Commons has supreme power, and that
             What the Commons enacts has force of law
             Even if King and Lords do not consent.
             The people through the Commons have now charged
             The King as tyrant, traitor, murderer,
             An enemy of the Commonwealth who
             Abused his trust as governor by wielding
             Tyrannical power, who made war against
             Parliament twice, and who as a tyrant
             Must be deposed for good with his office.

Charles   (*aside*). This Cook's a moral, self-righteous windbag.
             Where is the substance of his verbose charge?

Cook.   The principal charge is of high treason.

             (The KING *taps* COOK's *arm with his cane to protest. The silver end falls
             off. No one picks it up. Charles has to bend and retrieve it himself.*)

Bradshaw.   The King will now answer the charge just made
             On behalf of the Commons assembled
             In Parliament and England's good people.

Masked lady (*shouting*). That's a lie. On behalf of a quarter

Of England's people, even less than that.
Oliver Cromwell is a traitor.

(COLONEL AXTELL, who is in charge of troops, fires into the public gallery.)

Axtell.   Out!

(*The* MASKED LADY *is seized by* TROOPS. *Her mask is removed.*)

Charles.   Lady Fairfax.

(FAIRFAX'S WIFE *is hustled out.* FAIRFAX, *who has turned pale, leaves.*)

Bradshaw   (*rapping the table*).
                          No more interruptions.
                  The King.

Charles.   By what authority have I
                  Been brought to this bar? There are no lords here,
                  You're not a Parliament. There's no lawful
                  Authority here, so I won't answer.
                  And nor will I therefore remove my hat.

(*Laughter in the public gallery.*)

Bradshaw.   We have authority from the people
                  Who elected you King.

Charles.   Kings inherit
                  Their crowns. In England they aren't elected.

(*Laughter in the public gallery.* BRADSHAW *raps.*)

Bradshaw.   How do you answer the people's charges?

Charles.   The charges weren't levelled by the people
                  But by an Army group that's seizing power.

Cromwell.   Your answer. You must answer the people.

Bradshaw.   How do you answer?

Charles.   I don't. You do not
                    Represent the people, that is a lie
                    As Lady Fairfax said. You're not lawful.
                    You have no authority. You invoke
                    The people, but I know that crowds want me
                    Restored to my hereditary throne.
                    Your people's a shibboleth, a smokescreen.

Bradshaw.   It is not for prisoners to justify
                    Why they won't plead.

Charles.   I am no ordinary
                    Prisoner.

Bradshaw   (*to clerk*).
                              Record the King's default. Adjourned.

Charles   (*aside*). They hiss like a gaggle of frightened geese.

SCENE 14

(*26 January 1649. A room near Westminster Hall.* CROMWELL *and* JUDGES, *including* IRE-TON *and* INGOLDSBY.)

Cromwell.   A King's breach of trust must be punished more
                    Secretly than that of his own subjects.
                    The King made a contract with his subjects.
                    He broke his contract and must be punished.
                    We all signed the National Covenant that
                    Binds us to preserve the King, but the King
                    Obstructed a religious settlement.
                    We're released from our oath. We are excused
                    From the rules of common morality
                    Because we have been called to great service
                    And like Samson and David in great deeds
                    We are freed from moral constraints. We must
                    Put him to death. I have already signed
                    The death warrant, as have most of you as
                    The people's representatives.

(CROMWELL *studies the death warrant.*)

        Richard
Ingoldsby has to sign.

Ingoldsby.   I'd rather not.

Cromwell   (*shouting*). We have, and you're in this as much as us.
I insist you sign.

Ingoldsby.   I refuse. I won't.
I have freewill, I will not be coerced.
You're all like hounds surrounding a trapped deer.

(CROMWELL *rushes across the room, forces a pen into* INGOLDSBY's
fingers and guides his hand.)

Cromwell   (*reading*). Richard Ingoldsby. Good. You have now signed.

Ingoldsby.   That was the act of a tyrant worse than
The King we're killing because he taxed us.

(SIR RICHARD INGOLDSBY *is hustled out. Enter* THOMAS WAITE.)

Waite.   He does not look happy. Is Lord Grey here?

Cromwell.   No.

Waite.   He wrote me a note.

Ireton.   So you can sign
Along with all of us Commissioners.

Cromwell.   You see Lord Grey's name, second to Bradshaw's
Just above mine. You have to sign just there.

(WAITE *signs. Exeunt all save* CROMWELL.)

(*Aside.*) I wrote the note with Ireton, not Lord Grey.
I knew Waite would not sign if I asked him
To come to this room. Signatures absolve.

The execution must not seem my act.
I am God's instrument, and God requires
The people's representatives to sign.
Like a battlefield commander I urge
My people onward and lift their morale.
I facilitate God's purpose and if
I trick hesitaters into signing
I'm just pushing them to be decisive.
The end – the people – justifies the means.
My conscience is clear before God and man.

SCENE 15

(*27 January 1649. Westminster Hall.* BRADSHAW *and* COURT JUDGES. CHARLES *sits impassively. A* GUARD *passes him and mocks him with an elaborate bow.*)

Bradshaw   (*rapping*). There are sixty-two Commissioners here.
We have a quorum.

Charles.   Yesterday, there were
Forty-six and the quorum is fifty.

Bradshaw.   Forty. The prisoner will not interrupt.

Charles   (*aside*). He stares like a crow, portending my death.

Bradshaw.   The court will now sentence Charles Stuart. In
The name of the people of England –

Lady.   Not
Half the people!

Bradshaw.   Remove the lady.

(THE LADY *is removed.*)

                                 We
Voted yesterday, and the judges were
Unanimous for his death, and they all

	Recommended yesterday that he should
	Be put to death for being a public
	Enemy to the English Commonwealth.
	A committee has now withdrawn the charge
	Of high treason but recommended that
	Charles Stuart, tyrant, should be put to death
	By severing his head from his body.
	That is the sentence of this people's court.

Soldiers   (*crying out*). Justice! Justice and Execution! Death!

Bradshaw.   Does the prisoner wish to say anything?

Charles.   The sentence was very predictable.
                  I wish to address both Commons and Lords.

Bradshaw.   Out of the question.

                  (JOHN DOWNES, MP *leaps up*.)

Downes.   I support the King's
                  Request.

Cromwell.   Are you yourself?

Downes.   This court is quite
                  Illegal.

Bradshaw.   I will adjourn next door and
                  Hear John Downes through. Please wait.

                  (BRADSHAW, CROMWELL, IRETON *and* DOWNES *go to a corner of*
                  the stage.)

Cromwell.   Have you gone mad?

Ireton.   How can a people's court be illegal?

Downes.   It doesn't include lords –

Cromwell.   We're dealing with
                  The hardest-hearted man on earth.

Downes.	But I –
Cromwell	(*jeering*). And you're the most naive man on earth. You Are making a laughing-stock of yourself.
Bradshaw.	I've heard this peevish fellow's point of view. We will return to court.

(*They return to their places in court.*)

	This court's legal. We'll ignore the unsubstantiated Interruption just now. We will proceed To sentence, but before the clerk reads it I want to add some thoughts. Sometimes sovereigns Are deposed or dispatched –
Charles.	I will be heard.
Bradshaw.	Silence! Edward the Second and Richard The Second, and Mary, Queen of Scots all –
Charles.	I will not be sentenced without being heard.
Bradshaw.	Were sovereigns who had to be put to death. There's precedent for this court's sentence. Clerk!
Clerk.	This court's sentence is that Charles Stuart should Be put to death by the severing of His head from his body.
Charles	(*with dignity*). If I am not Allowed to speak at such a time, what hope Have others, what justice will others have?
Soldiers.	Death! Justice! Justice and Execution!

(CHARLES, *trying to make himself heard above the soldiers' chant, is hustled from the court protesting.* CROMWELL *confers with* BRADSHAW.)

Bradshaw	(*to the judges*). We need more signatures on the warrant.

SCENE 16

(27 January 1649. Night. London, Fairfax's quarters. FAIRFAX *and* OFFICERS.*)*

Army Officer 1.   General Fairfax, we want to save the King.
He's changed, he won't return to his old ways.

Army Officer 2.   Will you help us?

Fairfax.   How? An Army *coup*?

Army Officer 1.   Yes.

Fairfax.   I am unhappy about the sentence
As is my wife, but feeling is too strong.
I don't want to stir up the Army's wrath.
However, in this case –.

(There is a commotion. Enter CROMWELL *and* IRETON *with* SOLDIERS.*)*

Cromwell.   We know your aim.
An informer has revealed this meeting.
Any attempt to snatch the prisoner will
Result in deaths. (*To Fairfax.*) You must support us now.

Fairfax.   I've a letter from Louis the Fourteenth.

Cromwell   (*contemptuously*). So've I –

Fairfax.   And from the Dutch States-General too.

Cromwell.   So've I. Interfering busybodies.
Times have changed and Providence has disposed.
I've prayed and fasted for the King. Not now.
I've done everything possible for him.
We overlook your wife's outburst, but you
Must not retreat from our tyrannicide.
It would confuse the Army. They'd unleash
Anarchy on the nation. We must now
Steady its nerve. There must be no reprieve.

Fairfax.	You've raised expectations you're now stuck with. You should not have used Levellers' language. But what's done's done. I don't want more bloodshed. Events will take their course as they unfold. I will take no more part in state affairs. I shall retire to my Yorkshire estate And tend my garden, and my lily pond.
Ireton.	The main thing is, you don't interfere now. And you officers, back to your units Or we'll have you arrested and then shot.

SCENE 17

(29 January 1649. London, St James's Palace. CHARLES *and* BISHOP JUXON.*)*

Charles.	It's like stripping the Tree of State of leaves, Lopping branches, then felling the whole oak. There will be no tradition when I'm gone.
Juxon.	Many prominent men want to see you.
Charles.	I won't see anyone save my children. I fear for them. A magpie kills ducklings.
Juxon.	They are here.

*(*HENRY *and* ELIZABETH *are ushered in.)*

Charles.	Dear Henry, Elizabeth. I have to say goodbye, for tomorrow....
Henry.	We know, Papa.
Charles.	You must not feel badly Towards the men who're doing this. They think That Parliament's more powerful than the King. You must not dislike Parliament. They think That their religion's better than the Church

Of England. You must not be Puritan –

Henry.   Never.

Elizabeth.   We'll always be Church of England.

Cromwell.   You must forgive the men who'er doing this.
It will be hard, but no bitterness.

Henry.   No.
I love you, Papa.

Elizabeth.   And I love you too.

Charles.   And I love you. You've both been good children.
Now take these letters I have written you
And both be brave for me. No, very brave.

(*They kiss their father and leave with their letters.*)

Juxon   (*aside*). He sings serenely, like a nightingale.
(*Aloud.*) Are you all right?

Charles   I feel so peaceful now.
I have relaxed my grasp on life, honour
Is more important than saving my life.
I die for a principle. The monarch's
Above the people's law, he's appointed
By divine right, not human agency.
If I have fallen short, God will judge me.
But I am God's anointed, my nation's
Shepherd. I've raised funds to lead it forward.
I'm no more tyrant than a shepherd is.
The people will learn that the usurpers –
Cromwell, Ireton, Bradshaw and all the rest –
Are working with Dutch Rosicrucians who
Are seizing our Kingdom with virtuous
Protestations, as pirates deep in prayer
Resolve to storm aboard a ship of State.
A monarch cannot be abolished by
A people without a massive change in

The constitution, for man then leads man
As pirates lead the crew they have captured,
Divorced from God's great purposes and Light.
The monarch's the illumined leader of
A nation that needs guidance. Puritans
Think they receive guidance from God by prayer.
They are deluded if they think that God
Is inciting subjects to regicide.
The monarchy in England will survive.
No Cromwell can abolish King or Queen
Just as no pirate can the captain's rank –
The people will restore a Prince of Wales.
I must be martyred for the monarchy.

(BISHOP JUXON *makes the sign of the cross.*)

Juxon.   Let us go into our chapel and pray.

SCENE 18

(*30 January 1649, 11 a.m. London, an apartment in Whitehall Palace. Sound of banging as the scaffold is erected. CROMWELL, IRETON, HARRISON, HUNCKS and HACKER at a window.*)

Cromwell.   The King's walking across the frosty grass
                To this Whitehall palace, like a blackbird
                Hopping into a trap. He too can hear
                The scaffolding being erected. Now
                The Commons has passed an Act forbidding
                The monarch to have a successor. Look,
                He's shivering like us this icy day.
                We're freezing, this is no time to delay
                Signing the warrant.

Ireton   (*from under a bedcover*). Huncks must sign.

Huncks.   I won't.

Hacker.   I'll take his place.

692

Cromwell.	Brave man. Not a coward.

Huncks.	I'm no coward, I just don't think it's right.

A sudden social change is unnatural
Like jumping from lushness of summer leaves
To winter bareness and ribbed land without
Passing through autumn's gradual reddening
And golden ripeness of corn being reaped.

Hacker.	But can't it be like jumping from winter

To summer bloom without the April showers
And the first chilly inklings of the spring?

Huncks.	No, Cromwell's plunging us from high summer

To darkest Arctic shivering winter.

Hacker.	Out or be killed! I'll not stand idly by

While you insult our resolute leader.

(*Exit* HUNCKS. HACKER *signs.* CROMWELL *moves to one side.*)

Cromwell	(*aside*). Now I must be resolute one more day.

I have pushed all into this course – Ireton,
Fairfax, Bradshaw, the judges, many more –
And now I must carry through my design
Which began before the First Civil War
And has brought me to the brink of sole rule,
Of Kingship, which through guidance from Holland,
The Lord I should say, is now in my grasp.
I must be as calm as a watching owl
That calculates his silent swoop and strikes
With a prolonged and terrifying shriek
That's out of character for a wise bird,
And clutches a rat in his sharp talons.
I must be a sly as a fox near hens.
The executioner will wear false beard
And wig to conceal his identity.
It will seem I'm absent from the scaffold,
As it will appear Ireton is also.
I must steel myself for this final act.
It must not be botched, I need nerves of steel,

As keen as the sharp edge of a block-axe.
It's no more than striking the final blow
To fell a rotten oak that has leaf-blight.
From the outset this has been a contest
Between Charles Stuart and myself. Now I
Must smite the final blow and kill him clean.

SCENE 19

(*30 January 1649, 2 p.m. London, Whitehall Palace. A procession.* CHARLES, *his beard grey, his hair silver, wearing a white shirt under a black doublet and cloak and a white skull cap*; BISHOP JUXON; COL. HACKER; *and* COL. TOMLINSON.)

Charles   (*to Juxon*). I'm wearing two shirts lest I shiver and
                 Appear afraid, but still my teeth chatter.

Juxon.   This cold's bitter.

                 (JUXON *reads from the Book of Common Prayer. They pass between two
                 lines of troops and spectators, who pray aloud and make the sign of the
                 cross, unstopped by soldiers.* CHARLES *pauses and looks at the ceiling.*)

Charles.   The apotheosis
                 Of my father James the First by Rubens.
                 Now all witness my apotheosis.

                 (JUXON *continues reading from the prayer book. They step out of a window
                 onto the scaffold.* EXECUTIONER *in beard and wig, and his* ASSISTANT,
                 similarly disguised. A cloak touches the axe on the block.)

Charles.   Take heed of the axe! Don't blunt the axe or
                 It will hurt me. The block is very low.
                 Can it be raised?

Executioner.   You must lie on your front.

Charles   (*aside*). And grovel? Never! Somehow I will kneel.

                 (CHARLES *steps forward and addresses the vast crowd.*)

People as far as I can see. (*Aloud.*) I say
To the people that I regret nothing.
I am innocent, I did not begin
A war with the Houses of Parliament.
Their militia began the war on me.
Ill instruments have come between them and
Me and are the cause of all the bloodshed,
The conquerors of world imperialism,
Rosicrucian Freemasonry. Conquest
Is never just. Alexander the Great
Was a bigger robber than a pirate.
He and the pirate were two of a kind
And separated only by degree.
The refuge from imperialism is
The Church of England kept in good order.
I wanted the people to be prosperous.
I desire the people's liberty and
Freedom as much as anybody, but
They cannot have liberty and freedom
Without government and laws, that make sure
Their lives and goods are untouched by others,
And are safe from pillaging imperialists.
The people should not share in government.
A subject and sovereign are clean different.
It is to make this point that I am here.
I am the martyr of the people, I'm
Their shield of sovereignty from all robbers.

(CHARLES *turns back.*)

Juxon.	You will soon pass from earth to Heaven, the prize You hasten to, to a crown of glory.
Charles.	I go from a corruptible to an Incorruptible crown.
Juxon.	You're exchanging A temporal for an eternal crown. (*Aside.*) Like a blackbird and a rapacious owl.
Executioner.	Your hair under your cap.

Charles.   I know that voice.

(*The* EXECUTIONER *tucks Charles's hair under his satin cap.* CHARLES *takes his cloak off, removes his doublet, then puts his cloak back on over his shirt. He takes off his gold ring and gives it to* BISHOP JUXON.)

(*Aside.*) I know that tone of peremptory command.
(*Aloud.*) Bishop Juxon, take this gold ring, set in
Precious rubies, with a picture of me.
Hold this for my son Charles, the Prince of Wales,
And give it to him when he is restored.
(*Aside.*) "Your answer. You must answer the people."

(CHARLES *turns to the executioner.*)

Usurping is not clean, but now strike clean.
When I put out my hands! Wait for the sign!

(CHARLES *kneels and lays his head on one side on the low block, as on a pillow. He winces, then prays. He puts out his hands. The* EXECUTIONER *strikes off his head. There is a groan from the crowd. The* EXECUTIONER *picks up the severed head.*)

Executioner.   Behold, the head of a traitor!

Man in crowd.   Martyr!

(*The* EXECUTIONER *flings down the King's head with emotional force, bruising its face.*)

SCENE 20

(*30 January 1649. London, Harrison's rooms. A prayer-meeting of the Army Council, led by* FAIRFAX. *All are silent in prayer. Enter* CROMWELL *and* IRETON, *tiptoeing quietly.*)

Fairfax.   We will be criticised if the King dies.

Cromwell.   We should seek God to know his mind on this.

696

	(*All pray.*)
Cromwell.	O Lord, please tell us what we should now do. Should we behead the King or let him live?
	(*Enter* MESSENGER, *who speaks at a nod from* CROMWELL.)
Messenger.	The King is dead.
Cromwell.	Our prayer is answered. It Has not been the will of God he should live.
Fairfax.	This is dreadful.
Cromwell	(*to the messenger*). We will give orders for The King's burial speedily.
	(*Exit* MESSENGER.)
	We are all The instruments of God's will.
	(*All rise.*)
Fairfax	(*looking aghast*). Where were you And Ireton at the start of our meeting?
Cromwell.	We had some business to complete.
Fairfax.	Who was The headsman? Who assisted him?
Cromwell.	Not known. They were disguised, it will never be known.
Fairfax.	How did you know what they wore? You were here.

SCENE 21

(31 January 1649, 2 a.m. Whitehall Palace, the Banqueting House. CHARLES's *body on a velvet pall, watched by the* EARL OF SOUTHAMPTON *and the soldier* BOWTELL.*)*

Southampton.   I feel very melancholy. What will
Become of England now? The Royal Oak
Of Britain with its four crowns – the Bible,
Magna Carta, statute law and green peace –
Has been felled by a usurping woodman
Who had no right. What now?

Bowtell.   Republican
Commonwealth tyranny, dictatorship.

Southampton.   What's that?

Bowtell.   The stairs.

(Enter A MAN *muffled in his cloak. He approaches the body and puts out his finger as if to see if the head is completely severed. He shakes his head.)*

Cromwell.   Cruel necessity!
He'd have lived longer if he wasn't King.
Providence guided this, it was God's will
That the King should no longer live. We have
Freed the people and sought the public good.
Tyrants! Providence and necessity.

Bowtell.   What government do we have now?

Cromwell.   The same.

Bowtell.   A King?

Cromwell.   A better King.

Southampton.   Is it Cromwell?

(Exit the muffled figure back down the stairs.)

SCENE 22

(*9 February 1649. Windsor Castle. Snow.* BISHOP JUXON.)

Juxon.   Snow, the colour of his innocency.
      We are not allowed to use the service
      In the *Book of Common Prayer* or bury
      Him in Westminster Abbey. He will lie
      In this Windsor vault with Henry the Eighth,
      Who made the Church of England that he loved.
      May Charles the Martyr be received in Heaven.

SCENE 23

(*19 March 1649. House of Commons.* CROMWELL.)

Cromwell. The Commons have voted to abolish
      The House of Lords, which one MP described
      As a "great inconvenience". You all know
      That as Chairman of the Council of State
      Which runs the Republic of the British
      Isles, our Commonwealth people's republic,
      I did not want this, and voted to keep
      The Lords in some form. But, now it's happened,
      I accept that it is the will of God,
      The working of God's Providence. The Lords
      Weren't elected and did not represent
      The people any more than Charles Stuart.
      So though I did not seek it by my deeds,
      I now support a people's state in which
      There is no monarchy or House of Lords.

ACT FIVE

SCENE 1

(*13 May 1649. Burford, Oxfordshire. An encampment.* CAPT. THOMPSON *and* LEVELLERS.)

Thompson.   We're not going to Ireland, that's final.

          (*A cheer from other Levellers.*)

          There may be Royalists there, and Charles's son,
          But this regime's done nothing for us troops.
          Cromwell's a cuckoo who's pushed out the King.
          He couldn't have pinched his nest without us.
          Cromwell couldn't have killed the King without
          Us Levellers. We wanted a great change,
          Not just in the country – our conditions.
          The Army pay's an insult.

          (*More cheering.*)

                        Instead of
          Taking the King's arms from public buildings,
          Renaming ships with Stuart names, selling
          The King's paintings, they ought to do something
          For the common soldier, us.

          (*More cheering.*)

                        So we from
          Reynolds' regiment at Banbury will join
          Up with the Salisbury troops of Ireton and –

          (*Enter messenger,* MAJOR WHITE.)

White.   Message from Generals Cromwell and Fairfax.

          (THOMPSON *reads the message.*)

Thompson.   A peaceful mission of mediation!

Good news, lads. Generals Cromwell and Fairfax
Will not follow up this approach with force.
There's nothing doing, Major. We're resolved,
We Levellers ain't going to Ireland.

White. You'll regret it.

Thompson. With no force at your heels?
Don't make me laugh. You're talking to Levellers.

(*Exit* WHITE.)

Come on, lads, let's drink the night away, for
We're going nowhere till our pay is right.

(*Cheering. Suddenly they are under attack. A short battle, during which*
THOMPSON *escapes. Several mutineers are killed. The survivors are*
rounded up.)

Army Officer. You're going to be locked up in the church.
Ringleaders will be shot in the churchyard.

(*Enter* CROMWELL *and* FAIRFAX.)

Cromwell. Well done, men. We're not tolerating these
Levellers. They're giving us all a bad name.
They're mutinous, they won't do as they're told.
We're suppressing them all over England.
Burford will be a lesson to them all.
God's Providence has stopped the Levellers
From continuing in our republic.

Fairfax (*to Cromwell*). You look tired. Back to Burford Priory,
Where Speaker Lenthall awaits us. To bed.

(*Exeunt.*)

SCENE 2

(*June 1649. Whitehall, London.* CROMWELL *and* HARTLIB. *A specialist audience of esoteric*

Rosicrucians.)

Cromwell. Samuel, I've admired you. Your Andreaen
Society, Antilia, inspired
Your Rosicrucian pre-Fall Paradise,
Macaria, which follows on from More's
Utopia and Bacon's *New Atlantis.*
You brought Comenius to England to found
An invisible college that's become
A focus for Rosicrucian exiles
From the Palatinate at the Hague and
Robert Boyle's new Rosi-scientists.
You formed a group round Bacon, Milton, Fludd
And many others, and implemented
Francis Bacon's advancement of learning,
And have shaped policies for poor relief,
Agriculture, education and trade,
Industry and medicine. You're our ideas.
You've dreamt of a State-funded Paradise
And inspired me with your unique vision.
Splendid Utopian, I appoint you
State Agent for Universal Learning.

(*Applause.* HARTLIB *bows.*)

Hartlib (*softly*). And now, good luck in Ireland, Oliver.

SCENE 3

(*September 1649. The siege of Drogheda, Ireland. Enter* FIRST MESSENGER.)

1st Messenger. We've got in near the Gate and stormed the church,
But they're driving us back.

Cromwell. I'll hold the breach
Till Ewer brings up his reinforcements.

(*Exit* FIRST MESSENGER.)

Royalists everywhere – England, Holland
(Killing Dorislaus, our envoy), Scotland
And especially Ireland, teaming up
With the priest-ridden, drunk, barbarous Irish,
Popish Catholics we Puritans detest,
As if the choppy crossing weren't enough!
The Irish are savage, they massacred
The English settlers eight years back, and now
There must be no quarter. Put to the sword.

(*Enter* SECOND MESSENGER.)

2nd Messenger.   We're pouring through the walls, we've seized the church
And their trenches. They're fleeing to the hill.

Cromwell.   Pursue them. Kill them all. No survivors.

(*Enter* THIRD MESSENGER. TWO MEN *hold* A MAN *with a wooden leg.*)

3rd Messenger.   We've captured Aston, and we now suspect
His wooden leg is stuffed with gold pieces.
What should we do?

Cromwell.   Kill him. With his peg-leg.

(*The* TWO MEN *tear* SIR ARTHUR ASTON's *wooden leg off his knee and
bludgeon him to death with it. Enter* FOURTH MESSENGER.)

4th Messenger.   Sir, what happens to Drogheda's friars and priests?

Cromwell.   Kill them.

4th Messenger.   And those in the steeple at St
Peter's who won't come down?

Cromwell.   Set pews alight,
Burn them down. Make the church their funeral pyre.
Show what's fit for Popish Catholics. Burn them!

(*Confused sounds. Enter* EWER.)

Ewer.	It's been a massacre. No one's survived.
	Our eight thousand men roam deserted streets.
Cromwell.	It was God's Providence that none should live.
Ewer.	I have not seen you like this before, so
	Ruthless.
Cromwell.	Am I not self-controlled?
Ewer.	We must
	Not become tyrants like the King –
Cromwell.	We aren't.
	An effusion of blood will purge Ireland
	Of Royalists and subjugate this land.
	We've done this for the people of England.
	(*Aside*.) I will be Viceroy and Mrs Cromwell
	Vicereine, now she's set up home in Dublin.
	(*Exit* CROMWELL. *An owl shrieks*.)
Ewer	(*aside*). He has an owl's acute hearing, pin-points
	The slightest sound, swoops on unsuspecting
	Prey and devours it, fur, feathers, bones, all,
	And disgorges them as vile pellets. He
	Tears his foes to pieces and lives amid
	The disgorged mess of their swallowed remains.
	"Pure" Cromwell lives in filth like a barn owl.

SCENE 4

(*6 October 1649. Wexford, Ireland. The Market Cross. Slaughter in progress. Non-stop executions.* CROMWELL *and* EWER *stand by*.)

Ewer.	Captain Stafford betrayed the Castle. When
	Our men stood on top, Catholics left the walls
	And ran to the market-place. Our men stormed
	The town with ladders, and put to the sword

| | Near one thousand. Three hundred Catholics piled |
| | Into two boats, which sank – |

Cromwell.   God's Providence.

Ewer.   All drowned. Now at the Market Cross, we are
                     Finishing the task.

Cromwell.   Who are these prisoners?

Ewer.   The friars and priests of Wexford –

Cromwell.   Enemy
                     Soldiers in Catholic uniform, they should
                     Be treated no differently from the rest.
                     They've harried our troops for years. Governor
                     Sinnott is responsible for their fate.

                     (*The English run amok killing Irish by-standers.* CROMWELL *and* EWER
                     make no attempt to stop them.)

SCENE 5

(*Summer 1650. Whitehall, London.* ANDREW MARVELL *waiting. Enter* CROMWELL.)

Cromwell.   You're Andrew Marvell, poet?

Marvell.   Yes, sir.

Cromwell.   I've
                     Read your 'Ode to Cromwell'. I detected
                     Traces of sympathy towards the King,
                     But not many. And you've become tutor
                     To General Fairfax's daughter, Mary?

Marvell.   Yes. At Nun Appleton House.

Cromwell.   I'd like you
                     To keep an eye on General Fairfax, please.

He's refused the main command in Scotland.
I'd like to know why. Is it as he says,
That he's against an offensive campaign?
Or are there other reasons? I'm aware
He fought for the Dutch, who are close to him.
If any Dutchman approaches Fairfax,
Inform me. I will make it worth your while.

Marvell.   Thank you, sir.

Cromwell.   But principally you're the best
Tutor that he could find. Don't disappoint.
Oh, keep writing. Poetry's Milton and you.

Marvell.   I wish you luck in the Scottish campaign.

SCENE 6

(2 September 1650. Night. Dunbar, Scotland. LAMBERT and WHALLEY.)

Lambert.   We could do with Fairfax right now. It's such
A shame he would not be Captain-General.
We're trapped here in Scotland. Up on the heights
Twenty-three thousand Scots and Royalists,
The Pretender Charles' troops. The other side
Of us the cold North Sea. We can't attack,
The escarpment's impregnable. Cromwell's
Praying that they come down!

Whalley.   They're coming! See?

(Enter CROMWELL.)

Cromwell.   God is delivering them into our hands.
They're forming in an arc. And lying down.

(Enter a messenger, FLEETWOOD.)

Fleetwood.   The Scots outnumber us by two to one.

706

They've unsaddled their horses. They're sleeping
In the corn.

Cromwell.   We'll surprise them before dawn.
We'll take six cavalry regiments and
Three and a half of foot. I'll spend the night
Visiting the regiments on my nag.
We'll be in silence till we charge, and then
Our battlecry will be "The Lord of Hosts".

SCENE 7

(*3 September 1650, 6 a.m. Dunbar.* SIR JOUN HODGSON *and* OFFICER.)

Hodgson.   Cromwell's watching the sun rise from the sea.
He's chanting Psalm sixty-eight, "Now let God
Arise and his enemies be scattered."

(*Both men peer.*)

Officer.   The horse are through, the Scots are now in flight.

(MEN *cheer "Hurrah". Enter* CROMWELL.)

Cromwell.   We have won the battle of Dunbar. We
Have killed perhaps three thousand and captured
Ten thousand. The Royalists in Scotland
Are no more threat. The Lord of Hosts be praised!

SCENE 8

(*1 January 1651. Scone, Scotland.* CHARLES II, *Scottish prelate and* SCOTTISH LORDS *at coronation.* CHARLES *sits above the stone of Scone.*)

Charles II   (*aside*). Now Cromwell's in Edinburgh, whose castle's
Shamefully surrendered – Governor Dundas
Is a traitor – the Scots can best oppose

The New Model Army by supporting
My Royalist cause. I have not been slow
To see an opportunity. All who
Are not enemies of the Covenant
Are now friends of Scotland, allies in war.
When the crown sits on my head I will have
A Scottish army to challenge Cromwell.
For that I'd travel to Scone any day.

Prelate.   I crown you Charles, King of Scotland.

All.   Long live
Charles the Second! God save Scotland's new King!

SCENE 9

(*July 1651. Scotland.* CROMWELL *in bed.*)

Cromwell   (*aside*). I cannot subjugate Scotland, which is
Obstinately Royalist and proclaims
Charles the Second as King. My armies march
Round Scotland with Geneva help and try
To crush the resistance, but all in vain.
Now I've accepted Presbyterian form
For Scotland, England's going the same way –
And wants to return to being Royalist
And looks to restore King Charles the Second.
I feel unwanted, my Commonwealth rule
Will soon come to an end. I can feel it.

(*Enter* DOCTOR *escorted by* SERVANT.)

Servant.   Lord General, the doctor has come at last.

(*Exit* SERVANT.)

Doctor.   It's dreadful out, the mist is very thick.

Cromwell.   I fell ill after a Scottish snowstorm,

Then had three relapses. I've been shaking.
I just can't seem to get my health back. I
Know Royalists are hoping I will die.
The Hague and Rotterdam, that's where they talk.
They've spread rumours in Holland that I'm dead.

Doctor.   You will be if you go out in these mists.
             You've got to stay in the warm. You're not young.

Cromwell.   I'm not old – fifty-two. I have to trounce
             The pretender who's cheekily been crowned.
             I have to rid Scotland of Royalists.

Doctor.   You can't yet. You've been ill four months. You must
             Be sensible. This Scottish weather's bad.

Cromwell.   You talk as a Royalist doctor would.
             The Lord has plucked me from my grave – to fight.
             I must push north to Perth, catch the young man.

SCENE 10

(*6 August 1651. Near Carlisle.* CHARLES II, SCOTTISH PRELATE *and* SCOTTISH LORDS.)

Charles II   (*aside*). I've dived down into England at the head
             Of my Scottish army and left Cromwell
             Bogged down in Perth. I can't raise more Scots, so
             I'll raise an English army to join mine.
             Once I am King of England, the English
             Will rally to me and drive Cromwell out.
             I will march on Worcester and take the town.

Prelate.   I crown you Charles, King of England.

All.   Long live
             Charles the Second! God save England's new King!

SCENE 11

(3 September 1651, morning. Worcester, a command post near Perry Wood. CROMWELL, FLEETWOOD and LAMBERT.)

Cromwell.   We've moved with speed, some twenty miles a day
To Worcester, where Charles has mustered a mere
Sixteen thousand men. They've blown four bridges.
We've ringed him with thirty-one thousand troops
Who block his flight to London south or east.
We will attack from the west's open fields,
Crossing the Severn on a bridge of boats.
We'll take him by surprise. To it! To it!

SCENE 12

(3 September 1651. Worcester. CHARLES. Enter MESSENGER.)

Messenger.   We've been attacked to the west. The fighting
Is very fierce. The Scots have been pushed back.
Cromwell is riding up and down our ranks.
Promising quarter if our men defect.
We're shooting at him. He's taking a risk.
He seems to think he's indestructible.
There's a rumour he took the first captain
Of his own regiment, Colonel Lindsay,
Into Perry Wood and met an old man
Who held a roll of parchment, who promised
He'd have his will today and in all things
For seven years. In return the Devil would have
Mastery of his soul and body. Cromwell
Argued for twenty-one years but took seven –

Charles II.   Tosh! Cromwell's made no pact with the Devil.

Messenger.   It's said that Colonel Lindsay's told the tale –

Charles II.   It suits our propaganda but it's false.

710

And he's not indestructible. I will
Lead a charge uphill to the eastern heights
Where half his army can be stormed. It will
Not expect us up there. Muskets! And pikes!

SCENE 13

(*3 September 1651. Worcester. Sound of bombardment.* CROMWELL.)

Cromwell. Onward! We have forced the Royalists back,
Taken their Fort, turned their guns on Worcester.
The streets are full of Royalist corpses
And dead horses.

(*Enter* MESSENGER.)

What's the news from Worcester?

Messenger. Some four thousand Scots poured through the north gate.
We've killed perhaps two thousand. All the rest,
Some nine thousand, are our prisoners. The King
Has fled. You've won.

Cromwell.   The Lord of Hosts be praised.

SCENE 14

(*3 September 1651. Worcester.* CHARLES *with mud-grimed face and* ENTOURAGE.)

Charles. The day is lost and with it our great cause.
The Royalists did not rise, the Scots have gone.
Perhaps he *had* made a Faustian pact
With the Devil, and sold his soul for power.
There's nothing I can do save head for France
And oppose Cromwell from a new exile.

SCENE 15

(Autumn 1651. Amsterdam. JOHN THURLOE, secretary to Oliver St John, Cromwell's relative, and MENASSEH. They greet each other warmly.)

Menasseh.   Welcome to Amsterdam, friend of the Dutch.

Thurloe.   I'm secretary to Oliver St John,
Who is discussing Anglo-Dutch union
With the Dutch government. Cromwell has given
Me a message for you. Please now apply
To the Council for Jews to be settled
Again in England. His Highness will sit
On the committee that sifts your request.

Menasseh.   Good. The Jews can now become real Christians.

SCENE 16

(Autumn 1652. London, St James's Park. CROMWELL walking alone.)

Cromwell   *(aside)*. I have been left alone. First Fleetwood gone,
Then Ireton dead of the plague in Ireland
As the Lord-Lieutenant in place of me,
Then Bridget marrying Fleetwood, the new
Lord-Lieutenant in Ireland, where she reigns.
Lambert, who wanted Fleetwood's role, is miffed,
And furious with Parliament. That is good.
I have a task for him. Yes. Ah, Whitelocke!
You too are strolling in St James's Park.

Whitelocke.   Lord-General.

Cromwell.   Walk with me. This Parliament
Has outraged the Army with its delays
And perpetuation of its own powers.
Some of the MPs are from Royalist days.

Whitelocke.	The Army must be kept at peace.
Cromwell.	It wants
	The Rump restrained.
Whitelocke.	But we acknowledged it
	As the supreme power without King or Lords
	To check its laws. How can it be restrained?
Cromwell.	What if...a man...should become King?
Whitelocke.	I think
	That remedy is worse than the disease.
	A monarchy can drift to tyranny,
	Whereas a Commonwealth rules by consent
	Of the people, whom it protects. As long
	As the protection lasts, it's tyrant-free.
Cromwell.	Kingship would prevent legal reprisals
	If the monarchy is ever restored.
Whitelocke.	Should we negotiate with the young Charles?
Cromwell.	No. I did not mean he would become King.
	The Rump has stopped protecting the people.

SCENE 17

(19 April 1653, 10.45 a.m. Whitehall, London. Cromwell's lodgings. CROMWELL *in plain black coat and grey worsted stockings, and* ARMY OFFICERS, *including* MONK.*)*

Monk.	The clamour from the Army is intense.
	The Army want to dissolve Parliament.
	It's in uproar now soldiers' pay's been cut
	And sailors' pay increased. The naval war
	Against the Dutch has not improved its mood.
Cromwell.	The Army wants to dissolve. So do I.
	The Rump is full of the King's appointees.

It's like a plate of yesterday's left steak,
Left-overs that have now begun to smell.
The Rump's corrupt. It must not be prolonged.
But what holding Council will replace it?
That's what I cannot see.

(*Enter* MESSENGER.)

Messenger. The Rump's begun
To discuss the Bill of Elections which
Will prolong its own power, keep it supreme.

Cromwell. It's broken its promise, it's seizing power.
I need some soldiers with muskets. Quickly.

Monk. Aren't you going to change?

Cromwell. There isn't time!

SCENE 18

(*19 April 1653, 11.15 a.m. The House of Commons. Enter* CROMWELL. SIR HENRY VANE *is speaking. He stops.* CROMWELL *sits, then rises and speaks increasingly furiously.*)

Cromwell. Some of you've had the public good at heart,
But among you are men who have not cared.
Your behaviour is treacherous and wrong.
You're a rabble, some whoremasters, some drunk,
Some corrupt and unjust. You should not sit
As a Parliament any longer, you
Have sat too long. You are no Parliament.
I'll put an end to your sitting. Come in.

(*Enter* MUSKETEERS *from Cromwell's regiment of foot.*)

Fetch the Speaker down.

(*The* MUSKETEERS *drag away the* SPEAKER.)

Vane.	This is not legal Or moral. Parliament's not consented To its end.
Cromwell	(*quietly to* VANE). You supported my actions When the New Model Army was proposed.
Vane.	You did not then conflict with Parliament. You had not then become a dictator, A tyrant!
Cromwell.	The Lord deliver me from All turncoats, apostates, defectors and Sir Henry Vane. Take this bauble away.

(MUSKETEERS *remove the mace.*)

You've forced me to do this. It's all your fault.

(SCOBELL, *Clerk of the House, rises.*)

Scobell.	This House is to be let, now unfurnished.

(*Enter* JOHN BRADSHAW. CROMWELL *has moved away from the Speaker to the front of the stage.*)

Bradshaw.	What you have done all England will soon hear, But you are mistaken. Parliament's not Dissolved. No power under Heaven can dissolve It but itself. Please take notice of that.
Cromwell.	The spirit of God was strong within me. This is God's wish, I would not consult men, Fallible flesh and blood. God wants virtue In our MPs, not vice; public spirit, Not self-interest. God wants MPs to be An assembly of saints, not of sinners. (*Aside.*) Now the Kingship is mine. I will be King. But first a new Assembly of Saints must Be nominated – not elected – and

A Puritan republic established.

SCENE 19

(21 July 1653. Whitehall Palace, London. CROMWELL and DUTCH AMBASSADOR.)

Cromwell   *(aside).* Now is the time to challenge the Dutch War.
             I did not want to fight Holland, and now
             I want to deliver to Menasseh.
             (Aloud.) I've watched with dismay the growing naval
             Conflict between England and Holland, which
             I did not want or seek. Our two nations
             Represent the Protestant – Puritan –
             Hope for a better world. God gives victories
             To those who understand his glorious work.
             He has given victories to us, but we
             Must do God's work, joining with our allies.
             I appeal to you, please make peace and join
             With us in an Anglo-Dutch union.

Ambassador   *(aside).* My government will never accept that.
             It would seem that we have been swallowed and
             Devoured by the hungry British Empire.
             (Aloud.) I will consult my government but do
             Not hold out much hope in view of the war.

SCENE 20

(11 December 1653. Whitehall, London. Cromwell's lodgings. Enter MAJOR-GENERAL LAMBERT.)

Cromwell.   What's the Army's latest view of the Saints?

Lambert.   As leader of the Army party I
             Have come to say, as you already know,
             The Army are fed up with the Barebones
             Parliament. It's too radical and speaks

Against the Army's interests.

Cromwell.   I agree.
It's too hasty in abolishing tithes.
I set it up so virtuous MPs
Could rule in place of Christ as Chosen Ones,
But there has been dissent and they have not
Implemented my call for Anglo-Dutch
Union, one Protestant state – what a dream!
I know the Dutch resisted but they could
Have pressed for union more wholeheartedly.
But what do you think the Army should do?

Lambert.   I've known your thinking from our discussions.
With your encouragement I'd like to move.
We'd dissolve the Assembly. You should rule.

Cromwell.   You're offering *me* sole rule?

Lambert.   There's no other
Alternative. The Army will want you –
Once the Assembly of Saints has been closed.

Cromwell   (*aside*). I detect his dear wife in this approach.
Sweet Frances suggested as much to me.
(*Aloud.*) I cannot close it and then rule. *You* could
Dissolve it and return the mace to me
Who gave it to the godly in April.

Lambert.   All right. It's not good for the Commonwealth
That they should sit any longer. They must
Hand back to you the powers that you gave them.

SCENE 21

(*13 December 1653. Whitehall, London. Cromwell's lodgings.* CROMWELL *and* LAMBERT.)

Cromwell.   You carried through your *coup.*

Lambert.	Yes. Some members

Lambert.   Yes. Some members
Refused to move, but in the end they went.
I'd like to base the running of England
On my *Instrument of Government*, which
Proposes there should be a Lord-Governor.

Cromwell.   Me.

Lambert.   Yes.

Cromwell.   I'd rather be called King.

Lambert.   No, no!
The Army would not accept that. It's full
Of republicans. "King" 's too permanent,
Has too many connotations: "tyrant".
No, your mandate should be more temporary.
What about "Protector"? You'd sign yourself
"Oliver P", not too unlike "Charles R".
You would be treated as a Head of State
And called "Brother" by Louis the Fourteenth.
You'd be addressed as "Your Highness". The Dutch
Deputies would greet you caps in their hands.
I would give you the Palace of Whitehall
And Hampton Court. You'd live just like a King.

Cromwell   (*musing*). "Protector". That is good. The supreme power
Protects the people. I'll be "Protector".
Reluctantly I accept Providence
Has chosen me, one of the Elect, to rule.

SCENE 22

(*16 December 1653. London. A procession.* SOLDIERS, ALDERMEN *in scarlet, the* LORD MAYOR. CROMWELL *in a plain black suit and black coat, wearing a black hat with a gold hatband. The procession stops and a ceremony begins.*)

Lord Mayor.   I present Your Highness with the Great Seal.
The sword of State. The cap of maintenance.

(CROMWELL *accepts them, then returns them*.)

I name you Lord Protector of England,
Scotland and Ireland. Your Highness, welcome.

(*All applaud*.)

SCENE 23

(*3 September 1654. London. An English* COMMON MAN.)

Common man.   Cromwell in his two palaces, guarded,
Holds weekly dinners and attends events –
Wrestling, hurling – and of course goes to church
Prayer-book in hand, and now he's chosen his
First Parliament, and has designed a "throne",
A gold-trimmed chair in the Painted Chamber.
It's said the *Instrument of Government*
Was found in Mrs Lambert's petticoat.
He told the MPs he's been called by God
To wield power. Now he says the Levellers
Have stirred up the Royalists. I dunno.
To cap it all he's said, "I've prevented
Anarchy and social revolution."
He who revolted against King Charles says
He's *prevented* revolution. That's rich!
If you ask me he's a huge hypocrite
Who puts a fine gloss on all his actions.
He's King but not King, pure but not quite pure
As the silver, sewer-fed Thames shimmers
Near his Whitehall and Hampton Court windows.

SCENE 24

(*November 1654. London, Whitehall Palace.* CROMWELL *receives* MANUEL MARTINEZ
DORMIDO, *a Marrano merchant*.)

Dormido.	Your Highness, Excellency, Lord-Governor,
	I've come from Amsterdam, from Menasseh.
Cromwell.	You are welcome.
Dormido.	We seek your help against
	The Spanish Inquisition. Dutch Jews are
	Suffering persecution. It's set out
	In these three petitions I'll leave with you.
Cromwell.	I'll pass them to the Council. You are not
	Hoping that we will send troops against Spain?
Dormido.	No. Menasseh and the Amsterdam Jews
	Who contributed to the setting-up
	Of your New Model Army hope you can
	Now sanction the resettlement of Jews
	In England, as Menasseh discussed with
	John Thurloe before the Anglo-Dutch war.
Cromwell.	I will do my best for resettlement.
	I could have got it through three years ago
	When I was pressing Anglo-Dutch union
	But then the naval war set back my plans.
	The Dutch government forced me into war.
	I did not want it, and though it's ended
	And the Dutch government's promised to pay
	Damages for the loss of merchant ships,
	The Council still resists Dutch proposals.
	It will be harder to persuade it now.
	The war's made it stubborn towards the Dutch.

SCENE 25

(*9 August 1655. London, Whitehall Palace. Lord Protector* CROMWELL *in the Council of State.*)

Cromwell	(*aside*). The Council has refused resettlement.
	Unless I deliver what I promised
	The Dutch Jews will reveal the pact I made.

Council and Parliament resist the Jews
And so it's now military government.
There is no other way but martial law.
I cannot make the British Israelite
Without Major-Generals running England.
It's the biggest gamble of my career.
I'll blame the last uprising for the change.
(*Aloud.*) The Penruddock rising destabilised.
The rebellion itself was a small thing:
Penruddock opened up the Salisbury jails,
Took the Sheriff hostage and marched out with
Four hundred men. We crushed it easily;
Fifteen ringleaders have been put to death.
But we need strong regional government
To stop the taking of such liberties.
By my order twelve Major-Generals
Will have new powers in twelve regions. Each will
Be an overlord to maintain order –
To supervise laws and public morals –
In one region, and will have cavalry
Troops paid for by a new ten-per-cent tax
Now levied on known Royalists. I have
Set up new customs duties. Anyone
Who does not pay is to be imprisoned.

(CROMWELL *pauses.* TWO SOLDIERS *turn and talk to each other.*)

Soldier 1.   I'm a Leveller, I deplore this tax.
It's like Ship Tax which Charles the First ordered
And was not sanctioned by our Parliament.

Soldier 2.   For that Charles lost his crown and head. Would that
This King would lose his Great Seal and his head.
I speak for the English majority.

Soldier 1.   He's become a military dictator
Ruling through Major-Generals and muskets,
Not an elected Parliament's ideas.

Cromwell   (*resuming*). We'll close all ale-houses, stop bear-baiting,
Cock-fighting, horse-racing, performances

Of plays, punish swearing. Adultery
Will from now be a capital offence....

SCENE 26

(September 1655. London, Whitehall Palace. COUNCIL OF STATE *, and* COUNCIL CHAIR-
MAN. *The* CLERK TO THE COUNCIL *rises.)*

Clerk.   Menasseh ben Israel from Amsterdam
To present his petition, as you know,
To resettle the Jews in England.

(Enter MENASSEH, *a man of charm and energy, with* THREE RABBIS *and
a small library of books.)*

Chairman.   We
Dismissed a similar petition from –
Who was it?

Clerk.   Dormido.

Chairman.   Yes, Dormido.

Menasseh.   Good morning, gentlemen, I hope you're well?
Is your Protector here?

Chairman.   No.

Menasseh.   That's a shame.
He's lodged us in the Strand, near to Whitehall,
In a house opposite the New Exchange.
I want to thank him for his excellent
Hospitality. Thank you for your time.
I want to read my petition. These books
Support the references. I'd like to cite
Each one. You have the whole day free?

Chairman.   No. Five
Minutes.

Menasseh.   You are joking? That was a joke?
                             The Jews were all expelled from England by
                             Edward the First in 1290, and now
                             After three hundred and sixty-five years
                             There's a petition for their return which
                             Has the blessing of your Protector – bless
                             His Highness – and you allow five minutes
                             To consider the greatest injustice
                             In your history? There must be some mistake.

Chairman.   We will discuss your petition when we
                             Are ready, and with His Highness, once he
                             Has passed your petition to us, and we
                             Will decide what's appropriate for Dutch
                             Citizens –

                             (MENASSEH *begins to protest.*)

                             Dutch Jews are Dutch citizens –
                             Who forced a costly naval war on us.
                             We will use the Dormido decision
                             As a guideline in this new case. We wish
                             You a good stay in your Strand house. Good day.

SCENE 27

(*September 1655. Whitehall, London. Cromwell's lodgings.* CROMWELL *with some members of the Council. Enter* MENASSEH *and* THREE RABBIS. MENASSEH *presses Cromwell's hands and kisses him and begins to touch his body with care, standing back to look at him. He gives no indication that they have met.*)

Menasseh.   I came from Amsterdam just to see if
                             His Highness is of flesh and blood, because
                             His superhuman deeds suggest he is
                             Of more divine composition, and is
                             Perhaps the Messiah we Jews await
                             At God's will. *Deuteronomy* suggests
                             (Twenty-eight, sixty-four) that the scattering
                             Of the Jews will be complete when they've reached

The "end" of the earth, which suggests to Jews
"*Kezeh ha-Arez*", the "angle" or "limit"
Of the earth which Jews associate with
Angle-terre, or Angle-land, the land of
The Angles, none other than this England.
Many Jews believe that when they have reached
The end of the earth by settling here,
Then a Messiah will appear and lead them
Back to the Holy Land, Zion, and then
The thousand-year reign of Christ and his saints
Will begin. The millennium is next year –
Sixteen fifty-six may see Heaven on earth.
Utopia!

Cromwell.   Dinner is served. This way.

Menasseh.   But first I must say the English people
Are kind-hearted and not racist, and grasp
That when God banished Jews from their country
He gave them the gift of making money
To help them survive during their exile.
Their use of that gift in this country led
To their expulsion in 1290, and
Your Highness will see God's Providence in
The money-making skills that preserved them
And that such skills will be an asset in
This new commercial England that you rule.
I give you my assurance. I've not come
To create any public disturbance
But to express the hope that my nation
Can live under your gracious protection,
And trade with the English as Providence
Guides and directs.

Cromwell   (*warmly*).   Providence disposes.
Thank you for that assurance. Know that we
Are well-disposed to your petition. Come
Through to the table and explain it more.

Menasseh.   One of us is going to Huntingdon
To see if your lineage links with Israel.

If so, you have a claim as our Messiah.

(*They all go to the table just off stage.* TWO OF THE COUNCIL *lag behind. One is the* COUNCIL CHAIRMAN.)

Council member.   A bit oily, isn't he?

Chairman.   Dreadfully so.
There's a report that Jews want His Highness
To sell them St Paul's for a synagogue.
A million pounds. There's talk of Jewish gold –
Two hundred thousand – to sweeten the deal.
If it's not for St Paul's, it's for something.
We represent the sane English, we must
Veto this "British Israelite" nonsense
And stop our England being overrun
By Jews who'll breed and take our jobs and trade
Like rats that decimate by spreading plague.

Council member.   His Highness has surrounded himself with
Rosicrucian Freemasons who have made
His Revolution more Masonic than
Puritan, Protestant. It's a disgrace.

(*They join the others at the table.*)

SCENE 28

(*4 December 1655. London, Whitehall Palace.* CROMWELL. *Enter* THE COUNCIL, *including* THE CHAIRMAN.)

Chairman.   His Highness will address us regarding
The petition to resettle the Jews.

Cromwell.   The 1290 expulsion of the Jews
Was an act of royal prerogative
And therefore only applied to the Jews
Expelled at that particular time. We
English are the noblest and most esteemed

Merchants in the world. We won't be undone
By the influx of some Jewish traders....

(*We leave this debate and rejoin it a fortnight later.*)

SCENE 29

(*18 December 1655. London, Whitehall Palace.* CROMWELL *and the* COUNCIL. *The* CHAIR-
MAN OF THE COUNCIL *is objecting.*)

Chairman.   If Jews were once again permitted to
Land freely in England, I would protest
Most strongly on behalf of the Council
Of State's sub-committee. Their arrival
Would be a grave menace to State and Church.
The people are against resettlement.
Preachers in pulpits, merchants in markets,
Workers at looms or ploughs are happy with
Things as they are. If Your Highness demands
That Jews be readmitted, decayed ports
Are the best locations, and they should pay
Customs duties on imports *and* exports.
The Council of State will write a report
Stating the arguments and advising
Rejection of the petition, and then
Leave Your Highness free to do as you please.

Cromwell.   That is the best course. The outcome should be
Left in my hands. The Jews do not want us
To find a compromise that treats them as
Second-class citizens. They are the same
As us and all God's people in this land
Or else it's best that they're not here at all.
They're our equals. The matter's in my hands.

SCENE 30

(*6 May 1657. London, St James's Park.* CROMWELL *walking alone.*)

Cromwell   (*aside*). I'm not well. I've had my fair share of pain.
Down there. I have bladder trouble. A stone.
I've had a painful boil on my breast. It's
Been cut out. I am sick in mind as well.
I'm full of cares. I am like Job. I shan't
Live much longer. My son will take over.
Dick. There will be a Cromwell dynasty.
Dick's debts and incompetence torture me.
He's weak and gentle, I've been strong as steel.
The Major-Generals have disappointed –
My experiment to rule the country
Without Parliament. They're unpopular
And haven't found the funds I need, and I
Have had to call a Parliament to raise
Sums for the Spanish War. On every side
I see Royalists return with increased strength.
Why did I kill Charles? So his son can oust
Mine after I am gone? Menasseh is
Here broken-hearted from Amsterdam, and
I'm no nearer to getting the Dutch Jews
Legally readmitted. Outwardly
My authority's increased, but I'm tired.
I shan't live long. Perhaps it's a pity
The Leveller Colonel Sexby could not kill
Me as he planned. I'm ready for my grave.
Now I have to decide. Will I be King?
The House of Lords first offered me the crown.
A week later the Commons Speaker did
At the Banqueting House. I've played for time.
I would accept if my health were better.
It's an office, not just a title, and
I can pass it on to Dick. A King first
Settled Christianity in England.
But my health's played up and I have cancelled
Several meetings with the committee, and
I've dithered for a month, keen to accept

But mindful why I cut off Charles's head.
Now I have to announce my decision.
King Oliver the First. It has to be.

(*Enter* FLEETWOOD, LAMBERT *and* DESBOROUGH.)

Lambert.   We've heard that you will announce tomorrow
                      That you will accept the title of "King".
                      We all oppose this and we will resign
                      From all our employments if you do this.

Desborough.   Colonel Pride says he'll get a petition
                      Drawn up against the idea. The Army
                      Is against you taking the title "King".

Fleetwood.   "King" has unfortunate connotations.

Lambert.   "King" suggests a great chestnut tree like that
                      Which tyrannically shades the plants beneath
                      And slows their growth by obstructing sunshine.
                      A "King" retards a Commonwealth's progress.

Cromwell.   You followed me to say this?

Lambert.   It's as if
                      The soothsayer'd lain in wait for Caesar
                      And told him the triumvirate would resign
                      If he crowned himself King. That's all from us.

(*Exeunt.*)

Cromwell   (*aside*). Lambert has turned. Has Frances talked to him?
                      They mean it, and, having chosen my course,
                      I am thwarted, and must go back again,
                      Retrace my steps. If those three are against,
                      I can't carry the Kingship through. Can I?

SCENE 31

(Friday 8 May 1657, 11 a.m. London. The Painted Chamber, Palace of Westminster.
CROMWELL. *Enter the* COMMITTEE ON KINGSHIP. *The* COMMITTEE CHAIRMAN *speaks.)*

Com. Chairman. Your Highness, we came yesterday evening.
We waited a very long time.

Cromwell.   I thought
The House had risen before my message reached
You and you had not tried to speak with me.
I've thought deeply for two and a half months.
I cannot undertake this government
With the title of "King". I am sorry
It's taken me so long to say, and that
Your work has been held up while I have thought.

Com. Chairman. You have refused the crown?

Cromwell.   I have. No crown.
It is the will of Providence that guides
All things and does not want me to be King.

Com. Chairman. We will invest you as Lord Protector.
You may name your successor. Parliament
Must become more powerful than the Council.
Who will your successor be?

Cromwell.   My son Dick.

SCENE 32

(June 1657. London, Whitehall Palace. CROMWELL *and* LAMBERT.*)*

Lambert.   I expected to succeed you. Now you
Have chosen your successor, heedless of
The help I gave in dissolving the Saints,
Without which you would not be Protector,

I've lost my appetite to be away
From my dear sweet Frances's petticoat,
My home and my plants.

Cromwell   (*thinly*).   You will surrender
Your commissions to the Council at my
Request.

Lambert.   I denied you the crown, and now
I'll retire to my Wimbledon garden
With my dear sweet wife who'll tend plants with me.
We'll purge the rose-beds of all slugs and snails.

Cromwell   (*quietly*). You'll lose six thousand pounds a year from your
Commissions. I will grant you two thousand
Pounds a year from my personal monies.

Lambert.   I am touched by your generosity
To me and my wife in our retirement.

(LAMBERT *coolly nods at* CROMWELL.)

SCENE 33

(*Friday 26 June 1657, 2 p.m. London, Westminster Hall.* CROMWELL.)

Cromwell   (*aside*). I sit in Westminster Hall in the chair
Of Scotland, the coronation chair. There
Eight years ago stood King Charles, deposed from
This throne on which I sit. I could be King.

(*A fanfare. On the table in front of* CROMWELL *is a purple velvet robe lined
with ermine; a gilt, bossed Bible; a sword of state; and a sceptre.* THE
SPEAKER *steps forward.*)

Speaker.   I invest you with this robe, sword, sceptre.

(CROMWELL *puts on the robe, and takes the sword and sceptre.*)

I invest you as the Lord Protector
Of England, Scotland and Ireland. Welcome.

(*All applaud*.)

SCENE 34

(*September 1657. London. Menasseh's lodgings.* MENASSEH, *ill, sitting by the body of his son* SAMUEL, *and* CARVAJAL.)

Menasseh.   We have got nowhere. Cromwell says he wants
To readmit the Jews but he will not
Make it an issue with the Council.

Carvajal.   But
We succeeded in petitioning for
A cemetery in Mile End.

Menasseh.   That's just sad.
We're resettled when dead, but not alive.
I can't wait any more. I've no money.
All the synagogue raised we spent on arms.
I appealed to Cromwell. He authorised
First twenty-five pounds, then a pension of
One hundred pounds – brilliant if it's paid, but
The Treasury paid nothing. They are like
The Council of State, they impede his work –
And mine. Now I have lost Samuel, my son,
My only surviving son, I am broke.
The Treasury has promised to pay me
Two hundred pounds on the condition that
I surrender my pension rights. What can
I do? I've accepted, but do you think
They've paid? Not a penny. I have no rights
To a pension and they have paid nothing.
I'm tired of waiting, I am going home,
Back to Amsterdam. I'll bury Samuel
There. I'm exhausted. Resettlement is
No nearer, and I know I'll die quite soon.

I won't be long in following Samuel.
We thought we had done well. We influenced
The English Civil War, we did a deal
With Cromwell: cash for arms, King Charles's head.
But he hasn't been able to push through
Resettlement. And I've given up hope.

Carvajal   (*quietly*). I'll carry on the fight after you've gone.
There will be an official charter that
Grants protection to English Jews. There will!

SCENE 35

(*3 February 1658. London, Whitehall Palace.* THURLOE *knocking.* CROMWELL *within.*)

Cromwell.   Who's there?

Thurloe.   John Thurloe with important news.

(*Enter* CROMWELL *in his nightshirt.*)

Cromwell.   I was asleep.

Thurloe.   Your Highness, I'm sorry,
But the new Parliament's defying you.
They're reconvening the House of Lords. Some
Royalists are in with them, Some oppose you.
Sir Arthur Haselrig speaks of your....

Cromwell.   What?

Thurloe.   Usurpation.

Cromwell.   Arthur, my relative,
I knighted him.

Thurloe.   You should be at the House
Tomorrow morning.

Cromwell.	Roads are thick with snow.
	The Thames is frozen with islands of ice.
	It's the coldest winter in memory.

| Thurloe. | You can go by coach. |

| Cromwell | (*aside*). | I'll dissolve the House. |

SCENE 36

(*4 February 1658. London, Westminster Hall. LORDS and CROMWELL.*)

| Lord. | Ale and a piece of toast for His Highness. |

(CROMWELL *waves the offer aside and strides into the Commons. He begins speaking.*)

Cromwell.	You granted I should nominate a new
	House. I nominated honourable men.
	And now you're bringing back the House of Lords.
	It's high time your sitting's brought to an end.
	I dissolve this Parliament.

| Voice. | You've no right. |

| Cromwell. | Let God judge between you and me. All out! |

(*Outside CROMWELL coughs. He is still ill. The effort has drained him.*)

| Voice. | It's just like Charles. He dissolved Parliaments |
| | Without their consent. At least he was King. |

(SOLDIERS *move in the direction of the speaker to silence the voice.*)

SCENE 37

(*6 August 1658. London, Hampton Court. Sick-room. CROMWELL with his daughter*

ELIZABETH. DOCTOR *and* SERVANT. *Elizabeth gasps in pain.*)

Doctor   (*to servant*). The cancer's stifling her. There is no hope.

Cromwell.   Is it painful, Bettie?

Elizabeth   (*lying*).   No, Papa.

Cromwell.   Sure?

Elizabeth.   Sure.

(*She hides a grimace of pain.* CROMWELL *hides a look of anguish.*)

You should get some sleep. You musn't watch
All night. You've got England to run.

Cromwell.   I'll stay.

(*She dozes and dies of cancer.* CROMWELL *has also dozed, and he wakes
with a jolt and bursts in inconsolable grief.*)

Oh Bettie, Bettie, Bettie. Don't leave me.

SCENE 38

(*3 September 1658. London, Whitehall Palace.* CROMWELL *in bed.* RICHARD. FIVE
MEMBERS OF THE COUNCIL *surround the bed.* MRS CROMWELL..)

Cromwell.   Please read the *Bible* aloud. St Paul to
                          The Philippians, chapter four.

                          (RICHARD *reads the* Bible *to him.* THE DOCTOR *talks to* MRS
                          CROMWELL.)

Doctor.   It seems
                          He's dying of a broken heart. When she
                          Died, his mirror cracked. Yet the real cause
                          Is the pains in his bowels and his back

And the fits that he's had.

Cromwell   (*overhearing*).   It's the ague.
Some had this near the marshes of the Fens,
But I caught it in the swamps of Ireland.
I was bitten to death by mosquitoes.
I've got malaria. I know the cause.
(*Aside*.) I had a vision of a pure stream and
A clean land rid of tyranny and tax,
A Utopia, a Paradise. But I
Had to compromise as a leader and
Do things I now regret. Utopia
And military rule are opposites.
And my clean land became a marshy swamp.
My soul was part-fetid with a foul stench.
I got malaria through compromise.

(CROMWELL *lapses into silence. He signals to* RICHARD *to stop reading the* Bible.)

(*Aside*.) This is my punishment for Drogheda and
All the battles when I gave no quarter.
I had to do it to keep my kingdom
United. Only strong leadership could
Achieve unity. I'd go hot and cold,
I'd sweat like now. Suffer a drowsy fit.

(*He sits up restlessly, then flops back*.)

I think I see Menasseh, who is dead,
Who died last year in Amsterdam, standing
At my bedside, his ghost reproaching me.
This is my punishment for breaking my
Promise to resettle the Jews, my pact
With Menasseh, who gave me my Army.
I broke my word and must pay with my life.

(*Enter the Independent minister*, DR. GOODWIN.)

Dr Goodwin.   Lord, we do not ask for his life for we
Are sure of it. We ask that he may serve

You better than before.

(*There is little response from* CROMWELL. *The* FIVE COUNCIL MEMBERS *whisper to each other.*)

Chairman.   Your Highness, we
On the Council must know your successor.

Cromwell   (*eyes closed*). I told the Committee of Kingship.

(CROMWELL *lapses into unconsciousness.*)

Chairman.   They
Have not told us. We need to know, and soon.
Is your son Richard to succeed you? Yes?

(*They all listen, including* RICHARD.)

He hasn't answered. I will ask again.
Your Highness, is Richard to succeed you?

Cromwell   (*eyes closed*). Yes.

(RICHARD *has been bending. He slowly pulls himself upright.*)

Chairman.   It's Richard. You all heard that.

Cromwell.   I shall
Not die for an hour. Go on cheerfully.
Don't be sad. Hear my chatter as you would
A working man's. Lord, Lord though I am but
A miserable and wretched creature, I,
I am in covenant with thee through grace.
I saved England from becoming Catholic
Under the Stuarts, I'll be thanked for that.
I wanted England to be Israelite
Under Sion. Europe. The Rosy Cross....
I belonged to a Holy Brotherhood.
My thought was always guided by the Light,
Reason by the perceptive intellect,
Thinking by the intellectual vision.

I was true to the vision of the Light.
My work is done. God be with his people.
Pardon such as desire to trample on
The dust of a poor worm, for they are thy
People too.

(CROMWELL *dies*.)

Dr Goodwin.   He's gone.

Chairman.   The Protector's dead.
Long live the Protector. Your Highness, we....

(*All* FIVE COUNCIL MEMBERS *bend on one knee and kiss* RICHARD's *hand. Then the* COUNCIL CHAIRMAN *moves away with a council member*.)

Chairman.   Who will protect us now from what's to come?

Council member.   A time of anarchy, and little Light.
We shall not see his kind again, from now
The English sensibility's fractured,
Reason will have no contact with the Light.
His Puritan vision was inspired by
The medieval monasteries and now
The world will be a more secular place.

Chairman.   Was his Light from God or from Lucifer,
From Kabbalism and the Rosy Cross?

EPILOGUE

(*10 December 1660. London. Bell-ringing. Enter* ARCHBISHOP JUXON.)

Juxon.   Cromwell was embalmed, yet his coffin stank.
His filth broke through. He was swiftly interred.
A wax effigy filled his coffin at
His lying-in-state. It had glass eyes, and
After some ten days it was stood up, and
A crown was put on its head to suggest

His soul had passed from Purgatory to Heaven –
A Popish custom Cromwell abhorred when
It was used at James the First's funeral.
A kingly, Popish end – the hypocrite!
After Charles the Second's restoration
Broke on the land like a warm summer day
After the misery of a cold spring,
And all the churchbells pealed and all rejoiced,
In fact just six days ago at Captain
Titus's suggestion, his body was
Exhumed with Ireton's. Both corpses were lodged
Overnight at the Red Lion Inn, Holborn,
And joined by Bradshaw's corpse, which had been found
(Unlike Colonel Pride's). At dawn all were dragged
On hurdles to Tyburn, and hanged, Bradshaw
(President of the court that killed the King)
In the centre, from ten till four, and then
Had their heads hacked off by the hangman, who
Threw their trunks into a pit dug beneath
The gallows. Their heads were then taken to
Westminster Hall and stuck high up on poles,
Where they will stay throughout our new King's reign.
Cromwell's changes were all reversed by Charles.
The Protector's institutions perished
With him and his work ended in failure.
The monarchy and Lords will last centuries.
The British don't like change, and they don't like
A foreign power ending our monarchy
And closing down our ancient House of Lords.
Let this be a warning to all men who
Sweep away English institutions: their
Heads will end up on poles in Westminster.
Cromwell strengthened the English monarchy.

(*Exit* JUXON, *shuffling – he is over eighty.*)

(*August 1664. London. Enter* CHARLES II *at the back of the stage. He turns and speaks formally to a gathering off stage.*)

Charles II.   Carvajal's widow has petitioned me
                     That Royalist Jews supported our cause in

Holland, when we were in exile in France,
Waiting for the tyrant Cromwell to die.
I grant a charter to protect all Jews,
Who are now legally readmitted
Into England, after three hundred and
Seventy-four years of exile like mine.

(CHARLES *moves to the front of the stage. He addresses the audience.*)

That old fool Juxon, my Archbishop, 's dead,
He really believed in conspiracies
And thought my father was plotted against
By foreigners, rather than just pushed out
For overtaxing the people's patience
With ship money for his grandiose schemes.
He left me this bauble my father wore
When he went to the scaffold.

(*Enter* NELL GWYN.)

Let's not be
Solemn about the last two harsh decades.
Nell, pretty Nell, this ring is yours. Keep it
For our son when he comes of age. Now I'll
Make as many eyes at you as are on
A peacock's tail when raised. Let me express
The new vitality of our nation.

(*He hands* NELL *the ring, then pursues her off stage. She squeals coquettishly, holding the ring.*)

APPENDIX:

THE WARLORDS

Abridged Version

(For performance in one evening)

DRAMATIS PERSONAE

SPEAKING CHARACTERS IN ORDER OF APPEARANCE

Eisenhower
Montgomery
Churchill
Brooke
King George VI
Bradley
Patton
Dawnay
Corporal
Chef (Montgomery's)
Dempsey
Stagg
Tedder
Ramsay
Leigh-Mallory
Rommel
D-Day Soldier
Hitler
Bormann
Butcher
Dönitz
Göring
Howard Marshall
Henderson
Kay Summersby
Burgdorf
Poston
Stenographer (Hitler's)
Rundstedt
Aide (Hitler's)
Browning
Speidel
Von Stauffenberg
Haeften
Orderly (Keitel's)
Freyend

Witzleben
Wartenburg
Hansen
Bedell Smith
Strong
Goebbels
Blumentritt
Urquhart
Lucy Rommel
Maisel
Manfred Rommel
Hodges
Stalin
De Guingand
Eva Braun
Ilse Braun
Guderian
Antonov
Speer
Everett Hughes
Tex Lee
Aide (Marshall's)
General Marshall
Krebs
Simpson
Staff 1 (Goebbels's)
Staff 2 (Goebbels's)
Semmler
Earle
Hunter
Keitel
Jodl
Ernie, a private
Wagner
Gerda Christian
Magda Goebbels

Dr. Morell
Fromm
Soldier (German)
Williams
Himmler
Kaltenbrunner
Freisler

Günsche
Junge
Zhukov's voice
Interpreter
Matusov
Chuikov
Kiselyov

German voice
Abyzov
Heinersdorf
Friedeburg
Kinzel
Warren
Aide (Truman's)
Truman

Total: 94

MAIN CAST (all speaking roles)

94 parts distributed among 25 actors:

Eisenhower
Montgomery
Churchill
Hitler
Brooke + Hansen + Wagner + Tex Lee + Keitel
Bradley + Matusov + Warren + Marshall's aide
Patton + General Marshall + Guderian + interpreter
Dawnay + Kaltenbrunner + Browning + Staff 1
Henderson + Ramsay + Hitler's aide + German soldier
Dempsey + Chef + Speidel + Fromm + De Guingand
Stagg + Howard Marshall + Kiselyov + Ernie
Tedder + Rundstedt + Himmler + Wartenburg + Strong
Kay Summersby + Eva Braun + Junge
Leigh-Mallory + Dr. Morell + Urquhart + Hughes + Abyzov
Rommel + Stalin + Friedeburg
Bedell Smith + Dönitz + Speer + Earle + Freyend
Butcher + Jodl + Haeften + Maisel + Truman's aide

D-Day soldier + stenographer + Krebs + Simpson + Freisler
Bormann + orderly + Heinersdorf
Williams + Witzleben + Staff 2 + German voice + Kinzel
Göring + Antonov + Hunter
Burgdorf + Truman + Blumentritt + Zhukov
George VI + Poston + Semmler + Günsche + Manfred Rommel
Stauffenberg + Chuikov + Goebbels + Corporal + Hodges
Lucy Rommel + Ilse Braun + Magda Goebbels + Gerda Christian

This abridged version can be performed in one evening.

A few – very few – scenes have been moved from their position in the full version to make staging easier, to prevent actors from being on stage in successive scenes as a result of cuts in the text.

Recommended Interval: at end of Scene 7.

SCENES/PARTICIPANTS

SCENE 1

(a)   Eisenhower, Montgomery, King George VI, Churchill, Smuts, Brooke, Bradley, Patton & assorted officers
(b)   Montgomery, Dawnay
(c)   Montgomery and Churchill
(d)   Montgomery, King George, Corporal, Chef
(e)   Montgomery
(f)   Montgomery, Dempsey, Crerar, Bradley, Patton
(g)   Montgomery, Eisenhower
(h)   Stagg, Eisenhower, Montgomery, Tedder
(i)   Stagg, Ramsay, Eisenhower, Leigh-Mallory, Montgomery, Tedder
(j)   Rommel, Speidel
(k)   Montgomery, Eisenhower, Chef
(l)   Stagg, Eisenhower, Ramsay, Tedder, Leigh-Mallory, Montgomery
(m)   Montgomery, Montgomery's batman, Dawnay
(n)   Chorus of the Occupied
(o)   D-Day Soldier
(p)   Rommel, Lucy Rommel
(q)   Hitler, Keitel, Bormann
(r)   Eisenhower, Butcher
(s)   Montgomery, Eisenhower, Butcher

SCENE 2

(a)   Dönitz, Göring, Hitler
(b)   Montgomery, Howard Marshall, Henderson
(c)   Butcher, Eisenhower, Kay Summersby
(d)   Burgdorf, Bormann, Hitler
(e)   Churchill, Smuts, Brooke, Montgomery
(f)   Churchill, Henderson
(g)   Montgomery, Brooke
(h)   Montgomery, Poston
(i)   Eisenhower
(j)   Chorus of Londoners
(k)   Montgomery, Eisenhower, Tedder
(1)   Tedder, Coningham
(m)   Hitler, Rommel, Rundstedt, Jodl, Schmundt, Stenographer, Hitler's Aide
(n)   Eisenhower, Butcher
(o)   Chorus of Auschwitz prisoners
(p)   Rundstedt
(q)   Eisenhower, Bradley
(r)   Montgomery, Henderson, Browning
(s)   Rommel, Speidel
(t)   Henderson, Montgomery

SCENE 3

(a)   Butcher, Eisenhower
(b)   Stauffenberg, Haeften, Orderly, Freyend, Hitler, Dr. Morell
(c)   Fromm, Stauffenberg, Olbricht, Haeften, Quirnheim, Soldier
(d)   Hitler
(e)   Montgomery, Henderson, Chef, Churchill, Williams
(f)   Himmler, Kaltenbrunner
(g)   Eisenhower, Bedell Smith, Brooke, Churchill
(h)   Henderson, Montgomery, Eisenhower, Kay Summersby, Bradley
(i)   Freisler, Witzleben, Hoepner, Stieff, von Hase, Bernardis, Klausing, Hagen, Wartenburg

SCENE 4

(a)   Hansen, Eisenhower, Bradley
(b)   Bormann, Hitler
(c)   Eisenhower, Butcher
(d)   Montgomery, De Guingand, Henderson
(e)   Montgomery, Bradley
(f)   Montgomery, Eisenhower, Bedell Smith, General Gale
(g)   Eisenhower, Kay Summersby

(h)   Brooke, Montgomery
(i)   Churchill, Brooke
(j)   Churchill, King George VI
(k)   Henderson, Montgomery, James Gunn

SCENE 5

(a)   Eisenhower, Bedell Smith, Morgan, Gale, Strong, Whiteley
(b)   Hitler, Goebbels
(c)   Eisenhower
(d)   Montgomery, Dawnay
(e)   Eisenhower, Tedder, Montgomery
(f)   Eisenhower, Bedell Smith, Kay Summersby
(g)   Rundstedt, Blumentritt
(h)   Williams, Montgomery, Urquhart
(i)   Bormann, Hitler
(j)   Eisenhower, Montgomery, Brooke, Ramsay, Bradley, Patton, Dempsey, Crerar, Hodges
(k)   Montgomery, Dawnay
(1)   Rommel, Lucy Rommel, Burgdorf, Maisel, Manfred Rommel
(m)   Montgomery, Bradley, Gen. Marshall, Hodges
(n)   Dawnay, Montgomery

SCENE 6

(a)   Hitler, Rundstedt, Model, Göring
(b)   Montgomery, Bradley
(c)   Hitler, Burgdorf
(d)   Eisenhower, Patton, Bradley
(e)   Montgomery
(f)   Eisenhower, Bedell Smith, Strong, Whiteley
(g)   Dawnay, Montgomery
(h)   Eisenhower, Bedell Smith
(i)   Montgomery, Hodges
(j)   Montgomery, Bradley
(k)   Eisenhower, Tedder, Strong
(1)   Stalin, Rokossovsky
(m)   De Guingand, Eisenhower, Bedell Smith, Tedder
(n)   De Guingand, Montgomery

SCENE 7

(a)   Hitler, Rundstedt, Göring, Bormann
(b)   Eva Braun, Ilse Braun, Hitler, Bormann, Burgdorf, Guderian, Ribbentrop
(c)   Chorus of Berliners

(d)   Chorus of Dresdeners
(e)   Stalin, Antonov
(f)   Eisenhower
(g)   Burgdorf, Hitler, Speer
(h)   Everett Hughes, Tex Lee, Bradley, Eisenhower, Kay Summersby
(i)   Brooke, Churchill, Montgomery, Dawnay

SCENE 8
(a)   Churchill, Montgomery, Brooke, Eisenhower, Bradley, Simpson
(b)   Bedell Smith, Butcher, Eisenhower
(c)   Montgomery, Dawnay
(d)   Brooke, Churchill
(e)   Gen. Marshall, Aide
(f)   Bedell Smith, Eisenhower
(g)   Stalin, Antonov, Shtemenko

SCENE 9
(a)   Hitler, Krebs
(b)   Montgomery, Dawnay
(c)   Bedell Smith, Eisenhower, Kay Summersby
(d)   Simpson, Bradley
(e)   Goebbels, Staff 1, Staff 2, Semmler
(f)   Stalin
(g)   Burgdorf, Hitler, Bormann, Goebbels, Ribbentrop, Speer, Himmler, Jodl, Göring, Krebs
(h)   Chorus of Berliners
(i)   Hitler, Bormann, Krebs, Keitel, Jodl
(j)   Montgomery, Earle
(k)   Earle, Poston
(1)   Dawnay, Montgomery
(m)   Henderson, Hunter, Tindale, Montgomery
(o)   Keitel, Hitler, Jodl
(p)   Bormann, Hitler
(q)   Chorus of Berliners
(r)   Krebs, Hitler (plus daily conference attendees)
(s)   Chorus of Berliners

SCENE 10
(a)   Burgdorf, Junge, Hitler, Goebbels
(b)   Goebbels, Hitler
(c)   Montgomery, Ernie, Henderson, Belsen men
(d)   Hitler, Eva Braun, Wagner, Bormann, Goebbels, Gerda Christian, Constanze Manziarly,

Krebs, Burgdorf, Axmann
(e)   Hitler, Eva Braun
(f)   Junge, Gerda Christian, Günsche, Eva Braun, Hitler, Magda Goebbels, Krebs, Burgdorf
(g)   Chorus of Berliners

SCENE 11

(a)   Stalin, Interpreter, Zhukov's voice
(b)   Matusov, Chuikov
(c)   Kiselyov, German, Abyzov
(d)   Chuikov, Matusov, Heinersdorf
(e)   Montgomery, Henderson, Dawnay, Warren, von Friedeburg, Kinzel, Rear Admiral Wagner, Friedl
(f)   Montgomery, von Friedeburg, Kinzel, Rear Admiral Wagner, Friedl, Pollok, Col. Ewart
(g)   Strong, Eisenhower, Jodl
(h)   Dawnay, Montgomery

SCENE 12

(a)   Chorus of Londoners
(b)   Truman, Aide
(c)   Churchill
(d)   Eisenhower
(e)   Stalin
(f)   Montgomery

SCENE 1

(15 May 1944. St. Paul's School, lecture theatre. EISENHOWER, MONTGOMERY, KING GEORGE VI, CHURCHILL, SMUTS and BRITISH CHIEFS OF STAFF sit on chairs in the first row. GENERALS and their STAFF sit on wooden benches behind. Several hundred are present. Blackboard, map.)

Eisenhower. Today we present the plan for Operation
Overlord so that every commander has
A last chance to understand the strategy.
It is vital we are honest. It is the duty
Of anyone who sees a flaw to say so.
I now invite General Montgomery,
Allied Land Forces Commander, to come forward.

(MONTGOMERY rises in battledress. He speaks in a tone of quiet emphasis, addressing the audience. As he starts there is a hammering on the door and PATTON swaggers in and sits down. MONTGOMERY looks round angrily.)

Montgomery. General Eisenhower has charged me with the
Preparation and conduct of the land battle.
There are four armies under my control.
First American, Second British: assault.
Third American, First Canadian: follow-up.
The enemy. Last February, Rommel took command
From Holland to the Loire. It is now clear
That his intention is to deny any penetration.
Overlord is to be defeated on the beaches.
To this end he has thickened his coastal crust,
Increased his infantry, and redistributed
His armoured reserve. Fortress Europe has
Become more and more formidable. There are
Sixty German divisions stationed in France,
Of which ten are *élite* Panzer divisions,
And four of these are in the Normandy area,
(Pointing with pointer) At Caen, Lisieux, Rennes and Tours. Rommel
Is an energetic and determined commander,
He has made a world of difference since he took over.
He will try to force us off the beaches

And secure Caen, Bayeux and Carentan.
The Allies *must* seize and hold fast these three
Nodal points, in which case Rommel will revert
To his Alamein tactics of counter-attacks.
Now there are several hundred of you here,
And I want to give you all a clear idea
Of the problem we face, and the solution.

(*Later.*)

Montgomery.　　So, to sum up, the plan is straight forward
And simple. We hold the enemy at Caen,
Like a boxer holding off his opponent
With his left fist, and then with our right flank
We deliver a terrific surprise blow
From the peninsula around Cherbourg, through Rennes,
To Paris and the Seine, like a boxer
Swinging with his right and hitting his opponent
In his solar plexus, and send him reeling against
The ropes – the river Seine. Is that completely clear?
We're *not* knocking him out at Caen with our left,
We're holding him off with the British and Canadians.
The knock-out comes with our right, the Americans.
I remind you, these phase lines show where we expect
To reach in the ninety days after D-Day.
Now morale is very important. The soldiers
Must go in seeing red. We must get them
Completely on their toes, with absolute
Faith in the plan, infectious optimism
And offensive eagerness. Nothing must stop them.
If we send them into battle in this way
Then we shall succeed, and we'll show Hitler
Who is really Overlord of Europe.

(*Later. Audience standing and chatting.* THE KING, CHURCHILL *and* BROOKE *talk.*)

Churchill.　　It was like Henry the Fifth before Agincourt:
Confident, optimistic, but grave.

Brooke.　　　　　　　　　　　　　He
Has pressed me for *Overlord* since forty-two.

Churchill.	He returned to Britain a hero, the conqueror of Rommel.
	There's been nothing like the popular acclaim
	Since Wellington returned from Waterloo.
	When he began going round the country
	Speaking to thirty thousand men in a day,
	Wearing the beret of a tank soldier
	And being cheered for his charisma, I
	Thought he really might be after my job.
King.	I thought he was after mine.
Eisenhower.	I hope not mine.
Churchill.	Monty would make a good Prime Minister.
Bradley.	A brilliant presentation, clear and convincing.
Patton.	You were very confident, you radiated confidence.
Eisenhower.	Without notes, you were totally in charge,
	A very convincing estimate of the situation.
Montgomery.	Ike, you handled it well. You said little
	But what you said was on a high level.
Bradley.	You inspired your King to speak. That was unexpected.
Montgomery.	What he said was just right, short but just right.
Patton.	Smuts was pessimistic about German ruthlessness,
	But Churchill made a stirring speech at the end.
Montgomery.	He was more full of life than the last occasion.
Eisenhower.	He looked quite dejected then, and when he spoke
	He said "I am *now* hardening to the enterprise."
	That shocked me, I realised he had not
	Believed that *Overlord* would succeed till then.
Montgomery.	He does now. He has faith in the plan now.

(*Days later.Broomfield House study, Montgomery's TAC HQ.* MONTGOMERY *and* DAWNAY.)

Dawnay.   A letter from Churchill's military assistant,
General Ismay. Churchill was "much concerned"
By some of the statements made at Monday's
Conference, for example, two thousand clerks
Are to be taken to keep records, and at
D plus twenty there will be one vehicle
To every 4.84 men. Ismay writes:
"The Prime Minister would like to have a discussion
With you and your staff on the whole question
Of the British tail", before dinner on Friday.

Montgomery.   It's interference. But I'll have to see him.

(*Days later.* MONTGOMERY *and* CHURCHILL.)

Montgomery.   I understand, sir, that you want to discuss
With my staff the proportion of soldiers to vehicles
Landing on the beaches in the first flights.
I cannot allow you to do so. I took
An unsound operation of war as I
Told you in Marrakesh on New Year's Day,
With the organisation of command and frontage wrong,
And recast it into a clear plan that
Everyone can have faith and confidence in.
Nothing has been left to chance or improvisation.
The staff have done a terrific job preparing
The invasion. After months of meticulous planning
The whole of southern England is an army depot.
There are queues of tanks and lorries and guns
All waiting to be shipped, all checked by SHAEF.
The work is now almost completed. We
Have just enough vehicles, the right number.
All over England troops are moving towards
The assembly areas, prior to embarkation.
To make a change now would cause tremendous
Disruption, and shake their confidence in the plan.
In the last two years I have won battles
At Alamein, Tripoli, Medenine,
Mareth, Wadi Akarit, Sicily,

	And Southern Italy. The invasion of Normandy Has the confidence of the men. Besides commanding A British army I will command a Canadian And two American armies. Do you want to come Between a battlefield General and his men, his staff? I could never allow it, never. If you think That is wrong, you have lost confidence in me. And you must find someone else to lead the expedition.
Churchill.	Get the troops ashore, that's the main thing to me. I will make it an issue of confidence if you don't Allow me, as Prime Minister, to have my say. I want the invasion to succeed, I must Be sure we have made the right preparations.
Montgomery.	You cannot talk to my staff. At this stage For you to address the Twenty-first Army Group Would be unwarranted interference. I cannot allow you to do so. My staff Advise me and I give the final decision. They then do what I tell them.

(CHURCHILL *breaks down and weeps.* MONTGOMERY *offers* CHURCHILL *his handkerchief.*)

Churchill.	I'm sorry, Monty. I'm tired and overstrained, I don't mean To interfere.
Montgomery.	Let's go next door, where I Will present my staff.

(*Days later. Broomfield House caravan.* MONTGOMERY *and* KING GEORGE *walking outside.* CORPORAL, CHEF.)

Montgomery.	We only use the House during the day For meetings and formal dinners. Only the chef Sleeps in, the rest of us sleep in tents in the field Round my three caravans which are TAC HQ, And we eat in the dining marquee. We have To toughen the minds of the men, and their physique,

Get them used to living in the battlefield.
I'm afraid there are no exceptions. Tonight,
Sir, you will sleep in my caravan, in there.
My batman will bring you water. Corporal
Fetch hot water from the kitchen.

Corporal.   Sir. Sir, the new chef
Would like a word. (*Exit.*)

Montgomery.   Yes, Paul.

Chef.   I'm standing in
For Sergeant Wright. Is tonight's menu to be
Different? I mean, is rationing suspended?

Montgomery.   No, we have strict food rationing, this is
The Army, not Windsor where game, fresh fruit,
Vegetables, rabbits, I have heard, are brought
By loyal subjects for your family, sir.
Here like any commoner the King makes do.
There can be no extra rations because
The King has come.

Chef   (*embarrassed*).   Very good, sir. (*Exit.*)

Montgomery.   We eat
At half past six in the House. My bedtime's nine.

King.   Can I bath?

Montgomery.   No, sir. The water supply was hit
In the Portsmouth bombing raids, it's been off since
We moved here. We receive water from a wagon
That calls, or take jerry cans to an army
Tanker. The men cannot take canvas baths,
Nor we.

King.   What are those trenches?

Montgomery.   Toilets, sir.
As there is no water, we don't use the House.

(DAWNAY *appears.*)

I'll meet you by the cedar, on the lawn.

(THE KING *goes gingerly into the caravan as the* CORPORAL *arrives with water.* MONTGOMERY *turns away with* DAWNAY.)

Kit, I shall want to give the King my *Notes*
On High Command in War, and a photograph
Of myself. Can you get them ready? Wavell,
Auchinleck, Marshall, Mountbatten, Fraser,
Mackenzie-King and Smuts have had copies
And so should the King who, not long ago,
Was in favour of appeasing Hitler
And did not want Churchill to be PM.
It will be educative. You have heard me say,
I have three superiors – God, Churchill, Brooke
In that order – and to none other defer.

(*The following week.* MONTGOMERY *speaking to troops. He addresses the audience.*)

Montgomery   (*beckoning*). Gather closer, you're too far away. That's better.
Now all of you are soon going to be involved
In D-Day, when we invade France
And deliver the enemy a terrific blow
From which he will not be able to recover.
Now I am travelling about and meeting all
The troops who will be going, and I say to you
We have spent several months perfecting our plan,
Everything is prepared, nothing is left to chance,
And I will only move when I know it's safe.
We have to fight, but I don't want to lose lives.
We have done everything we can on the organisation.
Now it's up to you, and you can do it.
I know you can do it, and I believe in you.
And you have seen me and met me, you've seen
I wear a beret, the same as you, and you
Can now believe in me. I've already
Beaten the Germans in seven battles,
I know how to beat Rommel yet again,
And with your help and the Lord Mighty in Battle

On our side, we will drive the Nazis out of France
And out of Germany and win the war.

(*Broomfield House dining-room.* MONTGOMERY *at dinner with his four army commanders:*
DEMPSEY, CRERAR, BRADLEY *, who is shy and quiet, and* PATTON, *who is boastful. A*
convivial atmosphere.)

Montgomery.   It's done, I've written it in my betting book.

Dempsey.   And I bet General Bradley five pounds that the war
With Germany will end by November the first.

Bradley.   You're on. I'm optimistic, but I'm not
That unrealistic.

Montgomery.   That's in my betting book.
And that's *my* target date to end the war
By reaching Berlin by November the first.
(*Rising.*) Commanders, thank you for flying down here
And attending our final conference before D-Day,
Our final look at the plans, and for staying on
For this last supper before the historic invasion.
It has been a very convivial occasion.
And though I only drink water or orange juice,
I want to toast you and the success of
Your four undertakings. To the success
Of *Overlord.*

Patton.   I suppose I should reply
As the oldest army commander present,
And previously Bradley's boss. If everything moves
As planned there will be nothing for me to do
As Bradley will be doing it. I would like to toast
The health of General Montgomery, and declare
Our satisfaction at serving under him.

(*The* FOUR COMMANDERS *rise and toast* MONTGOMERY.)

(*Aside.*) The lightning did not strike me for my lie.
I have a better impression of Monty
But Dempsey's a yes-man and Crerar doesn't impress.

Montgomery	(*aside*). Bradley is diffident and he abhors
	The swaggering Patton, who is a sabre-rattler,
	Ignorant of battle but good at thrusting.
	Dempsey is imperturbable, but I have doubts
	About Crerar as a battlefield leader.
	(*Aloud.*) Here we are, leading the greatest invasion
	In history, and I am reminded of
	A scene in *Antony and Cleopatra*
	Before Actium when Lepidus is carried out.
	Patton. That will be Brad, the quiet ones drink the most.

(*The next day.* MONTGOMERY *dining with* EISENHOWER.)

Montgomery.	A Commander has to be many-sided.
	He must assess a situation and
	Make a clear plan and communicate it clearly
	To all his subordinates. He must have great
	Authority and inspire trust. He must make
	Men eager to follow his commands. He must take
	Account of ever-changing situations
	And simplify the complexity so
	It is comprehensible. A Commander
	Is like an artist who reveals the One
	Behind the surface many, in all its forms,
	The unity behind multiplicity.
	A Commander reveals the aim behind a war
	At every twist and turn of a long campaign.
	And the men sit in their camp and do not know
	How definite the Commander has to be.

(*Silence.*)

Eisenhower.	Bushey Park is like an armed camp, canvas
	Tents under every tree, GIs sitting
	And all round a red wall, sentries at the gate.
	Today I wrote my Order of the Day
	At Southwick House. It begins: "Soldiers, Sailors
	And Airmen of the Allied Expeditionary Force:
	You are about to embark on the Great Crusade,
	Towards which we have striven these many months,
	The eyes of the world are upon you."

Montgomery	(*reading*). "You will bring about

Montgomery   (*reading*).   "You will bring about
The destruction of the German war machine,
The elimination of Marxist tyranny
Over the oppressed people of Europe, and
Security for ourselves in a free world."
It's very eloquent. You know, Ike, you're
Just the man for the job.

Eisenhower.   I support you
Firmly, Monty.

Montgomery   (*aside*).   I like him immensely.
He has a generous lovable character,
And I would trust him to the last gasp.
I do like him tremendously. He is
So very genuine and sincere.

(*Evening. Southwick House mess room.* EISENHOWER, HIS COMMANDERS *and RAF Group Captain* STAGG. *Bookcases and French windows, large map.*)

Stagg.   Bad news. High pressure is giving way to a low
As a depression over Iceland spreads south.
The weather on June the fifth will be overcast
And stormy with Force Five winds. It's getting worse.

Eisenhower.   Thank you. Please leave the room. (*Exit Stagg.*) Well, what do we think?
What do you think, Monty?

Montgomery.   I have laid the plan
And prepared the armies. It is for you
As Supreme Commander to say if the armies should go.
A decision to cancel must be made
Twenty-four hours before the landings as
The invasion fleet of five thousand ships
Will assemble then.

Tedder.   I don't think we should go.
You can't have an invasion through mountainous seas –
Look what happened to the Spanish Armada –
And low cloud which does not allow air cover.

Montgomery.   I am in favour of going. Everything is ready.
                     A huge operation is co-ordinated.
                     The morale of the men has been lifted.
                     If we don't go now, we must wait a month,
                     And morale will flag, and the Germans may find out.
                     They think we have an army around Dover,
                     Operation Fortitude may be discovered.

(One hour later. EISENHOWER with STAGG and the others.)

Eisenhower.   No irrevocable decision has been made.
                     The American Navy with Bradley's troops
                     Should leave for Omaha and Utah beaches,
                     Subject to a possible last-minute cancellation.
                     I will make the final decision at the weather
                     Conference at eight tomorrow morning.

(Early next morning. EISENHOWER and STAGG.)

Stagg.   Sea conditions will be slightly better than
                     Expected, but low cloud will ground air forces.

Ramsay.   The sky is practically clear, when do
                     You expect cloud and wind?

Stagg.   Five hours from now,
                     Sir.

Ramsay.   I think we should go.

Eisenhower.   Leigh-Mallory?

Leigh-Mallory.   I'm against. Air forces could not carry out the plan.

Montgomery.   Some of the air programme would be cancelled,
                     But most could go ahead. We must go, for
                     Each hour's delay makes the troops' ordeal worse.

Eisenhower.   Tedder?

Tedder.   I must disagree with Monty.

We need full, and not partial, air support.

Eisenhower.   *Overlord* is being launched with ground forces
That are not overwhelmingly powerful.
We need the help of air superiority
Or the landings will be far too risky.
If air cover cannot operate we must postpone.
That is my casting vote. Any dissentient voices?

Montgomery   (*aside*). The sky is clear, dawn glows, yet we postpone
Because of dissenting meteorologists,
But I have myself revered air supremacy,
And there must be unity of purpose and decision
Under the Supreme Commander. Be silent.

(*Silence.*)

Eisenhower.   D-Day is not June fifth.

(*Pause.*)

Monty, perhaps
You and I should walk down to the Golden Lion.
Fruit juice?

(*La Roche Guyon.* ROMMEL *and his Chief of Staff General* HANS SPEIDEL.)

Rommel.   There won't be an invasion in this weather.
The Straits of Dover are even worse than here.
If they come they won't get off the beaches.
It's my wife's birthday. I'm going to take
A short vacation, I shall drive to Herrlingen
And give Lucy her present, these new shoes,
Then visit the *Führer* in Berchtesgaden
And press him to move Panzer Group West to
The coast rather than hold it in reserve
As von Schweppenburg and Rundstedt want.
We need three more divisions in all.
Look after the *château* for me.

(*Broomfield House. Wind and rain.* EISENHOWER *and* MONTGOMERY *over dinner in the din-*

ing-room. PAUL *the chef, serving, overhears.*)

Montgomery.	If we don't go on June the sixth, we can't Until the nineteenth, and to stand men down And bring back ships will damage their morale And blow their secrecy. We have to make it work.
Eisenhower.	You're right. If we have air superiority, We have to go.
Montgomery.	Thank God you banned Churchill, Banished him to a train near Southampton.

(*Early next morning. Southwick House. Mess room.* EISENHOWER *and* COMMANDERS *all in battledress,* MONTGOMERY *in fawn-coloured pullover and light corduroy trousers. Coffee,* STAGG.)

Stagg.	The rain will clear within a matter of hours. Look it's already happening now.
Eisenhower	(*pacing, shooting out his chin*). Who's for go? Monty. Smith. Ramsay?
Ramsay.	I'm concerned about Spotting for naval gunfire, but will take the risk.
Eisenhower.	Tedder?
Tedder.	I'm ready.
Leigh-Mallory.	Air conditions are Below the acceptable minimum.
Eisenhower.	Thank you, Stagg.

(*Exit* STAGG.)

The ships are sailing into the Channel.
If they have to be called back, we must do so now.
The Supreme Commander is the only man

Who can do that.

(EISENHOWER *thinks. Time stops.*)

OK, let's go.

(*A cheer. Everyone rushes to their command posts.* EISENHOWER, *alone, sits on in immense isolation.*)

Eisenhower   (*reflecting*). The fate of thousands of men hung on my words,
And the future of nations. I had power
Over the whole world, and was still; but now
It is too late to change the decision.
The invasion cannot be stopped – even by me.
Overlord now has a life of its own.
It is in the men, not me, that power resides.

(*Same day, 9 p.m. Broomfield House.* MONTGOMERY *by his caravan, his* BATMAN *and* DAWNAY.)

Montgomery.   Everything possible has been done to ensure the success
Of the landings. We've done everything possible.
It is now in the hands of God. It'll be
All right. I'm turning in at the usual time.
Wake me at the usual time. No, not before.

(*He goes into his caravan.*)

It seems only yesterday that I led, in rain,
My company in a charge at Meteren
At the start of the First World War, and as
I stormed the village was shot through my chest
And knee by a sniper, and the soldier
Dragging me to safety was shot and killed
And fell on top of me. For three hours in
The lashing rain I lay, bleeding. They dug
A grave, and as they picked me up and dumped me
In a greatcoat to sling me and drop me in
An orderly called "Hey, this one's still alive."
If I had died then, who'd have redrawn *Overlord*?
I feel I was saved by Providence for this moment.

(*Praying.*) O Lord, Eisenhower has entrusted to me
The conduct of Overlord, which is now in my hands.
I have launched the biggest invasion ever,
A hundred and seventy-six thousand men
Are now in the air or on the waves, to land
In Fortress Europe, breach Hitler's Atlantic Wall
Which is in the hands of my old adversary,
Rommel, from whom I captured this caravan.
Lord many will die on both sides, scarring your earth.
Forgive me Lord for destroying your world,
Your hedgerows, wild flowers, chestnut trees and fields,
With tanks, with flame-throwers – forgive me for
Taking part in the killing of men, but if
I don't, what will happen? Hitler will continue
His murderous campaign, his guards will press on
With the Final Solution. I have a just cause,
But Lord, let me not kill unnecessarily.
I will be cautious, to win with minimum loss.
Perception of evil is a point of view,
Lord, let me see within the harmony of the One
That shows this war has meaning in relation to Good.

(*He pauses.*)

O Lord, in this situation I must kill.
You do not want me to. I am like Arjuna
In the *Bhagavadgita.* Let me act without
Interference from my rational, social ego,
Let me act from my soul and I will be in harmony
With your will, and those who die as a result
Of my decision will die at the behest
Of your divine will. O Lord, I am troubled
At the thought of those who will die. I commit them to you,
To the whole, the One. And may you absolve me
From this necessity. For to remove Hitler
And his Final Solution men must die,
And it is worse for them not to die, and for more
To die. O Lord, Overlord.

(*Chorus of the* OCCUPIED.)

Chorus.   The Allies have landed, there is hope again.
                   No longer shall we walk with sullen faces.
                   A spring is in our step, liberation
                   Cannot be far away, freedom from the yoke,
                   From helmeted Nazis driving by our squares,
                   From *Gestapo* questionings and firing-squads,
                   Freedom from the noose in public places.
                   Once again we can live without fear – soon.
                   Come, Montgomery, liberate us, but
                   Without smashing our towns and killing our men.

(*D-Day* SOLDIER.)

D-Day Soldier.   For two nights we tossed on the choppy sea.
                   It was full of ships and craft, surely the Germans
                   Would see us and bomb us from the air?
                   The storm soaked us as we huddled on deck.
                   No one said much, we waited, seasick. Then
                   At H-hour a barrage from our Navy ships.
                   We scrambled down long ropes, packs on our backs,
                   Clutching rifles near tied gas masks, and jumped
                   Into assault craft, a ribbon of shore ahead
                   Gleaming in the early morning sunshine,
                   With little puffs of smoke from our Navy's shells.
                   Dipping, swaying, we crouched all tense and looked,
                   We approached through fire, bullets whipped up the waves
                   And clanged our sides. We nosed through floating bodies
                   Towards the smoke. A German plane roared down
                   And strafed the crowded beach, men and vehicles.
                   In that moment each one of us was afraid.
                   Yet we all showed courage. Bang! Down went the flap,
                   Out, we jumped into three feet of cold waves
                   And waded through the bullets and corpses
                   To the sand at the lapping water's edge,
                   Then dived as the plane whined down and raked our path.
                   "Mines," someone shouted, "stick to the matting."
                   We ran doubled-up under sniper fire.
                   The man beside me on the landing craft
                   Fell at my side, shot through the head. We gathered
                   At a muster point at the top of the beach,
                   And I saw a German soldier dead in a tree.

We were given provisions, and then ran on
Towards a house and fields, we advanced.

(*Rommel's house.* ROMMEL *and* LUCY. *Speidel rings.*)

Rommel.   Speidel. It *is* the invasion? Are you sure?
I will leave immediately.
(*To Lucy.*)   The invasion has come,
It is confirmed, out of high seas and storm,
And I was not at my post. Montgomery,
Who defeated me at Alamein, seems to know
My movements and when I am three divisions short.
The only way to repulse him was to drive
Him off the beaches into the sea. If he now has
A foothold, I fear it may be too late.

(*Later the same morning. The Berghof, Hitler's HQ in Berchtesgaden.* HITLER *and* KEITEL.)

Hitler.   Again and again I have warned Rommel and Rundstedt
The first invasion will come in Normandy.
In March I several times warned the Generals,
On May the sixth I telephoned Jodl
That I attached particular importance
To Normandy. But Rommel and Rundstedt
Remained convinced the invasion would take place
In the Straits of Dover. Now I can attack
London with my flying bombs. Now the enemy
Is where we can get at them.

(*Silence. Exit* KEITEL. *Enter* BORMANN.)

                        I am not worried.
I do not believe that this "invasion"
Is anything other than a diversion.
I have always said that the main attack will come
In the Pas de Calais. I speak as Will.
The Atlantic Wall will repulse them,
There will be another Dunkirk.
We are invincible, I am a will
To conquer, I have a personal destiny
Within the historical process.

Bormann.	Providence

Has saved you to lead Germany
Through this time of trial.

(*Silence.*)

Hitler.
There must be no let up
In the solution to the Jewish problem.
By expelling Jews from their privileged positions
I have opened up their positions to the children
Of hundreds of thousands of working-class Germans,
And I am depriving the revolutionary movement
Of its Jewish inspiration: Rosenberg,
To whom Eckart introduced me, my mentor,
Brought out of Bolshevik Russia a book,
The Protocols of the Elders of Zion,
The secret plans of the international
Jewish conspiracy for world domination.
I read it shortly after Zionists
Brought America into the First World War.
It shows that the Jewish doctrine of Marxism
Seeks the destruction of all non-Jewish
National states, and plans to hand the world
To the Jews. Russia has been captured by the Jews.

Bormann.
Through Bolshevism and the Jewish Trotsky
The Jews seek to achieve world domination.

Hitler.
And to spread through Germany as the Thule Society taught.
The Jews are a race, not a religious persuasion,
They foment revolution with Freemasons
And democrats from Britain and the US.
The Final Solution is the removal
Of Jews altogether. I am the Messiah
Who will save man from the Jewish Antichrist.

Bormann.
Zionism has driven the Bolsheviks
To butcher millions in the Soviet Union.

Hitler.
And is now driving the Allies' war-efforts.
Hungary is rotten with Jews everywhere,

Right up to the highest level, and a network
Of agents and spies. We must make a clean sweep.
We must do this while we are still able to.
Two days after the Americans entered Rome,
An invasion in Normandy. It is a diversion.
But it is also impudence. Launched from Britain.
Pah, I will pay Britain back with reprisal weapons.
I have eight thousand flying bombs, each one
Twenty-five feet long with a one-ton warhead,
Each pilotless with a jet engine. Prepare
To send the first of these to London.
I will rain destruction from the sky.

(*Early evening. Near Southwick House.* EISENHOWER, *pacing outside his trailer.*)

Butcher.
The landings have been successful. We have now
A hundred and fifty-six thousand ashore,
And two thousand five hundred casualties,
Mostly at Omaha. We have Bayeux,
The seat of William the Conqueror, who
Is the only man besides Caesar, and now you,
To command a successful cross-Channel assault.

Eisenhower.
We have not got Caen.

(*The next day. HMS* Apollo. EISENHOWER *and* MONTGOMERY.)

Montgomery.
Ike, in view of the American difficulty
On Omaha beach, on the whole US Army front
The immediate tactical plan has been altered.
The Utah and Omaha beach troops must link up
Or the Panzer Divisions will obliterate Omaha.

Eisenhower.
All right, I will signal the Combined Chiefs of Staff
In Washington to that effect, and will say
That after that adjustment, the original conceptions
Will be pursued.

(MONTGOMERY *rises to move away.*)

Oh, Monty, I'm concerned

That Caen has not been captured.

Montgomery.   It's clear the enemy
                     Intend to hold it strongly and to drive into
                     My eastern flank. Dempsey will have to envelop it
                     Rather than take it by a frontal attack,
                     And then pivot on Caen and swing his right flank
                     As the plan provides. I am well satisfied
                     With today's fighting.

                     (MONTGOMERY *moves away.*)

Eisenhower.   I'm not satisfied.

Butcher.   I find
                     Him insufferable. He almost made out that
                     Americans had messed up his plan on Omaha,
                     He seemed to derive some satisfaction from
                     Re-arranging the whole American front.
                     I find his self-satisfaction irritating.

Eisenhower.   He can be self-righteous and rather rigid.

Montgomery   (*aside*). I am in theory responsible to Ike
                     Who is in turn responsible to the Combined
                     Chiefs of Staff, and beyond them, to two governments,
                     But I look to Brooke for guidance, I am
                     The senior British officer in Europe and
                     I am responsible for my nation's interests.

SCENE 2

(*June 1944. Berghof, Hitler's HQ. Hitler,* DÖNITZ *and* GÖRING.)

Dönitz.   The invasion has succeeded. The Second Front
                     Has come.

Göring.   The Navy assured us the enemy
                     Would not risk his best ships in a sea invasion.

Dönitz. Discussion of such matters is not opportune
At present. There should be more air-strikes.
The enemy flew over ten thousand on
Invasion day, our *Luftwaffe* three hundred.
Hitler. I have warned since March that the first invasion
Would come in Normandy, not the Pas de Calais.
No one would listen to me. Send the 9th
And 10th SS Panzers to the Normandy front.

(*He goes out to his balcony. Bavarian Alps ahead of and below him.*)

(*Alone.*) From this high point in the Bavarian Alps
I look down on the slopes and paths of the world
And think how I have climbed to this great height
From Braunau in Austria, where I was born.
I left school without a certificate,
I lived in a doss-house in imperial Vienna,
I was a corporal in the First World War,
And saw my country humiliated, shrink
And then in Munich, in beer-cellars, the Hofbrauhaus,
I stood on tables and spoke and they echoed.
Eckart taught me I had a destiny,
After my rise to Chancellor, it was inevitable
That I would take the Rhineland, Austria
(My home country), and the Sudetenland,
Then Czechoslovakia and finally Poland;
I made my choice and carried out my free act.
I was driven not by personal ambition
But the will to purify the German race
Of all its Jewish blood. I made a pact
With the Bolshevik Devil to take Poland
And cleanse it of its ethnically degenerate past.
Chamberlain was a well-intentioned fool,
He was no match for my diplomacy.
How I despised him when he waved his paper.
I did not seek war with Britain and Russia,
But I blitzkrieged Britain and invaded Russia,
And my Atlantic war drew in Britain's supplier,
The Zionist US. I committed aggression
Against these three powers, beyond good and evil;
Because I sought to impose my vision

Of a pure race of god-men on the world,
And Jews and Bolsheviks were the obstacles.
Now two powers attack me on the west, and I
Am pressed on the east. And this Montgomery,
Who beat Rommel in North Africa and Italy,
Is now poised like some agent of the divine,
To strike and repay me for my cleansing.
But I do not believe in a moral universe,
That aggression leads to destruction, but in power.
I sought like Augustus and Constantine,
Like Charlemagne and Napoleon to rule
Europe and dominate the whole world,
Not for personal ambition, but so that the idea
I embody could find universal expression:
The supremacy of the Aryan race,
The Germanic people's mission to rule the world.
I am a German imperialist, I seek
To destroy the British Empire and inherit it,
To be crowned Kaiser of a world empire
Where German ideas are followed throughout the world,
Where God is dead as Nietzsche said, and where
Beyond good and evil, all is will to power.
I have to become the Christian Antichrist
To reject the *Old Testament* of the Jews
And the Christian code that says "Thou shalt not kill" –
Did not Napoleon reject its good –
In order to combat the Jewish Antichrist
Who seeks to destroy Germany and rule.
I have remade good in a nihilistic world.
Christians see me as the Antichrist, but I am
The Messiah who saves mankind from Jewish rule.
And so Montgomery does not frighten me.
Providence rules by power, not by what is good.

(*Creullet. TAC HQ, Montgomery's caravans.* MONTGOMERY *sitting outside with the BBC rep,*
HOWARD MARSHALL. *Beside him, a chamber-pot.*)

Montgomery.   Our first location after landing at Sainte Croix-sur-Mer
                Was a totally unsuitable place for my TAC HQ.
                It was a crossroads between fields with German trenches
                And under artillery fire. Colonel Russell

Must have taken it from a map. My Canadian
Assistant, Warren, scouted round and found
Me this lovely *château*. It was occupied
This morning by fifteen Germans whom he took prisoner.
So here we are. We arrived this afternoon.
I have everything except a chamber-pot.
I tried to gesticulate what I wanted,
And Madame de Druval has produced one,
After bringing vases, and look, you see its crest.
Montgomery. For my ancestors came
From Sainte Foy de Montgomery near Falaise.
Roger de Montgomery was number two
To William the Conqueror. I landed near Dives,
The spot from which William sailed. My family invaded
Britain, and now are liberating the
Conqueror's Norman homeland from the Saxon yoke.
Everything is going well. Rommel's Twenty-first
Panzer Division has arrived at Caen
And half have been destroyed, and half of the rest
Have been sent to retake Bayeux, weakening their thrust.

Marshall.   Was it over-optimistic, faulty thinking
To expect troops who landed yesterday morning,
Many seasick, to march on foot to Caen
And capture it by nightfall, without armoured
Troop carriers that follow tanks, of the kind
The Germans have? And why was the British
Tank advance so slow?

Montgomery.   Everything is going to plan.

(HENDERSON *and* DAWNAY *are in the "A" mess tent.*)

Henderson   (*to Dawnay*). He's tired and on edge, nothing's gone right
But now he's in the field, all is confidence
And he has time for relaxing anecdotes
About chamber-pots.

(*Days later. Telegraph Cottage, near Bushey Park.* EISENHOWER, BUTCHER *and* KAY.)

Butcher.   There's no information from Montgomery

Who agreed to cable every night.

Eisenhower.   That's too bad.
How can I evaluate what's happening
In Normandy if I don't have any cables?
Monty is slow. Bradley's disappointed,
Taking Caen was supposed to shield his troops,
American troops, and now they're exposed.

Kay.   You know,
Montgomery is the only person in
The whole Allied Command whom I dislike.
He's like a desert rat, with his pointed nose
And his quick eyes which dart to either side.
How can you stand not hearing from him? Tell him off.

Eisenhower.   I feel angry and frustrated, cut off.
I need to be the field Commander in charge
Of Twenty-first Army Group. Then I'd know
What the situation is.

(*Berchtesgaden*. HITLER, BORMANN *and* BURGDORF.)

Burgdorf.   Rommel plans to divert his counter-attack
From the British armour driving on Caen
To the American drive on Cherbourg,
And then return to stop Dempsey's advance
Which is already near Villers-Bocage.

Bormann.   Rommel is letting the British advance on Caen.
Hitler. Caen is nearer to Paris than Cherbourg.
I veto Rommel's plan. Army Group B
Will attack the British bridgehead from Caen,
Using the reinforcements we have supplied.
Send Rommel an *Enigma* signal now.

(*Creullet, Montgomery's TAC HQ. Operations trailer.* CHURCHILL, SMUTS, BROOKE,
MONTGOMERY, *who stands before a map. They have just had lunch.*)

Churchill   (*excitedly*). And the enemy are only three miles away?
Why, German armour may roll through our lunch.

Montgomery.	That is unlikely, Prime Minister. But to resume.
	My main strategy is to draw the Germans
	Onto the British east flank so the Americans
	Can break out from Cherbourg and wheel round.
	We shall exploit all German mistakes at once.
	For example, they've concentrated their
	Panzer strength to hold Caen and block what they
	Think is a thrust towards Paris and the Seine,
	But we have an excellent chance of encircling
	Their Panzer corps and capturing prisoners.
	The Allied aim is to defeat the German
	Armies in the West, not break out towards the Seine.

(*Later*. CHURCHILL *and* HENDERSON.)

Churchill   (*curious*). So what is Monty's day?

Henderson.   Here in "A" Mess
                 His day is simple. He rises in time
                 For breakfast at eight and is out by nine
                 In two jeeps with four redcaps, visiting
                 Headquarters, front line troops. At four he returns
                 Takes his uniform off, puts on his grey
                 Sweater and corduroy trousers. From five
                 Till six he has his main meal. Then he sits
                 In the open air with his LOs,
                 His young Liaison Officers who act as scouts,
                 His eyes and ears for different parts of the front,
                 And report what they have seen in the battlefield.
                 They sit with mugs of tea. Each will have been to
                 A different battle zone. He took the idea
                 From the Duke of Wellington – some say Napoleon –
                 Who had eight Liaison Officers in the field,
                 And his way of fighting, in caravans near the front,
                 Is not unlike the method of Waterloo.
                 From seven he reads and thinks, he goes to bed at nine.
                 Then he must not be disturbed for
                 Any reason. I know he prays every night.
                 In his caravan. I have seen him, heard him.

(*Later*. MONTGOMERY *and* BROOKE *briefly alone.*)

Montgomery.	Thank you for covering my back in London, With Churchill and Tedder. I wish you could Do something about Ike. His approach to war Differs fundamentally from my own. I am amazed he has commanded the only Cross-Channel invasion since Julius Caesar And the Conqueror. Of course it was my doing.
Brooke.	For a Caesar he is genial, but behind The friendly exterior is a ruthless mind That balances conflicting national interests And appears to lead by compromise, but may Favour his masters' interests, not blatantly But indirectly, at one remove, so that At surface level all seems reasonable And there are sound military reasons For what may at heart be political. Beware of him. He has a restlessness That latches on to any new idea And seeks to integrate it within the scheme, Always for a military reason, you follow. There is something in him that reminds me of a fox. He is a great man, and a simple one, Both at the same time. I find it hard to understand How a great man who leads like William the Conqueror Can while away his time with Western novels. There's a disparity between his decisions, what he gives out, And his tastes, what he imbibes. Perhaps his mind Is more advanced than his culture, or perhaps He is quite simply, just an American.
Montgomery.	He is pulling against me the whole time.

(*The next day.* MONTGOMERY *and* POSTON, *one of his Liaison Officers.*)

Montgomery	(*thinly*). What happened at Villers-Bocage?
Poston.	The Desert Rats Entered the cheering village and some tank crews Got out. Some Cromwells pushed on. Just outside Five Tiger tanks of 1 SS Panzer Corps

Lay in wait, commanded by Michael Wittmann,
The ace who destroyed a hundred and thirty-eight
Tanks on the Russian front. He set off alone
And destroyed four of our tanks in the village
With eighty-eight millimetre shells, blocking
Retreat. He returned and attacked our column.
He destroyed the first tank, then went down the line.
By mid-morning his one Tiger destroyed
Twenty-seven tanks and twenty-eight armoured
Vehicles and killed eighty infantrymen.
His own tank was disabled but he escaped.
Bucknall then withdrew. Dempsey was not consulted.

Montgomery. Rommel has given us a bloody nose.
My Desert Rats. I will see that Bucknall
And Erskine are sacked.

Poston.   And his counter-attack
Has taken Carentan, the junction between
The two American armies. He ignored Hitler.

(*London, Eisenhower's HQ at 20 Grosvenor Square. EISENHOWER.*)

Eisenhower. What's the matter with Monty? Why won't he attack?
The Germans should be kept off balance, but he
Needs supplies, and doesn't make any gains,
And even retreats. He hasn't taken the airfields
South of Caen, as he promised Leigh-Mallory,
And the air commanders at this morning's meeting
Spoke of "a state of crisis". Even Tedder says
The present situation has the makings of
A dangerous crisis. Leigh-Mallory's
Going to visit Monty today.

(*Chorus of* LONDONERS.)

Chorus. What is that whine that suddenly cuts out?
What is that crash, that devastation as
Houses crumble, bodies are strewn in the street?
What weapon has been unleashed upon us?
What are these flying bombs, that without pilots

Can be fired across the Channel at random,
To fall anywhere, any time, with no more warning
Than a stopped whine? We are all terrified.
Death hovers in the air and we do not know
Where it will strike. May it not be us. Not us.

(*Creullet, Montgomery's TAC HQ.* EISENHOWER *and* TEDDER *waiting. Enter*
MONTGOMERY.)

Montgomery.   Come to the operations caravan
And I will put you both in the picture.

(*Later, in the caravan.* EISENHOWER *is taking notes.*)

The conduct of war is like a game of chess.
Both players must think ahead and have a plan,
A strategy, to feint on the left and slice
Through on the right. To play by simply reacting
To the other player's moves is ragged, chaotic,
Suicidal, and yet some would have us do that.
War is fought in the mind, and the victor
Is the one who is the more mentally tenacious.
I must stress, Caen is the key to Cherbourg.
Rommel, and Hitler, must be made to believe
That the British are attempting to break out
In the east towards the Seine, so they dare not
Release the four Panzer divisions to block
The American thrust to Cherbourg. Villers-
Bocage has helped to create that belief,
It has not imperilled Bradley's drive at all,
It is the key to his success.

Eisenhower.   Monty,
We're impressed. There is no crisis.

Tedder.   The idea of a crisis was over-stressed.

Montgomery.   My Normandy strategy is succeeding.

(*London.* TEDDER *and* CONINGHAM.)

Tedder.	Power has gone to his head. He tells the great
	Who he will see and who he will not, and when.
	He keeps the Supreme Commander waiting all day
	Who has just been escorted by thirteen fighters.
	We sent him a message before we arrived,
	He could have come back early from Bradley,
	Indeed, cancelled his visit. He tells the PM
	Not to come, he speaks to the King with a cold contempt.
	He tells Liddell Hart he is "too busy"
	To see him, he offers a Napoleonic image.
	He is on a pinnacle, and it is *hubris*,
	It will surely tempt the gods to fling him down,
	To cause him to fall.

(*Margival, near Soissons, Hitler's reserve HQ, Wolfschlucht 2.* HITLER, ROMMEL *and*
RUNDSTEDT. JODL, SCHMUNDT *and others.* STENOGRAPHERS.)

Stenographer.	This man is the terror of the world. Four Focke-
	Wulf Condors flew him and his staff to France,
	The entire fighter force along the route
	Was grounded, anti-aircraft batteries
	Shut down. As he drove from Metz airport to here,
	Luftwaffe fighter planes patrolled the highway.
	He has come to boost the Field Marshals' confidence
	After the reverses in the battlefield.
	All men tremble at the power his conquests brought.
	I look forward to seeing what the man is like.
	I am sure he will have Rommel quaking too.

Hitler.	Soissons is near the battlefield where I
	As a corporal won my Iron Cross.
	Rommel and Rundstedt have asked for an urgent
	Conference on the situation in France.

Rommel.	The situation does not improve. The troops,
	Both Army and SS, fight like tigers,
	But the balance of strength tips against us.
	Reinforcements are not getting through,
	The Allied Airforce and warships bombard us
	Every day. The British are trying to break out
	Towards the Seine, the Americans –

Hitler	(*radiating confidence*). Are you losing your nerve?

Rommel.	I know Montgomery from the desert.
	He will press relentlessly till our cordon breaks,
	Then nothing will stop him. It is only days
	Before the front caves in. Rundstedt agrees.

Rundstedt.	I asked permission to withdraw my forces
	From the peninsula to Cherbourg port
	And fortress.

Hitler.	Yes. The fortress should hold out
	As long as possible and until mid-July
	To hinder the enemy's sea-supply.
	The withdrawal is part deception, as there will be
	A winter attack by four Panzer divisions.

Aide.	Air-raid warning.

(*The stenographers leave.* ROMMEL *and* HITLER *stand together in the air-raid shelter with* RUNDSTEDT, SCHMUNDT *and* CHIEFS OF STAFF.)

Rommel.	My *Führer*, please believe
	Politics will soon have to play a part,
	Or the situation will deteriorate
	Too far to be salvaged.

Hitler	(*snapping*). The time is not ripe
	For a political decision. One sues for peace from strength.
	To do so now would be to admit defeat
	In Normandy. I have often spoken
	Of my "secret weapons", and already London
	Has been bombarded by V-I rocket bombs
	And is reeling as under the blitz. Britain will now
	Sue for peace.

(*London.* EISENHOWER *in an air-raid shelter with* BUTCHER.)

Eisenhower.	I'm cooped up in these cramped conditions because
	Hitler still has the buzz-bomb rocket sites.
	Monty should be hurrying to reach them, but no,

He's postponed an offensive yet again. He's slow.
I'm ordering *Anvil* in Bordeaux, I know
There will be no landings till mid-August,
But at least we're doing something. He's like a snail.

(A *whine cuts out, a crash of a doodlebug.*)

(*Chorus of Auschwitz* PRISONERS.)

Chorus.   What will become of us? Who will help us.
We hear that Montgomery has landed,
Normandy is a long, long way away.
How many months will it be before his troops
Have captured Berlin and reached here? Where are
Zhukov's men? Last month, eight thousand were killed.
This month, some two hundred and twenty-five
Thousand, mostly Jews sent from Hungary.
We know, we've seen them, we drag the bodies
From the gas chamber into the crematorium
Next door, we burn them and bury the surplus.
Each day prisoners are taken out and shot
Before the killing wall next to block eleven,
And more are hanged on the portable gallows.
Montgomery, make haste, help us, help us.
We cannot wait more than a few more weeks.
It will be our turn soon. Help us, help us.

(RUNDSTEDT *is on the phone at the HQ of the Commander-in-Chief in the west – OB West –
in Paris.*)

Rundstedt.   Keitel? Rundstedt. While Rommel and I were away
The British IIth Armoured crossed the Odon.
When General Dollmann heard this, he poisoned himself.
Officially he died of a heart attack.
Caen is now undefendable. You say
"What should we do?" Make peace, you idiots.
That's what I will be advising Hitler.

(*Blay, TAC HQ.* EISENHOWER *and* BRADLEY *outside the map caravan.* MONTGOMERY *still
inside.*)

Eisenhower. I am stunned by the clarity and logic
Of his plan. In London he seems too slow,
Over-cautious, but here, I've fallen under
His conviction, his professionalism, his
Physical presence, his spell. He has a certain
Charisma, and I can see you and Dempsey
Cannot go any faster. This bocage
Is not tank country.

Bradley. Collins told me,
The British were in the war nearly three years
Before us, and took heavy casualties in
North Africa. It's natural that they're cautious.

Eisenhower. But the fact remains, the British have failed to expand.
I still want, nay demand, an offensive.
I wonder why he's not mentioned *Anvil*.

(*Two weeks later. Blay, Montgomery's HQ.* MONTGOMERY *and* HENDERSON.)

Montgomery. I'm alarmed that Ike's signal is euphoric.
No commander can have done more to avoid raising
Expectations. I've sent Kit to the War Office,
Written seven pages to Brooke, and sent
De Guingand to brief Ike, to simplify
The complex issues, to stress with simplicity
We are making the *enemy,* not the British or SHAEF,
Believe that we are breaking out to Paris;
And that our true aim is to dent Rommel's armour,
To muck up his plans and kill enemy troops.
Rommel is the objective.

(*Enter* GENERAL BROWNING.)

Browning, sit down.

Browning. As commander of all airborne divisions
I have dropped parachutists, and we have found
Rommel's HQ, and know where he goes to fish
And shoot pigeons. Would you like us to kill him?

Montgomery   (*aside*). How strange that what I have heard in my deepest thoughts
             And do not allow to surface should now be
             Externalised in this proposal. What is right?
             To say Yes and help the British break out
             Or say No with the Christian code? He is
             My old adversary at Alamein and elsewhere,
             I would rather beat him face to face, fairly
             As in a duel with pistols. But fair play
             Has no place in war. War is war.
             (*Aloud.*)   Yes, I would.

(*La Roche Guyon.* ROMMEL *and* SPEIDEL.)

Rommel.   The German front in France will collapse
             In a few weeks. We have tried to convince Hitler
             To surrender. He will not. Yesterday
             I warned him in my dispatch of a grave crisis
             And told him the proper conclusion must be drawn,
             That I must speak plainly. We must now surrender
             On our own responsibility and open
             Independent peace negotiations with the Allies
             As soon as possible.

Speidel.   I agree. But will you now
             Join the movement against Hitler?

Rommel   (*shocked*).   No, no.
             I have my soldier's oath, which is ancient
             And holy in the German tradition.
             I am a professional. I disapprove
             Of any movement against our Head of State.
             To make a change in Berlin is not the way.
             The Commander-in-Chief, West, who is now Kluge,
             Should negotiate for the Allies to march,
             Unopposed, across the Seine and into Germany.
             We will talk further when I return tonight.

(*Blay. Montgomery's HQ.* MONTGOMERY *and* HENDERSON.)

Henderson.   A report that will interest you. Rommel
             Was in his staff car on a country road.

Two of Broadhurst's fighter bombers strafed it.
The driver lost an arm, Rommel was thrown
Out of his car and is now in hospital
With a severely fractured skull and splinters
In his face. Your enemy is out of the war.
The village near where the attack took place
Was Sainte Foy de Montgomery.

Montgomery.   My ancestor's.
If I am Achilles, he was my Hector.

(MONTGOMERY *turns away and goes to his caravan.*)

(*Praying.*) Lord, my enemy has been removed from the war,
And if that is your will, then I thank you.
But if I am responsible – if he was targeted
By Browning's men, and the name of the village
Suggests this, or else it is an amazing coincidence –
Then I am sad, for he is a noble man
And deserved a better end to his career.
Lord, be with him now, help him to recover,
Remove his pain, support his family.
And now, Lord, I put him out of mind for good.

(*Silence.*)

I feel it may have been better for the war
If Rommel were still in charge, but I don't know why.

(*He rises and slowly takes Rommel's picture off the caravan wall.*)

SCENE 3

(*July 1944. London, Bushey Park, SHAEF's HQ. BUTCHER on the phone.*)

Butcher.   Ike's lying down. His blood pressure's up,
He's had ringing in his ears, it's the mental strain
Of being frustrated at Monty's slowness.
He's been in bed all day.

(EISENHOWER *appears.*)

It's Tedder, sir.

Eisenhower   (*taking phone*). The British armoured units have withdrawn.
You say Monty stopped the armour going further?
How dare he.

Butcher   (*nervously*). Your blood pressure, sir, let me –

Eisenhower   (*waving him aside*). The British air commanders are disgusted.
You are now telling me "I told you so".
You say the British Chiefs of Staff would support
Any recommendation I make. The sack?
Huh huh. Let me make sure I've got that now.
I take over field command, Alexander
Replaces Monty in charge of Twenty-first,
Chief Big Wind, you say, will be made a peer,
And you take Leigh-Mallory's place and command
The air forces. I'll have to think about that.
I'll call you.

(*Rastenburg, Hitler's HQ or Wolfsschanze, the "Wolf's Lair". Keitel's sitting-room.* VON STAUF-
FENBERG *with a briefcase.*)

Stauffenberg   (*alone*). Now is the moment of my destiny.
For nine months I have plotted to restore
Germany's greatness from a tarnished regime.
Ever since I became Olbricht's Chief of Staff,
And Olbricht promoted me to be Chief of Staff
To Fromm so I could activate his Reserve Army
And impose martial law when the *Führer* dies.
All my life has led up to this moment,
To kill the man who has shamed Germany
And operate *Valkyrie*; and I have been
The leader of the plotters – politicians, Generals.
Though I am crippled and have no right hand
And only three fingers on my left hand, yet still
I can carry a briefcase and prime a bomb.
Twice I marched the troops of the Reserve Army
To take Berlin, and twice I aborted the plan,

The first time because Göring was not there,
The second time because Hitler left early.
Now I have the best opportunity of all
As Hitler wants me to attend a staff conference.
It should be in the underground concrete bunker
But has been transferred to a wooden hut.
I have a wife and children. If I fail
I will put them at risk, and many others.
But I must act, this tyranny cannot go on.
Hitler's atrocities shame all mankind.
By ending the war now I will save, what? –
Twenty or thirty million lives, bring peace
And freedom to our sacred Germany.

(STAUFFENBERG *moves to disclose* VON HAEFTEN, *sitting.*)

(*To Haeften.*) Two two-lb packages of explosive.

Haeften.   They're here.

(STAUFFENBERG *stoops and breaks the fuse capsule of one of the packages with pliers held in his three fingers. The door opens. Stauffenberg starts.*)

Orderly.   Keitel wants you to hurry up.

Stauffenberg.   Coming.

(MAJOR JOHN VON FREYEND, *Keitel's adjutant, appears.*)

Freyend.   Stauffenberg, do come along now.

Haeften.   You've only primed one of the packages.

Stauffenberg.   One will have to do. It should be enough.

(*Exit* STAUFFENBERG, *leaving* HAEFTEN *holding one of the packages.* STAUFFENBERG *reappears.*)

Stauffenberg.   Now I will put the briefcase close to Hitler.
I will lay the bomb under his conference table,

Then the *Wehrmacht* will have a *putsch*, and then
We will arrange to surrender to the Allies
And stop the senseless conduct of the war.

(*He enters the hut and puts the briefcase under a heavy oak table near*
HITLER. COL. BRANDT *moves it to the other side of the table's leg.*)

Haeften.   Colonel Stauffenberg, phone call from Berlin.

Stauffenberg.   Excuse me.

(*He goes out and waits with* GEN. ERICH FELLGIEBEL. *They watch. The*
hut explodes in smoke and flame. Two bodies fly out of the open windows.
One is Brandt's.)

                    No one could have survived that.
I will telephone Berlin to activate Valkyrie.
Then von Haeften and I will bluff our way
Out of the compound and drive to the airfield
Where our Heinkel is waiting.

(*They leave.* HITLER *staggers out, his trousers and hair on fire. He beats*
out the flames.)

(*A few minutes later.*)

Hitler.   I am invulnerable, immortal.
                    My survival is a great miracle.

Dr. Morell.   You have some badly torn skin on your legs
                    And a hundred splinters from the oak table. Your face
                    Has been cut by splinters, a timber has bruised
                    Your forehead. Your eardrums are perforated.

Hitler.   This was the work of cowards. If they had drawn a gun
                    On me I might respect them, but they didn't dare
                    Risk their own lives. I shall make an example of them
                    That will make anyone else think twice before betraying
                    The German people. My own life is not
                    Important, but anyone who lifts a hand
                    Against the German State during a war

Must be destroyed, must be executed.
Guards, search for hidden fuse cable and for
Additional bombs. Now I shall have lunch.
Call in the secretaries or I will be late. I meet
The *Duce* from his train at two-thirty.

Dr. Morell.   You can't possibly meet the *Duce* now.

Hitler.   I must. What would the world's press say if I didn't?

(*Berlin, Bendlerstrasse, 2nd floor.* COLONEL-GENERAL FROMM *in his office.*
STAUFFENBERG, OLBRICHT, HAEFTEN, QUIRNHEIM.)

Fromm   (*to guards*).   Take these four down
To the courtyard.

Stauffenberg.   Goodbye my loyal friends.
We will rise above their guns and hold ourselves
Erect, for our idea was right, to stand
Against atrocities. What we thought we
Will act, our self-control will show we still
Hold our beliefs, our self-mastery in
The face of wrong. We will call others to
Complete our task. Our Germany thanks you.

(STAUFFENBERG, OLBRICHT, HAEFTEN AND QUIRNHEIM *are marched
under guard and stood against a mound of sand. Dim light from a row of
army lorries with hooded headlights. The* FIRING-SQUAD *appears.*)

Fromm.   Execute them. They shame our Fatherland.

Stauffenberg   (*standing straight, shouting*). Long live our sacred Germany.

Haeften   (*shouting*).   Not him.

(HAEFTEN *dives in front of* STAUFFENBERG *and takes his bullets. The
crash of the firing-squad reverberates. Three fall. Stauffenberg is still
standing. Perplexed, the firing-squad reloads. The crash of the firing-squad
again. Stauffenberg falls back on the sand.*)

Soldier.   Did he shout "sacred" or "secret" Germany?

Fromm.   Send a teleprinter message to the *Führer:*
                "Attempted *putsch* by irresponsible Generals
                Bloodily crushed. All ringleaders shot."
                Take their bodies to the local churchyard.

(Martial music on radio, then Hitler's voice.)

Hitler.   I am speaking to you, first, so you may know
                I am unhurt and well, and second so that
                You may hear details of a crime unparalleled
                In German history. A conspiracy
                To eliminate me has been hatched by
                A tiny clique of ambitious, irresponsible,
                Stupid and criminal officers. I was spared
                A fate which holds no terror for me, but would
                Have had terrible consequences for
                The German people. I regard this as a sign
                That I should continue the task imposed
                Upon me by Providence. The criminals
                Will all be ruthlessly exterminated.

(Blay, Montgomery's HQ. The dining marquee. MONTGOMERY alone.)

Montgomery   *(aside).* Brooke has told me Churchill has an order
                In his pocket, dismissing me. All TAC HQ
                Know this rumour. I will meet fire with fire. Brooke
                Says Ike told him I am keeping him from France,
                Which made him furious. I will welcome him
                Although I regard his visit as meddlesome.
                He likes canaries, I will charm him with mine.
                A General must be confident to all.
                I will radiate optimism and boost his nerve.

                *(Enter HENDERSON and CHURCHILL wearing blue coat and cap. There is
                a frosty atmosphere. PAUL the chef is listening behind a tent-flap.)*

                (Aloud, shaking hands.) Prime Minister, I'm delighted and honoured
                To welcome you to near the Cerisy forest,
                And I'm greatly looking forward to briefing you.
                Have you seen my dogs and canaries, sir?

Churchill	(*sitting*). I have A canary that sits on my head. Henderson, Would you mind leaving us?
	(*Exit* HENDERSON *to the kitchen tent, with* PAUL. *They listen.*)
	Monty, SHAEF – Ike and Tedder – want you dismissed. We've had setbacks –
Montgomery.	Setbacks? What setbacks? The battle is going Excellently.
Churchill.	They say we're losing the war And you're panicking, they want Alexander To take over. And I'm Defence Minister And Prime Minister, and I've a right to be here, Monty.
Montgomery.	It's dangerous, sir.
Churchill.	Let me be the judge Of that.
Montgomery.	There's no panic here, come into The operations caravan and I'll show you a map. The Germans are doing exactly what we want. Tedder doesn't understand my plan, I don't want To take Caen but to keep pressing on it To bring the Germans to me, then Patton can Swing round.
	(MONTGOMERY *and* CHURCHILL *walk to the caravan.*)
Montgomery.	I am not fighting the Germans and the Italians Alone, but the Americans and British as well, The only people I'm not fighting are The Russians.
Churchill.	Monty, I know the feeling well.
Montgomery.	In four to five weeks you will have all France

In your pocket.

(*They enter the caravan.*)

(*Later. Enter* BRIGADIER BILL WILLIAMS, *Intelligence Officer. He knocks on the caravan door.* MONTGOMERY *opens.*)

Williams.   Sir, we have gleaned from scraps of *Ultra* there's
Been a sort of revolution in Berlin.

Montgomery.   How intriguing. Sir, do you know anything
About this?

(CHURCHILL *holds keys on a long chain and opens two red boxes.*)

Churchill.   There's something about it in here.
See what you can find.

(MONTGOMERY *and* WILLIAMS *rifle through the dispatch-boxes.*)

Williams.   These are *Ultra* signals. Sir, have you read this?

Churchill.   No.

Williams.   This could mean a sudden end to the war.

Montgomery.   There could be a surrender this morning.
The American *Cobra* attack may not be needed.
We've got the Germans on the run.

(*They emerge from the caravan,* CHURCHILL *beaming.*)

Churchill.   Monty,
I must be off.

(*Exit* WILLIAMS.)

Montgomery.   Whenever you get angry
In the future, sir, you're to send me a telegram
And find out the truth.

Churchill.   I promise I will.

Montgomery.   And this bottle of cognac is a peace offering.

                   (*They shake hands. Exit* CHURCHILL. *Enter* HENDERSON.)

                   He is volatile, he's up and down, and love
                   Can turn to rage, but that was very friendly.

Henderson.   You've bought yourself another month, I would say.

Montgomery.   Things will have improved by then.

(*Berlin, Prinz Albrechtstrasse,* Gestapo HQ. HIMMLER *visits the cellars with* ERNST
KALTENBRUNNER.)

Himmler.   Take me to a cell where I
                   Can see an interrogator at work.

Kaltenbrunner.   Hundreds of officers have been arrested,
                   Including General Fromm. We are getting names.
                   Generals include von Tresckow and Wagner
                   And Field Marshals Rommel and von Kluge.
                   Also von Stulpnagel. We suspect Canaris,
                   Moltke, Dohnanyi, and Bonhoeffer.
                   There will be thousands of names. This is how they talk.

                   (*He opens a door. There is a muffled shriek, a groan.*)

                   His legs are in metal tubes with sharp spikes,
                   That are screwed into his flesh. There are more spikes
                   In his fingertips. A helmet and blanket
                   Muffle the screams. He will talk, they all do.

Himmler   (*nodding and turning back*). The Army has been purged. Guderian,
                   The new Chief of Staff, has pledged its allegiance
                   To the *Führer*. The army salute will be
                   Abolished for the party raised arm. All
                   Chiefs of Staff will be party men, and teach
                   The tenets of Hitler. This will be announced.

(London. Churchill's underground HQ. Dinner. EISENHOWER, BEDELL SMITH, BROOKE, CHURCHILL.)

Churchill.   Over lunch yesterday, you expressed dissatisfaction
With Montgomery, and I have asked you to repeat
These criticisms in the presence of my Chief of Staff,
And now I would like to hear his reply.

Brooke.   The criticisms which the Supreme Commander
And his Chief of Staff have again expressed
To the Prime Minister are defeatist and
Do not accord with the picture I have received
From General Montgomery today. He is fighting hard
On the eastern flank to assist the Americans
On the western side. I am quite certain that
Montgomery's strategy is about to pay off,
And anyone who doubts that knows nothing about strategy.
If the Supreme Commander has any criticisms
Of the way his Land Forces Commander-in-Chief
Is directing the battle, he should return
To Normandy and put them to his face
And not complain to others behind his back.

Eisenhower.   I am shy of doing that in a sensitive matter.
I want to maintain the best relations between
The British and Americans and win the war.

Churchill.   We cannot make a public statement about
Our strategy in making the Germans believe
The British are trying to break out when they're not,
As this would be read by the enemy. Silence is best.

(Two days later. Bradley's HQ in France. MONTGOMERY *and* HENDERSON.)

Henderson.   Ike's with Kay, his Irish driver.

Montgomery   *(scathingly).*   You mean,
His floozie.

Henderson.   It's her first time in Normandy.

(*Enter* EISENHOWER, KAY SUMMERSBY *and* BRADLEY. MONTGOMERY *ignores Kay, who talks aside with Bradley.*)

Eisenhower.	Did you get my signal, that I am delighted That your basic plan has begun to unfold Brilliantly with Brad's success?
Montgomery	(*nodding*). Yes, I did.
Eisenhower	(*elated*). I've told the American censor, General Surles, That I am responsible for strategy And major activity in Normandy And that any criticism of you Is criticism of me.

(EISENHOWER *and* BRADLEY *turn away.*)

Montgomery	(*to Henderson*). O-o-oh, did you hear that? Now he smells triumph, he's taking the credit.
Henderson.	It's time to meet Bradley, sir.

(*Eight conspirators before Freisler's People's Court:*VON WITZLEBEN, HOEPNER, STIEFF, VON HASE, BERNARDIS, KLAUSING, HAGEN *and* VON WARTENBURG, *all army men, ranks ranging from Field Marshal to Lieutenant.* FREISLER *is in a blood-red robe. Swastika flags.*)

Freisler	(*shouting*). Witzleben, you were a Field Marshal, why Are you fiddling with your trousers? You dirty old man.
Witzleben.	My belt has been taken away.
Freisler.	Can't you speak?
Witzleben.	My teeth have also been taken away.
Freisler.	Wartenburg, you wanted to tell the Court something?
Wartenburg.	Of my contempt for National Socialism. Man has a moral and religious duty To oppose any regime which lacks respect For the sacredness of human life.

Freisler.   Enough.

(*He has signalled to the cameras behind a swastika to stop filming.*)

I won't have any more of these irrelevant
Speeches.

(*He signals to the cameras to resume.*)

You say you are guilty. The Court
Accepts your confession. We have now heard
The evidence. This is the last day of this trial.
The Court finds all the defendants guilty.
It denies them the honour of beheading
And sentences them to death by hanging.
Sentences to be carried out at Plotzensee
This afternoon, film to be sent to the *Führer*.

SCENE 4

(*August 1944. Fougères. Bradley's HQ.* EISENHOWER *and* BRADLEY; HANSEN, *Bradley's aide.*)

Hansen   (*to Eisenhower*). Sir, a communication from General Marshall.

(EISENHOWER *takes it and reads.*)

Eisenhower.   Hey, Brad, listen to this: "The Secretary",
That's Stimson, "and I and apparently all Americans
Are strongly of the opinion that the time has come
For you to assume direct exercise of command
Of the American Contingent." He says that
"The astonishing success of the campaign"
Has evoked "emphatic expressions of confidence
In you and Bradley". He doesn't say the same
About Monty. I'm taken aback.

Bradley.   Me too.

(*Rastenburg. Hitler's HQ.* HITLER *and* BORMANN.)

Bormann.

My *Führer*, Kluge is dead. Army doctors
Say it was a cerebral haemorrhage.
He was still shocked by the failure of his
Counter-attack on Avranches, and then Falaise.

Hitler.

It is scandalous that the Canadians have
Taken Falaise. This was largely Kluge's fault.
He was defeatist and pessimistic.
But could he not have committed suicide?
He was linked to the putsch, along with Speidel.
I want a second army autopsy.
Model is to be congratulated on
Saving the German forces from encirclement.
He does not know the meaning of surrender.

(*Tournières. Eisenhower's HQ.* EISENHOWER *and* BUTCHER.)

Eisenhower.

Marshall wants me to command, and I have here
A letter from Monty to Brooke, which arrived after
Brooke left for Italy, saying the two
Army Groups should keep together. However Brad
Favours an eastward drive to Germany,
Not north via the Lowlands, and the Red Army
Yesterday launched its offensive to Romania.
The balance of Allied troops has changed.
On D-Day America had fewer troops than Britain.
Now America has twice as many,
No three-quarters of all forces. It is
Impossible not to change the command structure.
I have now decided to change the system of command
On September the first. I will take command
Of the two Army Groups, and Bradley's Twelve Group
Will drive for Metz and Saar. The British can
Go north to destroy V-bomb rocket sites
While the Americans go into Germany.
The Army Groups will separate. Send a cable
To the Combined Chiefs of Staff, and a directive
To Monty.

(The same evening. Condé, Montgomery's new TAC HQ. MONTGOMERY and DE GUINGAND.)

Montgomery   *(devastated)*. Tomorrow the battle of Normandy will be won.
I do not agree with the decisions reached.
I am sending you back to General Eisenhower
With some *Notes on Future Operations.*
You are to tell General Eisenhower that
These *Notes* represent my views and that Bradley
Has expressed his agreement with them.
Ask the Supreme Commander to lunch with me
The day after tomorrow. He should come and see me.
(Aside.) Eisenhower will read in the *Notes* that I want him
To abdicate command over both Army Groups.

     (Exit DE GUINGAND. Enter HENDERSON.)

Henderson   *(gently)*. I said you'd bought a month.

Montgomery.   But when I' ve just won.
Eisenhower wants to scoop the reward.
I thought he was too decent to do this.
I was wrong. This, in the hour of my greatest triumph.
It is dangerous to swap horses in mid-stream.
And when the Germans are on the run, and the war....
(Aside.) O Brooke, would that you were in the War Office
And not on a long visit to Alexander.

(Days later. Laval, Bradley's new HQ. MONTGOMERY and BRADLEY.)

Montgomery.   On August the seventeenth you agreed with me
That both Armies should go north.

Bradley   *(dropping the "sir")*.   No, I did not.
I see that the British should go north because
Of the V-I sites, but I have always wanted
To go east to Germany.

Montgomery   *(thinly)*.   You have been got at.
Yesterday, when you went to visit Ike.

Bradley.	No. The American army has put behind it
	The poor performance at Kasserine Pass,
	Salerno and Anzio, and has a new confidence.
	We're pouring fifty divisions into Europe
	While fighting in the Pacific, we've come of age.
	We have double the troops, we want to go east
	To Germany. We can do it on our own.

Montgomery	(*sadly*). I trained you, and now you want to race off
	Like Patton. It's a mistake to split the Armies.
	It will not shorten the war but prolong it.

| Bradley. | We don't see it that way. And as regards training, |
| | I'm "the military Lincoln" in the press back home. Good day. |

(*Later the same day. Condé, Montgomery's HQ. As* MONTGOMERY *returns,* EISENHOWER *arrives with* BEDELL SMITH *and* GENERAL GALE.)

Montgomery	(*to Eisenhower*). I must see you alone and get your decision
	On certain points of principle. The staff
	Should not be present.

(EISENHOWER *and* MONTGOMERY *go alone into the map caravan.
Montgomery stands before the map, feet apart, hands behind his back,
eyes darting.*)

You know I want a northward
Thrust of both Armies, who would be so strong
They need fear nothing. The immediate need
Is for a firm plan. I think it's a mistake
To split the Armies, and for you to take command
In the field. The Supreme Commander should be on high,
On a perch with a detached view of land, sea, air,
Civil control, political problems. He should
Not descend into the intricacies of
The land battle, someone else should do that.
And it is a whole time job for one man.
Today the Falaise trap is closed, we are now
Bombing the Germans caught inside. We have won
A great victory because of land control,
Not in spite of it. If American public opinion

| | Is the problem, let Bradley control the battle, |
| | Put me under Bradley. |

Eisenhower.   No, that's not my intention.
I don't favour a single thrust to the Ruhr.
The Germans are in confusion, I want two thrusts
With the flexibility to reinforce either,
Depending on which is succeeding the most.

Montgomery. I don't think either will be strong enough, alone.
The British, alone, need additional forces
For the northern thrust to the V-I sites.

Eisenhower (*deliberately*). They can have American assistance, but
It should be kept to a minimum.

Montgomery.   Who should command
The northern thrust?

Eisenhower.   There must be one commander. You.

Montgomery. Twenty-first Army Group only has fourteen divisions.

Eisenhower. How many American divisions would you need
For your thrust to the north?

Montgomery.   An American Army
Of at least twelve divisions on our right flank.

Eisenhower (*speechless*). If that happened the Americans would only have
One Army, and public opinion would object.

Montgomery. Why should public opinion make you want to take
Military decisions which are definitely unsound?

Eisenhower. You must understand, it's election year in the States.
I can take no action which may sway public
Opinion against the President, and lose
Him the election. And so we must now separate
The two Army Groups, I must take command
Of the ground forces and send the two Army

Groups in different directions so there is
No question of the Americans being under
The operational control of a British General.

Montgomery.   Military logic does not base itself
On public opinion.

Eisenhower.   The American Army Group
Will become two armies, so we have three
In all: an Army Group of the North, of the Centre
And of the South. And I will be Generalissimo
In the field. Bedell Smith and I will draft
A directive I will show you before it goes out.

(EISENHOWER *leaves the caravan.*)

Montgomery   (*alone*). This is the reality of war. Meetings,
Signals, modifications of the plan,
Developments, bickerings, and the Generals
Are all isolated from the main action.
They are like instruments in an orchestra.
Each has its own position, plays its own note,
But together they sound a great symphony
Like the *1812* with cannon and mortar fire
That ends in triumph to cheers and applause.
But each remains quite separate, alone,
And only the score – the plan – holds them together;
And if that is changed, there is cacophany.

(A *week later. Avernes, Montgomery's new TAC HQ. MONTGOMERY and* BROOKE.)

Brooke.   It's a pity this all happened while I was away.
It will add three to six months to the war.
But you can look back on a staggering victory,
Perhaps the most outstanding military victory
In the whole of human history, and all through your plan.
Our political chief, Grigg, thinks the same.

Montgomery   (*tiredly*). We killed ten thousand Germans in the Falaise pocket
And took fifty thousand prisoners. You
Could walk for hundreds of yards stepping on dead flesh.

The stench was awful, and many horses died.
The men who got out were stragglers without vehicles
Or equipment. It was a terrific blow.
Paris has fallen – I declined Eisenhower's
Invitation to go there – and Dieppe will soon fall.
Overlord has reached a successful end.
But what now? I go north with six or eight
American divisions under Hodges,
In all less than half what I have had. Patton
Says it's a mistake for Hodges to turn north,
That he could end the war in a few days
By driving eastwards. I am now out of
Telephone communication with Bradley.
And the Germans are not finished by any means.
I have isolated myself to perfect the art
Of field command from the front, keeping TAC HQ
Separate from Main, and I see with military
Eyes, not political or national antennae.

Brooke.   We are seeing the rise as a great power
Of the United States, to whom events now pass.
I fear we shall see the decline of the British Empire.

Montgomery   (*depressed*). War happens when nations' interests conflict.
Either through misunderstanding or aggressive greed,
Which must be checked; and Tightness is settled
By a challenge of strength as in a tournament
Two knights jousted with lances while kings watched
And territory was ceded by the fallen
Giant in armour. So jousted Rommel and I.
Such a contest is primitive, and unless
Providence is with the winner, not always just.
Councils and conferences are better, but
Words must be enforced. If national interests are
Behind war, it is better that there should be
Large regional blocks or a world government.
And I dream of a world in harmony,
In which my battlefield skills are not required,
In which men and women go about their lives
Without seeing their homes and families knocked to bits
By tanks and heavy bombers and artillery.

I deploy fire-power, but the great need is
For a new system of international law
And universal harmony under
A benevolent, benign authority,
And a single, decent, humane, good World Lord
Who represents all regions of the world.
Then greed and territorial dispute
And racial or historical aspiration
Can be sorted out without recourse to all this
Planned carnage, chaos and destruction
Which when I stop and think fills me with disgust.
Brooke.It doesn't do to stop and think like that.

Montgomery. Right now, I can see into the depth of things
And I am filled with horror and despair.
I know that all the wars and leaders' plans
And all the territorial gains they made
Are not worth one sentence of a philosopher
Who has seen truth and reflects the hidden One,
Or one memorable line of an epic poet
That reveals how the universe really is,
And all my skill in battles is as worthless
As tantrum fisticuffs in a school playground.
Brooke.You need a good night's sleep. You'll look on things
Differently in the morning when you're less tired.

(*London. Churchill's underground HQ.* CHURCHILL *in bed in blue and yellow dressing-gown.*
BROOKE.)

Churchill. I've got a temperature of a hundred and three.
Pneumonia. Did you see Monty?

Brooke.   I did.
He's bearing up, but pretty devastated.

Churchill. I want to make him a Field Marshal on
September the first, to mark the approval
Of the British people for his leadership.

(*Next day. Same scene.* CHURCHILL *in bed and* GEORGE VI.)

Churchill.	I have the submission ready, sir. Could you Sign it now, using my pillow as a table.
	(*The* KING *signs.*) It is the highest rank in the British Army. It puts him on a par with Wellington, Haig, Kitchener – and Brooke. He is paying The penalty for being unable to Communicate with his superiors.

(*Dangu, Montgomery's new HQ.* MONTGOMERY *sitting alone on a canvas chair, being painted by* JAMES GUNN. *They are observed by* HENDERSON.)

Henderson.	He looks like a medieval English king Surveying his lands at Crécy or Agincourt.
	(*The session is over.* MONTGOMERY *rises and goes into his caravan.*)
Montgomery.	Demoted. Elevated to Field Marshal But demoted as Commander, from Land Forces To Twenty-first Army Group. And by a man Who had not seen a shot fired in his life Before Overlord, does not understand strategy, Has failed to impose a clear strategic plan On the battlefield, squandering all our gains, And is therefore useless as a field commander. He's completely and utterly useless. Demoted after the greatest invasion ever And a three-month battle resulted in victory, And me, across the Seine, heading for Brussels. Where is the justice in that? What is the meaning? (*Praying.*) O Lord, I asked for your help for Overlord. You gave it, and we were victorious, But the task is only half-done, and now the command Is in the hands of a man who will lengthen the war. Is this what you want? Is this part of your purpose? If it is, I am content, though I cannot see The benefit to the Allies, the troops, or The German people of prolonging the war. Is it time for America's Grand Design? Is it time for the British to hand over

Their imperial rule and their world role?
O Lord of Light, I accept my demotion
If it is a part of your greater plan.
We warlords tussle for power but over all,
Our Overlord, is your Providential Light
Which knows the whole tapestry of history,
The past, the future, why events happen,
When one power rises and another declines,
Why one General rises and another is demoted.
What is baffling in nineteen forty-four
May be clear fifty years later, part of a pattern.
Shine into my soul, for I do not understand.

SCENE 5

(*September 1944. Granville, Eisenhower's Forward HQ. Meeting with* BEDELL SMITH,
FREDDY MORGAN, HUMPHREY GALE, STRONG, JOCK WHITELEY. BEDELL SMITH *is talking as he is handed a telegram.*)

Bedell Smith.   The German army is retreating along the coast.
    Antwerp has fallen, but not the approaches
    To Antwerp harbour from the North Sea. Should you
    Give the order for these to be taken?
    (*Reading telegram.*) Telegram from Montgomery. He says
    One thrust to Berlin can now end the war,
    And it should go through the Ruhr rather than Saar
    As the American plan states. I'll pass it round.
    He wants to meet you, sir. He wants a decision
    By tomorrow.

Eisenhower   (*sighing in exasperation*). He hasn't spoken to me
    For nearly three weeks, and now he wants a decision
    By yesterday. No, I've got too much on:
    My broadcast to the peoples of North West Europe,
    Linking the Italian campaign with *Overlord*,
    A conference with General Devers on control
    Of the Franco-American forces. And there's Greece.
    He's four hundred miles away, and my knee....
    What should we do?

Strong.   Speaking for Intelligence,
I vote for one strong thrust through Belgium to
The Rhine.
(EISENHOWER *looks at* STRONG.)

Eisenhower.   Can we go outside?

(*They go out,* EISENHOWER *limping, in pain.*)

                          Read this telegram.
It's from Stimson, our Secretary of State for War,
Urging me to take control. What can I do
In the face of this? I have to take account
Of the political ramifications. If I put
Monty in charge of the British and Americans,
Stimson will be angry, besides Brad and Patton.
There must be two thrusts, for political
If not military reasons.

(*They return to the meeting.*)

(*To Bedell Smith.*) Draft a written reply
To Montgomery. Say I like his idea
Of a powerful and full-bloodied thrust towards
Berlin, but that I do not agree it should be
Initiated at this time to the exclusion
Of all other manoeuvres. There can be
No question of a thrust to Berlin until
Le Havre and Antwerp harbours are operating.
The Allies will advance to both the Ruhr
And the Saar. I believe Montgomery's thrust
To the Ruhr will be via Aachen, and this can be tied
To Patton's thrust via Metz.

Strong.   Sir, shouldn't you
Meet Montgomery?

Eisenhower.   And be insulted by
The new Field Marshal? No, the telegram will do.

(*Rastenburg. Hitler's HQ.* HITLER *is in bed with jaundice. Hitler and* GOEBBELS.)

Hitler.	Why have my Generals withdrawn from France
	In defiance of my orders that they fight on?
	My telegram to the German HQ in Paris
	Said: "Paris must only fall into the hands
	Of the enemy as a field of rubble."
	Although the Eiffel Tower, the Elysée Palace
	And forty-five bridges were wired with charges
	That would cause a firestorm and burn the city down,
	Choltitz did not act, and the Allies are in Paris
	And all its cultural treasures are intact.
	I do not trust the officer corps. They withdraw.
	I want more party men who will observe
	My orders to the letter.

Goebbels.	My *Führer* you are
	A thousand miles away from the action,
	And cannot appreciate that the German force
	Is short of fuel and ammunition.
	The British and Canadians under Montgomery
	Have covered two hundred miles in four days
	And are in Belgium, have taken Brussels
	And Antwerp. Hodges has moved as far
	And is in South-East Belgium, and has Liège.
	Patton has reached the Moselle and has linked
	With the French American Army from the Riviera.
	We need to prepare the defence of the Fatherland.
	The Siegfried Line is largely unmanned,
	The West Wall, and many guns have been stripped.
	The British and Americans are four hundred miles
	From Berlin. The Russians a mere three hundred.
	In three months since D-Day we have lost
	A million and a quarter men, dead, wounded,
	Missing – fifty divisions in the east,
	Twenty-eight in the west. We have no guns,
	Tanks, lorries, our allies have deserted us.
	Germany now stands alone. The Allies have
	Two million men in Europe, the Soviets have
	Five hundred and fifty-five divisions.
	We need a defensive plan. I will raise
	A new army of a million men, and all
	German industry will produce the arms

	And equipment we need to repulse our enemies.
Hitler.	No withdrawal. We must keep on fighting
	Until, as Frederick the Great said, one
	Of our enemies tires and gives up.

Goebbels	(*aside*). Hitler's very name is terror, he is seen
	As a wolf who has gobbled up the countries round him,
	But somehow he's acting that part, calling
	His headquarters "the Wolf's Lair", for the man within
	Is really quite gentle, awkward, hesitant
	Even, and watching him fumble his way
	To his decisions I marvel that so uncertain
	A man should have thousands of helmets, planes,
	Tanks, ships hanging on his slightest word.
	Of course he is not now, since Stauffenberg's bomb,
	As he was before, when his hand did not tremble
	And he rode, standing in his car, his right arm out,
	Through hundreds of thousands of soldiers in miles of ranks
	On both sides of Berlin's East-West Boulevard,
	On his fiftieth birthday, in the most awesome
	Display of power mankind has ever seen,
	But even then in his quieter moments he
	Was not the tyrant the world dreads. But he
	Is able to open to a current of energy,
	Which fills him and radiates conviction, faith.
	It is not a good energy, it cannot be
	Seeing where it has led him and his people.
	He thinks it's a demonic energy,
	An evil power that has come from Lucifer.
	But he's not possessed by this for much of the time.
	When he is possessed by it, even I fear him.
	But the more vulnerable he becomes, the more
	I know I must follow him to the end.

(*Granville, Eisenhower's HQ. EISENHOWER alone.*)

Eisenhower.	Stalin has personal rivalries to endure.
	Zhukov and Koniev hate each other, I have heard
	And Rokossovsky is not easy. How is it
	That when he sets them to compete, they do,

Whereas when I do the same, Monty, Patton
And Bradley demand priority over each other?
Monty is the worst. He thinks he is a better
Commander in the field and planner than me.
His overweening egotism and self-esteem,
His vanity and brashness and arrogance
Make him insubordinate. He writes,
"One really powerful and full-blooded thrust
Towards Berlin is likely to get there and thus
End the German war." He demands all the
Funds and transport, and says Bradley
Can do the best he can with what is left.
I know I try to keep everyone happy
And to tend to compromise, but I bristle
When he weighs the Ruhr and Saar and writes, "If we
Attempt a compromise solution and split
Our maintenance resources so that neither
Thrust is full-blooded we will prolong the war.
I shall reply that a thrust to Berlin
Should not be initiated at this moment
To the exclusion of all other manoeuvres.
There will have to be a compromise: a broad front,
Resources split between Monty and Bradley.
We must take the ports of Antwerp and Le Havre
Before we go to Berlin. All SHAEF agrees.

(*Everberg, Montgomery's HQ. MONTGOMERY and DAWNAY.*)

Montgomery	(*angrily*). I have received Ike's reply in two parts,
	The second part two days *before* the first part.
	Now, four days after my message, signal:
	"Providing we can have the ports of Dieppe,
	Boulogne, Dunkirk and Calais, and in addition
	Three thousand tons per day through Le Havre
	We can advance to Berlin." Tell Ike I
	Must see him in Brussels tomorrow, please
	After my 9 a.m. conference with Dempsey.

(*Next day. Brussels airport. Eisenhower's aeroplane. EISENHOWER, TEDDER, MONTGOMERY in the cabin with others.*)

Eisenhower.   I hurt my knee last week when we landed
               On a beach in a high wind, and we had to push
               The plane away from the sea. I can't move. It's
               Been as much as I can do to fly to Brussels.

Montgomery.   I want everyone to leave the cabin including
               Tedder.

               (EISENHOWER *gestures, all leave.* TEDDER *is still in the plane but out of earshot.*)

                    Ike, I have your signal here. It
               Arrived in two parts, the second part first.
               The first part two days later, so I didn't get
               The drift till yesterday. How can we run
               A war if we can't communicate where we're
               Going? I had no orders from you for a fortnight.
               There's no communication apart from telegrams
               Written four hundred miles away from the front line.
               There's no plan, we in the field don't know what we're
               Doing, we're making it up as we go along.
               It seems that Patton, not you, is running the war.
               The double thrust will end in certain failure.
               You've dispersed the Allied war effort, there's no
               Field command or grip –

               (EISENHOWER *puts his hand on* MONTGOMERY's *knee.*)

Eisenhower.   Steady Monty. You can't
               Talk to me like that. I'm your boss.

Montgomery   (*humbly*).   I'm sorry, Ike.
               A new weapon hit London yesterday,
               The V-2 rocket, which is silent and
               Arrives without warning. It came from Holland.
               We need to go through Holland to capture the sites.
               The British Government wants me to find and destroy
               The V-2 sites near Rotterdam and Utrecht
               And that means I need to get to Arnhem.
               If I can do that I must have priority
               Of supplies over Patton and command in the north

Over American supplies and troops. I think you're wrong,
But I'm not insisting on a thrust to Berlin.
Arnhem is the gateway to the Ruhr as well
As to the V-2s, and after that Berlin.
But I need fuel and tanks. Give me these now
And I can get there.

Eisenhower.   Monty, you must understand
There are certain things that I cannot change.
The Allied armies must be kept separate;
You cannot command American troops in the north;
Your Ruhr thrust cannot have priority
Over Patton's Saar thrust as regards supplies.
I am now running the war, and that's my view.
And as I said in my signal, we cannot start
A thrust to Berlin now. But we can look
At your bold plan for a bridgehead over the Rhine
At Arnhem, which I wholeheartedly support.
If you can achieve that, you can cut off the Ruhr
And advance into northern Germany.
There can be a combined Anglo-American
Airborne drop. I'll wire you. Now if you'll call
Tedder, my knee is hurting.

Montgomery   (*aside*).   This man is no
Commander. He's a genial fellow,
He talks to everyone and is popular
And then works out a compromise all like
That pleases everyone. He has no plan.
He finds out what his subordinates think,
Collects their ideas and then reconciles them.
He visibly flinches from bold moves, he is
Timid and fearful in the teeth of pain, like a boy
Who winces at the whine of a dentist's drill.
He holds conferences in order to liaise,
I to give orders.

(*Next day. Granville, Eisenhower's HQ. EISENHOWER and BEDELL SMITH. KAY
SUMMERSBY, going.*)

Bedell Smith.   There are now three armies, and the Germans,

808

Fighting on three fronts, are far from beaten.
The way to the Saar is blocked by good divisions.
I can see a drop to seize Walcheren would
Control the approach to Antwerp the Navy want,
And help open the port. Montgomery's
Arnhem thrust would secure a Rhine bridgehead
And be most useful to our present cause.

Eisenhower   (*aside*). I am torn this way and that. It is not easy
To be a Supreme and a Land Commander.

(SMITH *receives a paper.*)

Bedell Smith.   A signal from Montgomery. He has postponed
The Allied airborne drop across the Rhine
For twelve days, because he lacks supplies.

(EISENHOWER *buries his head in his hands.*)

Eisenhower.   Do I accept it? Or do I keep the drop?

Bedell Smith.   It will be useful.

Eisenhower.   Go and see Monty,
And give him all he needs. We will stop the thrust
To Saar in view of the German opposition.
Give priority to the Ruhr and the Arnhem drop:
Operation Market Garden on the seventeenth.
(*Aside.*) I am giving Montgomery what he has urged.
I hope I am not making a strategic blunder.
If Arnhem fails, I should have said No.

(*Rundstedt's HQ. RUNDSTEDT and his Chief of Staff, GENERAL GUNTHER BLUMENTRITT.*)

Blumentritt.   Why have the Allies not gone for Berlin?
There were no German forces behind the Rhine
At the end of August, the front was wide open.
Berlin was the Allies' target, Germany's strength
Is in the north. Berlin and Prague were there
For the taking. Why did the Allies not take them?

(Eindhoven, Montgomery's HQ. MONTGOMERY, depressed and deep in thought. WILLIAMS.)

Williams.

You were very close to victory at Arnhem.
The largest airborne landing in history,
And the road for our troops was wide open.
There's an *Ultra* message from the German
Commander-in-Chief on the twenty-fourth, asking
Hitler for permission to withdraw all forces
In Holland to the Meuse (or Maas) and Waal.
Hitler refused and ordered von Rundstedt
To counter-attack. It's been suggested
Market Garden was betrayed by Bernhard,
That ex-SS man who took refuge in London.
He knew the plan.

Montgomery

(philosophically). The target was not Arnhem,
But the Ruhr. Urquhart was to threaten to seize Arnhem
While O'Connor's 8 Corps turned eastwards towards
The Ruhr. We have advanced our Ruhr campaign.
Here we are now in Eindhoven, we have
A bridgehead across the Waal at Nijmegen,
Enough life was lost across the Neder Rijn.
We did the best we could, given the lack
Of American support, which made it
A British effort; given that Eisenhower
Reinstated the Saar's equal priority.
There are many ifs – those two German armoured
Divisions, the rain – but we must put a brave face
On Arnhem, and consider what we gained.

(Enter GENERAL URQUHART, exhausted and downcast, with HENDERSON.)

(Gently.) My good fellow.

Urquhart.

                    I'm sorry. I failed.

Montgomery.

                              You're
Worn out, you've had no sleep, you're exhausted,
You'll spend tonight in my caravan. I only move out
For Winston Churchill and the King, but tonight it's yours.

Tomorrow I'll ask you what went wrong at Arnhem,
But tonight, you sleep in there. Where's my batman?
(*Exit* MONTGOMERY, *looking for his batman.*)

Urquhart   (*to Henderson*). I'm overwhelmed. Such a gentle reception.

Henderson.   He calls "A" Mess here his family, and he's like
                  A caring father concerned for his children.

(*Rastenburg, Hitler's HQ.* HITLER *and* BORMANN.)

Bormann.   My *Führer*, I have a report on Rommel.
                  You recall, Speidel testified on October the fourth
                  He knew of the plot against you from Hofacker
                  And passed the information on to Rommel.
                  You arranged for Keitel to summon him here.
                  Rommel pleaded his head injury. He
                  Has recovered from the crash, the *Gestapo* report
                  He goes for walks "leaning on his son", and I have
                  Reports from local party officials who say
                  He is still making mutinous remarks.
                  He should be told to see you if he's innocent,
                  Or behave like a Prussian officer
                  And gentleman, or face the People's Court.

Hitler.   Send Burgdorf and his chief law officer
                  To Rommel's villa with such a request.

(*Bradley's HQ.* EISENHOWER, MONTGOMERY, BROOKE, RAMSAY, BRADLEY, PATTON,
DEMPSEY, CRERAR, HODGES. *A conference for all commanders.*)

Ramsay.   We are an Allied force, as for *Overlord*,
                  I don't defend operations on national grounds.
                  Arnhem was a British undertaking. Perhaps
                  There could have been more American support,
                  But the plan was Field Marshal Montgomery's
                  And any criticism he should accept.
                  I am concerned that he didn't choose to secure
                  The approaches and port of Antwerp, rather than
                  Undertake this risky drop behind enemy lines.

Montgomery	(*thinly*). There were no orders from the Supreme Commander
	To take the approaches and port of Antwerp.
	What does the CIGS think?

Brooke.   I have to say
I feel that for once Field Marshal Montgomery's
Strategy was at fault. Instead of advancing
On Arnhem, he should have made certain of Antwerp.
I have been a supporter of the Field Marshal,
Who won a brilliant victory in Normandy,
But on Arnhem I have to agree with
Admiral Ramsay. The port of Antwerp first.

Eisenhower.   To conclude, we have had a reverse at Arnhem.
For this the blame is entirely mine as I
Approved Field Marshal Montgomery's plea
To operate an airborne drop at Arnhem.
Any blame belongs to me alone and is
My responsibility, and no one else's.
Now we need to get on with the war, and our thrusts
Into the Ruhr and the Saar against an enemy
That is not as defeated as we thought a month ago.

(*The conference breaks up into talking groups. BROOKE and RAMSAY
stand together. MONTGOMERY stands alone, isolated.*)

Ramsay.   That was spoken like a military statesman.

Brooke.   Whatever his shortcomings as a battlefield
Commander, he has great personal stature.

Ramsay.   He has a nobility that I admire.
And Montgomery has now been marginalised.
Brooke (*sadly*). He has been the victim of an American *coup*,
But he has also contributed to his undoing
And has to some extent marginalised himself.
After Arnhem, and with only a quarter of
The Allied troops, Britain has a junior role.

(*Next day. Eindhoven, Montgomery's TAC HQ. MONTGOMERY alone.*)

Montgomery.	I am in gloom. I know I could have ended The war in three weeks from my Normandy victory, Which left me invincible in the German mind If not in SHAEF's. And now, in this vacuum, Without my single thrust I have been defeated By the Germans at Arnhem, and the Americans. I will open the port of Antwerp, but I am full of scorn at the useless Eisenhower And Bradley, who want to show the world the power Of American might, and blunder in their decisions, Dispersing the Allied effort on too wide a front. And I am powerless to alter the course Of the shambles they have created, and so the war Will last through winter till next spring. My men Visit mistresses in Brussels. I turn a blind Eye. Not much happens. It's cold and damp.

(*Enter* DAWNAY.)

Oh Kit.
I am sending you to England, to Phyllis Reynolds.
You will take my summer wear – vests, pants and shirts –
And bring me my winter clothes: thick vests and pants,
Woollen pyjamas and my dressing-gown.
You wouldn't have had to do this if I'd been in charge.

(*Rommel's villa near Ulm.* ROMMEL *in his study and voices.* LUCY.)

Lucy	(*nervously*). Two men to see you. They're from the *Führer*.

(*Exit.*)

(*Gen.* BURGDORF *and Gen.* ERNST MAISEL *appear.*)

Burgdorf.	Field Marshal. A letter from the *Führer*.

(ROMMEL *reads it.*)

Rommel.	Does Hitler know about the two statements. By Speidel and Hofacker?

Burgdorf.	Yes, he does.

If you don't go to Rastenburg to contest
The evidence of Speidel and Hofacker,
The choice is the People's Court and execution –
Maisel. Sequestration of your house –

Rommel.   Or?

Burgdorf.   Poison,
Not pistol, and a State funeral with full
Honours, your reputation still intact.
No one will know. You will have died of your injuries.
And there will be a guarantee of safety
For your family, which will be revoked
If you choose the other way, the People's Court.

Rommel.   It is "die now" and save my family
Or "die later" and put them both at risk.

(BURGDORF *nods.*)

I need time to think.

Burgdorf.   We'll wait in the garden.
We will leave in your staff car. You will say
Goodbye to all who wait downstairs, then go.

Rommel.   Send up my wife.

(*Exeunt* BURGDORF *and* MAISEL.)

                    The moment I have expected,
For three months has arrived. There is no choice.
Disgrace and poverty for my family,
Or this, oblivion, and my family keep
This house and all I have mustered for them.
I knew of the plot, was shocked and would not join,
But I wanted our surrender and an honourable peace.
Speidel's testimony has done for me.
He was trying to save himself. I am innocent,
But cannot disprove the evidence, and I
Will not stoop to plead or beg for mercy.

There is no choice. Just the furtherance of
A legend. Montgomery, you wanted my end
But you never dreamt it would be at Hitler's command.
I think you will be sorry. And I hope
That one day, there can be reconciliation.
Perhaps our sons will be friends.

(*Enter* LUCY. *He holds her.*)

My dearest Lucy,
You must be strong and look after Manfred.
I have to say goodbye.

(*He gives her the letter.*)

Lucy.   But it's not true,
What Speidel has said. You can deny it, and prove –

Rommel.   No, it will be execution, and you will lose
Everything and Manfred.

Lucy.   There's no other way?

Rommel.   The choice is clear. They are waiting for my cap,
My Field Marshal's cap and baton.

(*Enter* MANFRED.)

Manfred.   Papa.

(ROMMEL *hugs* MANFRED.)

Rommel.   You must be very strong. I have to say goodbye.

Manfred.   Those men?

Rommel   (*nodding*). I have to go with them. It is for the best.
My first thoughts are of you, and of the life you will have.
Remember me as an honourable officer
Who fought well but couldn't stand the casualties,
Who when he knew we had lost the war, sought peace,

And pulled the front line further and further back.
I love you both very much.

Manfred.   You're going
With those two men?

Rommel.   Yes. They are waiting for me.
I will be going in my staff car. But you
Will remember.

Manfred.   Yes, Papa.

Rommel.   I love you both.
Now, goodbye. Be strong.

(ROMMEL *embraces both.* LUCY *escorts* MANFRED *out. Rommel is briefly alone. He puts on his greatcoat and cap and picks up his baton.*)

Montgomery, a Prussian officer's salute.

(BURGDORF *and* MAISEL *return.*)

Rommel.   Where?

Burgdorf   (*holding a packet*). On the back seat of your staff car. You
Died from your injuries. There will be no pain.
Believe me, this is the best way. I am sick
At what has happened to our culture. (*Exeunt.*)

(*Eindhoven, Montgomery's HQ.* MONTGOMERY *and* GEN. MARSHALL, BRADLEY *and* HODGES.)

Bradley.   General Marshall, Chief of Staff of the US
Army.

Montgomery.   General, could you spare me a few moments
In my office caravan? Would you mind Generals?

(MARSHALL *looks at* BRADLEY *and* HODGES, *shrugs and follows* MONTGOMERY *into his caravan.*)

I feel you should know that since the Supreme Commander
Took personal command of the land battle
As well as forces on the sea and in the air,
The armies have become separated
Nationally, not geographically.
There is a lack of grip, of operational
Direction and control. Our operations
Have become ragged, disjointed, and we
Have now got ourselves into a real mess.

Marshall.   Field Marshal, I have listened.

Montgomery.   And?

Marshall.   There is
More than one view in such complex matters.

Montgomery.   I can see that you entirely disagree.

Marshall.   There has to be a balance of national effort.
General Eisenhower is the Supreme Commander.

(*Silence.*)

(*Days later.* MONTGOMERY *and* DAWNAY.)

Dawnay.   A reply from Eisenhower. He's threatening you
With dismissal.

(MONTGOMERY *reads the signal.*)

Montgomery.   On October the ninth
He urged me to take Antwerp or Allied
Operations would reach a standstill. I
Replied reminding him that at Versailles
He had made the attack in Holland the main effort.
He replied it was now Antwerp, and Beetle Smith
Rang and demanded when there would be action
And threatened through Morgan I would lose my supplies.
I wrote back blaming the failure at Arnhem
On lack of co-ordination between Bradley's troops

And mine, and I asked to be given sole control
Of the land battle. Now he threatens to go
To the CCS, and he will win. I have pushed
Him as far as I can and must now promise
A hundred per cent support, and give Antwerp
Top priority, when I can wind down Holland.

SCENE 6

(October 1944. Rastenburg. HITLER *and his Generals.* RUNDSTEDT, MODEL, GÖRING.*)*

Hitler.

While I was in bed with jaundice in September
And recovering from the bungling Stauffenberg's bomb,
I studied maps and have found the weak point
In the American front line. The Ardennes!
Where Manstein and I struck in May 1940.
The Americans have three weak divisions there,
If all goes well, my offensive can annihilate
Twenty or thirty divisions, and drive them back.
I shall amass twenty-eight divisions.
My Panzers will cross the Meuse and take Antwerp,
Drive a wedge between the British and Canadians,
And the Americans. It will be another Dunkirk.

(The GENERALS *protest.)*

Hitler.

No, I will have no objections. I have drawn up my plans
With Jodl, and I have given Rundstedt instructions
That they must not be altered. The British
Are worn out, the Americans will collapse. We can defeat
Them in the west and then turn our forces to the east
And attack the Red Army on the Vistula.

(The GENERALS *protest.)*

Generals.

But sir –

Hitler.

I will hear no more. I have two Panzer
Armies, six hundred thousand men. I shall wait

For bad weather when Allied planes cannot fly.

(*Maastricht. Conference of commanders.* BRADLEY *and others.* MONTGOMERY.)

Montgomery.   First Army is struggling forward, but there are no reserves.
Everybody is attacking everywhere,
With no reserves anywhere. I propose Patton's
Third Army should be moved north for the Ruhr
Offensive, and that Brad should be Commander-
In-Chief of Land Forces, as General Eisenhower
Is simply not doing the job. Or at the least,
That Brad should command all Allied forces north
Of the Ardennes, so that the Allies can fight
With one effort, under one unified command.

Bradley.   That is not a good idea. There should be separate
National armies, with me as Commander
Of the American forces, and they should fight
In separate places.

Montgomery.   Then how do we deal
With the Sixth SS Panzer Army, which is now
Strengthening German lines according to reports?

Bradley.   Those Panzers are to plug holes that will be made
When Hodges and Patton attack the Ruhr and Saar.
Patton's new drive will start December nineteen.

Montgomery.   So although the present plan has failed, we must
Consider it has not failed and stick with it?

(*Rastenburg, Hitler's HQ.* HITLER *has just woken up.* BURGDORF *has a report from Model.*)

Hitler.   What is the news from the Ardennes? The Allies?

Burgdorf.   Taken totally by surprise. An artillery
Bombardment rained down on the American line,
So fast it seemed it hailed mortars and shells.
Then came the tanks out of mist over forty miles.
The American First and Ninth Armies were
Driven back.

Hitler.   Providence be praised!

(*Verdun. Eisenhower's conference.* EISENHOWER, BRADLEY, PATTON. *Not Montgomery or Hodges.*)

Eisenhower.   I'm very worried about the German offensive.
                     I've reinforced Bastogne to hold the line.
                     I'm tempted to take field command myself
                     But am turning to George. Can you go to Luxembourg
                     And counter-attack with at least six divisions
                     In three days' time? You will have to turn your
                     Entire army from eastwards to northwards.

Patton.   Sure, I can do it. But three of the six
                     Divisions have been overrun.

Eisenhower.   Oh, yes.

Patton.   I've only three divisions.

Eisenhower.   So you will abandon the thrust to Saar.

Patton.   That's no problem.

Eisenhower   (*aside*).   He spoke so bitterly
                     Against Monty's single thrust in August,
                     Yet he is happy now to support it
                     Because he has a star role.
                     (*Aloud.*)   I will issue
                     A directive ordering Devers to
                     Cease his offensive in the south and relieve
                     Patton's Third Army so it can move north.
                     Once this German offensive has been blocked
                     Bradley's Twelfth Army will mount a single offensive
                     To the north.

Bradley   (*tensely*).   That is what Montgomery proposed
                     At Maastricht, and I opposed.

(*Same day. Zonhoven, Montgomery's HQ.* MONTGOMERY *on the telephone to* DEMPSEY.)

Montgomery.	There is no doubt about it, my Liaison Officer
	To Bradley, Tom Bigland, went to Hodges' HQ
	This morning, and found no one. Breakfast was laid,
	The Christmas tree decorated. A German woman
	Said they went down the road at 3 a.m. –
	Without telling anybody. I have heard nothing
	From General Eisenhower, the Commander-in-Chief
	In the field, from Versailles; and Bradley's
	Out of telephone communication in Luxembourg.
	So I have arranged for you to have four divisions
	From dawn, to stop the Germans from crossing the Meuse.
	My LOs report there are no Americans
	Garrisoning the Meuse bridges, so I have sent
	Tank patrols fifty miles into the American sectors
	Under cover of darkness. I shall tell Mather
	To find Hodges and "order" him to block
	The Meuse bridges with farm carts. We're ready for Rundstedt –
	Despite the confusion, lack of information
	And faulty command we have to operate in,
	I have told Whiteley at SHAEF, and Brooke, that I
	Should be in operational charge of the northern front.
	The question is: will someone now compel
	General Eisenhower to accept, three months too late
	What he should have accepted three months ago?

(*Next day. Versailles.* BEDELL SMITH *knocks on Eisenhower's door.* EISENHOWER *calls in Bedell Smith.* STRONG *and* WHITELEY *wait outside.*)

Bedell Smith	(*to Eisenhower*). I am concerned at the situation in the Ardennes.
	The Germans are on the Meuse with many divisions,
	Two thrusts may have linked up, and General Bradley
	Has lost contact with Hodges, who seems to have left
	His HQ. All the details are in this report.
	Montgomery is on the spot. Bearing
	In mind you can't go out because of the paratroops,
	I reluctantly recommend that he is given
	Command of the northern forces, two of Bradley's
	Three armies.

| Eisenhower | (*astonished*). I can't go along with that. |
| | The American press would never accept it. |

Bedell Smith.	The press doesn't know how serious the situation
	In the Ardennes is. And there's wartime censorship.
	And I remind you again, you and General Bradley
	Are targets for Skorzeny's assassins.
	If Montgomery takes over, they'll switch to him.
Eisenhower.	I'm shocked. I need to question General Strong
	And General Whiteley about the latest picture,
	And their intelligence and operational reports.

(*Same day. Zonhoven, Montgomery's HQ. MONTGOMERY. DAWNAY, Montgomery's military* ASSISTANT, *answers the phone.*)

Dawnay.	It's General Eisenhower.
Montgomery.	Hello? Yes. Yes.
	You're speaking very fast and it's difficult
	To understand what you're talking about. (*To Dawnay.*) I don't know
	What he's saying, he's very excited.
	(*To Eisenhower.*) It seems we now have two fronts? And I am
	To assume command of the northern front.
	That's all I want to know. (*Shouting.*) I can't hear you
	Properly. I shall take command straight away.

(*He puts down the phone.*)

	He's still talking wildly about other things.
	I want the largest Union Jack that will go
	On the car bonnet and eight motor-cycle outriders.
Dawnay	(*quietly*). Congratulations, sir. (*Exit.*)
Montgomery	(*aside*). Field Commanders
	Are least important to governments when they sense
	Victory, most when they start to smell defeat.
	I have control, albeit temporarily,
	Of Allied forces north of the Ardennes,
	Of Hodges' First Army and Simpson's Ninth
	North of Bastogne, and Coningham commands
	All supporting American air forces.
	While the Supreme Commander cowers in his Hotel

And Bradley vacates his bedroom, fearing attack
From Skorzeny's assassination squad,
I will show a commander has no fear,
I will boost the morale and self-confidence
Of the American commanders in the field.
Let them call me a showman. It will work.

(*Next day. Versailles, Eisenhower's HQ. EISENHOWER and* BEDELL SMITH.)

Eisenhower   This Montgomery crows like a rooster,
I have had to give him command, there's no one else
Up there. But the man is impossible.
I have just received this message: "In a press
Statement Monty is claiming his new command
As a personal vindication." He seems to forget
Who is fighting this war. Tell General Marshall
That either Monty or I will have to go.
We're going to win, we're going to push the Germans
Back where they came from.

(*Next day. Zonhoven, Montgomery's HQ. MONTGOMERY and* HODGES.)

Montgomery.   No, you must withdraw, don't think what Bradley will say.
Bradley and Patton think of counter-attack,
But there are now twice as many German troops
In the Ardennes as we landed on D-Day –
Three hundred and thirty-five thousand – and more
Than nine hundred tanks in the ice and snow,
And Bradley, in his Luxembourg Hotel,
And Eisenhower, locked and shuttered inside
His Versailles Palace, and swashbuckling Patton
Talk of counter-offensives, and do not know
The picture I have from my LOs. They wage
Their war by telephone, I mine by scouts
Who each day visit the entire front line
And bring back sightings of enemy movements.
Bradley underestimates German strength,
And so, therefore, in Versailles does Eisenhower,
And optimistically thinks that Patton
Is about to finish the Germans off completely.
Bradley draws lines on maps with a brown crayon

Which indicate advances to be made
But does not know where the men are who will make them.
Let him call me over-cautious, but I honour
The fighting man, and I say "Hodges' troops" are
Tired, have been under strain and should now withdraw
And become reserves, which will be most useful.
No more American lives should be lost
Than is necessary.

Hodges.   I agree to be overruled.
I will order the withdrawal.

(*Christmas Day.* MONTGOMERY *in full battledress, Christmas cards.*)

Montgomery.   Inside the Bulge Hundred-and-First Airborne,
Encircled at Bastogne, were asked to surrender, their
Commander said "Nuts" and beat the Germans back.
Skies cleared and Allied planes strafed the Germans
And Patton began his thrust towards Bastogne
To lift the siege. And now, having been out of touch
Since December the seventh, almost three weeks,
Bradley has come out of his Hotel, has braved
The assassins, and is flying up here to be briefed.
I have not sent a car.

(*Enter* BRADLEY, *in an old combat jacket, looking tired.*)

Brad, you found the way.

Bradley.   In a staff car provided by General Hodges.

Montgomery.   I haven't seen you since Maastricht, when I
Proposed one unified command, and you
Preferred to command the American army.
Come up to my study, and I'll brief you.
I know what's going on in the American sector.

(*Later.*)

Montgomery.   So the Germans have given the Americans a bloody nose.
And the Americans deserve this counter-attack,

It's entirely their own fault for trying two thrusts
At the same time, neither being strong enough.
If there'd been a single thrust, none of this
Would have happened. Now we are in a muddle.
I always advised against the right going so far.
You advised in favour of it and General
Eisenhower took your advice. So we must withdraw.
If Patton's counter-attack is not strong enough
Then I'll have to deal unaided with Fifth and Sixth
Panzer armies, in which case General Eisenhower
Will have to give me more American troops.
Do you agree with my summary?

Bradley   (*uncomfortably*).   I do.

Montgomery.   Then what does General Eisenhower propose to do?
He hasn't spoken to me since giving me command
Of the main battle in the Ardennes. The Supreme
Commander has given no orders. So I ask
You, what does he propose to do?

Bradley.   I don't know.

Montgomery.   Don't know? Don't know? A commander has to know.

Bradley   (*uncomfortably*). I have not seen Eisenhower recently.

Montgomery.   But you and he agreed a better way
Than a unified command at Maastricht.
Surely he has been in touch?

Bradley.   Skorzeny
And his paratroops in Allied uniform
Are trying to kill him and me –

Montgomery.   And I have been
Riding round the front line in a Rolls Royce
With a large Union Jack, and I haven't seen them.

Bradley.   The security problem has hindered communication,
And my telephone lines were cut.

Montgomery.   Because you went
                        Too far, and in too weak a second thrust.

Bradley   (*aside*). He is humiliating me, shaming
                        Me like a Headmaster shaming a naughty boy.
                        I shall not forgive him for this. I shall demand
                        That Ike returns the First and Ninth Armies
                        To my command.

(*Versailles, SHAEF conference.* EISENHOWER, TEDDER *and* STRONG.)

Eisenhower.   I believe the German divisions in the Bulge
                        Are understrength and pummelled, and that their
                        Supply lines are poor. I want to hit them
                        Hard and quickly. The Allies are running late
                        In their counter-attack.

Tedder.   The good weather
                        Will not last much longer, and we must attack
                        While our planes can still fly.

                        (A *message is received.*)

Strong.   Montgomery
                        Has a new plan for attack, involving two corps,
                        Seventh US and 30th British.
                        A northern counter-attack, Twenty-first say.

Eisenhower.   Praise God from whom all blessings flow.

(*Moscow. Stalin's Kremlin office.* STALIN *and* ROKOSSOVSKY.)

Stalin.   The Soviet general staff have now drawn up
                        A plan for the greatest campaign in history,
                        An offensive that will take the Red Army
                        Forty-five days, and start between the fifteenth
                        And twentieth of January. It will cover
                        The entire eastern front from Barents
                        To the Black Sea, eight countries, and its aim
                        Is the lair of the Fascist beast, Berlin.
                        There will be three fronts to Operation Berlin,

It is vital that you, Rokossovsky,
Zhukov and Koniev should put aside
Rivalries and work together, co-ordinate.
Your three fronts will end the war in the west.
If you and Koniev don't advance, Zhukov
Will not either. You will approach from the north,
Koniev from the south, Zhukov from the east.
I attach such importance to the drive
That I will direct it, not my Supreme
Command staff, the Stavka, or army general
Staff – I will co-ordinate the three fronts,
First and Second Belorussian and First
Ukrainian and a fourth front, the Third
Belorussian, which will help the northern flank.
The commander in the field will be Marshal Zhukov,
Who stopped the Germans at Moscow and then
Defeated them at Stalingrad and Kursk.
He will spearhead the offensive, and take Berlin.
I want no arguments, no defiance.
You were sentenced to death seven years ago,
Though still under sentence I made you a Marshal.
And I look to you to co-operate
In our great undertaking as we kill the beast.

(*Versailles, SHAEF HQ.* EISENHOWER, BEDELL SMITH *and* STAFF, DE GUINGAND.)

De Guingand.   I've spoken with Montgomery, and he confirms
That the proper strategy is to let the Germans
Exhaust themselves with one final attack
Before an offensive.

Eisenhower   (*angrily*).   But he definitely
Promised to attack on January the first. Tomorrow.

De Guingand.   You must have misunderstood.

Eisenhower.   And Bradley's attacked
In the belief that Montgomery is attacking then.
If he doesn't, the Germans will move Panzer divisions
From the north to the south. We want an attack now.
Montgomery's timing in military

Operations is seriously flawed.
He's unable to see things from SHAEF's viewpoint. He's welched.

De Guingand.   He's written you a personal letter.

(DE GUINGAND *hands over the letter.* EISENHOWER *reads it.*)

He says my policies are wrong and demands
Control of the land battle. He says there must be
A single thrust to the north to seize the Ruhr,
With Patton held, or else the Allies will fail.
He sends a directive along those lines
For me to sign.

(*General indignation and outrage. "O-o-h. "*)

(*Aside.*)   I've lost control of him.
But he's gone too far. My credibility
Is at stake. He is insubordinate. I must
Keep my staff together.

Tedder.   It's outrageous,
It makes me seethe. Sack him.

Eisenhower.   Bedell, cable
General Marshall and the Combined Chiefs of Staff,
Saying it's Monty or me. And if it's me,
Then I want Alexander.

Tedder.   I'll help you find
Some appropriate words.

(BEDELL SMITH *receives a signal.*)

A signal from General
Marshall, Chairman of the Combined Chiefs of Staff.
It says you have their complete confidence,
That you're doing a grand job, and are not to pay
Attention to British press reports that call
For a British Deputy Commander – Monty? –
To lighten your task as this would be resented

Back home.

(*He hands* EISENHOWER *a paper.*)

De Guingand   (*aside*).   If Ike sends his cable, Monty will go.
(*Aloud to Eisenhower.*) Please don't send your cable for a few hours,
Until I've spoken with Monty in Zonhoven.

Eisenhower.   All right. But I'm now issuing my directive
Which contradicts Montgomery's on every point.
First Army is back in Bradley's control,
There must be a double thrust into Germany.
We must seize the initiative at once,
We must act quickly, with speed and energy
Before the Germans move in more Panzers.
Now draft a covering letter to Montgomery.
I do not agree there should be a single ground
Commander. I don't want to hear any more
About putting Bradley under his command.
I have planned an advance to the Rhine
On a broad front, and will no longer tolerate
Any debate. Say I don't want to take
Our differences to the CCS, but if necessary I will
Even though it damages the goodwill between
The Allies.

(*Later the same day. Zonhoven, Montgomery's HQ.* DE GUINGAND *is drinking tea with*
MONTGOMERY *in "A" Mess.*)

De Guingand.   The fog is really thick.

(MONTGOMERY *rises.*)

Montgomery.   I'm going upstairs to my office.
Please come up when you've finished your tea.

(*They go up to* MONTGOMERY*'s study.*)

                                                                  Well?

De Guingand.   The feeling against you at SHAEF is very strong.

Eisenhower has drafted a signal to Marshall
Saying it's him or you. He's set to resign.
Marshall has cabled the CCS's support.
Smith's very worried. They think you'll have to go.

Montgomery.   It can't be that serious?

(DE GUINGAND *hands over* EISENHOWER'*s letter and directive*)

De Guingand.   The Americans
Now have three-quarters of the war effort.
If the CCS sack you, there is little
That Churchill can now do.

Montgomery.   Who would replace me?

De Guingand.   Alexander. His name is in the draft signal.

Montgomery.   Alexander? He's a weak commander
Who knows nothing about field operations
And is unable to give firm and clear decisions.
He's ineffective in Italy, he'd be a disaster.
What a team: Eisenhower, Bradley and Alexander.
The Germans would push them back to Normandy.

De Guingand.   He's in the signal.

Montgomery.   What shall I do, Freddie?
What shall I do?

(DE GUINGAND *pulls out a letter from his battledress pocket.*)

                Sign this. It's a letter
Of apology to Eisenhower. It says
There are many factors "beyond anything I realise",
That he can rely on you "one hundred per cent",
And that you're "very distressed" your letter
Upset him, and that he should tear it up –
The one about you having sole command.

(MONTGOMERY *signs the letter.*)

Montgomery	(*aside*). I humiliated Bradley in this room
	And Eisenhower on his train, but now it's me.
	I've had to swallow my pride and humble pie
	To keep my job.
	(*Aloud.*) I shall begin my attack
	Twenty-four hours early, at dawn on the third.

De Guingand.	I'll take this straight back to SHAEF. Good-bye, sir.
	(*Aside*.) He looks nonplussed and so terribly lonely,
	I feel sorry for him. He knows he's lost.

SCENE 7

(*January 1945. Bad Nauhem, the Adlerhorst, or Eagle's Nest, Hitler's western field HQ.*
HITLER, GÖRING, RUNDSTEDT, BORMANN.)

Rundstedt.	*North Wind* has failed. The enemy nearly
	Evacuated Strasbourg, but sidestepped.
	Montgomery's new offensive in the north
	And Patton in the south are attacking the Bulge.
	We have destroyed one thousand two hundred tanks
	And taken twenty-four thousand American prisoners,
	But it is now time to cut our losses. Model
	Has requested we pull back on our western flank
	The 47th Panzer Corps. I ask you
	To authorise this move.

| Hitler. | And also the south |
| | Panzer Army, which should now be in reserve. |

| Rundstedt | (*aside*). He has indirectly admitted that |
| | He has lost his Ardennes gamble. |

(HITLER *withdraws*. BORMANN *follows him*.)

| Bormann. | The war is not lost because we are pulling back. |

| Hitler | (*depressed*). The war was lost two years ago. |
| | But still the killing must go on. It is a crusade |

Which must take precedence over everything,
Including the war effort, so that there are no Jews
Left to worship the Satanic Jehovah,
The demiurge who created the evil world.
So that a New Order can prevail for
The Aryan Sixth Root race, a race of Supermen.
Jodl did not understand this. He said
That in Warsaw the SS were proud of
Their killing, "their murder expedition",
But he did not understand that genocide
Is how we cleanse the earth, change the world.
Genocide can transform the world for good.

(*Berlin.* EVA BRAUN *and her sister* ILSE *are dining in the Chancellery library, white-gloved* SERVANTS *serving from silver dishes.*)

Eva.

The *Führer* left the Adlerhorst nearly
A week ago. He came into Berlin
Early in the morning with the blinds pulled down
The car windows, because the bomb damage
Upsets him. He was shocked to see how badly
The Chancellery was damaged. Every window
Broken, the west wing with our private apartments
Collapsed. General Rattenhuber of the
SS advised him to move his office
And our residence into the bunker
Under the garden outside. This was his study,
Where he holds his conferences. He has his SS
Guards round him all the time following the
Wicked attempt on his life in July.

Ilse.

I cannot believe the luxury in Berlin,
When in the countryside, the snowy roads are lined
With fleeing refugees who have nothing.
There was one train at the station, and several
Froze in open wagons, waiting for it to leave.

Eva.

I shall join you in Breslau in two weeks' time.

Ilse.

Breslau is lost. Do you not understand?
The Russians have taken Silesia, Germany

Is finished. As I travelled here I saw
Columns of hungry refugees and the Russians
Are burning and plundering and raping all.
Your *Führer* is responsible for the invasion.
He's destroying our country, and you, and us.

Eva.

You're mad. Crazy. How can you say such things
About the *Führer* who is so generous?
He's invited you to stay at his house at Obersalzberg.
You should be shot.

Ilse.

You need to open your eyes.

(*Enter* HITLER *briefly. He is a wreck, his left hand trembles, his left side shakes, he stoops, hunchbacked, with a pot belly. He shuffles.* BORMANN *is with him.*)

Eva.

My sister will gladly stay at your house.

Hitler

(*nodding, to Bormann*).   I want
Eva to follow her. She is a distraction here.

Bormann.

Jawohl, mein Führer.

(*Fade on* EVA *and* ILSA.)

Hitler

(*to Bormann*).   I have decided,
In view of the failures of my Generals
In the Ardennes, that every General should inform me
In advance of every movement in his unit,
In time for me to intervene in their decisions
If I think fit, and for my counter-orders
To reach the front-line troops.

(HITLER *goes to* Führer *bunker. Below, conference room or map room and Hitler's office or study/living room in which is Anton Graff's life-sized portrait of Frederick the Great. Hitler sits by dim candlelight and stares at the painting.*)

(*Alone.*) Frederick the Great, you expanded Prussia,
You fought Russia and Austria and France
And your luck turned when Tsarina Elizabeth died.

You are called "Great" because of what you endured.
Your spirit is with me, help me, help me.

(*He lights another candle and performs an occult incantation.*)
O power that I first contacted when Dietrich
Eckart opened my higher centres, power
Whose Will has carried me from the Munich
Beer-cellars to the highest point in the world,
Power which has filled me with an electric current
Of dynamic energy when I needed it,
Power which I have summoned through ritual magic,
And human sacrifice as Eckart taught,
Power you knew, Frederick, in your illumined search,
Do not desert me in my hour of need.
I have done your Will, I have speared Jehovah,
Whom there will soon be no Jews left to worship.
I am the chosen spear of the Antichrist,
The man chosen to wield Longinus' spear
Which I took from the Vienna Hofburg
And hid in sacred safety in Nuremberg,
And, inspired by Lucifer, to conquer the world
And lead the Aryan race to glory as
A race of Supermen - do not abandon me,
Your foremost Superman, *your* Overlord,
Fill me with your power, but more importantly
Strike down my enemies, give me a sign
That you are still supporting my world rule.
Strike dead Stalin or Roosevelt, my Overlord.

(*A knock on the door. Enter* BURGDORF *and* GUDERIAN.)

Burgdorf.   Sir, The Chief of the General Staff, Heinz
                 Guderian, who you summoned.

Hitler.   Ah yes.
                 My Generals continue to defy my orders.
                 General Hossbach has withdrawn his Fourth Army
                 From East Prussia after it was overrun
                 By Rokossovky. Did you know this?

Guderian.   No sir, but I know Hossbach wants to save

	As many men as possible, and keep a corridor open
	For the East Prussians –

Hitler.	Pah! The man is a traitor.

Guderian.	He cleared the withdrawal with Colonel-General
	Reinhardt –

Hitler.	Commander of Army Group North,
	But not with you – or me. I demand that
	You now dismiss Hossbach and Reinhardt and
	Their treacherous staffs, and court-martial them.

Guderian.	Sir, I'm an East Prussian, born on the Vistula,
	And I do not consider these men traitors.
	Hitler. I will dismiss Reinhardt immediately.
	Replace Reinhardt with Colonel-General Rendulic,
	He is a National Socialist.

Guderian.	But sir –

Hitler.	And Army Group Centre is now in the command
	Of Colonel-General Schörner.

(GUDERIAN *leaves and meets* RIBBENTROP *in the corridor.*)

Guderian.	Foreign Minister, the war is lost. I urge
	You to negotiate an armistice in the west
	And transfer troops to face the Russians.

(RIBBENTROP *enters Hitler's office or living room,* GUDERIAN *waits. Then* HITLER *appears.*)

Hitler	(*shouting*). Anyone who tells anyone that the war is lost
	Will be treated as a traitor, with consequences
	For himself and his family. I will take action
	Regardless of rank and reputation.

Guderian.	My *Führer*, I do not mean that the war *is* lost,
	Only that it *will* be lost unless we transfer more troops.

835

Hitler.	No.

Guderian.	My *Führer*, we need a new emergency
	Army group to support Army Groups North
	And Centre and stop Zhukov's advance.

Hitler   (*calming*).   Yes,
                That is good.

(*Chorus of* BERLINERS.)

Chorus.   The American bombers have filled the sky.
                For two hours the ground reverberated.
                Craters, fallen trees, roads filled with rubble,
                Fragments of walls, no lights or water.
                Hitler was unharmed in his bunker,
                Freisler the judge was killed by shrapnel.
                We queue at standpipes to fill saucepans, pails.
                We now have one loaf a week and most shops
                Are ruined or boarded up, and money is worthless.
                After each air-raid we just carry on
                Alas, what will become of us? Alas!

(*Chorus of* DRESDENERS.)

Chorus.   Alas! Dresden is flattened. The Allies
                Rained bombs from the night, first the British with
                Eight hundred bombers, setting the city on fire
                With high explosive bombs and incendiaries,
                And then a wave of American bombers when
                We were fleeing the firestorm, heading west.
                Refugees choked the roads, German reinforcements
                Could not get through the burning city to
                The eastern front, as Stalin no doubt wanted,
                But at what cost! Sixty thousand of us,
                Sixty thousand civilians have been killed,
                And all to choke the roads and slow down
                The German reinforcements, to the Red Army's
                Advantage. Alas, we are homeless, widowed, orphaned.
                Alas, Dresden is no more, and we've nowhere to go.

(Moscow, Stalin's office in the Kremlin. STALIN and ANTONOV.)

Stalin.   My Generals have now submitted reports and plans.
Where do they all stand? Start with Koniev.

Antonov.   Koniev's First Ukrainian Front broke through
The German defences in snow with non-stop shells
And advanced along a two hundred mile line,
And with the sun glistening on snow, took Lodz
And the same day Krakow, the capital
Of Poland's kings and of the Nazi "General
Government", in the rear. The Germans fled
And Hans Frank's city fell without damage.
Koniev has pushed on and taken Silesia
And has crossed the Oder.

Stalin.   And Zhukov?

Antonov.   Zhukov's
First Belorussian Front, led into battle
By Chuikov, the hero of Stalingrad, bombarded
The Germans and advanced south of Warsaw,
And cut the city off from the west, then
With another artillery barrage, tanks smashed through
The Germans in the south while the 47th
Army crossed the Vistula to the north
And surrounded the city. The Germans destroyed
Warsaw, shooting, hanging and burning thousands
Of Poles, and evacuated the city.
And Posen is now surrounded. Zhukov
Is crossing the Oder.

Stalin.   And the defiant Rokossovsky?

Antonov.   Rokossovsky's advance to the north of Zhukov
Has been slower because of the Masurian lakes,
And the ice of the River Narcis was not thick
Enough to bear tanks. The Imperial
Russian Army was defeated in that terrain
In the First World War, at Tannenberg. Even so
Rokossovsky is near the Baltic, he has

Advanced along the Vistula towards Danzig
And has cut off Germans in the Baltic
And East Prussia, and forced them to dig up
The remains of Hindenberg and his wife
Who were buried at Tannenberg.

Stalin.   Good. But
Rokossovsky has not advanced as fast
As the others who cover fifteen, eighteen,
Twenty-five miles a day. Tell him to turn
Towards East Prussia and support Zhukov.
He will not go down in history as
The Soviet General who took Berlin.
What is Zhukov's plan?

Antonov.   In February, a new
Non-stop offensive, smashing across the Oder
And into Berlin with one gigantic thrust.
Stalin. And Koniev's plan?

Antonov.   Destroy the German forces
At Breslau, and reach the Elbe, then join Zhukov
And capture Berlin.

Stalin.   Both men seek to become
The "conqueror of Berlin". Let them race each other.
The one will spur the other.

(*Reims.* EISENHOWER *in his HQ.*)

Eisenhower   (*alone*). My broad front in the west is now ready.
Monty has smashed nineteen German divisions
And ninety thousand men, and has occupied
The west bank of the Rhine from Nijmegen
To Düsseldorf. From there Bradley has cleared
Eighty miles on the west bank down to Koblenz,
Southwards and Hodges has captured Cologne,
And taken out forty-nine thousand men
And Collins has crossed the Rhine at Remagen
And established a bridgehead several miles deep.
Patton has reached the Rhine from Moselle.

We are all in place to advance into Germany.
The Ruhr is now within the Allies' reach.
I have told Marshall and Roosevelt, the Red Army
Is fifty miles from Berlin, while we are
Two hundred and eighty-five miles away.
I have asked: do they want us to take Berlin?

(Berlin, the Führer *bunker.* SPEER *waiting in the corridor ante-room or reception room.*
BURGDORF.)

Burgdorf.   The *Führer* rose at midday, he is on the phone.

                   (Enter HITLER.)

Hitler.   To Goebbels about the daylight air raid.

Speer.   Two thousand American planes filled the air,
                   Glinting in the sunny Sunday morning,
                   There was some opposition, our Messerschmitts
                   Shot some down, but the *Luftwaffe* is short of fuel.
                   Aircraft and pilots, and the bombs thundered down,
                   Everywhere now there are fires, and the people suffer.

Hitler.   The Allies' air raids are assisting our
                   Scorched earth policy. The Soviets will have nothing.
                   They will find rubble, as they found Warsaw.
                   I will destroy Berlin and the whole country –
                   Its industrial plant, power stations, water and gas works,
                   All stores, bridges, public buildings, ships, trains –
                   Rather than hand them over to the Soviets.

Speer.   I built your new Berlin and your Third *Reich*
                   To last a thousand years, I beg you, please
                   Do not do this. I have brought a report.
                   The economy will last one month or two,
                   Then the war must stop. Please think of the people.
                   They need electricity, gas, water and bridges
                   To continue their food supply so they survive.
                   Führer, on human grounds, do not raze Berlin.

Hitler   *(contemptuously)*. If the war is lost, the nation will perish.

And the nation will not be the good ones, who will have been killed,
But inferior ones and cowards who did not die.
If the war is lost, Germans do not deserve
To have the essential services, and they will not.
Tomorrow I issue my Nero Order
To destroy all installations and services.

Speer   (*quietly*). Nero burned Rome and is now considered mad.
I tell you, German civilians will fight
Kesselring's men as they implement your will.
(*Wearily*.) But Allied air raids will accomplish all
Your order seeks. You and the Allies will leave
A pile of rubble for the advancing Soviet tanks,
The rubble of what I built, of my life's work.

(*Cannes*. EISENHOWER *and* BRADLEY *in conference*. KAY *and* THREE WAC GIRLS *playing bridge*. EVERETT HUGHES *and* TEX LEE.)

Hughes.   Ike's back to himself today. He's slept two days.
Yesterday Kay suggested bridge. He said
"I can't keep my mind on cards at present,
All I want to do is sit here and not think."

Lee.   The stress of great men's jobs and lives.

Hughes.   You share
An office with Kay. Do you think Ike sleeps with her?

Lee.   No, I don't. He's always writing to Mamie.
He's cooling towards Kay. She's fun to be with,
Someone he can talk privately with. That's all.
He knows there's no place for Kay in his life.

Hughes.   I disagree. I think he does. But one thing's sure,
There is nothing we can do about it.

(*Fade on* HUGHES *and* LEE.)

Bradley.   You ask me about the risks of taking Berlin.
Even if Monty reaches the Elbe before
The Red Army reaches the Oder, fifty

840

Miles of Lowlands, with lakes, streams and canals
Would still lie between the Elbe and Berlin.
It would cost us a hundred thousand casualties.
For a prestige objective, then we'd have to fall back
Because Yalta gave Berlin to the Russians.

Eisenhower.   Brad, you were my friend and classmate at West Point.
I want you to lead the final victorious assault
Against Hitler. A SHAEF directive will
Instruct you to send Third Army over the Rhine
Near Mainz-Frankfurt and advance to Kassel.
Hodges will push east from Remagen and link
First and Third Armies, encircle the Ruhr.
I shall take the Ninth Army from Monty's command,
Remove it from Twenty-first and give it to you,
And shift the main thrust from the north to the centre.
I have decided not to take Berlin
But to leave it entirely to the Russians
And go for Dresden and Leipzig instead.
This is for your ears only at this stage.
We all have our masters, mine are Marshall
And Roosevelt, who agreed at Teheran
And Yalta to draw a line down the map of Europe
And place Berlin on the Russian side.
In the prevailing political climate
Of Yalta, and of those who control
Our President and Stalin, it is wise
To leave Berlin to the Russians. But Brad,
Political considerations aside,
I have been coming round to this view on my own
For military reasons I find sound.
Since January I've wanted to strengthen your front.
I first saw your front as a diversion, then
As a secondary thrust to help Monty,
Then as a major thrust if he gets bogged down
As he did near Caen. But now I see it as
The main thrust, and Monty's as secondary.
I have decided, I will not be lectured
Or dictated to by Monty any more.
He has been so personal, denying the Americans
And me credit, that I have stopped talking to him.

I know Monty wants to lead the armies
Into Berlin, and I know I should explain
This change of strategy to Churchill.
But I shall follow my masters and keep silent.

(*He rises and moves away. Fade on all except* EISENHOWER.)

(*Aside.*) General Marshall has pointed out again,
Berlin's in the Russian occupation zone
As agreed at Yalta, and we should not interfere.
Berlin is in the Russian sphere of influence.
There will be a problem if we take Berlin
At a cost of a hundred thousand Allied lives
And then withdraw under the Yalta terms,
Hand part over to the Russians. At home
They'll say, "Why were so many Americans killed
To hand Berlin over to Russian occupation?
Was this what we voted for four months ago?
Let the Russians take the casualties, not us."
I'll secure Marshall's approval to cable
Stalin and suggest the Americans meet up
With the Russians at Dresden, well away from Berlin,
A token meeting-place this side of the Elbe
That will justify the bombing Stalin sought.

(*Straelen, Montgomery's HQ.* MONTGOMERY, CHURCHILL *and* BROOKE *leave Montgomery's caravan in moonlight by the Rhine. Churchill is in the uniform of 4th Hussars. Sound of artillery barrage.*)

Brooke.   It's good news that Eisenhower has approved
                 The Whiteley plan that will put you north of the Ruhr
                 And Bradley south. You'll be in a good position.

Churchill.   That was a good dinner, and now we have
                 Studied the maps, all that remains is to watch
                 The boats and pontoons drift to the other side,
                 Which is, what, five hundred yards, would you say,
                 As we put a quarter of a million men
                 Across the Rhine, the first military crossing
                 Since Napoleon, the first time British troops
                 Have fought on German soil since the battle

Of Leipzig in eighteen thirteen, against the French.

Montgomery.   Have you seen my message to the troops?

Churchill   (*reading*). "Over the Rhine then let us go. And good hunting
               To you all on the other side. May 'The Lord
               Mighty in battle' give us the victory
               In this our latest undertaking as He has done
               In all our battles since we landed in
               Normandy on D-Day." Very eloquent.

Montgomery.   There go the first commandos across the river.
               Do you see their green berets?

Churchill   (*excited*).   Yes.

Montgomery.   Through the night there will be landings along
               A twenty-mile front, in ten places, two
               Airborne divisions –

Brooke.   They've started.

(DAWNAY *approaches*.)

Dawnay.   Sir, Patton
               Is across.

Montgomery.   What?

Dawnay   (*handing him a message*). We've just heard, the Americans
               Crossed near Mainz at ten last night. Bradley gave
               Patton permission to cross in assault boats
               By stealth – no barrage or paratroop drops –
               And has put ten divisions into the new bridgehead.
               He has given Hodges ten divisions to break out.
               The US Twelfth Army Group plan to race
               Your Twenty-First Army Group into the *Reich*.
               Patton has said, "I want the world to know
               Third Army made it before Monty starts across."

(*Silence. Exit* DAWNAY.)

Montgomery.	Ike is behind it.

Churchill.	And Roosevelt behind Ike.

Montgomery.

Even now the Americans are fighting their own war.
But for them, we would be in Berlin now.
It is time I retired to bed.

Churchill.	You can't leave this.

Montgomery.

Nothing disturbs my routine. Well, good night.

(*Exit to caravan.*)

Churchill.

How can he go to bed at such a time?
Despite the ominous news about the Yanks
I am exhilarated, let us walk
In the moonlight and watch and talk until
I return to my red boxes in my caravan.
What do you think the Americans plan to do?

(*Fade on* CHURCHILL *and* BROOKE. MONTGOMERY *in his caravan, praying.*)

Montgomery.

O Lord, who helps the righteous in peace and war,
O Lord of Love and Light, O mighty Lord,
I have flung a quarter of a million men
Across the Rhine to thrust towards Berlin
And root out the Nazi evil around Hitler's power.
O Lord of Light, fill me with your wisdom,
O God of Light, come into me now, come.
Purify my thinking, so my decisions are right,
Exonerate me from the deaths I cause.
I submit to you the power I have over men.
Guide me with your power, you ah! bright Light,
Guide me with your Providence. Thy Will, not mine,
Be done. If it is Thy will, let me have
The victory, let the Germans surrender to me
As your chosen instrument doing your will.
Not to the Americans, but to me.
Let me cleanse the earth with the Light you give me.
And after its moral cleansing may the soil

Return to your beauty, devoid of tanks
And guns and shells, the machines of war
Which so disfigure your simple paradise.

SCENE 8

(*March 1945. Rheinberg Castle, Simpson 's 9th Army HQ overlooking the Rhine.* CHURCHILL, MONTGOMERY *and* BROOKE *sitting with* EISENHOWER, BRADLEY *and* SIMPSON.)

Churchill.   We have come from a Palm Sunday Service.

Eisenhower.   I rested in Cannes, then flew to Wesel
And watched Simpson's Ninth Army cross the Rhine
Virtually unopposed. The plan's going well,
Under Monty's leadership.

(*He exchanges pointed glances with* BRADLEY.)

(To Brooke.)   Do you agree
With the new plan, with going north and south
Of the Ruhr, and in the south, pushing for Frankfurt
And Kassel?

Brooke.   I see no danger in it.
The Germans are crumbling and we should push
Them wherever they crumble.

Churchill   (*showing a note*). Ike, read this.
I received this note last night from Molotov.
He accuses Britain and America
Of lying, of going "behind the back
Of the Soviet Union, which is bearing
The brunt of the war against Germany," by
Opening negotiations for a separate peace
In Switzerland and in Italy. The accord
Between the three powers at Yalta is strained.

Eisenhower.   These are unjust and unfounded charges
About our good faith. They make me angry.

We will accept surrenders in the field
When they are offered. In political matters
We will consult the heads of governments.

Churchill.　　　　　I think the Allied Expeditionary Force
Should beat the Russians to Berlin and hold
As much of east Germany as possible, until
My doubts about Russia's intention have been cleared away.

(EISENHOWER *exchanges glances with* BRADLEY.)

Eisenhower.　　　　The truth is, we're five times as far from Berlin
As the Russians are. You want me to think
Less about the Germans than the Russians,
But I don't believe the *Wehrmacht* is finished
Until it has surrendered unconditionally.
It can set up Headquarters in the Austrian Alps,
With Hitler as its guerilla leader.
I want a quick end to the war. That means
Capturing the Alps, moving towards the south:
The Alps are a more important objective
Than Berlin, or racing the Russians there.

(*There is a silence with exchanged glances.*)

Churchill.　　　　　The Kremlin has stressed the importance of the Alps
To direct our attention from their goal of Berlin.

Montgomery.　　　　But the main thing is, the objective is still Berlin.

Eisenhower.　　　　These are political considerations
But our assessment is primarily military.

Churchill.　　　　　Berlin is our priority objective.
It is a political centre and if we can
Beat the Russians to it, the post-war years
Will be easier for us. We must look ahead.
(*There is a silence with exchanged glances.*)

Bradley.　　　　　　Political considerations can complicate the war
With political foresight and non-military objectives.

Eisenhower.   The Ruhr should be surrounded and mopped up
                     Before any advance to the east begins.

(*Days later. Reims, Eisenhower's Forward Headquarters. BUTCHER and BEDELL SMITH.*)

Bedell Smith.   He really needed his holiday in Cannes.
                     He had flu, his back hurt where the cyst was cut out,
                     His knee was badly swollen, he had bags under
                     His eyes, his blood pressure was high, I said
                     To him, "You can hardly walk across the room."
                     He slept most of the time for a couple of days.
                     He was really run down, physically. Since Cannes
                     He's been travelling: to Namur to see Brad,
                     Then he crossed the Rhine at Remagen with Brad,
                     Hodges and Patton, then back here to Reims
                     Yesterday, then to Paris with you. He's got new zest.

Butcher.   His press conference in Paris was a peach,
                     And then he had some R and R: a preview
                     Of a D-Day film in the Champs Elysées,
                     And don't tell anyone, but he spent the night
                     With Kay at the Raphael Hotel incognito –
                     I booked them in myself – and I think you'll find
                     He wasn't impotent for once, he's got
                     Untired, he's bodily fit. And now back here.

                     (*Enter* EISENHOWER.)

Bedell Smith.   Sir, a signal from Montgomery. You're not
                     Going to like it sir. He has ordered
                     His army commanders to go for the River Elbe
                     "With all possible speed and drive", and then Berlin.
                     He says he feels SHAEF will be "delighted".
                     Your Rheinberg directive of yesterday
                     Laid down that the Ruhr was to be surrounded
                     And mopped up before any advance to the east.

Eisenhower   (*stunned, reading*). He's ordered his British Second Army
                     And Simpson's US Ninth to Magdeburg.
                     He ends: "My TAC HQ moves to the north west
                     Of Bonninghardt on Thursday 29th March.

Thereafter my HQ will move to Wesel,
Munster, Wiedenbruck, Herford, Hanover –
And thence by *autobahn* to Berlin, I hope."
(*Blowing up.*) It's open defiance of my orders.
He thinks he's Supreme Commander, not me.
Of all the imperious and tactless things he's done,
This tops the lot. My reply will show my anger.
My message will be clear and uncompromising.
I will think it out while I lunch with Brad.

(*Later.* EISENHOWER *and* BEDELL SMITH.)

Eisenhower.   Brad says again that capturing Berlin
Would cost us a hundred thousand casualties.
If Brad were to the north, I might say Yes.
But it's Monty, after his slowness in the Ardennes.
The American armies are having great success.
I am determined to do right by Brad
Regardless of the British Chiefs of Staff,
And give him back his three US armies.
I've talked with Brad, it's time to block Monty.
I will be decisive. Say, "There will be no drive
For Berlin." Say, "Simpson's Ninth Army will
Be under Bradley's control once it has joined
With US First Army and encircled the Ruhr."
Say, "Bradley will deliver his main thrust
On the axis Erfurt-Leipzig-Dresden
To join hands with the Russians." Dresden
Is the shortest route to the Red Army, it will
Cut the German forces in half. Say, "Bradley
Will swing well south of Berlin, the mission
Of your army will be to protect Bradley's
Northern flank." Say, "My present plans
Are co-ordinated with Stalin." Cable Stalin,
Tell him of my intentions, ask for Soviet plans
To harmonise the operations of our two armies
Which are advancing from east and west.
Make it a personal message to Stalin
Via the Allied Military Mission
In Moscow. Say I am encircling
The enemy in the Ruhr until late April,

That I'll then seek to divide the enemy
By joining hands with Russian forces on
The axis of Erfurt-Leipzig-Dresden,
The focus of my main effort, and later in
The Regensburg-Linz area to stop
All resistance in a southern redoubt.

(*Surprised,* BEDELL SMITH *hesitates.*)

Bedell Smith.   Sir, are you sure –

Eisenhower.   It's all right, I know what I'm doing.
Don't question me about this cable. Do it.

(*Later the same day. Straelen, Montgomery's HQ.* MONTGOMERY *and* DAWNAY, *his senior staff officer.*)

Montgomery   (*devastated*). I am stunned by Eisenhower's cable.
I am shocked. "My present plans being co-ordinated
With Stalin." And no mention of Berlin.
I am speechless. "The mission of your army group
Will be to protect Bradley's northern flank."
I am devastated, fuming at his folly.
Why are they so hostile to me at SHAEF?
Who are my enemies? Public opinion?
Simpson's Ninth Army, taken away from me
And reverting to Bradley to mop up the Ruhr.
Bradley having the main role, and to Dresden.
And nothing of this said to us at Rheinberg.
And co-ordinating with Stalin, a Commander-in-Chief
With a Head of State. And did Tedder know?
Not going to Berlin, I can't believe it.
Is he blind, does he realise what he's giving Stalin?
The US and Russians must have made a deal.
There is very dirty work behind the scenes.
Until I know what Eisenhower is doing
With Stalin, the wisest counsel is silence.
(*He goes to his caravan.*)

(*Praying.*) O Lord, I do not understand your ways,
But if it is your will that Stalin should have

Berlin, and control free elections there,
Then I'm happy to accept that Bradley should
Lead Simpson to Dresden. Thy will, not mine
Be done. But how, Lord of Light, how, how, how
Is your will served by Stalin having Berlin?
By Communism ruling eastern Europe?
By a regime as bad as Hitler's controlling Poland?
Please give me an answer, for I do not understand.

(*London, underground war rooms.* CHURCHILL *and* BROOKE.)

Brooke.

A wire from Monty: "I consider we
Are about to make a terrible mistake."
He hopes Eisenhower's order can be rescinded.

Churchill.

Ike did not consult his Deputy Supreme Commander,
Tedder, about his change of plan, nor did
He mention it to the Combined Chiefs of Staff.
He said nothing of this to us at Rheinberg,
And for a General to communicate directly
With a Head of State, and so untrustworthy a one
As Stalin, leaves me speechless. It signals
To Stalin that his troops can take great tracts
Of Germany, a danger I foresaw
In Yalta, and tried to prevent. I ask myself,
It must have been premeditated, he
Must have known this when we talked at Rheinberg?
And Stalin. He must have cleared it with Marshall.
Not even Monty would cable Stalin
With a change of plan without contacting us.
But given that he cleared it, the question is,
Did Ike act alone, or was he under orders
From higher up? Let us try to find out.

(*Exit* BROOKE.)

(*Aside.*) In every time there has been an eruption:
The French Revolution, the guillotine and
Napoleon, which came out of a suppressed
Bavarian movement; the Bolshevik
Revolution, Lenin and firing-squads,

Which have been funded by the Rothschilds' banks;
Now the Nazis, Hitler and extermination camps,
Which came out of Eckart, Rosenberg and the Thule
Society in Munich, Bavaria.
What if this seismic movement against government
And religion which kills in different times
Has one volcanic source which is behind
The hand of Robespierre, Napoleon, Lenin,
Stalin, Hitler - and Roosevelt? What if Eckart,
Lenin, Baruch and Marshall are all connected?
What if there is one single idea behind
All the warlords who have shaken our century?
It's a nightmare I prefer not to think about.

(*Washington. Gen.* MARSHALL, *US Chief of Staff, with* AIDE.)

Aide.   A protest from the British to Roosevelt.

Marshall.   Now the President is sick I have taken charge
Of the conduct of the war. I will reply.
Ike is the most successful field Commander.
It is incredible that the British
Do not trust his military judgement now.
Churchill has phoned Ike at SHAEF to protest,
He's urged our forces to turn north, not east.
It is not clear whether he wants the Ninth
Army back, or the capture of Berlin.
Churchill says the fall of Berlin will send
A signal to the German people and will have
A psychological effect on German resistance.
Ike here denies he has changed his plans.
He says the British have called for one big thrust
Which he gave to Bradley; that his aim
Is to defeat the German forces, not turn aside
With many thousands of troops; that he has one thought:
The early winning of this war. It makes sense to me.
Only Ike is in a position to know
How to fight his battle, and exploit the changing situation.
Montgomery is slow, overcautious.
He wants to be sure before he attacks.
He'll mass hundreds of tanks when thirty will do.

He won't take risks. Eisenhower, for all his faults,
Is the best Commander the Allies have.
(*Exit* AIDE.)

(*Alone.*) The young American civilisation
Like Rome after two Punic wars, is poised
For a world role: involved in Europe and
Controlling the older Russian civilisation
Financially, American money will
Undertake urban reconstruction and spread
American influence and use Moscow
To end the European empires before
Our coming world rule. I wanted to squeeze
Europe, contract it to the east.
I did not want the Allies to take Berlin.
And I made sure, through Ike, they did not, so
The post-war world is America's, not Europe's.
Baruch did well when he identified Ike
And promoted him as the instrument
For our larger long-term, global purpose.

(*Reims, Eisenhower's HQ.* EISENHOWER *and* BEDELL SMITH.)

Bedell Smith.   Sir, a wire from Churchill: "Why should we not
Cross the Elbe and advance as far eastward
As possible?" He says the Russian Army
May take Vienna, that we must not give
The impression the Russians have done everything,
That we must avoid "the relegation
Of His Majesty's Forces to an unexpected
Restricted sphere". He says Britain is being
Relegated to an almost static role
In the north, and that the British cannot now enter
Berlin with the Americans. He says, "I do not
Consider that Berlin has yet lost its
Military and political significance."
He's very critical.

Eisenhower.   I am upset by that.
Say, I have not changed my plan. I still intend
To send Monty over the Elbe, but towards

Lübeck, not Berlin, to keep the Russians out
Of Denmark, an important objective.
Say I am disturbed and hurt that he should suggest
I have "relegated" his forces, or "restricted" them.

(*The Kremlin, Stalin's study. STALIN, ANTONOV and SHTEMENKO.*)

Stalin.   Cable Eisenhower that Dresden is the best place
For the AEF and Red Army to meet.

(*He chuckles quietly.*)

Add, "Berlin has lost its former strategic significance,
The Red Army will allot secondary forces
To capture the German capital in
The second half of May." Do not add that
Berlin is our primary objective,
We have allotted a million and a quarter men,
And aim to take it by mid-April; or that
I want it taken now in frantic haste.

SCENE 9

(*April 1945. Berlin, the* Führer *bunker. The conference room.* HITLER *with* KREBS, *Guderian's replacement.*)

Hitler.   The Soviet preparations for an attack
On Berlin are simply a deception,
A secondary thrust. The main attack
Will come round Prague, which we must defend.

Krebs.   But *Führer* –

Hitler.   No, Schörner has written:
(*Reading.*) "Remember Bismarck's words 'Whoever holds
Prague holds Europe.' " Schörner is loyal to me,
He is facing Koniev, he has been hanging
Deserters from trees with placards round their necks.
I promote him to Field Marshal, and transfer

Four of Heinrici's divisions from the Oder
To defend the Reich in Czechoslovakia.

(*Rheine, Montgomery's HQ.* MONTGOMERY *with* DAWNAY.)

Montgomery.   Write to Ike: "It is quite clear what you want.
                   I will crack along on the northern flank.
                   One hundred per cent, and will do all I can
                   To draw the enemy forces away
                   From the main effort being made by Bradley."

Dawnay.   Right, sir.

Montgomery.   We are moving fast, and as we move
                   I am shocked at the scenes of destruction I see.
                   Civilisation reduced to rubble, ruin.
                   At Munster, tank tracks crunched the carved faces
                   And limbs of medieval stone statues.
                   Here at Rheine, bombed shells of houses
                   And a pervading stench of decay and death.
                   We are driving through a Hell, and though I am pleased
                   We are liberating the wretched, I feel sad
                   That American mistakes have prolonged it all,
                   That we are not now in Berlin, and at the end.

                   (*Silence. Exit* DAWNAY.)

                   (*Aside.*) A civilisation is a gathering
                   Round an idea that can be found in its new religion.
                   It grows and expands, it has a style or art
                   And architecture, maintains an ordered life
                   In cities, an economy, fine manners.
                   Civilisation is the highest aspirations
                   Of the finest minds in a civilisation.
                   Barbarism is the lowest expression
                   Of the sickest minds in a civilisation.
                   Something went wrong in this one. All this rubble.
                   We caught the illness of barbarism.
                   A disease had to be cured, and at what cost.
                   Is the price of civilisation to purge
                   A civilisation from time to time?

Is the idea it grew round still here, your Church?
O Lord, your cathedrals round which Europe grew?

(*Reims, Eisenhower's HQ.* EISENHOWER, *sombre, with* BEDELL SMITH.)

Bedell Smith.   Sir, General Bradley on the phone for you. (*Exit.*)

Eisenhower.   Brad, how are you? I'm just recovering.
I've been to the concentration camp near Gotha,
I've never experienced an equal sense of shock.
What? The bridging operation's a success?
I'm glad to hear that. Brad, what do you think
It might cost us to break out from the Elbe
And take Berlin? You could take it fairly easily.
But once there lose a hundred thousand men?
Say that again? A high price to pay
For a prestige objective and then fall back
To let the Russians take over? That's what I think.
But Simpson thinks he can beat the Red Army there.
Huh-huh. Bye Brad.

(*He puts down phone.*)

Kay.   Can I join you, General?

Eisenhower.   Not just now Kay. I have a decision to make.

Kay.   You always have a decision to make.

Eisenhower.   But this
Is some decision. If I get it wrong,
It will return to haunt me. Send Beetle in.

(*Exit* KAY.)

I am in agony, for I must make a choice
That will have a universal application,
Affect all mankind, and men still unborn,
Shape history, and if I become President,
Tie my wrists with the rope of my own decision.
Should Berlin be American or Russian?

Militarily, I have only fifty thousand men
Who have advanced two hundred and fifty miles
In two weeks, and have already stretched
Their lines of communication. Racing them
Are two and a half million men, who are fresh,
Who have prepared two months, and are twenty miles
Away, and who must surely get there first.
To try and lose is worse than not to try.
Politically, if I win, I present Truman,
A new President, with the choice of rescinding
The Yalta agreement, that Berlin is Soviet,
And, worse, I raise doubts in Stalin's mind
About American good faith over Yalta.
He is anyway quick to say we are misleading him.
Then a hostile Soviet army, like a tidal wave,
Two and a half million men against our small force,
May keep going into Normandy, to the Atlantic
And swallow all that we have won from Hitler.
It is better not to anger the Russians.
It is wiser to stick to our agreement
And not risk what our hard-won efforts have gained.
Politically, I know, since the First World War,
There have been men in Washington, and London,
Who seek to promote Communist world rule,
Who would dearly love Stalin to have Berlin.
They follow their own agenda, not SHAEF's.
I have my suspicions about some men, including
Two who promoted me from nowhere to
This pinnacle from Lieutenant-Colonel
To Supreme Commander within three years,
Two years nine months. My career progressed
When, like Churchill, I wrote to Barney Baruch.
Now I must choose on military grounds,
As the voice of SHAEF, and shut out all interests.
I am in anguish as I must decide
A course I know to be politically wrong,
But militarily right. Judgement is like love,
You weigh everything up, and then choose heart
Or head. I must choose head, but my heart yearns.
Berlin, Kay. A leader reviews, decides,
Communicates, inspires, and then defends,

And I will have a lot of defending to do.
(*Enter* BEDELL SMITH.)

Bedell Smith.   You sent for me, sir?

Eisenhower.   Telegraph the Combined
Chiefs of Staff. I intend to hold a firm front
On the Elbe; to undertake operations
To the Baltic at Lübeck, and to Denmark;
And to thrust in the Danube Valley to join with
The Russians and break up the southern redoubt
So Hitler can't continue the war in the Alps.
As the thrust on Berlin must await the success
Of these three operations, I do not include
It as part of my present plan, the essence of which
Is to stop on the Elbe and clean up my flanks.

(*Next day. Wiesbaden, Bradley's HQ. BRADLEY and SIMPSON, who has just stepped off a plane.*)

Simpson   (*shaking hands*). You have received my plan to take Berlin?

Bradley.   Simp, I have to tell you right now. You have to stop
Right where you are on the Elbe. You are not
To advance any further towards Berlin.

Simpson.   I could be in Berlin in twenty-four hours.
Where did this come from?

Bradley.   From Ike. My orders
Are to defend the line of the Elbe. The supply
Columns are being attacked with German tanks
And assault guns, round Hanover and elsewhere.
We hold the bridgehead as a *threat* to Berlin.

Simpson   (*depressed*). So this is the end of the war for us. This is
As far as we go. We're not going to Berlin.

(*Berlin, Ministry of Propaganda. GOEBBELS returning to his office just after midnight.*)

Goebbels.   Ribbentrop has asked diplomats to leave Berlin.

I have visited Busse near Küstrin,, and I told
The officers of the miracle that saved
Frederick the Great, and urged them to believe in fate.
What are those fires?

Staff 1.   The Adlon Hotel, and
The Chancellery, both hit in the evening raids.

Staff 2   (*calling out*). *Herr Reichsminister*, Roosevelt is dead. It is true.

(*Enter Goebbels'press officer,* RUDOLF SEMMLER.)

Semmler.   It is confirmed. Truman is the new President
Of the United States.

Goebbels.   This is the turning-point.
Is it really true? Open the best champagne.
I must telephone the *Führer. (On phone.)* My *Führer*,
I congratulate you. Roosevelt is dead.
You recall the horoscope. The stars proclaim
That the second half of April will be our turning-point.
Providence has struck down your greatest enemy
On Friday the thirteenth, it is like the death
Of Tsarina Elizabeth for Frederick the Great.
(*Putting down phone.*) The *Führer* is overjoyed. It's the miracle.

(*Moscow, the Kremlin. Stalin's study.* STALIN *is on the phone.*)

Stalin.   Zhukov. Chuikov has the Heights and has broken
The Germans' first line of defence? Good, good.
The cost, *thirty* thousand men? They gave their lives
For their motherland.

(*He puts down the phone.*)

                              Thirty thousand,
That's war. Hitler attacks me with Barbarossa,
Seeking to eradicate all Soviet Jews.
And fifty million die in repelling him.
Thirty thousand to drive towards Berlin.
This blood will achieve territory, our rule.

I took over from Lenin a divided land,
I killed six million to unify it,
Reshape its borders, rule a vast expanse
From the Baltic to the Pacific from a strong centre,
A union that will now expand westwards,
As far west as the Allies allow my troops.
If they weaken, I am ready to push on
Till the whole continent, from the Atlantic to the Pacific,
All Euro-Asia, will be under Red rule.
The Byzantine Russian civilisation
Is in its greatest extent under my Tsardom.

(*He stands before a picture of Ivan the Terrible.*)

Ivan the Terrible, I look to you.
You approve of everything that I have done.
You know our Byzantine Russia must expand
At the expense of the Holy Roman Empire
And the Habsburgs, and their successors,
And the British Empire, the non-Orthodox faiths.
You know Russia's Byzantine destiny
To rule the world through a creed that captures minds.
Autocracy, through Communism, is our way.
I keep the tradition of the Russian Tsars,
I unite our lands and cultures with the glue of power,
And keep it stuck together by repelling force.
Thirty thousand is a small price to pay.
A human life is material which the State
Can remould into a peasant or a soldier.
It *is* while it is alive and then, is nothing.
Death is like a curtain drawn across a window.
It is nothing, it has no significance.
It is the end of life, as evil is the end of good.
There is no sacredness, men have bodies
That can be used like shell cases. There is nothing
Sacred about life, no good. Ivan *you* knew.
We have millions of material units
To sacrifice, to expand our empire.

(*Berlin, the* Führer *bunker. The refreshment room outside Hitler's office.*
HITLER *in greatcoat and peaked cap with* BORMANN, GOEBBELS,

RIBBENTROP, SPEER, HIMMLER *and* JODL, *all in uniform.* GÖRING *arrives in plain olive uniform.*)

Burgdorf.

The *Führer* rose at eleven and is greeting
Well-wishers on his fifty-sixth birthday.

Göring.

My *Führer*, congratulations on your birthday.
I passed Goebbel's banners on my way here.
One, stretched across a ruined building, says
"We thank our *Führer* for everything."

Speer.

I was just saying to the *Führer*, there are posters
On doors, walls, windows, saying "Should Berlin
Share the fate of Aachen and Cologne? No!"
The early morning shelling of Berlin has brought
Out resistance. What news of the air raid?

Göring.

A thousand American bombers, silver
Planes glistening in the blue sky, too high for flak.
We have no German fighters to attack them.
They had a clear run and have knocked out
The city's water, gas, electricity and sewage
Supply. There is no power. The bombardment
Ten minutes ago was from Zhukov's long-range guns.
The Allies' "Happy birthday" to our *Führer*.

Goebbels

(*taking message*). My *Führer*, the news is bad. Weidling, Heinrici
And Busse have been overrun, as you know.
Reymann says it is no longer possible to defend
The capital. All possible troops must be
Dispatched to the front.

(HITLER *nods tiredly.*)

Göring.

My *Führer*, you should leave Berlin.
You should fly south and go to Berchtesgaden.

Speer.

Führer, he is right, you should leave today.

Hitler.

No, I will remain. I must inspect the parade.

(*He climbs the stairs to the wrecked Chancellery garden with* BURGDORF, AXMANN, KREBS, FEGELEIN *and the* OTHERS. GÖRING *goes to a phone.* SPEER *returns.*)

Speer   (*to Göring*). I can remember when, for his birthday parade,
Forty thousand men and hundreds of tanks
Took three hours to salute him while he stood
On a dais. On his fiftieth birthday
I rode with him in his car as he stood,
Arm raised in salute; slowly we passed hundreds
Of thousands of soldiers standing silently.
He was like Tamberlaine in a chariot.
The Army had increased sevenfold in four years,
The Rhineland, Austria, Sudeten and Czech lands
Behind, Danzig, East Prussia and the Polish
Corridor ahead, and who could stop him?
Each man had sworn an oath to his Napoleon.
He was magnificent. I knew then it was war.
When he spoke the world trembled, and we were all proud
To follow him. Now a few SS men and
A few boys from the Hitler Youth. He's trembling
Fumbling for their hands, patting their cheeks, pinning
Iron Crosses on those Axmann points out,
He's staggering unsteadily, saying
The enemy will be destroyed outside Berlin.
It's pathetic. I couldn't bear to watch any more.
I know Stauffenberg's bomb began the decline,
And Dr. Morell's syringe has played a part,
But I can't help feeling power festers in the flesh
And infects the blood till the health corrupts.
I've seen it in other leaders. Power ruins
Like a drug an athlete takes to enhance
Performance; soon the body craves for more
And is addicted, and the doses must be increased,
And his health is past its peak. So it is with him.
Amid the trappings of power, he is impotent.
He was the mightiest in the world, and now
He looks like a drug addict who's terminally ill.

Göring.   It's finished, you are right. I am leaving Berlin.
This morning I learned that Rokossovsky is

Twelve miles from my estate in north-east Berlin,
Karinhall. I have packed my possessions –
Things I brought back from countries we conquered,
Souvenirs, you might say – into twenty-four lorries
And blown up the building. I could hardly bring
Myself to press the plunger, but I did.
That beautiful castle is now rubble.

Speer.   And the lorries?

Göring.   Parked at the *Luftwaffe* game park
Near Potsdam. I'm joining them now. We will drive
In convoy to my house at Obersalzberg.
Do not be trapped in Berlin.

Speer.   I certainly won't.

(HITLER *returns down the steps. The* Führer'*s conference begins in the*
conference room.)

Krebs.   The overall picture shows Berlin is
Half encircled. In the north, Rokossovsky
Has cut Manteuffel from the rest of the army.
Zhukov is in the north-east suburbs and
Will attack to the north-west. On the Oder,
Busse is encircled - but not Weidling's Panzers -
And Koniev has cut it off from the south.
Koniev is attacking the north and at Zossen,
In the south. Four hundred aircraft have been destroyed.
The Americans have trapped Model in the Ruhr pocket
With over three hundred thousand troops, while
Montgomery is attacking Bremen and the Elbe.
The Americans have taken Leipzig and Nuremberg,
The French Stuttgart and the Poles Rothenburg.
Berlin can only survive if Busse's Ninth Army
Is pulled back from the Oder.

Hitler.   No withdrawal.
I refuse to allow any withdrawal.

Krebs.   Heinrici

	Reports that all along the line, men are retreating,
	On foot and in vehicles. He is trying
	To prevent them, but he now needs more troops.

Hitler.   Send the Muller Brigade from Wenck's Twelfth Army.

Krebs.   *Führer*, without transport will they arrive in time?

Hitler.   Heinrici must take Reymann and Berlin
          Under his command.

Göring.   My *Führer*, I am now convinced
          You must leave Berlin. Planes are standing by
          At Tempelhof to fly out you, Keitel
          And Jodl.

Hitler.   If the Russians and Americans
          Cut Germany in two, the northern half
          Will be under General Admiral Dönitz, and I
          Transfer the command to him now. The southern half
          Will be under Kesselring, but I retain
          The command in case we fight on from the Alps.

(*Chorus of* BERLINERS.)

Chorus.   We have extra rations for Hitler's birthday:
          A pound of meat, half a pound of rice and beans.
          We leave our shelters and queue outside food shops,
          At every water pump or standpipe.
          The Russian guns are shelling our city.
          We live in cellars and come out for food.
          When will our misery end? When will Hitler give up?

(*Berlin,* Führer *bunker. The conference room. The daily conference.* HITLER, BORMANN, KREBS, KEITEL *and* JODL *in the ante-room or reception room.*)

Keitel.   The *Führer*'s face is yellow and expressionless.

Jodl.   He's sacked his doctor and has withdrawal symptoms.
          He can't concentrate. He needs amphetamine.

(*In the conference,* HITLER *twice gets up and goes to his private office and returns, abstracted.*)

Krebs.

The situation is grim – Koniev has taken
Our main munitions depot, Busse's army
Is trapped. Weidling has retreated to the Olympic village.
We are trying to arrest him.

Hitler

(*not listening*).   Where is Steiner?
Steiner's Army Detachment. How is his attack?

Krebs.

Führer, Steiner has not yet given the order
For an attack.

(*Silence.*)

Hitler.

                Everyone is to leave the room
Except Keitel, Jodl, Burgdorf, Bormann
And you Krebs.

(*The others leave.* HITLER *then raves, trembling.*)

                I ordered Steiner to attack.
Why has this not happened? I am surrounded
By cowards, traitors, incompetents and Generals
Who are insubordinate and disloyal.
Even the SS cannot be trusted, and tell lies.
Everything is collapsing. The war is lost.
I will stay here and lead the final battle.
I shall not fall into the hands of the enemy.
When the last moment comes, I will shoot myself.

(*He crumples into a chair.*)

(*Sobbing.*) It's over. The war is lost. I shall shoot myself.

Bormann.

There is still hope. You must remain in charge.
But you should move to Berchtesgaden, and
Continue the war from there.

Hitler.

                You can all leave

Berlin. I will stay and go down with my troops.
I have taken my decision.

Keitel.   This is madness.
You must fly to Berchtesgaden tonight
So there is continuity of command
Which can no longer be guaranteed in Berlin.

Hitler.   You go. I order you to go. I stay.
East Prussia held while I was at Rastenburg,
It collapsed when I moved back to Berlin.

Keitel.   I will stay with you.

Jodl.   And so will I.

Hitler.   I want
Keitel, as Commander of the armed forces,
Göring, my deputy, and Bormann to fly
Down south tonight.

Keitel,Borm.   We refuse.

Hitler.   If there is negotiating to be done,
Göring is better at that than I am.
I told Schörner, my death may now remove
The last obstacle that prevents the Allies
From making common cause with Germany
Against the Russians. Either I fight and win
Here, or I die here. That is my final
And irrevocable decision.

(*Soltau, Montgomery's new TAC HQ. MONTGOMERY and EARLE.*)

Montgomery.   Dempsey fears he can't cross the Elbe until
May the first after he takes Bremen.
I want you to go forward to Lüneburg
And visit General Barker and obtain his plan
For crossing the Elbe with 53rd Division.
But be careful, there are enemy troops
On the edge of Lüneburg Forest.

Earle.   I'll take
                    The shortest route north of the Forest, I'll
                    Take John with me, we'll be back by nightfall.

(*Later that day.* EARLE *and* POSTON *in jeep, Earle driving.*)

Earle.   This route is nearer the Forest, we'll be back by dark.
                    (*Shooting.* POSTON *fires back with a sten.*)

Poston.   I'm out of ammunition.

                    (EARLE *drives the jeep at the machine-gunner, killing him.* POSTON *and*
                    EARLE *are thrown out of the jeep and are surrounded by boys in German
                    uniform. Earle tries to wipe a location map and is shot in the back and falls
                    three yards from Poston, who is lying unarmed, hands above his head.*)

                              N-no. Stop -stop.

                    (POSTON *is bayoneted above the heart and is killed. The German boys
                    remove a watch and valuables and go.* EARLE *is still alive and is found by
                    a farmer.*)

(*The next day. Soltau.* MONTGOMERY *by his caravan.* DAWNAY.)

Dawnay.   Sir, a signal from Peter Earle.

Montgomery.   Ah, he hasn't been captured.

Dawnay.   Sir, it's bad news. Earle is alive, but Poston.
                    (*Reading.*) "Regret to report John Poston killed at
                    Eighteen hundred hrs Saturday twenty-one
                    April." Earle's in 212 Field Ambulance
                    Station. Poston was last seen in a ditch.
                    I'm sorry, sir.

Montgomery.   Kit, send my physician,
                    Hunter, to check Earle's condition, and then
                    Recover Poston's body.

                    (MONTGOMERY *turns on his heel and goes into his caravan.*)

(Later. Meadow by trees. Poston's funeral. MONTGOMERY weeps by Poston's grave. TINDALE, a Scottish Presbyterian padre. HENDERSON talks with HUNTER, the doctor, away from MOURNERS.)

Henderson.   There was a touching message from Churchill.
                  He's like a father weeping for a son.
                  John was Monty's youngest LO, and had been
                  With him longest. Twenty-five, and he had
                  A Military Cross and bar. Did you know he
                  Fell in love with a girl in London, and asked
                  Monty what he should do, as there was competition
                  And he needed some leave to propose,
                  And Monty said "Take my plane, fly to London
                  And keep the plane there till the girl says Yes."

Hunter.   He was a vivid fellow with a current
                  Of energy. He was always up to something.
                  Monty was very devoted to him, I think
                  He represented something Monty couldn't be
                  Because he's so disciplined, on a tight rein.
                  A meadow on the forest edge, with full
                  Military honours....

Henderson.   He's still weeping openly.

Hunter.   It's a kind of breakdown. He's been inconsolable.
                  He's suffered so many blows and disappointments –
                  His command being taken away, then given back,
                  Then taken away again – and he's no family,
                  And for a long time he's suppressed his hurt feelings
                  And carried on and let some out in prayer.
                  "A" Mess has been his family, and I'm sure
                  You're right, he's looked on Poston as a son,
                  And his death has brought out what should have come up
                  Months ago. It's cleansing, healthy, cathartic,
                  It's good. I predict he'll snap out of it now.

Montgomery   *(to the padre).* He would certainly have sailed with Drake.

(Berlin, the Führer bunker. The conference room. HITLER and KEITEL at the end of their conference.)

| Keitel. | *Führer*, can I persuade you now to leave Berlin? |

| Hitler. | No. |

| Keitel. | You may find yourself cut off. I need
To know of any peace negotiations. |

| Hitler. | It is too early to talk of surrender.
It is better to negotiate after
A local victory, such as the battle for Berlin. |

| Keitel. | I am not satisfied with that answer. |

| Hitler | (*tiredly*). I have approached Britain through Italy
And Ribbentrop is coming here on this.
I will not lose my nerve, you can rest assured. |

(KEITEL *and* JODL *leave the ante-room.*)

| Keitel. | He will die here. |

| Jodl. | Göring is the only hope
I have sent Roller to the Berchtesgaden
To tell Göring of Hitler's collapse and tears
And to ask him to intervene. |

(*Evening of the same day.* HITLER *and* BORMANN.)

| Bormann. | A cable from Göring. *(Reads.)* "My *Führer*, in view
Of your decision to remain in the fortress
Of Berlin, do you agree that I take over
The total leadership of the *Reich*,
With full freedom of action at home and abroad,
As your deputy, in accordance with your decree
Of 28th June 1941?
If no reply is received by twenty-two hundred hours
I shall take it for granted that you have lost
Your freedom of action, and shall consider
The conditions of your decree as fulfilled,
And shall act in the best interests of our country..." |

(*He hands the cable to* HITLER.)

Hitler   (*stunned*). What do you think of this?

Bormann   (*softly*).   It is treasonous.

Hitler.   Göring?

Bormann.   *Führer*, I have a radio message
From Göring to Ribbentrop, ordering him
To go to Berchtesgaden if nothing
Is heard from you by midnight. Göring wants
To start peace talks at once

Hitler.   Göring, Göring

(*Pulling himself together.*) Tell the SS to arrest him. Strip him
Of all offices and titles. Göring. A traitor.

(*Bormann's eyes gleam as he leaves* HITLER. *Fade on* HITLER.)

Bormann   (*alone*). A word here, a raised eyebrow there, no more.
I do not have to suggest my rivals come down.
Kluge, Rommel, Rundstedt, Model, I've seen them fall.
Göring, Himmler, I have had them in my sights
For months, no years. And others too. Burgdorf,
Guderian, Krebs, Jodl, Keitel, Goebbels.
I remember things and bide my time, put on
An oafish air so they do not suspect
My cunning, my deviousness. The way
Of advancement is to be at hand, of use,
To flatter the confidence of a great man,
And knock out the others one by one, secure
Their confidence by taking their side, suggest
A course of action here, an indiscretion,
Then undermine them by subtle reports
Which parade the misdeed unobtrusively,
Then arrange for them to have a disaster,
Then bring it, reluctantly, to the great man's eyes,
And then dispatch them on his authority,
Until in the end all have gone save you and him.

But what if I have to flee before the prize?
And flee I shall. There will be no trace of me
If the Russians put an end to my grand schemes.

(*Chorus of* BERLINERS.)

Chorus.   Germany is cut in two, Koniev and Hodges
                 Have met on the Elbe. At dawn this morning
                 As we cowered in cellars, the Russian attack began.
                 A barrage of artillery, pounding
                 Our houses into rubble, starting fires,
                 Raining shells onto our squares and gardens.
                 Then the tanks, crushing barricades, blowing
                 Apart any building which had a sniper.
                 Then the infantry, not down open streets
                 But under cover of ruins, creeping
                 To cellar doors with grenades and flame-throwers.
                 Half a million Russian troops, and hundreds
                 Of tanks against sixty thousand of us,
                 Pounding our city to a pile of rubble,
                 And a thousand fires and columns of thick smoke.
                 We are frightened of what the Russians will do to us.

(*Berlin, the* Führer *bunker. The conference room. The daily conference.*)

Krebs.   We had some good news yesterday, the disunity
                 Between the Americans and Soviets
                 About the sectors to be occupied.
                 And now Wenck has launched his attack
                 And Busse is fighting towards him.

                 (HITLER *is holding a torn map.*)

Hitler.   And Steiner?

Krebs.   He has not started his attack.

Hitler.   He is useless.

Krebs.   And there is a report that Soviet troops
                 Are using the U- and S- Bahn tunnels.

Hitler	(*in a rage*). The tunnels must be flooded immediately.

Krebs.	But *Führer*, our own troops use them, and trains
	Take the sick and wounded to hospitals,
	And thousands of refugees –

Hitler.	Blow up what keeps
	Out the Landwehr canal and flood the tunnels.

Krebs.	It will be a human disaster. A wall of water
	Will pour through the tunnels, many will be killed.

Hitler.	Flood the tunnels. They do not deserve to live.

(*Chorus of* BERLINERS.)

Chorus.	Misery, there is no end to it. We crouched
	In our underground command posts in the stations,
	A cascade of water swept through, people fought
	Round the ladders, many were trampled. The
	Torrent rose a foot then dropped. Many had drowned.
	There were floating bodies, screams, cries in the dark.
	Where can we shelter if not underground?
	Who has done this to us? Who flooded us?

SCENE 10

(*April 1945. Berlin, the* Führer *bunker. The conference room.* TRAUDL JUNGE, *who has been asleep for an hour, goes to* HITLER *with her secretary's dictation pad.* BURGDORF *is outside.*)

Burgdorf	(*to Junge*). He's been sitting in his private quarters,
	Not moving, his face quite expressionless.
	He's thinking about Himmler's betrayal.

	(*The table in his study has a white cloth with AH on it. Silver dinner service, eight champagne glasses.*)

Hitler	(*alone*). I made European civilisation
	Replace its weak, impure, democratic way

With a stronger, purer stance. But Churchill and
Montgomery stopped me, calling in two
Outside civilisations like starving wolves –
America and Russia – to feed on
The sides of Europe's dying carcass. Both
Have torn off lumps of flesh: Paris, Warsaw.
Europe will now be weak, and as she bleeds
Her wounds will be impure, perhaps gangrenous.

(*Enter* JUNGE. HITLER *winks at her. He stands at the map table.*)

I will now dictate my last political testament.
More than thirty years have passed since I made
My modest contribution as a volunteer
In the First World War, which was forced upon the *Reich*.
In these three decades, love and loyalty
To my people alone guided me in all my thoughts,
Actions and life. I never wanted war,
But it was forced upon the world by the machinations
Of international Jewry. The sole responsibility
For all the subsequent death and horror, including
The death of many Jews, lies with the Jews themselves.
But now the end has come I have decided
To remain in Berlin. I die with a joyful heart
In the knowledge of the immeasurable deeds
And achievements of our peasants and workers
And of a contribution unique in history
By our youth which bears my name.
I cannot, however, speak admiringly
Of the German officer corps which unlike me,
Has failed to set a shining example
Of faithful devotion to duty, till death.
Two of my most trusted Generals have let me down.
I expel Göring and Himmler from the party
And strip them of all office. They have brought
Irreparable shame on the whole nation
By negotiating with the enemy
Without my knowledge and against my will.
When I am dead, Grand Admiral Dönitz
Will be President of the Reich, and Supreme Commander
Of the *Wehrmacht*. Goebbels will be *Reich* Chancellor.

Bormann party Chancellor.

(*He hands* JUNGE *a paper.*)

Traudl, I have written
Who will hold the other offices of state.
I urge my successors to uphold the racial laws
To the limit and to resist mercilessly
The poisoner of all nations, international Jewry.
During the years of conflict, I was unable
To commit myself to a contract of marriage
So I have decided the day before the end
Of my earthly life to take as my wife the young
Woman who, after many years of faithful friendship,
Has of her own free will come to the besieged capital
To link her fate with my own. She will, according
To her wishes, go to her death as my wife.
For us, this will take the place of all that was
Denied us by my devotion to the service
Of my people. My wife and I choose to die
To escape the shame of flight or capitulation.
It is our wish that our bodies be burned at once,
Here, where I have performed the greater part
Of my daily work during the twelve years I
Served my people. That is all. Now type it, please.

(JUNGE *looks at him, rises and goes through to her office and starts typing.*
Enter GOEBBELS, *tears running down his cheeks.*)

Goebbels   (*to Junge*). Hitler has ordered me to leave Berlin
But I don't want to leave the *Führer*. My place
Is here, if he dies my life has no meaning.
He said to me, "Goebbels, I didn't expect
You to refuse to obey my last order."
I want to dictate my own will, which should
Be attached to Hitler's as an appendix.

(*Later. The conference room.* HITLER *and* GOEBBELS.)

Goebbels.   No one in the bunker is legally
Empowered to hold a marriage ceremony.

Hitler.	I must have a legal authority. I have been
	Married to Germany. She is not worthy
	Of me, she has failed me, and so I have divorced
	Her, and by marrying Eva I will demonstrate
	That I have rejected Germany for good.

Goebbels.   I know a registrar who is in Berlin.
            His name is Wagner.

Hitler.   That is appropriate
            We are approaching the *Götterdämmerung*.

Goebbels.   I will send SS men to find Wagner.

(*Belsen*. MONTGOMERY. HENDERSON *and* ERNIE, *a private*.)

Henderson. The Chief's upset. He ordered cameramen
            To record "German bestiality" and he's made
            The people in the neighbouring villages
            Parade through the camp so they can see what was done
            By their own countrymen.

Ernie.   Yesterday we saw
            Some Canadians so incensed that they took
            The women guards to the edge of the camp where there
            Are supple trees, they pulled two down and tied
            A woman's legs to each and then let go
            So she flew into the air and was torn apart.
            They did several. I cocked my Browning, but
            My commanding officer said, "Don't interfere
            Or they'll turn on us."

(*Enter* MONTGOMERY. ERNIE *withdraws saluting*. HENDERSON *is at hand*.)

Montgomery.   I don't like to see
            The realities of war, the blood and bone.
            It upsets me. I avoid seeing wounds.
            A commander deals in fit soldiers, and this
            Makes me ashamed to be European.

(THREE BELSEN FIGURES *have tottered near him*.)

We knew the Final Solution was happening,
Ever since D-Day we've hurried the best we can.
But this was worse than I ever imagined.
If I had had sole command, the war would have
Been over last September, and those corpses would be
Alive. Their deaths are a German responsibility,
Of course, but if Eisenhower, Bradley and SHAEF
Had made better decisions, hundreds of thousands
Who are now dead would now be fully alive.

(*Exit* HENDERSON. *More* BELSEN FIGURES *gather.*)

(*Aside.*) War is the Devil's game. He inflates egos,
Urges land-grabbing, feeds envy and hate,
Delighting in the ruin that follows,
The destruction and sense of injustice
Smiling at a Paradise on earth destroyed,
At rubble and these puny, thin-armed men
Who resemble walking skeletons in Hell,
More cadaverous skulls with sunken eyes than what
I think of as starving human beings.
The Devil's onslaughts must be repelled, rebuffed
And my skills do this, but my skills, such as they are,
Are of a diabolical order, and for that
I feel self-disgust. The only cleanness
Is in my caravan after nine o'clock,
When I can be pure, and open my self, my heart
And be filled with the health-giving Light of God
And I do not know how it can help you now.
Poor wretch, you tear my heart with your cupped hand.

(THE BELSEN MEN *kneel at his feet.*)

(*Aloud.*) Get up.

Belsen man.   Thank you, Montgomery, thank you.

Belsen men.   Montgomery, thank you, Montgomery.

(MONTGOMERY *turns away, his eyes filled with tears.*)

Montgomery   (*aside, moved*). Not a cupped hand, he's blessing me. He wants
Nothing, only to give his thanks – and I,
Six months late, am not worthy of his gratitude.
I would like to embrace him to demonstrate to all
Our common humanity, but a commander can't.
He is isolated from his fellow men
By the barrier of his command and decorum.

(*Re-enter* HENDERSON *holding a jug and a chipped mug. He offers it to*
MONTGOMERY.)

(*Aloud*.) Give each of these men a drink.

(*Later. The conference room,* EVA *in a long black silk dress;* HITLER *in uniform;* WAGNER,
BORMANN, GOEBBELS; GERDA CHRISTIAN, *now senior secretary;* CONSTANZE
MANZIARLY, *Hitler's vegetarian dietician;* KREBS, BURGDORF, AXMANN.)

Wagner.   I shall not ask the usual questions about
Aryan origins and hereditary disease.

Goebbels   (*impatiently*). That's quite all right.

Wagner.   And after the ceremony,
Two witnesses must sign.

Goebbels.   Bormann and me.

Wagner   (*nodding*). Do you Adolf Hitler, take Eva Braun,
To be your wife?

Hitler.   I do.

Wagner.   Do you, Eva Braun,
Take Adolf Hitler to be your husband?

Eva.   I do.

Wagner.   I have the pleasure to pronounce you at law
Man and wife. Please sign the wedding contract.

(HITLER *and* EVA *sign, followed by* BORMANN *and* GOEBBELS. *Arm in* arm, *Hitler and Eva go to the refreshment room before the office or study and offer the guests champagne and sandwiches.*)

Eva (*chatting happily*). It's so good of you to witness our marriage.
I am so honoured to be the *Führer*'s wife,
And so pleased that our long association
Has ended like this, I am so happy my *Führer*.
O look, Bormann has the gramophone.
I am afraid there is only one record, you know it.

(*The gramophone plays "Red Roses".*)

I must go outside to greet the others who
Have not been invited to our private party.

(*She appears in the corridor outside, or reception room, and greets* JUNGE, WOLF, SCHRÖDER, BOLDT, LORINGHOVEN *and others who say* "Congratulations".)

(*The early hours of the morning. Eva's sitting-room/bedroom.* HITLER *sitting alone on the settee,* EVA *asleep on her bed.*)

Hitler. In 1940 I offered the British peace
On generous terms. I ruled from Norway to Spain.
I still don't understand why the British
Used up their imperial resources
By fighting a power that did not threaten them.
I said in July, only the US and Japan
Would profit from the end of the British Empire.
I was depressed when Japan took Singapore.
As we approached defeat, I became more
Ruthless, to make our soldiers fight harder.
Someone sitting watching me now, as if
I were talking in a doctor's waiting-room,
Must think I am pitiless, without remorse,
But Britain made me snarl like a wolf at bay,
That intransigent Churchill who threw away
The British Empire to corner me, when I
Did not want to threaten the British Isles
For which I, as a German, have a deep respect.
What did Britain do mostly in the war?

Killed Italians in North Africa and
Bombed German civilians. Why? I know why.
Bankers were behind us all, Churchill, Roosevelt,
Stalin and me, and wanted our cities destroyed
So they could lend their billions to rebuild.
Bankers and Zionists rejected my peace.

Eva   (*stirring*). Adolf, my husband, my lord, my Overlord,
                    I love you very much. I adore you.

(HITLER *embraces her.*)

(*Later.* HITLER *sitting,* EVA *sleeping.*)

It is the Feast of Beltane, the thirtieth,
Walpurgisnacht, when witches meet on the Brocken
And revel with the Devil, the pagan day
Most suited to favourable reincarnation.
And now I must face my own fate. It was
Not supposed to end like this. Many times
I stood in the Hofburg Treasury and gazed
At the spear of Longinus, which pierced the side of Christ,
And called me to war and to rule the world,
And when I took Vienna, I went there
With Himmler, and held it in my hand, certain
That my destiny was to rule the world;
And to be crowned Kaiser Adolf the First,
Of a Third *Reich* that would last a thousand years;
And to destroy Jehovah by liquidating
The Jewish millions who worship him, so that
The power I serve could fill the vacuum.
It seems only yesterday that Eckart
And I discussed the Final Solution,
How we'd be on the side of divine good
Against the Jewish Satan, the demiurge
Jehovah who is responsible for all
The ills in the world, how we'd be
On the side of a power that opposes
The Jewish Satan and its Christian mask,
And do its work in this impure, tainted world.
My work's incomplete, three million more must die.

But the power that has vitalised my great will
And made me more feared than Napoleon
Is still abroad and still possesses me
And rejoices in universal destruction.
In Vienna I read Nietzsche and Schopenhauer,
And I have tried to bring in the Superman.
My will to power has dominated the will
Of my people and has possessed them all,
And I have left mankind more pure through it.
My power, I know, is a power of darkness, which
Has pierced Christendom and Jewry with its spear.
Lord of Darkness, I am ready for you.

Eva   (*stirring*). Adolf, I love you, adore you, my husband.
Come to bed now, you have shed your burden.
You can be virile now you've put down your cares.
Now you have been released from your bond with
Germany, by the betrayal of your Generals,
You can love me without any sense of betrayal.

(*Later in the day.* HITLER *has finished lunching with his* SECRETARIES *in the bunker's refreshment room.*)

Traudl Junge   (*smoking*). Look what Eva has given me. This coat.

Gerda Christian   (*smoking*). Her silver fox coat with four-leaf clover
Entwined with her initials, E.B. It's beautiful.

Günsche.   The *Führer* wants to say goodbye to all his staff.

(JUNGE *and* CHRISTIAN *put down the coat. In the corridor, or reception room, outside the refreshment room* HITLER *walks down the line and murmurs a few inaudible words to each.* EVA *is with him, her hair done up and in black with pink roses on either side of a square neckline.*)

Eva.Traudl, try to get out of here, you might
Make it. Give my love to Bavaria.

(HITLER *and* EVA *go through the refreshment room into Hitler's office.* GÜNSCHE *stands outside the door. Hitler sits on the left of the settee, picks up his gun and cyanide capsule and stares into space. He speaks more to himself than to Eva, who is more concerned about the practical business of dying.)*

(*Aside.*) And yet, and yet, now that the time has come,
Now that the time has come for me to die,
To release the vapour some call the soul,
What if I find, on the other side, millions
I have put before a wall, waiting to judge me?
I blew up Warsaw – only two houses
Remained standing – and so many places,
And all the extermination camps. Auschwitz-Birkenau,
In one month alone two hundred thousand Jews
From Hungary, one month alone.... The vision I had
In the First World War, of eliminating Jews –
And five out of eight million are now dead,
European Jews, that is, not the world's –
What if Jews too have an immortal *soul*
That comes from a divine web, a *good* whole?
Was I wrong? Will history judge me adversely?
For thirty years, I believed in power over men,
The Thule Society, Ariosophy.
I saw men as unclean souls, to be crushed
So that the world could be cleansed and transformed
For the pure souls who will channel the power.
And now that I must die, I wonder if
When I am the vaporous body in this flesh
I must pay for all I have done on this lower plane.
Why did I not think more about these things
When I heard the applause echo my words
In the Munich beer-cellar, the Hofbrauhaus,
As I first announced the name "National Socialism",
When my mentor Dietrich Eckart urged me
To give myself to the occult for power?
Lord, fill me now with your power. Nothing.

Eva   (*summoning him back to the situation*). Adolf.

Hitler   (*aside*). I had a vision of a new Europe
                    Led by Germany, and in every state free peoples
                    Going about their business, living free.
                    There had to be a transitional phase –

Extermination camps and the rule of the gun –
But at the end, under one Overlord,
A great *union* of free democratic peoples
Who are anti-Communist, with a strong centre.
This may still come to pass, people may come to see
That even though my racial ideas are
Repudiated, I brought it into being,
It came out of my anti-Communist vision.
Every leader must keep things developing,
Must have something ahead to aim for, some goal,
To keep the support of his followers. If
There is nothing ahead, or a contradiction,
Then he is lost. My death is necessary
To release all German soldiers from their oath to me,
And so that Dönitz can negotiate a peace
And win the Allies over to oppose the Russians.
By this sacrifice, I will make possible
A German-Allied front against the Bolsheviks.
My sacrifice will turn the war around,
Will save Germany, wrest victory from defeat.
I had a vision and I improvised.
Nothing ahead. Nothing.

Eva   (*holding him*). What are you thinking?

Hitler.   I am remembering
How clean the air is in Berchtesgaden
And you reclining like a beauty queen
On the stone veranda in the sun, knee up,
Your bikini on, the mountains behind you,
Smiling above the green slopes while I loll,
My head on a cushion, and gaze at Paradise,
And there is nothing you could not make me do.
I, the master of the world, am bewitched by you,
I am your obedient and devoted slave.

Eva.   You will do as I say, you will be my slave.
I will bite to commit suttee like an Indian's wife.
Then you will bite and fire. We will be together.

(EVA *embraces* HITLER. *Fade on* HITLER *and* EVA. *Outside* MAGDA

GOEBBELS *rushes down the corridor into the refreshment room and pushes past* GÜNSCHE *into Hitler's office.*)

Magda.

Please leave Berlin, I don't want my children
To die beside me in this bunker.

Hitler.

No.

Leave us.

Magda

(*weeping*). He will not speak to me.

Günsche.

Too late.

Junge.

Have your children had lunch? No? I will make
Some sandwiches. There's fruit. Cherries.

(*A shot is heard.* GÜNSCHE *waits and enters, arm raised in the Nazi salute.* HITLER *is on the sofa, left, leaning over the arm, his head hung down, blood dripping on the carpet. He has shot himself in his right temple with his 7.65 mm.* EVA *is curled up on the sofa, right, her small unused revolver lying on the table next to her pink chiffon scarf.*)

Günsche.

Cyanide.

He shot himself in the head to make sure.

Magda

(*picking up a capsule like a tube, to* GÜNSCHE, *of Eva*). Cyanide.

(GÜNSCHE *picks up a knocked over vase of flowers. He examines* HITLER *and* EVA *quickly.*)

Günsche

(*shouting*).   Orderly, Linge. Bormann.

(BORMANN, GOEBBELS *and* AXMANN *enter, arms raised in the Nazi salute, and view* HITLER.)

GOEBBELS.

My *Führer* dead. I want to go out on
Wilhelmplatz and stay there till I am hit.

(GOEBBELS, BORMANN *and* AXMANN *follow as an orderly,* GÜNSCHE *and Hitler's valet,* HEINZ LINGE, *wrap the bodies in blankets and carry them out.* MAGDA *stands and stares until Günsche returns.*)

Magda.   So. Our world has ended. Well?

Günsche.   We carried them
                Up the stairs and out to the park above,
                And laid them in a shallow trench. Then Kempka,
                Hitler's chauffeur, came with three soldiers,
                And sprinkled petrol on them from jerry cans.
                Shells were falling round them, some very close.
                And they tried to set fire to it, but it would not light.
                Kempka made a spill from paper and set it alight
                And threw it into the trench, and up it blazed
                And black smoke rose above the funeral pyre.
                We put out arms in a Nazi salute,
                Then ran back inside. It's not safe up there.

Magda.   So died the man who would be Overlord
                Of the whole world, feeling betrayed
                By all he had trusted, doubting Göring and Himmler,
                Save the noble woman who died at his side
                And instead of a State funeral through Berlin
                This Napoleon received a hurried bonfire
                On a patch of waste ground under exploding shells.
                A pitiful end.

(*Fade on* MAGDA. KREBS *and* BURGDORF *have appeared at opposite ends of the bunker.*)

Krebs   (*alone*). He was a chancer. He restored German pride
                After the humiliation of the First World War.
                He took power by fairly constitutional means.
                He did not plan war with Britain and the U.S.,
                It somehow happened as a consequence of what he did.
                His name is terror, under him there was terror
                But at the centre was a fumbling man
                Who lived from event to event, reacting mostly,
                Blaming his Generals for the inadequacy of his plans.
                His name is terror, he was responsible
                For terror on a colossal scale, but
                For all the amphetamine injections there was
                Something indecisive at the heart of his vision.

Burgdorf   (*alone, scathingly*). So ended the life of a man who shamed

Germany, and its noble Prussian tradition,
Who dabbled in the occult, mixed weird ideas
From the drunkard drug addict "poet" Eckart,
The crazy anti-Semitic Rosenberg
And the "root race" nonsense of Theosophy,
And thought his foul butchery was doing good.
He never grasped that as all are from the One,
Souls are droplets from the divine thundercloud
Which veils the radiant often-hidden sun,
And return to it as raindrops evaporate.
His racist philosophy conflicts with the One
And how the universe in practice works,
And can now be reduced to ashes, like himself.
I speak from a noble German tradition,
I think all Fascists and racists are to be pitied
For they are separated from the One
And therefore have a false view of the world,
Which they infect with their odious inadequacy.
I despise myself for having joined the army
And been caught up in such a foul episode,
And I am filled with self-disgust that I
Did not join Stauffenberg's plot and rid the earth
Of a creature who was a disgrace to humanity.

(*Chorus of* BERLINERS.)

Chorus.   We have heard the good news. Our trials are over.
The dictator is dead, by his own hand,
Leaving a ruined Germany, ruined buildings,
Smashed plant and services, a heap of rubble.
We are overjoyed, the Russians and Allies
Will liberate us from all senseless war.
The Jews are safe, no more the killing wall.
Gone the extermination camp, gas chambers
And chimneys. We are free once more.
We can come out of our cellars and breathe the air.

SCENE 11

(*May 1945. Kuntsevo, near Moscow. Stalin's dacha.* STALIN *in bed takes a call from* ZHUKOV. *His telephone system allows him to hear the caller as he lies in bed.*)

Stalin.   Zhukov, I was asleep, it's four o'clock.

Zhukov's voice.   The Red Flag is flying over the Reichstag.
We cannot clear Berlin by the May Day parade,
But Hitler is dead. Suicide.

Stalin.   So that's the end
Of the bastard. Too bad we could not take
Him alive! But where is Hitler's body?

Zhukov's voice.   Burnt.

Stalin.   Hmm. You have Krebs, you say, at Chuikov's place.
Relay this to Krebs. Ask him directly now,
Is your mission to achieve a surrender?

Zhukov's voice.   The interpreter will interpret Krebs' reply.

Interpreter.   No, there are other possibilities.
Permit us to form a new government
In accordance with the *Führer*'s will, and
We will decide everything to your advantage.

Stalin   (*angry*). There can be no negotiations, only
Unconditional surrender. No talks with Krebs
Or any Hitlerites.

(*That night. Berlin, Chuikov's HQ.* CHUIKOV *tries to sleep with a blanket over his head. Distant noise of merriment. An officer, Lt. Col.* MATUSOV, *enters.*)

Matusov.   Sir, a message received by 79th Guards division
In Russian language.

Chuikov   (*sitting up*). What are they doing up there?

Matusov.	Roasting an ox,

And dancing, the poet Dolmatovsky
Is reciting patriotic verse.

Chuikov   (*scoffing*).   Dolmatovsky!
Poets meddle in wars and use their horrors
To scan their lines as Homer did. But how
Did poets change the world? It is Generals who
Change it by smashing armies.

Matusov.   Poems outlast
Empires, and poets understand their Age
And fix it in the pattern of history
And the universe, and make the world aware
For all time, in all places, universally
Of the horrors of wars, so men think twice
Before starting what we've finished.

Chuikov.   Pah! There are
Always wars.

Matusov   (*sadly*).   The world does not listen to poets,
And resists being changed. Sir, the message.
(*Handing it over.*) German envoys are on their way to Potsdamer Bridge.

Chuikov.   Ceasefire around Potsdamer Bridge.

(*The next morning, 12.50 a.m. Berlin, a cellar. KISELYOV is waiting to attack.*)

Kiselyov   (*shouting into the darkness*). Who is asking for a Soviet officer?

Voice.   Truce envoys. We have a statement of the
Berlin garrison commander, addressed to
Marshal Zhukov.

Kiselyov.   Come over with your hands up.

(GERMANS *appear under a white truce flag, holding a brown folder, with a Hitler Youth boy in a steel helmet. ABYZOV covers them with submachine guns. KISELYOV takes out two papers.*)

German.	One is in German, the other is in Russian.

Kiselyov.	The light is too dim.

(*He hands the Russian text to his comrade.*)

Abyzov	(*reading, choking with emotion*). The German command Is prepared to negotiate an immediate Ceasefire. Weidling.

(*Silence.* KISELYOV *puts the papers back in the folder. A Young Communist League* ORGANISER *arrives.*)

Kiselyov.	Take the envoys at once To Potsdamer Bridge.

(*They leave.*)

Abyzov.	I can smell lilacs.

(*Later that morning.* CHUIKOV *is still trying to sleep.*)

Matusov.	There has been a call from Dr. Goebbels.

(CHUIKOV *jumps up and splashes his face with cold water.* THREE DELEGATES *appear, one with a pink folder.*)

Heinersdorf.	I am Senior Executive Officer Heinersdorf Of the Ministry of Propaganda. This letter is from the Director, Dr. Frische.

Chuikov	(*reading*). "Former *Reichsmarschall* Göring cannot be reached. Dr. Goebbels is no longer alive. As one of the few remaining alive, I request You to take Berlin under your protection."

(*The phone rings.*)

Yes, yes, I see. Weidling has just surrendered
In person. Berlin has fallen to the forces
Of Marshal Zhukov. Our war is over!

(Lüneburg Heath, Montgomery's last TAC HQ. Flagpole without a flag. MONTGOMERY *and* HENDERSON *before breakfast.)*

Montgomery   *(with satisfaction).* We beat the Russians to Lübeck by twelve hours
                  And sealed off the Schleswig peninsula and Denmark.
                  I was just thinking, TAC HQ has done well
                  As the nerve centre of four Allied armies
                  In Normandy, and then three, and now two.
                  Yet we've doubled in size: from twenty-seven
                  Officers to fifty, from a hundred and fifty
                  Other ranks to six hundred, and two hundred
                  Vehicles. We're not so much gypsy nomads now
                  As an army within an army.

                  (Enter DAWNAY.)

Dawnay.   A phone call
                  From Colonel Murphy, Dempsey's Intelligence Officer.
                  He's received four German officers who wish
                  To negotiate surrender terms.

Montgomery.   Tell Dempsey to send
                  Them here, then report back.

                  (Exit DAWNAY. MONTGOMERY *pushes a buzzer in his caravan.)*

                  (Aside.)   If they come to seek
                  Unconditional surrender, they must be made
                  To believe in my personal authority
                  And command, and my determination
                  To fight the war relentlessly to the end
                  Unless they obey me. I must be on a pedestal.
                  They must see me as the Montgomery who
                  Took on Rommel in the Egyptian sands
                  Near the pyramids that marked the limit of
                  Napoleon's power, and fought him to Tripoli,
                  Invaded Sicily and southern Italy,
                  Threatening Rome, and then, as Overlord,
                  Swept through Normandy, France, Belgium, Holland
                  And Germany, to the Baltic and the Elbe
                  Without losing a battle. I must be

The invincible Montgomery they fear,
A man as awesome as Napoleon.
I must be Overlord.

(*Enter* TRUMBELL WARREN *with* DAWNAY.)

Four German officers
Are coming and may have power to surrender.
I want you to get the Union Jack up,
And when they arrive, line them up under it, facing
The office caravan. Get everyone else
Out of sight, get your side arms and stand at ease
To the side about here and don't move till I say.
Get Colonel Ewart and his interpreter.

(DAWNAY *and* WARREN *raise the Union flag, and, with rifles, escort in four German officers, two from the Navy in long black leather greatcoats, and two from the Army in grey greatcoats, one – a General – with red lapels. From right to left: General Admiral* VON FRIEDEBURG, *Commander-in-Chief of the Fleet; Gen.* KINZEL, *Chief of Staff of the German Army, North, who is in his late forties, 6 foot 5 inches and wears a monocle; Rear Admiral* WAGNER, *Flag Officer to the Admiral of the Fleet; Major* FRIEDL, *Gestapo, 6 foot 2 inches, 28, with a very cruel face. They represent Dönitz and Keitel. They wait a long time facing closed doors of the three caravans. They are uncomfortably hot in their greatcoats. The door of the centre caravan opens and* MONTGOMERY *appears, dressed in battledress and black beret. The four Germans immediately salute, Friedl keeping his arm down until Montgomery has finished his salute, which takes a long time and is then nonchalant and casual.*)

Montgomery   (*bellowing austerely*). Who are you?

Friedeburg.   General Admiral von Friedeburg,
Commander-in-Chief the German Navy, sir.

Montgomery.   I have never heard of you. Who are you?

Kinzel.   General
Kinzel, Chief of Staff of the German Army,
North, sir.

Montgomery.	Who are you?
Wagner.	Rear Admiral Wagner, Flag Officer to the Admiral of the Fleet, sir.
Montgomery.	Who are you?
Friedl.	Major Friedl.
Montgomery.	Major? How dare you bring A major into my Headquarters.
Warren	(*whispering*). The Chief's putting on A pretty good act.
Dawnay.	He's rehearsed this all his life.
Montgomery	(*barking*). What do you want?
Friedeburg.	We have come from Field Marshal Busch, Commander-in-Chief, North, to offer the surrender Of the three German armies facing the Russians In Mecklenburg, withdrawing between Rostock And Berlin.

(*Col. EWART interprets Montgomery's words into German.*)

Montgomery.	Certainly not. The armies concerned Are fighting the Russians. If they surrender To anybody, it must be to the Russians. Nothing to do with me. But I will naturally Take prisoner all German soldiers who come Into my area with their hands up. I demand that you and Field Marshal Busch Surrender to me all German forces on My western and northern flanks, from Holland to Denmark.
Friedeburg.	We refuse to agree as we are anxious About the civil population there. We wish to reach an agreement to look after it.

Then we can withdraw our forces as you advance.

Montgomery.   You talk about your concern for civilian life.
               Six years ago you bombed Coventry and
               Wiped out women, children, old men. Your women
               And children get no sympathy from me,
               You should have thought of them six years ago
               Before you Nazis blitzkrieged England. You
               Have mistreated your own civilians appallingly.
               Near here in Belsen there are Germans like skeletons.
               You caused their suffering. There are concentration camps
               All over Germany, you have systematically
               Killed millions of Jews who were civilians.
               Don't talk to me about your Nazi concern
               For your German civil population.
               I reject any agreement regarding civilians.
               Unless you surrender unconditionally
               Now, I will order the fighting and the bombing
               To continue, and German civilians will die.

               (MONTGOMERY *turns his back on them. The Germans salute. Montgomery
               goes to* DAWNAY.)

Montgomery.   They need to reflect on what I've said. Put on
               The best possible lunch in the Visitors' Mess
               And supply all the drink they want.

(*The next day. Lüneburg Heath.* MONTGOMERY *in his caravan.*)

Montgomery.   Warlords expand into their neighbours' land
               As pain expands into a healthy limb,
               Sending waves of troops like bacteria.
               They unify their civilisations through hurt,
               Or defend them against a spreading sore
               Like inoculations that control disease.
               Warlords are aggressors or defenders,
               Attackers of civilisations or preservers
               Like germs or antibodies which cause pain
               Or bring relief. I cauterised the wound,
               I acted to preserve the whole body.
               Civilisation swells into barbarism

As a healthy body erupts into a boil
That infects the circulation of the blood
And turns septic with putrefying matter,
The squeezing out of which restores its health
So the limb can move as freely as before.
Is not all mankind one body with many limbs?
Warlords, stern men whose authority controls
Front lines on wall-maps without pity, and moves
Armies and orders thousands to their death,
Embody their nation's ego in their own,
Harangue the people forward to their whim
Or just defence. The worst poison the whole
Until they are lanced by the best. I, a jousting
Knight and preserver, have pierced the German boil
And now squeeze out the puss that oozes from
The inflamed mound, plaster it back to health,
Immunise the diseased flesh so it's free from germs.

(*Enter the* FOUR GERMANS *with a fifth, Col. Pollok.* VON FRIEDEBURG *climbs the steps and enters the caravan.*)

Montgomery.   Will you sign the full surrender terms as
                I demanded?

Friedeburg.   Yes.

Montgomery.   In that case, come with me.

(*They go into a newly erected surrender tent where there are Allied* PHOTOGRAPHERS, SOLDIERS *and* WAR CORRESPONDENTS, *all very excited. A trestle table covered with an army blanket, an inkpot and army pen. Two BBC microphones. The German delegation salute* MONTGOMERY, *who salutes back.*)

I shall now read the *Instrument of Surrender.*

(*He puts on tortoiseshell-rimmed reading spectacles.*)

"The German Command agrees to the surrender
Of all German armed forces in Holland,
In Northwest Germany including the

Frisian Islands and Heligoland, and all
Other islands, in Schleswig-Holstein, and
In Denmark, to the C-in-C 21 Army Group."
Unless the German delegation sign
The document in front of me, I will order
Hostilities to resume at once.

(*Col.* EWART *translates. The German delegates nod.*)

(*Rising.*) The German officers will sign in order
Of seniority.

(VON FRIEDEBURG, KINZEL, WAGNER, *then* POLLOK *sign.*)

        And Major Friedl
Will sign last. (*Pause.*) Now I will sign on behalf of
The Supreme Allied Commander, General
Eisenhower. That concludes the surrender.
(*Aside.*) The war is over, and they surrendered to *me*.
I have appeared a ruthless commander
Who will not be disobeyed. I took a million
Prisoners in April, making three million since D-Day,
And I have just saved two million civilians in
Schleswig-Holstein from starvation, while Bradley,
In Wiesbaden, has said we may be fighting
A year from now. I have just saved millions
From suffering and have ended the war.

(*Reims, SHAEF. Eisenhower's office. STRONG enters with JODL. EISENHOWER sits behind his desk, Jodl bows and then stands to attention.*)

Strong.   All the signatures are here. Jodl, Friedeburg.

Eisenhower.   Do you understand the terms? Are you ready to
                    Execute them?

Jodl.   Yes.

Eisenhower.   If the terms are violated
                    You will be held personally responsible.

(JODL *bows and leaves*.)

I'm dead beat.

(*He rises and goes outside.* PHOTOGRAPHERS *appear. Newsreel camera*.)

Eisenhower.   Message to the CCS. "The mission of
This Allied force was fulfilled at 02.41
May 7 1945."

(*Champagne is opened*.)
I haven't been
To sleep for three days. The war's ended.

(*Everyone cheers and shouts "Hurrah"*.)

(*Same day. Luneburg Heath, TAC HQ.* DAWNAY *to* MONTGOMERY.)

Dawnay.   The surrender to Eisenhower has been signed at Reims.
The Russian one will be signed in Berlin
Tomorrow by Jodl and Keitel.

Montgomery.   Not before time.
If Eisenhower had seen the emissaries,
And not left Bedell Smith to negotiate
While he waited in the next room, three days
Would not have slipped by, allowing German units
Facing the Russians to escape westwards.
True to the end in his incompetence.

SCENE 12

(*8th May 1945. V.E. Day. Chorus of* LONDONERS.)

Chorus.   Victory in Europe Day. Huge crowds in New
York, where ticker-tape and confetti snowed
Through the air; in Paris, where citizens cheered
From their balconies as Allied planes flew past;

And in Moscow where crowds hoisted Russian soldiers
High above their heads. And here in London,
Standing, leaning from windows, hanging from lampposts,
Crowds filled the streets waiting for the expected news,
Silent as the official announcement came.
In London we heard Churchill speak at three:
"The German war is therefore at an end."
There was a gasp as he spoke of "the evil-doers
Who are now prostrate before us".
The war against Japan has yet to be won
But Japan is far away, the threat is over,
No more will V-Is and V-2s rain down
From the skies, bringing death and destruction to our cities.
We heard the words, he ended "Advance Britannia,
Long live the cause of freedom. God save the King."
We cheered with relief and hope and renewal.
We massed in front of Buckingham Palace and sang
"We want the King" and he came out with the Queen
And his two daughters and we waved and sang
"For he's a jolly good fellow", and they waved back.
Churchill came out with the King and Queen;
The King, bare-headed in naval uniform,
Churchill in a civilian, parliamentary suit.
We cheered and waved, and crushed into Whitehall
And Churchill came out on the balcony
Of the Ministry of Health and we all sang
"Land of Hope and Glory", he too. Then he spoke.
"This is your victory," he told us. "No, it's yours,"
We roared back. He said, "In all our long history,
We have never seen a greater day than this."
He gave the V-sign, and that night we danced
In the streets and drank and embraced strangers,
London was floodlit, searchlight beams played
In the sky, ships' sirens sounded from the Thames,
There were bonfires, fireworks, and we drank and laughed,
We revelled and sang and danced and cheered till late,
We were joyful, for danger had passed, we had
Survived the Blitz and the flying rocket bombs.
Europe was free from Nazi tyranny,
There was a great hope, a new world had been born!

(The cruiser Augusta *returning from Potsdam.* TRUMAN *and* AIDE.)

Aide.   I have an eye-witness report from Hiroshima.
The uranium bomb was two thousand times the blast
Of the heaviest bomb ever used before.

Truman.   Describe what happened.

Aide.   A flash and with a roar
A yellow and orange fireball rolled and shot
Eight thousand feet into the sunny air
And turned into a ten-mile high column
Of black smoke, a mushroom cloud rose and hung,
And as the great wind dropped, on the ground
A flat desert where there had been a city,
The roads like tracks across endless waste ground:
Hiroshima has disappeared, and in its place
Rubble, ruin, twisted metal and people
Horribly burned, lying still, stirring or
Groaning and crawling or just sitting dazed.
Over ten square miles a thousand fires blazed,
And a hundred thousand may have died at once.
Birds had burnt up in mid-air, and people's brains,
Eyes, intestines burst, their skin peeled, and some
Burned to cinders as they stood. Others had
The print of their clothes burnt onto their naked backs.
It was awesome. Sir, this new weapon which
Makes a thousand-bomber firebomb raid look
Insignificant, has in one blast outmoded
Six years of war, which must now be strikes like this
That can wipe out half a country without warning.
A new terror has arrived, that makes one yearn
For the sort of world war we have just seen
Where hatred has a limited radius,
That of a conventional high explosive bomb.

Truman   *(with awe).* This is the greatest thing in history. We had
To drop the bomb, I had a report that
Half a million Americans would be killed
If we were to invade Japan. General
Marshall and I are quite clear it will stop

The Pacific war before the Russians reach
 Japan, which we can occupy alone.
We have learned from Berlin, where the Russians
Occupy half to our quarter. The hope is that
This bomb will abolish war because no one will
Invade another's territory and risk its use.
Aide. So long as Stalin doesn't steal it from us.

(*Silence. They exchange glances.*)

(*London.* CHURCHILL *alone.*)

Churchill.   Now that I am in the wilderness again
I ponder that had I remained Prime Minister
I would have persuaded the Americans to use
Their new power, which is drawn from victory and
The atomic bomb, to confront Stalin,
To make him behave decently in Europe;
And I cannot help wondering, Truman has been weak
Towards Stalin, was this deliberate,
Has Marshall an understanding with him,
Is that why Eisenhower sent Stalin that cable?
I am better placed to judge than most,
And I see the hand of Zionism in the war.
At Yalta Roosevelt told Stalin he was a Zionist
And Stalin said he was one "in principle".
The Jews will have a new state in Palestine
For which I spoke in 1939,
In accordance with the Balfour Declaration
Which was made in exchange for Rothschild's guarantee
He'd bring America into the First World War
On the British side and save us from defeat.
So America entered the First World War
In return for Balfour's promise to a Rothschild
That there would be a homeland for the Jews
In the British mandate of Palestine,
And now the German Jewish Rothschild family
Have seen the Nazis fall and will have their state,
And if I were suspicious I might think
That Hitler was lured into war with Zionist money
Through House, Baruch, Schacht, Wall Street and I. G. Farben,

Vast sums that reached the Nazis through Warburg banks
So that Nazis could massacre Jews and swing
International opinion behind this new state.
But I cannot be suspicious. That way madness lies.
That way history is not what it seems, and leaders
Who appear to do their best for their nations
In fact work to another agenda, luring
The unsuspecting into catastrophic wars
That suit their own interests that remain hidden
From view. And what the history books describe
Is wrong, for history is what a cabal intrigued.
I do not want to believe that, I prefer
The view that leaders do their best for their peoples
Without pressures they know nothing of.

(*Silence.*)

I want to believe that Eisenhower chose
On military grounds not to go to Berlin –
Not that there has since Lenin been
A Zionist-American-Communist joint front
Which engineered the rise of Roosevelt
And, also, the succession of Stalin,
And that Eisenhower was under orders
To make sure that Russia's post-war position
In Europe will be the dominant one,
That he therefore had a political objective
In making sure that Stalin was first to Berlin
By vetoing my wish to attack the soft
Underbelly of the Reich, and then Monty.
I rose after writing to Baruch in thirty-nine,
And after speaking in the House of Commons
In favour of setting up a Zionist state
In Palestine. I fell at the hands of
Public opinion, which can be manipulated.
I do not want to think I fell through a plot,
Because I tried to stand up to Stalin
And was felt to thwart a hidden alliance
Between Zionists, Americans and Russians
Who influenced public opinion against me.
I prefer not to believe that Zionism

Was behind my rise and engineered my fall.
I want to accept the surface of history
And not stir the muddy depths which cloud the reflection.
I prefer not to know "groups" that would run the world.
I stood up to the two most terrible tyrants
Mankind has ever suffered; and I fell.
I am full of questions that will echo
To the end of this century and beyond,
As we regroup in a United States of Europe
And eventually in a United States of the World.

(*Frankfurt, the office of I.G.Farben.* EISENHOWER *alone.*)

Eisenhower.   America won the war and rules the world
As the only power to have the atomic bomb,
Having fought in Europe and the Pacific.
I led America to victory and
Like Octavius see greater things ahead.
As Commander I found life exciting,
I had an appetite for each day's news.
I find administering Germany tedious,
Here in the office of I. G. Farben.
Marshall is going to China to sort out
The civil war, the Communist threat to Peking,
And I can succeed him as Chief of Staff
And judging from the cheering as I rode
In triumph in an open car, and waved,
I could then become Augustus in the White House.
I long for the States. But what do I do about Kay?
In June I wanted to divorce Mamie,
But Marshall told me it would ruin my career
And refused permission, and I now want to live
With Mamie and not with Kay. Away from war
And exhausting hours and tension, I can be myself,
Vital, virile again, with my natural flow,
Which power has blocked, restored. Kay feels alone
And deserted. And I know I've failed her.
I've got her a job in Berlin with General Clay.
Now I will dictate a business-like letter
Explaining she cannot work for me any more,
And go to Paris at once, and then the States.

I do not want to visit the ruins
Of our relationship, like a smashed city,
And wander in the rubble of our streets
Where once there were avenues and green parks,
And say goodbye amid broken memories
Of when it was sunlit and magical,
I would rather slip away without despair.
There is a waste in my heart, a devastation.
I am as shattered as this Germany.

(*Moscow, Stalin's Kremlin HQ.* STALIN *alone.*)

Stalin (*satisfied.*) I did it. All along I had my own agenda
To transform the Soviet Union from a nation
Of backward peasants with horses and carts
Into a major world power all would fear.
I terrified them into the twentieth century,
Then I allied with Hitler to carve up part
Of Poland. I made overtures to Britain to
Keep pressure on Hitler from the western side.
I counted on Hitler to attack me.
He fell into my trap, he readily obliged.
Then my main thought was a Soviet empire
In eastern Europe and the Balkans. I delayed
Taking Berlin until I had overrun
Eastern Europe. At Yalta, I used their fear
Of Hitler, who was already finished, to redraw
Occupation zones and Poland's borders,
Knowing my stooges would seize power, invite
Russian troops in and give me indirect control.
The Allies were too trusting, they believed my words.
I made them honour their mistake, and took
Berlin. If I were Montgomery I would feel
Aggrieved, but imperial diplomacy
Is about power and achieving your interests.
The Russian civilisation is in a stage
Of union, of reunifying its own lands.
It has expanded to control its parts,
All its territories. It has always claimed
Poland and Eastern Europe, there has been no conquest
Of the European civilisation, which is younger than ours,

Merely a readjustment of our borders.
I secured the Soviet Union's interests –
I needed less than a week to invade
Japanese-held China and secure our
Interests at Port Arthur and at Dairen –
And will go down in history as the ruler
Who, like Ivan the Terrible, held the union
Together and expanded it to its greatest extent.
I have been a Genghis Khan, a Tamburlaine
Over a greater area than they conquered.
Berlin was the key, for with it came Poland,
Czechoslovakia, Hungary, and all the rest.
Occupation is nine points of the law.
And now, thanks to Niels Bohr, though he barely
Knows it, I am about to have the atomic bomb.
I shall challenge America and spread
Soviet influence throughout the rest of the world.
Man is material, which can be raised
Like clay a potter shapes on a turning wheel.

(*Lüneburg Heath.* MONTGOMERY *standing alone on the heath.*)

Montgomery.   So many times during the last eight months
I have longed to feel this heather under my feet.
Travelling around Germany on my train,
Which I captured from Hitler, I longed to see
Lüneburg Heath again, the place where I
Ended my long campaign from the Egyptian sands
And my command of the Americans
By receiving the German surrender.

(*He falls silent and looks around.*)

Marginalised, I was marginalised,
And with me Britain, and as a result
It's an American-Russian world now.
Did the Americans do it deliberately
To advance their power, or were they just blind?
In not going to Berlin, was Eisenhower
Just being fair, too trusting and naive?
Or honouring a deal that Roosevelt made

At Teheran with Stalin, to secure
A Russian offensive that would coincide
With my *Overlord*: Berlin in return for attack?
If I had led the Allies into Berlin
Before Churchill met Stalin at Yalta,
I could have held back the Communist tide,
All Europe would be Anglo-American.
Now the Soviet Union surrounds Berlin
And controls Poland. If my way had prevailed,
This would not be so. Does it matter now?
Yes, for many millions will not be free.
Or is there a stability I don't know about,
Is there now a secret east-west accord?
I can't believe that. Once again, I have been proved right.

(*Silence.*)

I sometimes question what my battles were for.
Was the world a better place for what I did?
Yes. I pushed back Fascism in North Africa
And Italy and North Europe. But as fast
As I rolled it back, Communism took its place.
Hitler was Overlord of Europe till
I invaded Normandy. Who's Overlord now?
Not Eisenhower; not Churchill, nor me, we
Were marginalised. Europe is now divided
Between Truman, all-powerful with his new bomb,
And Stalin, whose huge Red Army has occupied
The east and who cannot be dislodged by
An atomic bomb. Stalin is Overlord –
Apparently, for the real Overlord is you,
My guiding, Providential, loving Light
Without whom Hitler would have won this war.

(*Silence.*)

Now America is an atomic power
Thanks to German scientific insight,
And Russia will soon be one too, warfare
As I have known it is of the past, finished:
Operating from mobile caravans through scouts

Close to the battle front, like Marlborough
Or Wellington or Napoleon. War
Is now a distant nuclear missile threat.
And where does that leave Great Britain? Not great.
The body of our European civilisation
Has suffered a malignant cancer, which has been cut out
With our consent by the surgery of two other
Civilisations: the American and the Russian.
Now, after our civil war, we are convalescing
And our health will be restored.
But no more have we the energy for empire,
No more is our role in Africa or Asia.
Empire is at an end. We have ended
An imperial phase in our long history.
If that had to happen, then the civil war had to too.
Now the British Empire will collapse for we've
Bankrupted ourselves to recover from Hitler,
And a new Europe will grow out of this ruin.
I, who rule a quarter of Germany, consent
That German people should be in our new Europe
In which Britain, an island, will be different.

(*Silence.*)

Now, hearing the birds, watching the butterflies,
I know Nature's content. Rabbits, flowers, bees,
Birds, fish, grass, leafy trees, the universe
Just grows despite titanic wars like storms,
Which wreak havoc and uproot. After a storm
The air is so sweet, the earth is so pure,
Unsullied by the blot of tanks and guns.
I love the earth, the trees, the sky, the sun,
And you, my Overlord, who manifests
Into bud and blossom and lambs in the spring
And copper leaves, hips, haws, berries in the autumn.
I love the clear blue sky, the vast seas
The green hills and forests and mountain streams
And valleys and pure rivers. Your storms
Serve a purpose, they shake what is dead,
Blow off crinkled leaves, smash down the old
To prepare for the new. Lord, may there be

No more war. But I know, there must always be
Renewing storms. I would gladly live
In my caravan to be near your world,
At one with your will, in union with Oneness.

(*Silence.*)

Civilisations go through seasons, we are
In a new season now, a season of winter,
A bleakness and clearing up of devastation,
And then a new growth. I can feel it ahead.
A cold time as we recover, and then,
Though I may not live to see it, spring.
I accept your universe, with its storms and growth.
Through contradictions harmony prevails.
Life is an endless gush of opposites.
A tussle between darkness and light,
Pain and joy, hate and love, and war and peace.
All are manifestations of the One Light
You are, which I know at nine each night,
Which guided me to this point. And now I see
That evil swells like a dark thundercloud
That must grow darker for the rain to burst,
But it is always temporary in your scheme.
Hitler laid waste like a great hurricane;
Now Stalin is gathering like a tornado.
Of his own accord he will blow himself out.

(*Silence.*)

I see I was not meant to reach Berlin.
That was the will of the one Great Harmony,
And, Providence, with Ike as its instrument
(And Patton and his "niece", who are both now dead),
Blocked me, and in my self-will, egotism,
Vanity and national pique, I did not see this.
And complained, not understanding. But now I see.
The earth is made leprous by volcanic wars,
Happy is the place that does not erupt,
Where opposites live at peace, in harmony,
Which is not disfigured by the disorder of war.

Lord, your ways are magnificently strange,
And the loving spirit in your universe
Endlessly brings new shoots from desolation.
And reconciles all diverging views in
A latent harmony that is often obscured.

(*He pauses.*)

I said goodbye to the other kind of love
When an insect bite took my wife from me.
I sat with her, she looked so calm, peaceful.
I rose and gently kissed her serene face.
Then the men came in and screwed down the coffin lid.
Since then I've had no use for that kind of love.
I've preferred the cheering of crowds, as when I rode
In an open horse-drawn State landau, and waved.
As a German bomb had destroyed my flat.
I asked the King for a grace and favour home,
But gratitude did not extend that far.
And so I must live in a "borrowed" home, alone.

(*Silence.*)

For over a year I implemented a plan.
Now there is no need for it any more
I feel slightly lost, a warlord without a war.
I must live again without a plan, I must find
My meaning in God's world, beneath reason.
I must look for the plan in the universe,
Rather than Rommel's, and there is as much
Deception and subterfuge, God is a General
Who guards his secrets from his troops' eyes.

(*Silence.*)

Under the atomic bomb the world will draw together.
There is a need for a new philosophy
Which embraces all mankind, all
Under the atomic bomb the world will draw together.
There is a need for a new philosophy
Which embraces all mankind, all religions,

A metaphysic for the United Nations.
The only way I can live without a plan
Is to piece the potsherds of the universe
Into the tessellated urn from which they came
And, like an archaeologist, know its pattern
In the fresh air of the universal sunshine.

(*He pauses.*)
I understand that Brooke and I will be
Made peers in the New Year Honours, and I will be
Viscount Montgomery of Alamein.
But I have moved beyond war and conflict,
I look for opposites being reconciled.
I hope my son and Rommel's become friends.
And I ask of future generations
Not glorification or triumphalism,
But sober assessment, and credit where due.
More than Lawrence of Arabia, like the moon I drew
Tides of men, and flung them like a stormy sea
Up the beaches across the Channel, towards here.
Like Marlborough, I never lost a battle.
I stood for a Britain that had greatness.
I was a potsherd in the larger pattern,
A fragment, an episode, a chain of events
In the unfolding process of our history;
But I am proud of what our deeds achieved,
How our courage transformed our time, our Age,
And in the stillness of the trees, round this heather,
In the ghostly moaning of the winter wind
Which sounds as if the dead are gathering,
I hear the million men of *Overlord*
Roar their approval for a job well done.